LISTEN...

OUR LAND IS CRYING

Australia's Environment: problems and solutions

White, M.E. (Mary E.)
Listen-our land is crying: Australia's environment:
problems and solutions

Bibliography.
Includes index.
ISBN 0 86417 844 1.

1. Environmental protection - Australia. 2. Environmental management -
Australia. 3. Conservation of natural resources - Australia. I. Title.

33.720994

Cover photograph courtesy of Alcoa of Australia Ltd

Designed by Linda Robertshaw
Maps and Diagrams by Barbara Eckersley
Photographs, etc in book as credited in captions

© Mary E White 1997

First published in 1997 by Kangaroo Press
an imprint of Simon & Schuster (Australia) Pty Limited
20 Barcoo Street, East Roseville NSW 2069 Australia

Reprinted in 2001

Printed in Singapore by Kyodo Printing Co.

LISTEN...

OUR LAND IS CRYING

Australia's Environment: problems and solutions

MARY E. WHITE

Kangaroo Press

Kangaroo Press and the Author acknowledge with gratitude a grant from Fuji Xerox Australia (part of their Gold Sponsorship of Landcare Australia) which enables the retail price of *Listen…Our Land is Crying* to be kept at a figure which makes it more affordable for all interested in Australia's environment.

LANDCARE AUSTRALIA

Landcare Australia's charter is to marshal our national concern for the environment and direct it into positive action. Its aim is to make the care of our land a national cause in which all Australians, individuals, groups, communities and companies have roles to play.

The concept of landcare, a movement of community based action groups working in partnership with government, grew out of pioneering work in Victoria and Western Australia in the 1980s when farmers were attempting to deal with extreme land degradation resulting from generations of inappropriate farming techniques. The proposal for Landcare came from the Australian Conservation Foundation and the National Farmers' Federation and was accepted by the government of the day. The 1990s were announced as the Decade of Landcare and a financial package was provided to help the aim of achieving sustainable land use by the year 2000. At the same time, Landcare Australia was formed as a non-profit public company, to raise community awareness and participation in Landcare and to attract corporate funding for campaigns and Landcare group projects.

With the help of Landcare Australia's famous *Caring Hands* logo, awareness campaigns like the Uncle Toby's *Let's Landcare Australia* and the *Angry Anderson Challenge* have been highly successful; National Landcare Awards have promoted the National winners as ambassadors for Landcare, a name now recognised by three out of four Australians.

The value of sponsorship and fund raising activities has increased over time, bringing the total funds raised (cash and kind) by June 1996 to $21.6 million. The Landcare Foundation, established in 1994 to support Landcare projects, reached its initial pledge target of ten million dollars in May 1997.

FUJI XEROX AUSTRALIA PTY LIMITED

Fuji Xerox is a company with a worldwide commitment to the protection of the environment and the health and safety of its employees, customers and neighbours. Their environmental initiatives have already saved hundreds of millions of dollars internationally, showing that what is good for the environment is also good for business.

An integral part of their commitment to the environment is their Gold Sponsorship of Landcare Australia, which provides $200,000 a year for four years. The company's ethic—to use resources wisely and sustainably, to minimise pollution and to cut down waste—is the same as Landcare's. A key element of this programme is their remanufacturing programme where used machines and machine parts such as print cartridges are saved from landfill and are totally remanufactured to new.

Another important component of the Landcare sponsorship is the Officecare programme which was launched nationally in 1995. Officecare aims to get the millions of Australians who work in offices also to become committed to saving the environment by saving resources, reducing waste and reusing or recycling materials.

THE DOCUMENT COMPANY
FUJI XEROX

David Stringfellow, Chairman and Chief Executive Officer of Fuji Xerox Australia and New Zealand said, '*Our major external activity—supporting and working with Landcare Australia—is integrated with our major internal activities—recycling and remanufacturing. Landcare represents the most important "grass-roots" movement in environmental education that this country (and possibly the world) has developed. We are proud of all these activities as they demonstrate, at a local level, Fuji Xerox's on-going commitment to the environment.*'

CONTENTS

PREFACE
'GEOPHYSIOLOGY'

James Hutton, father of Geology, wrote in 1795 of the need for a science to look after the well-being of the Earth. He saw the degradation caused by the Industrial Revolution in Britain, in particular the pea-soup fogs resulting from coal burning. He coined the words *Planetary Physiology* and *Geophysiology* for a proposed new discipline whose province would be the understanding of the natural processes which keep the Earth's life-support systems in balance and where *Planetary Medicine* would maintain all its systems in good health. He was ahead of his time. The almost universal concept of a bountiful Earth with unlimited resources, with self-healing properties — coupled with a philosophy that everything in the world was put there for exploitation by the all-powerful human species — has resulted in the critical global situation in which we find ourselves now.

James Lovelock, in *The Ages of Gaia*,[1] described as Geophysiology his attempts to understand and explain his concept of the Earth as a living organism in which Life and the inanimate environment were inseparably linked, evolving together through geological time and maintaining life-friendly conditions on our planet.

As I write, two hundred years on from the time of James Hutton, the pressures of global over-population are reaching crisis point in a world where soil and water degradation, air pollution, ozone depletion, build-up of greenhouse gases, depletion of natural resources and loss of biodiversity tell of an increasingly sick planet.

These environmental problems are of two domains: one encompasses global atmosphere and climate and their optimum states for life; and the other the local balancing of the resource triangle of water, land and life. Plants form the basis for food chains in this trinity. Since the first cooling of the Earth there has been an inter-connection between life and the physical environment, a co-evolution so fundamental that, in the course of geological time, it has created the oxygenated world and the life-forms which it supports today. In nature, a dynamic balance is maintained and the carrying capacity of each ecosystem is determined by the interaction of local environmental factors. In our human-dominated and technologically controlled world we operate outside the rules which govern natural ecosystems — hence the crisis in planetary health which people all over the world are affected by today.

Approximately two hundred years of European settlement in Australia has resulted in this continent today showing the same symptoms of ill-health as the rest of the world. The problems are now so pressing that each of us needs to know enough *geophysiology* to understand what has gone wrong, how it might be fixed and how we as individuals can make a contribution to the remedies.

This book is intended as a treatise for Australia's environmental healing. It explains the unique nature of the continent — how its evolution through geological time had made it what it was when the Aboriginals came 60 000 years (or more) ago, and how much altered it was already by the time of European settlement. Why the imposition of agricultural practices which had proved satisfactory in the Northern Hemisphere led to rapid degradation here is explained when the history of our ancient and time-worn land is understood.

The extent of the environmental problems — the symptoms of a continent whose health is deteriorating rapidly — is outlined so that the urgency of situation can be appreciated by all of us. We need to see the big picture with the extent of environmental degradation in context so that we may judge for ourselves if the piecemeal media reports which increasingly come to our notice are balanced and not merely alarmist. It will become clear that our current practices — urban, rural, agricultural and pastoral — and the rate at which we are using up our resources, are unsustainable.

When we know what the problems are and how serious the situation is, we, the lucky inhabitants of an island continent, have reasons for optimism. Australia still has choices to make while many nations are so weighed down by their multitudinous human populations that the immediate needs of their people are the only consideration. It becomes almost impossible to give priority to maintaining biodiversity in natural ecosystems when the pressures of human survival are paramount.

At a national level, we have a moral responsibility, because we are fortunate and do still have choices, to do what we can about planetary health (where our contribution may seem relatively insignificant, though every little bit helps) and about maintaining biodiversity (where our contribution is vital and can be enormous). To achieve these larger scale aims, we have to put our house in order, stop the degradation and repair the damage, and achieve some measure of sustainability.

Australia leads the world in grass-roots movements which aim to remedy the environmental degradation which results from human activities. This book celebrates the efforts of Total Catchment Management Schemes, Landcare, Greening Australia, Waterwatch, Bush Regeneration, and a host of other enterprises where ordinary Australians are doing their bit towards putting their environment in order, with their own effort. It shows how each and every one of us can be involved, for we are all equally responsible for the problems, however indirectly. It is our land, our future and the future of our children and grandchildren that is at stake.

Introduction

We have become, by the power of a glorious evolutionary accident called intelligence,
the stewards of life's continuity on earth. We did not ask for this role,
but we cannot abjure it. We may not be suited for it, but here we are.

Stephen Jay Gould, Harvard University

WATER, LAND AND LIFE

A GLOBAL AND AN AUSTRALIAN PERSPECTIVE

The most essential of the world's primary resources are water and soil. Our human-dominated world, where technology has allowed that domination outside the natural rules which govern dominance by other species, has been brought to a situation where we are up against the finite limits of freshwater resources and where the soil resource base is seriously degraded.

It is the balancing of the resources of soil and water and the life which depends on them that is the challenge facing the world today. The rapid increase in the human population is no longer being matched by our ability to keep pace by the technological means at our disposal. For a while the 'Green Revolution' of plant and animal breeding, improved pastures, fertilisers, irrigation, modern machinery and other technology-related innovations enabled production to keep up with population growth. A combination of the results of over-exploitation of resources, of the degradation consequences to land and water, and of the emerging evidence of the unsustainability of the current agricultural and pastoral systems saw the Revolution running out of steam in the 1980s. The brief honeymoon was over. We had thought we were clever enough to 'manage' nature on a grand scale for human benefit; we now find, when we are trying to repair the damage done to our life support systems, that we do not have the knowledge or the wisdom required, and many of us are haunted by the fear that we are rapidly running out of time in a globally deteriorating situation.

The **Total Water Budget** for Planet Earth is estimated to be 1386 million cubic kilometres, a figure beyond reasonable comprehension. Much more

Sheet erosion near Mt Oxley.

M.E.W.

comprehensible, however, is the 3.5% of the total which is freshwater (not seawater) of which a large amount is locked in ice, or otherwise not readily available, leaving just $9000 \, km^3$ for human use. A world expert on water resources, La Riviere,[2] estimates that this amount is enough to sustain a global population of 20 billion people and on that basis half the water should be in use by 2000 AD. However, two-thirds of the world's total available freshwater is already used in some way by humans, and uneven distribution means that many lands are already short of water.

A **water crisis** has crept up on an unnoticing world and now no longer creeps but is ready to leap into everyone's consciousness. Worldwide, the demand for water is increasing twice as fast as human population growth. Global water use increased by a factor of ten in the 20th Century. Much of the water is degraded by silt and salt which result in large part from human activities. The fact that human cities, towns and settlements of all sorts are congregated on rivers or in their catchments means that most rivers in populated parts of the world are polluted by sewage and high-nutrient effluent from animal production; by industrial pollution and chemicals; and by agricultural run-off from fertilisers and pesticides. Increased nutrient levels can lead to algal blooms and toxicity of the water in rivers and lakes. *Per capita* availability of good drinking water is falling in all developed as well as developing countries.

Worldwide, water use has become so excessive that the implications for irrigated food production are serious. It takes $5000 \, kg$ of water to produce $1 \, kg$ of rice — so one can see where the problem lies. World population is set to double in the next 50 years or so, and the world economy is expected to expand fivefold.

This will put enormous stress on soil and water. So far, up until the mid 1980s, the Green Revolution was able to keep pace with population increase because there was enough water. Now land degradation problems and the current level of population demand new approaches and technologies to sustain it. No more fresh water is available so the equation of less water and more people can only result in food deficits.

Australia today, with its current management practices — agricultural, urban, commercial — is already functioning at the limit of its water resources, and therefore at the limit of its carrying capacity in terms of human numbers (at our present living standards). According to Dr Wasson, Assistant Director of the CSIRO Division of Water Resources and chairman of the committee assessing the health of our inland waterways for the Commonwealth SoE 96 Report,[3] our water resources are already fully committed, apart from those in Tasmania and the monsoonal north (where factors other than amount of available water are constraining). Against the increasing backdrop of virtually unstoppable degradation in a large percentage of our arable land, this limitation by freshwater resources has to be the criterion on which a sustainable population number is based.

The world's resources of **arable land** are finite. It is estimated that only 3190 million hectares (Mha) of land is potentially arable, and of this about half is already under cultivation, representing most of the best land. Further expansion is constrained in many parts of the world by shortage of water for irrigation in arid regions and by the problems associated with irrigation in marginal lands. It is a combination of soil quality, climate and terrain which determine whether land is arable or not.

NATIONS MAY GO TO WAR
TO BALANCE THE TRIANGLE OF WATER, LAND AND LIFE

The fact that global freshwater supplies are finite and that population increases in the next half century will result in severe shortages of drinking water and increasingly restrict the availability of water for irrigation is sobering. Added to the limits imposed by water, the finite nature of the extent of arable land, and the loss of increasing amounts of it by desertification caused by human exploitation, adds a further dimension. Conflict over decreasing natural resources would seem to be inevitable, especially as already there are 'water wars' in many arid parts of the world, between conflicting States within Nations, and between Nations. The great river valleys of the world are sites for escalating conflicts between all the different interests which are contending for dwindling resources as population and economic growth increase. Experts consider that in the 21st Century, the growing scarcity of water and its primary product, food, will result in violent disputes. To mention only a few:

In Asia as a whole, *per capita* availability

of water has declined by between 40% and 60% since 1955, suggesting that most countries will be experiencing serious shortages by 2025 and disputes will result. In the Middle East, already there is conflict over the waters of the River Jordan and its underground aquifers by Israel, Jordan and the Palestinian State. Turkey, the Kurds, Iran and Iraq are disputing over the Tigris and Euphrates, and the resources of the Nile are a source of conflict between Egypt and Ethiopia.

In Europe, conflicts have arisen between countries because of damming of the Danube. The Colorado River in the USA is a present-day battlefield between States and so much of its water is being diverted to supply urban and rural needs that it no longer flows into the sea. (Very recently a program has been put in place to release water from a major dam and cause brief annual flooding in the Grand Canyon, in the hopes of restoring its natural ecosystems.) A huge dispute is looming between India and Pakistan because India would like to divert some tributaries of the

Indus for its exclusive use. Pakistan, where 80% of the food is produced under irrigation, has stated that it is prepared to go to war to defend its right to its share of the water. Apart from major conflicts, on a smaller scale anarchy is seen as inevitable as shortages of land and water become threats to survival.

The time may not be far distant when no country will be able to be complacent about its inability to produce food for its population, reasoning that it does not matter provided it can make money from its manufacturing industries, enabling it to buy in food from elsewhere. (Please note this, Australia, for the not-so-distant future when wheat can no longer grow because of salinisation of our major grain-growing regions, and our remaining arable soils are decreasingly productive.) Where desertification is added to water shortage, fewer and fewer people will be sustained, living standards will plummet and nature (or Gaia) will restore the balance with famines.

GLOBAL ASSESSMENT
OF LAND DEGRADATION (GLASOD)

In 1991 a global map was made to show soil degradation which resulted from the previous 45 years of human intervention (omitting any damage caused by earlier activity). The map covers an area of 13 billion hectares between latitudes 72°N and 57°S. Almost two billion hectares were shown to be degraded (1.2 billion moderately to severely, 0.75 billion lightly). All categories of soil degradation were mapped: erosion by wind and water resulting in displacement of soil material; changes in physical properties and soil structure by compaction, waterlogging, loss of nutrients and/or organic matter; chemical deterioration by salinisation, acidification and pollution by toxins. Water erosion accounted for 56% of the degradation (1094 Mha); wind erosion 28% (548 Mha); chemical 12% (239 Mha); physical 4% (83 Mha). The causes of the degradation were given as: Deforestation and removal of native vegetation, 579 Mha; over-grazing, 679 Mha; improper agricultural management, 552 Mha; over-exploitation of vegetative cover for domestic use, 133 Mha; industrial activities leading to chemical pollution, 23 Mha.

Land degradation on a global scale has been estimated to cost world economies about US$42.2 billion a year in income foregone, at 1990 prices.[4] **In a world where population is exploding, arable land is a resource which must be preserved at all costs.** Yet each year 1.6 million hectares of arable land becomes lost to production. Expressed in terms which are more comprehensible, this represents 10 ha lost each minute — 5 ha from erosion, 3 ha from salt, 1 ha from structural change, 1 ha from non-agricultural uses. Desertification is inevitable over large parts of the arid and semi-arid regions of the world under present-day management systems and expectations. All arid lands (and Australia is the driest vegetated continent) have greatly increased risks of being rendered non-productive by human activities. **Current best estimates of global desertification show that 3.5 billion hectares or 69% of the world's agriculturally used drylands are to some extent degraded. Rangelands have fared worst, with 73% showing moderate degradation or worse. For rainfed croplands the figure is 47%, and for irrigated drylands 30%.**

DESERTIFICATION

The 1992 Rio Conference (Earth Summit Agenda 21: Programme of Action for Sustainable Development) defined desertification as:

Land degradation in arid, semi-arid and dry sub-humid areas resulting from various factors, including climatic variations and human activities.

This is a widening of an earlier definition, which had used the word only to imply human-related degradation. It now includes the adverse impact of climatic desiccation and of prolonged and more frequent droughts.[5]

Using the Rio definition, much of the serious land degradation from whatever cause occurring in Australia can be classified as **desertification**. It is a useful name as it tells it as it is — continuing degradation by erosion, salination or other means is leading to the **creation of deserts**, and the extreme El Nino–Southern Oscillation (ENSO) climatic fluctuations to which much of Australia is subjected serve to compound the problems. ENSO, described in Chapter 3, is the climatic pattern responsible for the unpredictable droughts and flooding rains which make land management so difficult. (In *After the Greening* I asked the question 'are we turning Australia into a 'desert island'? and the answer was in the affirmative.[6] All the research I have done since for the more comprehensive coverage in this book has served only to reinforce that view.)

On the global scale, desertification is now a direct threat to survival of over 250 million people. The famine in the Sahel, in sub-Saharan Africa, where a 30-year drought has brought decreased rainfall to all lands to its south in Africa, is the most frightful example. A further 750 million people are affected adversely and only slightly less directly by desertification. While the phenomenon was one of arid and semi-arid lands originally, in the last 25 years it has become apparent in dry sub-humid regions where the rainfall is between 750 and 1500 mm, and where most of the human inhabitants of the drylands now live. Manifestation of this trend in Australia is the increasing problem of the spread of dryland salinity northwards along the western slopes of the Great Divide.

Soil degradation is a major global problem. And one of the more easily recognised forms, **soil erosion**, is estimated to cost the global economy $400 billion a year in lost production. Other forms of degradation are being increasingly recognised as of equal significance. These include soil **salinisation, acidification, compaction, loss of soil structure and a decline in microbiological health, lack of bioturbation by worms and other animals, lack of humus and nutrients, development of water repellence, pollution causing toxicity, and sometimes waterlogging.**

The seriousness of declining productivity and the running down of what is, with water, the most fundamental of all resources, at a time when the human population is exploding, cannot be over-emphasised.

The human-related factors which lead to desertification are all concerned with disturbance

An abandoned farmhouse near Quorn in South Australia, in a man-made desert. The only green on the ground after rain is from weed seedlings germinating. Erosion following inappropriate cropping, over-grazing and the inevitable droughts has reduced the biodiversity in the landcover (soil and vegetation) to a point where the ecosystem has collapsed.

M.E.W.

SHOULD THE SITUATION IN THE SAHEL IN AFRICA ACT AS A WARNING FOR AUSTRALIA?

A UNESCO investigation into the causes of the devastating desertification which has resulted in famine in the Sahel established that the land has become a desert as a result of the activities of people. It had been thought that the desert encroachment was due to the Sahara spreading southwards. Instead it is due to agriculturalists and pastoralists moving northwards into what were **fragile arid lands**. The over-grazing and clearing for agriculture, which resulted in rapid erosion, soil loss and mobilised sand, made it impossible for the land to withstand and recover from drought. It does not take long for a situation to be reached where the problems are compounding and self-perpetuating. The Sahel is not the only modern example of frighteningly rapid desert advancement. In Western Sahara, villages are being engulfed by advancing sand dunes; parts of Somalia have lost all their topsoil and the nomadic people have less grazing available for their goats and camels. The establishment of much of the desert round the

Mediterranean in North Africa and the Middle East tells of past times when land-use practices did not take into account the fragility of the arid country in which wheat was being grown for the Romans. Well-vegetated lands rapidly became dune deserts when they were over-exploited for economy-driven reasons.

Australia, the most arid of lands, with fragile ecosystems, highly saline water-tables, and climates where drought is an ever-present concern, persists in producing for export: grains in quantities sufficient to feed (at our level of consumption) 200 million people; sugar for 85 million, and meat for 30 million. In terms of a balanced diet at western levels we currently support 80 million people, only 18 million of whom live on this continent. As for fibre, we produce enough wool for 500 million and cotton for 100 million. (These estimates are made by Dr Henry Nix of CRES, who is also the originator of the Triangle of Water, Land and Life concept.)

The pressures being placed on our primary resources of soil and water are enormous and unsustainable. We are mining and degrading the soil and water. The desertification processes can be slowed by band-aid measures, but the progress towards desert continues. We cannot be complacent when the Final Report of the Select Committee into Land Conservation in Western Australia says they were:

*... shocked to learn of the extent and severity of the deterioration of Western Australia's environment: its soils, water resources and flora and fauna. **The primary cause of this deterioration of the environment since European settlement is the development and use of land for primary production.***

The study covered the winter rainfall south-western region and the arid and monsoonal rangelands, and recognised the fragility of all regions of the State.[7]

of the natural balance in ecosystems. **The more arid the land is, the more fragile the balance.** As well as the direct effects of land use and management practices, indirect and compounding effects result from government policies and socio-economic pressures. Over-exploitative land-use practices are often driven by political, global economic and national policies; or on a more human scale by things like high interest rates which cause farmers to be locked into a system which does not allow them the luxury of thinking about the environment first and their financial survival second.

Farmers struggling to meet short-term financial

commitments may be unable to afford to institute changes to land management practices requiring investment in soil conservation. In most cases, those operating viably today have made improvements to land degraded by previous generations who did not have today's knowledge and who had often been implementing government requirements and policies when they cleared timber and bush on a grand scale, often being subsidised to do so. In the post Second World War boom in allocation of farming leases in Western Australia, for instance, one of the requirements for retaining the land was that it had to be totally

GLOBAL ARIDITY ZONES

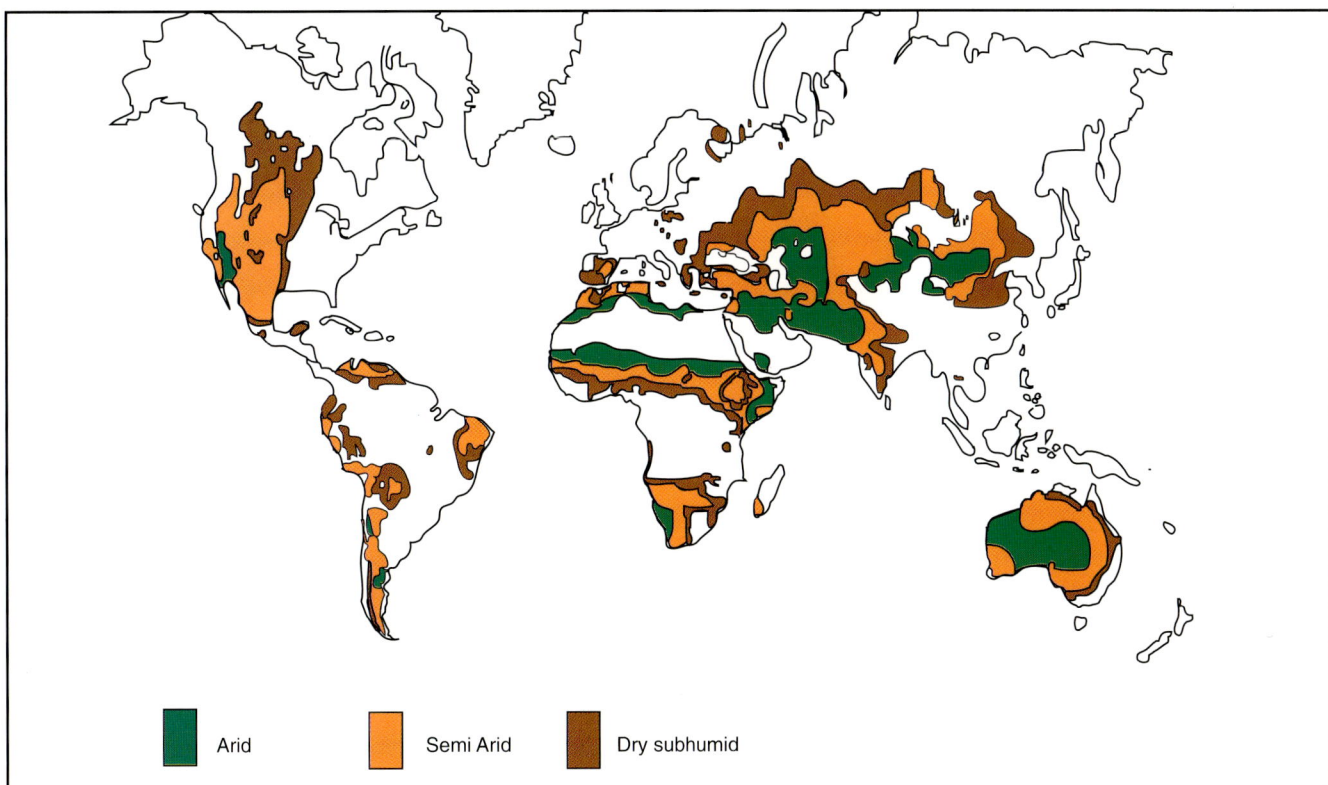

Arid   Semi Arid   Dry subhumid

GLOBAL STATUS OF DESERTIFICATION
Relative proportions of degraded land by continent

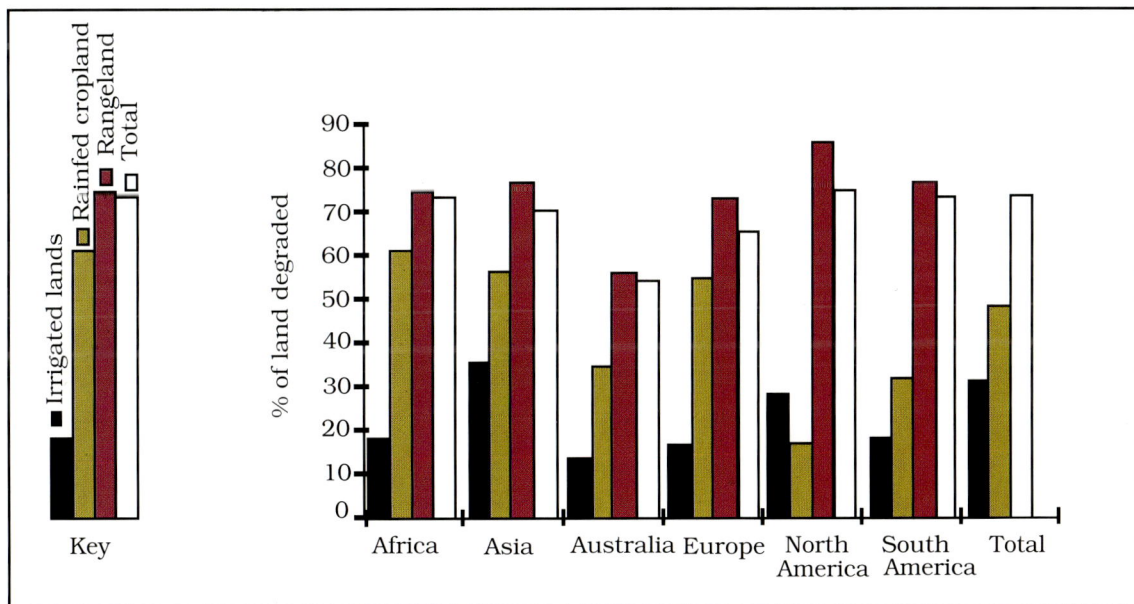

Irrigated lands Rainfed cropland Rangeland Total

% of land degraded

Key   Africa   Asia   Australia   Europe   North America   South America   Total

cleared within a year or two of taking up the lease.

Today's farmers are too often blamed for the land degradation which they inherited and have been battling with throughout their tenure. The waves of early settlers probably did more damage in the early days of settlement, in their headlong rush and enthusiasm to tame this land of perceived limitless resources and golden opportunity, than result from the cumulative effects of management practices of the last half century. Nowhere is this more evident than in the fragile arid lands of South Australia where in the 'good' years towards the end of last century the saltbush plains were ploughed for wheat far north of the Goyder Line, and desert was created when drought returned.

The human-induced factors leading to desertification in Australia are:

THE FORMULA FOR DETERMINING HUMAN IMPACT ON THE ENVIRONMENT

The complex relationship between population and environment has been expressed as a formula:[9]

$$I = P \times A \times T$$

where I = environmental impact; P = population size; A = affluence (per capita consumption of goods and services); and T = technology (quantity of resources consumed and pollution generated during production and consumption per unit of goods and services). The true causes of severe environmental impact — political, economic and social — are not reflected in this formula, but it emphasises that the more `developed' a society is, the greater its impact on the environment.

It also might be used to emphasise that the more affluent the developer, the greater the impact on the environment. The cotton industry in Australia is as an example, a not-politically-correct-to-mention one, where billions of foreign dollars are spent on building gins, landowners in surrounding regions are seduced into producing cotton in vast quantities for quick economic gains, and perhaps 10 years hence the black-soil plains, may well be on the way to becoming useless badlands and the rivers may be dying.

SPREAD OF SETTLEMENT IN SOUTH AUSTRALIA

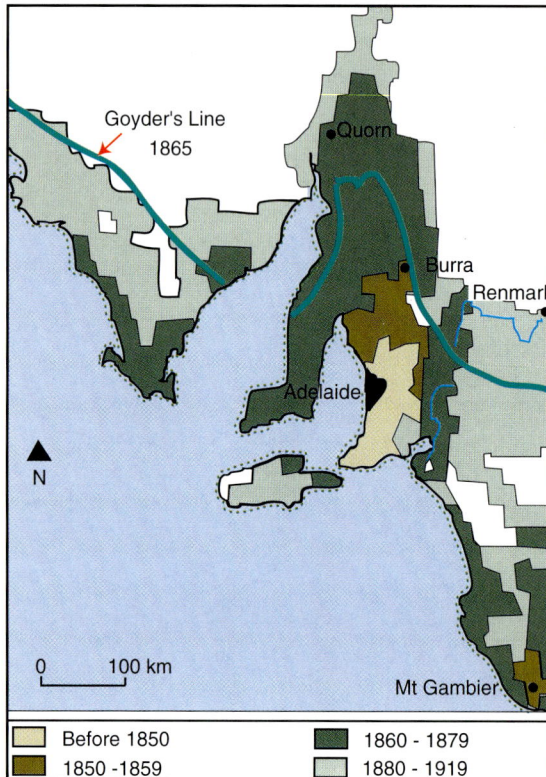

After Young [10]

Spread of settlement in South Australia. In 1865, a severe drought occurred in South Australia north of the Adelaide Plain. The Surveyor General, G.W. Goyder, mapped the area of drought and produced the line which seperated the drought-stricken northern lands from those less affected to the south. The line followed the boundary of semi-arid vegetation and was to be the limit, written into the law, beyond which land could not be ploughed up for wheat. When allocation of land south of the line was complete and there were no more selections available, attempts were made to discredit the line, and in the late 1870s, a time of better than average rains, there was a rush to take up land to its north. Ploughing for wheat resulted as far as 200 km north of the line. There was a belief that 'rain (or prosperity) follows the plough' and farmers were to find that in Australia desert, not rain or prosperity, eventuated.

- **Removal of natural vegetation, cultivation of the land, and planting of crops, which affects the hydrology of a region.** The quantity of water transpired by trees and native perennial

pastures is not matched by the evapo-transpiration of the system which replaces it. Water-tables rise, and when close to the surface, salinisation often follows (and waterlogging in some cases). Rivers become increasingly salty. Bare soil after cultivation and during fallows results in wind and water erosion, with mobilisation of sand in some marginal lands, and with siltation of rivers. Mechanised farming and over-cultivation result in a decline in soil structure which affects water permeability and results in compaction and increased susceptibility to erosion. Over-exploitation results in decline in soil nutrients and organic matter with the loss of the microbiological and invertebrate soil fauna and flora (a decrease in a less visible component of overall biodiversity).

- **Over-grazing** causes loss of biodiversity and reduction in vegetation cover, which results in bare patches and may affect the hydrology and lead to salinisation. Increased wind and water erosion follow, compounded by either the breaking up of the soil by the hooves of the grazing animals, or its compaction, which leads to excess run-off. Damage to the living biotic crusts which are a protective layer on arid-land soils in Australia is another consequence of grazing by hoofed animals. (See Chapter 3)

- **Replacement of forest and woodland with pasture** for grazing affects the hydrological balance of catchments. The effects — salinisation and waterlogging — may be felt in places quite remote from the altered areas which are causing the problems, and water quality in rivers deteriorates.

- **Fires**, too frequent or at the wrong time of year, cause degradation by damaging the vegetation, reducing ground cover and laying bare earth open to wind and water erosion. Fire also affects soil structure and its microbiological and invertebrate faunal content, as well as its organic content. Fire management in Australia is one of the most vexing of all the management problems. (See Chapter 11). In this dry land, the evolution of the natural vegetation has been in the context of environmental factors including natural fire, and

Farina, a ghost town in South Australia, is a monument to the unrealistic expectations of early settlers. Extraordinary rainfall for a number of years at the end of last century saw land ploughed for wheat in central South Australia, and Farina (whose name is the Latin word for flour) was destined to be the milling and baking centre for a profitable industry. The good years ended abruptly. Much of the ploughed land was never planted, the rest of the crops failed and wind erosion took over. Heavy over-grazing of fragile native pastures, the activities of rabbits and the drought years between 1922 and 1935 saw sand drifts threatening to engulf Farina (and Parachilna, Mannahill and some other small settlements). Conservation reserves, from which stock was excluded and rabbits were eliminated, were established round the towns, and with better years the drifts stabilised. The landscape was well and truly desertified, however. Now the bakehouse with its underground ovens stands among the ruins.

M.E.W.

for the last 60 000 years or more Aboriginal fire has been an added determinant and a selector and promoter of fire-tolerant species. Some fire is necessary to maintain biodiversity in most ecosystems as a result, and exclusion of fire, coupled with over-grazing, has been responsible for the conversion of some arid savanna rangelands to 'woody-weed' degraded lands. (See Chapter 10)

- **Mismanagement of irrigation**, with over-use of water and insufficient drainage has led to rapidly rising water-tables, waterlogging and salinisation of soils, as well as greatly increased salinity of rivers.

All the factors referred to above amount to **landcover** disturbance. The term landcover is a useful one for the combination of vegetation (or snow or water) and soils within a topographic context,[11] and satellite mapping of Australia has been carried out by the CSIRO to show the broad-scale alteration which results from 200 years of European land use. The degree of landcover disturbance can be roughly equated to the **biotic erosion**, or run-down in biodiversity of the major ecosystems defined by their landcover status. (Biodiversity, as we shall see in Chapter 3, is the key to ecosystem health and sustainability; loss of biodiversity is the fundamental reason behind all the desertification

processes and the unsustainable land-use practices which are described throughout this book.)

On the basis of human-induced landcover disturbance as mapped by satellites, the continent is divided into two regions:

1. Intensive Landuse Zone (ILZ),
   2 983 908 km^2 — 39% of the continent
2. Extensive Landuse Zone (ELZ),
   4 708 092 km^2 — 61% of the continent.

The satellite monitoring of Australia has been part of the **Global Land Cover Change Project**. Dr Dean Graetz and other officers of the CSIRO Division of Wildlife and Ecology, and the Australian Centre for Remote Sensing have compiled satellite images which enable the comparison of the vegetation cover of the continent during the last 20 years.[12] The ongoing satellite monitoring is a useful tool for measuring the extent and frequency of fire and drought on a continental scale; for observing the rate at which land is being cleared; and for observing the spread of major environmental weeds like prickly acacia. With an eye-in-the-sky we can no longer plead ignorance of the extent of environmental problems.

Dust storms were frequent during the early days of settlement when the Mallee lands were being cleared in Victoria.

DEAN GRAETZ

A very hot fire late in the dry season in the East Kimberleys leaves soil bare and unprotected with the monsoon only weeks away. An open invitation to erosion.

M.E.W.

Division of the continent according to the landcover consequences of landuse. The red region comprises those areas where the principal landcover disturbance threat is clearing for crops, pastures and forests (ILZ). However, not all of this is cleared. The green region comprises the areas where principal landcover disturbances result from grazing and burning (ELZ).

MAP SUPPLIED BY DEAN GRAETZ, CANBERRA[11]

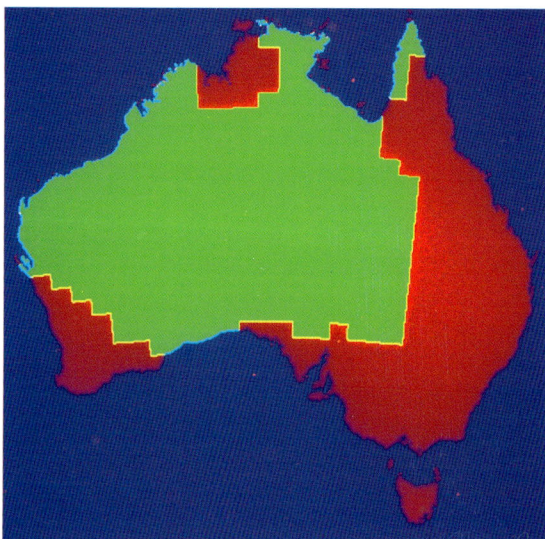

CLIMATIC FACTORS WHICH INFLUENCE DESERTIFICATION

The contribution to desertification of natural climatic fluctuations like ENSO and global climate changes, some of which may be attributable to the human-induced Greenhouse (see Chapter 1) is generally accepted, particularly when such natural climatic change is added to the damage directly caused by humans. However, it is less well known that regions which are degraded or greatly altered by human activities can actually have a climate-altering effect. It has been noticed that where badly over-grazed land has been separated by a fence from land whose native vegetation is in good condition, more rain falls on the good side than on the degraded side. To prove this scientifically has not been easy because of the scarcity of records.

Some interesting research carried out by the Flinders University Airborne Atmospheric Research group and teams working in Western Australia has shown that **massive clearance of land for agriculture can actually cause a local reduction in rainfall**. The 500 km of rabbit fence erected in the south-western part of Western Australia to keep rabbits out of the area cleared for agriculture is still maintained, though it was not very successful in its original aims. Now it separates the intensively farmed croplands to its west from the native vegetation to its east. The rainfall to the west has been decreasing over a 42-year period, to the east of the fence it has been increasing. The difference is the reverse of the natural rainfall pattern recorded before farmers cleared land nearer to the coast. Searching for a reason, the research group flew back and forth across the fence, measuring the radiation available for the energy transfer at the ground surface which is essential for the production of rain. They proved that the fence is a 'climate barrier' — the massive clearing directly affects the local climate.

A partial solution to the rainfall decline would be the planting of timberbelts (agroforestry) in the cropped land — a recommended way of decreasing salinisation as well. The calculated requirement of 50% to be replanted to trees to restore normal rainfall is unlikely to be acceptable to farmers (at least until their salinity and other desertification problems become so severe that they have no alternative).

This research, which has proved **that loss of native plant cover can affect climate**, gives an indication of what may be the compounding effect of El Nino droughts on climate. It would suggest that because of ENSO Australia was naturally set on a path towards an ever more dry (and fiery) state, and that human intervention has only greatly accelerated the process. Prolonged droughts in rapid succession, such as occur when El Nino events happen in series over a number of years, result in degraded vegetation and changed energy transfer, which leads to changes in rainfall — and that continues the drying cycle.

Land degradation in Australia is discussed in

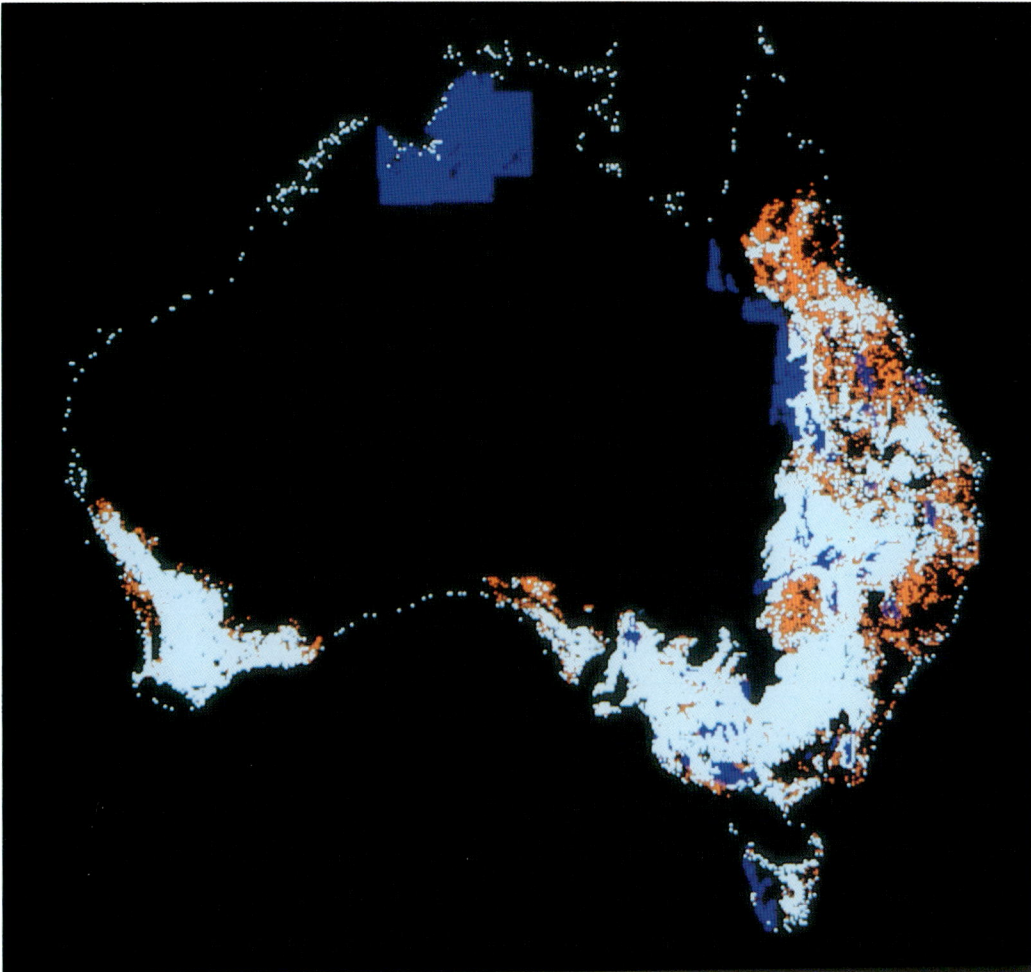

ILZ
The degree of disturbance caused by clearing. Uncleared areas are brown; thinned are orange; cleared are white; and indeterminate are purple.

MAP SUPPLIED BY DEAN GRAETZ, CANBERRA[11]

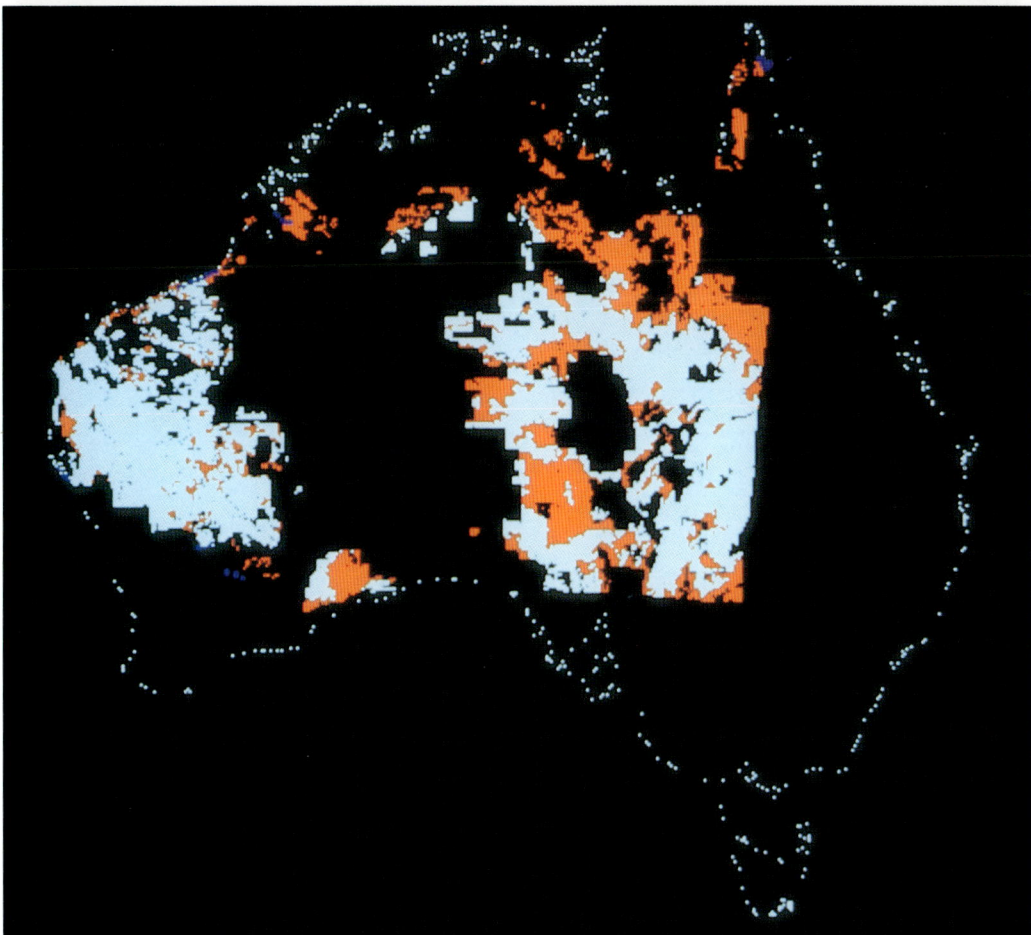

ELZ
The degree of disturbance caused by grazing and fire. Slight disturbance, brown; substantial, orange; significant, white; and indeterminate, purple.

MAP SUPPLIED BY DEAN GRAETZ, CANBERRA[11]

CSIRO

Global Change

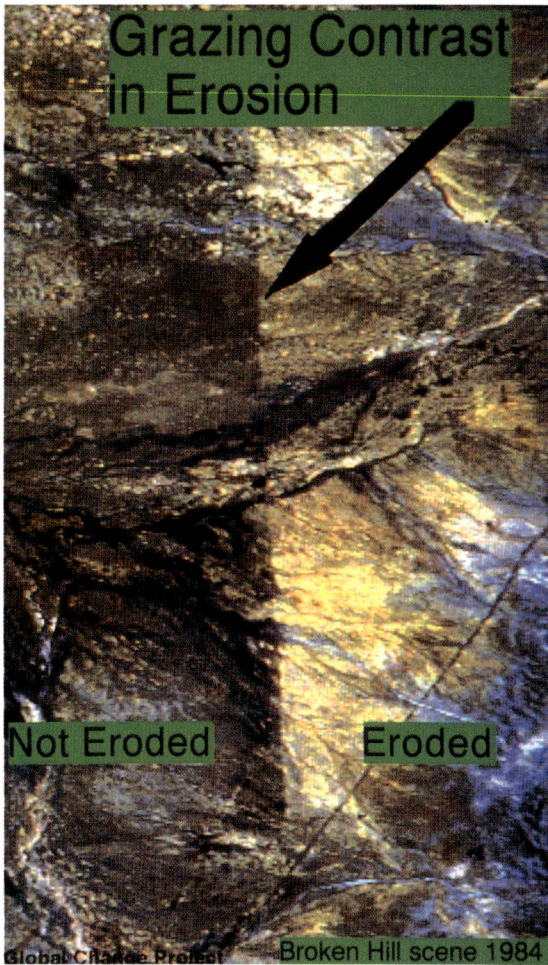

Grazing Contrast in Erosion

Not Eroded

Eroded

Global Change Project

Broken Hill scene 1984

Above: Satellite imagery of the continent in September 1991 reveals the 6% under crops concentrated in the Western Australian Wheatbelt and the Murray Basin.

Above right: The Global Land Cover Change Project, in which Australia participates, is a watchdog which monitors the destruction of forests and other changes to world vegetation. Satellites can produce pictures which show the rate of removal of Brazilian rainforests, and the rate of forest clearing which is taking place in northern New South Wales and southern Queensland. In 1995, the latter was proceeding at a greater rate than the former, a cause for alarm and dismay.

CSIRO

When landcover degradation is so severe that it can be seen clearly by satellites, as in this picture of land near Broken Hill where a fence separates over-grazed land from natural bush, the situation is obviously serious.

RAINFALL MAP

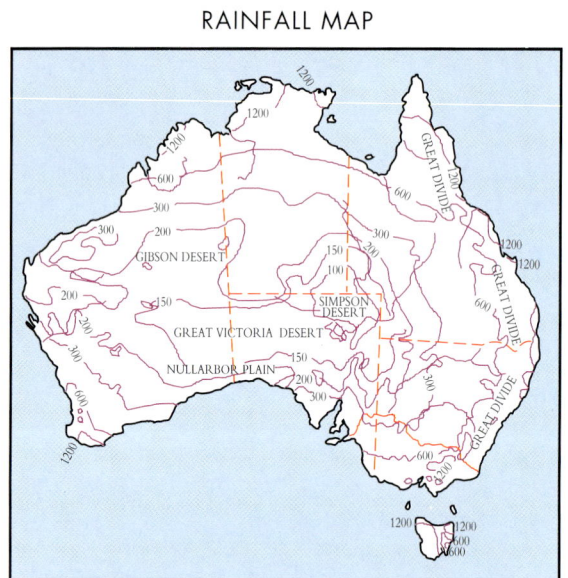

VEGETATION REGIONS WHICH HAVE SUFFERED THE GREATEST CHANGE

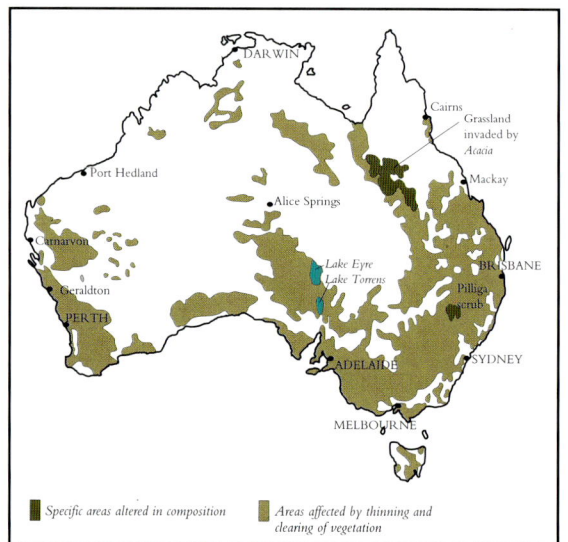

Specific areas altered in composition   *Areas affected by thinning and clearing of vegetation*

following chapters.

The reasons for the continent's susceptibility to all the processes of desertification are found in four areas:

- the fact that it is such an arid land, and arid lands characteristically have fragile ecosystems;
- the geological history of the land, which explains its nutrient-deficient soils, their erodibility;
- the underlying salty water-tables;
- and the magnitude of climatic swings, from drought to flooding rain, which are caused by ENSO.

DEAN GRAETZ

The magnitude of the task involved in assembling the big picture in this book is such that it can only be achieved by dealing with the main issues in detail and selecting carefully chosen case studies and examples which show them in the different contexts in which they occur all over the continent. By this means it seeks to explain and emphasise: what makes Australia unique; the current status of the environment and what are its problems, how they have arisen, and how they can be addressed; the successes and hopes in establishing more sustainable land-use practices; and all the side issues and bits and pieces which contribute to a well-rounded and comprehensive overview.

SNOW LEASES AND DEGRADATION OF THE HIGH COUNTRY

The **Kosciusko National Park**, under the control of the NSW National Parks and Wildlife Service, was declared in 1967.

The region has an interesting history, both on a geological time scale and in human time, in the uses to which its fragile ecosystems have been exposed within the period since people invaded it. In our old, flat land, the winter snowfields and the alpine vegetation and biodiversity are of unique significance and importance. Looking into the future, a time may not be very far off when there are no snowfields — the effect of Greenhouse will be most evident here.

Geological history

The High Country mountains were elevated by local block faulting during the Kosciusko Uplift, which was raising the south-eastern section of the Great Divide during the Tertiary Period. The Uplift rejuvenated the drainage and the rivers running to the coast cut deep valleys, which were later entered by the sea when sea-levels rose during the interglacial in which we are living today (creating the drowned-valley inlets along the south-eastern seaboard).

During the Pleistocene ice age (the last 2.6 million years), a small area of the highest land had a permanent ice cap during the more severe glacial stages, particularly at the peak of the last glacial stage 18 000 years ago. The area covered then was restricted to about 50 km², and the rest of the High Country would have had more extensive snow fields for longer periods each year than today. (Tasmania had Australia's only major ice cap during glacials, situated on the Central Plateau and connected to glaciers on the West Coast Mountains. In the last glacial stage it covered 4000 km² of the north-western part of the plateau. Ice age for most of Australia simply meant cooler, much drier and much windier climates than today.)

History of Grazing

The history of grazing in what is now the Kosciusko National Park extends over about 150 years. Parts of the area were freehold and subject to year-round use and various grazing practices; tenure of others was leasehold. The most controversial and damaging to the fragile environments were the '**snow leases**' which were an example of the imposition of practices well established in the Northern Hemisphere which proved unsustainable in Australia. Again, as with the introduction of European-style agricultural land use, a great deal of permanent damage was done in the very early years of Settlement. Virtually all of the alpine flora in the Kosciusko area has been modified by humans as shown by the changed plant distribution patterns which exist today compared with the early botanical records.

Aborigines had little if any effect on the High Country. Their annual visits in search of the Bogong moths were not invasive and it is unlikely that they altered the pattern of natural fires significantly. However, when Europeans came to the region in sufficient numbers in the 1830s and discovered that the alpine herbfields were ideal pasture for cattle and sheep, the degradation of the region began. By 1860 the practice of summer grazing was well established among the squatters whose presence in the surrounding areas was unofficial. It was common practice to burn the vegetation annually to promote fresh green feed and to clear some of the woodland and shrubland, promoting more grass.[13]

The 1861 Robertson Land Act allowed selection of land already taken up by early squatters, and the fact that landowners were now official and numerous, and confined to relatively small areas, resulted in a rise in the number of animals per hectare — and the damage escalated.

The **selective grazing** of plants by cattle and sheep over time has been the main problem. Livestock grazing, particularly in association with fires, is very selective both in terms of **species** and in terms of the **areas** preferentially grazed. It is obvious why animals graze species selectively — they seek out the herbs, particularly the daisies, eyebright, billybuttons and buttercups, which are relatively high in protein and easily digested. (The herbaceous plants, distinct from the grasses, comprise only 3% of the groundcover.)

Over-grazed land. Only unpalatable black blue bush remains on bare ground near Quorn.

M.E.W.

Ranunculus anemoneous, *the endemic mountain buttercup, which nearly became extinct when snow leases were causing widespread erosion in the High Country.*

Ken Green, NPWS

They avoid, for as long as they have an alternative, the snow grasses and shrubs which have low digestibility and low crude protein (unless frequently burnt).

A typical stocking rate in a former snow lease was only one sheep to one or two hectares, which would sound reasonable, but when the proportion of unpalatable components of the grazing is taken into account, the **effective stocking rate** approached four or five sheep per hectare (more than on most improved, managed pastures). The preferential grazing of selected areas affected swamps with their higher-nutritional plants; and some alpine herbfields, especially those below snow patches where the plants are particularly sweet. The heaths and regrowth snowgum patches were virtually avoided. By selecting areas on which to concentrate, the livestock also increased trampling pressure and soil-surface damage in the most used, and often the most fragile places (Costin, unpublished data).

The extremely high local grazing pressures which resulted from selective grazing of species and of areas led to reduction of biodiversity in the alpine ecosystems. Marked changes occurred in the relative abundance of species and in the composition of plant communities. A reduction in herbs led to bare soil between snow grass tussocks and other unpalatable plants, opening the way for weeds like sorrel to invade.

The infiltration of storm rain was shown experimentally to be greatly reduced when inter-tussock vegetative cover was reduced, and the amount of soil-eroding run-off was correspondingly increased. Frequent fire increased soil erosion; seedlings and resprouts of snow gums which appeared after fire were eaten, so when fire killed mature trees there was no replacement.

As early as 1887 it was noted by Victorian Assistant Geologist, James Stirling, who was based in the Lands Office in Omeo and who made collections of alpine plants which were identified by Ferdinand Mueller (Victorian Government Botanist), that livestock grazing was drastically reducing and even eliminating some species. *Ranunculus anemoneous*, the anemone buttercup, which grew on Mt Kosciusko and on Mt Hotham was 'fast disappearing from the summits of our Victorian mountains owing to the inroads made into native vegetation by stock as these alpine areas become increasingly occupied year by year'. The buttercup is now extinct in Victoria, and was on the verge of extinction on Kosciusko in 1944 when the alpine area was closed to grazing. Several other alpine plants were similarly endangered and have also recovered after protection from livestock.

By the mid 1860s the High Country was already being used for drought relief pasture. A Cooma landowner, William Bradley, sent 48 000 sheep and 2000 cattle into the mountains in the 1865 drought. Sheep were the predominant stock using the mountains, but cattle were assigned the rougher slopes to the south and west, partly because dingoes were numerous there and were a threat to sheep. Degradation due to grazing was already visible by the 1890s.

Ferdinand Mueller had begun research into the alpine flora in the 1850s, and his records provide a basis for knowledge of the changes to vegetation which have occurred since. Further work was carried out by Richard Helms in surveys in 1890 and 1893 and he recorded 'the desert-like look' caused by fire and the erosion of soil from the steep slopes. In 1898 the Government Botanist of New South Wales, J.H. Maiden, commented on the deterioration of the vegetation caused by grazing and burning. However, early attempts at control only resulted in trials of a number of different types of leases and permissive occupancies which made little difference.[14]

Seven-year snow leases (regulating the times of grazing, stocking rates and fire) were introduced in the 1920s for areas above 1300 m, but permissive occupancy in lower regions allowed year-round grazing. Many of the leases were held by western division landowners as drought insurance. Abuses of the system were widespread and no enforcing of stocking rates or burning practices took place until the 1940s when the snow leases were reduced in size and mainly reserved for local landholders. Administration (or non-administration) had been from Wagga Wagga; now it moved to Goulburn.

The turning point came when conservation started to enter the vocabulary in the 1930s and vegetation, alpine, montane or other, was starting to be recognised as having significance in its own right and not merely as fodder. Myles Dunphy (senior) was a pioneer conservationist whose vision saw the establishment of a National Parks and Primitive Areas Council. It proposed the reservation of 400 000 ha of the High Country of New South Wales and Victoria. A forester, Mr B.U. Byles, contributed to the argument for protection when his surveys of the Murray River catchment showed that severe damage was being done to the snow lease areas by fires, and that erosion was widespread. (Byles later served for many years on the Kosciusko State Park Trust.)

The River Murray Commission arose to oversee the use of the River and its tributaries as a result of concern about the erosion of the catchment. It was the possible effects of siltation of the Hume Dam (completed in 1936) which focused attention on the management of the High Country, and the Soil

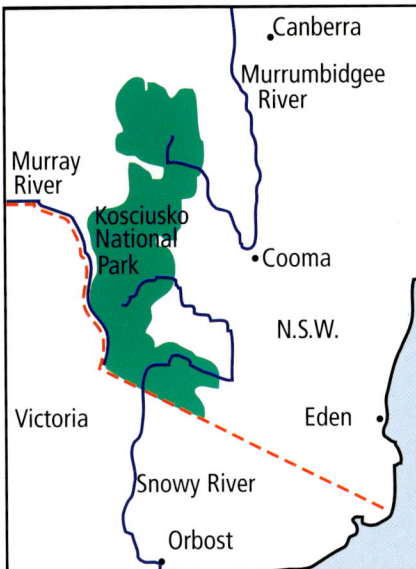

Map labels: Canberra, Murrumbidgee River, Murray River, Kosciusko National Park, Cooma, N.S.W., Victoria, Eden, Snowy River, Orbost

Revegetation works at the gravel pit near Seamans Hut.

NPWS, KOSCIUSKO HERITAGE UNIT

Conservation Service evolved in 1938 from the 1933 Soil Erosion Committee which had been formed to look at erosion there.

The declaration of the Kosciusko State Park in 1944 was a beginning, but its administration depended on rents from the snow leases. In order to accommodate tourist amenities and conserve water resources, 4000 ha of highest altitude leases were withdrawn in 1944. Further leases were withdrawn to enable occupation of land by the hydro-electric installations and towns built by the Snowy Mountains Hydro-Electric Authority during the Snowy Scheme, and it was proposed to eliminate all grazing above 1370 m, again because of worry about silting of dams, not primarily to preserve unique ecosystems.

The Authority was established in 1949 with the object of collecting the waters of the Snowy River and the Eucumbene and diverting them into the Murray and Murrumbidgee Rivers to allow irrigation of the dry inland, and to generate electric power. The vast engineering project included 145 km of trans-mountain tunnels, seven power stations, 16 large dams, one pumping station, 80 km of aqueducts, power transmission lines and access roads. The land degradation and threat to the natural ecosystems of all this activity in one of the most fragile regions anywhere is obvious. It was clear to the Authority that water conservation and quality for the Scheme and mountain livestock grazing were incompatible. A long and bitter battle ensued with proponents of continued grazing.

Though the Snowy Scheme in its day did much for national pride and contributed to the heady optimism of the Green Revolution in Australia with the irrigation schemes in the Murrumbidgee Irrigation Area and in the Murray Basin, with the wisdom of hindsight it can be seen to have been an environmental disaster. All over the world, such schemes which involve changing the direction of rivers, over-controlling their flow and upsetting their natural seasonal patterns and occasional floods which feed wetlands, are now recognised as unjustifiable interference with natural systems. In the driest vegetated continent, subject to the extreme climatic fluctuations of ENSO, man plays god at his peril.

WHAT HAS HAPPENED TO THE SNOWY RIVER SINCE THE SNOWY MOUNTAINS SCHEME STOLE ITS WATER?

The Snowy River is dying. From a wide, swift-flowing river, deep, full of fish, and home to the platypus, subject to floods which renewed the fertility of its floodplains, it has been reduced in parts to a trickle. This river's appeal to the imagination of every Australian is due to Banjo Patterson and the folklore which surrounds it. We visualise the rapids, wild waterfalls and deep pools in its gorges; and now we find that we have been cheated and the river of our imagination has become a shallow drain. On the NSW Monaro side, its banks are eroded and collapsing; its water downstream of Orbost is too salty to use in irrigation or for cattle to drink. The amount of water which feeds it below the dam at Lake Jindabyne is less than 1% of the River's original natural flow.

At its mouth, water levels are so low that the sea tides and salt water now penetrate 20 km upstream, turning the once-fertile floodplains into brackish flats where samphire replaces pasture. Thirty years of water starvation has brought the whole river ecosystem to the brink of collapse.

Only the restoration of `environmental flows' will save the Snowy. It needs to have at least 25% of its original flow in average seasons released, and to be given access to flood wash during the spring thaw if it is to stand any chance of restoration. This will come at a cost to the Hydro-electric power generation and, as usual, economics will dictate what happens. There are those who think that the advantages (economic) of the power and irrigated agriculture which flow from the Snowy Scheme justify the death of the River. (What has happened to the Snowy, a river fed by snow on high mountains and not by a semi-arid catchment much more prone to great fluctuations in rainfall, like, for instance, the Clarence, should stop any consideration of schemes to divert waters from other rivers to flow inland.)

In 1958 the State Cabinet agreed to terminate leases above 1370 m when they expired. **Up to 40% of the sub-alpine grassland had become bare soil by this time**. Debate had become so heated that the Lands Minister and the Conservation Minister, who held opposing views, threatened to resign if a decision went against them (neither resigned). Permissive occupancies continued, subject to annual renewal.

The Park Trust was deprived of much of its income by these changes and the Commonwealth offered funds on condition that half was delegated to the Soil Conservation Service for work in the mountains. This began a 25-year project to restore the most degraded parts of the alpine areas, above 1850 m. Grazing above 1370 m was still continuing illegally, or with unofficial sanction during droughts, until the declaration of the Kosciusko National Park in 1967 (the year in which the National Parks and Wildlife Act was passed, and the NSW NPWS came into being under the Minister for Lands). A report by Dr Graham Edgar in 1969 recommended the total abolition of grazing in the Park. It was accepted in 1972 and all leases were terminated, but the drought of 1973 saw 10 000 cattle allowed in on short-term agistment. The Park's first plan of management in 1974 ended the sorry story of grazing, over-grazing of specific plants including many endemics, soil erosion and loss of biodiversity, and destruction of whole ecosystems.

Research between 1976 and 1984 by the CSIRO investigated the impact of controlled burning, and grazing by native and feral animals (almost exclusively rabbits). Experimental plots on the sub-alpine Kiandra Plain were subjected to different fire and grazing practices and it was shown that the prescription for preserving the sub-alpine environment was **no burning**, **no livestock** and **no rabbits**. Rabbits greatly increase the amount of erosion-susceptible bare ground and they can have a devastating effect on alpine flower species.

Up to the time of these experiments, rabbits had not been seen as significant contributors to degradation because they were not present in alarming numbers. However, it was their selective grazing, just like that of introduced livestock, which had a drastic effect on some 39 palatable species (nine of which were completely eliminated from experimental plots). Their fondness for eating flower heads resulted in an overall decrease in seed setting; their preference for eating resprouting trees after fire and ring-barking burnt trees when green pick had not yet appeared after burning altered vegetation and reduced biodiversity; and the physical disturbance of soil due to their scratchings and burrows increased erosion.

The very presence of rabbits in the alpine country was shown by the experiments to be due to the 'unnatural' fire and livestock grazing which had made these areas (normally at the upper limits of their range) habitable for them. In dense shrub and tussock habitats, rabbits depend on fire to maintain their numbers. This implies that, left alone, the alpine country may rid itself of rabbits.[15] The impact of native mammals on the alpine environment was shown by the experiments to be sustainable, exerting no damaging grazing pressure on the vegetation.

Fire, of low intensity and relatively frequent (such as practiced during the snow lease era) was shown by the experiments to have brought about many changes. The decrease in biomass, and its corresponding effect on run-off, was found to persist for amazingly long periods. Twelve years after the last fire, biomass was still lower than that which approached the pre-grazing-burning status which gave soil stability and rainwater penetration without excessive run-off.

The fragility of the ecosystems of the high country is emphasised by these experiments. Because of the harshness of the climatic conditions, the precarious status of soils, the slow regeneration and recovery of perennials, and the vulnerability of the annual plants to selective grazing, balance is easily destroyed and very hard to restore. (As we shall see, the situation here on the roof of the continent is not unlike that in the equally fragile arid 75% of the land, for the same reasons.)

Rehabilitation and Regeneration: 'Thatching the Roof of the Continent'

Degradation was so severe when grazing ceased that it was realised that there was little chance that vegetation would regenerate naturally, and active reclamation and rehabilitation projects were started by the Soil Conservation Service and the Snowy Mountains Authority. The 'Summit Area Works Programme' began in 1957, concentrating on Carruthers Peak and the Mount Twynam area in the Main Range during the 1960s and 1970s.

Areas of active soil movement were stabilised by **hay-mulching (the 'thatching' of the area)**, fertilising and seeding with introduced (not native) species. A number of exotics were tested and *Lolium perenne* and *Agrostis tenuis* (rye and bent grass), and *Trifolium repens* and *T. pratens* (white and red clover) were found to be the best suited to the conditions. Fertilising with nitrogen, phosphorus and lime was found to be necessary to establish the exotics, but was found to be detrimental to the regeneration of native vegetation. The exotics stabilised the eroded areas, and by reducing the rate of fertiliser application over four years a transition to native plants was achieved.

Mulching was found to be a most important part of the revegetation process, protecting the soil from wind and water erosion and from frost heave. To prevent the mulch from blowing away it was mixed with bitumen emulsion or secured with wire netting. (Galvanised netting was found to produce toxic levels of zinc as it weathered, so black wire netting or jute mesh were substituted.) The amount of mulch required to achieve stability makes seed germination difficult, so there has been an increasing use of sods produced in nurseries and hardened to acclimatise to the harsh conditions. With the greater emphasis on native plants' introduction from the start instead of exotics, some

Revegetation works at the gravel pit near Seamans Hut.

NPWS, Kosciusko
Heritage Unit

MODERN AUSTRALIA

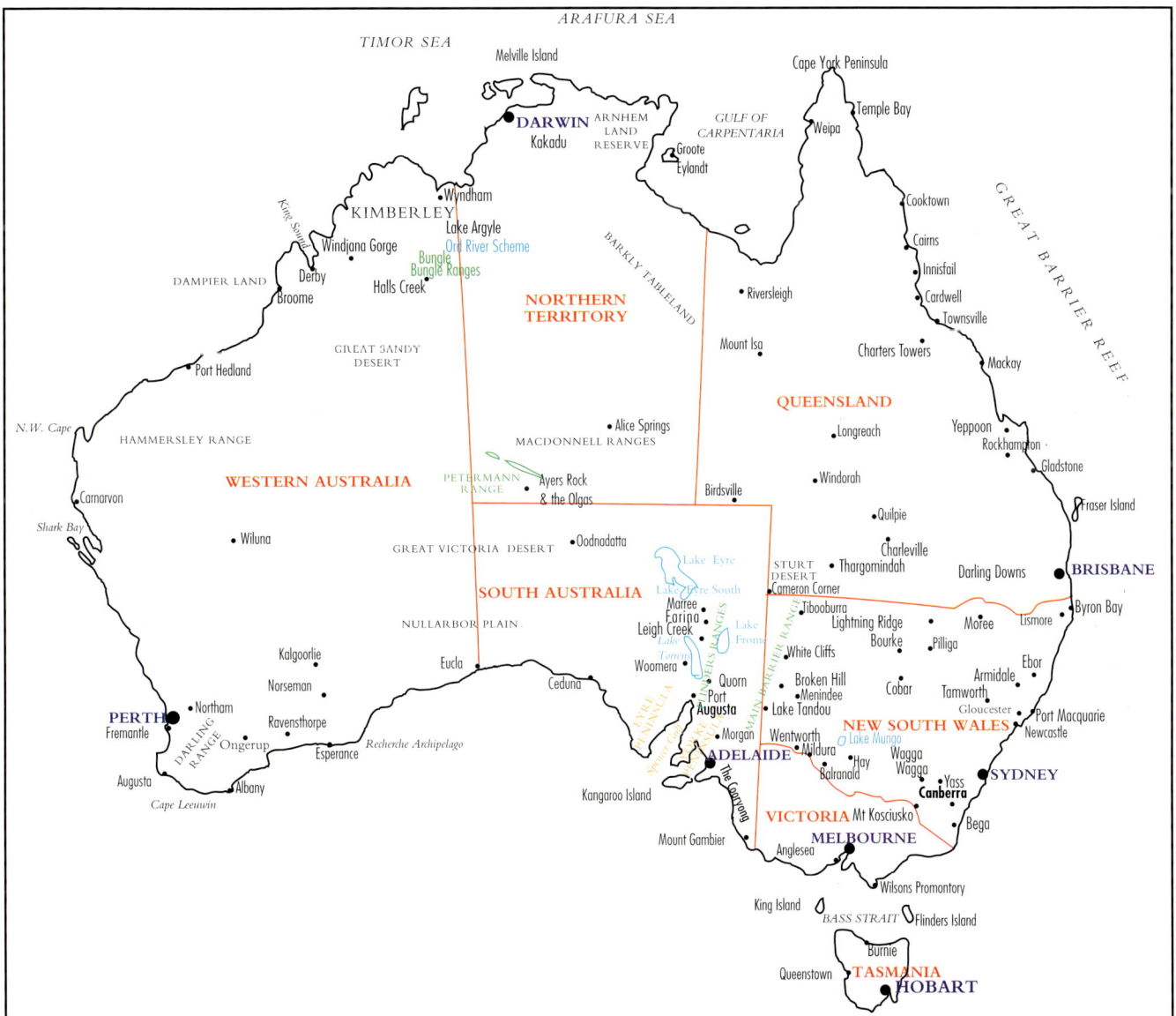

ARAFURA SEA

TIMOR SEA

Melville Island

DARWIN
Kakadu

ARNHEM
LAND
RESERVE

*GULF OF
CARPENTARIA*

Cape York Peninsula

Temple Bay

Weipa

Groote
Eylandt

Wyndham

KIMBERLEY

Lake Argyle
Ord River Scheme

Bungle
Bungle Ranges

Windjana Gorge

Derby

Halls Creek

DAMPIER LAND

Broome

King Sound

BARKLY TABLELAND

Cooktown

Cairns

Innisfail

Cardwell

Townsville

GREAT BARRIER REEF

GREAT SANDY
DESERT

Riversleigh

Mount Isa

Charters Towers

Mackay

Port Hedland

**NORTHERN
TERRITORY**

N.W. Cape

HAMMERSLEY RANGE

Alice Springs
MACDONNELL RANGES

QUEENSLAND

Longreach

Yeppoon

Rockhampton

Gladstone

Carnarvon

WESTERN AUSTRALIA

PETERMANN
RANGE

Ayers Rock
& the Olgas

Birdsville

Windorah

Shark Bay

Wiluna

GREAT VICTORIA DESERT

Oodnadatta

Lake Eyre

Lake Eyre South

STURT
DESERT

Cameron Corner

Charleville

Quilpie

Thargomindah

Darling Downs

BRISBANE

Fraser Island

Byron Bay

Marree
Farina
Leigh Creek

Lake
Torrens

Woomera

Lake
Frome

Tibooburra

Lightning Ridge

White Cliffs

Bourke

Lismore

Moree

Pilliga

NULLARBOR PLAIN

Eucla

Ceduna

Quorn

Port
Augusta

Broken Hill

Menindee

Lake Tandou

Cobar

Armidale

Tamworth

Ebor

Gloucester

Port Macquarie

Newcastle

Kalgoorlie

Norseman

Morgan

Wentworth

Mildura

Lake Mungo

NEW SOUTH WALES

PERTH
Fremantle

Northam

Ravensthorpe

Recherche Archipelago

DARLING
RANGE

Ongerup

Esperance

ADELAIDE

Balranald

Hay

Wagga
Wagga

Yass

SYDNEY

Augusta

Albany

Cape Leeuwin

Kangaroo Island

The Coorong

VICTORIA

Mt Kosciusko

Canberra

Bega

Mount Gambier

Anglesea

MELBOURNE

Wilsons Promontory

King Island

BASS STRAIT

Flinders Island

Burnie

Queenstown

TASMANIA

HOBART

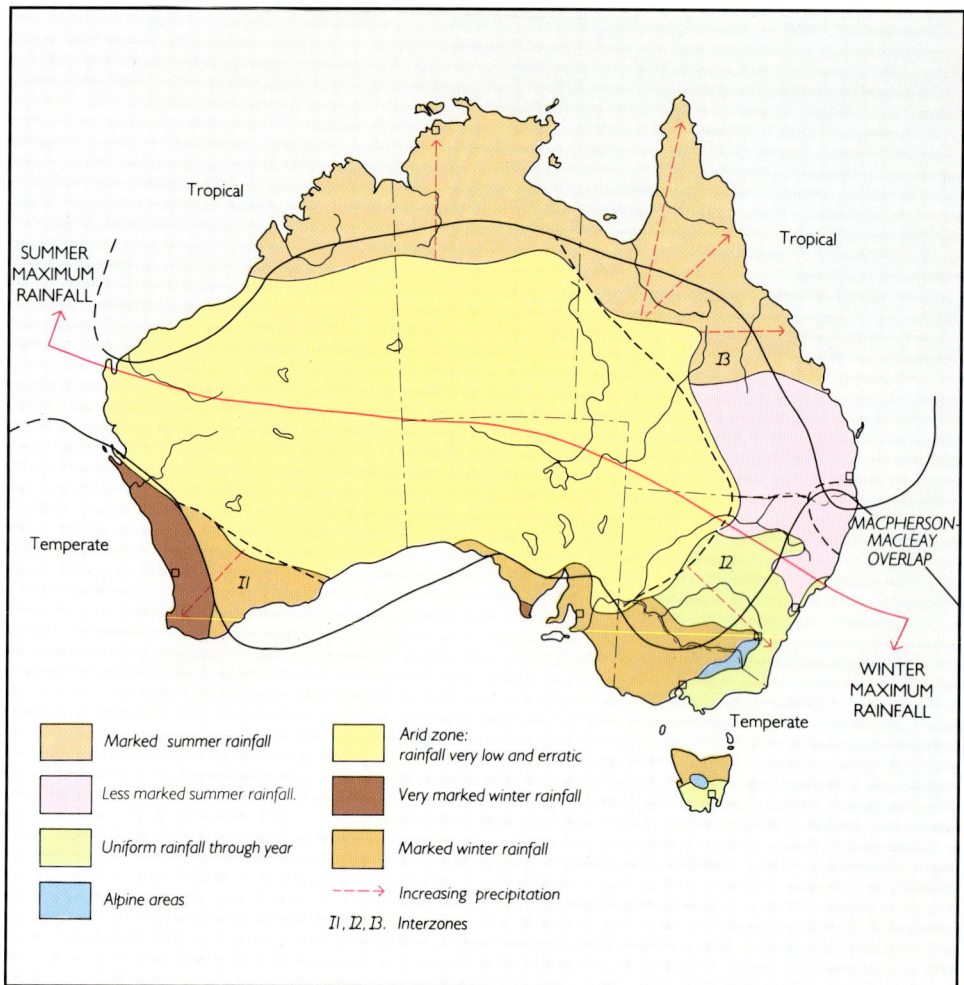

Tropical

Tropical

SUMMER
MAXIMUM
RAINFALL

I3

MACPHERSON-
MACLEAY
OVERLAP

Temperate

I1

I2

WINTER
MAXIMUM
RAINFALL

Temperate

	Marked summer rainfall			Arid zone: rainfall very low and erratic
	Less marked summer rainfall.			Very marked winter rainfall
	Uniform rainfall through year			Marked winter rainfall
	Alpine areas		– – – →	Increasing precipitation
			I1, I2, I3.	Interzones

native species like the mat-forming snow grass and a number of others are being used.

To re-establish snow gums it was necessary to plant nursery-grown seedlings in the many areas from which they had completely disappeared. In areas where they remained, regeneration is occurring naturally now that grazing has ceased. Ground cover, infiltration of rainwater, biodiversity and general amenity of the mountain pastures has greatly improved over the years. The process of rehabilitation has been slow and extremely expensive (up to $4000 a hectare in the most rapidly eroding bare areas) and the cost has only been met because of the necessity to protect the Snowy Scheme. Where similar severe erosion occurs in other parts of the continent there is no hope of the sort of funding needed for rehabilitation being made available. But at least we have to be grateful that an approximation of pre-grazing vegetation cover is being achieved and even if its composition is different its ecosystems have been pulled back from the brink of local extinction.

TOPOGRAPHICAL MAP

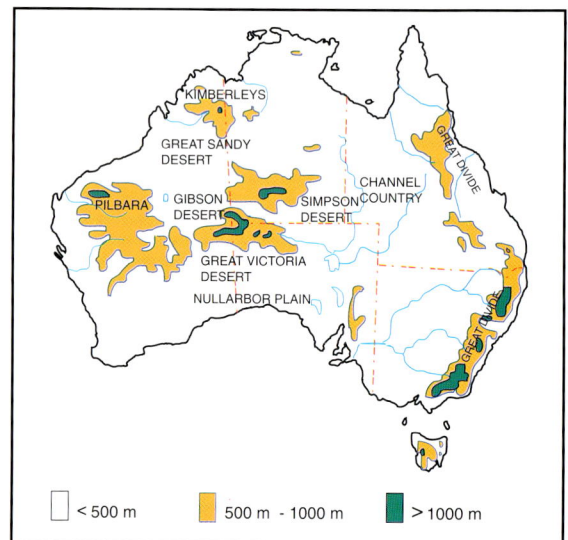

KIMBERLEYS

GREAT SANDY
DESERT

CHANNEL
COUNTRY

GREAT DIVIDE

PILBARA

GIBSON
DESERT

SIMPSON
DESERT

GREAT VICTORIA
DESERT

NULLARBOR PLAIN

GREAT

| | < 500 m | | | 500 - 1000 m | | | > 1000 m |

NATURAL VEGETATION

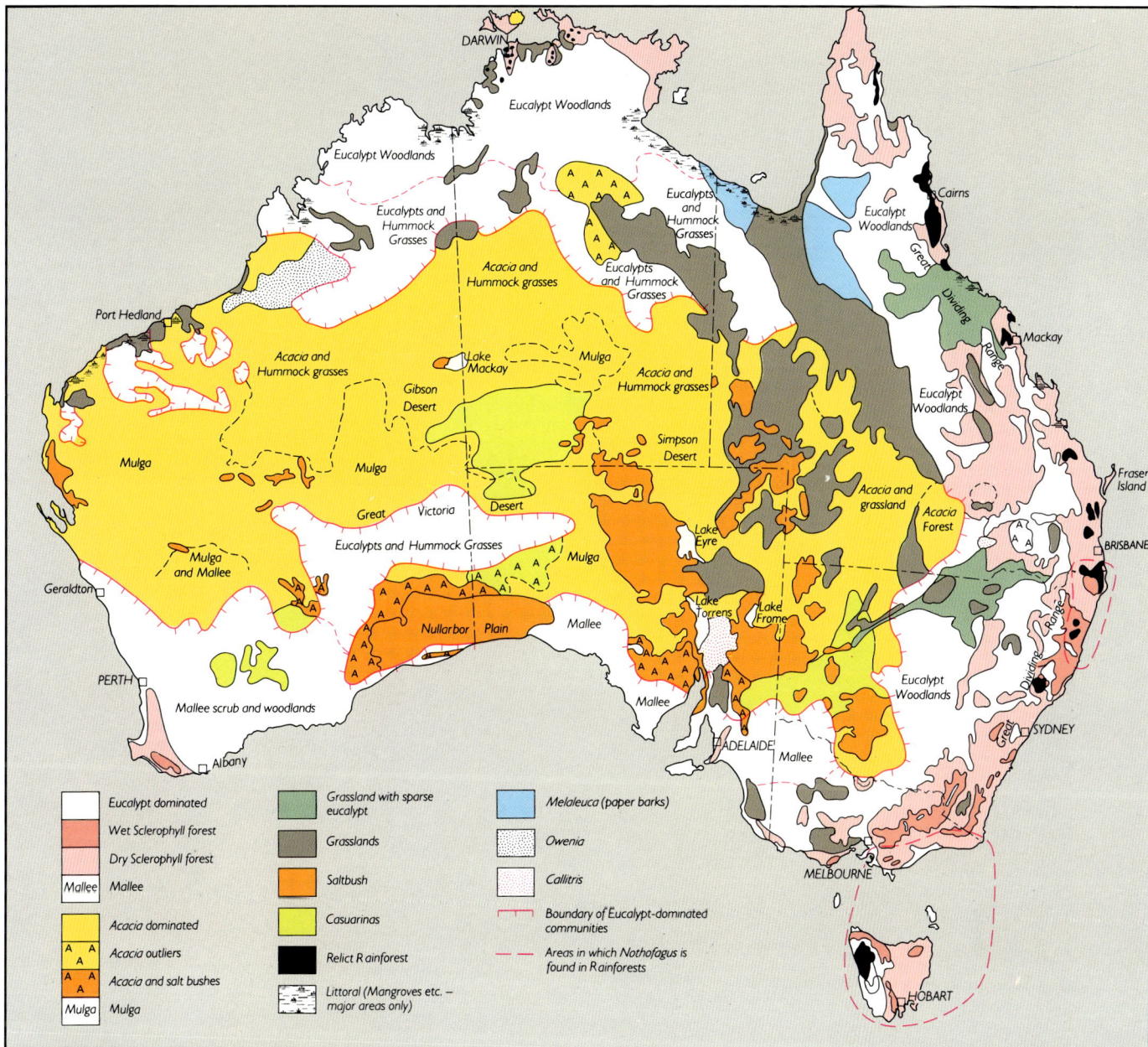

Legend:

- **Eucalypt dominated**
- **Wet Sclerophyll forest**
- **Dry Sclerophyll forest**
- Mallee **Mallee**
- **Acacia dominated**
- A A / A A **Acacia outliers**
- A A / A A **Acacia and salt bushes**
- Mulga **Mulga**

- **Grassland with sparse eucalypt**
- **Grasslands**
- **Saltbush**
- **Casuarinas**
- **Relict Rainforest**
- **Littoral (Mangroves etc. — major areas only)**

- **Melaleuca (paper barks)**
- **Owenia**
- **Callitris**
- **Boundary of Eucalypt-dominated communities**
- **Areas in which *Nothofagus* is found in Rainforests**

Map labels: DARWIN, Eucalypt Woodlands, Eucalypt Woodlands, Eucalypts and Hummock Grasses, Port Hedland, Acacia and Hummock grasses, Mulga, Geraldton, Mulga and Mallee, PERTH, Mallee scrub and woodlands, Albany, Acacia and Hummock grasses, Lake Mackay, Gibson Desert, Mulga, Great Victoria Desert, Eucalypts and Hummock Grasses, Nullarbor Plain, Mallee, Acacia and Hummock grasses, Mulga, Simpson Desert, Lake Eyre, Lake Torrens, Lake Frome, Mallee, ADELAIDE, Mallee, Eucalypts and Hummock Grasses, Eucalypts and Hummock Grasses, Acacia and grassland, Acacia Forest, Eucalypt Woodlands, Cairns, Mackay, Great Dividing Range, Fraser Island, BRISBANE, Eucalypt Woodlands, Great Dividing Range, SYDNEY, MELBOURNE, HOBART

CHAPTER ONE

AUSTRALIA'S CLIMATE, GLOBAL AND LOCAL

'GREENHOUSE', DEPLETION OF THE OZONE LAYER AND ENSO

GLOBAL WARMING: THE MAN-MADE GREENHOUSE EFFECT

For the first time in the history of life on earth, a species — the human species — has developed the capability of altering the global environment.

The sophisticated technology which has evolved since the mastering of the first technology — the use of fire — by early Hominids about 1.5 million years ago[16] has, among other things, modified the atmosphere to the extent that changes in its composition threaten to cause changes in global climate. It may be argued that global climate change, along with land and water degradation, is one of the most important issues facing human civilisation, with the potential to cause disruption and suffering on an unimaginable scale.

Two hundred leading scientists from 100 countries coming together under the auspices of the United Nations are a force to be reckoned with and a jury whose verdict may not be lightly dismissed. Such a gathering, in Madrid in November 1995, considered the evidence for global warming resulting from human activity and agreed that air pollution has begun to transform global weather patterns.[17]

There is no doubt at all that warming is occurring, although some doubt remains about how much is attributable to human activities and how much is natural — because the intricacies of climate and weather patterns are still so incompletely understood. Some leading scientists are still unconvinced that

climate modelling, the new discipline made possible by computers and used in predictions of climate change, is able to take all the necessary factors into account. Any human-induced effect on climate will be superimposed on the 'background noise' of natural climate variability. Volcanic eruptions and solar variability are the sort of external natural causes for changes; and we are living within the Pleistocene ice age and have no idea when our interglacial will start fluctuating towards the next glacial stage, or even what variability is 'normal' for this interglacial.

The concentration of carbon dioxide in the atmosphere has increased by 30% in the last 200 years; methane levels by 145% due to livestock increases and agriculture; nitrous oxide has been produced in dangerously significant quantities (15% increase) by burning fossil fuels (1992 values).[18] The theory of man-made Greenhouse is that these gases blanket the Earth and trap more heat, starting a progressive trend which is already having a measurable effect on global climate. According to the experts, records of temperature contained in ice cores from the Poles show that the last 100 years have been the warmest century for 600 years. Closer to home, Australia has seen overnight minimum temperatures increasing by between 0.1°C and 0.3°C each decade since 1950.

It is calculated that if the current rate of carbon dioxide emissions continues, levels will have doubled by the end of the next century, and average global temperature will have increased by between 2°C and 3.5°C, with the higher range more probable, altering climate and weather patterns considerably. (Considering the rapid emergence of the Third World as consumer societies one can see doubling as a possibility during the next generation.) In Australia, the most recent estimates of average temperature increases made by the CSIRO [16] indicate that **increases of 2.5°C may occur by 2030, and that by 2070 some parts of the continent may have warmed by 5°C. An increase in rainfall of 20% in the north and a corresponding decrease in the south is also** **considered likely by 2070**. Many greenhouse gases remain in the atmosphere for a long time (carbon dioxide and nitrous oxide, from many decades to centuries).

The microscopic air-borne particles (aerosols) which accumulate in the troposphere as a result of burning biomass (forest, bush and grass fires), fossil fuels and other sources, can have a local effect which offsets warming by Greenhouse gases. These aerosols are

ICE CORES FROM ANTARCTICA

A research project to find out how carbon dioxide levels have fluctuated in the last 30 000 years

The CSIRO Division of Antarctic Research is currently analysing the data obtained from an ice core taken from the Deep Ice Drilling Project on the Law Dome. The age of the ice can be estimated by counting annual 'rings' — layers whose composition changes throughout the year because summer snow has a higher proportion of oxygen-18 isotope than winter snow. Samples of known age are crushed and the carbon dioxide which was contained in bubbles of air in them is measured. A graph can then be made showing carbon dioxide content against age. Between the years 1600 and 1800 the carbon dioxide level is believed to have been about 280 parts per million (ppm) by volume.

CARBON DIOXIDE LEVELS OVER THE LAST FIVE CENTURIES

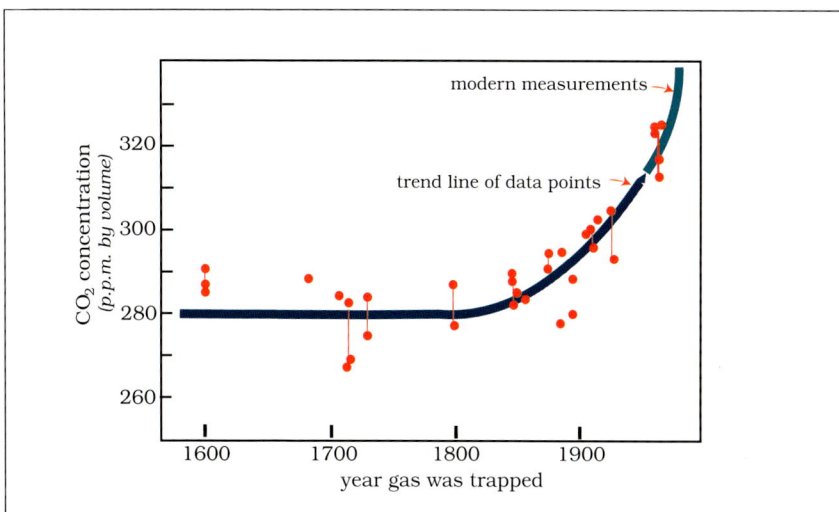

After Bell. [18]

CARBON DIOXIDE AND TEMPERATURE FLUCTUATIONS DURING 175 000 YEARS.

When information on levels is assembled for 175 000 years ago from ice cores and from marine sediment data (where carbon-13 content of tests of microscopic marine animals varies according to carbon dioxide concentration) it can be seen that there has been great fluctuation in carbon dioxide in the atmosphere through time. During glacial stages of the Pleistocene ice age levels were low; during warm interglacials, high.

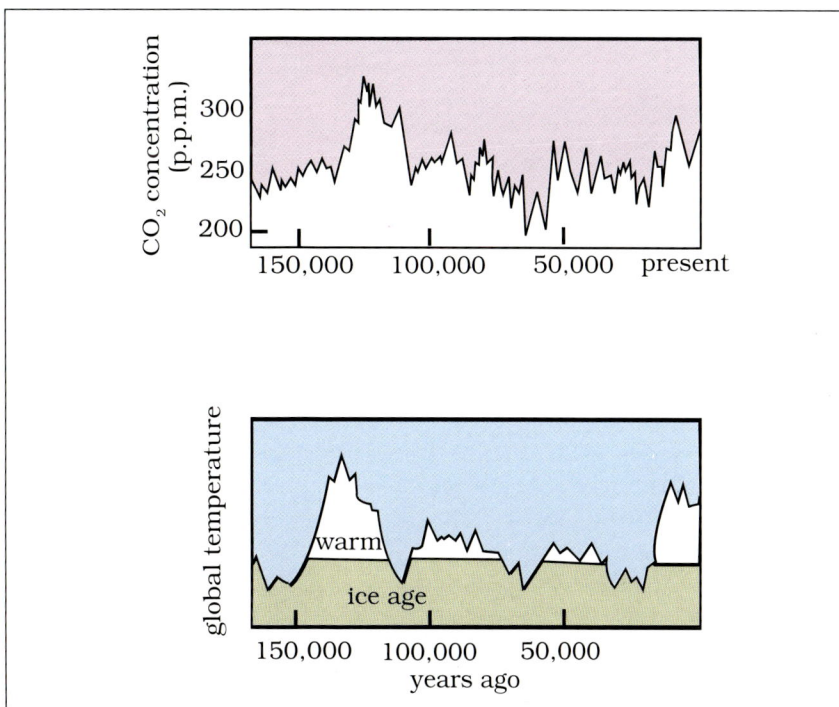

After Bell. [18]

short-lived. However, it is frequently stated that biomass burning, particularly in the tropical savannas, is a significant source of atmospheric trace gases contributing to global warming. This has been poorly quantified and, according to CSIRO scientists, cannot be readily assessed.[20] Their work in the Australian tropical savannas has seemed to show that frequent, low intensity and patchy fires are unlikely to make a substantial contribution to Greenhouse.

With Third World countries set to adopt more First World practices and with increasing global over-population, logic alone would tell us that the Greenhouse is inevitable and we had better start planning for it now. More people means more land clearing, and land clearing itself causes carbon dioxide increase. The benefits of any controls which act on the present situation and reduce the immediate risks must surely be out-weighed by the inevitable increases in greenhouse emissions that enormous increases in population will cause. The exponential nature of global population increase is a mathematical certainty. Future generations will be operating in a changed world, though how changed is not certain because of all the unknown factors in this Gaia-driven planet. (The concept of Earth acting like a living organism — **Gaia** — with all its systems, animate and inanimate, interacting and maintaining some measure of balance offers some hope that the effects will be modified.[1])

The value of actively growing vegetation in taking up carbon dioxide is demonstrated by calculations made at the Tropical Beef Centre in Rockhampton. About 60 million hectares of badly over-grazed land is currently being 'woody weed' invaded as a result of changed fire practices and the over-grazing, which has destroyed pasture and caused removal of most of the stock. A figure of 130 million tonnes is given for the carbon tied up in this re-vegetation of the region.

The consequences of global warming have been computer modelled and we know what to expect in addition to the higher temperatures.

- **Melting ice** will cause a global sea-level rise. (Melting ice releases methane itself, adding to greenhouse gases.) Sea-level changes are hard to measure as the Earth's crust is sensitive to loading and unloading. Isostatic uplift can outpace the tendency for sea-level to rise, and continental margins tend to tilt. For example: the eastern side of the Gulf of Carpentaria has risen about 3 m in the last 6000 years; shoreline of the Eyre Peninsula in South Australia has been stable over 6000 years, while at Port Augusta it has dropped 3 m, and at Port Adelaide it has risen 3 m — with little change in surrounding regions.
- **With the atmospheric heating engine running at higher speed, stronger air and ocean circulation will result.** Rain will come increasingly in storms with less gentle, soaking falls in warmer regions. Severity and frequency of hurricanes and cyclones will increase and their

range will be greater than now. There will be an increase in the occurrence of extremely hot days, and a decrease in extremely cold days.

- **Climatic zones will shift** with some regions becoming better watered, others drier. **Deserts will expand, and the heartlands of continents will become drier. Lands on the border of subtropical arid zones will be most affected** (which has great significance for Australia).
- **Increased carbon dioxide will promote plant growth** where water and soil are suitable. (Laboratory tests exposing plants to carbon dioxide levels such as are predicted for the mid 2000s resulted in up to 50% increase in wheat and rice yields, though nutritional value of the grain was much decreased.) An increase in carbon dioxide concentration changes the competitive balance between plants which use Carbon-3 (broad-leaved shrubs and trees) and Carbon-4 (warm-season grasses) nutritional pathways. This may already be making some contribution to the 'woody weed' problems which are increasing globally in over-grazed grasslands.

Although it is impossible at this stage to sort out 'normal' climatic fluctuations from man-made effects and to apportion the blame for observed changes which are increasingly giving cause for concern, the list of warming indicators increases steadily, making more and more plausible the proposition that greenhouse global warming has already commenced.

- Satellites have been measuring the **decrease in sea ice** around Antarctica and in the Arctic. Arctic sea ice was decreasing by 2.5% a decade in the 1980s but the rate of decrease now is 4.3%. (Eskimos, of whom 113 000 follow a traditional lifestyle in Greenland, Alaska and Northern

ANTARCTICA: RETREAT OF THE ICE

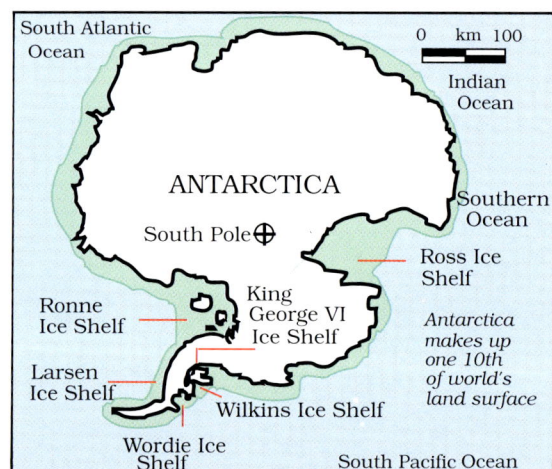

Antarctica is a very large landmass, comprising 10% of the Earth's land surface. Its enormous ice cap, three kilometres thick in parts, depresses the land with its weight, and much of the continent is below sea-level. Its ice shelves are beginning to melt with global warming.

THE SUB-ANTARCTIC AND ITS ISLAND GROUPS

Indicators of Climatic Change

THE SUB-ANTARCTIC REGION

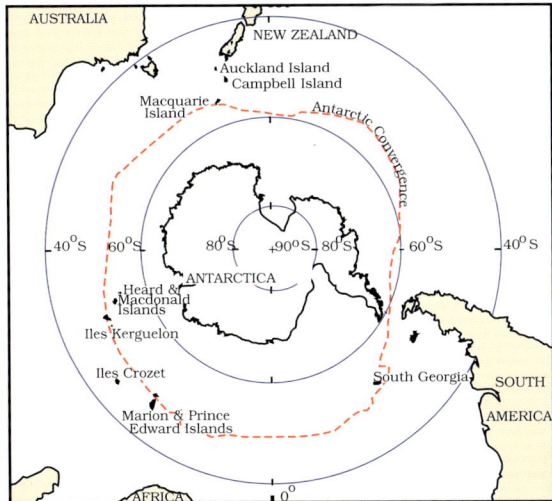

After Selkirk, 1992 [21]

The **Southern Ocean** occupies a vast region of the globe between 40°S and 60°S. An important oceanographic boundary, the **Antarctic Convergence**, lies within it. This is the zone about 150 km wide where cold Antarctic surface water (2°C) from the south meets warmer Sub-Antarctic surface water (4°C) from the north. The position of the convergence moves within about 4 degrees of latitude, its position being determined by the circulation patterns of oceanic water bodies. Atmospheric conditions may also affect its position.

Six island groups lie within the Sub-Antarctic zone, situated close to the Antarctic Convergence. To the north: Macquarie Island; Iles Crozet; Marion and Prince Edward Islands. Iles Kerguelon lie on the mean position of the Convergence. South Georgia and the Heard and Macdonald Islands lie to the south. (Islas Diego Ramirez, an island group which lies south of Tierra del Fuego and north of the Convergence is sometimes included to make a seventh Sub-Antarctic island group.)

It is usually cool, cloudy and windy on Sub-Antarctic islands. It is almost always wet, whether it be from mist, drizzle, rain, sleet, hail, soft hail or snow — according to Dr Pat Selkirk who spends a great deal of time on Macquarie Island.[21] Air temperature is close to that of the surrounding ocean (but wind-chill makes conditions unpleasant).

Vegetation on the islands is of tussock grasslands, herbfields, fernbrakes, mires, cushion-plant communities and feldmark (where mosses and lichens are very important components of the vegetation). The islands are without trees or upright shrubs. They are important breeding grounds for a number of ocean-based mammal and bird species like fur seals, elephant seals, penguins, albatrosses, petrels and prions. There are no indigenous terrestrial mammals, but introduced species like rats and cats are present on all except Heard and Macdonald, causing problems.

The Sub-Antarctic is a highly sensitive region where global warming is already clearly evident. Its ocean and islands are warming more rapidly than the rest of the world. The effects of higher temperatures on land vegetation and on the marine-based mammals and birds (whose feeding grounds, and their proximity to their breeding grounds, are dependent on ocean currents) are likely to be great.

Above top: Royal penguins in the vast rookery at Hurd Point. The slopes behind are covered in tussock grass (Poa foliosa).

Above middle: Elephant seal weaners lying on washed-up seaweed, Durvillaea antarctica on a Macquarie Island beach. The pups are fed incredibly rich milk for eight weeks and grow at an enormous rate. When they are weaned, like these babies, they are on their own and will feed themselves when they have mastered swimming and hunting.

Above: Moulting male elephant seals at Middle Beach in tussock grasses (Poa foliosa) with Macquarie Island cabbage (Stilbocarpa polaris) in the background. Stilbocarpa is a member of the family Araliaceae, a tropical family, apart from this genus, which includes Queensland umbrella trees.

DR PATRICIA SELKIRK

Feldmark on the plateau, a mosaic of gravel and stripes of vegetation. (The stripes are the product of the winds which blow strong and cold across the landscape.) The bright green patches are cushion plants (Azorella macquariensis) and the golden brown are moss (Rhacomitrium crispulum).

DR PATRICIA SELKIRK

An increase in ambient temperature would result in greater photosynthetic activity and perhaps increased plant productivity. Alien species would find it easier to become naturalised on the islands, and the risk of alteration to natural ecosystems would be greater. Some shrubby vegetation would soon become possible.

Macquarie Island, ENSO and Global Warming

Macquarie Island is a sensitive indicator of climatic trends because of its global situation. It lies in high latitudes like the other Sub-Antarctic islands, and shows the same warming trends as they do. Because it also lies at a longitude close to, but on the eastern side of, the boundary between the eastern (Pacific) and western (India-Australia) limbs of the Southern Oscillation, a region of frequent ridge formation and blocking in the Southern Hemisphere circulation, it is a valuable site for monitoring climatic variability. In terms of temperature, its record matches that of the area east and south-east of New Zealand, rather than that of Tasmania. Atmospheric pressures in the Southern Ocean to the east and west result in either warm north-easterly or cold southerly airflow over the island.[22]

Monitoring of mean temperatures in the region east and south of Australia and New Zealand has shown that the higher the latitude, the more pronounced the warming on a string of islands from the edge of Antarctica to north of New Zealand, including Macquarie Island.

The contrast between this region of the Southern Ocean and similar regions to the west is due to the fact that Macquarie Island is in a zone of cyclone decay, and no cyclones form east of it. One of the most

FIVE-YEAR RUNNING MEANS OF ANNUAL MEAN TEMPERATURE ON THE ISLANDS

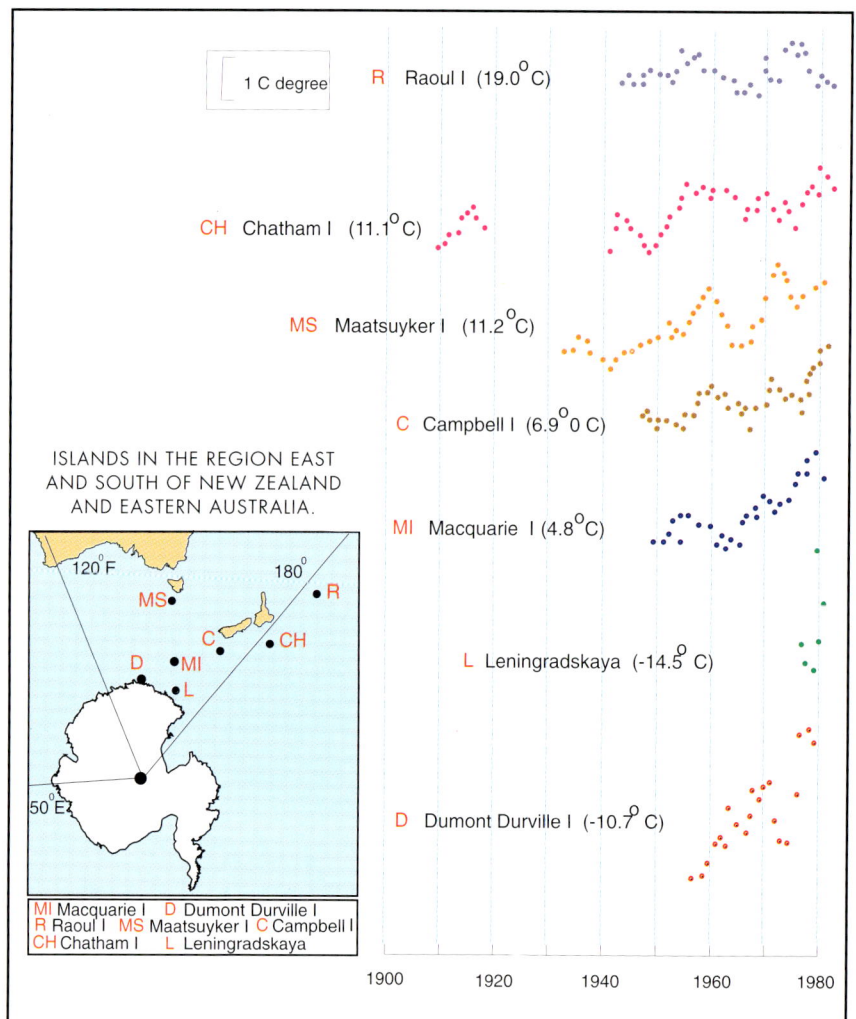

1 C degree

R   Raoul I (19.0°C)

CH   Chatham I (11.1°C)

MS   Maatsuyker I (11.2°C)

C   Campbell I (6.9°0 C)

MI   Macquarie I (4.8°C)

L   Leningradskaya (-14.5°C)

D   Dumont Durville I (-10.7°C)

ISLANDS IN THE REGION EAST AND SOUTH OF NEW ZEALAND AND EASTERN AUSTRALIA.

120°F   180°
MS•   •R
    C•   •CH
D •MI
   •L
50°E

MI Macquarie I	D Dumont Durville I
R Raoul I	MS Maatsuyker I C Campbell I
CH Chatham I	L Leningradskaya

1900   1920   1940   1960   1980

After Adamson et al. [22]

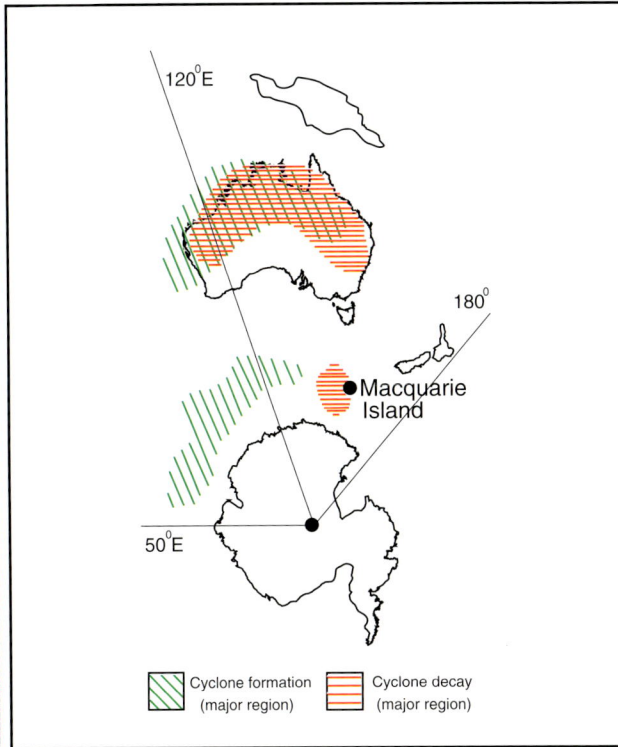
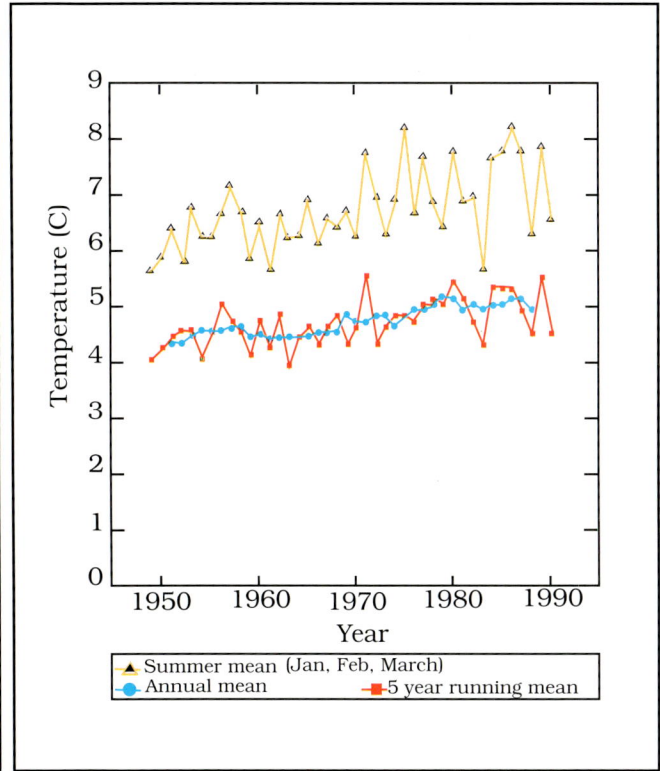
intense areas of cyclone formation is situated to the west, south of the Indian Ocean and Western Australia. The largest waves of the Southern Ocean are generated here. (It has recently been observed that the retreat of sea ice around Antarctica has been in this zone.)

The temperature record for Macquarie Island showed that it is warming at twice the global average rate, with a 1°C average warming trend in the period from 1949 to 1986. The trend accelerated in the last 20 years of the period with eight of the 10 warmest years occurring in the last decade.

The greatest average warming has occurred in late summer, the lowest in spring. In severe ENSO years the island cools. Considering that the annual mean temperature of Macquarie Island is 4.8°C, the warming is most significant and can be expected to cause alterations in the vegetation.

Canada, complain that the ice on which they hunt is becoming dangerously thin and the habits of polar bears and other wildlife are changing.) In the Antarctic, decrease has been at 1.4% a decade, and more than 8000 km² of ice shelf on the Antarctic Peninsula had been lost in 50 years as temperatures in the region have risen by 2.5°C. According to British Antarctic Survey scientists, massive disintegration of ice shelves took place in 1995 when, in just 50 days, 1300 km² of the Larsen Ice Shelf broke off, sending huge icebergs into the Weddell Sea. Retreat of the ice is far more widespread than had been thought and involves breaking up of the Wordie Ice Shelf between the Antarctic Peninsula and James Ross Island, and disintegration of the Muller Ice Shelf. The **Wilkins Ice Shelf** in Alexander Island just off the Peninsula is now also threatened. The **King George VI Ice Shelf** has been known for some time to be beginning to disintegrate at depth.

Melting sea ice does not cause significant sea-level rise as sea ice is floating and already displacing its own weight of water, but melting of ice on Antarctica and Greenland would add volume to seawater globally.

- Surface temperature of the Indian Ocean has increased by 0.5°C in the last 50 years.
- The annual average temperature on Macquarie Island is increasing at twice the rate of the rest of the world, while the average annual ocean temperature adjacent to the island has increased steadily from the 4.5°C measured by Sir Douglas Mawson's expedition in 1912 to more than 5.4°C. An alarming decrease in the number of penguins and elephant seals on the island is raising questions about whether the warmer sea and changed ocean currents has affected the food chain in high latitudes.
- Vegetation has been increasing in biomass on Sub-Antarctic islands.
- In Europe there has been a decrease in the day to day variability of temperature.

- 1994 was the eighteenth year in a row in which world surface temperatures were higher than the 1951–1980 average. Recent years have been among the warmest since 1860, despite the cooling effect of the 1991 Mt Pinatubo eruption.
- Regional changes are also evident. For example, the recent warming has been greatest over the mid-latitude continents in winter and spring, with a few areas of cooling, such as the North Atlantic Ocean (where higher waves and wilder storms have also been reported). Precipitation has increased over the land in high latitudes of the Northern Hemisphere, especially during the cold season.
- Temperatures in the South Pacific increased by between 0.4°C and 0.8°C from 1951 to 1993 and Australia has experienced up to a 1°C rise this century. The Australasian region is heating up faster than anywhere else. In Australia, 12 of the 15 hottest years recorded have occurred since 1978.
- The CSIRO Division of Atmospheric Research has recorded an increase in heavy rainfall events in 46 of its 53 meteorological stations in the tropical north since 1910, with an increase of 20% in quantity of rain, which bears out the predictions for rainfall behaviour under Greenhouse.
- Glaciers are retreating on mountains worldwide, particularly in the Alps.
- Fewer frosts are occurring in some parts of eastern Australia.
- The 1990 to mid-1995 persistent warm phase of ENSO was unusual in the context of the last 120 years. (ENSO is the acronym for the El Nino–Southern Oscillation climatic regime, see pages 37-42.)

The **remedies required to avert a Greenhouse crisis** — cleaner air by controlling emissions of greenhouse gases — are beneficial and improve the quality of life, so all possible measures should be taken now for this reason, particularly as they also serve as an insurance against future, more serious, consequences.

The problems of rising sea-level if Greenhouse warming has started must be considered seriously by governments worldwide. With the concentration of major cities along coastlines and realistic estimates suggesting a rise of 95 cm in the next 100 years,[17] policies must be put in place to minimise effects, particularly as the rate of rise may have been substantially underestimated. We now know that sea-level changes in the glacial-interglacial stages of the Pleistocene ice age were very rapid. It will be too late to start planning when rising sea-level has begun to affect peoples' lives, and to threaten the very survival of populations in Bangladesh and the Pacific Islands. Regional sea-level changes may differ from the global mean value owing to land movement and ocean current changes, and this added hazard must be taken into account.

Australia has reason to be concerned at the prospect of rising sea-level. It is the flattest of all the continents with coastlines sculpted by sea-level changes of the last 2.6 million years of the Pleistocene ice age. To select just a few examples: In the drowned valley systems like Sydney Harbour, even a small rise will cause inconvenience; coastal housing estates on sand bars and in estuaries will be more than 'canal' estates; the coastal lake systems protected now by sand bars, the low-lying swampy areas adjacent to the coast and mouths of major rivers are all at risk; in Western Australia the Swan Coastal Plain, which already has to be drained, will have major problems with even a modest change in sea-level; the floodplains of the major rivers in tropical northern Australia will be converted to salt-marsh country, and wetlands of Kakadu National Park will be affected; if water rise is more rapid than coral growth, the very survival of the Great Barrier Reef could be threatened.

Measurements of sea-level change over the last 50 years in Australia have shown a 2 mm per year rise. (New Zealand, with measurements made only over the last 25 years, records a similar rise.)

Climatologists predict that, for Australia, Greenhouse will mean, in addition to sea-level changes and overall rise in mean temperature, a number of other serious effects. The arid and semi-arid zones of central and western Australia will expand; in New South Wales the semi-arid zone will eat into valuable arable land. The southern fringes of the continent will be drier and less suited to agriculture. Western Tasmania will be wetter. Cyclones which now track across the top of Australia and down the northern quarter of the east coast will be more frequent and will travel further down the coast, possibly as far as Sydney. Rainfall, overall, will be more frequently in the form of storms with local heavy falls, with fewer rain days.

Changed rainfall patterns and amounts will have potentially serious consequences for dams which have been built with the 'worst case' flood in mind. Worst case under Greenhouse regimes may be considerably different and floods of great magnitude may come more frequently than the once in 100 or 200 years, and the ultimate super-flood once in 1000 years, which is the accepted probability under normal climate regimes.

Now when there is consensus about global warming (whether human induced or natural) beginning to affect world climate, it is surely already amoral to allow developments on low-lying coastal plains, in river mouths, adjacent to rivers which will flood when their waters back up against tides, and particularly in the 'canal estates' so favoured by developers. Waterfront property with buildings close to present tidelines will no longer be the most sought-after real estate.

Superimposed on all the changes due to global warming, ENSO will still add a further dimension of unpredictability. It is anticipated that **major swings in the Southern Oscillation Index will be more**

frequent. There may already be evidence that El Nino droughts will be longer and that the pattern of climatic swings may alter. The most recent El Nino drought (1992–95) persisted for 51 months (and continues into 1996 in some parts of western Queensland), making it the longest on record and much longer than the drought of 40 months between 1911 and 1916. Since 1976, El Ninos have outnumbered La Ninas by four to one, and this may have something to do with global warming. ENSO-related climate fluctuations make predictions and measurements of global warming difficult, masking the gradual and still small-scale changes.

Australia's contributions to the global problems of atmospheric pollution might be thought to be relatively insignificant compared to those of other lands because of our small population numbers. Our fortunate situation as an island continent means that we are not the direct recipient of air pollution caused by other lands. We are not reminded, like Canada is when its maple forests die because of acid rain blown in from Europe and the USA, of the serious world situation, and we are complacent in our imagined isolation. **Yet we cannot escape the global consequences of the man-made Greenhouse — one world, one atmosphere — and it is sobering to find that, measured on a per capita basis, Australian production of greenhouse gases is the highest in the world.**

In spite of United Nations Conventions aimed at a global reduction of greenhouse gases, to which Australia has been a signatory, there has been no improvement in the situation here. Not by one tonne has our estimated production of 572 million tonnes of carbon dioxide per year been decreased. At a government level, the supply of cheaper power to promote economic growth is in conflict with the urgent need to curb waste and use as little coal-generated electricity as possible while actively seeking solar and other alternatives. A proposed carbon tax was abandoned for political reasons in 1995, being too close to a Federal election for comfort, and we have yet to see whether the latest Inter-governmental initiative, 'Greenhouse 21C', will have any more results than its predecessors did. At a citizen level, each of us can be more responsible in our use of electricity, gas and the hydrocarbons which we consume in transport.

Air Quality in Cities

If we want cleaner air in our cities we can no longer countenance the increase in the vehicle kilometres travelled (VKT) index, which for the Sydney statistical district, for example, showed a rise of more than 30% in the last two decades. The single largest source of air pollution in cities is motor vehicles and it has been improvements in technology which have led, over the last decade and up to now, to a most welcome improvement in air quality. The point has now been reached where the increased number of vehicles and their increased use means that the improvements with current technology are no longer enough to hold the situation. Deteriorating air quality is inevitable. We now need fewer cars, each being used less, and new technology which will cut emissions further if we are not to see a return to photochemical smog in our large cities.

DEPLETION OF THE OZONE LAYER

While Australia's record in controlling greenhouse gases has been a non-event, the contribution we have made to measures to save the ozone layer has been exemplary.

The extraordinarily delicate balances in which the biosphere operates are epitomised by the ozone layer. The **biosphere** is the living skin on the inanimate planet which makes Earth unique in our solar system.

In the beginning, more than 3.5 billion years ago, first life was confined to the waters of the planet because it required a protective layer — water — to shield it from the harmful short-wave (UV) radiation of the sun. Early life-forms were busily making oxygen by virtue of their green pigment and the process of photosynthesis, and for the first 1.5 billion years or so the oxygen was being used up in oxidising materials in the watery environment. There was no oxygen in the atmosphere and no ozone layer. Then when saturation point was reached in the water, oxygen began to leak into the atmosphere. As oxygen levels rose over the next 1.5 billion years, an ozone layer formed from oxygen which had risen into the stratosphere.

At last, and only about 450 million years ago, the ozone layer was dense enough to filter out sufficient radiation to allow life to emerge from under the protection of water and start to colonise the land. Evolution since that dramatic leap forward has led to the establishment of the Plant Kingdom with all its divisions derived from the algae, the original single Division in the water; and to vertebrate evolution from fish in the sea to amphibians, then reptiles and mammals, and ultimately to humans — a species now capable of destroying the biosphere.

Ozone, the three-atom form of oxygen, forms in the upper atmosphere from the action of sunlight, and shields us from 90% of the sun's damaging ultraviolet radiation. A 1% loss of ozone would lead to a 2% rise in UVB — the type of radiation known to damage DNA, causing skin cancer and damage to certain plant and animal tissues. Ozone continually forms and breaks down in chemical processes, which are sensitive to a number of reactive gases, particularly the chlorine monoxide radical produced when chlorofluorocarbons (CFCs) break down in the upper atmosphere.

The evidence for ozone depletion is incontrovertible. In the last two decades, ozone levels in the Southern Hemisphere south of the Tropic of Capricorn, in mid-latitudes, fell by 4.9% as measured from satellites, and by 3.9% by ground-based

A FLOOD HISTORY RECORDED IN LIMESTONE GORGES OF THE KIMBERLEY REGION

Evidence of super-floods in the past

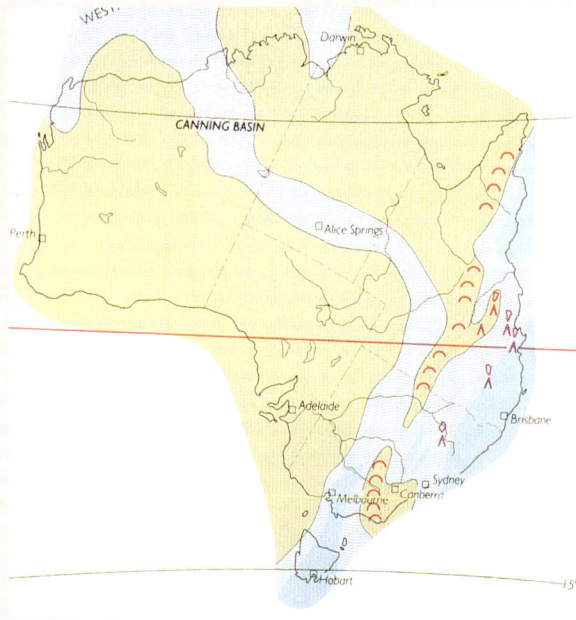

PALAEOGEOGRAPHY OF THE EARLY TO MID DEVONIAN
400 to 380 million years ago

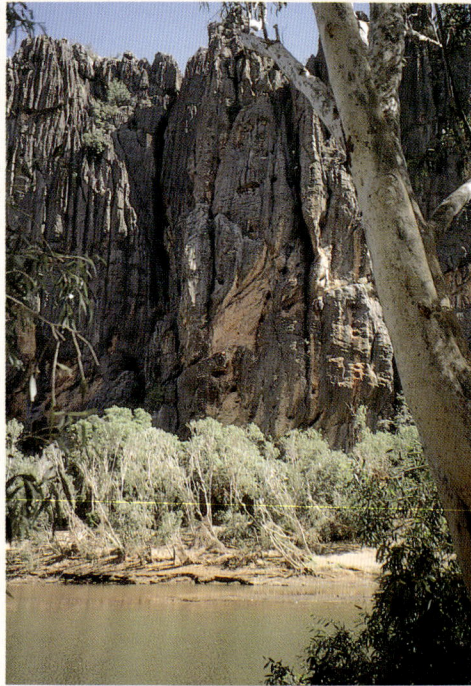

Far left: Palaeogeographic map of the Early to Middle Devonian, 400 to 380 million years ago. A seaway ran across Australia and its fringing reefs along the edges of the Kimberley and Pilbara blocks (ancient cratons) today stand like ramparts in the landscape.

Left: Winjana Gorge.

Below: A freshwater crocodile in the Lennard River in Winjana Gorge.

Bottom: Geike Gorge.

M.E.W.

As part of the Kimberley Research Project organised by the Royal Geographical and Linnean Societies, palaeo-flood studies were undertaken in gorges which cut through the Napier and Oscar Ranges, which are parts of a Devonian limestone reef complex.[23]

The Lennard River winds its way through Winjana Gorge in the Napier Range, which is a section of the Devonian reef which fringed the Kimberley Block when an epicontinental sea covered this part of Australia. Above the high-water mark left by average monsoonal floods, scientists have discovered less visible signs left by higher-than-average and 'worst case' floods, in the form of deposits of silt and debris (slack water deposits) in caves and on ledges in the walls of the Gorge. Four depositional levels for floods higher than the average have been recognised and dated.

The lowest of these slackwater deposits fall within the range of the mean annual flood and two of them are believed to represent the recorded high flood of 1983. Partial erosion makes for problems in stratigraphy and only six deposits have survived at the two lowest-level sites in 500 years. The next highest flood level is dated at 2000 years ago, and the highest remnant slackwater deposit was left by a super-flood 2800 years ago. Interpretation of the results is that only one flood in two thousand years has equalled the 1986 flood, and only one in 3000 years has exceeded it.

Such a record is of value in establishing what are 'normal' fluctuations in water volume in rivers as a basis for predicting height of floods under changed rainfall conditions.

The Fitzroy River cuts through the Oscar Range, part of the ancient Devonian fringing reef, along Geike Gorge. The towering limestone cliffs of the gorge show the regular high water mark of annual floods caused by the monsoon. The well-washed lower section of the cliffs is pink, while the part which is above flood-level is dark grey.

measurements. The vortex-like hole in the ozone layer over Antarctica, which develops each spring, was first recognised in 1985, and found to have concentrations depleted by up to 50%. The British Antarctic Survey found during 1995 that the hole was getting bigger and ozone concentrations within it had dropped by 63%. In addition, it persisted into January and February, exposing Antarctica to extra UV radiation during the summer. When the hole dissipated in early summer, 'filaments' with 10% ozone depletion come across southern Australia.

Tasmania and the South Island of New Zealand have some reason for concern, and what effect the southern hole will have on fauna in Antarctica, on the flora and fauna on the Sub-Antarctic Islands, and in particular on the planktonic life in the Southern Ocean has yet to be determined. Already it has been suggested that certain phytoplankton, and *Phaeocystis antarctica* in particular, are becoming more numerous. In laboratory experiments it has been found that increased exposure to UVB radiation leads to rapid proliferation of *Phaeocystis*, whose colonies produce a bladder-like protective shield containing an effective sunscreen protein, while diatoms and other forms decline in numbers.

The Southern Ocean represents 20% of the world's oceans. The micro-organisms in it are part of the lungs of the planet, processing carbon dioxide, and involved in the sulphur cycle where the release of dimethyl sulphide from natural die-off of phytoplankton supplies the nuclei for cloud formation. (A wonderful example of the nexus between life and the inanimate environment where their interaction makes Earth life-friendly.)

There appears to be new evidence of a second Southern Hemisphere hole developing over southern Australia and New Zealand in winter — June, July and August — distinct from the vortex over Antarctica in the spring. How serious it is and what effect it might have, bearing in mind that in winter solar radiation is less intense, has yet to be measured.

Recently a vortex-like hole has started to develop over Northern Hemisphere high latitudes, causing increasing anxiety because it lies over populated regions, unlike the South Polar hole whose major impact is on areas without people.

When it was realised that the chlorine in CFCs, used as coolants in fridges and air conditioners, as propellants for aerosols and in production of polystyrene; and halons, used in fire-fighting, were the main offenders in damaging the ozone layer, Australia became a world leader in their control and in eliminating them from production.

The good news is that global control of ozone-depleting chemicals should allow the ozone layer to start to recover by the year 2000. Growth in the concentrations of CFCs has slowed to about zero, though hydrochlorofluorocarbons (HCFCs) are still rising. Implementation of the Montreal Protocol is progressing. The CSIRO Division of Atmospheric Research has confirmed that chlorine levels monitored from Cape Grim in Tasmania are falling already.

The Cape Grim Monitoring Station is situated in a most remote part of Tasmania, far from contamination by urban or industrial pollutants, ideally placed on the edge of the lonely Southern Ocean. It has been researching levels of airborne sulphur particles which are vitally important as nuclei around which water vapour condenses to form rain-bringing clouds. The sulphur nuclei are believed to result from the action of sunlight on dimethyl sulfide, which is produced by the decomposition of marine phytoplankton and seaweed.

THE SOUTHERN OSCILLATION — EL NINO PHENOMENON (ENSO) WHICH MAKES AUSTRALIA THE LAND OF DROUGHT AND FLOODING RAINS

El Nino has been described as 'the world's most powerful weather warper'. The El Nino climatic pattern, related to sea-surface temperatures and responsible for droughts in Australia, and the Southern oscillation, which involves fluctuations in atmospheric pressure systems, are linked and together they are known by the acronym ENSO.

The great variations in climate, with such swings as to make at least the eastern two-thirds of the Australian continent into a land of 'drought and flooding rains' are now known to be orchestrated by ENSO. They add an extra dimension to the problems facing flora and fauna — and graziers and farmers. Australia is particularly vulnerable to the irregular climatic fluctuations to which it is subjected because two-thirds of its area is under arid regimes with long dry periods and irregular rainfall, both in quantity and timing.

The combination of ENSO-related rainfall fluctuations and European land-use strategies has resulted in some very rapid, unpredicted and undesirable changes in vegetation in the past two centuries. Land degradation has resulted from farms and rangelands being over-stocked when drought hits, resulting in over-grazing of plants and decreased groundcover, leaving the soil bare and subject to erosion. When fields are fallowed, crops have failed or already ploughed fields have not been planted, soil is left vulnerable to erosion. The rapid swing from drought to flooding rain (the La Nina phase) which occurs in some ENSO events, subjects over-grazed lands with damaged vegetation cover, and bare soil, to water erosion. **It is ironic that in this driest of lands, water is such an agent of destruction. The delicate balances of the natural ecosystems, in which native plants and animals are adapted to the vagaries of climate, are revealed by their sustainability — which is in stark contrast to the unsustainable nature of systems managed by people.**

THE SOUTHERN OSCILLATION BETWEEN 1940 AND 1992 FOR AUSTRALIA.

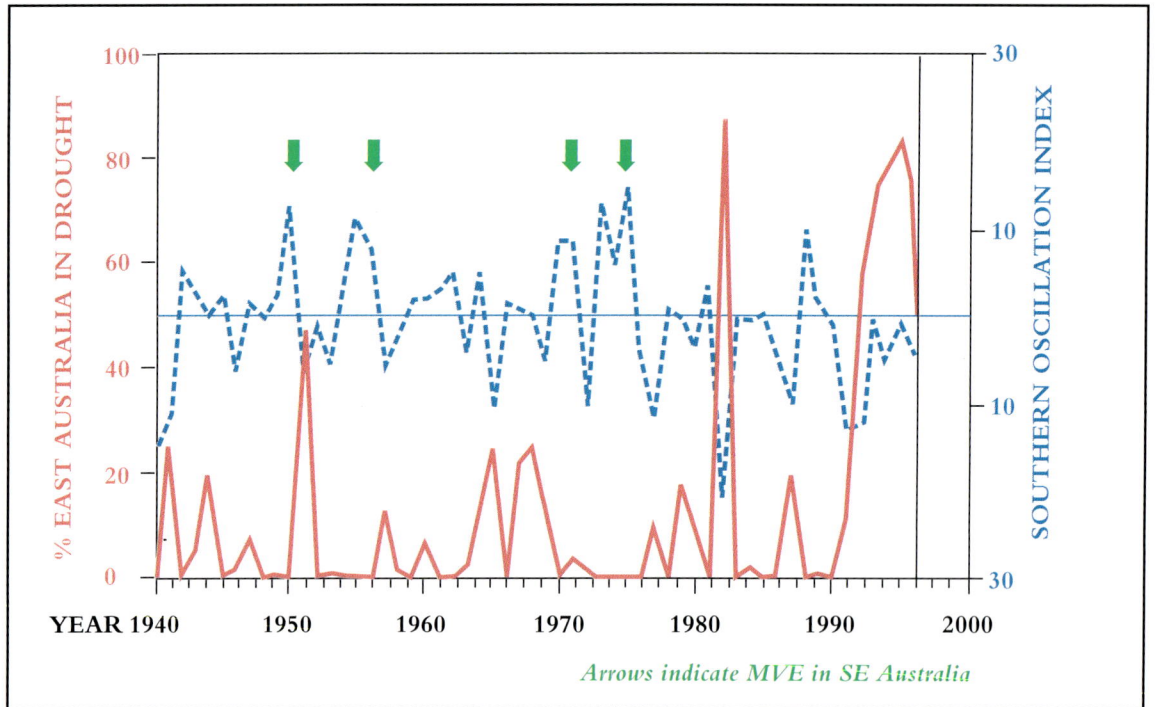

Arrows indicate MVE in SE Australia

Updated from graph prepared by Neville Nicholls.

THE RAINFALL OUTLOOK FOR JUNE TO AUGUST, 1995

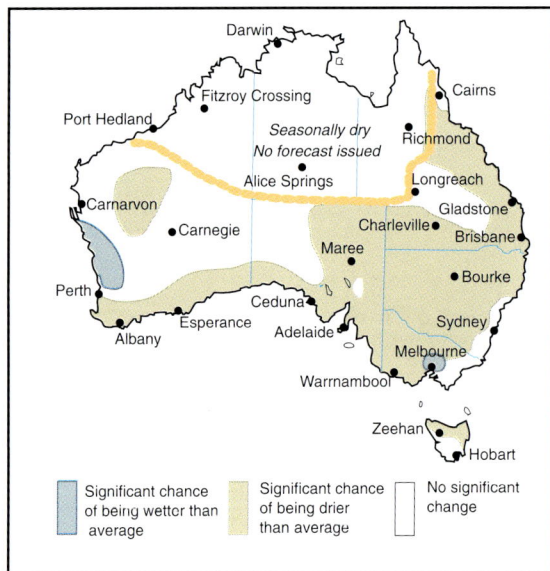

After Stevens [24]

The ability to predict climatic conditions will make a difference to land management, allowing planning for drought and enabling farmers to decide when they should plant crops or control pests.

It is at last becoming possible to predict with some confidence how weather patterns are going to change in the next season or year. Taking some of the unpredictability out of climate will make a difference to land management. The Bureau of Meteorology in Melbourne monitors all the factors involved in ENSO and puts out CLIMEX maps which take some of the guesswork out of farming. Even knowing what the rainfall outlook is **likely to be** can make a difference to

successful planting of crops. Pest control and many other functions can be performed with optimum results if it is known when conditions most favourable to germination of weeds or spread of insect pests is likely to occur.

How ENSO works

The El Nino phenomenon depends on a pool of warm water which normally lies near Indonesia and New Guinea. Strong trade winds usually blow from east to west across the Pacific, dragging surface water westward. During its passage the water is steadily warmed by the sun, and when it accumulates in the Indonesia–New Guinea warm pool it sits as a mound on the cooler, denser water in that region. (Some of the warm water overflows from the pool and becomes the warm **Leeuwin Current**, which flows down the coast of Western Australia.) If the easterly trade winds weaken, which happens in El Nino events, the warm pool elongates and flows 'downhill' from the mound, back east towards South America. Modern satellite technology has enabled photography of the '**Kelvin wave**' which carries this body of low-density, warm water 10 000 km back across the Pacific, taking two or three months for the journey.

When the wave of warm water approaches the South American coast, it over-rides the cold, dense waters of the Humboldt Current. This has a serious effect on the marine life dependent on this high-nutrient current, and on the local fishing industry. The Kelvin wave divides into two when its progress is blocked by South America. One branch travels north towards California and affects marine life and ocean

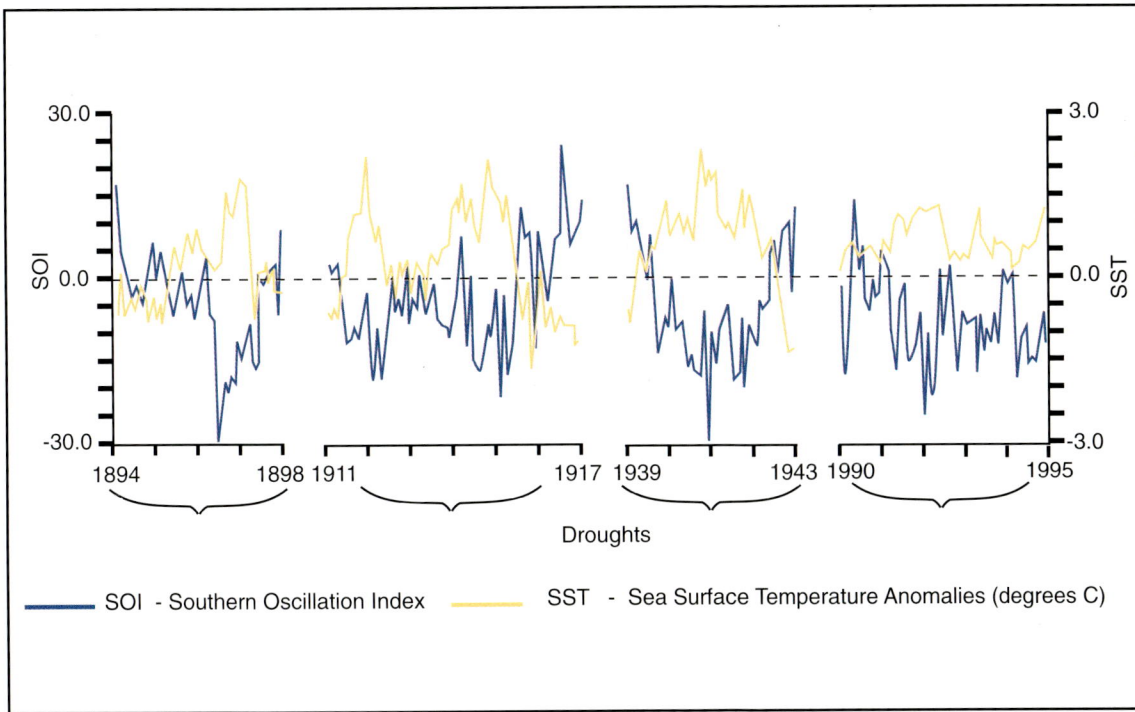

After O'Neill. [25]

The close relationship between the Southern Oscillation Index (SOI) and sea surface temperature (SST) is seen in this graph. The 'episodes' correspond to major droughts.

temperature as far north as Vancouver, the other travels south towards Chile.

The easterly shift of warm water has a dramatic effect on rainfall patterns. In South America the usually arid, barren west coast is deluged with tropical rain, leading to floods and mudslides.

The consequences of the removal of the warm water pool from the western Pacific are equally dramatic. Evaporation is less from the cooler sea-surface and rainfall decreases. The climate of the western Pacific becomes drier and drought affects the eastern two-thirds of the Australian continent. The El Nino recedes when the warm water pool is rebuilt with the return of the easterly trade winds.

La Nina events, when they develop as El Nino recedes, are due to an upwelling of abnormally cold water in the central and eastern Pacific, while sea-surface temperatures become unusually high in the western Pacific. Tropical rain is then centred over Indonesia and northern Australia, and systems spinning off this region give eastern Australia torrential rain and flooding.

ENSO-related fluctuations of rainfall in Australia are characterised by droughts and big wets having time scales of about a year, and having widespread influence; by being phase-locked into annual cycles; and by often being followed, or preceded, by the opposite rainfall anomaly. It is the occasional succession of weak or moderate El Nino episodes, with only short intervals in between, which results in major droughts. Such a sequence occurred in the 1991–95 drought.

La Nina and El Nino episodes may be separated by long periods of near-normal conditions. Alternatively,

THE EXTENT OF THE 1982–83 DROUGHT

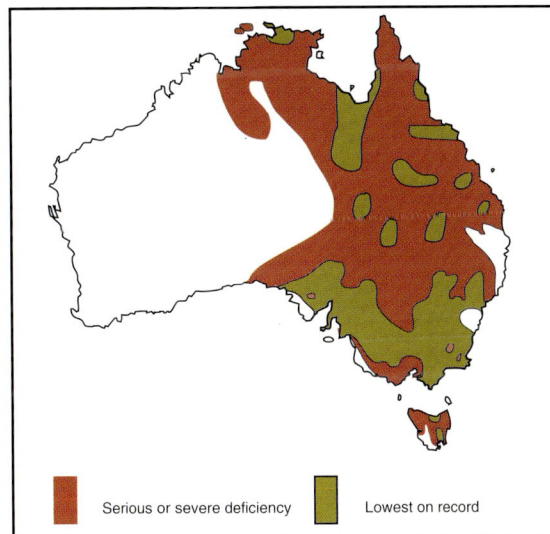

After Williams [26]

the climate system may swing between the two extremes for several cycles with either or both returning every few years. The **Southern Oscillation** causes the see-saw effect. The air pressure at sea-level is higher over Australia, New Guinea and South-east Asia during El Nino and lower over the south-eastern Pacific. The reverse applies in La Ninas. Fluctuations in pressure can be monitored by the Southern Oscillation Index, which records the see-sawing of atmospheric pressure between Darwin and Tahiti, giving warning of impending El Nino events.

When the world is coming out of an ENSO event,

OPPORTUNISTIC REPRODUCTION STRATEGIES

Birds

Australia has more nomadic birds than any other land. It is believed that about 30% of all species move from region to region in the semi-arid to arid inland, taking advantage of places where conditions are good. Waterbirds which survive drought in the Centre often travel to coastal areas in great numbers to wait for a return of satisfactory conditions inland.

Many species have **a-seasonal breeding patterns**, initiated by falls of rain; many can produce multiple broods in good seasons, or, on the other hand, produce smaller clutches in dry years or none in droughts; some, like zebra finches, can breed at a very young age, enabling them to contribute to rapid population growth in favourable years; and the widespread habit among many species in which the older offspring assist the breeding male in raising nestlings while the female lays and incubates the next clutch enables maximum use of good seasons.

Red kangaroos

The red kangaroo, widely distributed across the continent on arid and semi-arid plains, is an opportunistic breeder with no fixed seasonal pattern of reproduction. In a good season a mother may have a baby attached to a teat in her pouch or developing there as a pouch young, while a slightly older joey is at heel, though still being fed milk, by putting its head into her pouch to access a teat. The milk formula which the mother supplies to her two children is matched to their specific requirements, that of an infant being a different strength from that supplied to a bounding youngster. In addition, females are able to store fertilised eggs at a blastocyst stage, which enables them to have one ready to promote when a joey leaves the pouch. If the male is still around, she mates again at this stage, storing another fertilised egg. This adaptation enables an independent offspring to be produced every 240 days under good conditions, though each takes 600 days to develop from conception to complete independence. There is a high rate of mortality in the transition stage from pouch to independence, but when a number of good seasons follow each other, as occurs occasionally under ENSO-dominated

regimes, the young are ready to take advantage of the improved conditions.

Under prolonged drought conditions breeding ceases, and it is only recommenced when rain triggers a hormone response.

Other animals

Many other animals, like long-haired rats, are also opportunistic breeders which take advantage of good years to multiply and spread out from the refuge areas where they survive in small numbers during inhospitable times.

Plants

Mulga and saltbush are two major ecosystem dominants whose regeneration only occurs during La Nina wet phases of ENSO. Both are slow growing and only seed prolifically when there has been good rain to promote their flowering and seed formation. In order for seed to germinate and seedlings to become established, ongoing good rainfall is required, so it is only in the occasional times when several good seasons follow each other that any regeneration occurs. This explains why both ecosystems have been so vulnerable to grazing by introduced stock and rabbits. If young seedlings are eaten each time they appear there may not be any significant replacement. In the case of mulga, which like

Above top: Kangaroos and mulga, two species with opportunistic reproductive patterns.

JIM FRAZIER

Above: Bladder saltbush.

M.E.W.

many acacias has a fairly short life, this may mean their local disappearance. In the case of saltbush, the very heavy grazing of saltbush plains in the early days of settlement resulted in substantial permanent thinning of plant cover because seedlings were eaten and the slow-growing nature of the plants was not understood. Many of the bigger plants were up to 200 years old.

climatic anomalies appear and persist in some regions, particularly in parts of the Northern Hemisphere. They are characterised by warmer temperatures and extremes of rainfall. Conditions swing around much more from one extreme to another and the chaotic situation makes it difficult to determine if the El Nino is over.

It has been found that changes in sea-surface temperature in the Indian Ocean can affect rainfall across central and south-eastern Australia, and it is believed that Victoria escaped the drought which affected northern New South Wales and Queensland so badly in 1993 because of this linkage between Indian Ocean and Pacific ENSO patterns. The surface waters of the Indian Ocean off north-western Australia were warm and fed a band of rain-bearing cloud from north-west to south-east across the continent. Interaction between this cloud band and low-pressure westerly wind systems insulated Victoria from the drought.

However, the interaction between ENSO and

Indian Ocean anomalies is not always so benign. It is believed that when the Indian Ocean pattern was in 'drought favouring' phase during the major drought of 1982–83, its influence reinforced the drought in south-eastern Australia. In mid 1994, the expansion of severe drought from Queensland and northern New South Wales through all eastern districts right down into Tasmania was again due to the interaction of the Indian Ocean system in its drought-amplifying mode.

The question of how long ENSO has been influencing climate in Australia cannot be answered. Many of our plants and animals are apparently very sensitively adapted to the large, irregular climatic swings it creates, which might be thought to imply a very long time of co-evolution with ENSO. The adaptations have been taken as evidence for ENSO's long existence.[27] However, when one takes into account what the fluctuations of climate and conditions were like over the last 2.6 million years of the Pleistocene ice age, perhaps the adaptations were initially to the uncertainties of survival during hard times then. The selection of adaptations was strongly biased towards opportunistic behavioural patterns over those two million years or more, and it may simply be coincidence that they are as well suited to ENSO.

It is hard for us to comprehend how inhospitable this continent would have been during glacial stages in which rainfall overall was halved and windiness was doubled. At the last glacial maximum, only 18 000 years ago, and probably at several glacial maxima before that, 80% of the continent was covered by wind-blown sand. The desert dune fields would have been practically waterless and lifeless, the arid zone with unpredictable rainfall was enormous. Semi-arid savanna and woodland occupied much of the rest of the continent. Even the tropical north was much more arid. Devastating natural fires, and, by the last glacial maximum, Aboriginal fires, would have added an extra hazard. Survival would have depended on species becoming increasingly problem-tolerant.

Twice this century, massive wildfires have swept through forests in south-eastern Australia at the height of El Nino droughts, when climatic conditions may briefly have resembled those of a glacial maximum. Black Friday in February 1939 saw 1.4 million hectares of forest, including most of Victoria's mountain ash forest, destroyed. The Ash Wednesday fires in February 1983 destroyed 350 000 ha of forest, including many softwood plantations in Victoria and South Australia. Bushfires are always an additional problem during times of drought.

What is known about ENSO — that localised sea-surface temperature changes and associated atmospheric pressure systems have a profound and widespread influence on currents and climate — should make us cautious about reconstructing the distant past or predicting the future. We cannot assume that what may have applied during perhaps the last 3000 more or less stable years of our present interglacial would have been the situation in the more distant past.

How global warming will affect the ENSO climatic phenomenon is still uncertain. We may already be seeing some changes as a result of the slight warming which has so far been detected: In the last 20 years El Ninos have out-numbered La Ninas by four to one; and the most recent El Nino drought in Australia has been caused by a succession of El Ninos over 51 months, making it the longest recorded period with negative SOI.

The Effect of ENSO on Fisheries

The link between availability of fish species and climatic fluctuations due to ENSO is only now being recognised. So little fundamental research has been done that it is impossible to decide, when the catch of a particular species suddenly declines, whether over-fishing is to blame or whether the decline is a natural response to some climatic variable.

The oceans are largely unproductive deserts. The seas around Australia are nutrient-poor, being fed by nutrient-deficient run-off from an old and weathered continent. In good rainfall years, when coastal rivers flood, the resulting nutrient flushes are important for species which spawn and spend the early part of their lives in estuarine environments. El Nino droughts and low river levels can reduce spawning and growth of young. (Artificially reduced flow in rivers due to damming and irrigation must play a significant role in decreasing productivity of such species; and increased sediment loads, concentrations of salt and contamination with fertilisers and pesticides must also affect the natural balances.) A time lag of several years may occur between an event which decreased the number of young reaching adulthood and an observed decrease in the adult fish catch, which makes it difficult to know whether natural or human influences are to blame.

Fish which are at home in the deeper water off the edge of the continental shelf would be assumed to be less influenced by climatic variations than those more directly dependent on nutrients from the land. However, the orange roughy, one of the few fish whose circumstances have been sufficiently researched, provides evidence which suggests explanations for the drastic decline in catches as well as raising concerns about exploitation of marine life in general on several counts. So little is known about the ecology of the open seas, and the lessons which might have been learnt from, for instance, the complete collapse of herring and cod fisheries in the Northern Hemisphere, do not appear to have been heeded.

The orange roughy lives at depths of up to 1500 m in the darkness of the deep ocean and feeds in the nutrient-rich currents which flow as an intermediate depth layer. The currents originate in sub-Antarctic regions. Flow of ocean currents is determined by temperature differences between different layers of seawater and their differing salinity.

Changes to currents on which the orange roughy

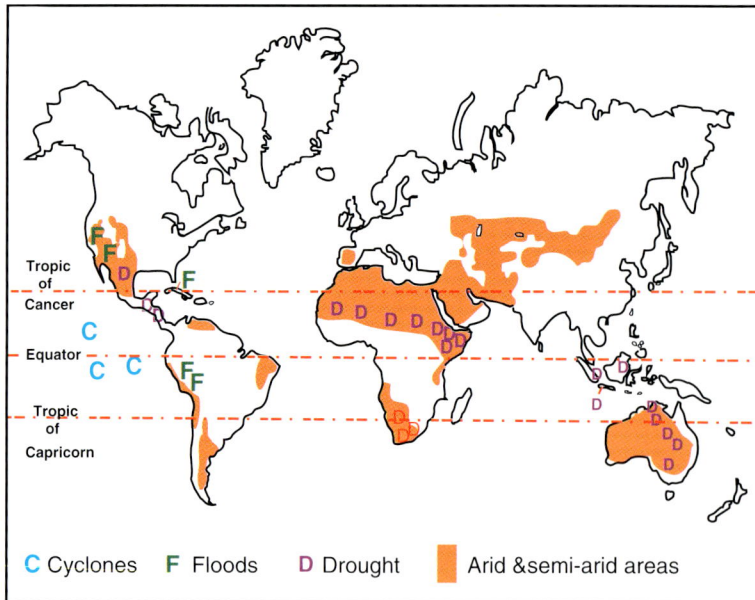

C Cyclones   F Floods   D Drought   ▮ Arid &semi-arid areas

After Williams. [26]

Deeply eroded land on the floodplain of the Burke River near Boulia in the Channel Country. Major floods in the Channel Country occur in La Nina years.

M.E.W.

reproduction are areas which meet all their requirements for spawning and the safe early development of their young.

In the 15 years during which New Zealand and Tasmania have been harvesting orange roughy, the average size of individuals has remained constant. There are very few small fish, and the adults of the average size are known to be very old — perhaps between 100 and 150 years. Once again, the analogy of these slow-growing, long-living creatures from the oceanic desert to their long-living, slow-growing land-desert counterparts (like old-man saltbush) is brought to mind. Over-fishing of a species whose survival is precarious because of the fragile ecosystem in which it functions has probably had a similar result to over-grazing of desert species dependent on rare climatic events followed by enough time without the grazing pressures to allow young to survive.

In the case of the uniformly old populations of orange roughy being caught, it is possible that the specific conditions needed for successful breeding have not occurred for many years (and may not occur again within their lifetime, and they may be heading for local extinction).

How ENSO affects other parts of the world

El Nino was originally seen as an oceanic event which only affected the west coast of South America. It is now recognised that in partnership with the Southern Oscillation its influence is extraordinarily widespread. It affects lands on the Pacific rim as well as around the Indian Ocean, and the Americas. ENSO's main impacts are in the tropics, but it causes changes to pressure systems polewards, more particularly in the Southern Hemisphere. Less directly it also influences weather patterns in central Europe and Asia. It affects the monsoon in India and inflicts drought on parts of southern Africa and Australia in El Ninos, while at the same time it generates high altitude winds as the Kelvin wave approaches South America. These winds disrupt budding storm systems which otherwise would often have developed into hurricanes in and around the Caribbean. (The hurricane season of 1995 saw exceptional numbers of violent storms, and the chaotic ending of the El Nino has been blamed, while global warming has been suggested as an added explanation.) The changed jet stream over North America brings torrential rains to California while Australia and southern Africa are in drought.

depends could affect the number of young surviving to replace dying adults. Their plight would then be similar to that of a land-based animal whose habitat was altered and restricted, and survival of a specialised species in the sea is as much threatened by habitat degradation and loss as is a land-living species with special requirements. **We tend not to think of free-swimming marine creatures as being part of distinct ecosystems within the ocean. Water is water to us but presumably to its inhabitants it is a mosaic of environments stacked according to depth as well as laterally as determined by currents. And central to their**

CHAPTER TWO

AUSTRALIA'S GEOLOGICAL HISTORY

HOW THE PAST HELPS TO EXPLAIN TODAY'S PROBLEMS

Australia is an ancient landmass. It has been stable through enormous lengths of geological time. Its land surfaces and its rocks have undergone continuous weathering under sun, rain and wind. It has some of the most ancient landscapes preserved anywhere in the world. The antiquity of landscapes of the old plateau of Western Australia, the Yilgarn Block, has long been recognised. There, ancient river channels, in which modern rivers or chains of salt lakes lie, date back to times when Australia and Antarctica were joined and rivers flowed from high mountain ranges in Antarctica into Western Australia, more than 150 million years ago.

Recently it has been recognised that some landscapes in the Southern Highlands of New South Wales are not the product of Quaternary erosion, as originally thought, but date back little changed to the Eocene, about 40 million years ago.[29]

The Ochre Pits near Leigh Creek in South Australia. Deep chemical weathering has turned the rocks to clay through geological time. Aboriginals used to travel from afar to obtain ochre for their ceremonies and paintings.

M.E.W.

THE GEOLOGICAL TIME COLUMN

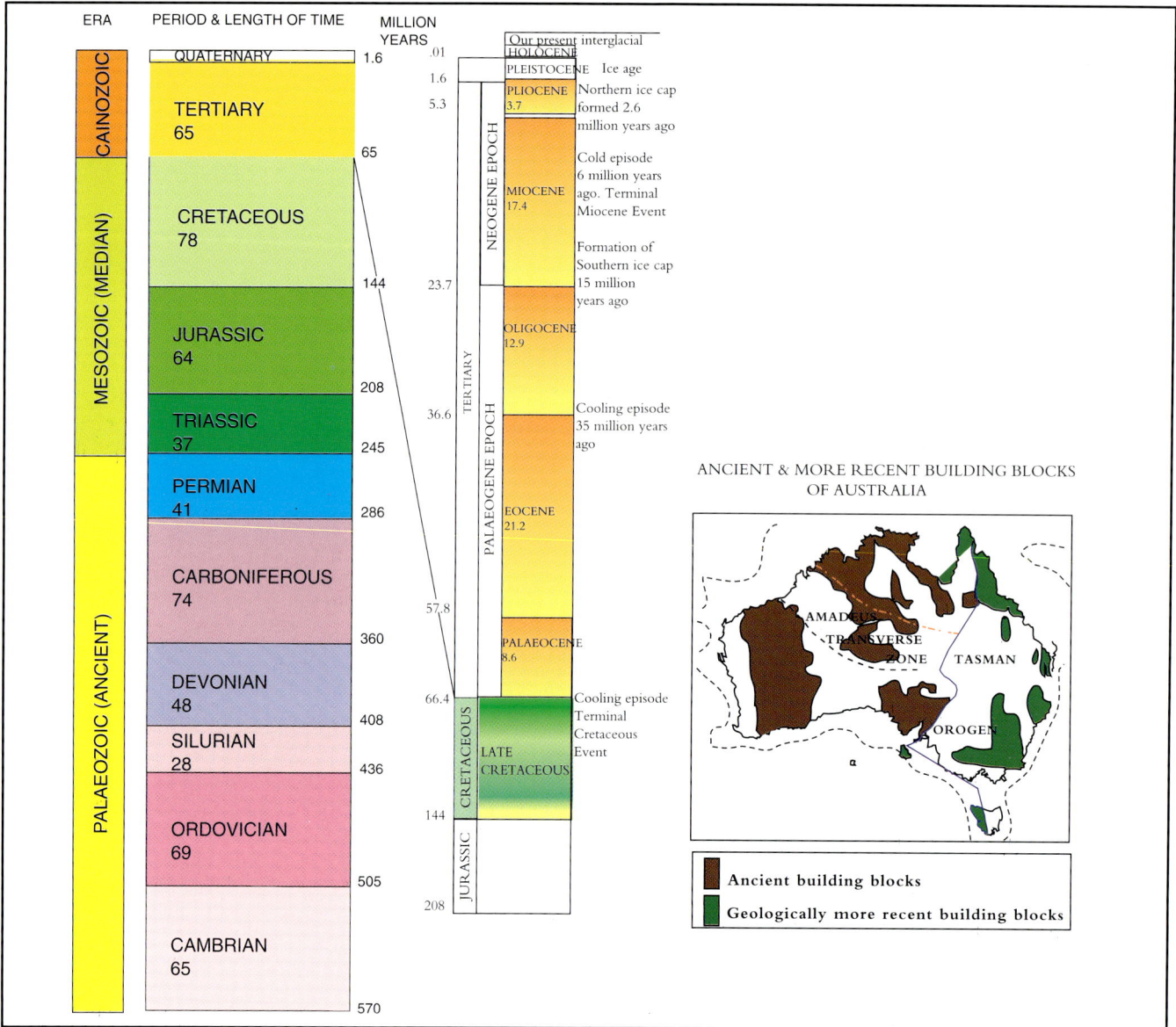

ERA	PERIOD & LENGTH OF TIME	MILLION YEARS
CAINOZOIC	QUATERNARY	1.6
	TERTIARY 65	65
MESOZOIC (MEDIAN)	CRETACEOUS 78	144
	JURASSIC 64	208
	TRIASSIC 37	245
PALAEOZOIC (ANCIENT)	PERMIAN 41	286
	CARBONIFEROUS 74	360
	DEVONIAN 48	408
	SILURIAN 28	436
	ORDOVICIAN 69	505
	CAMBRIAN 65	570

Our present interglacial
HOLOCENE — .01
PLEISTOCENE Ice age — 1.6
PLIOCENE 3.7 — 5.3 Northern ice cap formed 2.6 million years ago

NEOGENE EPOCH
MIOCENE 17.4 — Cold episode 6 million years ago. Terminal Miocene Event
23.7 — Formation of Southern ice cap 15 million years ago

PALAEOGENE EPOCH
OLIGOCENE 12.9 — 36.6
EOCENE 21.2 — Cooling episode 35 million years ago
57.8
PALAEOCENE 8.6
66.4

CRETACEOUS
LATE CRETACEOUS — Cooling episode Terminal Cretaceous Event
144
JURASSIC — 208

TERTIARY

ANCIENT & MORE RECENT BUILDING BLOCKS OF AUSTRALIA

AMADEUS TRANSVERSE ZONE TASMAN
OROGEN
a

■ Ancient building blocks
■ Geologically more recent building blocks

GONDWANA, THE GREAT SOUTHERN SUPERCONTINENT

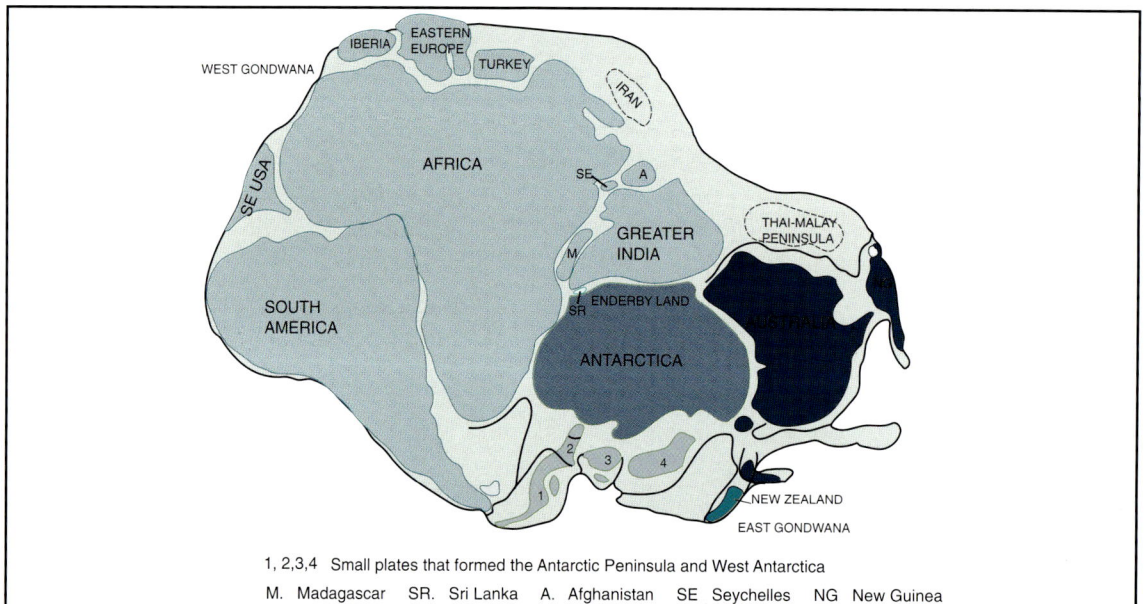

IBERIA EASTERN EUROPE TURKEY
WEST GONDWANA
IRAN
SE USA
AFRICA
SE A
GREATER INDIA
M
THAI-MALAY PENINSULA
SOUTH AMERICA
SR ENDERBY LAND
AUSTRALIA
ANTARCTICA
2
3 4
1
NEW ZEALAND
EAST GONDWANA

1, 2,3,4 Small plates that formed the Antarctic Peninsula and West Antarctica

M. Madagascar   SR. Sri Lanka   A. Afghanistan   SE Seychelles   NG New Guinea

Another view of the Ochre Pits near Leigh Creek in South Australia.

M.E.W.

POOR SOILS FROM WEATHERED ROCKS; NO RENEWAL BY VULCANISM OR GLACIATION

Erosion through the ages, deep chemical weathering and leaching of the continent 's ancient rocks, have resulted in their alteration and loss of many minerals. When they break down into sediments, the soils which result are nutrient-deficient, and presumably were so through great lengths of geological time.

The depth to which rocks can be weathered and altered by groundwater through time is dramatically, and beautifully, illustrated by the ochre pits near Leigh Creek in South Australia where rock has become ochre clay; and by the opal-bearing rock in the Three Mile Pit at Lightning Ridge.

The stable nature of the Australian landmass, as part of the Gondwana supercontinent and in the last 45 million years as an island continent, determined that volcanic activity has been limited. Australia separated from Gondwana by passive margin rifting and moved northwards independently while located in the middle of its Tectonic Plate. (The full story of its rifting, drifting and drying to become the driest vegetated continent, which it is today, is told in my book After the Greening[6]). Australia's position on its plate was remote from active zones of plate margins where volcanic activity and mountain building occur. Therefore its soils have not been renewed by the breakdown of fresh volcanic rocks except in the small areas where localised volcanic activity has occurred; and the absence of broadscale tectonic mountain-building results in there being little erosion rapid enough to reduce fresh, unweathered rock to sediment. Such volcanic activity as occurred was mainly from the

The Three-Mile Pit at Lightning Ridge. Deep weathering of Cretaceous rocks of the Great Artesian Basin has resulted in their alteration, and in the freeing of silica which, about 35 million years ago, formed opal.

M.E.W.

'hot-spot' volcanoes down the eastern continental margin, which poured out basalt.

The location of the remnant basalt volcanoes and the rich basaltic soils derived from them actually records Australia's movement as an island continent northwards away from Antarctica during the last 45 million years. The continent passed over a hot-spot, an area of weakness in the Earth's crust through which volcanoes erupt periodically. Dating of the volcanoes shows that

TECTONIC PLATES OF THE EARTH'S CRUST

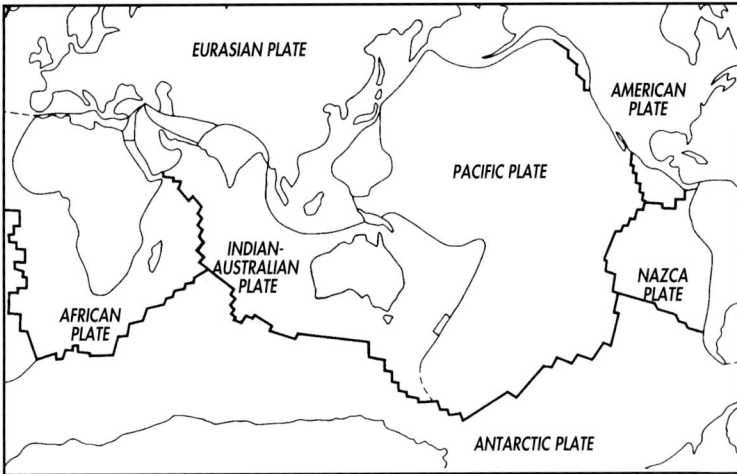

GONDWANA:
The extent of ice during the ice age about 300 million years ago in the Late Carboniferous to Early Permian.

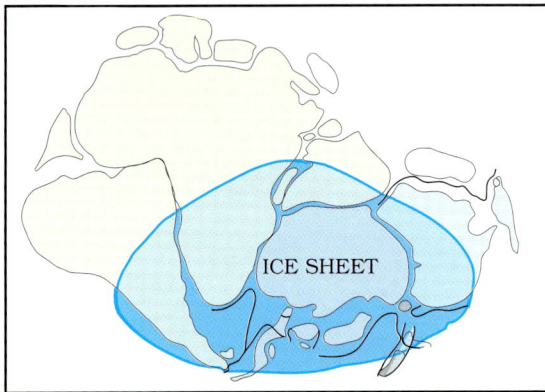

AUSTRALIA 18 000 YEARS AGO:
80% of the continent was desert

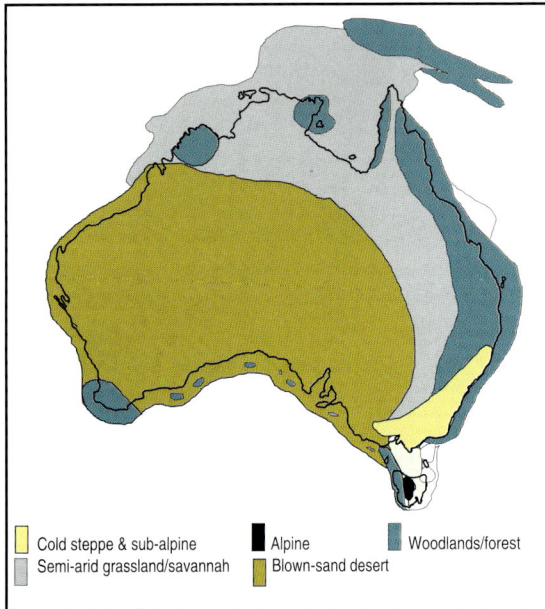

☐ Cold steppe & sub-alpine   ☐ Alpine   ☐ Woodlands/forest
☐ Semi-arid grassland/savannah   ☐ Blown-sand desert

After Hope & Kirkpatrick [32]

EXTENT OF POLAR ICE AT THE LAST GLACIAL MAXIMUM, 18 000 YEARS AGO

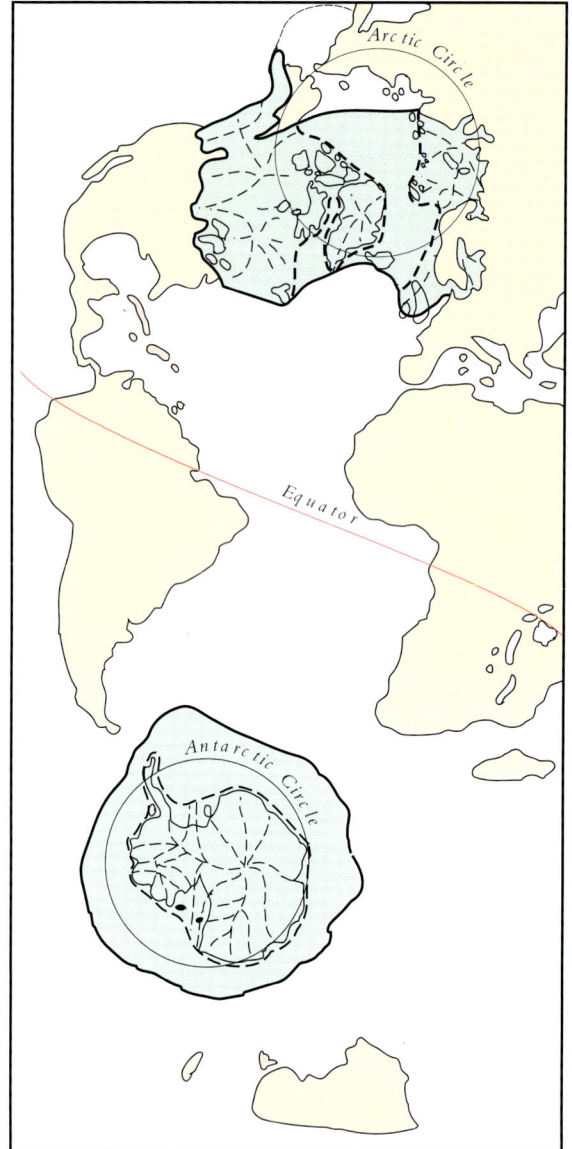

After Prentice & Denton [34]

The North-polar ice sheets spread across land, covering Canada and the northern part of the USA as far south as the Ohio River. The northern parts of Europe, including Britain, were also covered. Moving ice sheets ground up the country rock as they advanced, creating fresh, deep soil deposits. In the Southern Hemisphere the polar ice was restricted to Antarctica.

those in the northern part of the Great Divide are about 40 million years old, and that the volcanoes become younger southwards, with those near Melbourne only thousands of years old. Measuring the age of individual volcanoes and their distance apart enables a calculation to be made of the rate at which Australia has moved across the hot-spot. The figure arrived at is 6.7 cm per annum, and Australia is still moving northwards at that rate.

The areas of basalt soil are valuable for agriculture (where topography allows) in a land where most soils are nutrient-deficient as a result of their derivation from time-worn rocks.

(Australia's native flora is adapted to low-nutrient soils; many of its plants are adapted to different salt levels; most are drought tolerant. In contrast, introduced crops require added fertilisers and are salt and drought sensitive.)

CHANGES IN SEA-LEVEL, LAKE LEVELS IN SOUTH-EASTERN AUSTRALIA, AND TEMPERATURE IN THE LAST 40 000 YEARS.

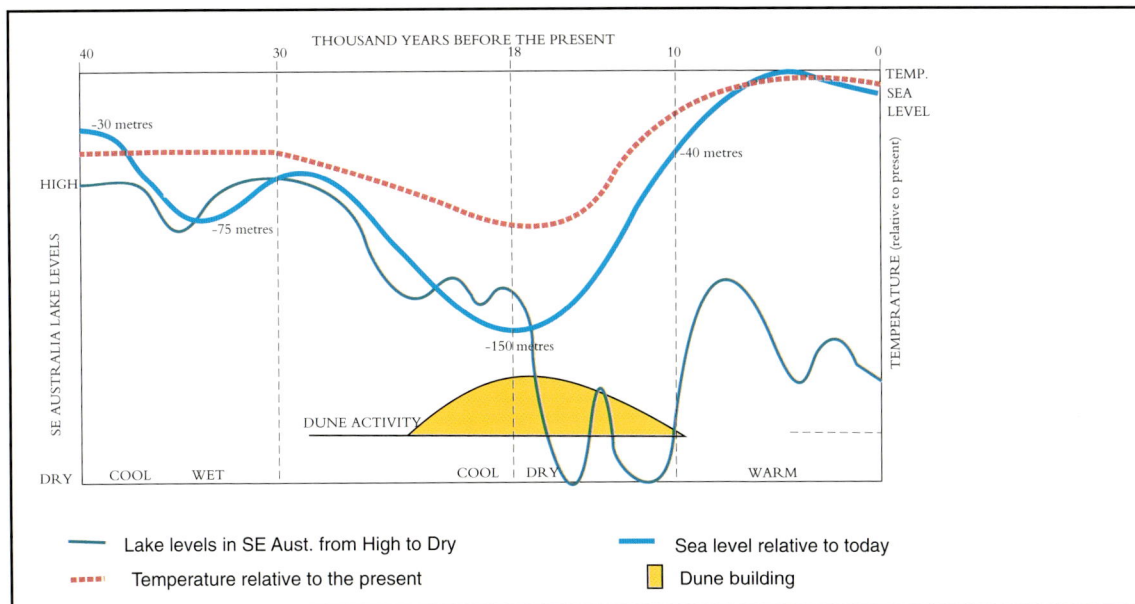

THOUSAND YEARS BEFORE THE PRESENT

-30 metres

-75 metres

-40 metres

-150 metres

DUNE ACTIVITY

DRY   COOL   WET   COOL   DRY   WARM

SE AUSTRALIA LAKE LEVELS

HIGH

TEMPERATURE (relative to present)

TEMP.
SEA
LEVEL

—— Lake levels in SE Aust. from High to Dry

----- Temperature relative to the present

—— Sea level relative to today

☐ Dune building

After Chappell [33]

Another major factor contributing to Australia's poor soils, and making them so different from those of Britain and Europe, was their different history during the Pleistocene ice age. No ice sheets moved across the Australian continent then, grinding up unweathered rock and making it into fertile soil, but this process happened repeatedly during the last 2.6 million years in parts of the Northern Hemisphere. The last time that ice sheets ground their way across parts of Australia making new soil was in the Late Carboniferous to Early Permian ice age of 300 million years ago.

The deep, fertile soils of northern Europe and North America and Canada result from the expansion of ice sheets across land, spreading southwards under their own weight and covering vast areas — down to the Ohio River in the USA, across Britain and northern Europe. The ice cap in the Southern Hemisphere was confined to Antarctica and ice shelves spread out around it, kept in check by the surrounding sea. At the peak of the last glacial stage, 18 000 years ago, sea ice extended far beyond the Antarctic Circle.

The huge polar ice caps tied up so much fresh water (and the Earth has a limited water budget) that the world was much drier, rainfall was halved, and winds were stronger and more active. Australia was little affected by ice. In Tasmania on the Central Plateau a small ice cap existed during the last glacial maximum (and probably in one or two other glacial stages as well) connecting to glaciers on the west coast mountains. The hollows scooped out by the ice now hold many small lakes. Only a small area, not more than 50 km², was glaciated on the Southern Highlands of the mainland. For the rest, Australia was a 'desert island' with blown dunes and sand covering 80% of the land during the last glacial stage, half the rainfall, probably intense fire activity, and was unimaginably inhospitable. Today, with 40% as dune deserts and 75% under arid

THE GREAT DIVIDE,
the Great Escarpment and the distribution of basalt on the elevated eastern margin of the continent.

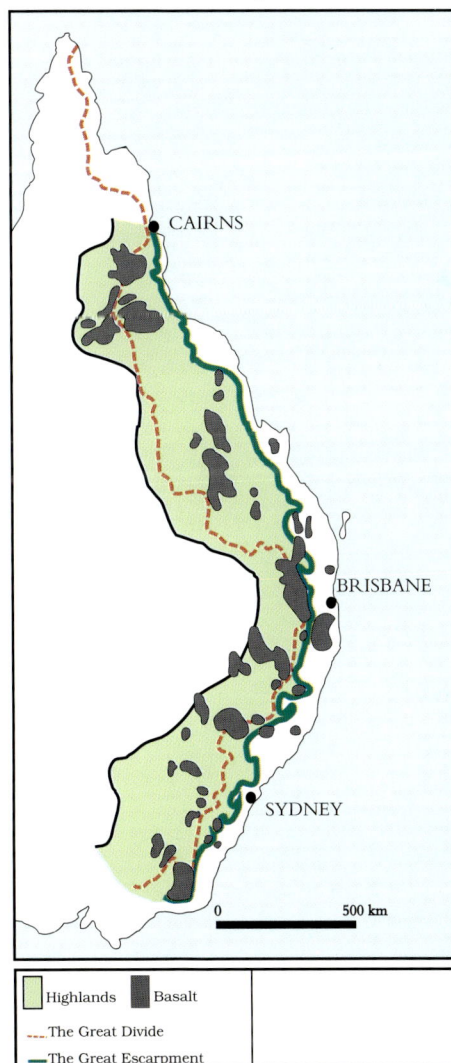

CAIRNS

BRISBANE

SYDNEY

0   500 km

☐ Highlands   ■ Basalt

----- The Great Divide

—— The Great Escarpment

After Ollier [30]

AUSTRALIA IN THE JURASSIC AND EARLY CRETACEOUS
(160 and 120 million years ago)

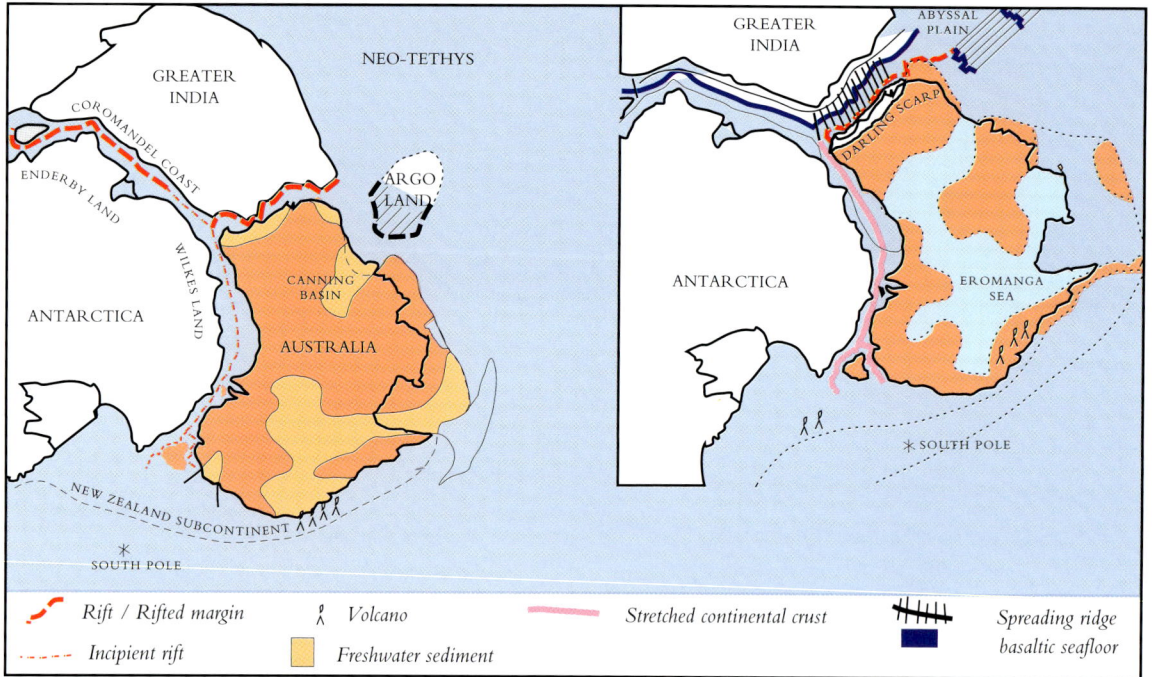

Rift / Rifted margin	Volcano	Stretched continental crust	Spreading ridge basaltic seafloor
Incipient rift	Freshwater sediment		

After Veevers et al. [34]

While rifting was starting in Eastern Gondwana, freshwater sediments were being laid down in the Great Artesian Basin in the Jurassic; and marine sediments laid down in the Eromanga Sea covered them in the Early Cretaceous. These sandstone layers are the aquifers of the Basin.

regimes it is the driest vegetated continent. It is almost surprising that it has become so much more friendly in only 14 000 years.

The extent of wind-blown sands on which shallow soils developed explains why parts of the continent, like the Mallee and the Riverine Plain of the Murray Basin, have such problems with wind and water erosion when their vegetation is disturbed. **The arid 75% of the continent which resulted from ice age climatic**

fluctuations comprises fragile ecosystems — their aridity, coupled with the degree of unreliability of rainfall, both in terms of quantity and distribution, which they endure, determines their fragile status.

The first settlers had learned their agriculture in non-arid, temperate lands with deep, productive soils and predictable weather patterns. The farming practices which they knew, and which were satisfactory in Britain, were transported and applied without question to Australia. The enormous degradation that resulted from early years of settlement, when people were 'taming' the wild land, is described in following chapters. Two hundred years have not made a great deal of difference to the philosophies which determine land-use in Australia, and the degradation of our primary, life supporting resources of soil and water continues and has reached crisis point.

THE INWARD AND EXTERNAL DRAINAGE OF AUSTRALIA

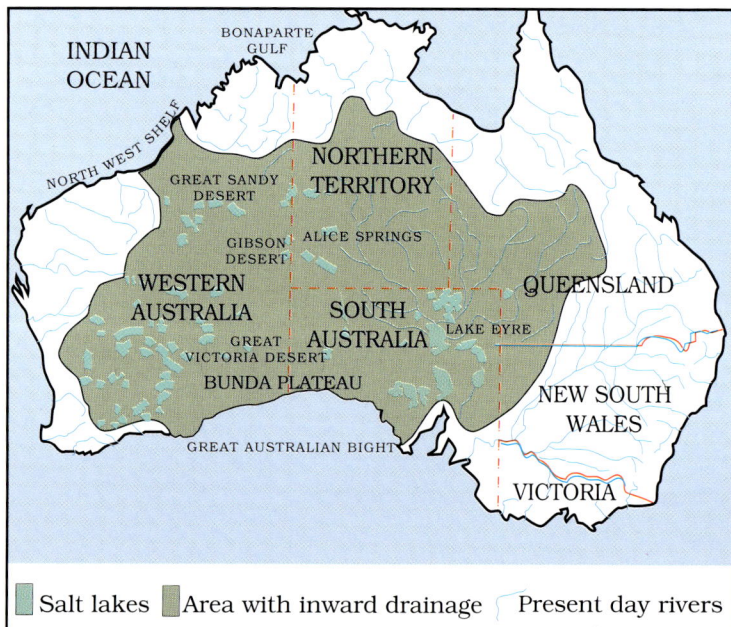

Salt lakes	Area with inward drainage	Present day rivers

A FLAT AND STABLE LANDMASS ERODING THROUGH GEOLOGICAL TIME, ACCUMULATING SEDIMENTS AND SALT

Australia today is the continent with the lowest relief and no high mountain ranges, characteristics which it has had through great lengths of geological time. Palaeogeographic maps, compiled from geological information, show that much of Eastern Australia was a floodplain in Jurassic times (about 160 million years ago), and rivers were pouring freshwater sediments into what is now the **Great Artesian Basin**. This had important implications for modern Australia, as the sediments are now aquifers (water-bearing strata) of the basin and the artesian water they contain has been essential for the development of much of the arid inland. In the Cretaceous, about 120 million years ago, a global sea-level rise resulted in vast areas in the continent's interconnected, sedimentary geological basins being flooded and becoming an epicontinental sea. Marine sedimentary rocks were laid down on top of the freshwater sediments in the Great Artesian Basin, completing and capping the water-bearing sequence. The high salt content of marine sediments contributes to the problems with salty water-tables which are widespread over the continent.

The processes of separation of Australia from the supercontinent Gondwana affected landscapes and started changes which have resulted in the modern conformation of the continent. The Western Australian coastline was created when the Indian Ocean opened as India moved away, from 132 million years ago; the southern continental margin was freed progressively from the west as the sea entered the rift valley between Australia and Antarctica after India had separated. (Tasmania and the South Tasman Rise formed the last connection to Antarctica until 45 million years ago.) The opening of the Tasman Sea between 80 and 60 million years ago moved the New Zealand Subcontinent away from the Eastern margin. The freeing of the margins changed drainage patterns, and rivers which had run into Australia from its neighbouring parts of Gondwana were deprived of their headwaters. New drainages, many in old valleys running backwards, formed when the edges of the land rose as it was freed from its supercontinent connections.

(A full account of all these changes is given in After the Greening.[6])

The eastern margin of Australia, the **Great Divide**, rose with the opening of the Tasman Sea. Its elevation was increased by the volcanoes which penetrated it as the continent passed over the hot-spot on its northwards journey after total separation from Antarctica. It became a drainage divide, with coastal rivers running eastwards to the sea, and westward-flowing rivers running inland. From the time of its elevation as a major catchment, run-off and river water entering the aquifers of the **Great Artesian Basin** acquired a head of pressure, becoming an artesian system. Water travels across the basin in the pores of the sandstone aquifers, at about a metre a year, and some of the water which emerges in mound springs near Lake Eyre, at the furthest point from where it fell as rain on the Divide, is about two million years old. Erosion of the tilted edge of the continent and headward retreat of its rivers created the ranges of the **Great Escarpment**.

The western margin of the continent also rose and the old, worn-down and weathered **Western Plateau** became so flat that it had no organised drainage and with the drying of the continent in the last 15 million

THE LAKE EYRE BASIN

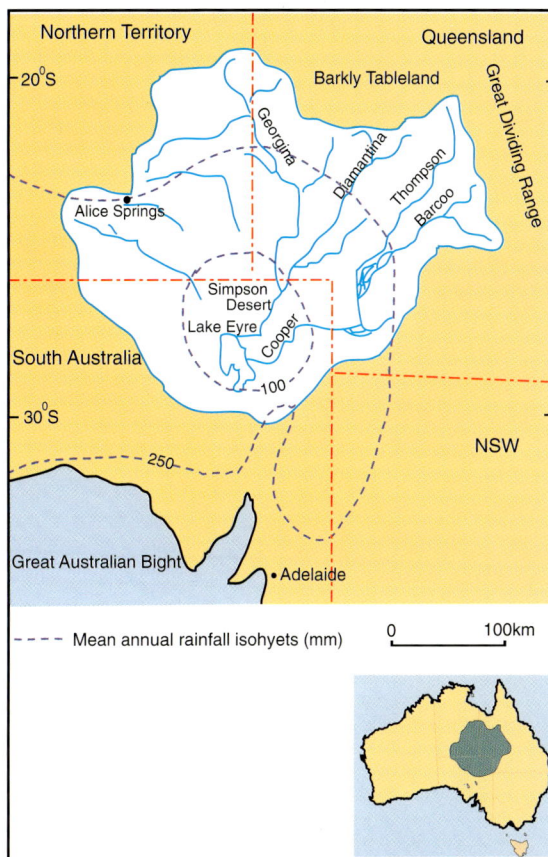

Mean annual rainfall isohyets (mm)

0   100km

THE GREAT ARTESIAN BASIN

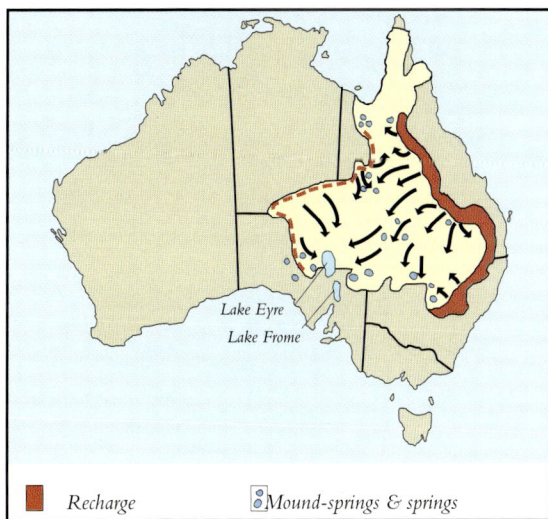

Recharge   Mound-springs & springs

After Habermehl [35]

years its rivers became ephemeral with chains of salt lakes in their beds.

Progressive sinking of the centre of the continent began when the Great Divide had risen. The **sinking of Lake Eyre Basin** has resulted in the centre of the continent becoming inward draining towards Lake Eyre, and the lake being 15 m below sea-level. The drainage prior to the sinking of the centre had been mainly right across the centre, with rivers running into the Great Australian Bight. Salt, which accumulates in all arid zones where evaporation exceeds rainfall, has no way of getting out of the system when drainage is

THE MURRAY BASIN

Late Eocene to early Oligocene, 40 to 30 million years ago.

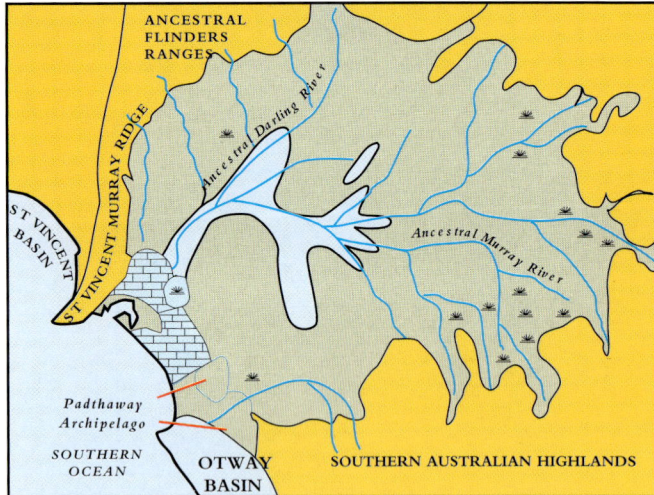

In the early Miocene, 24 to 16 million years ago.

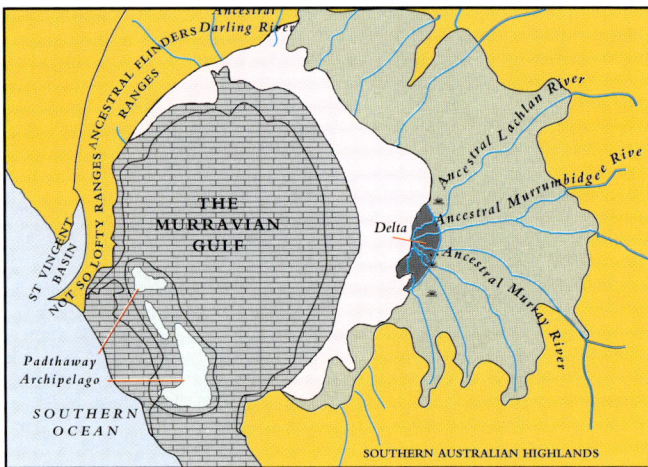

In the Pliocene, about 5 million years ago.

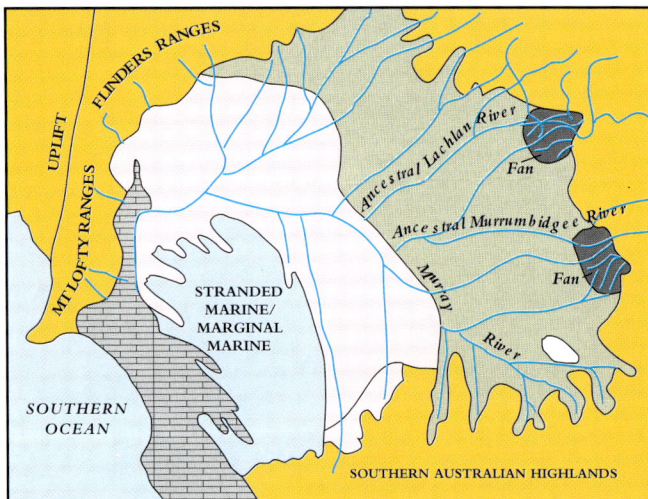

After Stephenson & Brown **36**

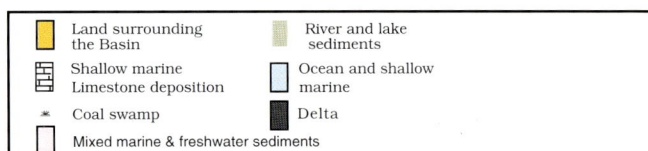

Land surrounding the Basin

Shallow marine Limestone deposition

Coal swamp

Mixed marine & freshwater sediments

River and lake sediments

Ocean and shallow marine

Delta

internal, so for about 30 million years it has steadily built up in the whole of the Lake Eyre Basin (which represents about one-fifth of the continent). To a lesser extent salt levels have built up steadily at the water-tables under all the flat and sluggishly drained parts of the continent — and that represents a large proportion of Australia.

During the extraordinary last glacial stage of the Pleistocene ice age 18 000 years ago, when the continent was twice as dry and twice as windy, the salt lakes and salt pans of the centre were dry and their bottom sediments and salts were blown across the landscape, resulting in a wide dispersal of salt. In the Murray Basin, now the food bowl of the continent, much of the area would have been a salt desert with the Mallee saltpans blowing across the land with the westerlies, creating the factors needed for the dryland salinity which we see today.

Some salt comes from breakdown of rocks, particularly marine sediments, but salt drifts from the sea onto the land in rain and when a landmass is as old as Australia it has acquired a vast tonnage. When drainage is poor it builds up in the regolith. It may be held in clay at the water-table, or dissolved in the underground water, or dispersed in the soil, and when the hydrology of a region is altered, water-tables rise, salt is mobilised and salinisation of soil and water result. The saline water-table which underlies parts of Australia, including some of our major agricultural regions, can be likened to a toxic waste zone.

When the southern margin of Australia had been freed from Antarctica, parts of it were subject to flooding by the sea at different times. During the Eocene, the sea flooded the Bremer Basin near the western end of the southern margin, and the Eucla Basin (Nullarbor), and penetrated up the river valleys in the Murray Basin. In the Miocene it again flooded the Nullarbor region (which was subsequently uplifted to become the Nullarbor limestone plain). The flooding of the Murray Basin in the Miocene created the Murravian Gulf, a large epicontinental sea; and flooding by the sea again occurred in the Pliocene, five million years ago. In consequence, marine sediments underlie the western half of the Murray Basin, the Mallee.

Sea-level changes associated with glacial and interglacial stages of the Pleistocene have sculptured Australia's shores. Acid sulphate soils now exist in coastal zones where mangroves grew when the sea-level was higher; the deep drowned valley systems like Sydney Harbour were carved out when sea-level was low and the rivers cut deep channels to reach the sea; the sand bars which protect estuaries and lakes along the east coast only formed when sea-level stabilised in the last 6000 years.

Opposite right: The Combo Waterhole on the Diamantina — where Banjo Patterson's jolly swagman camped by a billabong!

Opposite far right: Coolibahs at Coopers Creek. The river is a chain of deep pools in the dry season.

M.E.W.

THE LAKE EYRE BASIN AND WETLANDS OF THE COOPER AND THE DIAMANTINA

Some of the world's most remarkable wetlands are found in the far north-east of South Australia, in an area famous for its dunefield deserts, the Simpson, Tirari and the Strzelecki, and the gibber plains of Sturt's Stony Desert. The inward-draining Lake Eyre Basin receives the waters of the two great, wild rivers, the Cooper and the Diamantina, which are two of the most variable large rivers in the world. They may stop flowing for months, then flood at rates exceeding those of the Nile. Their floodplains extend over tens of thousands of square kilometres creating a myriad of swamps, salt and freshwater lakes, flooded woodlands, internal deltas, billabongs and channel networks. The whole landscape is repeatedly and magically transformed when they flood. Swamps become deltas, dunes become islands, dry pans become lakes and lakes expand into seas. The waters teem with life — algae, plankton, crustaceans, fish, tortoises, water rats and birds. Waders arrive from Siberia, and water birds, including hundreds of thousands of pelicans, congregate to feed and breed. The sunken centre of the continent is literally kept alive by the pulses of water brought to it by the floods.

The wetlands of the Lake Eyre Basin in northern South Australia are currently being assessed for World Heritage Listing. Lake Eyre itself and drainage systems of the lower Cooper and lower Diamantina (Warburton), the Coongie Lakes, Goyder Lagoon, and the mound-springs along the western margin of the Great Artesian Basin fulfil the criteria for world listing, which are to be:

- *An outstanding example representing major stages of Earth's history...including significant geomorphic and physiographic features.* The ephemeral nature, unregulated state, vast scale, inward draining nature, existence in a hot desert landscape, and arid catchments make the wetlands unique. Mound-springs also meet this prescription.
- *Outstanding examples representing on-going ecological and biological processes.* The northern wetlands provide an outstanding example of the evolution of such aquatic processes in an arid environment. They highlight the extreme variability of conditions, with millions of water birds during floods, almost lifeless conditions in droughts in surface aquatic systems, and the perennial nature of mound-springs.
- *Contain superlative natural phenomena or areas of exceptional natural beauty and aesthetic importance.* Anyone who has travelled in the central deserts and seen the contrasts between living oases and shimmering sand and gibbers, and experienced the soul-expanding vastness of the scenery at dawn and dusk will know that these criteria are met.
- *Contain the most important and significant natural habitats for in-situ conservation of biological diversity, including those containing threatened species of outstanding universal value...* While the marsupial fauna has suffered many extinctions, in common with the arid zone elsewhere, the significance of the wetlands for conservation of other fauna is unrivalled.

The Coongie Lakes are already listed by Ramsar Convention (set up at an international gathering in 1971) as *Wetlands of International Significance.*

The catchments and upper reaches of the Cooper and Diamantina in Queensland are vital for the health of the lower sectors of the rivers and their wetlands. Vegetation clearance, over-grazing, damage to river and stream banks, and all the rangeland-use practices that have degraded the Channel Country, have had downstream effects, including siltation and changes to river flow. Urgent measures are required in catchment management to reduce the impact, recognising that the life of ecosystems downstream depends on the catchments being restored to health. No irrigation or other schemes to divert water from such variable rivers can be tolerated and to start irrigated cotton production on the Cooper in western Queensland is unthinkable. (See p.178)

Much degradation has been suffered by floodplains and wetlands in the proposed heritage area, and more is threatened. Grazing and trampling by stock and feral animals destroys river-edge vegetation and silts up channels; oil and gas exploration and production brings roads, seismic tracks and pipelines; tourists in four-wheel drives behave irresponsibly and damage vegetation, cause erosion and disturb wildlife. World Heritage would bring protection; a managed tourism policy would bring visitors whose money would pay for the maintenance and conservation. Such protection cannot come too soon for one of the remaining areas with 'wonders of the world' status.

PROPOSED LAKE EYRE BASIN WETLANDS WORLD HERITAGE AREA

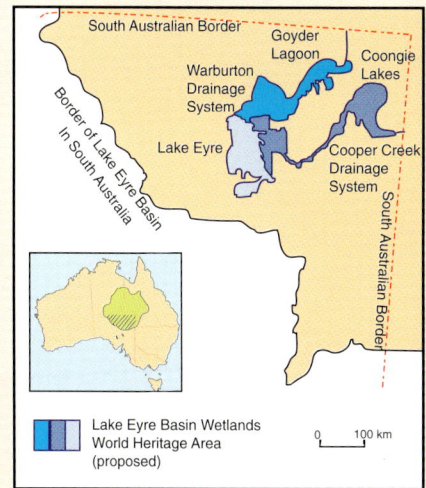

South Australian Border
Goyder Lagoon
Coongie Lakes
Warburton Drainage System
Border of Lake Eyre Basin In South Australia
Lake Eyre
Cooper Creek Drainage System
South Australian Border

Lake Eyre Basin Wetlands World Heritage Area (proposed)

0   100 km

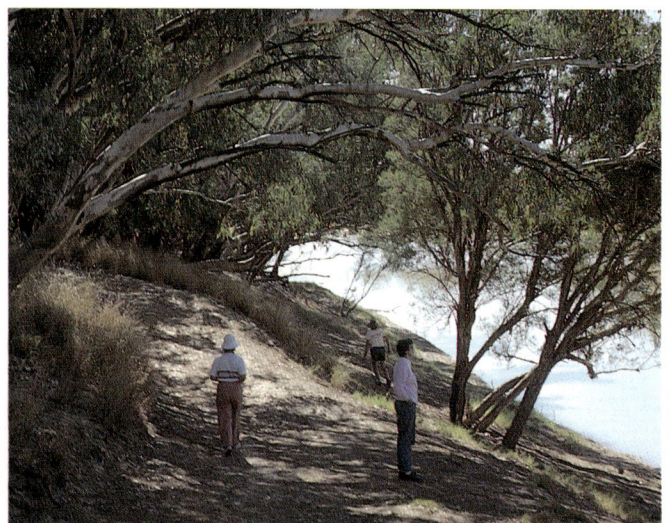

CHAPTER THREE

BIODIVERSITY

It is biodiversity, the multitude of living organisms which form the web of life and interact with the inanimate environment, that is responsible for the dynamic balance and sustainable functioning of ecosystems.

Biodiversity keeps the biosphere, the living Earth — the ultimate ecosystem — alive. It keeps a dynamic balance in our life-support systems, atmosphere, earth, water, enabling them to sustain life.

From the beginning, when first life started on our cooling planet about four billion years ago, life and its inanimate environment have been working together, inseparable. The end products of their vital partnership and their co-evolution through unimaginable lengths of time are the modern world and the life-forms it supports. Life itself has made Earth life-friendly, and it is the infinitely complex inter-relationships between all living things that maintain the health of the biosphere.

The evolution and enormous diversification of life in the oceans and waters of the planet preceded life on the land by about 3.5 billion years. Our human focus in today's world is on the biodiversity of the world as seen from a land-dweller's perspective. In each of the biosphere's component ecosystems, the inter-dependence of all the elements of its biodiversity is fundamental. We have come to realise that sustainable use of the land resources which support us involves understanding and maintaining the whole web of life from the microscopic soil organisms which recycle nutrients and maintain soil structure to the macroscopic plants and animals it supports.

In order to retain the full biodiversity of a continent like Australia, examples of all the different ecosystems (which are determined by climate, soils, specific requirements of individual plants and animals and local conditions) have to survive sustainably.

Loss of biodiversity destabilises ecosystems. Degraded ecosystems can only be rehabilitated by restoring biodiversity.

The word 'biodiversity' is a new one, coined in 1988 by Walter G. Rosen of the US National Academy of Sciences to encapsulate the topic to be discussed at a symposium on biological diversity.[37] Considering biodiversity as simply **species richness** immediately raises the question of how many species of living things exist on the Earth, how many have been described and how can it include the vast majority of life forms which are undiscovered, unnamed, and about which nothing is known. Suddenly it is obvious that science knows next to nothing about species diversity. Ignoring the 'impossible' realms of microscopic or barely visible creatures, plants and fungi, the size of the problem is highlighted when 480 'species' of beetles, nearly all undescribed, are found to inhabit $900\,m^2$ of Australian subtropical rainforest.[38]

From defining biodiversity on a global scale as the grand total of all the living organisms on Earth, the

The Kwongan sandplain ecosystem of the Swan Coastal Plain is threatened with extinction by agriculture and urban sprawl. It persists mainly as roadside vegetation. In terms of species richness it exceeds rainforest.

M.E.W.

concept has evolved to encompass biological variety at genetic, species and ecosystem scales.[39]

Living things are classified into **five Kingdoms**:

1. **Plants**, which are distinguished by their green pigment which enables them to photosynthesise.
2. **Animals**, which cannot synthesise their own food. Their foodchains start with plants.
3. **Fungi**, which are saprophytic, parasitic or symbiotic.
4. **Bacteria**.
5. **Protista**, which do not fit comfortably into any of the other Kingdoms. (Latest classifications replace this group with 'Protoctista' and in this arrangement include green algae — which is highly controversial.)

The biodiversity of a country, region or ecosystem includes all the representatives of the five Kingdoms that are present, but because so little is known of the less visible or microscopic elements, and most of them are not yet identified or classified, it is the obvious living things that are usually noted. Thus Australia is classed as a 'megadiverse' country and it has the highest rank for the number of endemic mammalian and reptilian taxa; the second highest rank for birds; and the third highest for amphibians, but no one knows how it ranks for its incompletely catalogued invertebrates or its soil bacteria or fungi. It has 20 000 described species of native plants, of which 90% are endemic.

Globally, biodiversity is being lost at an alarming rate, both in terms of species which are becoming extinct, and in terms of loss of natural

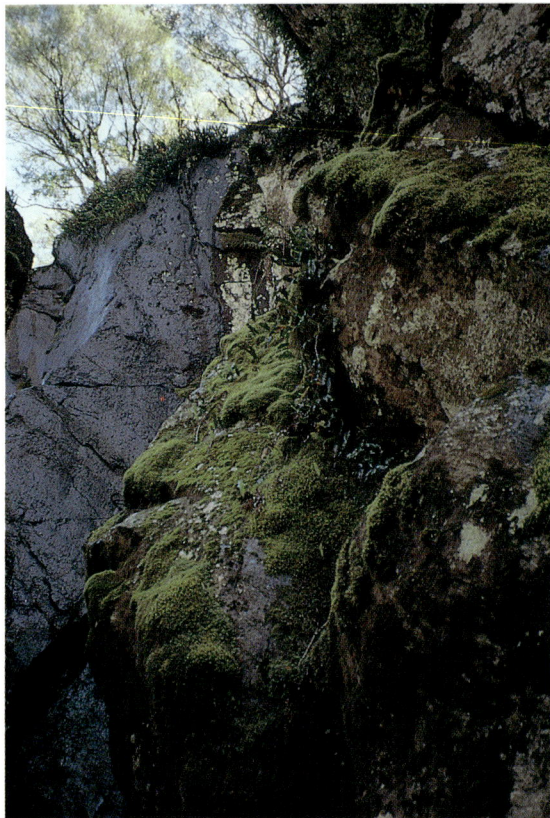

*A deep gorge on an
ancient volcano
provides a
topographical refuge
with a microclimate
suitable for rainforest.
The Ebor volcano in
north-eastern NSW.*

M.E.W.

present-day situation as the driest and flattest
continent with great climatic variability, have all
contributed to make it unique, and have also
contributed to its extraordinary biodiversity. The
nature of the land, where 75% is under arid regimes,
means that very large areas are relatively sparsely
populated. The concentrations of biodiversity in the
arid areas are in the more favourable patches (refugia)
created by local topography and other factors. That
these pockets are isolated from one another today, and
that the few habitable places that existed in the vastly
expanded arid zone during the last glacial stage of the
Pleistocene ice age were even more like islands in an
inhospitable sea, has contributed to the speciation
which results in high endemism and biodiversity. The
climatic and physical isolation of the south-western
province of Western Australia (a winter-rainfall corner
surrounded by arid terrain and separated from the rest
of the continent by desert) is a major island of this sort
with more than 80% endemism in its plant species as a
result.

In the better-watered 25% of the land, the
concentrations of biodiversity are in the best areas as
regards soil, water and climate and here they come into
serious conflict with agriculture and other land-use
practices. Often only topography has saved them from
local extinction.

REFUGIA AND BIODIVERSITY

In evolutionary terms, a refuge is a *region in which certain
types or suites of organisms are able to persist during a period
in which most of the original geographic range becomes
uninhabitable because of climatic change.*[41]

The Gondwanan flora and fauna which was in
Australia 45 million years ago when it became an island
continent (when it was a warm and well-watered land,
largely forested and green) was sorted and sifted in
response to the global drying which was occurring
during the continent's northward drift. Broadleaf forest
and rainforest, once widely distributed, were replaced
over most of their range by sclerophyll vegetation, and
the areas where they managed to survive, because of
microclimates and local conditions, became refugia —
isolated islands in a sea of terrain no longer suited to
their requirements. (*After The Greening* tells the full
story of Australia's evolution from a green and largely
forested land to the driest vegetated continent.[6])

The acute aridity during glacial stages of the
Pleistocene ice age created the central deserts and a
greatly expanded arid zone, and the biota which had
been widespread in the dry but not acutely arid
environments survived in refugia. In the strict sense
populations of refugia are relict or remnant.

In a wider sense, refugia are areas to which species
retract and are restricted for short periods by drought,
flood or biologically driven collapse of food supply.
Regions to which threatened species have retreated

communities. Australia is no exception. Twenty
mammal species; 10 species and 11 subspecies of birds;
and 97 vascular plant species (2.9% of the total flora) are
known to have been lost in the 200 years of our
stewardship. A further 3329 plant species are listed as
rare and endangered, which is 17% of the known flora,
a figure which should tell us that our current land-use is
unsustainable.[40] This is a sad record, and no one knows
how many less visible elements of our biodiversity —
the microscopic flora and fauna, invertebrates, non-
vascular plants and fungi — may have gone. **Our
temperate grassland ecosystems are facing
extinction**; and probably other ecosystems, which may
not even have been officially recognised, are lost
already.

**Australia's geological history, the evolution
of its climate through geological time, and its**

form a new category of refugia, created by the environmental changes caused by European land-use and destruction of natural habitat, as well as competition and predation pressures caused by introduced animals, domestic and feral.

Human activity has brought rapid change to Australia's terrestrial ecosystems in the last 200 years. The complete or partial removal of vegetation for cultivation, grazing, forestry, mining and urban development has contributed to loss of soils, habitats and species. Changed fire regimes have altered the structure of some ecosystems. The different forms of land degradation which have followed our use, or misuse, of the continent — soil erosion, salinisation, compaction, soil structure decline and acidification — have led to decline in water quality. The introduction of exotic animals and plants has caused massive disruption. All these factors have contributed to changes in biodiversity, and the distribution and abundance of many kinds of organisms have changed significantly.

If native species biodiversity is to be maintained, refugia have to be protected. Their occupants are at risk from clearing and livestock grazing, from feral animals, from fire (or sometimes from lack of it) and from tourists. Just as they are havens for wildlife, so they are magnets for tourists who seek out these 'interesting' special areas, particularly in the arid lands where ecosystems are the most fragile. Access roads, tourism infrastructure, competition between human consumption and needs and those of the fauna in times of drought, and stress and disturbance to the biota of the refuge are all invasive.

Where remnant natural vegetation provides habitat for scattered populations of native animals and birds in

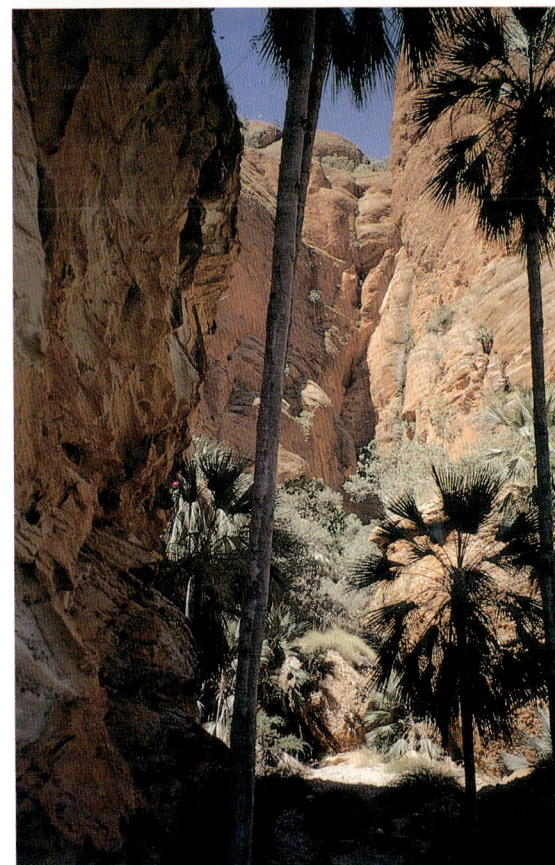

Top right and left: Outside the Flinders Ranges in South Australia, a dry, over-grazed desert landscape. Inside, Arkaroola — species-rich, green.

Above and left: The Bungle Bungles, dry savanna outside, gorges with palms inside.

M.E.W.

BATS AND BIODIVERSITY

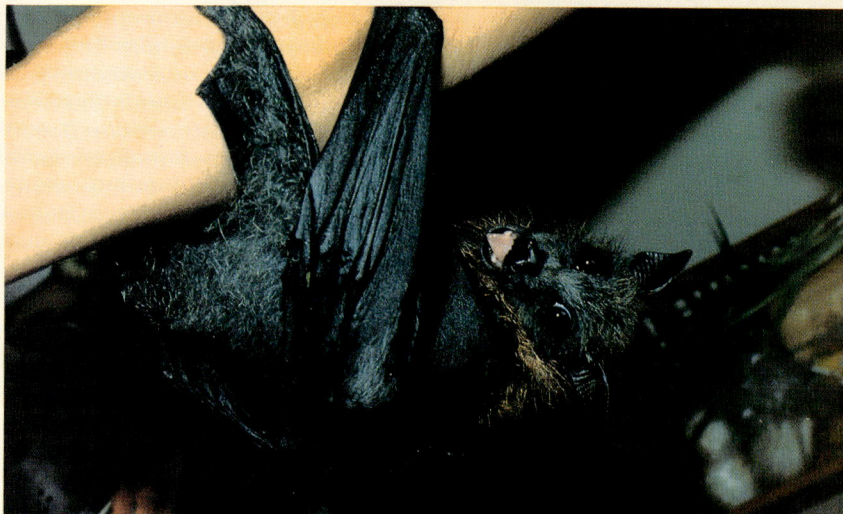

Flying-foxes are just 'hanging-in' in an upside-down world and they need protection. This orphaned baby was lucky, being raised by a carer, and he was successfully released and returned to the wild when he was big enough.

JOAN PUFFETT

A tiny baby hangs on his foster mother's pocket. Many flying-foxes are electrocuted on power lines. Sometimes when the victim is a mother carrying her baby clinging tightly to her abdomen, the shock which kills her when she short-circuits the power across two lines does not affect the baby. If the infant is lucky and it is found and rescued in time, it can be raised by a carer registered with organisations like FAWNA or WIRES (wildlife rescue groups have different names in different States and Territories).

JOAN PUFFETT

Grey-headed flying-foxes (*Pteropus poliocephalus*) are important distributors of seeds and pollinators of native trees and shrubs, thereby playing a significant role in maintaining biodiversity. They occur all along the east coast from central Queensland to Melbourne. Social mammals, they spend the day hanging high in the canopy of trees in their camp (where they can be detected by their smell before they become visible) and they fly out at dusk to feed within a radius of 30 km. Radio-tracking of individuals has shown that they can move over vast distances (in one instance, 800 km over several months), following the flowering of native trees — their preferred food is the nectar and pollen of eucalypts, turpentines, paperbarks and banksias. Congregations of several hundred thousand are seen periodically when mass flowering of eucalypts occurs.

Rainforest fruits, particularly many species of figs, are important in their diet. The fruit is chewed thoroughly, the liquid swallowed and the fibre spat out, minimising the weight carried in the gut and providing a high energy, easily digested liquid diet — important in a flying creature. Large fruits are carried away from the parent tree to be eaten, and the seeds are dropped. Smaller seeds are swallowed and later expelled in flight. Trees in rainforests depend on having their seed taken away from their immediate vicinity in order to have space to germinate and grow.

When fruit of native plants is scarce, flying-foxes (known also as fruit bats for this reason) can cause economic loss by raiding orchards. Entire orchards can be netted to exclude bats and birds — a practice which is proving to be cost effective.

Flying-foxes navigate and locate food using excellent vision and a keen sense of smell. They do not echo-locate like insect-eating micro-bats do. They are highly intelligent and people who have raised orphaned babies say that they are like dogs in their relationship with their carers. In their camps in the daytime they doze, or jostle and chatter, or groom their fur. In spring, females give birth to a single young, which is suckled for up to six months. The baby clings onto its mother when she flies with the colony for the first four weeks of its life; then it is left in the camp with other babies during the night while its mother forages. By four months old it is able to fly and it begins to feed with the adults.

Flying-foxes, like other native animals, have suffered from destruction of their habitat. Few breeding habitats remain in New South Wales, and where they exist they are increasingly threatened. One highly vulnerable colony's refugium is situated in a Sydney suburb and it is fortunate in having a protection society to ensure its survival.

The Ku-ring-gai Flying Fox Reserve

The reserve is a bushland valley surrounded by houses in the northern Sydney suburb of Gordon. A conservation agreement between the NSW Minister for the Environment and Ku-ring-gai Municipal Council safeguards this wildlife site and protects a maternity colony whose population fluctuates, sometimes reaching 50 000 depending on food availability in Sydney and elsewhere. Many of the trees are stressed and dying due to massive weed invasion and the climbing and landing of flying-foxes. Weeds prevent regeneration of the native trees. A plan of management was completed in 1995.

In 1985 the Ku-ring-gai Bat Colony Committee Inc. was established to inform the public of the ecological importance of bats, especially flying-foxes, and the need to conserve their habitat. In 1987 the committee began the long-term restoration of the habitat by removing weeds. This allows natural regeneration to occur, and some seedlings are planted. A contract bush regeneration team is currently funded by grants from the NSW Government, Ku-ring-gai Council, and by public donations. A volunteer team works each Tuesday. As with other volunteer bush regeneration programs, the activities are much enjoyed by all in the working parties, friendships are made and a great deal of satisfaction is felt in doing something positive to improve a local ecosystem.

The Committee organises other bat-related activities.

- Bat talks with hand-reared flying-foxes and illustrated with coloured slides can be arranged for schools and community groups.
- Bat walks through the reserve in summer can be arranged with *Chase Alive* (02 9457 9853).
- Volunteers are needed to count flying-foxes regularly.

agricultural areas, the planting of trees and shrubs to make wildlife corridors between remnants assists in conservation. Roadside and railway bush corridors and streamside revegetation serve the same purpose. Landcare groups are performing a valuable service to maintaining biodiversity by their activities of this sort.

Our northern **Gondwanan rainforests** are an example of relict vegetation in refugia. Their refuges form a chain of pockets along the eastern margin of the continent. The forests are so species-rich that on that ground alone they should all be given full protection. A proportion are World Heritage forests. The concentrations of species which belong to primitive families of flowering plants in them; the fact that they are closed ecosystems and little changed in their composition from the warm-temperate 'mixed' forests of Gondwana in the Early Tertiary; and their survival in the core areas, to which they are now confined, since the days of the dinosaurs, gives them a scientific significance additional to their value as a biodiversity resource. They are the only relatively unchanged and uncontaminated Gondwanan forests in the world — which makes them a scientific resource beyond price; a gene pool which the world may well need when humans have so changed the environment that they have to look for new plants to sustain their lifestyles; and an ecosystem whose antiquity and conservatism demands reverence.

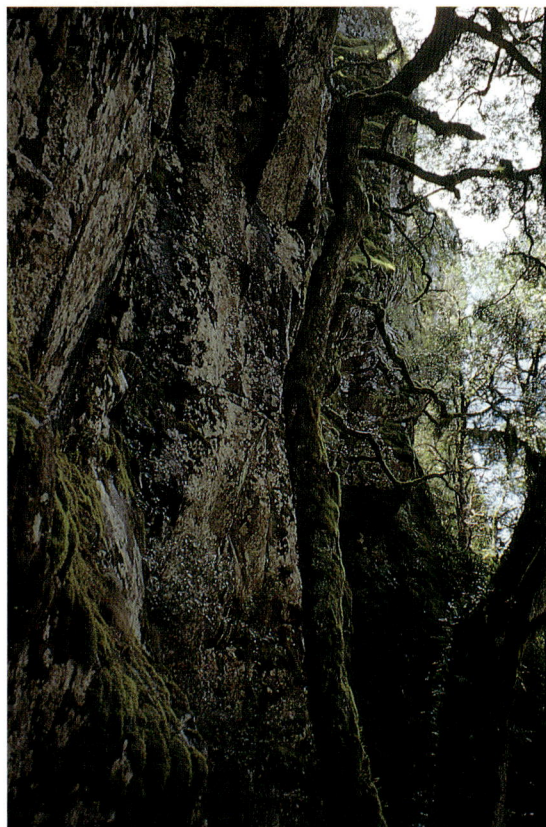

Remnant of Antarctic beech forest in a microclimate on the Ebor Volcano.

M.E.W

VERTEBRATE EXTINCTIONS IN AUSTRALIA

Australia's record in terms of conservation of its biodiversity is not good. Eighteen of its endemic marsupial species are now extinct, representing 30% of global mammal extinctions according to the 1992 census of the World Conservation Monitoring Centre. Much of this attrition has occurred within a specific group — the medium-sized marsupials or **meso-marsupials**, some of which are totally extinct, some extinct on the mainland, and many locally extinct over most of what was their range 200 years ago.

When New South Wales was first settled it was home to 131 native mammal species. Of these, 27 are now extinct in the State and another 50 are recognised as threatened. The pig-footed bandicoot and the numbat both disappeared from western New South Wales late last century, as did the burrowing and brush-tailed bettongs (whose importance in semi-arid ecosystems of the Western Division before European settlement is described below). Semi-arid regions of the State, like such regions worldwide, were least suited to the agricultural and land management practices which were inflicted upon them, and were the first to be drastically and permanently degraded. **As early as 1901 a Royal Commission was established to look into the condition of Crown land tenants in the western lands. Overstocking with sheep, invasion by rabbits, followed by drought and dust storms had taken an enormous toll.** The Royal Commission was concerned with the socio-economic plight of the farmers and the visible signs of vegetation and soil degradation, and no mention was made of loss of native fauna.

ARID ZONE EXTINCTIONS

Seventy-two species of mammals (excluding bats) were known to be living in the arid zone at the time of European settlement. Of these, 11 are now extinct; five

Perennial vegetation in the arid zone is often confined to run-on zones, as in this picture where bushes grow below the breakaway.

M.E.W.

have disappeared from the mainland and are now found only on offshore islands; 15 have suffered a great decline in their range, with several of these now confined to semi-arid fringes. It is the medium-sized mammals which have suffered most. Arid zone mammal species on the endangered list comprise 90% of the 28 land-dwelling Australian mammals whose survival into the next century is uncertain. No reptiles, birds or amphibians are known to have become extinct in the arid zone, although some have become rare, and this poses the question: why have the arid zone mammals been selectively affected?

When one understands the nature of arid-zone environments and the problems which face animals living there, the reasons for the extinctions becomes clear. Infrequent and unreliable rainfall, which characterises the region, is less of a problem than that of nutrition.[41,42] Most of the arid zone animals obtain their water from their food and it is the availability of an adequate diet that is the limiting factor. The infertile soils over most of the arid zone are deficient in nitrogen and phosphorus and the perennial native vegetation is low in nutrients. In fact, much of the vegetation has a high content of digestion-inhibiting chemicals, actively discouraging herbivores. The small patches of more fertile soil such as the 'run-on' zones caused by local topography, local changes in geology, and some clay-pans, produce plant material with higher nutritional value. These areas are enormously significant, acting like life-supporting islands in the generally infertile sea.

Added to the problems of almost universally infertile soils throughout the arid zone, the extreme climatic fluctuations caused by the Southern Oscillation introduce a new dimension into survival there. In the occasional La Nina years of good rains the countryside may bloom and animals may multiply, only to be culled by the return to the characteristic conditions of unreliable rains and high evaporation. During the long periods between rains and, in particular, during the El Nino droughts, survival depends on the fertile islands, which may be reduced to very small areas in an animal's home range, or may even disappear, causing local extinction. Medium-sized animals do not have the capability of larger ones to migrate over the distances required to find surviving patches of quality food, nor do they have the lesser requirement of the smaller mammals which enables them to persist in an area.

Ever since the establishment of a major arid zone in our continent, medium-sized mammals must have had a precarious existence there in its delicately balanced ecosystems. The zone is a feature of relatively recent geological time attributable to the global climatic changes of the run-down towards the Pleistocene ice age from perhaps six million years ago, and it acquired its present form and extent during the glacial stages of the 2.6 million years of the ice age.

During the last glacial stage, which had its peak 18 000 years ago, desert and arid zone extended over about 80% of the continent, so present-day conditions are benign compared with that time when rainfall was half what it is today and wind strength and frequency were double present levels. Add the Southern Oscillation to the equation and the probability is that life in core areas of the deserts was practically non-existent. Even during the present interglacial stage in which we are living there have been global climatic fluctuations with periods when life in the arid zone would have been easier and times when it would have been more precarious than now.

Seen in the context of the geological past and the delicate balance of present-day arid zone ecosystems, it is not surprising that medium-sized mammals have been so vulnerable to change. Introduction of the rabbit and of hoofed animals (stock and feral) which compete for limited food resources and cause soil erosion and degradation of vegetation by their over-grazing is enough to explain the selective extinctions. In addition, the introduction of predators — feral cats and foxes — preying on already embattled populations, has probably been the final straw in many areas. Birds and reptiles have not suffered the same extinctions because of the mobility of the former and the ability of the latter because of their cold-blooded nature to survive in an inactive state when conditions are bad.

Understanding the situation in the arid zone and its relationship to medium-size mammal extinctions should open our eyes to the problems which are increasingly faced by native animals (and plants) in our man-made deserts and degraded areas, and even in the areas where we have so changed the environment for our purposes, or as a consequence of our activities, that it no longer suits its original occupants. The balance in ecosystems becomes more precarious as they are degraded and their resilience decreases, species become endangered and extinction faces those whose range or specialised requirements are no longer met. Any species with a small home range is especially disadvantaged and at risk, while wide-ranging generalists are less vulnerable.

Local Extinctions

The **burrowing bettong** (*Bettongia lesueur*) and the **brush-tailed bettong** (*Bettongia penicillata*) are today very limited in their distribution — the former restricted to three offshore islands in Western Australia, and the latter surviving in four localities in south-western Western Australia. Both species were widespread, together covering about seven-eighths of the continent 200 years ago.

In eastern Australia these meso-marsupials (also

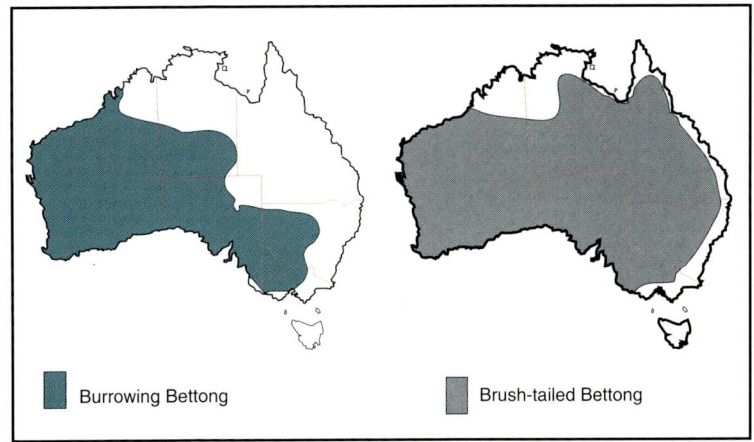

Burrowing Bettong

Brush-tailed Bettong

After Noble[43]

known as rat kangaroos) were rapidly eliminated *within two or three decades of European settlement*, through a combination of competition from introduced herbivores (including rabbits which invaded their burrows), predation from foxes and cats, and poisoning or hunting of 'bush vermin' by early settlers.[43]

In the Western Division of New South Wales the bettongs disappeared so fast that it is only from accounts by early naturalists and from remnant physical signs of their burrows that we know of their presence. The last specimen collected and held by the Australian Museum is dated December 1879. The burrowing bettongs left evidence of their occupancy of the semi-arid rangelands because they made substantial warrens, whose relict features, particularly in the 'hard red' soils, have recently been recognised. The brush-tailed bettong left no signs of its presence because it made surface nests

MARSUPIALS ON THE DANGER LIST

A Marsupial Research Centre has recently been set up at Macquarie University, Sydney, to coordinate programs aimed at saving species on the verge of extinction. Under the Co-operative Research Centre program funded by the Federal Government ($11.68 million over seven years) Macquarie University biologists will work with New Zealand's Landcare Research Institute, Perth Zoo, Queensland's Department of Primary Industry and the University of Newcastle. (New Zealand's involvement is not to save endangered species but, through research into reproductive biology, to find a way to control Australian brush-tail possums which are feral and present in alarming numbers in New Zealand.)

The animals involved are:

- The dibbler, *Parantechinus apicalis*, of Western Australia, which has not been seen since 1988 and may already be extinct.
- The numbat, *Myrmecobius fasciatus*: Scattered relict populations occur in

Western Australia. It breeds well in captivity and a program at the Perth Zoo has resulted in its re-introduction into forest in the Dryandra Reserve in the south-west, where a program of baiting had eliminated foxes and feral cats.

- The Proserpine rock wallaby, *Petrogale persephone*, of Queensland exists as a small scattered population in a fragmented area, making it highly vulnerable. It could be bred in captivity.
- The bridled nailtail wallaby, *Onychogalea fraenata*, of Queensland is reduced to a single population in a semi-disturbed area west of Rockhampton. Its survival is threatened by foxes and cats. Captive breeding has been fairly successful.
- The northern brush-tailed bettong, *Bettongia tropica*, of Queensland has a highly specialised habitat and food requirements and is at risk from clearing and predators.
- The northern hairy-nosed wombat,

Lasiorhinus krefftii, of Queensland is reduced to a single surviving population of about 70 individuals in a small remnant of habitat. It has never been bred in captivity.

- The Julia Creek dunnart, *Sminthopsis douglasi*: a single isolated population of a few individuals is the only one known to exist. It has never bred in captivity.
- Leadbeaters possum, *Gymnobelideus leadbeateri*, survives in Victoria in a small area threatened by logging, fire and climate change.
- The mountain pygmy-possum, *Burramys parvus*, of the mountains of south-eastern New South Wales and Victoria survives in two isolated remnant populations at risk from foxes, ski resort development and climate change.
- The long-footed potoroo, *Potorous longipes*, is found in isolated populations of unknown size in New South Wales and Victoria, where it is vulnerable to habitat destruction and predators.

Remnant bettong warrens on 'Glenora' in the Western Division.

JIM NOBLE

diameter, and they always have a horse-shoe-shaped perimeter mound on which white calcrete rubble is deposited in discrete patches, indicating the direction of individual tunnel drives. Even on lighter-textured soils, the basic warren geometry is still recognisable, despite extensive reworking by rabbits. Rapid spread of rabbits during the massive rabbit plagues of early days of settlement was in part enabled by the availability of warrens which they could occupy so readily.

A survey of relict burrows west of Louth on 'Glenora', adjacent to the CSIRO Lake Mere Research Station, established that the warren density was averaging seven per square kilometre. Colonies of 50 to 60 bettongs per warren are known elsewhere, though on the arid off-shore islands today numbers are very much lower. Using an average colony size of just 10 suggests a conservative population size of 70 per square kilometre. It is not unreasonable to suggest that brush-tailed bettongs probably existed in similar numbers. Therefore, the bettongs can be assumed to have had a significant impact on certain landscape processes, including patch dynamics, nutrient recycling, dispersal of diaspores and regulation of shrub seedling recruitment. Brush-tailed bettongs have recently been shown to be important distributors of ecto-mycorrhizal fungal spores in sclerophyll forest in south-western Western Australia.

The rapid extinction of bettongs in western New South Wales coincided with an equally rapid increase in density of native shrubs, according to an anonymous 1901 report which described the increasing abundance of *Eremophila* (emu bushes), *cassias* (Senna), *Dodonaea* (hop bushes) and *Callitris glaucophylla* (cypress pine). (The rufous bettong, *Aepyprymnus rufescens*, is known to be a voracious eater of seedlings of cypress pine and its local extinction led to the development of the Pilliga Forest in northern New South Wales. The quokka, another meso-marsupial, maintains post-fire vegetation as low heath on Rottnest Island by eating tree seedlings.)

It is customary to ascribe **woody weed invasion** to a change in fire frequency following excessive grazing pressures imposed by a combination of domestic, feral and native herbivores which eliminated potential herbage fuel. The significance of the removal of two widespread, numerous and influential species abruptly at an early stage in settlement (when so much serious land degradation took place) has been largely overlooked. Unbalancing brittle ecosystems by removing animals that had such important linkages in their web of interactions may have set in motion an unstoppable biodiversity decline. Periodic natural fire and bettong grazing habits probably maintained the Western Division as open savanna before rabbits, sheep and other introduced animals arrived.[44]

Re-introduction programs for the two bettong species are under way in Western and South Australia, restoring them to islands where there are no predators or to peninsulas which can be fenced and rendered free of foxes and feral cats by baiting.

beneath shrubs, using long strands of bark or grass residues which it carried in a bundle in its prehensile tail.

Large, circular surface-soil features in mulga country of western New South Wales conform to warrens built by the burrowing bettong still living on Western Australian islands. Surface soil has eroded away leaving a calcrete central dome and a radial pattern. The features often attain substantial size, up to 30 m in

BIOTIC CRUSTS—THE FIRST STABILISERS OF SOIL IN THE PRIMAEVAL WORLD

When life first started to colonise the land, the emergence of organisms from the green-scummy watery places onto the inhospitable dry land was an enormous evolutionary step. Microscopic fungi and bacteria; lichens and the earliest land plants — ancestors of mosses, clubmosses and the spore and seed-bearing vascular plants — created a living zone around the edges of water. From the very beginning an inter-dependence existed between the organisms that photosynthesised and manufactured food; those that ate them; those that recycled the nutrients and assisted plants in their uptake; and the ever-expanding web spreading out and becoming more complicated in its inter-relationships.

Probably the first land cover was essentially lichen crusts, which contained also an assortment of less visible and microscopic organisms. Lichens are the product of symbiotic relationships between fungi, which form their body structures, and green algae (and/or cyanobacteria) which live inside the structures and are able to synthesise their food requirements because they contain chlorophyll. Cyanobacteria, which had been the very first photosynthesisers in the earliest oceans, half way between bacteria and plants, would have been prominent soil dwellers. As colonisers of bare earth, stabilisers of the landscape, creators of soil from inanimate sediment, fixers of atmospheric nitrogen, and providers of food and shelter for invertebrates making the transition from water to land life, the living crusts were fundamental in establishing the basis for the evolutionary processes which have resulted in today's biota and environments. It should not surprise us, therefore, that fundamental biotic crust assemblages still play a significant, if generally little recognised, role in modern ecosystems. The amazing conservatism of simple life forms throughout geological time is always a source of wonder.

A further example of the fundamental inter-connectedness of living things, which goes back to the start of land-plant evolution about 425 million years ago, is the symbiotic relationship between mycorrhizal fungi and vascular plants. Some of the earliest known vascular plants like *Rhynia* (known from petrified material in Scotland) had mycorrhiza inside their root cells, assisting them in mineral and water uptake. The higher land plants evolved from green algae by processes of selection as they adapted to the changed requirements of a land world, by developing body structure of roots, stems and leaves, specialised tissues for transport of water (vascular tissue) and reproductive mechanisms suited to life on the land.

Today, cyanobacteria are stabilising the desert sands of the Red Centre and enriching them with nitrogen,[45,46] just as they used to do in the distant geological past. The high levels of nitrate in groundwater in our arid lands is related to cyanobacterial activity.

SOIL CRUSTS, PHYSICAL AND BIOLOGICAL, IN AUSTRALIA'S RANGELANDS

Rangelands account for more than 70% of the area of Australia, comprising pastoral land, areas under Aboriginal ownership, and national parks and reserves. Rangelands and aridity go together in this continent by its very nature. With 75% under arid regimes, the better-watered parts of the land are fully allocated for other uses.

The arid and semi-arid rangelands characteristically have low rainfall which is also variable in quantity and timing, and with frequent droughts. The mallee and mulga shrublands and tussock grasslands, the spinifex shrubland and hummock grasslands, all evolved with, and are adapted to, the dry, unpredictable climates. The tropical rangelands, the grassy savannas and dry eucalypt woodlands of northern Australia, have long dry seasons and short monsoonal seasons where the amount of rainfall is also variable.

Soils of the rangelands are generally shallow, infertile, weathered and highly sorted. Over the whole area of rangelands they have been much affected by the intense aridity and aeolian activity of the Pleistocene ice age, and they have only stabilised during the last 14 000 years — the interglacial in which we are living today.

Widespread areas of crusting, sealing and hard-setting soils occur throughout the rangelands. **Physical seals** and hard-setting surfaces affect infiltration, run-off and erosion processes and soil fertility, resulting in reduced productivity. **Biological crusts**, on the other hand, **are associated with healthy landscapes**.[47] The two types often occur together in areas which are degraded as a result of human intervention.

Soils liable to develop physical crusts are often those with a high dust-derived component;[48] and those with high clay content due to sorting when the country was blowing away to form sand drifts and dunes during glacial stages of the Pleistocene ice age. Scalds have always been part of the arid landscapes (since Australia became the driest vegetated continent), just as hard-setting soils have always been associated with the stony desert pavements, where the stones are what was left behind when the sandy portion blew away. Where wind and water erosion continues today when ground cover is reduced by over-grazing and fire management practices, the hard-setting layer is exposed and scalding increases. (Severe scalding can only be remedied by physical intervention — ripping contour lines to promote infiltration and water-ponding, and to provide areas where seeds and humus accumulate from run-off and start the spreading back of vegetation.) The cracking-clay alluvial soils of river floodplains in the rangelands develop hard surface crusts when dry.

Soil crusts develop on degraded land as a result of compaction and soil structure decline. Bare soil between plants results from selective over-grazing of vegetation; trampling of soil and a decrease in organic matter content result in compaction; and rain-drop splash and wind and water erosion all contribute to crusting. Very large areas of the rangelands have crusted soils because 50% of the tropical savannas and most of the mallee and mulgalands are degraded by over-grazing. When land is severely over-grazed, to the extent that large areas of bare earth exist between plants, the surface crust is the only thing preventing erosion of the soil (while at the same time it is

Mulga grove at the foot of the hill, scald with hard crust in front of it.

M.E.W.

A desert pavement with algal crust between the stones.

M.E.W.

preventing infiltration of rain and promoting run-off, and preventing germination of seeds). These conflicting effects create the situation frequently observed in degraded mulgalands where the vegetation structure becomes one of **groves and intergroves**. The bare, crusted ground of the intergroves is a run-off zone, shedding its water onto an interception zone, adjoining the run-on zone of the mulga grove.[49]

Management of degraded lands with crusting of the bare soil areas is controversial. There are those, like Allan Savory (the 'father' of Holistic Resource Management[50]) who advocate high intensity, short duration grazing practices in which the grazers' hooves chop up the crusts while the dung and urine fertilises the soil (effectively creating zones like the interception zone mentioned above). The more generally accepted strategy (as assessed by Eldridge *et al.*[47,51]) is to maintain very conservative stocking rates, with no build-up in good years, using only 20% to 30% of available pasture. The scientists advocating this approach say that there is *no Australian evidence to support Allan Savory's argument, and that the conventional wisdom is that this strategy leads to*

a decline in soil condition in the long term. Where the crusting of the soil is of a biological, not physical, type, its destruction by high intensity bursts of grazing, or by hooves during times of over-grazing pressures, is believed to be unequivocally harmful.

Biological Soil Crusts

(also called cryptogamic crusts, microbiotic crusts)

Biological crusts formed by mosses, liverworts, lichens, cyanobacteria, algae, fungi and bacteria, occurring together or separately, in intimate association with surface soils, are dominant surface features in arid and semi-arid landscapes which are not altered by human intervention or comprised of pure silica sands. Beneath the obvious surface organisms the structure of several millimetres of crust is felt-like, due to the mat of extremely thin fungal hyphae, the rhizoids of mosses and anchoring threads of lichens. Gelatinous algal sheaths and cements produced by the cyanobacteria and algae result in cohesion of sand grains and the organic material, contributing to the structured nature of the crust.

The living crusts survive prolonged desiccation and are rapidly restored to active life when they are wet. They occur in all vegetation communities and on most soil types, their component organisms varying according to site-specific requirements, successional stage and climate. They play a major role in infiltration processes through changes to the physical and chemical properties of the soil in the few upper millimetres of the crust they create, and through their effect of increasing soil-surface roughness which channels water flow and concentrates it in selected locations. The crust becomes like a filter zone, letting water through and protecting the soil below. Seeds are trapped in its rough surface; germination is enhanced by the nitrogenous fertiliser

Lake Mungo National Park. The ground in this picture is covered with a biotic crust.

Above left: A dry lichen crust, and left, shows how it came alive with one night's rain, with bright green moss and liverworts.

M.E.W.

supplied by the cyanobacteria in the crusts which are nitrogen fixers.

It has been shown that on badly eroded soils, infiltration increased greatly with increased cryptogamic cover.[52] The crusts are primary colonisers when land has been degraded, and in the early stages of colonisation it is the cyanobacteria which are responsible for stabilising the surface. Their gelatinous sheaths and algal gels bind soil particles and with fungal hyphae start to form the crust.

Biological crusts stabilise the soil against water and

Far left middle and bottom: Biotic crust on white sand dune at Lake Mungo.

M.E.W.

The stony ground between clumps of spinifex at Wilpena Pound in the Flinders Ranges is covered with a dense biotic crust of lichen, mosses and liverworts.

M.E.W.

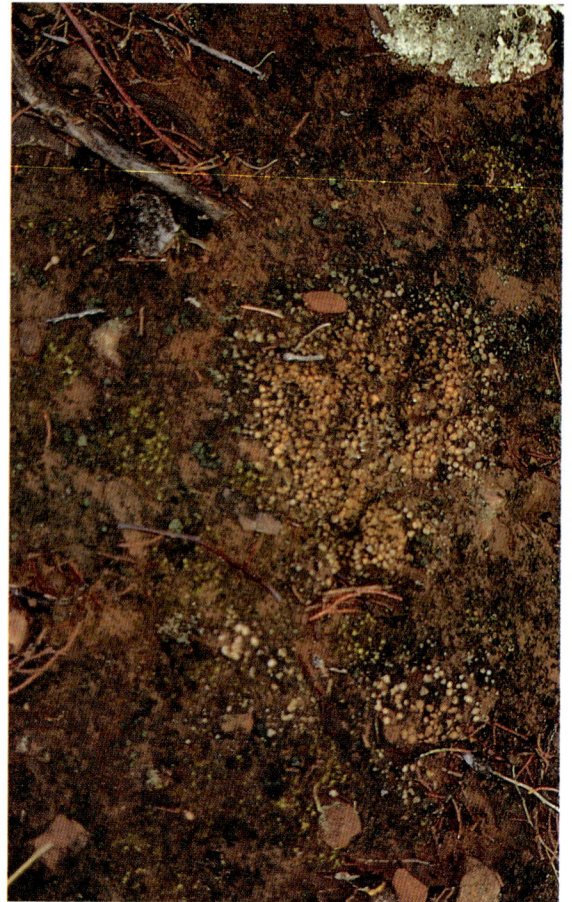

DISTRIBUTION OF LICHEN CRUSTS

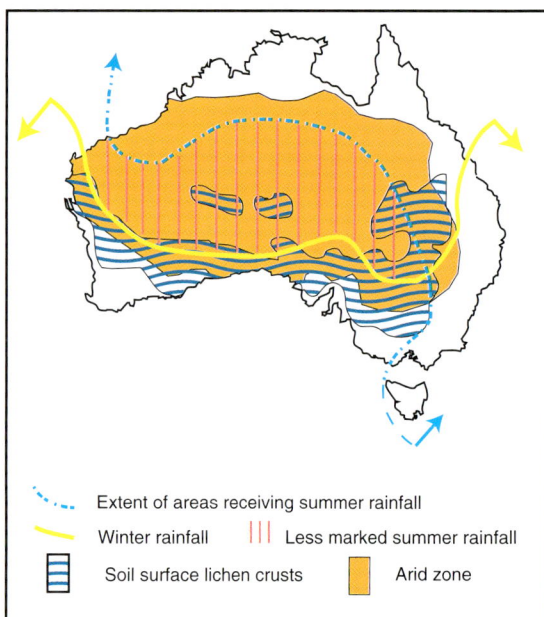

Extent of areas receiving summer rainfall

Winter rainfall ||| Less marked summer rainfall

Soil surface lichen crusts   Arid zone

After Rogers,[55]

wind erosion, thus increasing landscape stability, particularly when vegetation cover is reduced.[53,54] During droughts they may provide the only protection to the soil from wind erosion; and from water erosion when rain falls again on bare ground. Sediment loss was found to be from three to five times greater from rain splash on physically hard-crusted surfaces than on biologically crusted surfaces.

Lichens are prominent in the soil crusts in the winter rainfall regions, and are absent in crusts in the tropical, summer rainfall, northern part of the continent. Lichens can survive high temperatures when in a dry and inactive state, but when they are wet and active they are unable to tolerate excessive heat, which effectively limits them to the southern, winter rainfall, half of the continent.[55]

In the Bungle Bungle National Park in the Eastern Kimberleys, for instance, the biological crust is black and comprises cyanobacteria almost exclusively, and the dark staining on the alternating finer-grained, clay-rich layers in the sandstone in the wonderful pillars of Bungle rocks is cyanobacterial, not lichen. The layers of easily weathered ochre-coloured sandstone with no clay cement which alternate with the cyanobacteria-darkened layers, do not supply the necessary foothold for a biological crust and their surface erodes more easily, keeping its clean, fresh colour. Textural differences in sandstone layers are emphasised, creating the striped effect like a 'seersucker' fabric.

Biological crusts are susceptible to fire and are damaged or destroyed by trampling of livestock. Therefore management of degraded rangelands where they are important soil stabilisers has to be aimed at reducing grazing and trampling pressures and imposing fire regimes which can be tolerated by the crust. At Cobar in western New South Wales the recovery of the cryptogamic cover on a degraded soil took 15 years; at the Koonamore Regeneration Area in South Australia the lichen cover was still substantially reduced after 44

years of exclusion of grazers.[56]

Scientific evaluation of the impact of fire on biological crusts has mostly been from studies in the semi-arid woodlands of eastern Australia. There the cryptogamic cover has been shown to be essential for maintaining the hydraulic properties of these surface soils. Removal of the crust by fire adversely affects infiltration, and the increased run-off causes erosion. The removal of the protective vegetation by fire allows direct damage to the crust. Annual fires for seven years were shown to completely eliminate the lichens and mosses on the surface and also the fungal hyphae and the cementing gels and mucilaginous sheaths which form the felt-like layer of the crust.[57] The fuel load in semi-arid woodlands tends to restrict prescribed burning to low frequencies, and although biological crusts are destroyed and organic matter and soil structure are adversely affected, the effects of fire are temporary. A return to pre-fire levels is expected in about four years.[49]

In spinifex grassland on wind-blown sands, burning results in increased wind erosion due to destabilising of algal soil crusts. The frequent burning of the spinifex in Uluru National Park (Ayers Rock), guided by the 'wisdom' of Aboriginal Rangers, takes no heed of this factor and ecosystem degradation over time would appear to be inevitable for this, and other, ecological reasons. In the mallee lands it has been shown that fires more frequently than at ten-year intervals cause permanent damage to biological crusts.

In the tropical savannas, frequent fires are likely to

Above top: The dark, blackish biotic crust in the Bungle Bungle National Park is composed of cyanobacteria. Where the crust is broken between the grass clumps, erosion is occurring.

Above top left: The striped effect on the sandstone in the Bungle Bungles is due to the sandstone layers having different amounts of clay cementing the sand grains together in alternating layers. Some layers have virtually no clay and they erode rapidly, retaining their fresh orange colour; others are more resistant to erosion because their sand grains are locked together by clay, and they develop a crust of cyanobacteria which makes them blackish.

Above: Spinifex grows in discrete hummocks with bare soil between them. Algal sheaths and gels are important in maintaining stability of the soil between the plants.

M.E.W.

keep infiltration rates low and increase the chances of physical soil crusting. The annual burning which today occurs in much of the northern savannas must surely affect the biological soil crusts, though research into fire in the Australian wet-dry tropics has not focused on this aspect of ecosystem health. The fact that the rapid growth of the tall grasses of the savanna woodlands makes annual fires possible, unlike the situation in the semi-arid and arid woodlands where biomass restricts fire frequency, has led to the assumption that because the savanna will burn annually, it should burn annually.

Right: The spongolites in the Fitzgerald National Park were laid down in an Eocene sea about 45 million years ago.

M.E.W.

Above: View from East Mt Barren to the tombolo across the entrance to Culham Inlet on the road to Hopetoun. The coastal strip in the Biosphere Reserve has spectacular scenery and vegetation.

M.E.W.

BIOSPHERE RESERVES

The concept of biosphere reserves was developed by UNESCO, the United Nations body which had been set up after the Second World War, in response to growing concern about environmental degradation and extinction of species in many parts of the world. The first international use of the term **biosphere** referring to **all that part of the Earth which supports life** was at the 1958 UNESCO Conference *The Rational Use and Conservation of the Resources of the Biosphere* which also began a shift in thinking from conservation by pure protection towards ecologically sustainable development. In 1974 the Worldwide Network of Biosphere Reserves was established. Its primary aim was to protect representative areas of the world's major ecological units.

The **Man and the Biosphere Program** has evolved from the initially protective concept, and

sustainable land use became part of the program. All true biosphere reserves must now include development as well as conservation, research and education. Humans are clearly understood to be part of the biosphere, working with the environment for sustainability. Core areas must remain 'natural' and be of sufficient size to allow the fauna and flora of the ecosystems to self-perpetuate in a self-sustaining manner with minimum human management and interference. Surrounding buffer zones may contain human-modified examples of the ecosystems and also degraded areas which are to be rehabilitated.[58]

Australia has 12 biosphere reserves, of which The Fitzgerald Biosphere Reserve in south-western Western Australia and Macquarie Island, an Australian sub-Antarctic territory, have been chosen as examples.

The Fitzgerald Biosphere Reserve, Western Australia

The core area of this biosphere reserve is the **Fitzgerald River National Park** and it was selected in 1978 on the basis of its high nature conservation value and potential for research. In the last ten years it has attained the complete UNESCO requirements for biosphere status by incorporating a buffer and corridor zone and a surrounding Landcare zone with community involvement and cooperation. The area is sparsely populated with about 3000 residents mainly living on farms and in four small towns.[59]

Droughts of the 1980s had led to land degradation and soil loss by wind erosion on surrounding properties, and the clearing of vegetation had caused rising water-tables and salinity problems, so the landholders in the zone of cooperation were ready for Landcare projects. Catchment management, care of remnant vegetation,

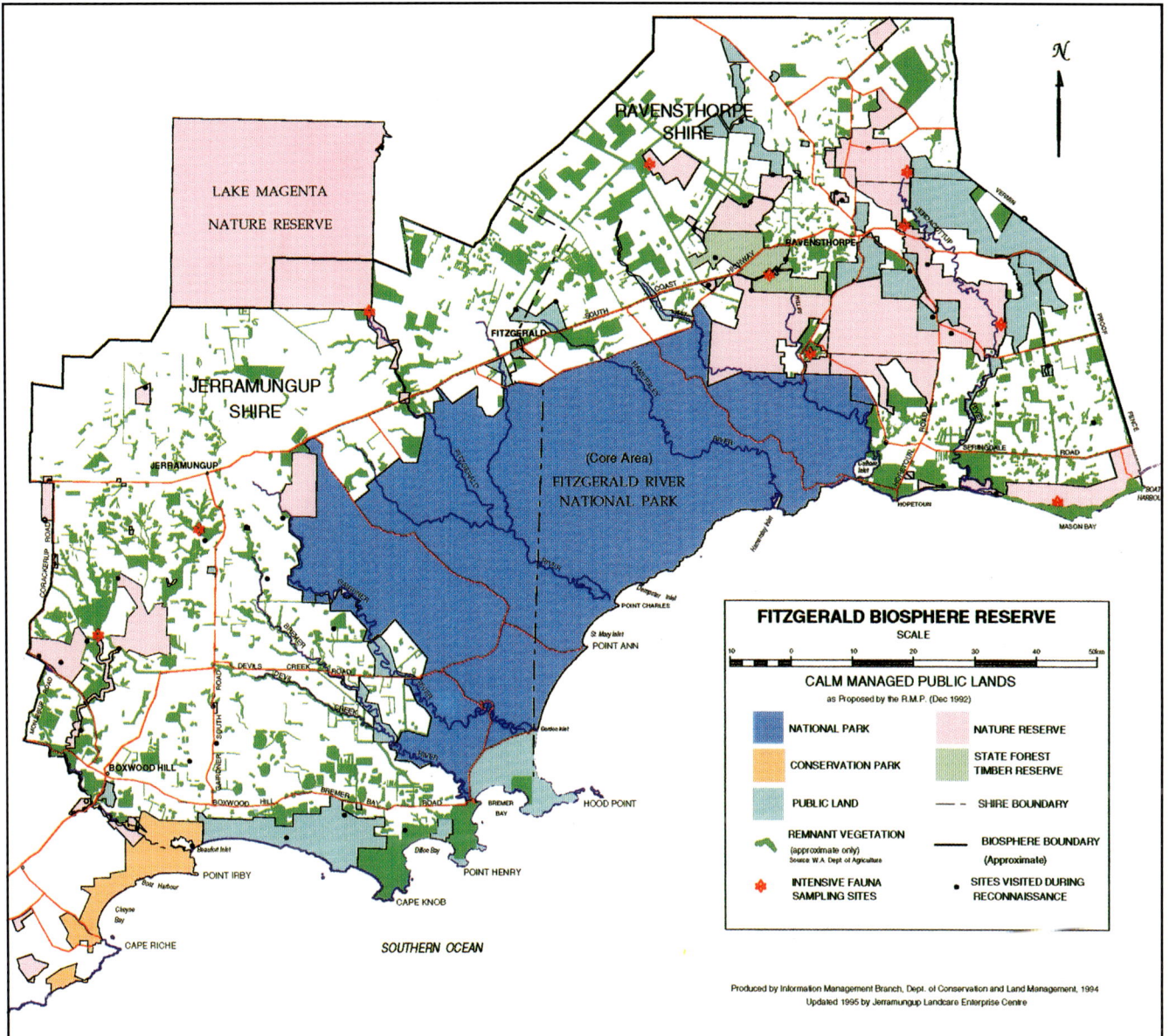

FITZGERALD BIOSPHERE RESERVE

SCALE

CALM MANAGED PUBLIC LANDS
as Proposed by the R.M.P. (Dec 1992)

NATIONAL PARK — NATURE RESERVE
CONSERVATION PARK — STATE FOREST TIMBER RESERVE
PUBLIC LAND — SHIRE BOUNDARY
REMNANT VEGETATION (approximate only) Source W.A. Dept of Agriculture — BIOSPHERE BOUNDARY (Approximate)
INTENSIVE FAUNA SAMPLING SITES — SITES VISITED DURING RECONNAISSANCE

Produced by Information Management Branch, Dept. of Conservation and Land Management, 1994
Updated 1995 by Jerramungup Landcare Enterprise Centre

Map kindly supplied by CALM, WA

Far left: Royal hakea and **Banksia baxteri** *in the Fitzgerald National Park.*

Left: The cauliflower bush, Hakea corymbosa, *and wildflowers.*

M.E.W.

re-establishing trees and changed land-use practices, like minimal tillage and replacing shallow-rooted plants with deep-rooted alternatives, were recognised as beneficial to farmers, and at the same time necessary for the health of the rivers that flow through the Park to the estuaries and wetlands on the coastal plain.

Activities of the Malleefowl Preservation Group in the Corackerup Nature Reserve and in privately owned remnant bushland within the Landcare zone have led to increased interest in conservation and research in the area. The bird is relatively common in the park and in the buffer zone, and especially in the Ravensthorpe Range. Its presence in the Bookmark Biosphere Reserve in South Australia offers opportunity for comparative research projects.

The National Park core area covers 330 000 ha extending from the central south coast inland on average about 40 km. Inclusion of the surrounding zones extends the area of the reserve to 1.3 million hectares.

The park contains a variety of diverse landforms including quartzite mountains with their drainage systems and associated estuaries, swamps and wetlands; a former marine plain with incised river valleys — formed from sediments, laid down in an Eocene sea about 40 million years ago, which contain abundant sponge spicules in some strata (the mountains were islands in this sea); upland plains; and 60 km of rugged coastline.

The biodiversity in the park core is astounding. It contains:

- 1748 species of plants, of which 75 are endemic and 250 are very rare or geographically restricted. The highest concentration of endemics is in the Barren Ranges. (Including the rest of the biosphere reserve where the importance of remnant vegetation, mostly on private land, cannot be over-stressed: the number of plant species becomes 2500, with 120 endemic and 300 rare or geographically restricted.)
- 193 species of birds, of which eight are threatened. The best long-term survival prospects of the ground parrot and the western bristlebird and western whipbird are offered by the park. (Numbers for the whole biosphere reserve are 209 species with eight threatened.)
- 22 native mammals, with six threatened, including the dibbler which is now part of the **newly formed marsupial research centre (managed by Macquarie University with a breeding program at the Perth Zoo)**. Other rare animals, the heath mouse, tammar, red-tailed wambenger, woylie and western mouse, are concentrated in the northern part of the park, on the ancient granitic shield section. (In the whole biosphere reserve the number of native mammal species is 27, with six threatened.)
- 12 frog species. (Including the whole biosphere reserve the number of frog species is 14.)
- 42 reptiles. (The total in the whole biosphere

reserve is 51, including one endemic skink in the Ravensthorpe Range.)

Management of the park has been complicated by the prevalence of the dreaded **die-back disease**, *Phytophthora cinnamomi*, to which members of the Proteaceae as well as some of the eucalypts are highly susceptible. Spores of the soil fungus can be carried in on vehicle tyres and on shoes. It has been necessary to prohibit entry into some areas where the disease is not present, and to confine traffic to maintained gravel roads in other parts. When restrictions were first introduced, they led to a certain amount of conflict with visitors, largely locals, who were used to free access. Fire management is also critical and fires more frequent than every 15 years are known to be detrimental to the fauna. The need to restrict access to parts of the coastal fringe was also a source of conflict because fishermen had always driven their 4WDs wherever they liked, and the fragile sandy ecosystems were suffering. Establishing good communication in the adjacent shires, involving everyone in projects and educating the general populace has seen these teething problems largely disappear.

CALM (the Department of Conservation and Land Management) and the Australian Nature Conservation Agency (ANCA) are jointly funding the first systematic biological survey of the buffer-corridor zone and Landcare zone. The project involves community liaison between organisations, private landowners and Landcare groups, coordinated by ecologist Angela Sanders, who also publicises activities, organises community workshops and associated field tours, and involves local schools. A pilot program with two schools was successful and now all six local schools are involved in studying remnant bushland, and vegetation and fauna studies are being incorporated into the school curriculum. UNESCO and the State Education Department have contributed financially to the biological monitoring program.

The Macquarie Island Biosphere Reserve

Macquarie Island is particularly interesting geologically as it has never been part of any continent and is composed of uplifted oceanic crust. It is part of the Macquarie Ridge, a major crustal feature which results from interaction of the Pacific and Indo-Australian Plates. The ridge extends from the South Island of New Zealand to near Antarctica.

The Macquarie Island is a unique example of well-preserved deep oceanic crust existing above sea-level and as such is of great interest to scientists studying sea-floor spreading and plate tectonics. Volcanic blocks (mainly pillow lavas), basalt dykes and various sediments compose about 80% of the island. It rose from under the sea about 500 000 years ago.[60] Tectonic activity still continues along the ridge and earthquakes of about 6.2 or greater on the Richter Scale occur about once a year; more major tremors, of 7.2 and above, occur approximately every decade.[61]

Macquarie Island lies 1500 km south-south-east of Tasmania and apart from seastacks and a few small islets (also on the Ridge) the nearest land is the Auckland Islands and Campbell Island, about 600 km away. It is 34 km long and 5.5 km wide at its broadest point, a long, narrow undulating plateau 100–350 m above sea-level, bounded on all sides by steep slopes or cliffs. It rises straight out of the deep ocean with no 'continental' shelf. The highest point on the Island is Mt Hamilton, 433 m, and several other peaks rise to over 400 m. Its plant life has come to it by long-distance dispersal, apart from species introduced by humans.

The island has a long and bloody history of commercial exploitation of seals and penguins from 1810 to 1919, eradicating the fur seals and decimating the elephant seal and king penguin populations. In 1933 it was declared a wildlife sanctuary, largely because of the efforts of (Sir) Douglas Mawson.

The first scientific station was established in 1911 by Mawson and was maintained until 1914, and various scientific expeditions visited for short periods up to the 1930s. The first permanent scientific station was established by the Australian Government in 1948. The Australian National Antarctic Research Expedition (ANARE) Station has been operating ever since, conducting multi-disciplinary research programs.

Macquarie Island became a conservation area in 1971; was upgraded to a state reserve in 1972, and in 1978 was renamed Macquarie Island Nature Reserve. In 1977, when the Biosphere Reserve Program was in its early stages, it was chosen as an example of a distinctive ecosystem to be protected. The revised UNESCO Biosphere Reserve Action Plan of 1984, which required the integration of areas with permanent residents as part of the biosphere reserve concept,

detracts from its full compliance. As a Tasmanian State Reserve it has been managed by the Tasmanian Parks and Wildlife Service since 1971.

Today it is one of the richest wildlife sanctuaries in the world, supporting huge concentrations of land-breeding marine wildlife, including about 100 000 seals

Above top: King penguins on Macquarie Island where they are now abundant and protected.

Above: Moulting male elephant seals on a Macquarie Island beach.

Left: Pillow lavas in an outcrop on Macquarie Island. The island was raised from the deep ocean where the basalts of the Macquarie Ridge solidified under water, resulting in the ropey structures.

Dr Patricia Selkirk

and 3.5 million seabirds, mainly penguins. While the mammal and seabird breeding and moulting sites on the island are protected, the surrounding seas, on which the populations are totally dependent for food, are not. This highlights the need for an ecosystem approach to conservation, and a marine reserve has been recommended. It would complement the terrestrial nature reserve/biosphere reserve and provide protection for the marine ecosystem components, at least during the breeding season of the island's land-breeding wildlife.[62] Nomination of Macquarie Island for World Heritage status is now underway.

A major management task has been the control of feral animals since 1978. (All the native mammals are marine.) Cats and dogs, introduced by sealers, were reported by the explorer von Bellinghausen in 1820. The dogs died out but feral cats multiplied, eating burrow-nesting birds until rabbits, ships' rats and house mice were introduced and became widespread. Rabbits were introduced in 1878, to supply food for sealers; the rat and house mice appeared in the 1890s, fugitives from ships. New Zealand rails, wekas (Maori hens), were introduced in the 1870s as a food source, and were largely responsible for the extinction of indigenous rails and parakeets. They were finally eliminated in 1988. Mallard ducks, introduced to New Zealand and Australia last century, made their independent way to Macquarie Island in the 1970s. Starlings and red polls also flew in. There were no native perching birds (passerines) before their arrival.[63]

About 1600 cats were destroyed between 1974 and 1994 and complete eradication is now a high priority. When their numbers were between 250 and 500 in 1974, they were estimated to be eating 60 000 burrow-nesting birds a year even though their main diet was rabbits. Rabbits have been controlled by myxomatosis and the new calicivirus may make eradication possible. As rabbit numbers decline, the impact of cats and rats on birds becomes more focussed, and it will be necessary to achieve full control of all feral animals eventually. Some smaller seabirds are confined to the islets and seastacks for breeding and will only be able to re-establish on the main island when feral animals are eliminated.

Five introduced species of vascular plants have become established on the island — two grasses, two chickweeds and a dock. An annual meadow grass and the chickweeds were brought in with straw packing last century. Every care is taken today to ensure that no further plants are introduced.

Today tourists travel to Antarctica and to the sub-Antarctic islands. Their potential impact on the fragile ecosystems is serious and already the wildlife of Antarctica at tourist-landing spots is stressed, fragile lichen and moss cover in dry valleys is damaged, and rubbish and waste are problems. No matter how stringent the regulations, people, expeditioners and tourists alike, do not necessarily comply.

Macquarie Island has a ship-based tourist industry. The money it brings in pays for the conservation and research. Shore visits are limited; landing areas are specified; small groups are accompanied by guides and are supervised throughout their time on land; stringent quarantine restrictions apply and every possible measure is taken to ensure minimum impact on the fragile ecosystems and minimal disturbance of the fauna.

THE MALLEEFOWL AND ITS PROTECTION

Imagine a male bird whose whole life is work, managing a huge mound for ten months of the year, dedicated to the well-being of his mate's eggs, never even being compensated by enjoying his children — and you have the malleefowl. He lives a nearly solitary existence — for although he mates for life, he has his work, his mate has her responsibilities. (Sounds like yuppies in the high-mortgage belt?) His life may last 30 years if he survives predators, fire and motor vehicles, and he is in breeding mood from the age of two.

To make his mound he first has to dig a hole up to 3 or 4 m in diameter and 1 m deep. Then he fills it to overflowing by busily kicking, scratching, and even sweeping up with his wings, a veritable mountain of leaf litter and sticks, hollowed on top so that it catches the rainwater which will ferment the plant material. He knows just how deep to make the egg chamber where heat from the composting and the sun will incubate the eggs, and he waits until rain has wet the heap before covering the whole edifice with sand. Each time his mate appears on the mound ready to deposit an egg he has to move tonnes of sand and dig down through the rotting vegetation to the egg chamber. He has to be an expert at temperature control, monitoring it, moving sand on and off, keeping it constantly at 33°C. He arranges the eggs neatly in an upright position (necessary for the safe development and escape of the chick) in layers within the egg chamber.

DISTRIBUTION OF MALLEEFOWL
Past and Present

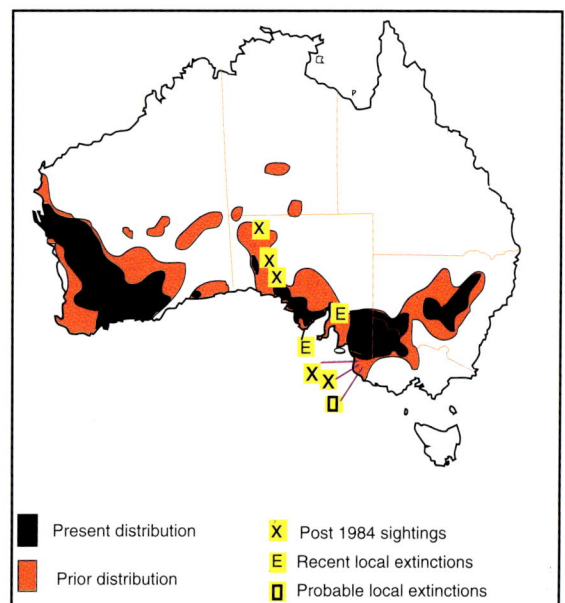

■ Present distribution	X Post 1984 sightings
■ Prior distribution	E Recent local extinctions
	□ Probable local extinctions

After Copley & Williams[64]

*Left: Mallee
woodland — an
unlikely place to find
mound-building birds.*

M.E.W.

It's not much fun for the female either — she is an egg-laying machine producing a couple of dozen or more very large eggs each year, and to obtain sufficient nutrients to do that in the dry and sandy places where she lives means an endless search for seeds, buds of herbs, and insects. The sugary covers of lerps (psyllids) which infest the leaves of mallee eucalypts are a significant and important part of her diet in autumn and winter. How many eggs she lays and how long the laying period is will be determined by rainfall. In dry years she lays few eggs at long intervals. In a good season she produces an egg every five days over a five-month period, each five times the weight of a hen's egg, and equivalent to 10% of her body weight. Each egg takes about seven weeks to hatch, but that is of no interest to the egg-machine, she just makes them and she is totally involved in keeping up her strength eating for two (up to 30 times) throughout the breeding season.

The poor little chick emerging from this malleefowl factory receives no TLC. It pecks its way out of the egg, struggles through sand, emerges exhausted on top of the mound, rolls off, and with what strength it has left it heads for shelter of the mulga, mallee or broombush scrub. It may have had to burrow through a metre of sand, and one case has been recorded where the chick took 22 hours for this epic struggle. In about an hour after its arrival in the wide world the chick has collected its wits and is ready to face life on its own, feeding itself, hiding from predators, and it can even fly — though its body is covered in down, it has wing feathers. Within a day it can fly up into trees to roost at night like its unknown parents do.

Survival must have been difficult enough in a malleefowl's world unaffected by humans. How slim must be its chances of survival now that its habitat is restricted and it has to escape foxes and feral cats and compete with introduced grazing animals for meagre food supplies. It is believed that only 1% of chicks survive to adulthood, and 80% (in New South Wales) are taken by foxes within two weeks of hatching.

The malleefowl (*Leipoa ocellata*) belongs to the Megapode family of mound-building birds. Other representatives of the family in Australia are the scrubfowl of tropical forests from Cape York to Yeppoon in Queensland and of the Top End; and the brush turkey of tropical and subtropical forests along the eastern edge of the continent from Cape York down to the Manning River in New South Wales. The forests in which scrubfowl and brush turkeys live have deep and abundant forest floor litter, constant dampness to promote rotting, and liberal food supplies for the mound-builders. Little wonder then that thriving populations of both birds exist in areas where their habitat is undisturbed.

In contrast, the malleefowl is the only mound-building bird in the world whose habitat is in semi-arid regions where leaf litter is comparatively hard to find and where aridity makes fermenting of the vegetable matter within the mound

*Above: The
malleefowl.*

LYNN PEDLER

SURFACE-SOIL FEATURES IN SEMI-ARID MULGA WOODLANDS WHICH REPRESENT THE POSITION OF MOUNDS MADE BY MALLEEEFOWL

(which are now locally extinct in the region)

Research by the CSIRO as part of National Rangelands Program identified relict surface-soil features in the semi-arid mulga woodlands about 50 km west of Bourke as having been created long ago by malleefowl, which are now locally extinct in the region.[66] The features are circular and about 10 m in diameter, some having raised rims and well-defined central depressions with heightened fertility, supporting vigorous grass tussocks and acting as sites for mulga establishment. (Ancient mounds formed by the orange-footed scrubfowl have been identified on Melville Island in the Northern Territory and radiocarbon-dated at 8000 years ago, providing evidence of the potential longevity of earthen features built by such animals.)

Ring structure in arid mulga-land. Site of ancient malleefowl mound.

JIM NOBLE

THE MANTUNG–MAGGEA DISTRICT, SA

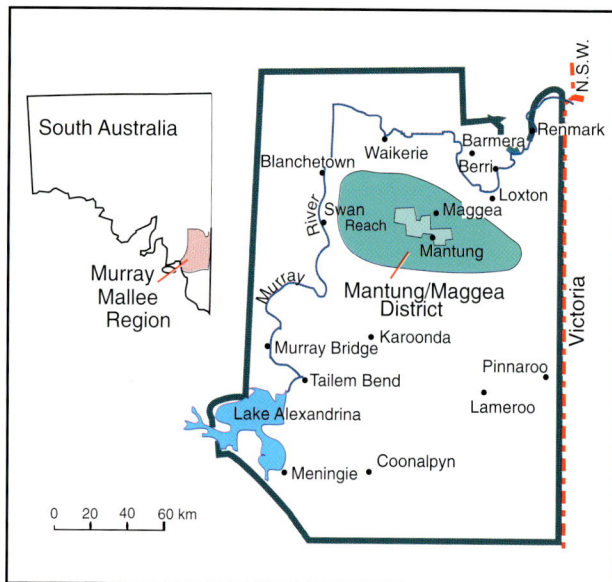

more chancy, while the nutrient-poor environment generally makes survival much more difficult. Where a species is operating like this at the edge of its ecological range, as it were, it is in a precarious situation and extinction is not far away.

Malleefowl used to be common, in the early days of European settlement, in the mallee and mulga lands of south-west and south-east Australia — semi-arid regions with sandy soils and vegetation which provides leaf litter. Their range is now very much restricted and they are becoming increasingly rare. Their present distribution coincides with heavily cleared agricultural regions in the Western Australian wheatbelt, in South Australia, the Murray Basin and southern New South Wales. Ground-dwelling birds with such specific requirements for survival — complicated incubation

rituals, the need for a large ground-based territory, no nurturing or defending of the young, and limitation to natural ecosystems which have been the hardest hit by farming and grazing activities — are obviously extremely vulnerable.

The malleefowl is listed as an endangered species under the Commonwealth Endangered Species Act of 1992, and the Action Plan for Australian Birds classifies it as vulnerable nationally. Because its habitat is most fragmented throughout its range in New South Wales, Victoria and South Australia, recovery action has been considered to be more urgent in the eastern States than in Western Australia where its range is comparatively large. Any finance available from the Action Plan being organised by the Victorian Department of Conservation and Natural Resources only benefits protection measures in the eastern States. Research is proceeding there into the behaviour and distribution of the birds. The Mildura-based Malleefowl Preservation Society recorded 130 mounds in the **Mallee Cliffs National Park** north-east of Mildura in 1994. Only 17 of the mounds were in use in the 57 000 ha expanse of mallee, native cypress pine and spear grass. The area was mapped and locations of mounds recorded using a satellite navigation device.

In the **Murray mallee** and the **upper south-east** region of South Australia farmers were asked to fill in a questionnaire to establish information on the numbers of malleefowl in scattered remnant vegetation. The birds are known to be threatened by foxes (which eat them and their eggs); by feral cats; by loss of habitat and rabbits competing for food; and by fire which removes the woodland litter which they require for their mounds.Malleefowl have acted as a catalyst for the adoption of conservation measures in the Murray mallee of South Australia.[65] As has happened elsewhere

THE FOSSIL HISTORY OF MEGAPODES

Does it explain why the malleefowl is a mound-builder in an unsuitable semi-arid landscape?

The Megapodes are members of the order Galliforme — the fowl-like birds — which were abundant and much more diverse in the Early Tertiary than they are today. A giant Megapode, *Progura*, is found fossilised in Pleistocene deposits in Australia (the Pleistocene is the ice age time of the last 2.6 million years) and Walter Boles of the Australian Museum has found it recently in Pliocene deposits. He also reports the recent identification of a very small Megapode from the Late Oligocene to Middle Miocene Namba Formation (25 to 15 million years ago) from a site near Lake Frome. Before these recent finds were made, there was no record of Megapodes from any strata older than Pleistocene in Australia. (The only fossil evidence that Megapodes were among Early Tertiary birds was from Eocene to Oligocene strata in France — 55 to 30 million years ago. A re-examination of these fossils now places them in another, closely related family.)

The gigantism shown by the megabeast fauna in Pliocene and Pleistocene times in Australia involved members of groups already in the continent attaining abnormally large size. On these grounds, before there was any fossil evidence of Megapodes older than Pleistocene, it was simply assumed that in order to have a giant Megapode there must have been normal-sized species preceding it. So the new finds come as a satisfying confirmation of the correctness of that assumption.

Although today Megapodes are considered highly characteristic of the Australo-Papuan avifauna, their limited range is regarded as relict in the light of the little evidence available from the disjunct distribution (in France and the Australia~South-east Asian regions) and in spite of their incomplete coverage in the fossil record. (More fossil Megapodes will undoubtedly come to light as more identification of bird fossils proceeds. It is still possible that Riversleigh, the world-famous fossil locality 250 km north of Mt Isa in Queensland, may provide such a break-through with its diversity of avian fossils.) All Megapodes except the malleefowl are found in rainforests, the sort of habitats which were widespread all over the world in the warm and wet Late Cretaceous~Early Tertiary when these birds presumably evolved.

Although the malleefowls show very advanced evolutionary traits in their sophisticated management of their mounds and in their adaptations to their present day environment, the mound building and incubation of eggs using heat from rotting vegetation and the sun is a direct link to the reptilian origin of all birds. The crocodile male who tends his mound and waits for his young to hatch may be less of a skilled artisan in mound building or neatly arranging the eggs, but in other ways he shows advances on malleefowl when he tends his young after they emerge from the mound and even carries them

to water and protects them during their most vulnerable early days.

Seen in the context of the prehistoric evolution of the Australian continent, the present situation of the malleefowl is explainable. The southern part of the continent remained largely forested, with parts rain-forested, throughout the Early Tertiary when Australia was separating from Antarctica and starting its journey northward as an island continent. Its mound-building birds were living under the generally warm and wet conditions which applied. Remnant rainforest was still fairly widespread during the warm and wet first half of the Miocene epoch. As global climate changed progressively with the development of the circumpolar current which isolated Antarctica from the warm waters which travel polewards from the Equator and started its cooling, the Australian continent started to dry out. Forest retreated and was replaced by shrubland and open grassland. Rainforest had disappeared from what has been the range of the malleefowl for at least the last two million years.

Successful adaptation of the malleefowl to the changing environment over geological time has seen it become fine-tuned to the semi-arid lands in which it now lives. As with all species in arid and semi-arid lands, any changes to its always somewhat precarious situation are liable to threaten its ability to survive, causing local extinction first and eventually its complete demise.

when people came together to protect a charismatic species (platypus in the Wimmera, hairy-nosed wombat in South Australia), the concern over the declining numbers of malleefowl resulted in a farming community joining forces with State and Federal government agencies, and in this case with an international conservation institution, to undertake conservation measures on their properties. The regenerative capacity of the native vegetation on their farms has been enhanced and increased farm productivity has resulted as a by-product of the measures which were primarily adopted to protect the malleefowl. The community has developed an understanding of the biodiversity of their district and a greater commitment to conservation.

Farmers in the **Mantung-Maggea Land Management Group** have protected remnant vegetation from stock grazing under the State's Heritage Agreement Scheme, providing secure habitat for malleefowl. (Management guidelines and plans for protecting native vegetation were supported by the Commonwealth Save the Bush Program and the South Australian Department of Environment and Natural Resources.) The farmers have gone to great lengths to

eradicate foxes and rabbits and they have found that the malleefowl has benefited greatly, but that they have reaped even more benefit than the birds have done. Their country is tough, with sandy dunes, sheets of limestone near the surface, low and erratic rainfall which averages about 250 mm a year. The removal of rabbits has resulted in pasture improvements which enable sheep to survive the dry times better; wheat yields have improved; and foxes no longer take lambs in large numbers. Fox control research was supported by the Chicago Zoological Society. Recently a feral cat eradication program has started as part of the integrated pest management program for wildlife conservation.

Dr Stephanie Williams of the Chicago Zoological Society (which is involved with the Bookmark Biosphere Reserve project and with malleefowl recovery programs) emphasises that the community involvement in providing necessary information on the breeding biology of the malleefowl has been an essential ingredient in the project. The regular surveys of fixed areas of malleefowl habitat to determine long-term changes in numbers of breeding pairs is essential to the national recovery program. In South Australia and Western Australia these data can only be obtained by

WILDLIFE REHABILITATION

All over Australia, countless native animals suffer through human activity every day. Destruction or disturbance of habitat, motor vehicles and machinery, fences, buildings, ravages of domestic pets or feral animals, poisons — all sorts of harmful agents and influences causing injury, pain, often death. Orphaned young often survive the death of parents but can't make it on their own — particularly the pouch young of marsupials — our kangaroos, wallabies, wombats and a host of others. Road kill victims may have living babies in their pouches, and all should be examined, just in case. It is a grisly task, and stopping on highways to turn corpses over to check requires fortitude (and road sense), but a rescued baby wombat is a reward beyond price.

In the wild, injured animals are often doomed — Mother Nature has no way of intervening. But caring humans can come to the rescue, and with so many animals now rare, and increasing numbers of species endangered, the more that is known about raising orphaned young and rehabilitating the injured, the better. It all helps in the captive breeding programs that are becoming increasingly necessary as more species need to be rescued from extinction.

Many Organisations, under many different names, coordinate the network of carers, advise and assist in all aspects of rehabilitation, train the volunteers and supervise activities. They also deal with wildlife that is causing stress to the public — like snakes in the house or possums in the ceiling. In New South Wales there are a number of Wildlife Rehabilitation groups licensed by the NSW National Parks & Wildlife Service. All operate on a voluntary membership basis to Rescue, Relocate, Rehabilitate & Release.

WIRES (Wildlife Information & Rescue Service) has headquarters in Sydney and 24 branches through the State; the **ACT Wildlife Foundation** looks after animals in Canberra and district: **Wildcare** operates in the adjacent Queanbeyan region; **LAOKA** (Looking After Our Kosciusko Animals) looks after the high country.

A brief account of one active wildlife rescue organisation follows.

FAWNA (NSW) Inc.

(For Australian Wildlife Needing Aid)

FAWNA operates throughout the mid-north coast region of NSW. It was licensed in 1990 to cover the Port Macquarie National Parks District, parts of the Hunter District and a small section of the Armidale district. Its boundary to the south meets **Native Animal Trust Fund**; to the north, WIRES Woolgoolga; to the west WIRES Tamworth and Armidale. Within this network there is a free exchange of information, advice and assistance and member training courses are shared.

Members of FAWNA come from all walks of life in the community. Junior members are encouraged, but can only care for fauna if supervised by an adult member. Members are covered by insurance, receive training in courses or by one-to-one training with individual experienced carers on different species. A minimum standard of training is required for carer members. FAWNA receives no government funding and relies solely on membership fees, private and public donations and its own fund-raising activities. It bulk-buys the special fauna care foodstuffs and sells to carers at the discount price, and pays veterinary costs (where they are charged — many vets generously attend to wildlife free).

FAWNA provides a 24 hour, seven day a week phone contact service, manned by a rotating roster of members. When a message is received from the public, a member nearest to the location of the call is contacted to arrange to collect the animal and take it into care. Vet attention is arranged if necessary and the animal is passed on to a carer who specialises in that type of animal. The carer aims to provide the correct diet, housing and care and treatment so that the animal may be released back to the wild when it is ready. Small pouch-young marsupial babies may require care for up to a year; concussed birds which have flown into windows or been hit by cars may just need a few days of cage rest and good diet before they can fly away again. Where possible, animals are released in the areas from which they came.

A very young brushtail possum needs a lot of tender, loving care. This tiny baby was even smaller and still blind when she was taken from the pouch of a roadkill mother.

She grew up to be a beautiful possum and eventually had a baby of her own.

the dedication of large groups of volunteers. Government agencies have neither the manpower nor the funds to carry out such surveys.

In the Mantung-Maggea District the malleefowl rescue project has shown the advantage of having a flagship species to increase awareness of the need for conservation, and to facilitate acceptance of changes to land management practices.

Aboriginal dreamings and art suggest that malleefowl were much more widespread into arid Central Australia in the past, and there were some records of sightings west of Alice Springs and elsewhere in those latitudes since European settlement and up until the 1950s. Since then, one mound with newly laid eggs was found in the Musgrave Ranges in South Australia where the species was thought to be locally extinct.

Against this background of a unique and marvellous bird which is on the list of rare and endangered species, is the equally unique and marvellous conservation effort of the **Malleefowl Preservation Group** in the Gnowangerup-Ongerup-Borden region of Western Australia. A full account of this group is given here as a case study in order to show other groups how they can protect *their* bird (or plant, or marsupial, or bit of forest or bushland, or whatever). It shows that in a few years an unsatisfactory situation can be completely turned around and in the process other environmental problems are recognised. And, most importantly, the strong community spirit and involvement lays the groundwork for successfully tackling all the basic problems which underlie the one originally being addressed.

The region involved is about 350 km south-east of Perth and is bordered by the Stirling Range to the west-south-west and includes the major drainage systems of the Pallinup River and the Corackerup Creek. Its marginal, semi-arid mallee lands were extensively cleared for agriculture as part of the call to clear a million acres a year by the State in the 1970s. Today many of the farmers of these fragile lands are almost as endangered as the malleefowl — with soil degradation, salinisation and erosion progressing under current land-use practices and making economic survival extremely difficult. Yet they comprise most of the membership of the preservation group, perhaps recognising that their fate and that of the malleefowl are linked, because if environmental problems are not dealt with, both will be forced out of the area.

Active mounds in the area are found in mallee woodland remnants with thickets of *Melaleuca uncinata* (broombush) and *Gastrolobium* spp. (poison bush which has natural poisons related to the commercially produced 1080). The factors threatening the malleefowl with local extinction are:

- the extent of clearing which has reduced their habitat to small, unconnected areas in which they compete with grazing stock and rabbits;
- the effects of fire (unburnt patches are required for breeding, highest breeding densities are found in land unburnt for 40 to 60 years, and density is reduced in land unburnt for less than 30 years according to studies in Victoria);
- predation by foxes and feral cats;
- lack of young birds reaching adulthood (most dying before reaching maturity).

It's Gnow or Never is the slogan that by the end of 1995, three years after the first meeting of residents of the Gnowangerup Shire to discuss the decline of malleefowl in the area, has about 700 people (270 members and their families) involved in the Malleefowl Preservation Group. That first meeting was held in one of the two remaining breeding areas in the shire. **Gnow** is the local Aboriginal name for the bird, and the name of the shire means the *place of the malleefowl mound*. (It probably helps, at the beginning of a project, when the species you are trying to save is the emblem of your shire and catches the interest and imagination of the public.)

The beginnings of the group are attributed to a resident woodcarver, John Davis, who had been commissioned to carve a malleefowl for the Shire Chambers. The bird being used as his model was suddenly taken by a fox, bringing home to him the plight of the birds, whose decline in the area had been widely noticed and lamented. He arranged a meeting of concerned local residents with representatives of the Threatened Species Network and the Perth Zoo. That was in August 1992.

By the end of 1992 the group had obtained a grant of $3000 from the Gordon Reid Foundation, enabling it to put together a display board to advertise its activities, and to start outlining its community action plan. It obtained media coverage in local newspapers, advertised its aims and activities through local outlets, and designed T-shirts with the local slogan as one of its fund-raising activities.

1993 saw great activity and progress. The Gnowangerup Shire donated $300 towards putting restricted access gates on a minor road which runs adjacent to a remnant bush area on private property where there is a breeding malleefowl population. This helped to protect the area from human interference and to cut down on road kills. The local advertising program had raised such interest that the Ongerup Museum, local primary school and Apex built a replica malleefowl mound in the Museum grounds — full size, with a glass panel to view its structure. (Builders developed a new respect for the male malleefowl which moves all that material with only his feet, and who is called upon to open, remake and adjust his mound constantly!)

A community awareness program saw volunteers travelling to local schools with a display and presentation, and two representatives attended the Landcare '93 Conference in Perth to advertise their project. A newsletter — 'Malleefowl Matter' — with a quarterly production, and paid membership to the group commenced. A children's book was published by a member and badges were designed for sale to raise funds. Malleefowl sighting forms were distributed to the public to encourage reporting of sightings to the group, thereby establishing population distribution and promoting community involvement.

A National Landcare — Save The Bush grant of $14 050 was received, enabling the group to employ a part-time project officer and to continue the community action plan program. The first field study site was established in a large 4334 ha Conservation and Land Management (CALM) reserve. An area of 300 ha was gridded using 'human chain' and compass readings to establish grid lines. The project was overseen by representatives of the Threatened Species Network and the Perth Zoo; accommodation in shearers quarters was donated by adjacent farmers for the 42 volunteers who came and went over a five-day period. An average of 1.6 active mounds per square kilometre were located and mapped in what proved to be a very happy and productive community enterprise.

1994 saw the erection of 'Malleefowl Crossing' road signs in the shire; the State government donated $3000; an aerial survey of the Corackerup Reserve mapped the location of mounds (in a joint project with the Stirling Range–Porongurup National Parks planning committee); more schools in a wider area were visited; and a local composer produced a malleefowl song.

Landowners were encouraged to take part in baiting programs for fox and rabbit control using 1080; to fence off remnant vegetation and ensure adequate firebreaks around it. The 'Why can't the Farmer and the Malleefowl be friends?' leaflet publicising these measures was another successful exercise in promoting public awareness. The use of 1080 as a bait poison is not a threat to wildlife in the southern part of Western Australia because fauna has become tolerant of the poison by being in *Gastrolobium* territory. Introduced foxes and rabbits have no such tolerance. A donation of $500 from *Australian Geographic* magazine helped with fox baiting costs. The poison is injected into hens' eggs which are buried for the foxes to dig up, and 90% of those buried have been eaten by foxes. Should a goanna eat one (and goannas are the only other animal likely to dig up eggs) it has about 400 times the fox's tolerance of the poison, so it will not be affected. An active cat desexing program in the shire and feral cat eradication on farms is bringing the cat problem under control.

A field study of the breeding ground in a privately owned mallee woodland remnant revealed a total of 59 active mounds, which was an average of five to six per square kilometre, confirming the area to have the highest breeding population anywhere in Australia. The bush remnant is surrounded by cleared agricultural land and its isolation raised concern about local over-population, prompting the start of corridor fencing to connect it to other remnant bush areas, and a campaign to obtain funds to complete the work.

In 1995 the application for funds for the corridor fencing project was approved by the Gordon Reid Foundation (State Lotteries) which will provide $31 000. As a result, 21 km of corridor fencing will connect the high density privately owned remnant woodland to a CALM reserve and another isolated malleefowl population. Ten local farmers and the Australian Trust for Conservation Volunteers will be involved in the voluntary work which began early in 1996. The CALM reserve has no active mounds to date, but recent sightings in it (the first for 30 years) are attributed to the regular fox baitings and the partial corridor fencing. The baiting programs are highly successful.

Evidence of a category 1 endangered species, the western mouse, *Pseudomys occidentalis*, was discovered in a survey of one of the CALM reserves recently, highlighting the way a program to save one species can have spin-offs for others. The South Australian Museum has recently sought the assistance of the group in its DNA testing of malleefowl, using road-kill birds.

Alcoa, the aluminium mining and processing company which has sponsored Landcare in Western Australia most generously, has provided the money for a Global Positioning System which will make the mapping of areas and the location of mounds much easier for the volunteers who survey each area. No longer will 'human chain' and compass gridding be necessary.

If anyone could question the economic effectiveness of a volunteer organisation like the Malleefowl Preservation Group, the figures presented at the Geraldton conference 'Nature Conservation: the Role of Networks' should dispel their doubts. The voluntary contributions in kind of the group and its supporters represents $15 for every dollar of the seeding grant, provided at no cost to the government or taxpayer. The way a campaign like this one starts out saving a bird and ends up raising awareness of general environmental problems in a region, and establishing a well-informed community network, is a marvellous bonus. **It is only by altering the value systems of the population, of a region first and then of the whole country, that time and money will be made available to deal adequately with the environmental problems which are in urgent need of everyone's attention.**

The inspiration given by the Malleefowl Protection Group's success to other groups intent on preservation of what they consider valuable in their area is another bonus.

WATERWATCH

Waterwatch is the only truly national program of its type in the world. It is one of the large and increasing number in which local communities are becoming involved, monitoring the state of *their* environment. Waterwatch fosters environmental awareness, bringing home the fact that every one of us lives in a catchment and each of us must realise our responsibility for the environmental problems which our continent suffers. Solution to the problems, however massive they might be, depends on the multitude of small local initiatives which will add up first to attitudinal changes, and then to finding ways to make our land-use practices sustainable.

Waterwatch began in 1992 when the Federal Government announced a three-year national support program for community-based water quality monitoring programs such as **Ribbons of Blue** (in Western Australia) and Streamwatch (in New South Wales). **Streamwatch** had started as a school and community-based water quality program but has since become much more than that, working with Councils, Catchment Management Committees and community groups to protect and improve local waterways.

The **National Waterwatch Program** is managed by a national facilitator based with the Australian Nature Conservation Agency (ANCA), who works closely with a national steering committee of State Waterwatch facilitators. State panels are responsible for directing Waterwatch activities and making funding recommendations to the Waterwatch Program to complement existing regional or catchment plans.

Growing public concern about water quality has resulted in increased water monitoring and stream reclamation activities in all States and Territories. By 1995, an estimated 32 000 people were involved. By 1996 the number estimated is 40 300 in 1441 groups in 107 catchments, comprising 444 primary schools, 699 secondary schools, and 298 Landcare and Catchment Groups. The involvement of children of all ages in the program is exciting and forward-thinking — empowering them to do something about the environment they live in today and helping to ensure that it will still be life-friendly for their children — and they find that involvement is fun and natural history and environmental science are important.

National Water Week, in October every year, aims to make communities more aware of their local waterways and to get them directly involved in hands-on action, in accordance with its ethos of '**Protect, conserve and get involved**'. The 1995, Water Week selected the two most popular activities — testing of turbidity and macro-invertebrate monitoring — as the focal themes. Turbidity testing alerts people to catchment degradation; 'bug surveys' are a great way to involve all ages in water monitoring. The abundance of small insects, crustaceans and molluscs in a stream is a measure of the water quality — good clean water is necessary for life and the more polluted the water, the less life it supports.

In most States, biologists involved with the **National Monitoring River Health Initiative** assist Waterwatch groups with training, program design and interpretation of results, and Waterwatchers team up with catchment groups and Councils to carry out a wide variety of tests. Most Waterwatch groups regularly monitor indicators such as pH, temperature, phosphates, nitrates, dissolved oxygen, turbidity, faecal bacteria levels, macro-invertebrates and river bank vegetation throughout the year.

Water Week activities involve the taking of 'snapshots' of water quality readings across a group's area at a specified time, as a survey of the health of the water body or waterway involved. In 1995 for the first time these individual snapshots were assembled to form a national snapshot. A brief account of activities in the States and Territories, summarised in their snapshots, follows.

- In the **ACT**, the survey concentrated on the major tributaries of the Murrumbidgee River, identifying sites where organic pollution and excessive sedimentation (the major concern) were a problem. It also revealed sites such as newly formed artificial sedimentation ponds and areas taken over by willows where water quality was good but bug numbers were low, due to lack of habitat. Follow-up actions by Waterwatch will include monitoring water quality after removal of

Streamwatch students from Narrabeen Sports High School collecting samples in Narrabeen Lake.

Sydney Water

Streamwatch students from Mackellar Girls High School testing water from Manly Lagoon.

STREAMWATCH

willows and their replacement with native trees; planting reeds around sedimentation ponds; and fencing off creeks from livestock.

- In **Western Australia** (where Ribbons of Blue is in its fifth year), Water Week saw great activity by school children from Geraldton, 500 km north of Perth, to the south-western corner of the continent. In the Blackwood Catchment, where children from 35 schools have been monitoring water quality for five years, the coordinator says the program 'deals in real community science' with children and adults participating in research alongside scientists and government agencies. Ten field assistants help in this work, providing consistency of testing and giving participants confidence. The Ribbons of Blue Facilitator says 'Waterwatch is like the Internet. There is no central starting point. It is accessible from everywhere — and every part has a life of its own'.

- In **Victoria**, Waterwatch is seen as an ideal partner to the Landcare program and over 300 groups comprise landholders as well as schools. The community support for the scheme is seen in the sponsorship which it attracts from water and river management authorities, local government and local business. More than 100 groups took part in Water Week activities.

- In **South Australia**, where surface water is scarce and quality fluctuates enormously from season to season, 80 groups were involved in sampling biodiversity in rivers. In the South Australian Riverland and on the Murray River, high salinity, high turbidity and feral fish account for poor water quality; in wooded catchments in the Adelaide

Hills water quality was better.

- In **Tasmania**, where water quality is mostly still good, Water Week saw 500 Waterwatchers (students, teachers, Landcare members, councils) sampling bugs. Some long-term problems were revealed at some sites by low numbers of macro-invertebrates.

- In **Queensland**, National Water Week was marked by Junior Landcare expos, catchment crawls, river cruises, poster competitions and displays, with the emphasis on everyone working together. The Queensland Facilitator, Lynne Turner, explains: 'Waterwatch is a universal catalyst. It helps people cross the boundary between thoughts, feelings and emotions to positive and corrective action. It empowers people because it is not just about water testing. It is social, it's fun, and it works! A special program, '**Kids, Coppers, Catchments and Companies**', the Police Citizen's Waterwatch Program, was launched on the Brisbane River, where local students then commenced a study of the city's waterways.

- In the **Northern Territory**, the challenge for Waterwatch is to help the community to maintain water quality in the face of increasing population and rapid development — most waterways in the Top End are in reasonably good condition. Activities are mainly concerned with clearing rubbish from urban creeks before the monsoon washes it to the sea.

- In **New South Wales**, Streamwatch now has more than 450 schools, community groups and local government groups in the network. The program is sponsored by Sydney Water in the Sydney, Illawarra and Blue Mountains area with support from the Hawkesbury~Nepean Catchment Management Trust and the Upper Parramatta River Catchment Trust. Outside this area, Streamwatch is run by the Department of Land and Water Conservation with support from the Hunter Catchment Trust. The Great Water Week Discovery Tour was a highlight of Water Week, with 350 canoeists taking part in a 12 km journey along the Nepean River. They met experts in riparian vegetation, local fisheries and water quality along the way and took water samples to be analysed at the end of the trip by 'Streamteam'. The Department of Land and Water Conservation intends to introduce a year 5-8 Streamwatch program into schools, which will add 100 000 students a year.

THE MANLY ENVIRONMENT CENTRE

Manly... there is no place like it in the wide, wide world
— according to the father of Manly, Henry Gilbert Smith in 1852

Manly's physical situation of 20 beaches and nearly 50 bushland reserves is reflected in descriptions of decades ago, 'pearl of the Pacific and Brighton of the South'. It attracts some eight million tourists a year to enjoy its variety of waterways, harbour and ocean beaches, creeks, waterfalls and the polluted Manly Lagoon. It is also home to the longest sewerage outfall in the world — 45 km from Blacktown in Sydney's west to the outfall end off North Head.

By the late 1980s, the intense pressure of development, tourism and pollution resulted in a groundswell of community concern. This was translated into a unique form of powerful and positive action when the community sought to work with council and local business towards common goals. Manly Council's Community Environment Committee recognised the importance of providing resources for community education on environmental issues. (Foundation members were Judy Reizes, now Director of the Manly Environment Centre; Dr Peter MacDonald, MLA; Ann Jones; Jim Corbett, ex CSIRO; and Volker Psannenberg. Local corporate sponsorship was obtained from Blackmores and Macquarie Pathology for a small shopfront in Manly's CBD. The centre was opened in March 1991 by local Peter Garrett with the symbolic planting on the beachfront of the Turnaround Tree, the first of the young Norfolk Pines planted to replace the famous trees along the promenade which were dying because of pollution (in aerosol from the sewerage outfall) and other factors resulting from development.

This unique example of council, community and corporate cooperation has continued to expand into its third set of premises with 10 m of shopfront window

and two full-time and a part-time staff member funded by council. It has won eight awards for community education and stocks over 1500 different environmental resources, including brochures, reports, videos, tapes and resource kits for schools. It has become the hub for many other community groups by giving them resources and providing them with a venue for their meetings, whilst at the same time working with council staff and committees on many successful projects.

The centre has become a dynamic force for change, bringing together the stakeholders from all levels of government, community and business to work together to harness energy on many projects. Its enormous success is largely due to the enthusiasm, hard work and dedication of Judy Reizes, and her loyal few regular helpers. Community education in Manly Warringah, particularly on water pollution issues, is so highly regarded that it is often used as a model at international, national and State level. This process has grown to embrace more and more sectors of the community and has involved many events, including expos at shopping centres, schools, main streets and the beachfront on reducing waste, energy and pollution.

GREEN AND OzGREEN

GREEN — The Global Rivers Environmental Education Network:

... is an international network committed to actively improving and sustaining the Planet's water on which all Life depends. The uncertain quality of water threatens the health of 70% of all people, and endangers countless other species. GREEN encourages positive attitudes, practices and people's active participation at all levels through education, global communication and cooperation. Programs foster environmental ethics, intercultural sensitivity and respect, thus contributing to a more caring and peaceful world.

Programs based on the GREEN model presently operate in 136 countries throughout the world, with international headquarters located in Michigan, USA.

OzGREEN — Global Rivers Environmental Education Network (Australia) Inc. is a non-profit organisation, founded and run by Sue and Col Lennox who established an international link-up for Australia through Pegasus in 1991, and was established as an incorporated association in 1993. It

... builds links between business and community, rural and city, local, state, national and international environmental projects to encourage Australian projects to be seen in a global context and global issues to be seen in a local context.

The organisation has grown rapidly from an initial water monitoring project in 1990 with Freshwater High School students, which was a response to the polluted state of the lagoon. That project, and a video 'Fresh Water' which was produced as part of it, won the World Environment Day Youth Award. A water monitoring program to clean up the Ganges took the Lennoxs to India, and the video which resulted has

KIDS, COMPANIES AND CREEKS

An example of community involvement in catchment protection

This project, in Sydney's northern suburbs, brought together three important elements in the community: kids, enthusiastic young people who care about their environment; **companies**, business and industry in a local community; and **creeks**, the environmental focus and reason for action. It may serve as a guide to what can be done elsewhere because in many urban situations (and Australia is the most highly urbanised society in the world) kids and companies and environmental problems, if not always involving creeks, co-exist.

Students and teachers at Freshwater High, Mackellar Girls High and Stella Maris College have been monitoring water quality in the Manly and Curl Curl Lagoons since 1990, as part of a Streamwatch program. Both lagoons have been shown to be polluted and the schools have organised a number of awareness-raising events. One of these, a successful Waste Information Forum, targeting the Brookvale industrial area, led to the kcc project which focussed on the Balgowlah Industrial Estate, an area with about 250 small and medium sized businesses and industries near Manly Lagoon. It was a joint initiative of **Blackmores Ltd** (a leading natural health products manufacturer, based locally), **OzGREEN** (Global Rivers Environmental Education Network — Australia Inc.) and the **Manly Environment Centre**.

The project brought together the Streamwatch students, environmentalists, industry, the local community and waste management experts to share information about ways to clean up local waterways through cleaner production processes and waste reduction. A community-based environmental education project, it aimed to make non-threatening contact with industry and business. By encouraging the adoption of practices which minimise environmental impact and increasing awareness about waste reduction, water pollution and catchment protection and involving all key stakeholders in the Manly Lagoon Catchment, it aimed to control pollution of the lagoon.

Students made personal contact with managers and proprietors, in a carefully planned and supervised program, inviting them to participate and explaining their aims. They planned a special event involving a display and entertainment to obtain the widest possible local involvement, guided in the planning of the event and the production of an action plan for the whole project by their three sponsors and Streamwatch. The number of participating schools had swelled from the original three to include Balgowlah Boys High, St Pauls College, St Mary's Primary, St Cecilia's Primary, Manly West Primary, Manly Vale Primary and visiting country schools Forster High and Muswellbrook High. The students were powerful ambassadors for the environment. Summing it up, Marcus Blackmore commented

It is rather ironic that with the kcc initiative we in business are responding to a challenge put to us by schoolchildren from our own community. Perhaps as business people we should have been more pro-active about our environmental responsibility before it got to this stage... we must congratulate 'the kids' for having the temerity and the enthusiasm to bring these environmental issues to our attention.

Such a project has a snow-balling and far-reaching effect beyond the local area where attitudinal change has occurred and environmental gains have been made. The hundreds of young people who move on after their school days continue as ambassadors because they know that they have the power to influence decisions and improve their world.

THE MANLY LAGOON CATCHMENT

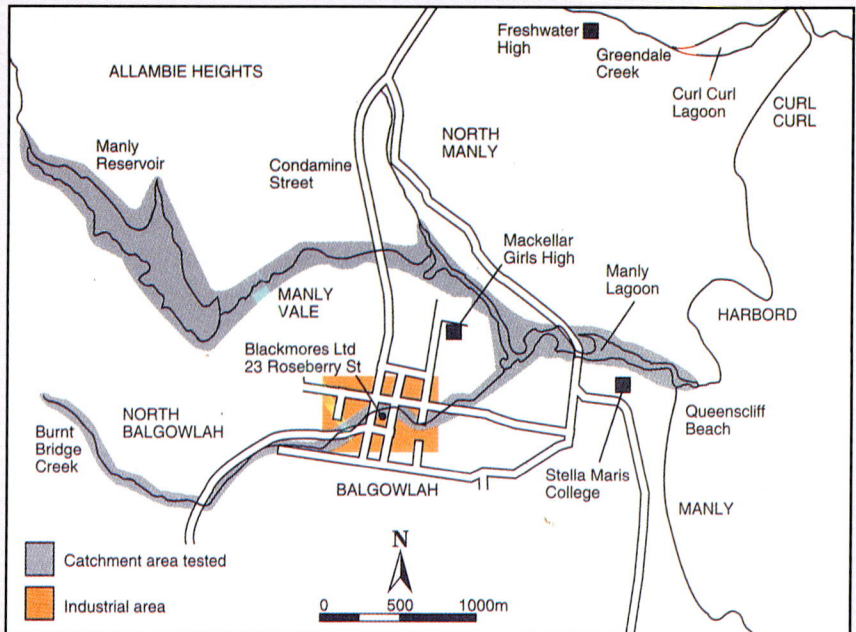

Children performing at the event at the Warringah Mall. Some of the quilt banners they made were used to decorate the stage.

MANLY ENVIRONMENT CENTRE

since won a United Nations award — one of a string of honours which have been bestowed on OzGREEN for its continuing work with students in water monitoring; with training programs for teachers and organisations; organising waste reduction seminars and expos; organising the first international congress for GREEN, held in Sydney in August 1995. The **kids, companies and creeks** project in which it was involved won the 1995 Gold Medal, NSW Government Rivercare 2000 award. (OzGREEN can be contacted at Box 57, Harbord, NSW 2096)

A competition to produce banners resulted in many wonderfully colourful and original quilts being made by children at the different schools which were involved in the project.

MANLY ENVIRONMENT CENTRE

CHAPTER FOUR

SOIL—

A NON-RENEWABLE

RESOURCE IN SERIOUS

TROUBLE

The eastern Darling Downs, some of the richest agricultural land in Australia, prone to heavy soil loss by water erosion in tropical storms.

DAVID FREEBAIRN

Revitalising soil requires revitalising the ecosystem which currently depends on it, re-activating the cycling of nutrients and reversing the trend towards further biodiversity loss. To leave a degraded landscape, like, for example, a seriously over-grazed mulga-land, to rehabilitate itself by simply removing the grazing agent almost invariably results in progressive degradation. This applies particularly in the fragile, semi-arid environments which characterise so much of the Australian continent.

Soil has to be regarded as a virtually non-renewable resource because it forms so slowly in an arid land. Weathering of rocks under arid conditions is slow; a minutely thin layer is added by dust; some redistribution results from normal erosion in stable ecosystems; and bioturbation (soil stirring), by ants and termites in particular, only barely keeps pace with the background erosion. It is imperative, therefore, that sustainable land management systems are adopted to slow the degradation and the running down of this vital resource.

That the process of converting inorganic sediment to soil is biogenic is graphically demonstrated by recent research into the effects of ants on sandy soils in semi-arid eastern Australia.[67] So much of the continent's soil comes within this category that the findings from this study in western New South Wales can be assumed to indicate that similar processes, probably involving different organisms, are widespread in the arid 75% of our land.

The activity of funnel ants (*Aphaenogaster barbicula*) was monitored on an aeolian soil (composed of wind-

'A nation that destroys its soils destroys itself'

(Quote from a letter from President Roosevelt to State Governors, in 1937 during the US 'Dustbowl' era.)

Soil, the resource on which all land-life depends because plants are the basis of food chains, is not a dead substance. The sands, clays, grits and other sediments which comprise much of its bulk are the inorganic matrix for the complex organic network whose components are still only partially understood, and far too frequently left out of studies on ecosystem health. Biodiversity and a healthy dynamic balance in the soil is the first prerequisite for soil stability and productivity. Degraded soils have lost some of their biodiversity, and rehabilitation efforts have to start by restoring it.

blown sand, resulting from the dry and windy glacial stages of the Pleistocene). These ants are common on sandy soils dominated by the *Callitris glaucophylla* association (native cypress pines) or mallee eucalypts, where they build nests with conspicuous funnel-like entrances. Multiple nest entrances of the same subterranean colony may extend over hundreds of square metres. A simple nest structure has a main shaft supporting an intricate assemblage of tunnels at depths ranging from 100 to 350 mm. During nest building the ants move large quantities of soil from the sub-soil to the surface and dispose of it by building the entrance funnels. In some cases there may be up to 40 entrances per square metre, covering 1% of the landscape. The study found that nest entrances remained active for about nine months. The bioturbation activity was equivalent to the annual development of a soil layer 0.28 mm thick.

It was estimated that 92% of the total volume of soil would be removed from the profile during the construction of nest entrances within 100 years. This bioturbation is calculated to be substantially greater than the estimates of water erosion in these soils in undisturbed environments (the 'background noise' erosion which is always going on), implying that over time the soil brought to the surface forms a new layer. The ants' activities also result in the incorporation of organic matter into the surface soils around the entrances. The benefits resulting from the marked increase in infiltration of rainwater to depth in the soil via the ant nest tunnels are obvious. When heavy rainfall washes the entrance funnels away, their soil material ends up mixed with plant debris in micro-swales, and the ants become frantically active, rebuilding their funnels and clearing out their flooded tunnels.

Australia's arable area, which includes both crops and sown pasture, represents **6% of the continent**. Although potentially arable soils are present over greater areas, the primary determinants of productivity and land use patterns involve climate and terrain as well as suitable soil. Where the three major determinants come together satisfactorily, the land is arable. Professor Nix, one of Australia's eminent land-

Mulga ants make large, raised collars around their nest entrances and decorate them with mulga phyllodes. Underground, the system of tunnels and storage chambers is extensive and the night-foraging inhabitants store seeds, fruits and scavenged insects.

M.E.W.

Termite mounds in recently burnt land in the Northern Territory. Termites, like ants, are also significant soil-makers, bringing material from deep down to the surface and enriching it with organic matter.

M.E.W.

use experts, produced maps of the land available for agriculture after successive imposition of constraints imposed by climate, terrain and soil; and of potential agricultural land still available for development.[68] In the years since his paper was published, some of the potentially usable land in the second map has been developed, but Professor Nix (personal communication)

LAND AVAILABLE FOR AGRICULTURE
after successive imposition of climate, terrain and soil constraints
(in million hectares)

POTENTIAL AGRICULTURAL LAND AWAITING DEVELOPMENT

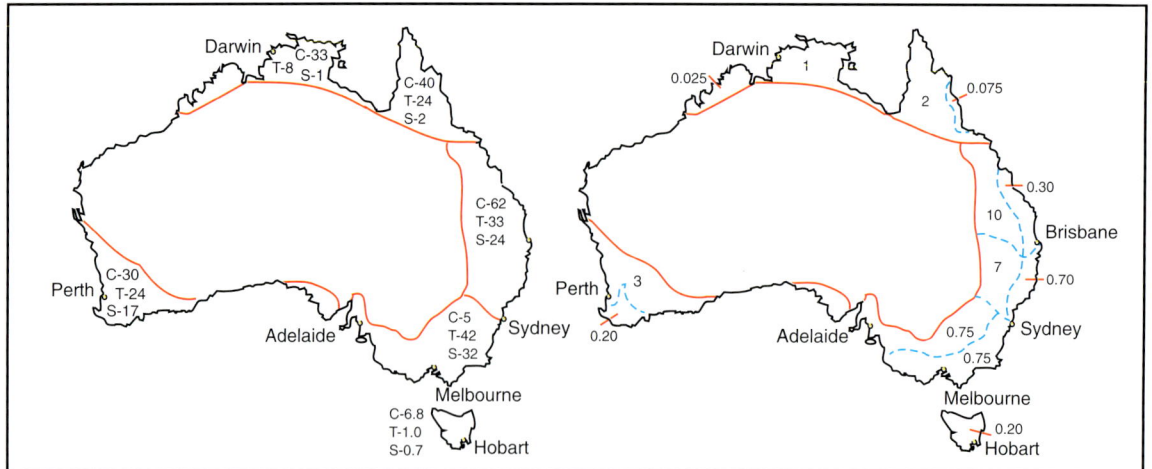

After Nix [68]

TO FEED THE PEOPLE...

To feed people an adequate, diverse diet, 0.5 ha of arable land is needed per capita. Already only 0.27 ha is available and over a billion of the world's population are hungry because of shortfall in local food production and inadequate distribution arrangements. In 40 years from now, both because of land degradation and population increase, only 0.14 ha per capita will be available. Worldwide, per capita production of grains (which make up 80% of food supply) has been declining since 1984 when the honeymoon of the Green Revolution came to an end.[69]

The **Australian `ecological footprint'** — the area of land needed to produce a person's food, housing, transport, consumer goods and services to maintain the current living standard — is **4.4 ha of productive land**. This figure was released by the Australian Bureau of Statistics in June 1996. It compares with 5.1 ha in the US and with 0.4 ha in India, reflecting the different standards of living and expectations in different countries. (On this basis, Australia is already over-populated.)

A census of soil resources in the US is interesting in that it was designed to show what had been the effects of 200 years of agriculture — so it corresponds to the time of European occupation and use of Australia's soil resources. It has to be remembered that because of North America's geological history it started off with a bank balance of soils that overall were far more potentially productive and less fragile than Australia's soil resources. An inventory of the soil biota of a hectare of arable US soil is: 1000 kg of earthworms; 1000 kg of arthropods; 150 kg of protozoa; 150 kg of algae; 1700 kg of bacteria and 2700 kg of fungi. These organisms recycle nutrients and promote soil structure, improving aeration and water penetration by bioturbation. (And who says soil is a dead substance made from sediments eroded from rocks?) Average Australian soils of semi-arid and arid regions have a very different and comparatively impoverished inventory, but an equally essential one.

WHAT HAS 200 YEARS OF AGRICULTURE DONE TO SOILS IN THE UNITED STATES.

In 200 years, **30% of farmland has been abandoned because of erosion**, salinisation and waterlogging. Today, wind erosion takes a higher toll than water erosion which is decreasing due to better management practices.

Croplands (according to Pimentel[69]) are losing topsoil at an average of 17 tonnes per hectare each year. This rate is unsustainable as soil is being made at one tonne per hectare a year (i.e. 1 mm thickness). Pastures lose an average six tonnes per hectare a year. About 90% of croplands are losing soil at above the sustainable rate, and 54% of grazing land is over-grazed and subject to high rates of erosion.

To give more down-to-earth examples: Iowa has lost half of its fertile topsoil in the last 150 years; and 40% of the rich Palouse soils of north-western US have been lost in the last century. Farm size has doubled in the last 50 years, and this has resulted in removal of hedges and shelter belt plantations, and in amalgamation of fields, making wind erosion more effective. The use of heavy farm machinery which affects soil structure also contributes to erodibility of soils. When topsoil

is lost, the most nutrient-rich part of the soil is removed. What is left usually has only a third as much nutrient, and its absorption of water is impaired.

Farming practices were shown to be important in decreasing or increasing the rate of soil loss. Living or dead plant material left on the land after harvesting substantially reduced erosion and runoff. In Missouri, barren land lost soil at a rate 123 times that of land covered with sod; and in Oklahoma, areas without rye grass or wheat cover lost up to five times as much water as land with cover. (In many third-world countries, crop residues are removed for use as fuel and even their roots may taken for this purpose — 90% of residues are removed for fuel in Bangladesh. It is obvious that erosion problems are compounded by such a situation, but where there is no firewood, what are the options?)

The US would have to invest $6.4 billion a year ($40 per hectare) to reduce erosion loss from 17 tonnes per hectare to a sustainable one tonne per hectare, and pasture conservation would require $2 billion ($5 per hectare).

has seen no reason to change his overall estimates, except to comment that major subtractions would be land occupied by infrastructure —- cities, settlements, roads, railways etc. which have a predilection for consuming arable land.

SOIL EROSION — A 'FORGOTTEN MENACE' — IN A GLOBAL CONTEXT

*Soil erosion is a major environmental threat to the sustainability and productive capacity of agriculture. During the last 40 years, **nearly one third of the world's arable land has been lost by erosion** and continues to be lost at a rate of more than 10 million hectares per year.*

*With the addition of a quarter of a million people each day, **the world population's food demand is increasing at a time when per capita food production is beginning to decline**.* (Pimentel[69])

On the world scale, one-third of the world's agricultural lands are used for crops and two-thirds for pastures for livestock. About 80% of agricultural land worldwide suffers moderate to severe erosion; 10% suffers slight erosion. Steep slopes are increasingly being used for cropping because of the amount of originally more suitable land put out of production by erosion, and the rapid increase in populations needing to be fed. Erosion is much more rapid on steep slopes. Croplands are erosion-prone because they are often bare and tilling exposes them to risk, so it comes as no surprise that they are degrading. However, the fact that over-grazed rangelands can lose up to 100 tonnes of topsoil from each hectare, each year, is a startling revelation.

SOIL EROSION IN AUSTRALIA

Wind Erosion

In May 1994 a cloud of dust 800 km long, 200 km wide and 200 m deep was entrained by the westerly wind from the Yorke Peninsula in South Australia and blown across the continent. It was such a large and thick dust storm that it was seen from satellites, and it represented 20 million tonnes of topsoil which had been left bare and ready to be blown away when fields covered in stubble were ploughed as a measure to control a mouse plague in drought-afflicted lands. The cloud dropped some of its burden and thinned as it crossed into western Victoria and New South Wales, but it picked up new dust from far-western regions of New South Wales and the drought-stricken Riverina and had plenty left to drop on Sydney and into the Tasman Sea.

Strip cropping on the Condamine Plain aims to reduce the run-off during storms and to prevent erosion.

DAVID FREEBAIRN

The Condamine Plain suffers serious water erosion during tropical storms if the land is left bare between cropping.

DAVID FREEBAIRN

Satellite image of the Simpson Desert showing linear dunes.

DEAN GRAETZ

AUSTRALIA'S DESERTS
the alignment of dunes and the major dust paths

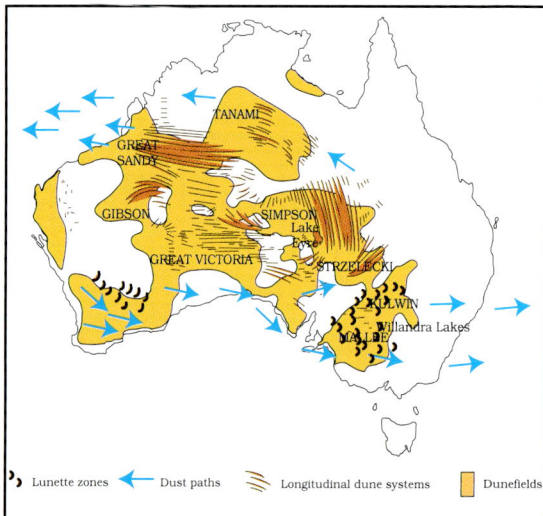

Lunette zones   Dust paths   Longitudinal dune systems   Dunefields

Dust paths after McTainsh [72]

Only when such an event occurs is the highly urbanised Australian nation reminded that there is an arid, inhospitable outback where wind erosion of bare earth is creating desert — and it makes the headlines in newspapers. Much less publicised is the fact that in the Western Division of New South Wales land degradation from wind and water erosion is on a par with the worst in the world and a third of the rangeland is so degraded by over-grazing that in some places it loses about 200 tonnes of topsoil per hectare annually.[70] When it is realised that nutrients are concentrated in the top centimetre of arid-land soils, the loss of topsoil becomes a disaster of another dimension.

In the early days of settlement, and right up until the 1950s, dust storms were commonplace in south-eastern Australia. The rapid over-stocking of grazing lands, compounded by rabbit plagues; the clearing of land for long-fallow cropping; and the droughts of 1895–1899 and 1901–1903 saw red rain and 50 tons of red mud deposited on each square mile over which the dust cloud passed, according to 1903 calculations (about

20 tonnes per square kilometre). The red dust which crossed the Tasman Sea and coloured glaciers in the South Island of New Zealand in the 1928 drought was still visible on the ice in 1930. (Long-distance travel of dust is a global phenomenon with fine sand from Africa recognisable when it is deposited in Brazil and Florida, and dust from China settling on Hawaii.) Melbourne was regularly darkened by dust in the 1930s and until the Green Revolution started to improve matters by the late 1950s in the mallee lands which had been cleared for wheat. Broken Hill was regularly dusted out and there was a real fear that the red dunes of the Corner Country would be activated and roll over New South Wales in 1935.

Although human activity was a large contributor to the dust storms during the first half of this century, and still contributes to the less frequent dust storms and the dust haze which still occur, **Australia has 'natural' dust phenomena strongly related to drought**. Dr Grant McTainsh of Griffith University has been researching aeolian deposits (blown sand and dust) and their relation to continental wind patterns. It is well known that the orientation of dunes in the central deserts follows an anticyclonic wind pattern, and that dunes and lunettes in the southern portion of the continent are aligned according to the westerlies. The dust plumes which result from these two wind patterns go out to sea off the Western Australian coast mainly in the region of the Great Sandy Desert, and off the east coasts of Victoria, New South Wales and Queensland.

During glacial stages of the Pleistocene, and particularly during the last glacial maximum 18 000 years ago, when the Australian continent was twice as dry as it is today and winds were twice as strong, great quantities of dust left the continent in the two plumes and are now sediment layers in the Indian Ocean and the Tasman Sea. (See Map of the extent of the continent covered by wind-blown sand 18 000 years ago, page 48.) Dr McTainsh argues that dust then was a significant contributor to soils under the path of the plumes, and that dust still adds a minutely thin layer of soil today. The main sources of today's dust are the fine sediments from the lower Lake Eyre Basin and the Riverine Plain and Mallee of the Murray–Darling Basin.[48,71-74]

Recent research into oxygen isotope ratios in quartz in soils in Australia[75] confirms that dust deposition has played an important role in soil formation. The new techniques even enable pin-pointing of the source of the dust. A soil on granite at Sutton on the Southern Tablelands of New South Wales was estimated to be 50% dust-derived, on the strength of the oxygen isotopes in its quartz (only half of which matched those in the underlying granite).

Dr McTainsh[48] believes that the nature and extent of wind erosion have been much underestimated and that big dust storms are only the very visible events while the process is continuing wherever the prerequisites of erosivity of wind, erodible soil type and the effective soil moisture level come together. The

A red dust cloud arriving at Thargomindah in south-western Queensland in January 1994.

GRANT MCTAINSH

dust storm record on which wind erosion is measured is incomplete and not all meteorological stations keep records. Droughts obviously provide conditions favourable for wind erosion, and agricultural and pastoral activities increase the problem.

Several areas of eastern Australia have been recognised as suffering major wind erosion.

- The Mallee-Riverina region of south-west New South Wales and north-west Victoria, plus the Darling River and Murrumbidgee floodplains in western New South Wales. The Murray-Riverina region covers the largest wind-erosion-prone area and is acknowledged as the most seriously wind eroded in Australia. Its highly erodible soils were largely developed from dust deposits, dunefields and alluvium laid down during the Pleistocene, which explains their vulnerability to wind erosion today. The long history of cultivation in the region has been a contributing factor.

- The Charleville region of southern Queensland, which corresponds roughly to the spatial extent of

WIND EROSION

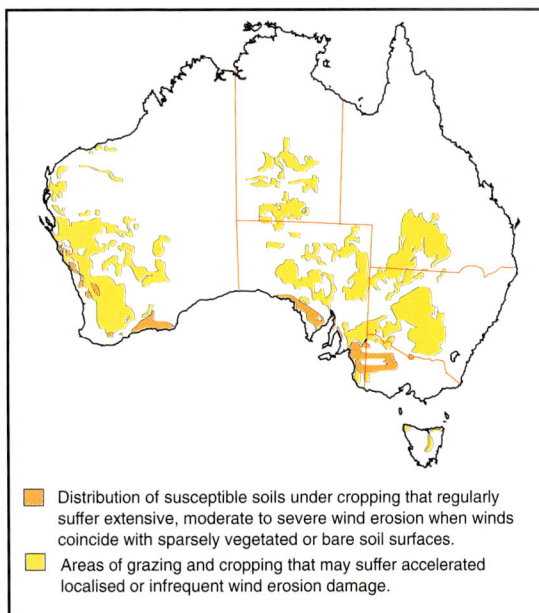

Distribution of susceptible soils under cropping that regularly suffer extensive, moderate to severe wind erosion when winds coincide with sparsely vegetated or bare soil surfaces.

Areas of grazing and cropping that may suffer accelerated localised or infrequent wind erosion damage.

After Decade of Landcare

the area around Urandangie and Camooweal in western Queensland, where there are extensive areas of cracking clays. Such heavy cracking clay soils are usually stable, but in the case of those in these areas the 'bull dust' in them, comprising sand-sized clay aggregates characteristic of the Cooper and Diamantina floodplains, makes them erodible, particularly in drought years. The dust-laden southerly winds which blow across the Channel Country are known as 'Bedouries' after the small town of Bedourie situated on Eyre Creek 250 km south of Urandangie.

An amazing storm with gale-force winds which caused dramatic erosion in the South-West Land Division of Western Australia was reported on by Dan Carter, Agriculture Western Australia, at Albany.[76] The May 1995 storm depression directed gales over the region for seven hours and a strip of land about 150 km wide along the south coast was affected by dust storms. Rain had fallen to the north and west of the area before the gale started, otherwise the wind erosion area would have been much larger.

The patterns of wind damage in this large, closely farmed area were varied and were related to the state of individual paddocks — their soil type, past seasonal conditions and management. In the western portion from Katanning to Ongerup only about one in ten paddocks blew, but visibility immediately down-wind was less than five metres. Progressively east of Ongerup the proportion of blowing paddocks increased to about nine out of ten, then decreased across to the eastern south coast where damage was less than on the central south coast.

The paddocks which were most affected were those that were almost bare with stubbles in their second year after cropping. The stubble roots had rotted during the winter and the wind blew them out of the ground, and all the bare soil with them. Canola stubble, deep rooted and having been less grazed because it is less palatable, afforded better protection; while patches of burnt stubble blew easily. All over-grazed pastures were affected to some extent. The central coast had been in drought and pastures were minimal with much bare earth, and how much erosion occurred was determined by the soil type with loose, powdery ones easily blown. Near Ongerup on grey clays, 3 mm of soil was scoured off, leaving a hard surface.

It was estimated that two million tonnes of topsoil left the continent in a south-easterly direction during the seven-hour storm, and this included 5000 tonnes of organic nitrogen. If the nitrogen had gone into wheat production it would have brought in $4.2 million. The same area had suffered a similar storm in the previous year, and such storms occur frequently (every two or three years) over much of the south-western region.

To prevent massive wind erosion of this kind a number of measures are indicated: planting windbreaks (alley farming) reduces the power and velocity of the

Above top: An aerial view of fields which suffered wind erosion at Jerdacuttup in the south-western division of Western Australia in a dust storm on 30 August 1991.

Above middle: Fields blown away during a dust storm in May 1988 at Chillinup in south-western Western Australia.

Above: Guest Road near Esperance, Western Australia after a wind-storm in April 1991.

DAN CARTER

the mulga lands, with their erodible sandy red earth soils, and with a history of intensive grazing.
- The Longreach area of central Queensland, and

Sheet erosion has created a vast scald on Mt Oxley Station, near Bourke in western New South Wales.

M.E.W.

wind in paddocks; improved perennial pastures and rotating stock so that they are not over-grazed eliminates bare ground; minimal till farming and stubble management reduce wind erosion; stubble burning is unacceptable; a variety of crops and opportunistic cropping can minimise risks.

For the most part, erosion proceeds far less visibly than dust storms and red-mud rain, its effects in cropped land masked by increased inputs of fertilisers, irrigation and improved crop varieties, and by the opening up of more land for agriculture as land already in use becomes less productive. But moderate erosion over 20 years takes a steady toll and reduces the potential of the land by about 20% — and when that stage is reached the benefits of the extra inputs are outweighed and productivity declines. This stage has been reached almost everywhere, worldwide, and the Green Revolution had ground to a halt by the mid 1980s. **With present technology, and no proven new technology, enormous problems are just around the corner.** (The high input of fertilisers, insecticides and irrigation water have the potential to create pollution of soil and water and to affect peoples' health, and they contribute to high energy consumption on farms, leading to economically unsustainable agriculture.)

Water Erosion

Everyone is familiar with the visible evidence of water erosion — the rills and gullies which scar the land; roadside erosion where water channelled from culverts carves canyons; scalds where all the topsoil has gone and only the clay-rich subsoil remains. Less visible is the steady washing away of topsoil from agricultural land. Figures for soil loss from agricultural land under land-use practices which do not put conservation first can be

MEASURED EROSION RATES

from several studies in eastern Australia (tonnes per hectare)

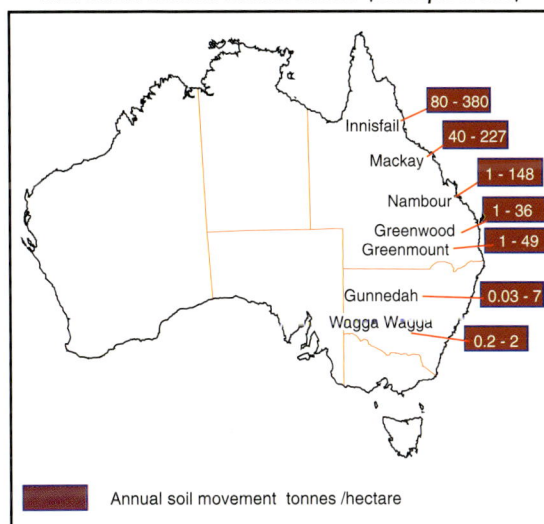

Location	Annual soil movement (tonnes/hectare)
Innisfail	80 - 380
	40 - 227
Mackay	1 - 148
Nambour	1 - 36
Greenwood / Greenmount	1 - 49
Gunnedah	0.03 - 7
Wagga Wagga	0.2 - 2

Annual soil movement tonnes /hectare

After Freebairn [77]

The correlation between heavy tropical downpours and erosion is seen in this map; also the unsustainable soil loss from sugar-producing regions at Innisfail and Mackay. The enormous soil loss possible from sugar fields is responding to reduced tillage systems.

hair-raising. This is particularly the case in the tropics, where rainfall tends to occur in big events with high erosive power.

A fundamental truth about desertification emerges from observations on land degradation in the semi-arid to arid Western Division of New South Wales.

When degradation is so severe that soil stability is lost, processes are set in motion which are progressive and heading for a new stable state at some time in the future. In this context, some of the arid-land degradation in Australia is

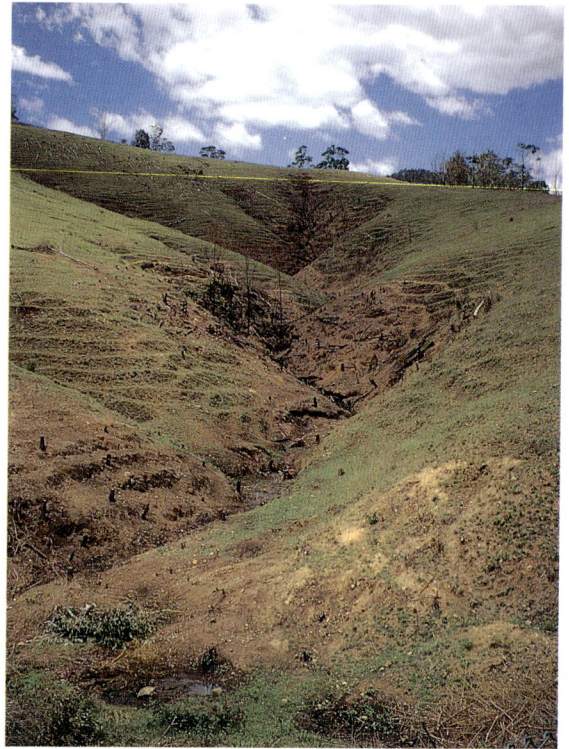

Clearing of all trees and bushes from deep gullies results in erosion, as seen in this photograph taken on the Nowendock–Gloucester road in a fertile, well-watered part of eastern New South Wales. The land was originally forested and it was cleared for grazing.

M.E.W.

Above top: Sheet and gully erosion adjacent to a main road in the Northam district of Western Australia.

Above middle: Erosion and bitou bush (boneseed) weed invasion at Lake Menindee in the western division of New South Wales. Bitou bush was introduced to colonise dunes on the east coast of Australia and has taken over and become a noxious weed in coastal areas. How it reached Lake Menindee is unknown. Weeds and erosion go together, however.

M.E.W.

virtually unstoppable and rehabilitation is impossible.

The marginal lands of semi-arid regions worldwide have been the most vulnerable to grazing, agriculture and other human-induced changes. Australia's arid ecosystems in their natural state were finely balanced and we now know that the balance depended on the interactions between so many animals and plants, the living soil and climate, that no human has the wisdom required to re-establish it.

The dynamics of the natural ecosystems allowed and catered for:

- the very slow growth-rate of saltbush, mulga and probably most perennial species;
- the comparative desert within arid soils in terms of micro-biological components;
- the slow rate of organic breakdown;
- the specific requirements of the termites and ants which are vital in nutrient recycling and soil formation;
- the restriction of nutrients to the top few centimetres of soil, which makes any soil loss serious;
- the biotic soil crusts which protect against erosion, create nutrients and act as seed beds but which are damaged or destroyed by hooved animals and too frequent fires; and

- the grazing by native animals (many of which are now locally extinct), and by invertebrates, to prevent 'stagnation' of perennial pasture without over-grazing of plants.

Degradation in the Western Division of New South Wales

There were 10 million sheep west of the Darling in New South Wales by 1890. The adequate rainfall and good markets in the early, heady days of settlement had seen a rush to take up land and tap the limitless riches of the new promised land. When the 1895 depression resulted in collapse of the sheep industry, more than loss of income for farmers was involved. **The land had been permanently damaged.** The Royal Commission of 1901, established to look into the plight of farmers leasing western division crown lands noted that salt bush (*Atriplex vesicaria*) and cottonbush (*Marieana aphylla*) had been eaten out over large areas, rabbits had prevented re-establishment by eating seedlings, and non-edible woody plants were spreading. In the first 30 years of settlement in other parts of the continent a similar pattern of rapid stock increase also led to land degradation — by cattle in the Centre; cattle and sheep in Queensland and Western Australia.

The rapid and serious desertification which resulted from inappropriate land use and excessive exploitation a hundred years ago is ongoing right up to the present, according to Patricia Fanning, a researcher

Erosion by water and wind on the Walls of China at Lake Mungo is taking place so rapidly that soon this marvellous feature will be eroded away. Sheep grazed the vegetation which stabilised the lunette dunes which lie on the downwind side of the dry bed of Lake Mungo, exposing the sands to erosion.

M.E.W.

studying erosion rates in the Homestead Creek catchment at Fowlers Gap, 110 km north of Broken Hill. Homestead Creek is an upland tributary of Fowlers Creek which flows in a north-easterly direction through the northern Barrier Ranges towards Lake Bancannia. The study area is located on the valley floor adjacent to Homestead Creek in 'badlands' which are almost bare, and the vegetation of the whole catchment is degraded, with copper burr (*Bassia*) and saltbush, and a little tussock grass in less-grazed areas. River red gums are present along the larger creeks.[70]

At the time of settlement the vegetation was mulga and belah and native cypress woodland (*Acacia aneura*, *Casuarina cristata* and *Callitris glaucophylla*) in savanna of tussock grasses and saltbush. The belah and cypress were largely felled to make fence posts. Over-grazing by sheep devastated the pastures, creating bare earth and destabilising the ecosystems.

The land has not been able to recover from the breakdown of soil structure which, by the turn of the century, had resulted in its inability to absorb rainfall and prevent excessive run-off, and through time the problem has merely compounded. The removal of the groundcover increased run-off on the slopes and increased creekline erosion. Valley floors were widened and incised, and the waterholes along the main channels, which had provided a reliable water resource for Aboriginal populations through great lengths of time, were destroyed. Headward retreat of gullies now threatens roads and watering points in the catchment. **The rates of erosion recorded are comparable to the highest quoted in scientific literature for anywhere in the world.** Rates of up to 209 tonnes per hectare, per year were recorded on rilled surfaces; 59.5 tonnes on flat surfaces; and 30.6 on vegetated remnants. This equates to a soil loss in excess of 6000

WATER EROSION

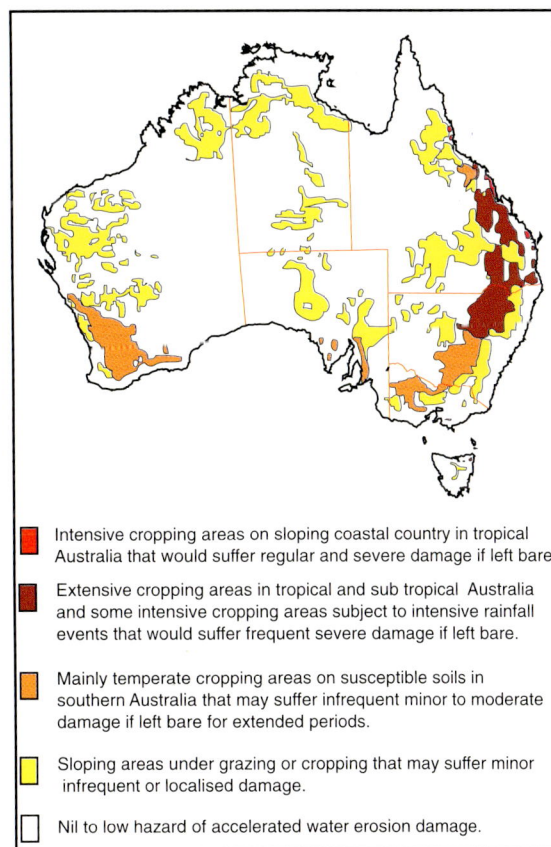

- ■ (red) Intensive cropping areas on sloping coastal country in tropical Australia that would suffer regular and severe damage if left bare.

- ■ (dark red) Extensive cropping areas in tropical and sub tropical Australia and some intensive cropping areas subject to intensive rainfall events that would suffer frequent severe damage if left bare.

- ■ (orange) Mainly temperate cropping areas on susceptible soils in southern Australia that may suffer infrequent minor to moderate damage if left bare for extended periods.

- ■ (yellow) Sloping areas under grazing or cropping that may suffer minor infrequent or localised damage.

- □ Nil to low hazard of accelerated water erosion damage.

After Decade of Landcare

tonnes a year on just 3% of the Homestead Creek catchment. It is estimated that at present rates of erosion the whole of the narrow valley-fill section of the Homestead Creek catchment will be removed by the processes of sheetwash, gullying and wind erosion within another 100 years.

Severely stripped land in other parts of arid

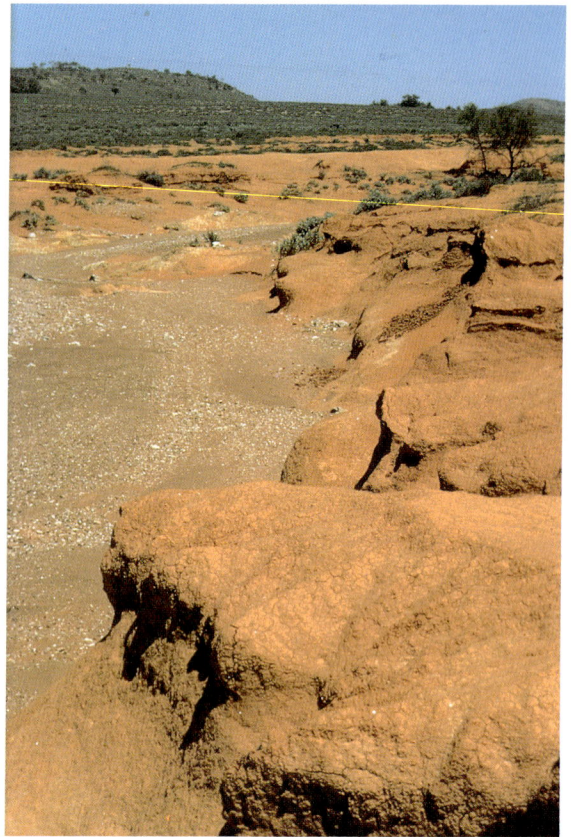

Above right: Bank degradation at Homestead Creek where massive erosion is occurring.

Above top: The whole catchment at Homestead Creek has been so destabilised by erosion that the processes will continue until a new stable state is reached at some time in the future.

Above: A massive bank collapse at Homestead Creek.

TRISH FANNING

rangelands have responded to rehabilitation by '**waterponding**' — a process by which low earth banks are made on contours so that water can pond behind them and penetrate into the soil, improving its moisture-holding capacity. Vegetation begins to creep back over the scalds from the ponds, which also serve to entrap seeds and humus. This technique has been used successfully on large areas of flattish alluvial land adjacent to the large river systems of the Darling, Lachlan and Murrumbidgee in western New South Wales, and in parts of Western Australia like the headwaters of the Ord River where land rehabilitation was necessary to stop serious silting of the Argyle Dam.

However, the incised nature of the main channel of Homestead Creek and the close-gullying of the land adjacent to the main channel means that the hydraulic slope is too great and the area of flat land on which ponds could be established is too restricted for waterponding to be a remedy here. The topography locally is such that when stability was lost, processes began which are heading for a new stable state at some time in the future. The stripping will ultimately be self-limiting, but not until up to half a million tonnes of soil have been lost in this very small catchment.

This is an example of a situation where geological forces, which in stable situations are operating as 'background noise', take over and move inexorably towards a changed landscape in which stability is restored. The example of Homestead Creek is not an isolated one. Unfortunately, severe stripping of the same sort is widespread throughout the Australian arid zone wherever the nature of the local landscape makes it vulnerable to progressive erosion after it has been destabilised. Millions of hectares of once stable rangeland have been destroyed and cannot be rehabilitated. Geological time, not a life-time, will be needed before productive ecosystems can be re-established on these run-away places. Woody weed-invaded areas represent a quasi-stable state attained where degradation of the ecosystem has not been completely destabilising like it has at Homestead Creek.

Soil Acidification

Acids enter natural ecosystems as carbonic acid in rainfall, as sulphuric and nitric acids produced by biological processes, and as organic acids. The large areas of naturally acidic soils in the higher rainfall regions of eastern and southern Australia may have been acidified under previous climatic conditions. A balance exists in natural ecosystems between vegetation and soil, maintaining soil chemistry in a relatively stable state.

Soil acidification has only been recognised relatively recently. Like other changing chemical reactions in the soil it has crept up on the Green Revolution, causing declining yields, lower stocking rates for improved pastures, germination failures, and restrictions on nodulation of legume roots.

In response to a serious and increasing problem of agriculture-induced soil acidification, the Land and Water Resources Research and Development

Corporation has launched a National Acid Soils Program. It has recognised that **90 million hectares of productive farmland are affected by soil acidity levels which are resulting in loss of productivity, with 35 million hectares highly acidic and 55 million moderately or slightly acidic**. Most of the nation's most productive soils are threatened by, or suffer from, serious acidification, including the south-west corner of the continent and the fertile green crescent of south-eastern Australia and much of the east coast. Soil acidification is costing Australia at least $300 million a year in lost production and it makes soils more prone to erosion.

The increase in soil acidity results from the use of superphosphate and other fertilisers, from the extensive use of legumes with nitrogen-fixing bacteria in their root nodules in crop rotations and improved pastures, and from the gradual removal of alkali in hay and other products. In southern Australia, nitrogen-producing plants like legumes die in the summer. Micro-organisms convert plant nitrogen to nitrate, a process which acidifies. In autumn the nitrate is leached deep into the soil before the new plants which follow can absorb it. Top layers of the soil become acidic and toxic aluminium and magnesium (and some trace elements) become increasingly mobilised and available to be taken up by plants.

Liming of the soil is the only chemical remedy for the problem. It is expensive because a great deal is needed where the acidification is serious. At present, 500 000 tonnes of lime are used annually, and that is regarded as one-tenth of what should be used. Depending on the nature of the soil, its acidity and what it is being used for, amounts necessary to restore full production vary between a light dressing every five to six years and annual heavy dressings (which may take many years before having any effect on productivity). To remedy the 1.5 million hectares of land where acidity is 'dangerously' high would take 2.3 million tonnes of lime, costing $120 million.

Research in south-eastern Australia has shown that removal of one tonne of lucerne hay from a piece of land has 20 times more acidifying effect on the soil than equivalent harvesting of a cereal grain crop, so it is evident that land-use can play a significant part in controlling the problem. Perennial pastures (or summer-active plants) are better than annual ones; deep rooted annuals recover more of the leached nitrogen, so crops with this attribute would reduce acidification. Some plants are more acid-tolerant than others, and selection of varieties which are less affected increases productivity but it does nothing for the underlying problem. Techniques like the lime-pelleting of legume seed, which helps the germination and production of nodules in young plants, can help when acidity levels are not too high. Judicious choice of crops, combined with liming at the rate required by specific areas, can restore balance to areas which are not too badly affected fairly rapidly.

Human health is under threat as acidification

INDUCED SOIL ACIDITY

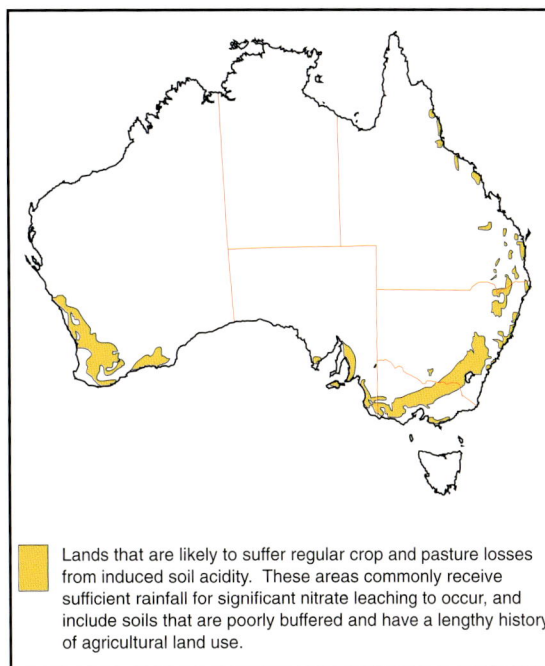

Lands that are likely to suffer regular crop and pasture losses from induced soil acidity. These areas commonly receive sufficient rainfall for significant nitrate leaching to occur, and include soils that are poorly buffered and have a lengthy history of agricultural land use.

After Decade of Landcare

Soils are either slightly acid, alkaline or neutral, depending on their geological composition and history. Those that contain lime (alkaline) are buffered against acidification from plants or fertilisers, while those that start off acid are at risk when cultivated. Most soils tend to become slightly acidic under cultivation and serious problems result from a build-up of acids.

proceeds. The increased solubility of aluminium, magnesium and some trace elements in acid soils results in their entry into the water-table, rivers and water storages, as well as into the foods we eat. In the case of soluble aluminium, which is already increasing in concentrations in some water supply dams, the link to Alzheimer's disease is a concern. Poisons like cadmium are mobilised by acid groundwater and their uptake by plants, particularly vegetables, increases the risk that toxic levels will be present in food.

Acid Sulphate Soils

Acid sulphate soils contain iron sulphides or their oxidation products. They are formed when sea or brackish water mixes with sediments containing organic matter and they are part of the world's natural sulphur cycle.

The presence of acid sulphate soils in low-lying coastal regions is related to the changes in sea-level which occurred in the Pleistocene, and those that are of most concern relate to the rise in sea-level which followed the last glacial cycle (14 000 years ago until stabilisation of sea-level at about 6000 years ago). As the sea rose and crept up the continental shelves it mobilised sediment and deposited it in coastal embayments, where it was colonised by mangroves. The mangroves stabilised the sediment and added organic matter. In the absence of oxygen in the waterlogged mud, bacteria breaking down the organic matter reduced the sulphate from seawater to iron pyrite or iron sulphide, at concentrations of up to 15% in the top metre or more of the sediment profile.

While the mud is covered by water it is insulated from the atmosphere and no oxidation takes place and the pyritic layer is an innocuous **'potential acid sulphate soil' — a PASS** in soil science jargon. When this land is drained or cleared for agriculture or development, oxygen can reach the iron sulphide and oxidise it to sulphuric acid.

When sulphuric acid starts to form, the soil is called an **actual acid sulphate soil (ASS)**. The soil itself can neutralise some of the acid, but the remainder acidifies the soil water, the groundwater and eventually drainage waters and streams. As it moves through the soil it strips iron, aluminium and sometimes manganese from the soil, creating an acid brew. It can be strong enough to corrode steel and concrete, and it is toxic to plants. When it reaches the streams it is lethal to aquatic life, especially fish. Because of the high concentrations of sulphides in acid sulphate soils, large volumes of acid can be released with devastating impacts on estuarine ecosystems.

Acid sulphate soils are widespread in estuarine floodplains, mangrove tidal flats, salt marshes and tea-tree swamps of coastal New South Wales and Queensland, where they cause most concern because so many areas along Australia's east coast are undergoing rapid expansion and development of rural and urban land uses. (With most of the population concentrated along the margins of the continent and major city and town expansion located right along the coast, coastal wetlands are increasingly involved.) The acid sulphate soils also occur adjacent to the coast in the Northern Territory, where vast areas of mangrove swamps existed far inland during the 'big swamp' phase between 7500 and 6000 years ago (see Chapter 11), and in isolated areas of Western Australia, South Australia and Victoria.

The Multi-Function Polis site near Adelaide is on swampy ground which has acid sulphate soil — a developers' nightmare where steel and concrete will be devoured by acid when the site is disturbed. On the fringes of the Homebush Olympic site in Sydney, the mangrove-lined wetlands no doubt pose similar threats. According to CSIRO research scientists, uranium mining on the Kakadu floodplain is going to run into problems with sulphuric acid when the wetlands are disturbed and very careful planning will be needed to ensure that ecosystems are not damaged.

It is estimated that more than two million hectares of acid sulphate soils occur in Australia, and that represents about a billion tonnes of iron pyrite. Each tonne of pyrite can produce 1.5 tonnes of sulphuric acid.

Because potential acid sulphate soil areas are waterlogged, they are often drained. Excavation leads to rapid release of large amounts of acid into waterways, and the excavated soil continues to leach acid. In New South Wales some acid sulphate soils which were drained 100 years ago are still leaching acid. In clay soils the oxidation process is slow, in sand it can be rapid. The best management is to avoid disturbing soils which are potentially dangerous. Lime can be used to treat the acidity, but the amount needed when the problem is severe is enormous.

Typical land uses associated with environments containing acid sulphate soils include grazing, dairying, sugar cane production, urban development and sand mining. Various aquaculture industries are also associated with these environments. Fishermen experience the off-site effects when heavy rains following dry periods flush extremely acid and aluminium-rich water into rivers and estuaries. **About 60% of commercial fish species spend part of their lives in estuaries**, which makes the problems of high acidity serious. Massive fish kills can result from sudden flushes of acid, and sustained high acid levels result in the fish disease red spot, which costs fisheries about $1 million a year in discarded fish. Fish also suffer eye, gill and tissue damage, calcium deficiencies leading to bone deformities and egg abnormalities, reduced growth rates and increased susceptibility to fungal and bacterial infections. It appears that fish can detect increased acid levels and may try to move to areas less affected. Where dams, weirs and other obstructions block their way in rivers they cannot escape. Oysters and crustaceans, and presumably very large numbers of less visible organisms also are affected by the acid.

Investigations have been made into land management practices which decrease the impact on rivers when acid land is drained. For example, sugar cane is growing on land at McLeods Creek, a tributary of the Tweed River in New South Wales, where acid sulphate soils extend to a depth of 9.7 m below the soil surface and the land is extensively drained. Here it has been found that it is best to let the acid water drain at a steady rate and at a height that leaves some surface water after heavy rainfall, by leaving flood-gates slightly open all the time. (It had been the custom to drain completely when the water-table was high after rain.) Sudden increases in acid entering the river are largely avoided and the amount of oxidisation is decreased when the cane is growing in saturated soil after rain, and both factors are better for the river and at the same time have been proved not to be disadvantageous to the cane.

Australia has a growing **prawn farming industry**, using low-lying coastal sites close to tidal flushing and a supply of prawn fry. Traditionally, 'tanks' are excavated, allowed to fill with salt water, stocked with prawn fry and flushed by tidal action. Problems being experienced start with the ponds being excavated into acid sulphate soils. In addition, fowl manure and fertiliser are added to produce the algal blooms on which the prawns feed, and 10 tonnes of feed are needed to produce 5 tonnes of prawns. This results in 100 tonnes of sediment over the period required to grow the prawns to marketable size. Because prawns only thrive in alkaline environments, lime is added to the ponds and as a result

Pattersons curse and capeweed in a paddock near Northam in Western Australia.

M.E.W

the oxidation of pyrite does not mobilise aluminium but produces soluble iron in great quantities. Then too, the sediment in the tanks which results from the intensive feeding is largely anaerobic and bacteria in it produce black iron monosulphide. The soluble iron also oxidises to form acidity, which strips carbonate and bicarbonate from the water. These conditions clog the prawns' gills and prevent moulting. Prawns have to moult to grow because they have rigid exoskeletons.

These interconnected problems have been limiting prawn production, but Dr Ian White of the CSIRO and Dr Mike Melville of the University of New South Wales have suggested remedies as a result of their research on a prawn farm at Logan River in southern Queensland. Constructing the tanks above ground and not excavating into the potential acid sulphate soil is the first requirement. Then the ponds should be lined with a layer of magnesium carbonate or calcium carbonate. If sulphuric acid comes into contact with carbonate compounds it transforms them to magnesium sulphate or calcium sulphate — neutral substances which prevent the build-up of iron monosulphides and maintain aerobic conditions so that sediment organisms can survive and provide an additional source of food for the prawns.

Pollution and Contamination of Soil

Market Gardens and Orchards

Soils of market gardens are liable to be polluted either by pesticides or with heavy metal residues from superphosphate fertilisers. Residues of DDT, dieldrin and other pesticides which are now banned persist in soils and in the water-table.

The Sydney region has particular problems in relation to high levels of **cadmium** because of the length of time that the market gardens in and around the greater metropolitan area have been in use, the nature of the soils, and the fact that the superphosphate used came from Nauru, Christmas and Ocean Islands, all of which have high cadmium levels. Recent studies have shown that the level of cadmium in some instances was as high as in the worst affected parts of Europe and the US. The situation has been compounded in many instances by the use of poultry manure as an additional fertiliser. For three decades, until a few years ago, chickens were often fed rock phosphate supplements and cadmium was being concentrated in their droppings. (Increased use of sewage sludge also has the potential to increase the heavy metal component in soils.)

Certain plants concentrate specific metals, and cadmium is taken up in greater quantity by leafy green vegetables — like lettuce, cabbage and parsley — than by root vegetables. The National Food Authority assures us that although cadmium levels in some of our foods greatly exceed the permissible levels under the Pure Food Act, this does not pose a serious health risk. When there is no known way that cadmium can be removed from the soil, and it may be 1000 years before lettuce grown in some areas would have levels approved by the Act (supposing that no more of the metal is added in the meanwhile) we can only hope that the experts are right.

The fertiliser industry claims that in the last decade much of its rock phosphate has come from sources other than those known to have high cadmium levels (again we must hope that we are being told the truth), while acknowledging that some commercial growers are using too much fertiliser, and that Sydney has a particular problem. The Agriculture Department has reported that most market gardeners have been using up to four times as much superphosphate as is necessary.

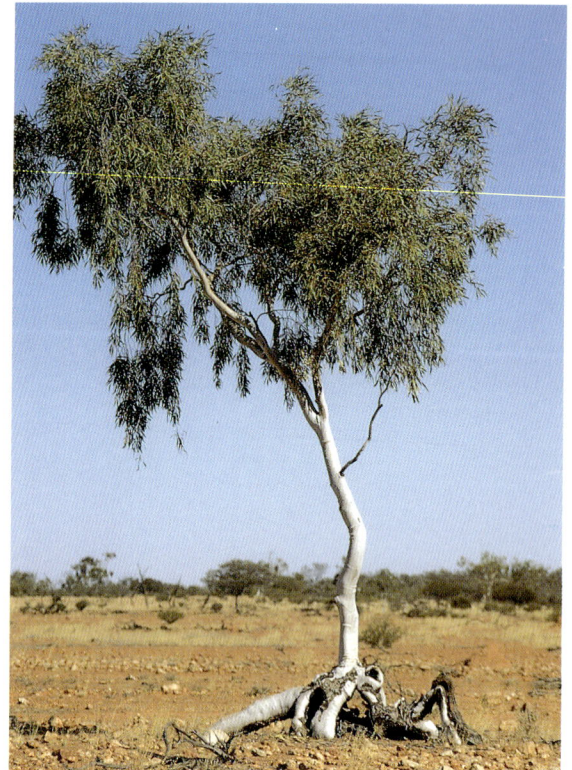

Right: Capeweed makes a field of gold in the Stirlings district of southern Western Australia.

M.E.W.

Far right: Over-grazing has resulted in soil erosion, which has lowered the landscape down to the subsoil, exposing the roots of this lonely Eucalyptus papuana.

JIM FRAZIER

The Sydney region supplies most of the city's vegetables and much of its fruit, and also supplies interstate markets. The risk to consumers posed by high cadmium levels may be reduced by liming soils to decrease acidity and thereby reducing solubility of the compounds containing cadmium (in the same way as liming acid soils decreases the solubility of aluminium). Cadmium uptake by plants can be reduced by adding zinc in zinc-deficient soils. In time it may be necessary to grow those plants which do not have a heightened ability to take up the metal, or to breed special strains of leafy vegetables suited to our contaminated soils (which will increase productivity but do little to address the problem of the soil's toxicity).

Improved pastures fertilised with high-cadmium superphosphate have the potential to result in milk and meat with higher concentrations of the metal than is desirable. This is particularly the case where capeweed is a significant component of pastures. **Capeweed** is a notorious concentrator of cadmium and mature plants can have high to toxic levels of cadmium. The widespread nature of this weed in pastures, combined with the equally widespread use of superphosphates high in cadmium, makes this a potentially serious problem.

The chemical interaction of different elements in the soil can lead to toxic concentrations or to certain necessary trace elements becoming unavailable to plants. **Cobalt**, which is necessary for animal health, may not be taken up by pasture where soils have a high manganese content, and it then has to be fed as a supplement. **Phosphorus** may similarly be unavailable to plants if the local soil chemistry results in it being held in an insoluble state.

Boron may be present in soils in quantities which

are actually toxic to plants. Soluble boron occurs in soils throughout South Australia, Western Victoria and the south-western part of New South Wales, and in parts of Western Australia. There is no way known to remove it, and where concentrations are high, boron-tolerant varieties of crop plants may be the only answer.

The chemistry of soils is complex and there is always the risk that additions of fertilisers, sewage sludge which often carries heavy metals put into the system by industry, and pesticides, will result in a new set of problems.

Decline in Soil Structure

The decline in soil structure which has occurred under European use of agricultural land for cropping or grazing results primarily from **loss of soil organic matter**. It is estimated that 75% of Australian soils now contain less than 1% organic matter, whereas 2% is needed for soil stability.

Symptoms of soil structure decline, which is estimated to cost Australia $300 million a year in lost production, are: rill and sheet erosion; crusting of soil (not to be confused with the living biotic crusts which protect arid-land soils); clodding of soil when it is cultivated; ponding after rain; poor water infiltration; hard soil; less organic matter; increased erodibility — up to five or 10 times as much soil is lost when structure is damaged.

We have seen how erosion over time has removed topsoil (both in cropped land and in over-grazed pastureland) and with it has gone organic matter. Organic matter contains much of a soil's reserve of nutrients, particularly nitrogen, and under natural conditions soil organic matter reaches an equilibrium

SOIL STRUCTURE DECLINE

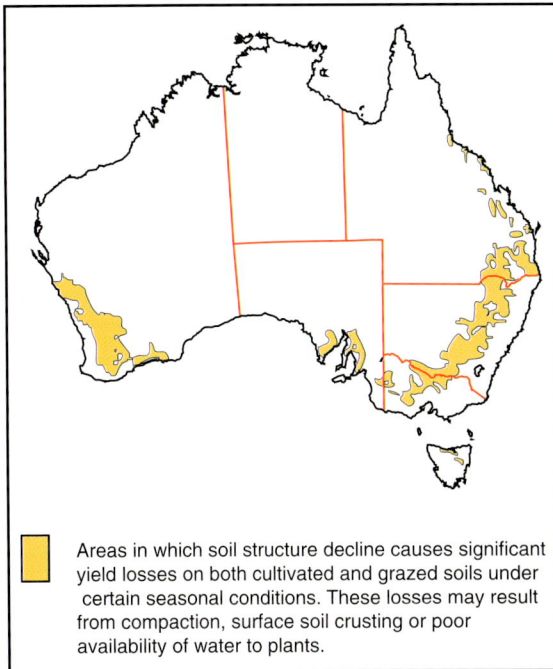

Areas in which soil structure decline causes significant yield losses on both cultivated and grazed soils under certain seasonal conditions. These losses may result from compaction, surface soil crusting or poor availability of water to plants.

After Decade of Landcare

controlled by climate, vegetation and erosion. Clearing, cropping and fertilising upset the natural balance and establish a trend towards a new balance which depends on the nature and magnitude of the changes. Soil fauna and flora and the paths and rates of organic matter turnover have been affected by the changes in vegetation cover as forest and woodland have given way to cultivation. Activities of termites and ants and other important components of the nutrient cycling systems have often been eliminated. Soil temperature change following conversion of shady woodland to open cropland is one obvious factor which influences microbiological activity.

Cultivation of the cleared land causes structural change to the soil which is related to smaller aggregate size, and decomposition of soil organic matter is stimulated by exposing additional surfaces to microbiological attack. In addition, repeated wetting and drying accelerates breakdown and leaching of organic matters, and stubble burning (which used to be a widespread practice) and long fallowing in crop rotations cause rapid loss of organic matter.

Soil compaction follows change in soil structure, loss of organic matter, decrease in bioturbation, and physical compacting by heavy machinery in croplands and by hooves of animals in pastures. Earthworms, so important in soils in the Northern Hemisphere as recyclers and bioturbation agents, though introduced into Australia, have not adapted to dryland farming, and native worms have not thrived under the cultivation of croplands.

Compaction affects mycorrhizal health and thus affects nutrient and water uptake by plants. (Symbiotic fungi act not only to enhance nutrient uptake but are now also known to enable water absorption.) At the same time, the unbalanced microbiological status of soils whose structure is affected leads to opportunities for invasion by undesirable fungi. The 'take-all' fungus *Gaeumannomyces* and the root-rot fungus *Rhizoctonia* cost Australian agriculture $100 million a year in productivity loss. (Healthy symbiotic mycorrhizas are known to create a protective barrier around roots.)

Soil compaction is recognised as being one of the factors which has contributed to die-back death of trees in New England and elsewhere.

The black soils of the Namoi irrigated cotton region have suffered severe compaction by the heavy machinery used in cultivation and harvesting. The fact that the soils are permanently wet has aggravated the problem. A yield decline has prompted a move to use wheat in rotation with cotton. The wheat crop takes up excess water, enabling cultivation of the soil before planting the cotton, and better yields result. (What the accelerated soil loss is under this system is not recorded.)

Water repellence is a characteristic which is strongly developed by certain soil types under cropping. It results in effective rainfall penetration being dramatically reduced, and run-off correspondingly increased.

This scene in the Yass district of New South Wales has all the elements of land degradation: an erosion gully has a salty crust in its bottom; the trees are dying of dieback disease because of soil compaction, salt and other pressures; weeds, in this case Patterson's curse, have invaded the over-grazed native vegetation.

M.E.W.

WATER REPELLANCE

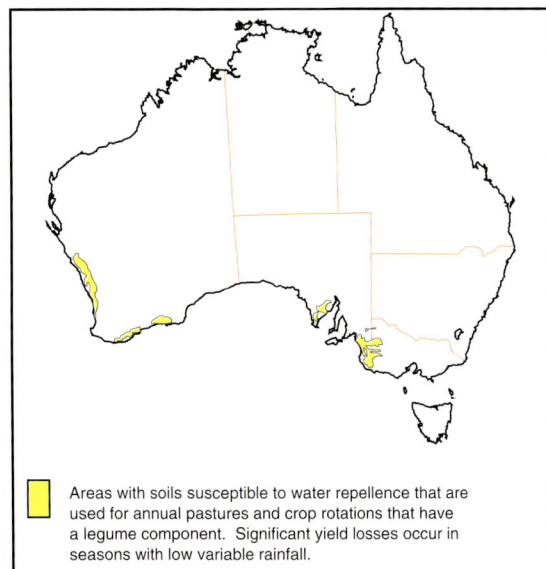

Areas with soils susceptible to water repellence that are used for annual pastures and crop rotations that have a legume component. Significant yield losses occur in seasons with low variable rainfall.

After Decade of Landcare

The eastern Darling Downs are a patchwork of contoured fields on the rich black soil. Grassed waterways along contours help to prevent erosion, though the rainfall pattern of heavy storms makes soil conservation a very difficult task.

DAVID FREEBAIRN

AGRICULTURE ON THE DARLING DOWNS, QUEENSLAND

Soil erosion in the rich agricultural regions of Queensland, of which the Darling Downs is the best known and most studied, continues at an 'unacceptably high rate' in some cases, in spite of the current agricultural practices which are aimed at sustainable use.[78-80] Annual soil losses of 30 to 60 tonnes per hectare have been recorded in cereal growing areas. Summer-dominant high-intensity rainfall, highly erodible clay soils and farming practices which result in bare soil are the recipe for massive soil loss.

It was estimated that eight million tonnes of the rich black soil was being lost a year, and that at that rate all the soil would be gone in 30 to 50 years.[81] The value of nutrients in soils washed down from the Downs in drought-breaking rains on 1983 has been estimated at $2 billion.

David Freebairn (personal communication) qualifies this estimate, saying that erosion rates of less than five tonnes per hectare per year under best management practices, while higher than those under pasture, are probably sustainable for most soil types. When poor management results in erosion rates of 10 to 50 tonnes per hectare, the life of the soils may be in the order of 30 to 50 years, and even though production can be sustained on deeper soils with increased inputs of fertiliser, off-site effects remain socially unacceptable.

Water stress is a major limiting factor in the semi-arid tropics. It is related to the high evaporation rates and the generally unreliable rainfall in the summer months, compounded by run-off which reduces effective rainfall, and by soil erosion which reduces the ability of the soil to store water.

On the eastern Darling Downs, crop yields are

LOCATION OF SITES IN THE EASTERN DARLING DOWNS

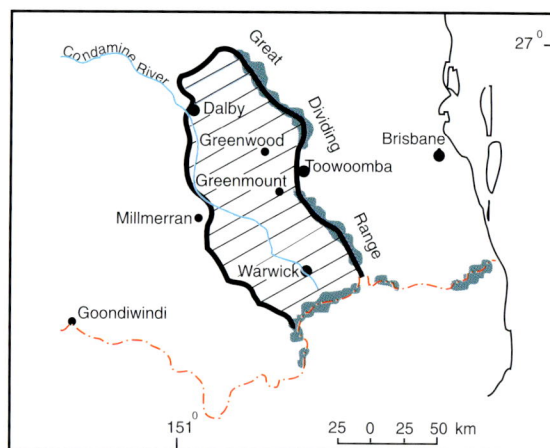

commonly limited by the water stress factor, yet 70 to 90 mm of the average annual 630 to 730 mm rainfall is lost as run-off. When it is realised that 60% to 70% of summer rain which falls on fallow is lost in evaporation, and when the erratic nature of the rainfall is taken into account, the reasons for water stress become clear.

In southern Queensland the main winter crops, wheat and barley, are planted in May-June and yield is strongly influenced by the amount of soil moisture at planting. Fallowing is practiced to conserve rainfall in the soil for the use of winter crops in particular, because winter rainfall is less reliable. The principal summer crops, sorghum and sunflower, are planted from October to January, while a range of cereal, legume and other crops are also grown. Annual cropping is the normal practice though some farmers grow two crops in a year if soil moisture allows; others maintain a fallow for 18 months while changing from summer to winter crop rotation. After harvesting, stubble is either burnt, cultivated or left standing.

Cover and soil loss
Darling Downs 1978-92

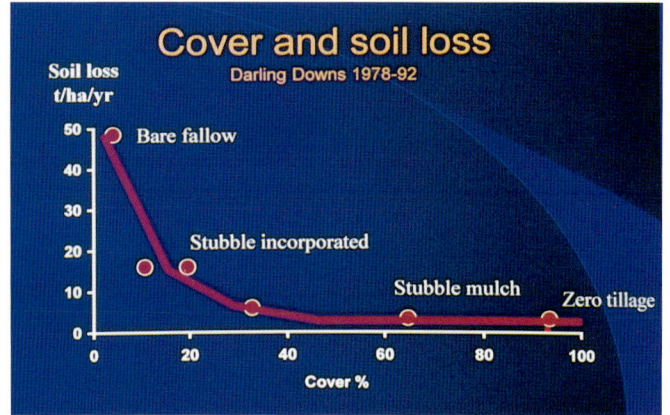

Soil loss
t/ha/yr

Bare fallow

Stubble incorporated

Stubble mulch

Zero tillage

Cover %

To combat the heavy soil loss which occurs by water erosion, mainly during the few severe storms between October and March, contour banks and grassed waterways have been installed over most of the eastern Downs. The contour banks trap 80% to 90% of the soil from the paddocks, and run-off from the banks is channelled along grassed waterways, further reducing soil loss. The black soil landscapes, with their patterns of contour banks and grassed waterways, are like patchwork quilts. In spite of all the earthworks, erosion still proceeds, and rills and gullies run at right-angles to the contour banks. In extreme events (which occur in more than one in 10 years on average) these structures often fail.

Extensive experiments have been conducted to determine what land management practices reduce erosion and increase the uptake of water by the soil. It has been found that stubble or crop cover reduced run-off volumes by 40% and peak discharge rates by 70% to 85% compared to bare soil. The suspended sediment discharged from contour banks into grassed waterways was reduced from a mean of 1.3% from bare soil to 0.2% when stubble was retained as surface mulch. Experiments with different crop rotations have also been conducted to determine which combinations of practices satisfy production requirements, decrease run-off and erosion, and are the most 'sustainable'. No-till or minimum-till farming has been shown here (as on the Liverpool Plains) to be the best option. Weed control is a challenge under these regimes and chemical control with 'safe' herbicides the usual option. Stubble burning is practically a thing of the past. Because of the seriousness of the soil loss, farmers on the Downs have made enormous changes in a relatively short time

Top left: Erosion gullies running at right angles to the contour bays after heavy rain.

Top right: Graph of the relationship between ground cover and erosion.

Above: Stubble burning on the Darling Downs, a practice which is losing favour as stubble retention decreases erosion.

DAVID FREEBAIRN

Right: A close-up of soil erosion in a field planted with sunflowers on the Darling Downs.

Below: Massive erosion of the deep black soil of the Darling Downs.

DAVID FREEBAIRN

(compared to the rate at which much agricultural innovation is usually accepted).

The continuing soil loss means that even at the very reduced rate of erosion under the best-case management practices, the deep black soils of the Darling Downs have a finite lifespan. How long will depend on how uniformly the better management practices are implemented, and probably on whether Greenhouse will bring more extreme events in which no management regimes can prevent heavy soil loss.

EROSION ON NORFOLK ISLAND

Erosion control under Bird Rock on Norfolk Island (which is an outlier of NSW and suffers from erosion just like the mainland).

DICK BURNS

Hillside erosion at Ansons Bay on Norfolk Island.

DICK BURNS

LANDCARE

A great deal of Australia's agricultural land and vast areas in its rangelands are severely degraded — but the Landcare movement, and other grassroots conservation initiatives, are reasons for optimism that sustainable land-use practices will be developed and implemented. Australia leads the world in the participation of its people in self-help schemes. Landcare is such a world leader, coordinating all the voluntary land and water conservation groups and providing them with the support they need to achieve their goals.

The **National Landcare Program** was modelled on Victorian LandCare groups established in the 1980s. In 1989, the Prime Minister issued a *Statement on the Environment* in which 1990 was declared to be the **Year of Landcare** and the decade to the year 2000 was declared to be the **Decade of Landcare**.

Commonwealth, State and Territory Ministers responsible for soil conservation agreed in 1990 to develop a **National Decade of Landcare Plan**, integrating actions by governments, individuals and the community to address land degradation in Australia until the year 2000.

The administrative umbrella for the Landcare movement at a national level is the National Landcare Program (NLP) within the Department of Primary Industries and Energy. The Program comprises **a community Landcare component** which assists community groups to work towards sustainable management of land, water and vegetation resources in their local areas; a **Commonwealth–State component** where a framework for Federal–State–Territory funding of projects is agreed upon; and a **national component** which funds Commonwealth initiatives for integrated land and water management.

Programs from other Commonwealth agencies which support community-based activities are also part of the National Landcare Program. These are the **Save the Bush Program** and **One Billion Trees** program administered by the Australian Nature Conservation Agency, and the community component of the **Natural Resources Management Strategy for the Murray–Darling Basin** (administered by the Murray–Darling Basin Commission). The One Billion Trees program is delivered by Greening Australia.

Andrew Campbell, the first National Landcare Facilitator, published *Landcare — Communities Shaping the Land and the Future* (Allen and Unwin) in 1994 — recommended reading for anyone wanting a complete account of the movement. I have included a number of Landcare case studies (in Chapter 5) to show how this remarkable community-based organisation works and what it achieves.

GREENING AUSTRALIA

Greening Australia is a community-based federation with eight State and Territory organisations and a National body. Its aim is:

... to assist the community to achieve sustainable land management through the conservation and establishment of vegetation for the environmental, social and economic benefit of all Australians.

Its energies and resources focus on activities which have a direct vegetation impact.

The Greening Australia Council is a body comprising 11 non-government organisations plus Federal Government observers. This body advises Greening Australia on policy and strategy directions and also offers advice to government.

Greening Australia was established in 1982. Its capacity and effectiveness in achieving its mission was enormously enhanced through the introduction of the **One Billion Trees Program** (part of the Federal Government's National Landcare Program in 1989). This program was contracted to Greening Australia.

Greening Australia has thousands of members, including individuals, 1339 community groups, over 200 local councils and many corporate sector companies; 175 full-time and part-time staff, and hundreds of volunteers (1994 figures). Income is derived from a combination of government and private contracts, sponsorship, membership and product sales.

Greening Australia activities include:
* Managing the **River Murray Corridors of Green Project** for the Australian Nature Conservation Agency (ANCA). The aim of the project is to establish an open web of vegetation in a 100 km wide band along the River Murray in three States.
* Assisting State and Territory organisations with projects in the **National Corridors of Green Program** which helps to link the corridor projects undertaken by scores of separate, local community groups around Australia during the last decade. These separate projects have involved protection of remnant bush patches; new plantings; linking remnant and new patches across farms with shelterbelt and alley plantings; and creating corridors along roadsides, stock routes and railway lines.
* Developing demonstration projects under the Regional Environmental Employment Program (REEP) for training long-term unemployed, with Corridors of Green on the Yarra and the Hawkesbury Rivers.
* Providing employment and training experience for hundreds of unemployed people through the Landcare and Environmental Action Program (LEAP) and Jobskills.
* Advising Aboriginal communities on land-use and rehabilitation through the Greening Australia's **Aboriginal Liaison Program**. (Aboriginal interests own and manage 15% of the Australian continent and much of the land is degraded.)
* Producing *Local Greening Plans: a guide to vegetation and biodiversity management for local Councils* and other publications; and creating public awareness of environmental matters through the media etc.

CHAPTER FIVE

SALT AND THE SALINISATION OF SOIL AND WATER

Salinisation in the Western Australian Wheatbelt.

ALCOA

Salinity of soils and water is a natural characteristic of arid climates. This **primary salinity** results from low and erratic rainfall and high rates of evaporation. An estimated 955 million hectares (Mha) of land worldwide has primary salt-affected soils where the rainfall is insufficient to leach the salts out of the soil. Flat terrain and, in particular, inward-draining regions like the centre of Australia which drains towards Lake Eyre, do not have the advantage of having rivers carrying salt run-off to the sea.

Australia is estimated to have 29 Mha of naturally saline land, of which salt marshes, salt lakes and salt flats cover 14 Mha. A further 15 Mha of land in arid and semi-arid regions has naturally saline subsoils, but no groundwater in the profile.

Human-induced salinisation — **secondary salinisation** — is related to inappropriate land use which causes changes to hydrology, and in the modern world it is second only to soil erosion as a degrader of soils. Secondary salinisation is the result of salt stored in the soil profile and/or groundwater being mobilised by extra water provided by human activities, directly in the case of irrigation, and indirectly by land-clearing, agriculture and alteration to natural vegetation and soils by over-grazing — activities which alter the water balance.

In Australia, damage to the nation's economy caused by salinity in the Murray Basin alone is estimated at $260 million a year in agriculture and $65 million in water supply problems. Costs of the effects of salinity to the community from degraded lands, deteriorating water quality, rising groundwater and loss

Lake Francis, near the Goyder Channel between Lake Eyre and Lake Eyre South.

M.E.W.

Natural salt deposits near Maralinga in South Australia.

DPI

of natural habitat through the Basin are many times greater. In south-western Western Australia losses are estimated as $62 million in agriculture, $90 million in waterlogging problems and $40 million in stream and river salinity.[83]

Associated with soil salinity is the secondary process of **alkalisation** in which the clay fraction of the soil becomes saturated with sodium. The sodium ions disperse the fine clay particles and cause the soil's crumb structure to collapse. The soil swells, pores are clogged and it becomes less permeable. Soils with high clay content are sensitive to alkalisation and waterlogging. Gypsum can be used to restore crumb structure to sodic soils (which, by definition, have a high proportion of exchangeable sodium.)

These days, with modern technology it is possible to map salt-affected land, using satellites as part of a remote sensing program. More importantly, it is possible to map salinisation-prone areas by using instruments mounted in small aircraft. In particular

HUMAN-INDUCED SOIL SALINITY

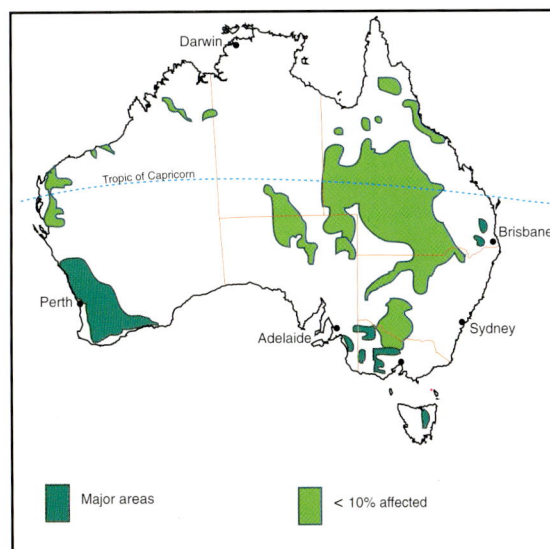

Major areas

< 10% affected

After Chartres et al.[82]

SALTMAP

A technological break-through in the battle against salinisation

The SALTMAP technique for 'seeing' underground and detecting saline water-tables also maps bedrock and soil type. It has been developed by the Australian company **World Geoscience Corporation Ltd** in collaboration with the CSIRO and the Cooperative Research Centre for Australian Mineral Exploration Technology. (It is a progression from techniques used in mineral exploration by remote sensing and is a example of the excellence of Australian research science.) Development costs for SALTMAP to date have been in excess of $4 million, including grants of $1.5 million from the Federal Government and $100 000 from the Western Australian Government.

A copper transmitter cable strung kite-wise on a small aircraft generates an electric current in sub-surface salt, which in turn creates magnetic fields which can be picked up by a sensitive electromagnetic detector mounted in the receiver 'bird' which is towed by the aircraft. Bedrock type and other underground structures are mapped by a sensitive magnetometer mounted in the nose of the aircraft, and soil characteristics are analysed using a gamma ray spectrometer. Information from the sources can be fed into a geographic information system on a computer. This allows the data to be related to other datasets, such as satellite images and topographic information. Problem areas can then be interpreted from the data. It is estimated that mapping a farm in this way would cost farmers about $5 a hectare when a whole catchment is being mapped. Compared with the on-ground alternatives of geological and soil mapping, drilling holes to sample soil and water-table — which has never been feasible on a large scale, let alone over a whole farm — this new technology is the breakthrough which has been needed if the salinisation menace to sustainable land use is to be reduced. It is the missing link in providing sub-surface information about salt to be included with surface information such as satellite images, aerial photos, etc.

World Geoscience kindly supplied the slides of the illustrations used in this account of SALTMAP (and Greg Street kindly checked this account to be sure that the explanation is correct).

The SALTMAP Aircraft in the air.

WORLD GEOSCIENCE

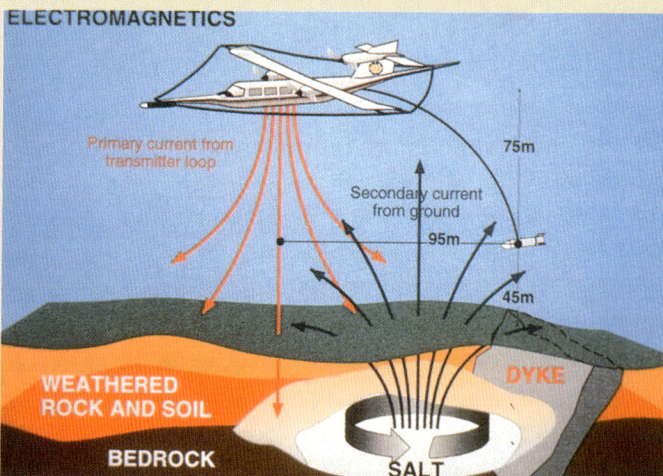

How SALTMAP works.

WORLD GEOSCIENCE

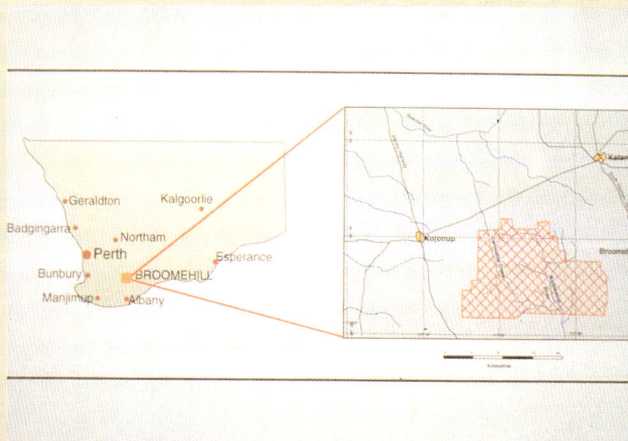

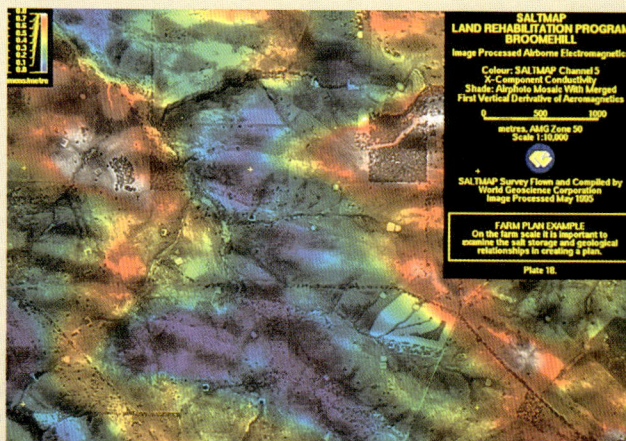

Above: The farm used in this project was Marty Ladyman's property, Chan Channup, near Broomehill. Above right: The scale in the top left corner shows the degree of conductivity which can be directly related to salt content in the sub-surface (salt storage) — red is very salty.

WORLD GEOSCIENCE

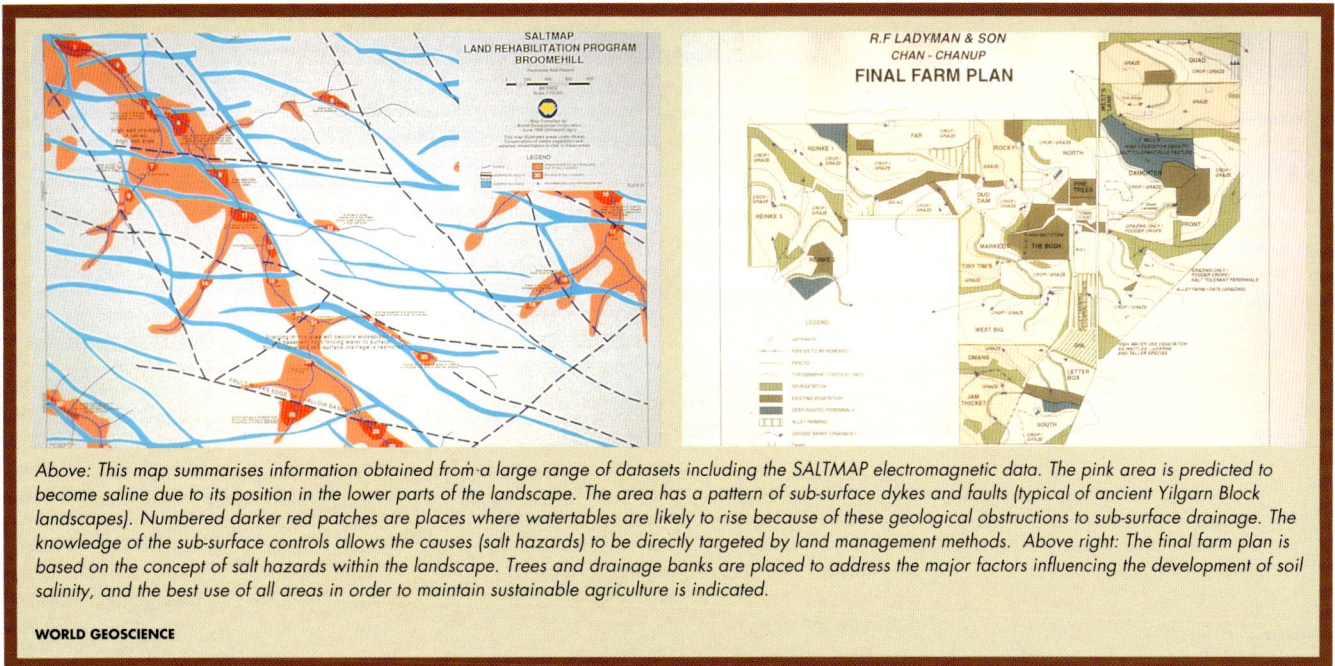

Above: This map summarises information obtained from a large range of datasets including the SALTMAP electromagnetic data. The pink area is predicted to become saline due to its position in the lower parts of the landscape. The area has a pattern of sub-surface dykes and faults (typical of ancient Yilgarn Block landscapes). Numbered darker red patches are places where watertables are likely to rise because of these geological obstructions to sub-surface drainage. The knowledge of the sub-surface controls allows the causes (salt hazards) to be directly targeted by land management methods. Above right: The final farm plan is based on the concept of salt hazards within the landscape. Trees and drainage banks are placed to address the major factors influencing the development of soil salinity, and the best use of all areas in order to maintain sustainable agriculture is indicated.

WORLD GEOSCIENCE

these instruments can accurately measure the ground conductivity which can be related to sub-surface salt storage. Having a tool and being able to predict problem areas is the first step towards prevention and control.

SALINISATION AND IRRIGATION

Secondary salinisation which is irrigation-related results from the water-table being elevated, bringing stored salts up into the rootzone of plants. Waterlogging of soil is often associated with salinisation. There is a **critical depth for the water-table**. A sharp increase in evaporation occurs above this depth, resulting in salt deposition in the soil. Mobilised salt can also move laterally or vertically towards watercourses. Increase in salinity of river waters results, and the whole situation is compounded when the increasingly salty river water is being used for irrigation. Much of Australia's groundwater has high concentrations of dissolved salts and irrigation using bore water instead of surface water from rivers can lead to rapid salinisation when the water evaporates.

The hydrology of a region can be substantially altered by the building of a dam. The pressure of the head of water which results causes groundwater to flow into the river downstream of the dam, raising the water level. In regions where salinity is a problem the associated raising of the water-table in surrounding areas causes salinisation of soils.

In a poorly drained region (or in a closed basin like the Murray Basin) even a deep water-table can be elevated to within one or two metres of the surface by irrigation. (See Chapter 7) Local topography and basement rock play a part in the movement of groundwater. Shallow basement rock, dykes and faults

can impede and confine it. Extra water in a confined aquifer creates pressure and there can be an upward leakage from a deeper zone, bringing more salt into the system. The local subsoil geological structure of a region should be understood before an irrigation plan is implemented so that sufficient drainage can be planned. The amount of water which can safely be added without causing dangerous alterations to the hydrology of an area should be calculated. This has not usually

Widespread salt near Renmark, South Australia.

DENSEY CLYNE

SALT AND ANCIENT CIVILISATIONS

For as long as there has been agriculture in the arid and semi-arid parts of the world, salinisation has been an insidious menace, and it has been held responsible for the demise of civilisations like the Sumerians and even the Aztecs.

Floodplains of the Tigris and Euphrates were being irrigated for wheat growing in the 4th millennium BC. By 3500 BC rising salt had made half the area no longer suited to wheat, and barley, which is much more salt-tolerant, formed half the harvest. By 2500 BC only one-sixth of the area was planted to wheat, and no wheat at all would grow by 1700 BC. The steady decline in fertility of soils as salinisation increased resulted in large areas being depopulated.

Early peoples had the option of moving to new areas as they made their lands unusable. In the over-populated world of today no such option exists.

SALT COMES TO TOWN: URBAN SALINITY

Waterlogging and rising salt affect far more than croplands in an area, as cities like Wagga Wagga have found. The elevated water-table beneath 60% of the urban area is already causing rising damp and salting of the foundations of buildings in about 5% of the area, with potentially huge expense to public and privately owned property. Damage to roads and bridges is already serious and expensive. At Frog Hollow, on the western approaches to Wagga, half a kilometre of the Sturt Highway had to be rebuilt, at a cost of $500 000, because of rising water-tables and salinity damage. The water-table is rising at half a metre a year and is already oozing in some places. Trees are dying, salt is killing gardens and people digging holes find water just below the surface of their land.

Underground, the rising salty water-table is rusting water pipes, telephone and power cables, and damaging concrete and clay sewerage pipes, particularly the mortar joints between sections of pipe. The city is the first to instigate an urban salinity action plan. This is a pilot program looking at the options available for urban salinity management and control. It involves State and Local Government agencies, Charles Sturt University and community groups. When salt becomes an urban problem, the full meaning of salinisation is literally brought home and no longer confined to the realm of impersonal agricultural matters.

The Wagga Wagga City Council is to be congratulated for its leadership. No city wants to admit to problems which might affect the value of real estate, but ultimately the exposure of the situation and the measures taken to remedy matters will pay off, and what is learnt there will benefit others.

Wagga Wagga was established on the alluvial floodplain on the southern side of the Murrumbidgee River. Today it occupies about 44 km², with 60% of its area spreading out on the hill slopes south of the floodplain. The alluvium of the floodplain is deep — up to 80 m — and 60% of the town water supply is from bore fields tapping the groundwater in the alluvium, with the balance taken directly from the Murrumbidgee River. Ordovician sedimentary rocks, much altered through time, and Silurian granites form the bedrock and outcrops of the hill slopes. The contact between the two units forms a north~south ridge which runs through the southern suburbs. Granite country lies to its east, and to the north of the floodplain; Ordovician rocks to the west. Most of the salinity problems occur in western parts of the city and result from groundwater backing up as it travels down-slope because of a thick clay sequence at the base of the slope adjacent to the floodplain. Once through this it percolates down through the deep alluvium. Higher up the slopes, perched water-tables, due to unevenness in bedrock trapping water and impeding downslope drainage, are also localised sites for waterlogging and salinisation.

Land clearing for agriculture in the Wagga Wagga–Narrandera region has caused groundwater to rise at 0.24 m a year in granite country, 0.34 m a year in the Ordovician sedimentary rock regions. Recharge of groundwater in the urban area which, compounds the problem, has been investigated and found to be greatly increased by: leakage from water pipes; rainfall run-off from house gutters being directed into rubble pits in back gardens; sewer leakage; and irrigation. Irrigation here comprises water use on domestic gardens, irrigation of public recreation areas, and of large open areas such as school grounds, and represents 44% of the area's water use.

Long-term management of urban salinity requires a permanent reduction in groundwater recharge. Whole catchment management and the restoring of deep-rooted vegetation is required for the underlying regional problems. In dealing with all the issues in the catchment and in the city, Landcare and other community-based involvement is essential. Urban problems are not easily or inexpensively addressed. In planning future development, existing vegetation and re-vegetation will have to be included. It is difficult to eliminate existing rubble pits and put in underground drainage for rainwater shed by buildings, which would immediately decrease recharge. But this issue is currently being addressed by the Wagga Wagga Landcare Group and individuals are being asked to become responsible for minimising their contribution to the problem.

To update water supply and sewerage pipes to stop leakage would be impossible on a large scale, so for the moment, short-term relief will have to be sought through management (cutting back on the irrigation component and making small advances with the other factors) and drainage, which itself poses problems in disposal of saline water.

The Wagga Wagga study is in its very early days and the estimates of the costs which will be incurred to deal with the problems of rising water-tables and salinity are incomplete. The value of this study to other communities facing similar problems is great — in bringing the subject out into the open, showing what factors are involved, and emphasising that only by the cooperation of a large number of government agencies and the whole local community can the situation be dealt with. It also emphasises

ANNUAL RECURRING COSTS OF SALINITY IN WAGGA WAGGA

Roads	$226,600
Footpaths	$4,400
Parks	$103,400
Housing-Severely Affected	$22,500
Housing-Minor to Moderate	$50,000
Industrial	$6,000
Total	$412,900

After Christiansen [85]

URBAN SALINITY: CONTRIBUTION TO RECHARGE IN WAGGA WAGGA

RECHARGE SOURCE	ESTIMATED VOLUME FOR 93/94 YEAR (KL)
Rainfall	
diffuse (1-3%)	29,750-89,250
rubble pits	53,120
Pipe leakage	
water supply (15-17%)	46,400-190,130
sewer (5-15%)	16,430-49,280
Irrigation (1-5%)	4,120-20,600

After Hamilton [84]

EXPENDITURE ON URBAN SALINITY TO DATE IN WAGGA WAGGA

PROBLEM AREA TREATED	COST OF TREATMENT
Juvenile Justice Centre	$30,000
Wagga Showground	$52,000
Wagga Golf Course	$25,000
Gas Supply Infrastructure	$75,000
Sturt Highway	$350,000
Railways	Unknown
Total	$532,000

After Christiansen [85]

that problems will not go away and the sooner a start is made on dealing with them, the better.

Wagga is not the only town affected by 'salt cancer', a manifestation of off-farm salinity problems in their regions. Towns across New South Wales, Victoria and Western Australia are known to be affected. A survey was recently conducted to find out what was the perception of municipal councils within the Murray Basin as regards salinity. In 1994, 50% of the councils recognised that they had problems with salinity, and 7% indicated that their problems were severe. Roads and bridges were identified as being most affected by salt and rising water-tables, and 67% of the councils expected problems, continuing or emerging, with them three years hence. The message about salinisation problems has not been getting through to the public uniformly, as 30% of councils throughout the whole Murray–Darling Basin were not well informed about the salinity problems which exist in adjacent municipalities.

been the case and the salinisation of irrigated land worldwide is suddenly visible — the 'white death' had crept up virtually unnoticed until it was so serious that productivity was greatly affected.

While the addition of irrigation water is a major cause of rising water-tables, **land clearing in the catchment** in which irrigated land lies can also have an influence. The removal of trees and deep-rooted native vegetation in parts of the catchment, even at some distance from irrigated areas, affects the amount of water which reaches the water-table. The native vegetation removed more water from the system by evapo-transpiration than the vegetation which replaced it does, which means that more groundwater recharge is occurring. There may also be more run-off from higher parts of the catchment if soil degradation has occurred. In addition, the crops grown under irrigation usually are not as deep-rooted as the native plants which they displaced, so they are less efficient at lowering the water-table.

Irrigation is obviously mainly practised where rainfall is insufficient overall for crops or pasture (as in arid or semi-arid regions) or where the wet season is confined to only a few months of the year (as in the monsoonal north of Australia). In places where aridity is a problem there is insufficient rain to leach salts out of the soil and artificial drainage is essential if rapid salinisation is to be avoided.

In Australia, 0.16 Mha of irrigated land has become useless because of salt; and 0.65 Mha has water-tables at depths shallower than two metres — which means that they are in acute danger of serious salinisation if the water-table rises further. Already the high rate of evaporation in the top two metres of some soil types is causing different degrees of salting.

DRYLAND SALINITY

Dryland salinity is a global phenomenon which causes major problems in Australia as it does in the Great Plains region of North America, in South Africa, Turkey, Thailand, India, Argentina and other places. It has been recognised as a major problem in Western Australia, South Australia and Victoria for a long time, and is now seen to be an increasing problem on the western slopes of the Great Dividing Range in New South Wales and Queensland.

Dryland salinity is a major threat to the resource base of many rural industries around Australia. Its impact is not only on the farm, it has the ability to generate downstream effects that also affect a wide cross-section of the community. These effects become progressively more severe at the lower end of the water catchment area. According to the Research and Development Corporation of the Department of Land and Water Resources in Canberra, two million hectares of productive land are already affected by dryland salinity and another million hectares are in danger. A figure of $300 million a year loss to production is estimated, based on these figures.

Dryland salinisation manifests itself as **seepage areas and scalds**. Seeps are areas downslope from recharge areas where groundwater is discharged at the surface. Scalds are produced when wind or water erosion removes topsoil from areas with saline or sodic

Salt scalding, erosion and saline water at Crocodile Creek near Northam in Western Australia. In the background, tree planting on the hillside is part of the rehabilitation program for the area, combined with the draining. All low points in the landscape in this region are salt seepage sites.

M.E.W.

THE EFFECTS OF LAND CLEARING ON THE WATER-TABLES OF TWO WESTERN AUSTRALIAN CATCHMENTS

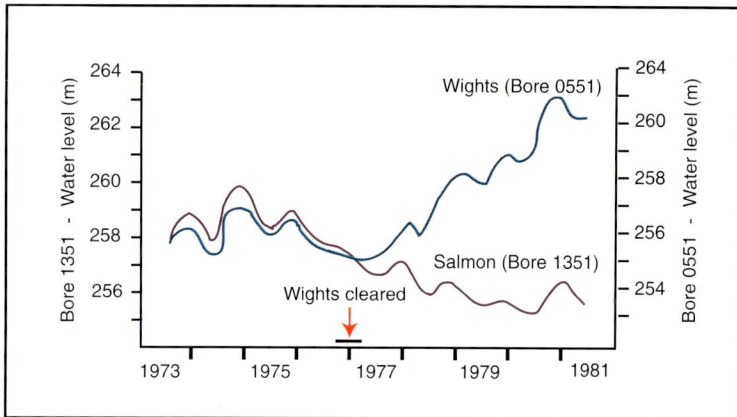

After Peck [87]

The Wights Catchment was cleared in 1976-77; while the Salmon Catchment remained forested.

subsoils, following degradation of vegetation by over-grazing, drought or fire.

Extensive removal of deep-rooted native vegetation has occurred in the south-western sector of Western Australia, in South Australia, in Victoria and southern New South Wales, and on parts of the western slopes of the Great Dividing Range northwards into Queensland. Its replacement with crops and pastures has upset the water balance over large areas. Rising groundwater has mobilised salts causing salinisation of soils. Seepage of groundwater into rivers has increased their salinity, polluting the major source of domestic and irrigation water supplies.

Just how the health of rivers has suffered is illustrated by a few examples.

- Murray River: salinity is 25 mg/L in headwaters, 480 mg/L at Morgan. In an average year 5.5 million tonnes of salt enter the sea; 30% of the salt is human induced. Adelaide depends on the Murray for 35% of its water supply (90% in the drought year of 1983) and major water treatment is required to make it potable.
- Glenelg River in Victoria: The river basin is grazed by cattle and sheep. Some 95% of the water is brackish and most of the water needed for stock, for domestic purposes and for irrigation is from groundwater.
- Rivers in south-western Western Australia: 36% of river water is too salty to drink; 16% is marginal.

Roadside salting and erosion near Northam.

M.E.W.

AVERAGE ANNUAL WATER BALANCE FOR A NATIVE VEGETATED AND AN AGRICULTURAL CATCHMENT NORTH-EAST OF NEWDEGATE, WESTERN AUSTRALIA

	Rainfall	Runoff	Evapo-transpiration	Interception	Recharge
Native vegetation	370 mm	0	359 mm	11 mm	0
Agriculture	370 mm	18 mm	319 mm	7 mm	26 mm

After McFarlane [86]

The Blackwood River water is unusable.

- Rivers in South Australia: 56% of water is fresh, 29% is marginal and 15% is unusable.

Salinisation of Coastal Land

Areas of land adjacent to the coast can become salinised by the entry of seawater into freshwater aquifers. In low-lying coastal regions a layer of freshwater lies on top of a brackish layer, which lies on a seawater layer at the water-table. If too much freshwater is drawn off by pumping, the aquifer becomes increasingly salty, sometimes to the extent that paperbark trees and mangroves in coastal swamps are killed. (Should a scheme like the one proposed to divert waters from the Clarence in northern New South Wales to add more water to the Darling go ahead, the salinisation of the lower reaches of the Clarence will be a consequence. Salt water will penetrate far up the river, killing mangroves, altering the salt–fresh balance in water-tables.)

WHAT CAN BE DONE TO REMEDY SALINISATION

Fundamentally, the solution or amelioration of salinisation depends on **restoring the hydrological balance** which has been upset by human activities. The rising water-tables which mobilise salt and bring it up into the root-zone of plants must be lowered by a combination of engineering (draining) and biological–agronomic means (restoring the sort of vegetation which efficiently decreases recharge of groundwater by evapo-transpiration, and by changing agricultural practices). The disposal of the salt which accumulates as a result of draining is a significant problem.

To restore the water balance and stop water-tables rising, and where possible to lower them, a broad-scale attack on the factors which cause salinisation is necessary. Whole catchments are involved though symptoms of the problem may only be visible in downstream parts. In response to the need to develop plans for whole catchments, **Integrated Catchment Management (ICM)** was born. It was intended to integrate biophysical, social and economic systems containing natural resources (land, water, flora, fauna), agriculture, industry, communities, government agencies, services and recreational facilities. By giving consideration to all resources and their uses within a catchment, degradation of soil and water would be minimised.

Increasing concerns for management of water quality and salinisation on a river basin scale (mainly because of the Murray River's problems and the state of rivers in south-western Western Australia) has since led to formulation of **Total Catchment Management schemes (TCM)**. They are now the basis for

USING THE MINERAL WEALTH CONTAINED IN SALINE WATERS

The idea of extracting industrial chemicals from salt lakes and saline groundwaters has been under investigation in Australia. Salts which are the cause of so much expense in our landscapes could be processed to produce the raw chemicals used to make fertilisers, food additives, glass fibre products, building materials, industrial catalysts and other valuable substances — turning a huge deficit into a nice profit.

Reclaiming the salts which run off the $4 billion irrigation industry alone would be economically rewarding, with markets in Asia, while replacing chemical imports worth many millions with home-grown alternatives would help the balance of payments.

Research continues but so far no satisfactory process has been developed commercially.

coordinating and planning, recognising as they do that a holistic approach is the only one which offers hope of success because catchments do not fall neatly within farm or State boundaries. Cooperation between State and Federal Governments has seen the development of The National Conservation Strategy; National Soil Conservation Program; National Tree Program; Murray–Darling Basin Initiative; Salt Action: Joint Action in Victoria; and the Decade of Landcare Program.

In the modern world we are no closer to a complete solution to the problems of soil salinisation than were the ancient civilisations which collapsed because of it. We can only slow the process in some areas and try to prevent it from developing in others. At the 'Making Catchment Management Happen' conference in Gunnedah in mid 1995, the chairman of the Land and Water Resources Research and Development Corporation, Dr Greame Robertson, concluded his address by saying: [00]

It is unlikely that there will ever be a total solution to the salinity problem in Australia unless we return the landscape to its original state. Even then it may take centuries to restore the original hydrological balance. The acceptance of this reality places the management of salinity in a new paradigm. One that acknowledges the impact land use has had on landscape processes. Further management will not be about simple fixes, but about making choices, choices between retaining farms or retaining forests; between saline land or foregoing income from wheat; between saline wetlands or foregoing income from wool.

The case studies which follow will illustrate the strategies being used to deal with a range of problems in different parts of Australia. A general introduction follows here as a background to the specific studies.

Many of the problems of salt and waterlogging associated with irrigation are the result of excessive and wasteful use of water. Surface irrigation leads to loss of 70% of water delivered in some cases, and to run-off water carrying not only salt but pollutants into the river systems. Pricing of irrigation water and its availability are highly political issues. The Murray Basin, with an irrigated area of 1.27 Mha has irrigation water costs subsidised to the tune of $300 million each year, which has undoubtedly contributed to over-use and waste. Therefore, in irrigated areas the management of the added water, suiting it to the needs of the crops or pastures without raising the water-table, is the first imperative. In addition, all those measures which have to be taken to deal with dryland salinisation are applicable.

Where land is already salinised to the extent that only the most salt-tolerant plants will grow there, planting of saltbush can give it a new lease of life and prove an economically satisfactory local solution. Research into salt-tolerant tree species has established that there are several species which will grow in waterlogged seep areas, including *Casuarina obesa*, and *Eucalyptus sargentii*, *camaldulensis* and *occidentalis*, and research is ongoing to select salt-tolerant genotypes, which are varieties better suited to salt conditions than others within the species.[89] Native trees planted in saline areas supply no direct commercial benefits. However, in well-drained saline areas *Pinus radiata*, suitable for timber and wood products, and *Eucalyptus globulus*, *viminalis* and *saligna* for pulpwood are commercially viable. *Pinus radiata* agroforestry in the Mangimup region of **Western Australia** will be more profitable than grazing alone in the long run. A Western Australian Government scheme to help farmers financially by overcoming the wait for returns from the timber crop pays an annuity and a share of the revenue on harvesting. This **Softwood Share-farming Scheme** is an inducement to change farming practice to agroforestry and combat land degradation while increasing productivity. In Western Australia, 20 000 ha of timberbelt plantations of *Eucalyptus globulus* are already controlling salinity and producing pulpwood.

Economic constraints often make it difficult or impossible for farmers to undertake the measures needed to combat rising water-tables in their catchment, especially when symptoms of salinisation may not be present on their land. Large-scale planting of trees may take up good agricultural land and may not be a chosen (economic) option. However, it is being increasingly found that planting trees in wide timberbelts combined with agriculture can bring unexpected improvements to productivity of crops, pasture and livestock.

In **South Australia** the Department of Agriculture is implementing a Rural Tree Planting Strategy, involving Landcare groups and support from the National Soil Conservation, the Natural Resources Management and the One Billion Trees Programs.

As part of the **Salt Action: Joint Action** program, **Victoria** has six agroforestry demonstration sites in the Lower Goulburn Valley where salinisation problems are serious and increasing, with the prospect that 80 000 ha could be salt desert in 50 years if current trends continue. Twenty-eight landholders are collaborating in establishing trees on 10% to 20% of their farms. Over the catchment, high-density tree planting (200 trees per hectare) is being done on 4000 ha of the recharge area; low density planting (20 trees per hectare) on 24 000 ha. Perennial grass and lucerne pastures are being established on high and moderate recharge areas. Rehabilitation of discharge areas is being carried out by planting salt-tolerant species. Cash incentives are being given to carry out the work and monitoring of results will enable polices to be developed for dealing with other regions.

Salt Action: Joint Action is based on community ownership of the salinity problems and joint action between the community and the government to manage the problem. Nine salinity control regions, based on major catchments, have been identified, with sub-regions in irrigated and dryland areas. Plans are

The 'trained' Avon River from a lookout on the Avon Ascent.

M.E.W.

prepared by committees whose representatives are drawn from the local community, farmers and conservation organisations, supported by inter-departmental advisers and independent consultants. Plans are drawn up considering a number of management options and outlining economic, environmental and social implications as well as cost-sharing arrangements between the community and the State. The management plans are released for public comment and discussion, and revised until approved. Only then does the government support the plan. The Victorian Government is to spend $900 million over the next 30 years on Salt Action: Joint Action projects.

New South Wales has a State Tree Policy and a Trees on Farms Program with the same aims of biological–agronomic control as the other States. As part of Total Catchment Management strategy it has a Salt Action program whose aim is to control existing land and water salinisation; prevent further degradation; rehabilitate affected areas; protect sensitive ecosystems; raise public awareness and understanding; and foster sustainable production methods.

LANDCARE IN THE SWAN–AVON CATCHMENT, WA

The Avon River descends from the Yilgarn Block plateau, which is one of the oldest landscapes preserved anywhere in the world, and rushes down through the ranges of the Darling Scarp when in spate. It becomes the Swan River as it crosses the coastal plain and its wide reaches are a feature of Perth's landscape, with the city development concentrated around it. About 80% of the Swan's water comes from the Avon and its tributaries.

The geology of the ancient landscapes of the catchment controls the different soils, and subsoil geological structures determine areas where a salt hazard exists because of restrictions to sub-surface drainage, as is shown in the SALTMAP information on page 104. The nutrient-deficient nature of soils in the region is explained by the antiquity of the land surface which has undergone weathering and leaching through enormous lengths of geological time. No part of the continent (or of any other continent in the world) is more time-worn than this. It has seen no renewal by vulcanism, no passage of ice sheets across it in 300 million years. And even the rivers today lie in ancient river valleys which used to contain rivers that had their headwaters in Antarctica — before the last connections between Australia and Antarctica were broken in the final stage of disintegration of the Gondwana supercontinent.

The Swan–Avon Catchment has been selected as an example of Landcare in an Integrated Catchment Management Program because the problems faced by farmers in this catchment cover the whole range of land degradation issues, the huge area (bigger than Tasmania) is a rich wheatbelt region, and half way through the

THE SWAN–AVON CATCHMENT

Major Land Zones of the Avon Catchment Program Area

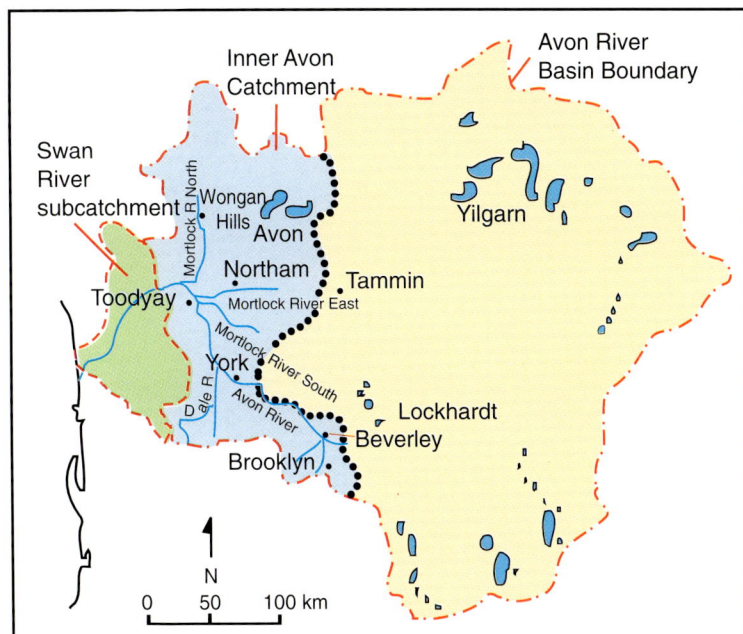

Initially, management groups of the Swan–Avon Catchment were developed in the Inner Avon Catchment. The Integrated Catchment Management Program for the whole Catchment started in 1995.

Decade of Landcare it already shows what can be achieved by community action.

This Catchment grows half Western Australia's wheat and a fifth of its barley, and these, together with wool and meat, produce revenue of $700 million annually. Of its 100 000 km² area, two-thirds is farmland which has been massively cleared (90% of natural vegetation has been removed). The remaining one-third comprises remnant bushland, the Swan Valley horticultural area, and the urban sprawl of Perth and lesser urbanised regions of towns.

The massive clearance and cropping have resulted in rising water-tables and 500 000 ha of once-productive land are already lost to, or badly impaired by, salinisation, with the salt areas increasing by about 11 000 ha a year. Water quality has been affected by salinisation throughout the region, and many areas have problems with waterlogging. In addition, massive soil erosion has resulted in soil loss and in soil structure decline, and in siltation of streams and rivers. Stream erosion has already filled most of the Avon's deep pools with silt and would ultimately stop its flow if nothing was done about catchment problems.

The large catchment and small river gradients contribute to the flooding which characterises the Avon Valley in the occasional very wet year, or when there is an exceptionally severe storm. In 1958 the Public Works Department decided to deal with the problem of siltation of the river, caused by land degradation in the catchment, which was increasing the frequency and height of flooding. A '**river training scheme**'(!) was instigated and bulldozers had excavated a central channel and removed obstructions along 187 km of the

Roadside erosion near Northam. Culverts and drains which divert water from the roadway frequently cause severe erosion.

M.E.W.

South Branch of the river between Toodyay and Brookton by 1970. A review in 1985 indicated that flood levels had been reduced by 60% and flow velocity increased by 70% as a result of the 'training' but that the deeper river pools had remained silted up. Revegetation of some of the river margins has occurred since the scheme was stopped, and some life has returned to its waters but silt from the degraded catchment continues to choke the waterway.

Soil acidification affects large areas of the catchment as a result of legume crops and nitrogenous fertilisers. Run-off from farmland has led to **high nutrient levels in waterways**, further adding to the problems of water already suffering from extra salt loads. **Algal blooms** in the Swan River are largely the result of nutrient run-off from the catchment. Remnants of native vegetation throughout the area are degraded by grazing, soil salinisation, weed invasion and other problems.

Small wonder, in the face of situations like these, that Landcare has attracted 1000 farmers (half the farmers in the Catchment) to form 70 groups based on local creek catchments (each averaging 20 000–30 000 ha and including 10–15 farms). The evolution of Landcare has been a real grass-roots, from-the-ground-up process as the experience of this catchment shows.

A number of farmers in the **Morbinning catchment** (about 20 km east of Beverley) formed one of the first management groups in 1989. They were concerned about flooding of gullies, increasing salinisation and the need for improved drainage — problems which could only be tackled by cooperative planning and work programs across farm boundaries.

In 1990 they were successful in attracting the sponsorship of Alcoa of Australia Limited, which, in a unique partnership with Agriculture Western Australia, was seeking to establish a wide range of community Landcare activities and demonstrations. The **Alcoa Landcare Project** provided a generous sponsorship of $6 million over six years towards the establishment of the Avon Catchment Project, as part of the National Decade of Landcare.

Six catchments were selected to demonstrate integrated catchment management and accelerate the implementation of on-ground works. They include a broad cross-section of farming systems and land degradation issues within the catchment, and provide examples in the higher and lower rainfall areas, in regions with differing topography, and on different soil types. The six groups chosen had also already shown a commitment to catchment management and were sufficiently organised to cope with the pressures of the five-year program. Development officers from Agriculture Western Australia were to provide guidance (financed by the National Landcare Program) and the rehabilitation work was to be done by the Landcare groups. Conservation and Land Management (CALM), the WA Water Authority and the Waterways Commission would supply support as needed.

In five years, and halfway through the Decade of Landcare, great progress has been made towards rehabilitation of degraded land, natural vegetation and water. (Brief outlines of progress by the six demonstration groups follow.) The next phase of the project will focus on using the demonstration groups to show farmers from other areas how to tackle problems in their own areas, and how to structure their groups and manage their programs. The aim is also to target the city audience and educate them about land degradation and the massive problems faced by rural people.

Alcoa's generous sponsorship has been well spent with $1.4 million going to implement catchment plans, including fencing off rehabilitation sites and remnant vegetation (including corridors between remnants); and contributions toward pasture improvement, drainage, saltland management, tree planting and bushland regeneration. Alcoa has also been involved in the project to save Lake Toolibin, the only remaining freshwater lake in the wheatbelt. (Salinisation of other lakes has been progressive since it was first noticed and reported on in the 1890s when land clearing was already raising water-tables.)

Management of the Beeliar Wetlands in the south-western part of the Perth metropolitan area has been another Alcoa-funded project; and Alcoa's educational program has resulted in publication of material about Landcare, as well as the establishment of the Tammin Alcoa Landcare Education Centre. An innovative educational idea — the Avon Ascent — involves the creation of a number of picnic areas which demonstrate examples of land reclamation for city people.

The Morbinning Catchment Group

The Morbinning Catchment Group won the State BP award at the Landcare '95 Conference in Perth for its achievements over the five-year program period. On 27 March 1996, the Group won a National Landcare Award — the inaugural **BP Landcare Catchment Award** and the National Party leader Mr Tim Fischer was quoted as saying:

The Morbinning Catchment Group is a stunning example of farming families working together to solve land and water degradation on a large scale.

Such success and recognition revitalises a group, and is an inspiration for others, while for all members of the 15 families involved in this catchment it is a personal triumph.

- A main focus of the group has been the drainage line running down the catchment. Redefining the channel over five properties and revegetating 160 km of creeklines has stabilised the banks and has led to substantial protection of remnant vegetation as a bonus. In all, 65 ha of bushland have been protected.
- Alley farming has been introduced on light sand soil to stabilise it and provide shelter for stock. More than 30 ha have been planted to alleys 25 m apart, containing three rows of trees and fodder bush. An amazing 210 000 trees have been planted by the group. **Tagasaste**, a tree-lucerne from the Canary Islands, has been widely planted as a fodder bush in areas needing soil stabilising. Being deep rooted and perennial it is useful for lowering the water-table.
- Shallow drains have been introduced in waterlogged areas, and lucerne planted after draining has proved to be economically viable.
- Saltbush has been planted on scalds in salinised valley floors (widespread problem areas in the wheatbelt) and grazing has been re-introduced into what was wasteland. An estimated 496 ha of saltland have been treated.

- Some 26 km of fencing have been erected. Changing the fencing on farms to match paddocks to soil types has proved profitable. Diversity of crops and changed land-use has started to show results. Farmers are experimenting with perennial pastures, minimal tillage of cropland, oilseed and floraculture instead of grains, and even with yabbie culture in dams.

A typical saline creekline at Tammin, and the same site four years after revegetation.

ALCOA

The Gabby Quoi Quoi Catchment Group

This catchment occupies 19 980 ha of the Avon Catchment, north of Goomalling. Water from farms in this area drains into the sea through the Avon and Swan Rivers.

Fourteen families formed the group in 1989 in

A deep sand ridge at Tammin, previously unproductive and an area of groundwater recharge, becomes highly productive three years after planting with tagasaste, which is a high water user.

ALCOA

The South Tammin Catchment Group

The South Tammin Catchment covers 18 200 ha of the Avon Catchment. Water from the area drains to the Avon and Swan Rivers. The group was formed by 15 families in 1989, and since 1990 they have re-vegetated 70 km of creeklines; stabilised 27 ha of deep sand; reclaimed 136 ha of saltland; built over 17 km of banks and drains; and planted over 194 000 trees.

The South Yoting Catchment Group

This Catchment covers 45 000 ha and the group involves 20 families. Since 1990, together they have re-vegetated 40 km of creeklines; reclaimed 137 ha of saltland; stabilised 115 ha of deep sand; protected 63 ha of bushland; and built over 8 km of banks and drains.

The Yeelanna Catchment Group

This group was formed by 14 families in 1991. Their catchment occupies 16 200 ha and in it they have re-vegetated 6 km of creeklines; stabilised 334 ha of saltland and 20 ha of deep sand; protected 7 ha of bushland; and built over 46 km of banks and drains.

When you add up the achievements of 66 families in five years:

They have planted about a million trees to lower water-tables and stabilise the land; reclaimed 1837 ha of saltland, creating saltbush grazing and drought fodder reserves; stabilised 280 ha of deep sand; protected 168 ha of native bush; built 107 km of banks and drains; and replaced vegetation along 375 km of creeklines. (And they have carried on their bread and butter farming at the same time, which one might think was more than a full-time occupation, making their achievements all the more wonderful.) When the focus catchments are only a fraction of the total Swan-Avon Catchment, and 1000 farmers in 70 groups are in fact involved, one cannot speak too highly of the Landcare movement and all who are contributing in their different ways.

The Corrigin Land Conservation District Committee are a particularly enthusiastic group who have achieved much over the past five years. They won the John Tonkin Greening Award for Community Groups in 1994.

Their activities include:
- Revegetating the Kunjin–Jubuk railway reserve as a bush corridor.
- Protecting and managing a local bush area, Hartley's Reserve, which was going to be sold and cleared.
- Setting up a Conservation Centre in the old railway building in the middle of the town for use by locals and visitors.
- Establishing a local herbarium.
- Working with research scientists to re-introduce

order to work together to combat land degradation in their catchment. Since 1990 they have re-vegetated 40 km of creek margins; stabilised 33 ha of deep sand; reclaimed 280 ha of saltland; built 16 km of banks and drains. They have planted over 200 000 trees.

The West Dale Catchment Group

Eight families were involved in forming this group in 1989. The catchment is only 9000 ha yet the farmers have re-vegetated 59.5 km of creeklines; reclaimed 454 ha of saltland; stabilised 84 ha of deep sand; protected 33 ha of bushland and built over 20 km of banks and drains.

the rare Corrigin grevillea back into the wild.

- Revegetating all roadside reserves within a 5 km radius of Corrigin with locally collected seed.

THE BLACKWOOD RIVER CATCHMENT

The Blackwood River Catchment has an area of nearly 3 million hectares and is the largest catchment in the south-west of Western Australia. The Catchment covers 18 shires, 15 of which are Land Conservation Districts with 60 catchment groups active. It is divided into three zones which reflect their topography, soils and land use.[90]

The **Upper Catchment** is the zone of ancient drainage which lies east of the Meckering Line on the Yilgarn Block, whose ancient granites and gneisses weather to white sandy clay, often 20–30 m deep, which is the main salt storage in the region. The granite has been intruded by swarms of dolerite dykes which form barriers to groundwater movement and are often associated with saline seeps. (See SALTMAP, p.104)

The landscape is a gently undulating plateau with broad valley floors where chains of salt lakes lie along the rivers which only flow in wet years. About 40% of the Upper Catchment drains into **Lake Dumbleyung**, which only overflows once every 20 years or so, making it an important buffer which intercepts silt and salt which would otherwise affect the downstream parts of the catchment. The flow regime of the Blackwood river is extremely variable from year to year. In general, water supplies in streams in the Upper Catchment are

Corrigin LCDC office — old railway building put to good use.

AGWA

unsuitable for use, being too salty. Farmers rely on dams on small natural catchments away from main creeks and rivers, to avoid excessive salinity.

The Upper Catchment zone has been extensively cleared for agriculture, mainly wheat, with smaller areas of lupins, barley and oats. In recent times some field peas, canola, faba beans and chick peas have been grown. Merino sheep are grazed for wool and meat production at low stocking rates (2.5 dry sheep equivalents per hectare). The clearing of 95% of the natural vegetation has led to the serious land degradation problems where water-tables are rising at 10 to 20 cm per year, causing dryland salinity; surface run-off causes waterlogging and sometimes flooding; streams are degraded; wind erosion is serious when land is bare; and remnant vegetation is declining. Average annual rainfall is from 375 to 450 mm. The present

THE BLACKWOOD CATCHMENT

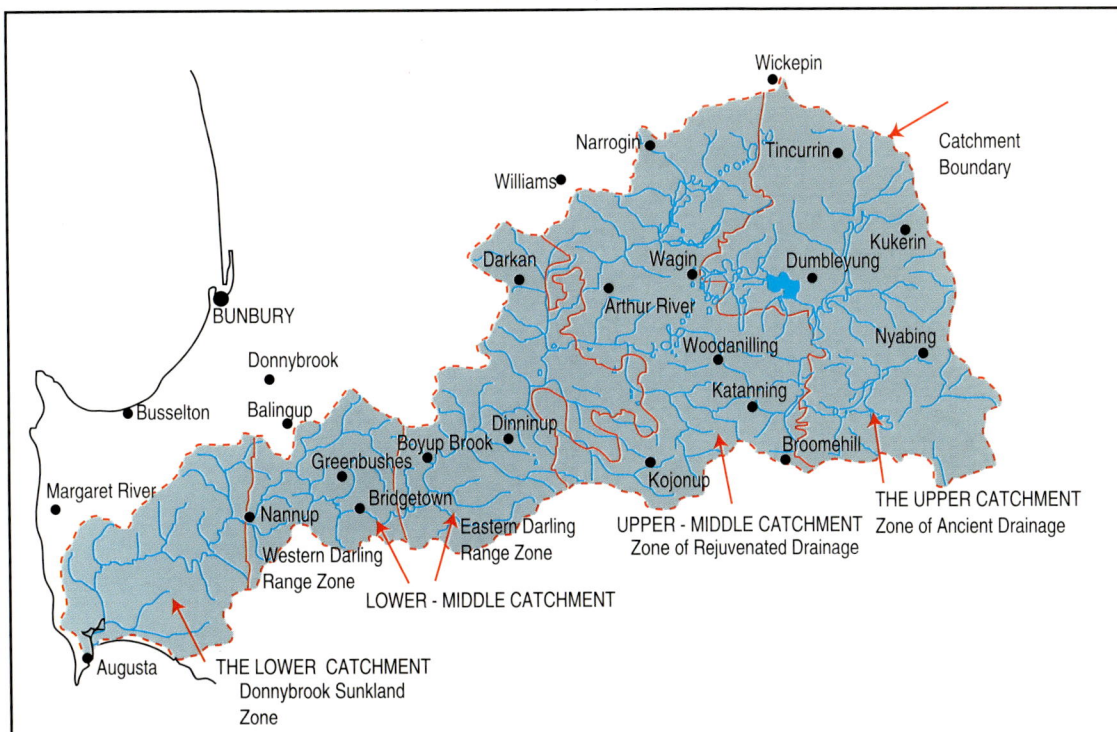

farming systems are clearly unsustainable.

The **Middle Catchment** is effectively two zones: the Upper-Middle and the Lower-Middle. Problems include rising **water-tables** (rising 50 cm per year) leading to dryland salinity; over-grazing leading to erosion, which also affects the streams; waterlogging; and remnant vegetation decline. Hillside salt seepages are widespread and salt finds its way to the river system.

The **Upper-Middle Catchment** is a zone of rejuvenated drainage about 45 to 75 km wide, lying between the ancient plateau of the Upper Catchment to the east, and the Darling Range Zone to the west. The area is extensively cleared and mainly used for merino sheep farming, but mixed farming is also important, mainly oats followed by barley and lupins to supply summer stock feed. Average annual rainfall is from 450 to 600 mm, and most rivers and streams are too salty to use.

The **Lower-Middle Catchment** is approximately 125 km wide, comprising the undulating lateritic plateau of the Darling Range.

The Blackwood River has cut down through the plateau forming a deep, steep-sided valley. Average annual rainfall is from 600 to 1000 mm. State Forests cover a major portion of the western Darling Range Zone, with clearing and agriculture (mainly sheep and cattle grazing and some horticulture) restricted to the valleys. The eastern part of the zone is the centre of the 'sheepbelt', with the highest stocking rates in Western Australia. Paddocks are frequently grazed bare in summer and autumn, exposing them to serious erosion during wind and thunderstorms. Devastating wind and water erosion occur every second year on average. Silt and organic matter, largely sheep manure, enter the streams as a result of the erosion and promote algal blooms.

The Darling Scarp drops 60 to 100 m to the Lower Catchment along the western edge of the plateau.

The **Lower Catchment**, the **Donnybrook Sunkland Zone**, extends westward from the Darling Scarp. The central part of the Sunklands consists of the gently undulating Blackwood Plateau Plains, formed on a cap of Tertiary laterite. The Blackwood River dissects the Plains with a shallow valley system. The Scott River Plains lie south of the Blackwood Plateau. Rainfall is between 900 and 1100 mm and much of the Sunkland remains under natural Jarrah–Marri forest, with farming communities around Nannup and Augusta–Margaret River. The problems in the Lower Catchment resulting from the farmland and forest zone are relatively few; siltation and increased levels of nutrients in the river are mainly downstream effects from the Middle catchment. Algal blooms at Bridgetown and Nannup are symptoms of nutrient enrichment, while silt from the Middle catchment is gradually filling the deep pools in the Lower Blackwood. The Lower Blackwood has low salinity levels. Local issues are mainly concerned with damage to river foreshores; weeds in native forests; and maintaining the amenity of this beautiful region.

The Blackwood Catchment contributes about $550 million to Western Australia's economy each year. (Agriculture $400 million; forestry $77 million; mining $19 million and tourism $53 million.) About 2000 farming businesses are involved in the agricultural section; forestry business is set to increase when a wood-pulp mill is built to service the growing agroforestry which is aimed at lowering water-tables; and mining is expanding, with the Beenup Mineral Sands enterprise coming on-stream. The total population of the Catchment is about 30 000 with main centres in the regional towns of Narrogin and Katanning, and smaller centres at Dumbleyung, Wagin, Kojonup, Boyup Brook, Bridgetown and Augusta.

Degradation of the catchment has reached a critical stage with 56 000 ha of good farming land wrecked by salinity[90] (an increase from 47 000 in 1979) and the river carrying 1.26 million tonnes of salt to the sea each year. Wind erosion is increasing on the sandy soils of the Upper Catchment, and is emerging as an increasingly serious problem on grazing land in the Middle Catchment. The 200 000 ha of surviving remnant vegetation on private land urgently need protective fencing to prevent its disappearance. It is currently being lost at 2% to 4% a year and not replaced. Most rivers and streams, and their riverine vegetation, are badly degraded by clearing, grazing, fire, erosion and salt in the Upper and Upper-Middle Catchments, where waterlogging is causing loss of crop and pasture yield and increasing salinisation of soil.

Because of the salinity of the river water, the towns of Narrogin, Wagin, Dumbleyung, Katanning and Darkan are supplied with water from the Harris River Dam near Collie, while Nannup, Bridgetown, Boyup Brook and Balingup have small schemes based on reticulation from surface water storages.

Many farmers have been trying to stop land degradation on their properties for the past 20 or 30 years, battling the consequences of the unsustainable land-use systems of the past 100 years. Land Conservation Districts formed since 1985 brought farmers together to form Catchment Groups to address their problems in a cooperative and coordinated way.

Many prepared whole-farm plans with the help of advisers from the Department of Agriculture. During the past five to 10 years, increased emphasis has been placed on remnant vegetation protection, planting windbreaks to control erosion and for stock shelter, and the revegetation of degraded creeklines and also of prime recharge areas.

In 1990, the first steps were taken to identify the Landcare problems of the Blackwood Catchment as a whole, and shortly afterwards the **Blackwood Catchment Coordinating Group (BCCG)** was formed to bring together the farmers, foresters, government agencies, conservation groups, local government and land conservation districts. Its major task was to develop an **Integrated Catchment Management Plan** for the whole catchment through wide community consultation.

According to the Chairman David Reid, when the first meeting had defined the size of the problems:

... it would have been easy for us to say that the job was too hard, that it was too costly, or that the government should do it. But we didn't. Instead we set to and formed a community-dominated steering committee which ultimately led to the formation and incorporation of the Blackwood Coordinating Group. I believe we can lay claim to being the first community drawn and oriented natural resources management group concentrating on a catchment in WA.

The **Blackwood Catchment Conservation Strategy** is a first step in documenting the major Landcare issues in the catchment.[90] It prioritises the issues and suggests action plans to achieve a reduction in non-sustainable practices and the implementation of sustainable ones. The strategy was developed through consultation with the community at public meetings on catchment water control (drainage) at Katanning in 1993; on remnant vegetation at Kojonup in April 1994; and river and foreshore management at Bridgetown in November 1993. These meetings included workshops which identified problems, issues and solutions.

In January 1995 the Blackwood Catchment Coordinating Group held a series of 10 meetings with Local Government and Land Conservation District Committee representatives throughout the catchment. Since then discussion group meetings have been held in a number of urban centres and participants have discussed the main land degradation issues, their current extent and the 'best bet' solutions. The BCCG has insisted that views of the community are of paramount importance and are incorporated in the strategy document. Government agencies, local government authorities and Land Conservation Districts were represented at workshops, meetings and discussion groups, or were consulted individually.

It is the philosophy behind the BCCG and the strategy that is the all-important ingredient which offers hope that the serious degradation of the catchment can be halted, turned around, and maybe eventually fixed.

Because this philosophical ingredient is, I believe, so essential for the success of Landcare initiatives everywhere, a selection of quotes from BCCG publications and other sources follows.

The philosophy is quite simple, according to David Reid, chairman of BCCG:

People living in the catchment should manage it ... Our group firmly believes that the only way to manage the environment is through a community representative group ... The hardest task is effective communication with the catchment's 30,000 people ... it is difficult to get that message across and to get a real understanding of what it means to a diverse community.

The BCCG's success has been in turning the debate around from '**What is the government going to do about it?**' to '**How can the community manage the catchment in a more sustainable way?**'

According to the Regional Initiative, it supports the *BCCG's aims of developing new ways to do things better and new ways to inspire community involvement*, recognising that it was the community's demand for action which resulted in the first public meeting, which led to the formation of the BCCG. The Initiative endorses the belief that *there needs to be change in natural resource management and **change in attitudes** to effectively reverse environmental degradation* and that **community ownership of catchment problems will produce appropriate solutions given adequate resources and expertise**. Integration is sought at all levels of the population, including local government and landowners, both urban and rural; and strong communication and direct involvement is essential with all the catchment stakeholders including shires, State and Federal agencies and Land Conservation District Committees.

In August 1995, Senator Collins, the then Federal Primary Industries Minister, announced a $2.5 million National Landcare Grant to the Blackwood Catchment. He stated: *This Initiative is unique because the BCCG is community-based and has developed the concept in partnership with the state agencies and the community.* The State (WA) Primary Industry Minister, Mr House, added: *The most important thing about the project is the **people power** that has gone into it and the coordinating effort.* Mr Reid predicted that the Regional Initiative would set *new national standards for community participation in catchment management.*

This Federal grant is the first major regional funding available to address the severe land degradation problems of the Blackwood Catchment. Seven projects are now to be implemented with shires, Land Conservation District Committees and farmers. Combined with the State's new **Remnant Vegetation Protection Scheme** and the Australian Nature Conservation Agency's **Corridors of Green** funding, meaningful resources are available for the first time to fight land and water degradation.

The Blackwood Catchment has recently received Federal recognition as a focal catchment. The CSIRO Division of Land and Water Resources Research and Development Corporation will be collaborating in research programs.

Much has already been achieved in the Catchment by community involvement over a number of years. A few examples follow to show the range of activities.

Ribbons of Blue Watercare Projects, sponsored by Bunnings Treefarms, has involved students of 35 schools in the Blackwood and Margaret River catchments, supervised by 10 field assistants, in their water sampling and other river ecosystem monitoring activities. Sampling of macro-invertebrates in rivers has also been done by schoolchildren. The Muja Power Station near Collie has given technological backup, providing calibration standards for measurements of salinity and the pH of water samples. Watercare leads people on to become involved in other projects like stream foreshore assessment and rehabilitation and tree planting.

The East Boyup Brook Catchment Group has been granted \$47 500 by the Lotteries Commission towards development of wildlife corridors which will link stream reserves and remnant vegetation shelter belts with public and private reserves. Fencing and revegetating 400 ha of Wandoo–Marri woodland is part of this project.

The **Catterick Catchment Group** (in the Bridgetown–Greenbushes Shire) has focussed on fencing off and replanting creeklines, financed by a National Landcare Program grant to purchase fencing and plant 55 000 seedlings. The group has also been planting trees in shelter belts, and has run workshops on timber trees. Group members have found that the increased buying power which they have as a group enables them to make great savings, bulk-buying plants and hiring machinery. REEP (the Regional Environmental Employment Program) has provided some labour for the tree planting.

Projects investigating sustainable use in the Blackwood Catchment

1. Waterlogging is calculated to cost graingrowers more than \$90 million a year in lost production in the Katanning district. A new five-year research project has just commenced on a local farm, owned by the Rundle family, to provide practical information on how land use affects the water balance.

The project is part of the Grains Research and Development Corporation's soil and water management program, and it involves researchers from Agriculture WA, CSIRO Division of Soils, Plant Industries and Forestry. The study is intended to show how effective deep-rooted perennial pastures and trees

are at improving the productivity of farm enterprises. The research is the first of its kind to evaluate the effects of trees on waterlogging, crop production and salinity on Western Australia's duplex soils.

2. Half of the Upper Blackwood Catchment is at risk of salinisation from rising saline water-tables, affecting 1500 landholdings. The downstream effects of salinity and related land degradation are of concern to communities in the region. Current farming systems, based on annual plant species with 60% as pastures and 40% crops, are unable to control recharge and salinity. Annual pastures cannot use all the rainfall during the growing season; annual crops use it all during the growing season but are unable to use out-of-season rainfall, which on average can be up to 25% of annual rainfall. Deep-rooted perennials use all rainfall and prevent recharge. Trees, tagasaste and lucerne are able to dry the soil out at depth, and this creates a buffer against periodic recharge events (mainly summer rainfall) which would otherwise cause groundwater to rise.

A groundwater model developed by researchers in Agriculture WA predicts that planting trees at 100 stems per hectare on all cleared land within a study catchment would in theory control recharge and salinity. Many farmers have already planted very large numbers of trees but there has been no scientific monitoring of the effectiveness of these high water users, or of whether the agroforestry is profitable, sustainable or sufficient to control recharge. The National Landcare Program has provided funding for a three-year project to find out how effective tree planting is in lowering groundwater on a farm in the Upper Blackwood catchment. A neighbouring farm will be monitored as a control and this experiment should provide some answers.

LAKES IN THE WESTERN AUSTRALIAN WHEATBELT

Freshwater wetlands were widespread throughout inland south-western Australia until clearing for agriculture occurred on a grand scale between 1890 and the 1930s. Rising water-tables since then have resulted in salinisation of most of the lakes and permanent waterlogging and salinisation of wetlands. Today **Lake Toolibin** is the only major lake which has not been destroyed by salt in the wheatbelt, and it still has extensive stands of swamp sheoaks and paperbarks growing across its floor. It is a major breeding site for waterbirds. The lake is one of a chain of seasonal freshwater lakes in the headwaters of the Arthur River near Narrogin (within the Blackwood River Catchment). It is listed as a *Wetland of International Importance* under the Ramsar Convention.

The graveyards of dead trees in **Lake Taarblin** and other originally freshwater lakes and wetlands in the wheatbelt landscape are visible and stark reminders of what could happen to Lake Toolibin. In the 1970s, Lake Toolibin appeared to be heading the same way. It was then that the local community began remedial action to save the lake. The two major threats to Toolibin are rising groundwater and the surface inflow of saline water.

The Department of Conservation and Land Management purchased and rehabilitated adjacent land, so that perennial vegetation now completely surrounds the Lake. Other actions taking place in the catchment include engineering projects, changed agricultural practices, protection of remnant vegetation and revegetation, sponsored by landowners, government agencies and private companies.

In 1992 it was decided that the most effective way of coordinating the many actions was to draw up a **Recovery Plan** which recognised that Lake Toolibin's problems were symptoms of the degradation of the 40 000 ha catchment. Since then, land management strategies and salt mitigation works have been undertaken in the catchment and on the lake floor to lower the water-tables and reduce salinisation. The latest works include the installation of pumps to extract groundwater from under the lake and the construction of a diversion channel to bypass saline surface flows round the lake. The Recovery Plan represents a coordinated effort between Landcare Groups, local communities and State government agencies. Its implementation will not only be beneficial to the lake, but will lead to rehabilitation of the catchment and to improvements in agricultural productivity in the region.

Resources and assistance from the following groups have contributed to the Recovery Plan's implementation: Alcoa, Australian Nature Conservation Agency, BankWest, *Landscope* Conservation Visa Card, CALM, Commonwealth Farm Forestry Program, Agriculture Western Australia, National Landcare Program, Toolibin Catchment Group, Toolibin Catchment Landholders, and Water Corporation Western Australia.

Lake Taarblin, killed by salt, is only 4 km downstream from Lake Toolibin.

CALM

The **Lake Toolibin Catchment Committee** won the inaugural Shirley Balla Wetland Award (1995) for their commitment and efforts towards the protection and improvement of the catchment. Development Officers of the Narrogin Office of Agriculture WA have advised and supported the Landcare Groups. The Narrogin Office of Agriculture WA produces a newsletter — *Farmer to Farmer* — funded by National Landcare, in which farmers give accounts of their approach to more productive and sustainable land use in the region. When you read how farmers like Keith and Kerry Parnell have turned 'gutless sands' into forage blocks with a grazing value equal to better class country by planting tagasaste, you realise how valuable this sort of communication is. People are so much more likely to follow and change their land-use practices when they see that someone else has proved it possible to do so profitably.

PROJECT PLATYPUS

Dealing with degradation in the Upper Wimmera Catchment in order to save the Platypus

The Wimmera River catchment is situated in central western Victoria, a land-locked catchment whose waters flow northward but do not join the Murray. The river and its tributaries drain from the Mt Cole-Pyrenees ranges in the south-east and the Grampian ranges in the south, to the terminal lakes of Hindmarsh and Albacutya and the Wyperfeld floodplains in the north.

The **Upper Wimmera Catchment** surrounds the major centres of Stawell and Ararat, and is a prime woolgrowing area which also supports other agricultural enterprises — fat lambs, cereal crops, beef cattle, vineyards, orchards and timber.

The upper catchment contributes 85 000 tonnes of salt a year to the river system. With no outlet to the sea,

Healthy vegetation on the lake floor in Lake Toolibin, photographed during a dry phase. It is essential for the health and productivity of shallow freshwater lakes and wetlands that they dry out occasionally. Permanent waterlogging kills their trees.

AgWA

all the salt and pollutants which enter the rivers build up downstream, affecting the river health and water quality. Fifty towns, with a population of 45 000 people, rely on the Wimmera River for their water supply, and none receive water of a quality which meets World Health Organisation standards. Declining water quality threatens the future existence of communities in the Wimmera–Mallee and also the sustainability of agricultural pursuits whose viability decreases as dryland salinity increases. The improvement of water quality requires changes in agricultural management which will result in economic advantages to farmers and at the same time lead to improvements in the whole Wimmera River catchment.

Erosion in the upper catchment has reached catastrophic proportions. In places, between 4 and 5 km of gully and streambank erosion have been measured per 100 ha of land. The resulting siltation in the hills around Navarre, Landsborough and Elmhurst has caused damage to roads, channels, dams, fences and remnant vegetation, as well as the loss of once-productive farming land. The increased run-off into watercourses choked with silt results in flooding, more frequent and severe, in the hilly country comprising much of the catchment.

Landcare groups have formed in the upper catchment and have been addressing problems. Now through **Project Platypus** a unified approach to solving them is about to begin. This is another example of the value of a **catalyst** — in this case the uniquely Australian, duck-billed, egg-laying, unbelievable platypus — in publicising the underlying problems which affect everyone in a catchment, involving all the

people in all the diverse communities in the region because they can relate to them. The platypus becomes the factor which changes attitudes, brings environmental degradation home to people as something for which every one of us is responsible, however indirectly; and shows us that as individuals we can do something and make a difference. It suddenly becomes a case of *'what can we do about the situation?'* instead of *'the government ought to be doing something about it'*.

The Landcare Groups which will collaborate and focus their activities towards improving the health of tributaries of the Wimmera in the upper catchment include Black Range, Concongella, Crowlands, Elmhurst, Great Western, Jallukar, Landsborough, Moyston, Northern Grampians, Navarre and the Upper Wimmera Farm Tree Group. Already much excellent work has been done by them using National Landcare Program grants. Now sponsorship from the corporate sector is being sought and considerable financial support for Project Platypus is already promised. The first scientific study ever undertaken of platypus in the Upper Wimmera Catchment has begun and will provide an effective monitoring device for the improving health of rivers in the catchment as remedial work proceeds.

In the first year of operation, Project Platypus has already achieved a lot. Four sub-committees produced guidelines for landcare work in the catchment to ensure that groundworks will meet the same high standards. An action plan targets, over five years:

- **Pasture program:** pasture improvement, with sowing of 10 000 ha, including 2500 ha in hill country; 20 km of fencing will ensure better pasture management.

- **Tree program:** planting 775 000 trees, including 180 km of fencing in high priority areas.
- **Vermin and weed program:** to undertake control programs on 150 sites, each of 20 ha, and to develop a weed control strategy for the upper catchment.
- **Remnant vegetation and wildlife protection,** included in the tree program.
- **Erosion control:** rectifying 20 eroded gullies on 200 ha, involving 100 landholders; and 10 eroded gullies on 250 ha, involving 50 landholders. Sponsorship from Wimmera Mallee Water enabled work to begin in 1995 with the rehabilitation of severely degraded hill country near Navarre.
- **Salinity control:** to restore 16 saline discharge sites per year, involving 800 ha and 80 landholders.

To quote from *Introducing Project Platypus*:

Project Platypus is a community based strategy which aims to put into practice the guidelines for land and water management which have been documented in the Wimmera River Integrated Catchment Plan, the Wimmera Catchment Salinity Plan and the Wimmera Regional Landcare Plan. A technical advisory system of officers from the Department of Agriculture and the Department of Conservation and Natural Resources is already working with us to implement this project. It will bring the message of landcare into the local towns and schools. Junior Landcare Groups and Secondary College students will have a role to play in growing and planting trees, monitoring water quality and wildlife, and by participating will learn to respect and care for the land.

THE WIMMERA RIVER CATCHMENT

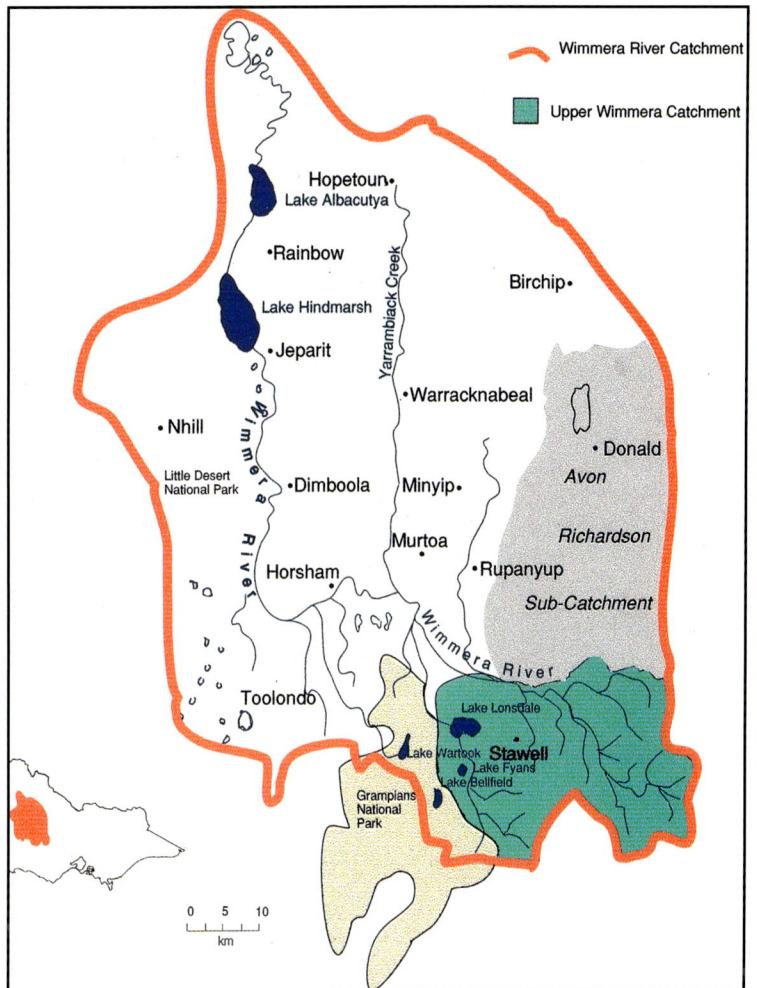

CHAPTER SIX

THE MURRAY–DARLING BASIN AND RIVER SYSTEM

The Murray–Darling Basin covers more than a seventh of the Australian continent. It consists of 26 major catchments. Run-off is highly variable, with 60% of the basin, mainly in the south-west and western regions, providing little or none. The Darling and its tributaries contribute 12% to the River Murray; the Murrumbidgee 13%; and the tributaries of the Murray upstream of the Murrumbidgee junction contribute 75%.

The Murray-Darling Basin is Australia's breadbasket, contributing about $10 billion to the economy.

The Murray–Darling river system is the largest in Australia and is internally draining in the sense that it arises in the humid regions of the Great Divide along the eastern margin of the continent and flows westward through the semi-arid regions of the eastern States before it reaches the sea. Only a very small proportion of its total sediment load ever reaches the ocean. On a global scale neither the Darling nor the Murray are very major rivers — the volume of annual flow of the system is about the same as the Amazon's flow per day. It is estimated that 85% of the Murray–Darling water is developed for use, with 70% used in irrigation. As a

The Darling at Wentworth where it joins the Murray.

M.E.W.

result only 20% of the natural flow ever reaches the sea.

The Murray–Darling is a perennial system because the main catchments are in relatively well-watered regions and the sub-catchments have different seasonality because of their latitudinal extent. The Darling is fed by summer rainfall in south-east Queensland and northern New South Wales, while the Murray receives the winter precipitation of the Snowy Mountains. The flow of both rivers is very variable as a result of ENSO.

IRRIGATED AGRICULTURE IN THE MURRAY–DARLING BASIN

Some 80% of Australia's irrigated agriculture takes place in the Murray–Darling Basin, involving 4.6 million hectares. Irrigated agriculture brings in a total of $6 billion each year, which represents 25% of the nation's agricultural income. When one realises that about 75% of all water used in Australia is used in irrigation, it becomes obvious that water use must be properly

AUDIT OF SURFACE WATER USE IN THE MURRAY–DARLING BASIN

RIVER SYSTEM	DISPERSION FOR IRRIGATION	DOMESTIC, INDUSTRIAL STOCK AND TOWN USE	TOTAL WATER DISPERSION	DIVERSION AS A % OF TOTAL BASIN DIVERSION
NSW				
Border Rivers	221	1	222	2.1
Gwydir	299	1	300	2.8
Namoi	244	4	248	2.3
Macquarie/Castlereagh/Bogan	465	6	471	4.4
Upper Darling	188	1	189	1.8
Lower Darling	128	85	213	2
Murrumbidgee	2424	19	2443	22.9
Murray	2024	29	2053	19.2
Total NSW	**5993**	**146**	**6139**	**57.4**
VICTORIA				
Upper Murray/Ovens/Kiewa	1531	36	1567	14.7
Lower Murray	264	20	284	2.7
Goulburn/Broken/Loddon	1656	54	1710	16
Campaspe	79	22	101	0.9
Total VICTORIA	**3530**	**132**	**3662**	**34.3**
SOUTH AUSTRALIA				
Private Pumped Diversion	235	4	239	2.2
Government Pumped Division	129	100	229	2.1
Reclaimed Swamps	106	0	106	1
Total SOUTH AUSTRALIA	**470**	**104**	**574**	**5.4**
QUEENSLAND				
Border Rivers	72	2	74	0.7
Macintyre Brook	10	0	10	0.1
Condamine/Balonne*	157	5	162	1.5
Total QUEENSLAND*	**239**	**7**	**246**	**2.3**
ACT	0	63	63	0.6
Total for BASIN	**10,232**	**452**	**10,684**	**100**

*Excludes water for harvesting
Key points to note from this table: Annual Diversion averaged 10,676 GL/year
Over 95% of diversions were for irrigation

(reproduced with kind permission of MDBC) 91

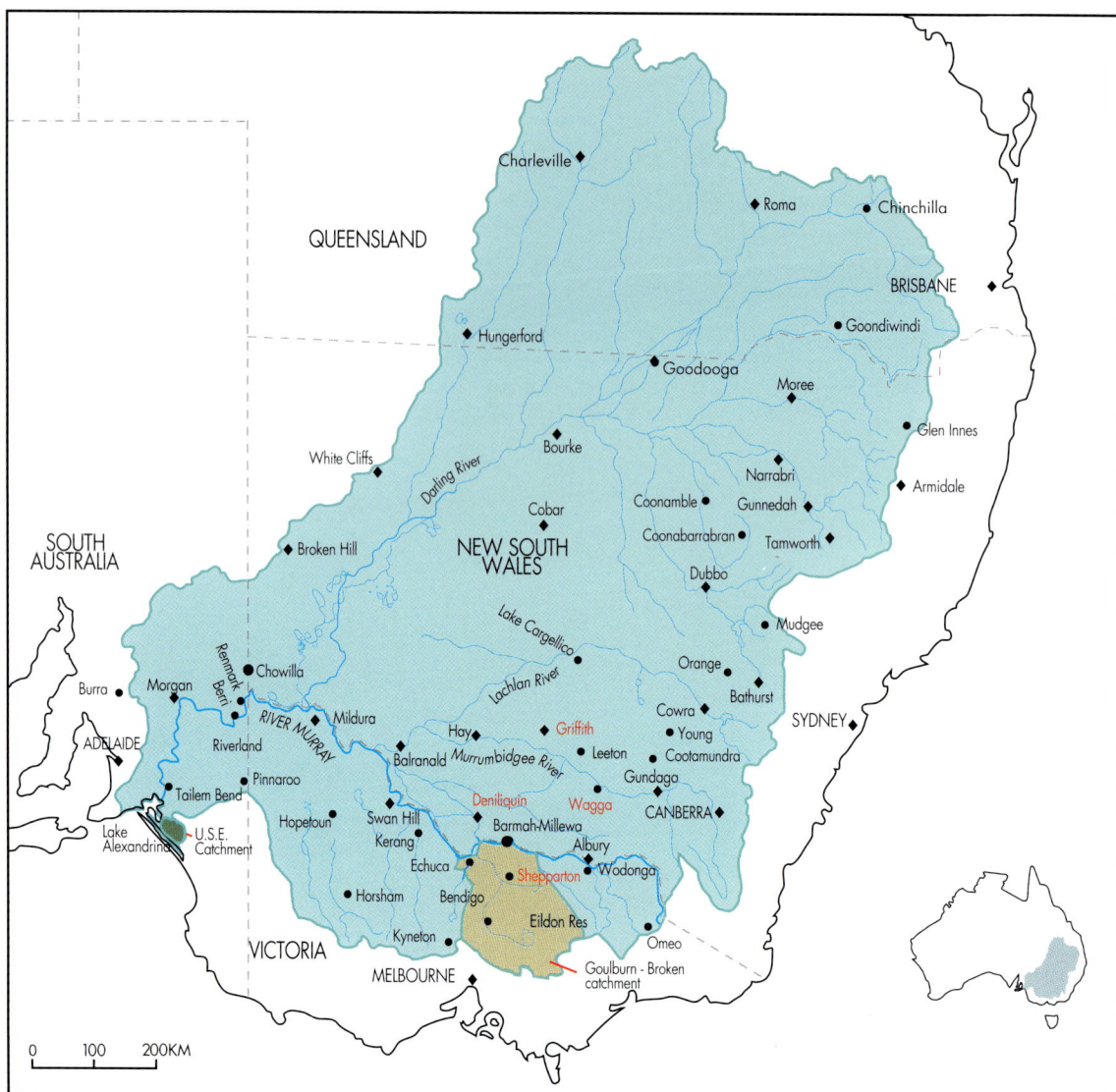

managed, without waste, in this dry continent. In the case of the Murray–Darling, annual diversion of surface water for 1988–89 to 1992–93 averaged 10676 GL per year and 95% of the diversions were for irrigation.[91] (Chapter 7 describes irrigated agriculture on the Riverine Plain.)

SALINISATION OF THE MURRAY–DARLING RIVER SYSTEM

The magnitude of the problem of increasing salinity in the Murray–Darling River System is only now being fully recognised. According to the Chairman of the Murray Darling Basin Commission, Professor John Lovering, salt levels in the rivers are rising, and will continue to rise over the next 25 years. The salt load in the Lower Murray is already so high that there are times when the water is unfit for drinking. This is despite the 11 salt mitigation schemes which are withholding 266 000 tonnes of salt a year from the river. According to Dr Wasson of CSIRO Division of

Water Resources, up to 2600 tonnes of salt is making its way into the Lower Murray each day as a result of agriculture, and just about every river in the Murray–Darling system is getting saltier. The increased salinity of the lower reaches of the river is a concern for Adelaide as it relies on Lower Murray water for a high proportion of its water supply.

The Murrumbidgee, Lachlan and the north-flowing rivers of central Victoria are all in trouble and will be particularly affected by rising salt levels. **Because of the nature of the problems of rising water-tables and the time-lags which apply in hydrological matters, the trend of increasing salinity in all rivers will continue. The increasing dryland salinity which is occurring in catchments is compounding the problem. According to Professor Lovering, the impact of dryland salinity on salt in the rivers had been underestimated in the salt management plan for the basin.**

The **Murray Basin** is a discrete geological structure, a basin-shaped depression filled with Tertiary sediments. (See Chapter 2 for the geological history of

EVOLUTION OF THE MURRAY BASIN

During the last 2.5my

THE MURRAY BASIN

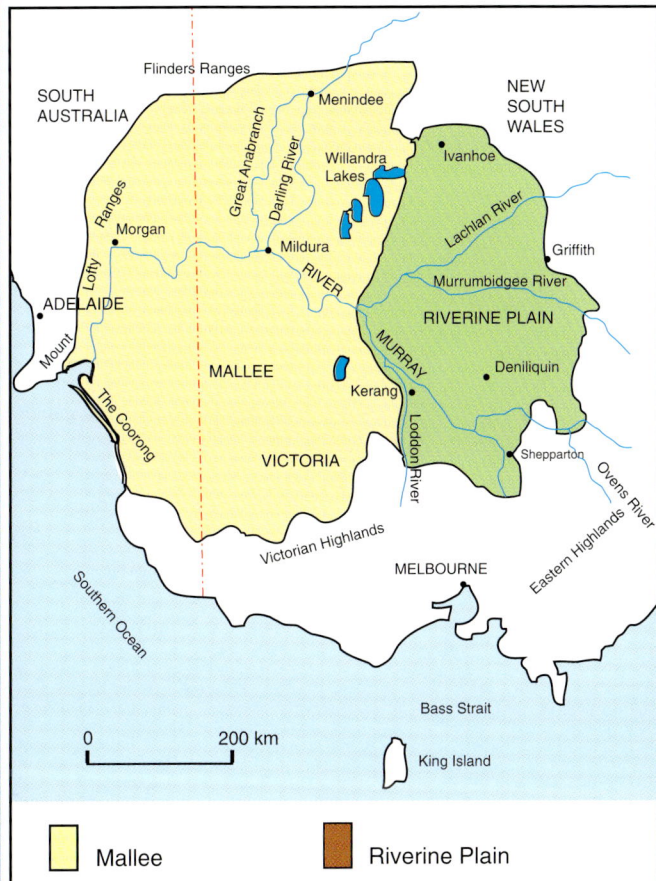

Mallee

Riverine Plain

The two major divisions of the basin are the **Riverine Plain**, comprising the river sediments spread by the prior river systems as the basin sank, with a wind-blown component added during glacial stages of the Pleistocene; and the **mallee lands** whose underlying sediments are mainly marine, with freshwater sediments from Lake Bungunnia on top in the area straddling the South Australian border, and wind-blown surficial sediments.

THE EXTENT OF LAKE BUNGUNNIA

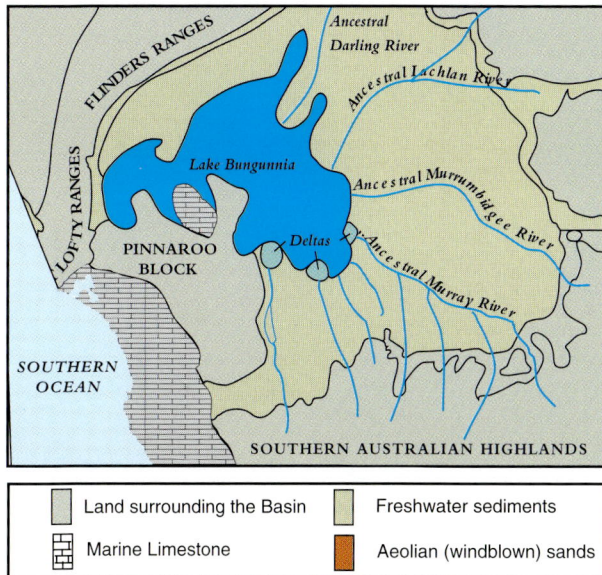

Land surrounding the Basin

Marine Limestone

Freshwater sediments

Aeolian (windblown) sands

A tectonic elevation of the Pinaroo Block blocked the exit of water from the Murray–Darling river systems and a large freshwater lake developed. About 68 000 km² were covered when the lake was at maximum extent. It started to fill about 2.5 million years ago, and started to drain about 700 000 years ago when the blockage was breached near where Morgan is today, and the outflow formed the direct north-south reach to the sea.

THE MURRAY BASIN IN THE LATE PLEISTOCENE
(600 000 to 100 000 years ago)

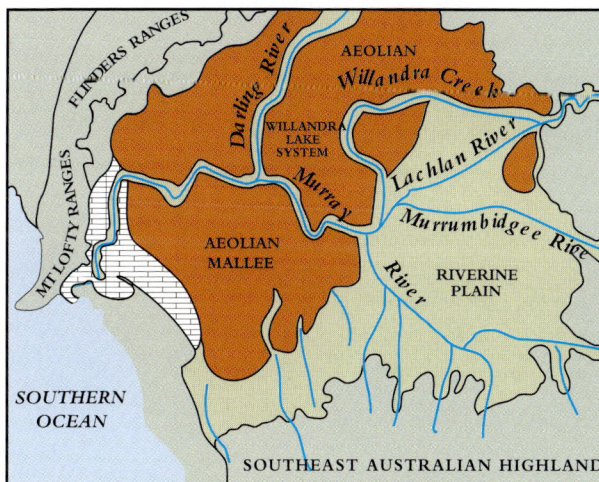

After Stephenson and Brown [36]

During glacial stages of the Pleistocene ice age, wind-blown sand containing a great deal of salt was deposited across the mallee.

the basin, the repeated invasions by the sea, the ancient rivers.)

The Darling River enters it through a breach in its most northerly margin in western New South Wales. It is the fact that it is a closed basin with only one outlet to the sea via the lakes at the mouth of the Murray that has contributed to its problems of rising water-tables and salinity.

The flatness of the basin landscapes determines the meandering course of the Murray River. At Mildura the fall is less than 5 cm/km; near the sea the gradient is only 1.6 cm/km. As a result of the flat terrain, water

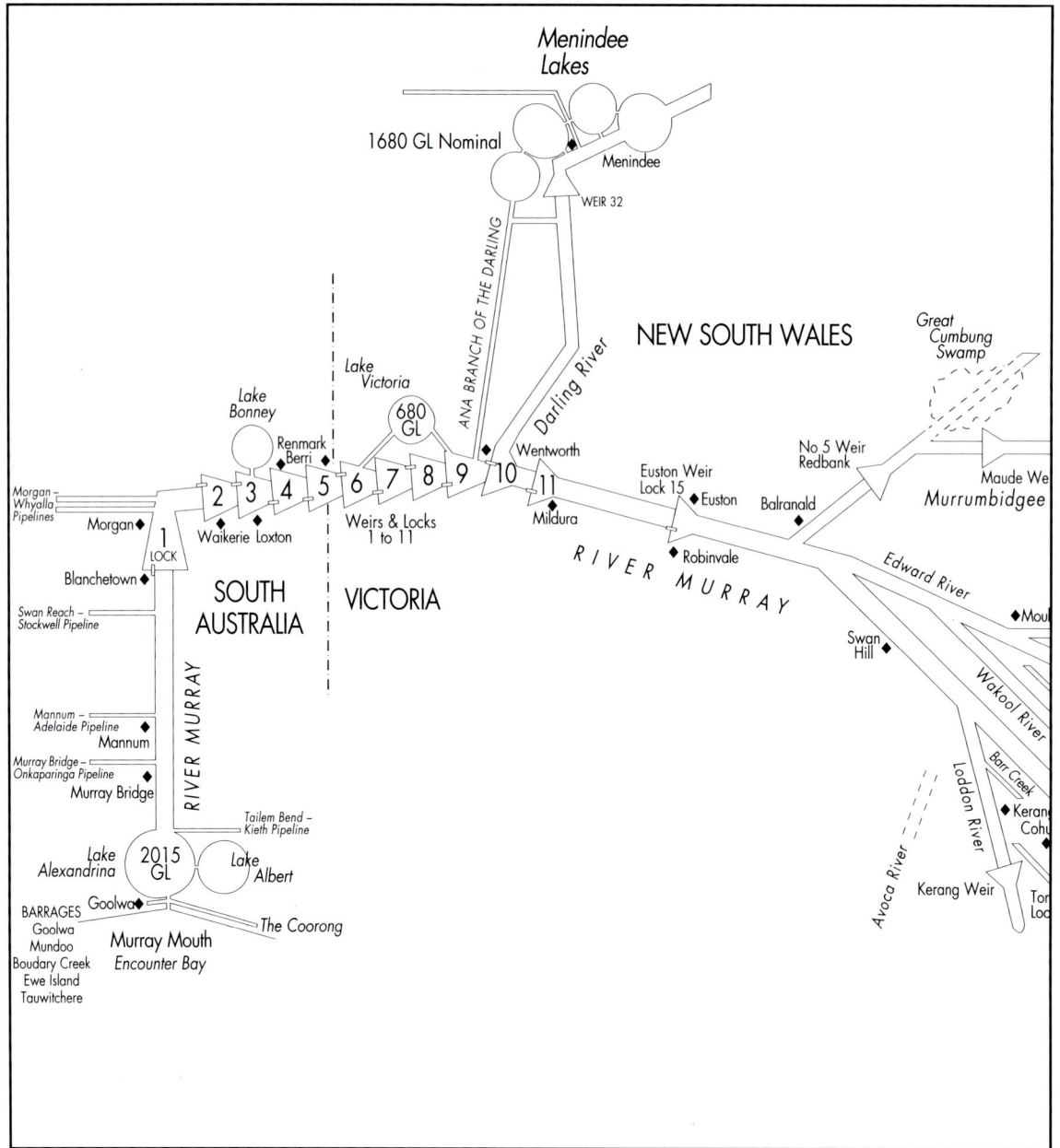

Menindee Lakes

1680 GL Nominal

Menindee

WEIR 32

ANA BRANCH OF THE DARLING

Darling River

NEW SOUTH WALES

Great Cumbung Swamp

Lake Victoria

680 GL

Wentworth

No 5 Weir Redbank

Murrumbidgee

Maude We

Lake Bonney

Renmark
Berri

2 3 4 5 6 7 8 9 10 11

Euston Weir
Lock 15

Euston

Balranald

Edward River

Morgan –
Whyalla
Pipelines

Morgan

1 LOCK

Waikerie Loxton

Weirs & Locks
1 to 11

Mildura

Robinvale

R I V E R   M U R R A Y

Wakool River

Mou

Blanchetown

SOUTH
AUSTRALIA

VICTORIA

Swan
Hill

Swan Reach –
Stockwell Pipeline

R I V E R   M U R R A Y

Barr Creek

Mannum –
Adelaide Pipeline

Mannum

Loddon River

Kerang
Cohu

Murray Bridge –
Onkaparinga Pipeline

Murray Bridge

Kerang

Tailem Bend –
Kieth Pipeline

Avoca River

Kerang Weir

Tor
Loc

*Lake
Alexandrina*

2015 GL

Lake Albert

BARRAGES
Goolwa
Mundoo
Boudary Creek
Ewe Island
Tauwitchere

Goolwa

Murray Mouth
Encounter Bay

The Coorong

Below left: Barren Box Swamp.

M.E.W.

Below right: Vineyards at Griffith.

M.E.W

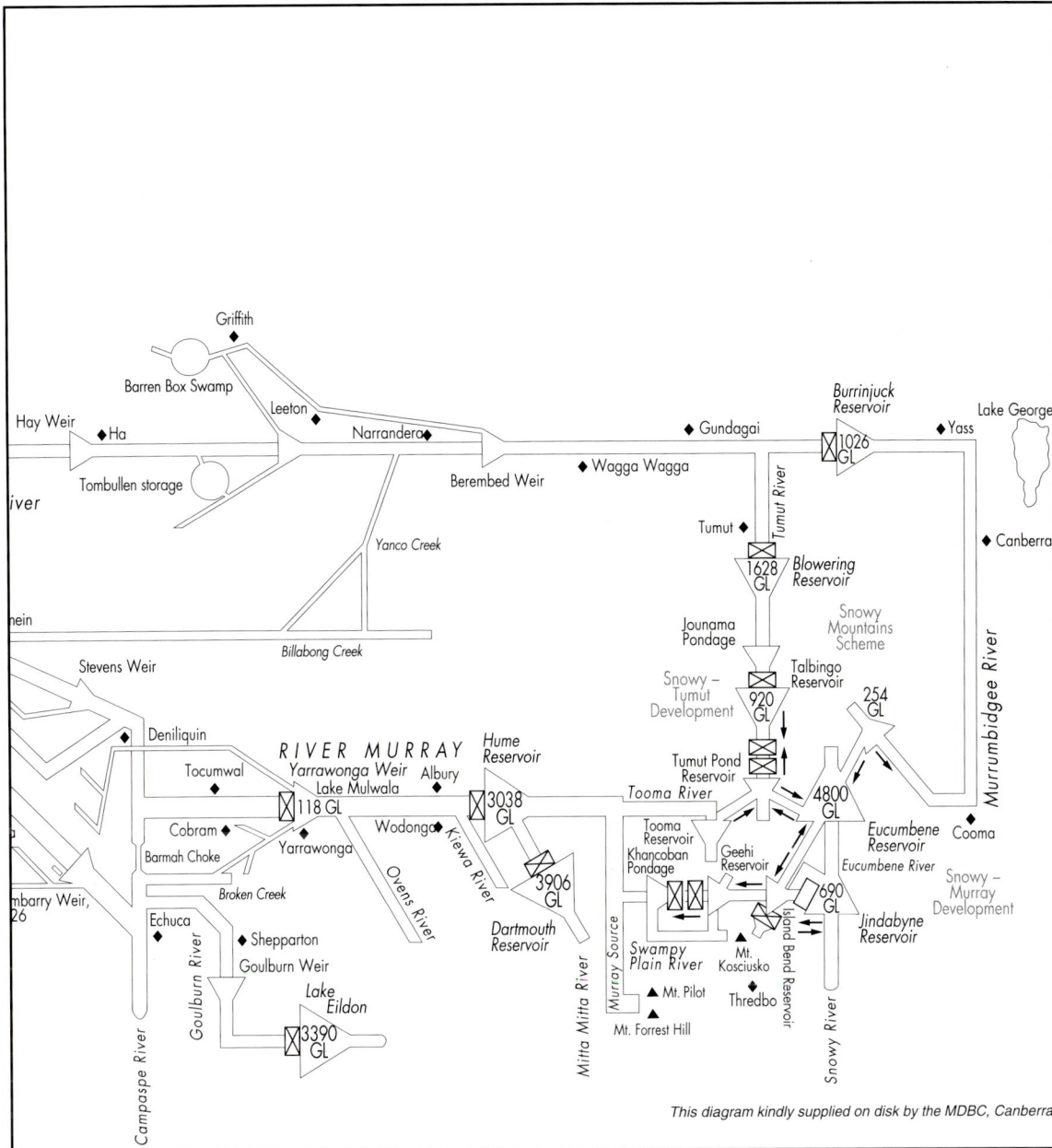

Griffith

Barren Box Swamp

Leeton

Hay Weir ◆ Ha

Narrandera ◆

Tombullen storage

River

Beremded Weir

◆ Wagga Wagga

Yanco Creek

◆ Gundagai

Burrinjuck
Reservoir

⊠1026
GL

Lake George

◆ Yass

nein

Billabong Creek

Tumut ◆

Tumut River

◆ Canberra

Stevens Weir

Deniliquin

Tocumwal ◆

RIVER MURRAY

Yarrawonga Weir
Lake Mulwala

⊠ 118 GL

Cobram ◆

Barmah Choke

Yarrawonga

Echuca ◆

◆ Shepparton

Goulburn Weir

Lake
Eildon

⊠ 3390
GL

Campaspe River

Goulburn River

Broken Creek

mbarry Weir,
26

Albury

Hume
Reservoir

Wodonga ◆

⊠ 3038
GL

Kiewa River

Ovens River

⊠ 3906
GL

Dartmouth
Reservoir

Mitta Mitta River

Murray Source

Tooma River

Tooma
Reservoir

Khancoban
Pondage

⊠⊠

Swampy
Plain River

◆ Mt. Pilot

Mt. Forrest Hill

Jounama
Pondage

⊠
1628
GL

Blowering
Reservoir

Snowy
Mountains
Scheme

Snowy –
Tumut
Development

Talbingo
Reservoir

⊠
920
GL

Tumut Pond
Reservoir

⊡

254
GL

4800
GL

Geehi
Reservoir

⬦
690
GL

Island Bend Reservoir

Mt.
Kosciusko

▲

Thredbo

Eucumbene
Reservoir

Eucumbene River

Jindabyne
Reservoir

Snowy River

Murrumbidgee River

Cooma ◆

Snowy –
Murray
Development

This diagram kindly supplied on disk by the MDBC, Canberra

*Below left: Control
weir at Lake
Mulwala.*

*Below right: Lake
Mulwala.*

M.E.W.

Right: The Murray, between Corowa and Berrigan.

Below: Spinifex and mallee near Pooncarie: the Darling runs through an arid landscape.

M.E.W.

KINDLY SUPPLIED BY MDBC

In November 1991, massive algal blooms developed along 1000 km of the Darling River and a State of Emergency was declared. Stock losses of 1600 sheep and cattle were attributed to the poisonous algal blooms. It is believed that stock exposed to the toxins suffer long-term effects of reduced condition and lowered productivity, so the effects were more widespread than the number of stock deaths imply. (No record exists of the impact of the poison on native animals.) One person was reported as suffering a severe reaction including skin rashes, breathing and gastric problems. The toxicity of cyanobacterial blooms is undoubted, and the toxins cannot be filtered out of the water. (Recent research by the CSIRO and Queensland University have found a way of breaking down the toxins, using bacteria. It may eventually be possible to treat affected water with cultured bacteria, making it safe to drink.) Algal blooms are a danger signal which tell us that the rivers are sick, and we ignore their warnings at our peril.

used to spread over vast areas across the floodplains (which vary from 2 to 10 km wide, and up to 25 km wide at one point) during years of high rainfall. The less dramatic seasonal flooding of average years maintained the wetlands and redgum forests, while drought years saw the river reduced to a trickle with permanent pools — natural cycles and pulses of life — but that was before regulation of the river. The Murray flows slowly, with water normally taking two months to travel from the Hume Dam at Albury (192 m above sea-level) along the meandering course of 2225 km to Murray Mouth.

The amount of water taken out of the major rivers of the Murray–Darling system for irrigation has altered flow patterns so that drought conditions occur in six years in every 10, instead of once every 20 years under natural conditions. Average flows now occur in one in 20 years, instead of about one in three as recorded early this century. Floods now occur one year in 14, where once they used to occur about one year in every three.

The figure (p.126-127) shows the extent to which the Murray, this natural artery supplying the life-blood of the most important agricultural region of our land, has been altered — with one object in mind, economic growth, but with no thought of the far-reaching environmental consequences (which we are now seeing and which are largely beyond our ability to remedy).

Regulation of the Darling, though it is not on a scale comparable with that of the Murray, has serious implications as well. Water flow in the catchment is limited and highly variable. Huge sums of money have been invested in dams, weirs, private diversions, on-farm storages and pumps to achieve greater reliability of supply. Since the 1970s, many private water diversion schemes have sprung up with the rapid expansion of the high-value cotton industry and other irrigation enterprises. Over-allocation of water has resulted in ecological consequences. The downstream effects were not taken into consideration when between 40% and 85% of water in some of the Darling's tributaries was diverted for irrigation, resulting in a serious cumulative impact. Irrigation water has obviously been too cheap, licences too easily come by. **There is simply not enough water in either the Murray or the Darling systems to meet the ever-increasing demand and to have enough over to maintain the healthy function of the rivers themselves or their wetlands.** Nutrient enrichment and rising levels of salinity of river water resulting from human activities are additional causes of river degradation.

The 1000 km stretch of bright green, cyanobacteria-infested, Darling River in the summer of 1991–92 (the longest stretch of poisoned river known anywhere in the world) should have frightened the Murray Darling Basin Commission into action. Less spectacular algal blooms are a regular feature of the river and its tributaries at times of low water and occurred also under natural regimes before settlement. The situation now is affected by the concentrations of phosphorus from sewage and nutriment from agricultural run-off which pollute the waterways and which are not flushed out because of the diminished flow caused by regulation of the rivers. 'Drought' conditions in the Murray and the Darling, due to too much water being diverted, leaving them impoverished, are now occurring every few years, instead of being related to long El Nino natural drought cycles.

In February 1996, unprecedented **bank collapses** occurred along a 2000 km stretch of the Darling, dumping enormous amounts of sediment into the river. The river bank failures coincided with record extraction of water from the river, 150 billion litres over December, January and February. At one stage there was a 4 m drop in water level in four days, and the banks are not able to dry out with such rapid falls and they slump into the river under the weight of the water they are holding.

There has been talk of **diverting the Clarence River** to add more water to the Darling so that irrigation can continue at even higher rates than now. There are always those in power who want to leave a legacy of a scheme with their name on it, regardless of the long-term consequences. History, even in this country with the Snowy Scheme, and everywhere overseas where such schemes have been implemented, tells us that we 'manage' nature on a scale like that at our peril. In the eastern half of the land, which is subject to ENSO climatic fluctuations, **it would be environmental vandalism to interfere with the Clarence** in order to prop up an unsustainable system

Bank collapse and erosion leave a coolibah's roots high and dry on the Barwon River.

M.E.W.

MAJOR TRIBUTARIES OF THE MURRAY–DARLING RIVER SYSTEM

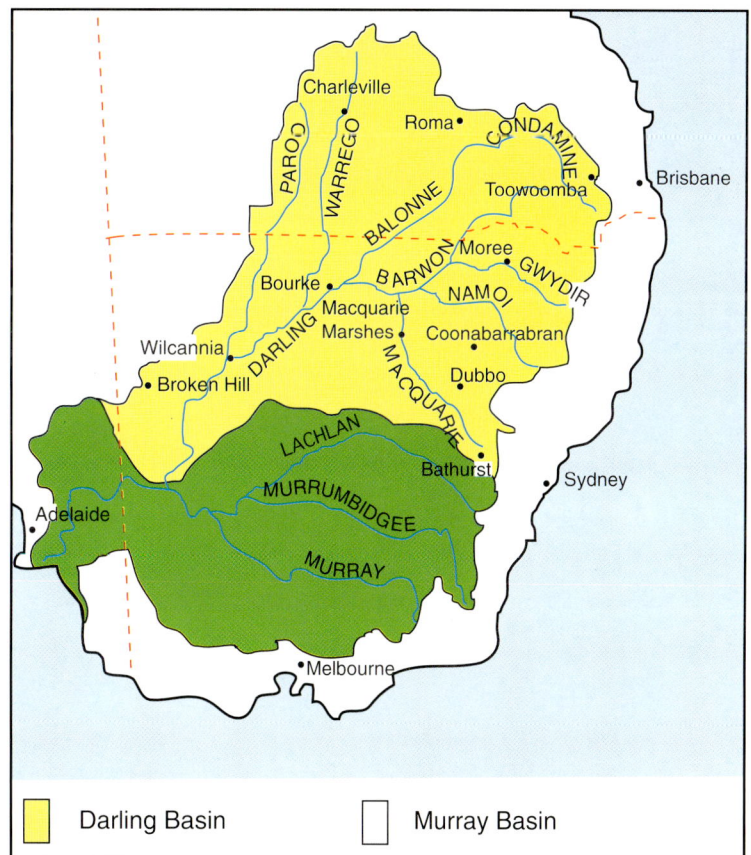

Darling Basin   Murray Basin

The Darling River at Bourke.

M.E.W.

elsewhere. Remember the Aral Sea disaster, the Colorado River! How can we think of allowing two State MPs, who want to increase Australia's role as the 'food bowl' for Asia regardless of the degradation and destruction of our resource base, even to go on with their subversive propaganda?

When river systems are starved and stagnant for long periods, and when floods are no longer of sufficient magnitude or frequency to flush out the system, algal blooms are one of the more visible signs of their failing health.

The **Macquarie Marshes** are an example of wetlands on a tributary of the Darling which are suffering from the reduced flow and pollution which results from the irrigation schemes which rely on the Macquarie River. This wetland complex spans a 100 km stretch of the lower Macquarie valley where the river forms a delta with shallow channels spreading out on the alluvial plain. Redgum forests, coolabah

CYANOBACTERIA (BLUE-GREEN ALGAE), INDICATORS OF DEGRADATION OF RIVERS

The Environmental Protection Authority of New South Wales has reported on the status of rivers of northern New South Wales and the Queensland border region.

- In the **Namoi Valley**, persistent algal blooms occur in Pian Creek in summer and skin irritations have been reported. Toxic algae are present in Chaffey Reservoir which supplies Tamworth, and there is concern about the poison in domestic water supplies. Both the Keepit and Split Rock Reservoirs have experienced blue-green algal blooms, and these problems are increasing throughout the valley. (Diversions in the **Namoi River** have varied from 60 GL a year in 1969 to 245 GL in 1987. Flow duration curves for natural and current river flows at the confluence with the Barwon River show that regulation has greatly increased the occurrence of low river flows. Those less than 250 GL a year occur 52% of the time, compared with 18% before regulation.)
- In the **Gwydir Valley** around Uralla and in Copeton Dam and other storages the frequency and severity of algal blooms has increased in recent years. The town supply for Inverell, which is pumped from the Copeton Dam, can be contaminated. (The **Gwydir River** system, including Carole Creek, the Mehi River, Moomin Creek, the Gingham Watercourse and the Gwydir River, has experienced an increase in total diversions between 1978 and 1987, ranging from 50 to 440 GL a year. A marked increase in low flows of less than 100 GL a month occurred 65% of the time, compared with 30% under normal conditions; the natural mean monthly flow of 14.2 GL a month is now

MEDICAL CHART OF A STARVING RIVER:
Natural and Current Median Flow in the Darling River upstream of Menindee Lakes

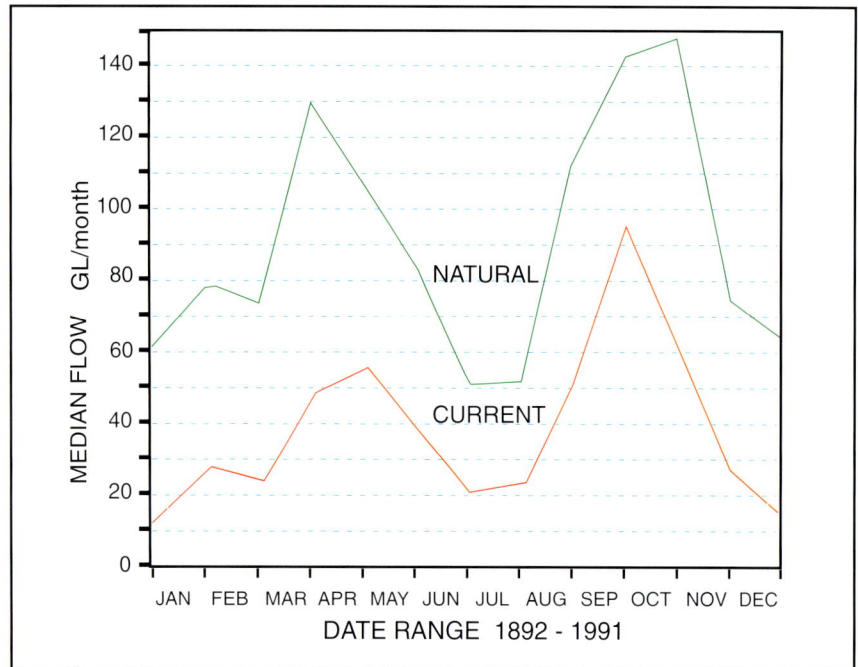

After Arthington [92]

Total Darling River Diversions *have increased from less than 50 GL a year between 1930 and 1960 to 1400 GL a year in 1990–91. This represents 40% of the mean natural flow or 84% of the median natural flow. Natural and current patterns of flow have the same monthly distribution of high and low flows but the absolute volumes of discharge are currently lower than natural flows in all months of the year.*

exceeded only 17% of the time; and the maximum of 680 GL a month has dropped to 230 GL a month.)

- Severe blooms of toxic algae have occurred in Windamere Reservoir on the **Cudgegong River** and in the major inflow arms of the Burrendong Reservoir (**Macquarie River System**). These blooms may affect water users of these storages, and there is concern for livestock drinking directly from the reservoirs.

impacts of unchecked high water-table and salinity in this region are frightening'.[94]

This assessment was made after five years of the Shepparton Irrigation Region Land and Water Salinity Management Plan which operated under the guidance of SPAC and its Irrigation Committee.

A new Strategic Plan for the five years 1995–96 to 1999–2000 has recently been launched. Its massive report and executive summary are politically correct and leave one with the impression that all is well and the results of all the strategies will mean bigger and better profits, a cure for salinity, and sustainable irrigation-based agriculture. Without wishing to decry the genuine efforts of government policy makers, agencies and all the other groups involved in trying to improve matters in this economically vital catchment, the exercise is not being looked at in the light of experience with irrigation elsewhere in the world in semi-arid zones. Trouble-free irrigation there has proved to have a life expectancy of only a few decades, after which time salinisation and other problems steadily decrease productivity and cause desertification. In the Murray Basin you have huge dryland portions of cleared catchments which are already heavily salinised, connected to the irrigated portions which lie in a confined basin structure whose only exit to the sea is via the Murray River, and **any large-scale irrigation-based agriculture is clearly unsustainable**.

The Introduction to the Strategic Plan refers to five successful years of implementation of the original plan in which:

.. implementation, policy development and dealing with community concerns through the SPAC decision-making process has provided comprehensive documentation and the progressive development of a Community-driven Salinity Management Plan for the Shepparton Irrigation Region. The decision making process has been supported by an intensive and highly focussed Research and Investigations program undertaken by Agriculture Victoria, Goulburn Murray Water and the Department of Conservation and Natural Resources. This activity has been strongly supported by the Salinity Bureau.

After all this bureaucratic effort the 'frightening' situation is unchanged after 'five successful years', and time is running out.

The problems have been around for so long one has to ask why have agencies waited until now to assess the situation, why has the basic accumulation of information only started recently in earnest, and will the day ever come when realistic thinking will replace the economy-driven planning which promotes continuation of irrigation when it is leading to complete desertification? Problems generated by the present unhealthy situation of the catchment are an accumulation from all the management practices of the past and will not be cured, and possibly may not even be significantly slowed, for a very long time by a change to better management practices. In matters affecting hydrology, significant time lags apply. It is not fair to blame the farmers who hold the land today.

According to SPAC, $54 million has been spent by landholders implementing the salinity action plan.

Twelve community Landcare groups have recently been formed within this catchment, giving hope that the change of mindset and attitudes which are required, and which follow real community involvement, will start to make a difference, however temporary.

It is not only officialdom which has not wanted to see the problems which have been escalating for a long time, hoping that they would go away, eyes fixed on the holy grail of profits. Farmers trapped in the system have until recently not been sufficiently informed of the big picture, and they are too constrained by the difficulties of making a living when the land is becoming progressively less productive to be able to do much about it. A recent survey has highlighted this dilemma. It found that 93% of farmers on the Tragowel Plains in the Kerang Lakes region have salinity problems on their farms and 52% have land areas actually going out of production. However, only about half of the farmers on the plains adopt any salinity management practices, which include channel improvements, drain construction, laser levelling and water reuse systems. Where land is already salinised there is a government grant available to fence off and try to rehabilitate the areas affected. Only 40% of the farmers who are dealing with their salinisation problems have used the grant. Salt-tolerant species have been planted on badly affected land by about 50%; about 30% have stopped irrigating salted land, and 25% have taken it completely out of production.

WETLANDS OF THE MURRAY RIVER

Seven thousand wetlands (covering more than 200 000 ha) were identified in the Murray Basin in a survey carried out by the River Murray Commission (forerunner of the Murray Darling Basin Commission) in 1983. The aim of the survey was to prepare an inventory and to find out how the changed regimes caused by regulation of the river's flow affected them. The number of dams and weirs that control the flow of the Murray result in many wetlands becoming permanently inundated, no longer subject to cycles of drying and refilling; while others have been destroyed by having no access to floods at all; and many have been used as evaporation basins for salt removed from the system.

Changes in water regimes have resulted in river red gums on the edges of the swamps being killed by drowning; or in wetland meadows being invaded by river reds where they are now less frequently flooded. The ecology of the famous Barmah river redgum forest has been drastically altered since the building of the Hume Weir in 1934 and then the Dartmouth Dam in 1980. Flooding is now infrequent in winter and spring and is replaced by summer floods when high river levels are maintained for irrigation.

When wetlands are permanently inundated, a species change occurs in ecosystems, favouring those suited to waterlogged conditions. The number of food organisms in the water is reduced — drying releases nutrients which become bound to waterlogged soils and these are released to the food chain on re-flooding. In addition, drying provides an opportunity for a flush of dry-land plant growth which becomes nutriment when the wetland floods again. Reduced waterfowl breeding results from the decrease in available food when this revitalising of the system is omitted. Agricultural run-off with its pesticides, herbicides, fertilisers and other nutrients has affected many wetlands; urban contamination with sewage and waste-dump effluent have damaged others.

Much of the Murray floodplain is grazed by sheep and cattle (and rabbits); feral pigs cause damage; the river redgum forests are still logged (although the surviving remnants are only a small fraction of what was there at the time of settlement); weeds like water hyacinth create problems; and introduced carp displace native fish, destroy water plants and cause turbidity. The boating and other activities of people on billabongs and lakes add pressures to already embattled ecosystems. Urgent action is required to protect and maintain the vital resources of the River Murray for the future.

The **Loveday Wetlands Complex** lies on a loop of floodplain enclosed by a River Murray meander near Barmera. The area has been heavily grazed by cattle and rabbits. Some of the wetlands have been used as evaporation basins to store saline irrigation drainage water; others have been kept in a permanently inundated state for over 70 years by the higher river levels maintained by the weir at Lock 3.

Since 1990, the **Barmera-Moorook Field and Game Association** has been undertaking rehabilitation works in the Loveday Complex, particularly rabbit control, grazing reduction or exclusions and planting of salt-tolerant species. From 1994, **Ducks Unlimited Australia** has provided expertise in wetland rehabilitation to the management plan, and flow control structures were installed to allow

Azolla in the water on the Murray floodplain about 5 km west of Tocumwal.

M.E.W.

Ecotone Project. These are the **Riverland Wetland Rehabilitation Sites** in South Australia; the **Chowilla Floodplain Complex** which straddles the borders between New South Wales, Victoria and South Australia; and the Barmah-Millewa Forest on the Victorian and New South Wales sides of the Murray.

Above left: Logged redgum forest at Gulpa Creek.

Above right: Murray pine regenerating in an area fenced off by the Southern Riverina Field Naturalists in the Gulpa Creek forest.

M.E.W

The Chowilla Floodplain Complex

The Chowilla floodplain is one of the last regions of Lower Murray floodplain which has not been developed for irrigation. It covers an area of 177 km² and it is dissected by more than 100 km of anabranch creeks which carry a significant portion of the River Murray flow since the construction of the weir at Lock 6 in 1930. This weir and the development of several large water storages upstream deprived the floodplain of flood flows and aggravated natural salt discharges in the area. Flooding in the lower-lying areas of the floodplain now occurs once every three years on average instead of annually, and is much reduced on higher areas. Where once the whole floodplain was inundated about

re-introduction of wetting and drying cycles.

In early 1995 the permanent wetlands were dried for the first time in 70 years. Thousands of adult carp were killed; fish barriers were installed to prevent re-entry of adult carp when the lagoons re-filled in spring 1995. A burst of plant regeneration followed the drying, and the removal of cattle and rabbits from most areas allowed the young plants to survive.

International concern about the health and sustainability of wetland systems has led to the inclusion of three sites in the Murray Basin in the UNESCO

THE LOVEDAY WETLAND COMPLEX

Above left: Massive river redgum and lignum regeneration in Big Mussel Lagoon, following the first drying phase in the Loveday Wetland Complex for 70 years (April 1995). Above right: The Loveday Wetland Complex filling on rising river levels in spring, September 1995. Big Mussel Lagoon is highlighted by bluer water, as the turbid river water reaches this part of the complex last. The drowned trees of the Loveday evaporation basin and causeway to the Loveday irrigation pumping station on the Murray are visible in the background, with Lake Bonney in the far distance.

ANNE JENSEN

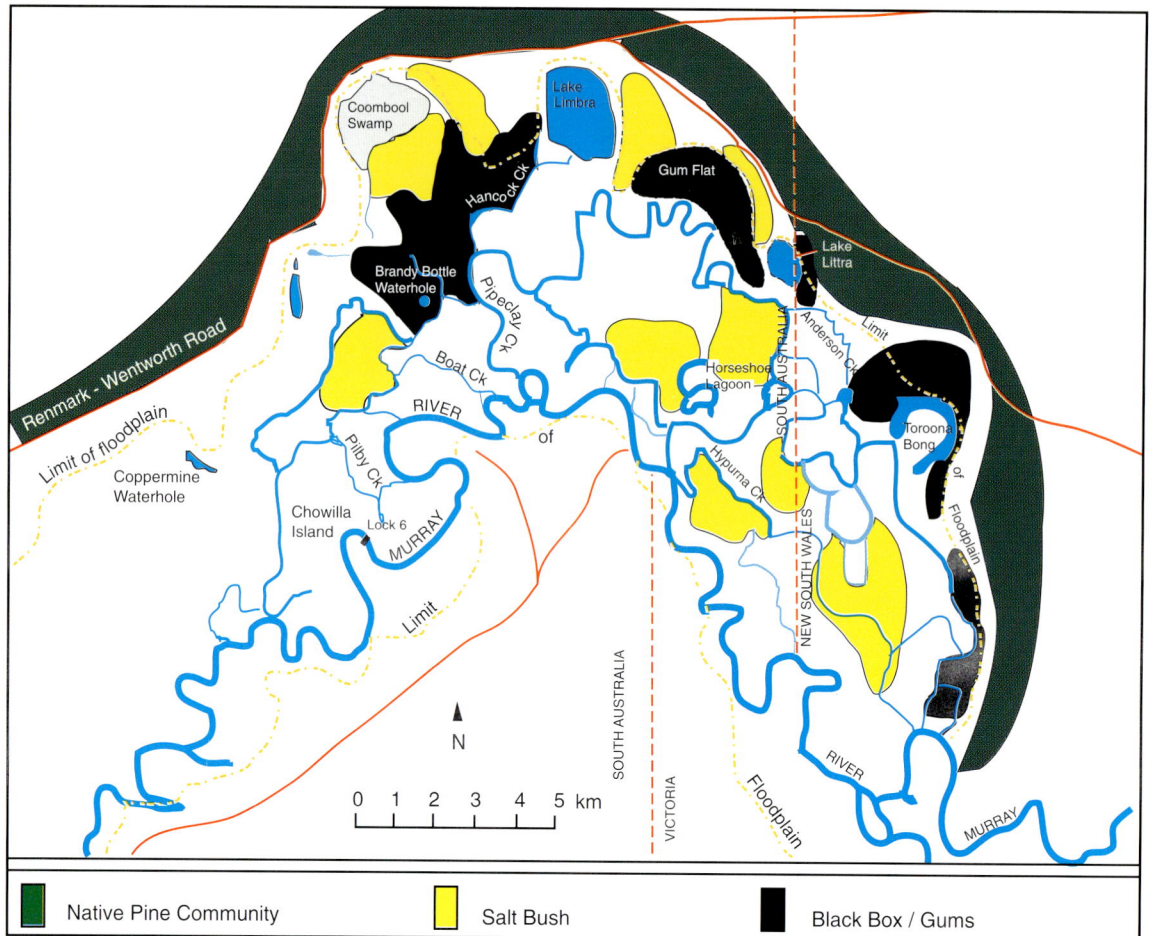

After Jensen **96**

Native Pine Community	Salt Bush	Black Box / Gums

Meandering anabranches of the Murray, oxbow lakes, flowing creeks, billabongs, floodouts, levees and lunette dunes, and ephemeral lakes around the margins of the floodplains, make this a place of high conservation value. It provides habitats for birds, mammals, reptiles and fish and contains magnificent redgum forest. It is an important area for recreation, agriculture and fish production. The Chowilla floodplain is an important nursery for Murray cod, and is a refuge for four species of small endangered fish, while the anabranch creeks are important routes for migrating native fish. Unfortunately the feral European carp is widespread here, as it is in the rest of the Murray. Foxes, rabbits and goats are other unwelcome ferals in the area.

CAPTION KINDLY SUPPLIED BY ANNE JENSEN

one year in four, this now happens one year in thirteen.

Two million tonnes of salt has accumulated in the floodplain and the region is now the largest contributor of salt to the river, particularly on the recession of a flood. Increased spring flows in the River Murray (over 35 000 ML per day) overflow the banks, filling wetlands and replenishing groundwater. However, as the flood recedes, saline groundwater from Chowilla enters the river system, causing concern to irrigators and other water users downstream. Because of reduced floods and rising groundwater levels, the salt is now in the root-zone of vegetation and trees are dead or dying in some places.

The South Australian portion of the floodplain was listed in 1987 as a Wetland of International Importance under the Ramsar Convention and is included in the **UNESCO Bookmark Biosphere Reserve**. Key areas have had stock excluded, and extensive rehabilitation is being carried out on the lunettes which had been over-grazed. Manipulation of flood peaks is now being evaluated to increase the frequency of floodplain inundation (releasing salt to the Murray when it can be best diluted) and this will significantly improve the overall health of the floodplain and its biota. New management strategies are being implemented to restore health to this wonderful and unique region.

The Barmah–Millewa Forest

The Barmah–Millewa forest occupies 70 000 ha of the Murray River floodplain upstream from Echuca — the largest remaining redgum forest in existence. The Barmah forest is on the southern side of the Murray, in Victoria; the Millewa forest on the northern, in New South Wales. Most of the river redgum forests along the Murray were felled for timber and to fuel the river boats which plied the Murray and the Darling as far

River reds in the Barmah-Millewa forest.

MARTIN DRIVER

north as the Queensland border in the early days of settlement. The boats had to refuel every 30 km or so, and huge piles of wood were maintained at stopping places, first from the trees on the river banks, and then from further afield.

The wetlands of the Barmah forest are *Wetlands of International Importance* under the Ramsar Convention. Regulation of the Murray has resulted in changes to the flood regimes, with flooding less frequent and widespread, but with some areas permanently inundated and flood peaks occurring later in the year. Changed water management programs have been proposed and are being implemented in order to restore more natural watering of the forests. These include new regulators to control flow into the forests; small capacity diversion works and low banks to spread water; commitment of water resources for forest watering; providing small environmental flows on a case by case basis as required. Water bailiffs will operate water regulators, scientific research will provide support information on water needs; a Geographic Information System will continue and expand mapping of the forest.

The Riverland Wetland Rehabilitation Sites

South Australian Murray Valley

`Six floodplain sites in the South Australian Riverland have been undergoing rehabilitation since 1990 under the Wetlands Management Program of the Department of Environment and Water Resources.[96] Three disposal basins, Disher Creek, Bulyong Island and Berri Basin, and three well-known wetlands, Ramco Lagoon, Lake Woolpolool and Lake Merreti, have all been receiving increased flows of water to remove the accumulations of salt and to revitalise the wetland systems. In order to promote revegetation, rabbit control has been intensive

THE BARMAH-MILLEWA FOREST:
Its situation during the 1917 big flood

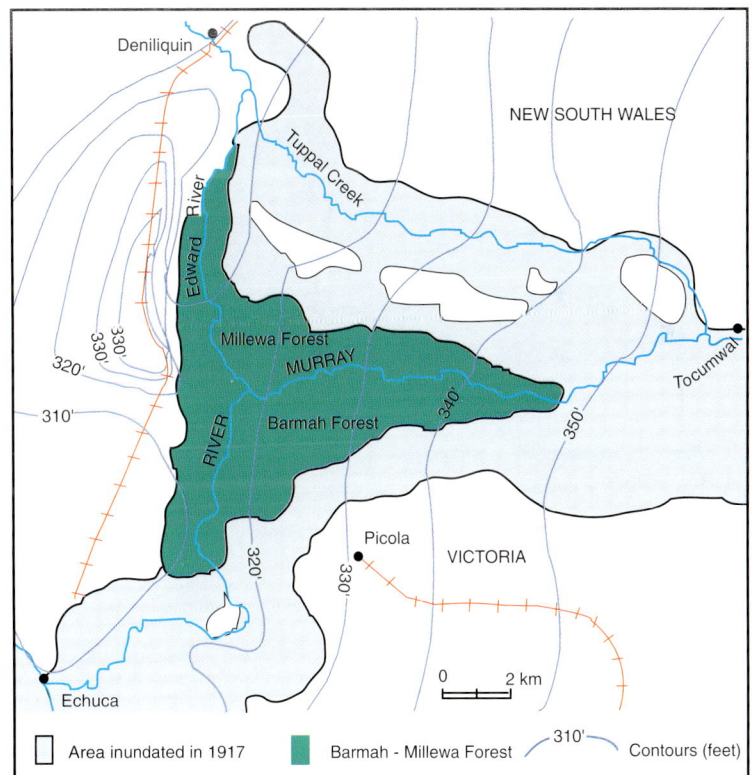

After Mackay & Eastburn [97]

A major flood in 1917 breached levee banks and spread out over the full extent of the floodplain. All of this area probably carried forest of some sort prior to clearing.

(and with the release of the new virus in 1996 the rabbit problem may be reduced), and fencing has excluded stock from areas which are regenerating naturally or being replanted.

At the two lakes, regulators have been used to fluctuate water levels for the benefit of the

LOCATION OF RIVER MURRAY WETLANDS MANAGEMENT PROGRAM SITES

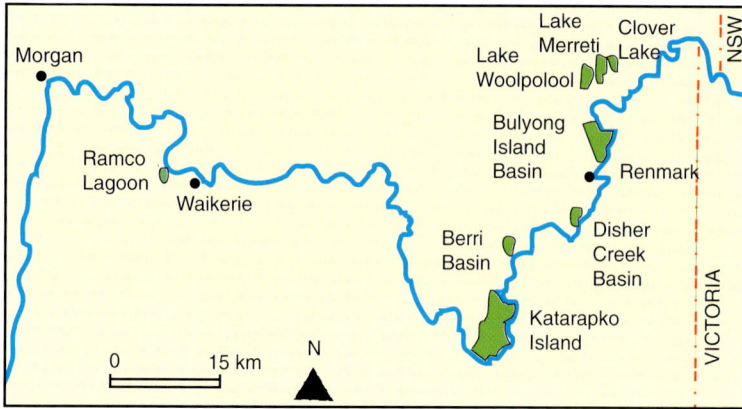

THE DISHER CREEK DISPOSAL BASIN

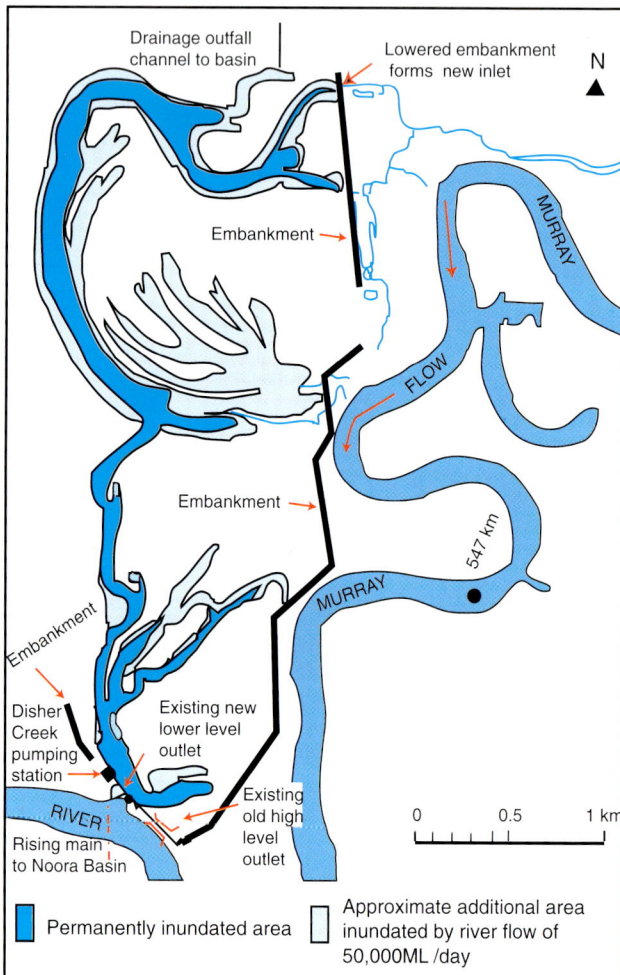

After Jensen [96]

Disher Creek was isolated from the Murray River by low levee banks in 1967 and used as a storage basin for saline irrigation drainage water from the district until 1984. The pressure of the stored water caused displacement of highly saline groundwater from under the basin into the river, so from 1984, water was transferred from Disher Creek to Noora Basin, outside the river valley. The levee banks were breached to allow high river flows to enter the basin more frequently, and the level of water held in the basin was reduced to 30% of former storage levels.

CAPTION KINDLY SUPPLIED BY ANNE JENSEN

Gulpa Creek in the redgum forest.

M.E.W.

environment, as well as to protect water quality for downstream irrigators. Manipulating the water level at Lake Merreti can be done in a way which reduces the salinity of water reaching the Chaffey Pumping Station on Ral Ral Creek, but which maintains water–levels to ensure the safe maturing of ibis chicks in the big rookeries in lignum stands.

Lake Woolpolool is also linked to the main stream by the anabranch Ral Ral Creek. Past irrigation of the lake bed had raised the saline water-table and caused severe salting. Local irrigators blocked off the regulator valve on the inlet creek in 1981 to prevent slugs of saline water flowing out of the lake and down Ral Ral Creek to the Chaffey pumping station. Since 1984 the regulator has been used to allow fresh water to flood the dry lake bed in spring if there are extra flows available from the river. This creates a rich temporary wetland which wets and dries in response to seasonal variations in river flows. The lake has been filled 11 times since 1984, supporting thousands of waterbirds when it is wet, and providing a demonstration of the benefits of wetting and drying cycles. Strong growth of reed beds has occurred, and river redgum regeneration is taking place at the edge of the wetted zone. The algal fibres which cover the lake bed when it is dry break down rapidly and, along with nutrients released from the dried bed, provide a burst of nutrients to stimulate the food chain in the next wet cycle.

LAKE WOOLPOLOOL

This aerial view of Lake Woolpolool, with neighbouring Lake Merreti in the background, shows the first experimental wetting in 1984. Salt encrustation on the soil surface is apparent in the foreground, and black box trees in this area appeared dead (they have since recovered, following good rains on the floodplain). A high levee in the foreground was built prior to the 1956 flood to exclude rising floodwaters from a valuable pasture crop. The pressure of water outside the levee forced saline groundwater up into the lake bed, destroying the crop and leaving a legacy of vegetation destruction.

Right: Lake Woolpolool in a dry cycle, showing matted algal fibres and a groundcover of Mimula repens. Strong reedbed growth (Phragmites australis) can be seen in the background, with young regenerating river redgums (Eucalyptus camaldulensis).

ANNE JENSEN

DISHER CREEK

Above right: Disher Creek Evaporation Basin, May 1992.

Above left: Disher Creek Evaporation Basin at the start of the diversion to Noora, January 1981.

ANNE JENSEN.

THE NATURAL HISTORY SOCIETY OF SOUTH AUSTRALIA INC.

Saving the Southern Hairy-nosed wombat

The Natural History Society of South Australia is an example chosen to illustrate how members of such societies are achieving conservation and preservation of indigenous Australian flora and fauna. Their voluntary work and dedication has led to saving the **southern hairy-nosed wombat**, one of our most engaging marsupials, from local extinction on two reserves in the arid mallee lands near Blanchetown.

The campaign to save the southern hairy-nosed wombat was nearly as unique as the animal itself at the time when it commenced, and is a success story which should inspire other groups to tackle similar problems in their vicinities. (And it should perhaps recruit more willing participants, who are looking for community projects in which their help can make a positive contribution to the society.)

The plight of hairy-nosed wombats in the Blanchetown area was noted as early as 1925. Competition with introduced grazers, degradation of vegetation by over-grazing, encroachment of agriculture and destruction of habitat, added to the already difficult arid environment with its droughts, made survival precarious for animals, even those as well adapted as wombats. Their sedentary nature requires

The southern hairy-nosed wombat, Lasiorhinus latifrons. This species is confined to localities west of the River Murray in South Australia. Its range and numbers have contracted greatly since settlement. Today it is confined to the Nullarbor Plain, to isolated localities in the Eyre and Yorke Peninsula, and to small remnant populations in the Blanchetown region. The northern hairy-nosed wombat, Lasiorhinus krefftii, now very rare and endangered, was once widespread in New South Wales and Victoria and ranged into Queensland. Almost, or perhaps totally, extinct, a few individuals are thought to exist near Jerilderie in New South Wales and in the Epping Forest National Park in southern Queensland.

A. CLEMENTS.

that they have to cope with the extreme local conditions — little or no water, and in summer grazing on pasture with high fibre and low nutritional content. They conserve moisture by resting in a burrow and letting their body temperature fall during the day; their metabolism is such that neither water nor nutrients are wasted.

An increase in adult population requires three consecutive years of effective rainfall, critical factors being the ability of the female to produce milk; the availability of suitable green feed at the time of weaning; and good pasture at the time of maximum growth of the juvenile. Along the Murray Valley in that part of South Australia effective rainfall has only occurred in 25 of the last 100 years, so the longevity of adults (more than 20 years in captivity) is an adaptation for a species in which reproduction is potentially low.

The hairy-nosed wombat was declared a protected species in 1935 but shooting and poisoning continued and habitat destruction and competition with introduced animals continued to take a toll. The first serious attempts at conservation came as a result of the intervention of two people, Mr and Mrs J.P. Conquest, who tried in vain to lobby government into creating a reserve for the remaining population near Blanchetown in the 1960s. They approached several preservation societies without success and eventually came to the Natural History Society of South Australia. (The Field Naturalists Society of South Australia had proposed the establishment of a large reserve but the government would not cooperate, the price of $300 000 being too high.) The drought of 1967–68 created a crisis situation for the wombats, 'taking a fearful toll of the last survivors of the species, now restricted to a few square miles near Blanchetown' according to the *Sunday Mail* of March 1968.

In 1968 an appeal was launched by the Natural History Society asking nature-lovers and members of the general public each to donate the price of an acre (0.4 ha), $4, and an extra $2 for fencing, to enable the purchase of 1215 ha of Portee Station at a cost of $18 000. The experiment in buying a reserve in this manner at that time was unique. It captured the imagination of people in the State, and was backed by major newspapers giving publicity, and by donations and support from many prominent citizens. Even the Duke of Edinburgh sent congratulations. The target amount was exceeded in just five weeks, so the fund was left open and a further 810 ha were added to the reserve. The **Moorunde Wildlife Reserve** came into being in 1968. (The South Australian government, through the National Park's Commission, then bought land and established two other small reserves in the Blanchetown region, riding the wave of publicity and public interest generated by the Natural History Society's success. These reserves, the Swan Reach National Park and the Ridley National Park, have helped to make the future of the southern hairy-nosed wombat more secure.)

Voluntary labour fenced the reserve and has

maintained it, and natural regeneration of vegetation has occurred, the wombats have bred up to satisfactory numbers and continue to thrive. The 1982–83 severe drought was a source of worry and alarm for members of the Society when it appeared that numbers had been decimated. However, when rain came in 1984 it was found that many wombats had survived by staying in their burrows in a state of suspended animation and the losses had not been as great as had been feared. Other wildlife has been returning to the reserve as the condition of the vegetation improves and because water has been made available at a couple of places by installing catchment roofing and watertanks. It has been found that the biotic soil crusts of lichens, mosses, liverworts and algae, which are such an important feature of arid landscapes, have returned with the exclusion of hoofed animals. Problems with feral goats still occur, because goats are notorious for ignoring fences.

Population studies have been carried out on the wombats over the nearly 30 years since the reserve was created. It was found that warrens were widely spaced or almost absent in the parts of the reserve where mallee scrub dominated; in the wilga shrublands (*Geijera linearifolia*) they were more abundant, particularly where a good grass understorey existed; and they were most abundant in the grassland areas. Photographic records kept by the Society over the years show the steady improvements in the vegetation which have occurred since the reserve was fenced and grazing pressures were reduced. The return of the biotic soil crusts has been documented photographically.

In 1994, the **Lake Short Conservation Reserve** was donated to the Society by the government. It

LOCATION OF MOORUNDE SANCTUARY AND OTHER RESERVES, SOUTH AUSTRALIA

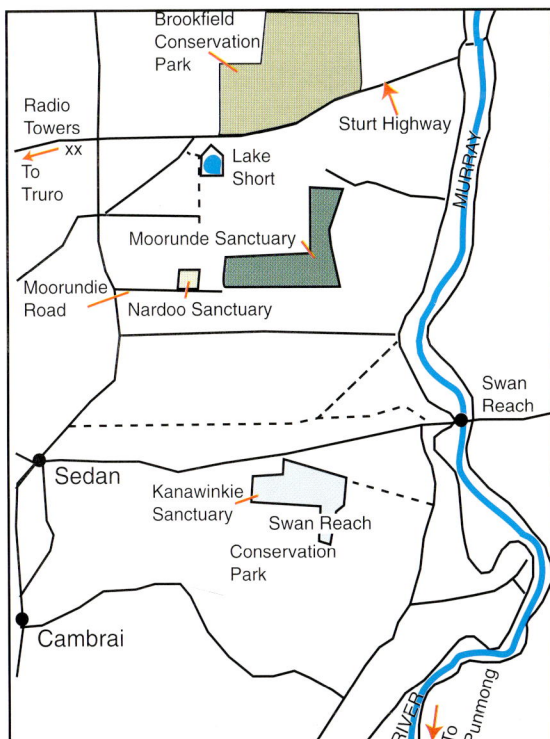

consists of 34 ha of wetland about 6 km from Moorunde. A 'Save the Bush' grant has enabled fencing of a hectare, and Society funds have been used to fence a few other small areas so that the vegetation (including swamp box) can regenerate and native grasses can be re-established. The Lake Short Reserve forms a wildlife corridor between the Brookfield Conservation Park and the Moorunde–Nardoo Reserves, and is another hairy-nosed wombat territory.

The Natural History Society of South Australia maintains two other reserves — Nardoo, near Moorunde, and the Cullen Reserve at Robe (on the coast between Beachport and Kingston in the south east). Regular working bees on all the reserves are happy social occasions; members are rostered to act as rangers inspecting the fences; and a great deal of satisfaction has resulted from the achievements of the Society in facilitating the regeneration of the natural vegetation and the creation of permanent refuges for the wombat.

Above top: A hairy-nosed wombat at a burrow in a degraded landscape.

Above: Regeneration of vegetation in the Moorunde Reserve since it was fenced.

A. CLEMENTS

A PHILOSOPHY FOR BALANCING WATER REQUIREMENTS FOR THE ENVIRONMENT WITH WATER REQUIREMENTS FOR OTHER PURPOSES IN THE MURRAY–DARLING BASIN

Parts of an address by David Mitchell are included here with his kind permission, because it encapsulates the problems behind agricultural land and water use in Australia.

By David Mitchell, Professorial Associate, Charles Sturt University, Albury

The conservation of surface water in reservoirs is essential for sustaining most forms of agriculture in the Murray–Darling Basin and for maintaining the socio-economic stability of the region and other associated areas in Australia. Such conservation measures in themselves need not cause major irreversible degradation to riverine and riparian ecosystems. Unfortunately however, the current **management** of the conserved water, together with the excessive consumptive use and some of the practices the stored water makes possible, have had severe adverse impacts on the welfare and sustainability of aquatic and related ecosystems in the basin.

These are exemplified by the losses in biodiversity, decreases in extent of wetland and riparian systems, changes in habitat promoting invasion of alien species, and degradation in water quality caused by eutrophication, addition of environmental toxins, excessive growth of blue-green algae and other related factors. Moreover, this situation is likely to continue under current management practices, because they are largely based on the needs of agricultural systems, which were developed in other parts of the world with very different environmental conditions and which utilise alien plants and animals that are not adapted to Australian conditions.

Consequently, current management approaches in the Basin do not take account of the basic characteristics of its natural environment and therefore continue to exacerbate the problems caused by past neglect of the water requirements of native ecosystems. In addition, the recent audit of the water use in the Basin has revealed that the current allocations of water have created unrealistic expectations in the agricultural industry and other sectors of the community which could have serious repercussions in the future.

There is an urgent need for a fundamental shift in the basic approach of all those whose decisions affect the quality of the Australian environment. Instead of persisting with attempts to alter the nature of this environment to suit imported agricultural systems and biota, attention should now be given to using transferable agricultural and land husbandry skills in the production of systems that accentuate the strengths of the Australian environment and its native biota. Such systems would be particularly suitable in areas which are only marginally suitable for traditional forms of agriculture and which are currently being progressively degraded by current farming practices. These new systems would also extend the versatility and resilience of Australian agricultural production and give it a leading edge in the development of new markets.

Factors contributing to the over-allocation and unequal distribution of water resources in the Basin have been excessive storage, regarding the portion which escaped to the sea as an opportunity lost; failing to recognise that the variability of the system was built into the sustainability of natural ecosystems and that the `surplus' being stored to reduce variability in agriculture was adversely affecting rivers and wetlands; and that heavy subsidisation allowed wasteful use as well as allowing the development of basically uneconomic enterprises.

The native flora and fauna had evolved with, and had become adapted to, the variability in the system, responding flexibly and opportunistically to a wide range of conditions. The 'average' flow allowed to them did not meet their natural requirements (like the flooding and drying cycles of wetlands, the requirement for fish of small fresh water flushes during otherwise low flows in summer).

A new policy for the management of surface water resources of the Murray–Darling Basin should emphasise the fundamental need to sustain the natural Australian environment, while promoting economic productivity in the basin. These two goals are potentially compatible if the needs of economic productivity are given priority access to stored water during the summer and if management of water resources in the basin gives first priority to the needs of the environment during the rest of the year by emphasising variability of supply wherever possible. There are elements of a compromise in this suggestion. It is not ideal for either system, but both should flourish most of the time.

A number of difficult decisions will have to be taken:

- Commitment to buy back irrigation licences, starting with sleeper licences, until a better balance is restored between a sustainable irrigation industry and a sustainable environment of acceptable quality; to consider drainage and rehabilitation of off-river storages; to control alien species; and to finance long-term research into ecology of the Basin in balance with more short-term applied projects.
- Allocation of generous amounts of water to the environment in years of high rainfall, when consumptive use is least.
- Recognition that land use practices on floodplains must be compatible with frequent flooding; and of the requirements for floodplains to be flooded and dried out if they and the river systems associated with them are to be sustained — with consequent judicious removal of levee banks.
- Recognition that many areas are climatically/geographically/environmentally unsuitable for intensive agriculture.
- Establishment of an interconnected system of research, development, demonstration, technology transfer, and training, involving both regional and basin-wide components, which recognises the relationship between public and private ownership of resources such as water, soils and native biota; and establishment of a system of appropriate incentives and disincentives that promotes wise and responsible management and use of natural resources with respect to both quantity and quality.

MAJOR COTTON-GROWING REGIONS OF AUSTRALIA

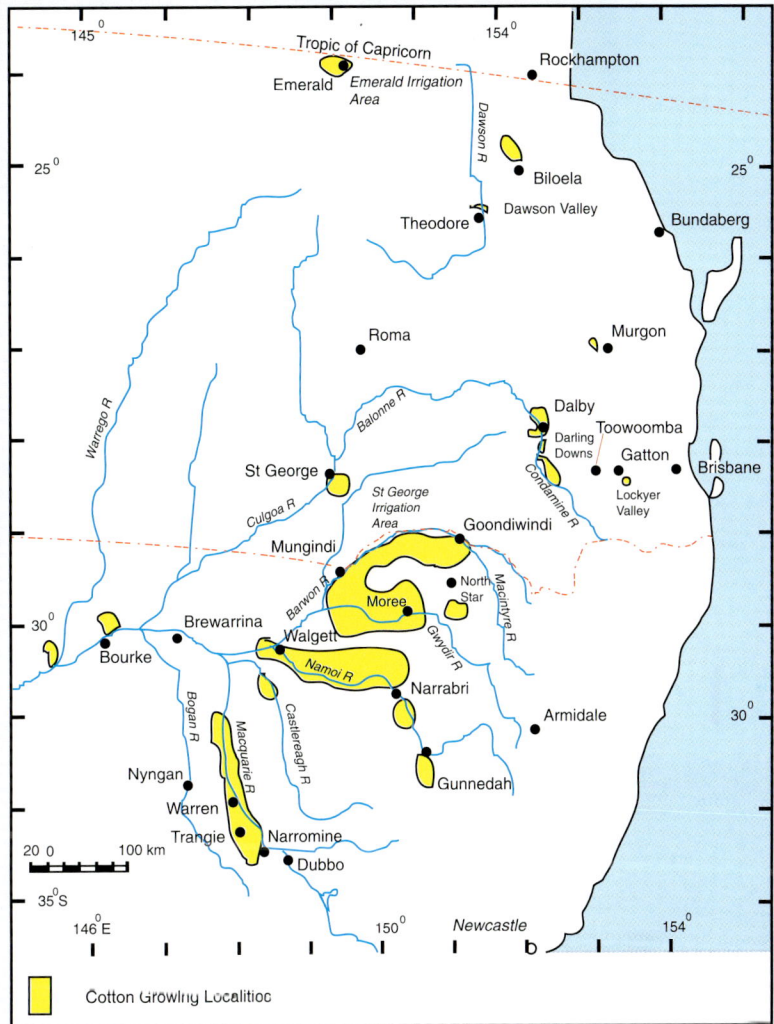

Most of Australia's cotton is grown on land irrigated by water from the Darling and its tributaries. A recent survey of rivers in cotton-growing areas has shown that pesticide contamination of river water is occurring in all major growing localities. *Endosulfan* was the dominant organochloride found in areas downstream from cotton farming. It is highly toxic to fish, and although it is non-persistent, breaking down quickly, its levels in surface waters are a serious threat to aquatic life and reflect its high usage on cotton. Surprisingly, DDT and its metabolites, which have not been used in the cotton industry since 1981, was the most common insecticide found in the Gwydir River, underlining their dangerous persistence. In all, seven different pesticides were detected; and several were found in tissues of fish and aquatic creatures in contaminated areas. Four herbicides, *atrazine, diuron, fluometuron* and *prometryn* were commonly detected.

The pesticides, herbicides and defoliant chemicals used in the cotton industry are not the only pollutants of rivers. The fertilisers used contribute high levels of phosphorus and nitrogenous material to the waterways, and it is such nutrient enrichment that contributes to algal blooms.

MAJOR COTTON-GROWING REGIONS OF AUSTRALIA

After Arthington [92]

Anabranch of the Darling at Menindee.

M.E.W.

Right: Redgum forest.

Below: Murrumbidgee at Balranald.

M.E.W.

CHAPTER SEVEN

THE RIVERINE PLAIN OF THE MURRAY BASIN IN NEW SOUTH WALES

IRRIGATED AGRICULTURE

The Riverine Plain of the Murray Basin occupies a large part of southern New South Wales (and extends south of the Murray River into the Shepparton and Kerang regions of northern Victoria). Two major irrigation districts have developed on the plain in New South Wales: the Murray Region is centred on Deniliquin; the Murrumbidgee Region has irrigation districts centred on Griffith and Coleambally.

Irrigation farms cover a total of 1.3 million hectares and are of two general types:
- Small area farms, averaging 15–20 ha, centred around Griffith and Leeton, with permanent plantings comprising vineyards and orchards of citrus and some stonefruit.
- Large area farms, of 200–300 ha, on which rice, winter cereals, row crops and pasture are the major crops.

Water-tables have risen, and are still rising rapidly, in irrigated areas of the Murray Basin due to the combined effects of clearing of trees and deep-rooted perennial vegetation in catchments and the addition of irrigation water. It has been estimated by the Water Resources Commission that **70%–80% of all irrigated land in the basin will eventually have water-tables less than two metres below the soil surface and that water-tables will fluctuate about an equilibrium level in response to climatic variations and land use practices**.

With current practices and no successful mitigation measures, the scenario is seen as bleak by many experts including van der Lely.[99]

He predicts that 20%–30% of agricultural land could become salinised and that these salt areas would essentially become **sacrificial discharge areas** where

New vineyards are springing up everywhere around Griffith, often replacing stone fruit orchards which have been pulled out to make way for the more lucrative grapes.

M.E.W.

WATERLOGGING IN THE BOOMANOOMANA BASIN

Above left: A low point in the landscape, through which Dry Creek used to run only occasionally, has become a salty lake ringed by samphires.

Above right: Salty water has crept right to the edge of a cultivated field.

Right: Dry Creek is now a broad, permanent water body, drowning trees.

M.E.W.

evaporation from the water-table occurs, balancing accessions and preventing further long-term rise in water-tables. (In other words, a stable state would be reached, having lost one-third of the productive land.) It is important to reduce and delay this 'no intervention' outcome by decreasing the recharge from irrigation.

In the Murrumbidgee and Murray regions of southern New South Wales, rice is a major crop, and **up to half the rise in the water-tables has been attributed to rice growing, 25% to channel seepage, and the remainder to other crops and pastures.**[98,100]

Case studies on the irrigation area centred on Deniliquin in the Murray Region, and on the Murrumbidgee Irrigation Area, centred on Griffith and Coleambally, follow. In general they share basic problems associated with their location in a closed geological basin within the driest vegetated continent, Australia, whose nature is unique — which makes the imposition of practices which work reasonably satisfactorily in other lands decidedly hazardous here. Flood irrigation on the Riverine Plain, in particular, is inherently incompatible with:

- the **geological structure** of the Murray Basin (see Chapter 2), a closed basin with only one outlet to the sea (Murray Mouth); with

small closed sub-basins superimposed and with problems of drainage associated with prior streams (now sub-surface) resulting from the previous courses of rivers on the Riverine Plain;

- the **rising saline water-table hazard** which results from removal of vegetation throughout the basin and is already progressive and serious, without adding flooding of vast areas for up to six months of the year;

- the **nature of the rivers in this arid continent** where removal of the amount of water needed for the crops leaves them impoverished;

- the **climatic swings** which make interference with the flow of rivers more damaging to their ecology and to that of the wetlands which they support;

- the salinity, nutrient enrichment levels, and **ecological degradation of the rivers** which are already at crisis point.

Truth is not always palatable. It is going to take advanced technology and engineering, and courageous and expensive experimentation to save a large part of the continent's breadbasket from desertification. One can only hope that wisdom will prevail in finding local solutions and that no grandiose scheme will be dreamed as a 'cure', like the suggestion about diverting the Clarence to enable more irrigation on the Darling!

THE MURRAY REGION IRRIGATION AREA

Deniliquin lies in the centre of one of New South Wales' most productive irrigation areas where crisis point is fast being reached because of rising water-tables and salinisation. Already 120 000 ha of this 750 000 ha Murray Irrigation Area are severely affected and the Department of Land and Water Conservation warns that half will suffer serious production decline in 25 years unless remedial action is taken. Water-tables have been rising by up to a metre every three years and are now at an average of 3–6 m below the surface. The rapidly deteriorating situation is due to the addition of irrigation water to water-tables already on the rise throughout the region because of the almost total clearing of the land. Production losses are already estimated at $13 million a year and many current land use practices, including intensive irrigated land use, are clearly not sustainable without improvements in technology and engineering.

As long ago as the 1930s it was recognised that Deniliquin is situated at a pivot point in local hydrology. Soils tend to get heavier towards the west; soil and groundwater salinities increase westwards, as do groundwater pressures.[101] A Canadian consultancy company advised the government not to irrigate west of a line due south through Deniliquin because this region was a discharge area, while the region to the east of the line was a recharge area. The advice of the consultants was not taken — so often unpalatable advice sought and paid for is ignored if it is not what government wants to hear.

In addition to the salinisation problems associated with irrigation, the Deniliquin area also suffers from serious vegetation decline over much of its dryland grazing lands. Its landscapes, as part of the ancient riverine plain where palaeo-rivers spread sandsheets and alluvial clay deposits throughout the development of the Murray Basin in the last 60 million years, are flat plains over which the modern rivers wander. The 'prior streams', remnant beds of the more geologically recent palaeo-rivers, are visible in the landscape and the 'sandhills' or ridges on the plains are on the leeward side of these and represent the ancient dune systems which were a product of windy and dry glacial stages of the Pleistocene. The clay-rich plains were also the product of the last glacial stage 18 000 years ago (and in previous glacial stages, no doubt) when wind-blown sediments covered the landscape. The way the mallee lands of the western part of the Murray Basin and sandy soils of the Riverine Plain blow away when their stabilising vegetation is removed is related to this comparatively recent geological history of the region.

It was the construction of the Hume Dam on the Murray River near Albury which enabled irrigation in the Murray Region. (The Dam was under construction during the 1920s and irrigation water only became available in the mid 1930s.) The Wakool Irrigation District was established in 1935, Berriquin in 1939,

THE IRRIGATION AREAS AND DISTRICTS OF THE RIVERINE PLAIN OF NEW SOUTH WALES

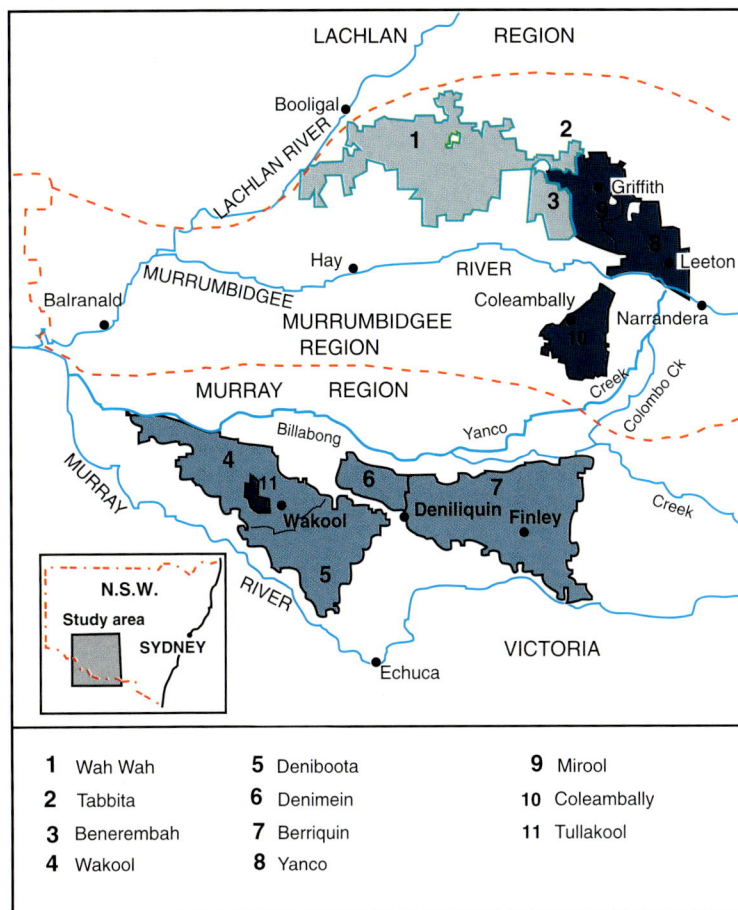

1	Wah Wah	5	Deniboota	9	Mirool
2	Tabbita	6	Denimein	10	Coleambally
3	Benerembah	7	Berriquin	11	Tullakool
4	Wakool	8	Yanco		

After Humphreys et al. [98]

THE EXPANSION OF RICE GROWING IN THE MURRAY REGION, THE MURRUMBIDGEE IRRIGATION AREAS AND DISTRICTS, AND THE COLEAMBALLY IRRIGATION AREA

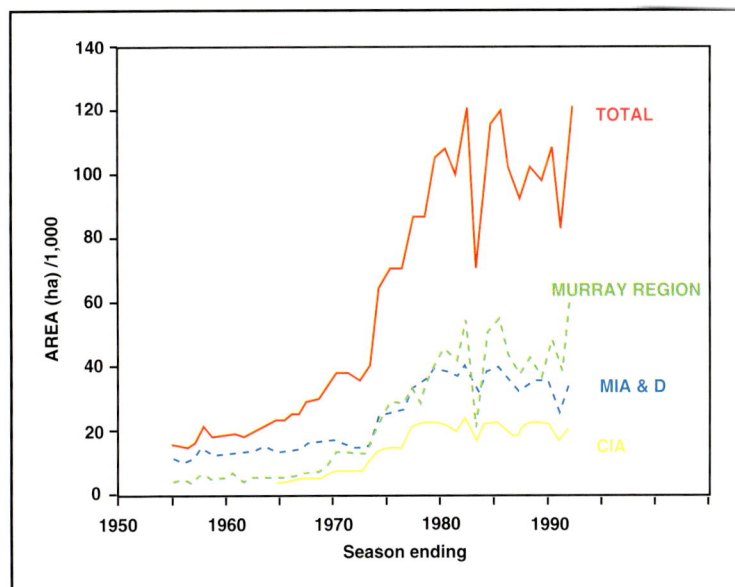

After Humphreys et al. [98]

Denimein in 1951 and Deniboota in 1957. The Dartmouth Dam on the Mitta Mitta River (in the Headwaters of the Murrumbidgee Catchment) was

Rice is the economic base of 'broad acre' irrigated agriculture in southern New South Wales, using water from the Murrumbidgee and Murray Rivers over the summer months. The industry represents 20% of the regional income, and directly and indirectly generates 18% of the total regional employment. (Within the national economy the rice industry provides employment for some 9000 people.) About 149 000 ha were sown in 1995 and over a million tonnes of unhusked rice was produced. The area sown is expected to stabilise at about this figure, limited by the availability of water, according to the Executive Director of the Ricegrower's Association (speaking on 25 July 1996 at the CSIRO in Griffith).

The Ricegrowers' Co-operative Ltd produces, mills, stores and markets the entire crop, this industry being a shining example of a value-added export industry. About 90% of the crop is exported and the *Sunrice* brand name is a guarantee of quality. **The industry is extremely efficient** and yields are the highest in the world, with overall production averaging about eight tonnes per hectare. Deniliquin has one of the largest rice mills in the Southern Hemisphere and the Co-operative owns five others as well and has a staff of 1000. **No wonder then, that an industry like this which brings in about $300 million a year at the farm gate will continue in spite of the environmental havoc which is looming and to which it is contributing in no small measure.**

The socio-economic compromise is to minimise the damage, using resources in the least harmful way — processes in which scientific research has an ever-increasing and vital role to play. (Obviously, a solution to rising water-tables and safe disposal of salt has to be found and implemented, and just as obviously it is an engineering problem of drainage, recycling of water, and ultimate transport of evaporated salt, or concentrated brine, to the sea.)

Everyone involved in irrigated agriculture, and the rice grower in particular, is aware of the problems of the rising water-tables and has been progressively improving water management by improved layouts and altered practices. While ricegrowers used to have a lot of water running off the bottom of their paddocks, surface drainage today is much decreased. The aim is to judge the amount of water as accurately as possible, supplying just enough for the crop to use it up, eliminating the need to drain for harvesting. Unpredictable weather makes this a difficult calculation. Scientific research is the key to finding more 'sustainable' management practices.

Production of the best rice crop in the world results from understanding the requirements of the plant, the management of soil and water, and the climate — all factors which have been established by research and development programs which have evolved

Above: Early flooding of rice bays with rice just emerging from permanent water.

Left: Rice bays, showing the check boards which are adjusted to raise the height of the water in the upper bay.

CSIRO, GRIFFITH

over time. (The cost for 1995 of research and development was $1.8 million according to the Executive Director of the Ricegrower's Association, with 13% spent on developing 'sustainable farming systems'.)

Rice seed is soaked in water and mainly sown from aircraft in October and November, straight into the flooded paddies. Nitrogenous fertiliser is drilled into the soil or broadcast on the soil surface prior to flooding, and additional fertiliser is spread over the paddies by planes in January if necessary. The seedlings grow in shallow water (5–10 cm) until the flowering heads start to appear, then the water depth is increased to 20–25 cm at around the time of their full expansion in January. At this time when meiosis (the specialised cell divisions involved in sexual

reproduction) occurs for the production of pollen, the temperature is critical. Cold snaps with night temperatures falling below the critical level of 15°C, in spite of the insulating water, result in a great reduction in the amount of grain set. This happened in 1995, reducing yields by an average of 25%, but in a very random manner. Some crops were not worth harvesting, others were unaffected. As the grain matures during February and March the water level is reduced, and the paddocks are dried out to allow harvesting from late March to June.

In New South Wales, rice has only one insect pest, bloodworm, and no diseases, so pesticide use is low. Weeds are the main pests and some herbicides are added to the supply water at point of entry. A new method of spreading chemicals (and fertiliser), using specially designed motorbikes which are driven through flooded bays, is becoming widely used.

The extent of flooded rice bays in the landscape in the CIA in November 1993 is seen in the Landsat image. The flooded paddies show up as dark-coloured or blackish. Subtle colour changes relate to the clarity or turbidity of the water. Satellite imagery is increasingly used as a tool to monitor land cover. An image of the same landscape in March 1994, is calibrated to show summer cropping. The orange fields are soybean crops.

'Landstat Thematic Mapper Data acquired by the Australian Centre for Remote Sensing (ACRES), Australian Surveying and Land Information Group, Canberra.'

THE CENTRAL AREA OF THE MURRAY REGION

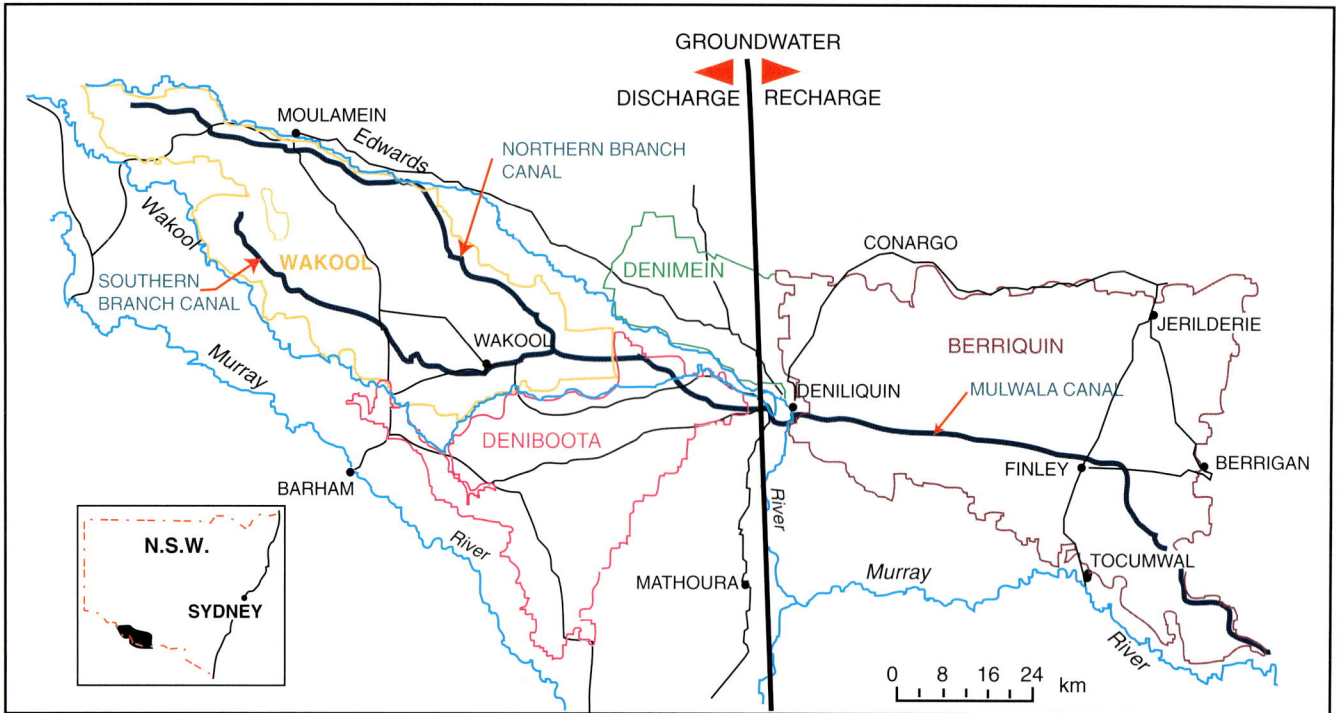

WATER-TABLE DEPTH BELOW SURFACE, BERRIQUIN & DENIMEIN IRRIGATION DISTRICTS

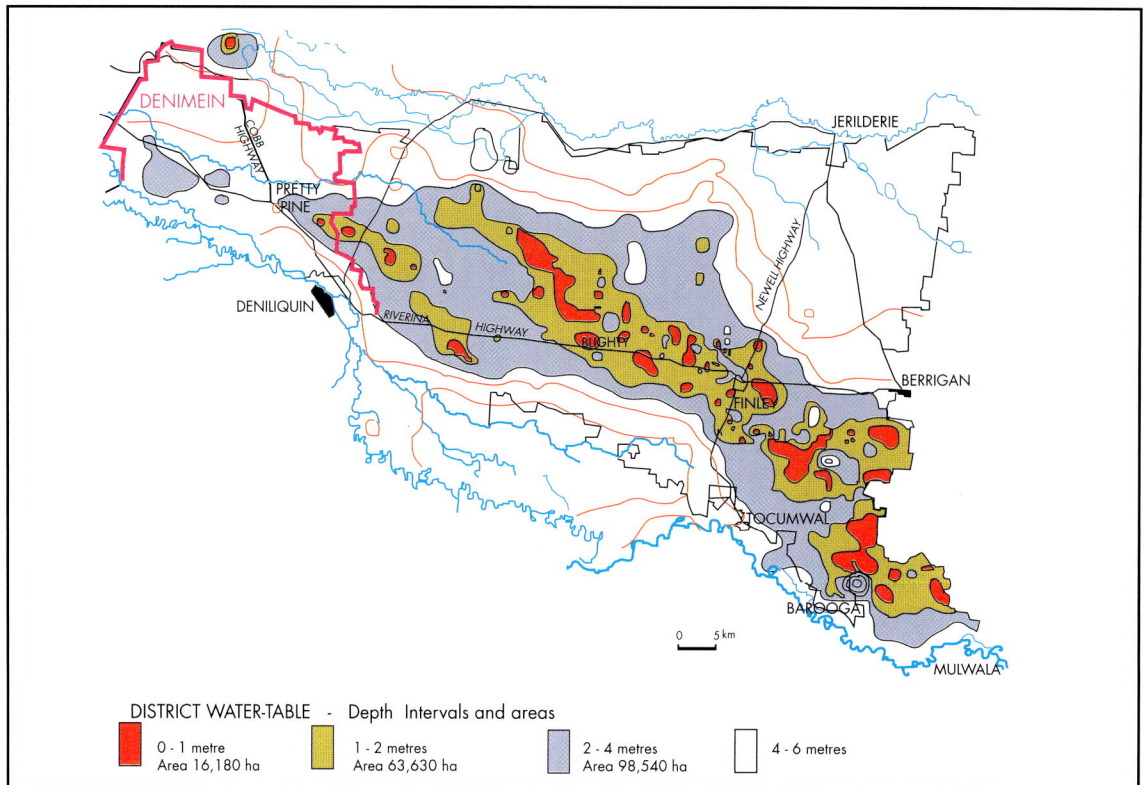

DISTRICT WATER-TABLE - Depth Intervals and areas

■ 0 - 1 metre Area 16,180 ha	■ 1 - 2 metres Area 63,630 ha	■ 2 - 4 metres Area 98,540 ha	□ 4 - 6 metres

After van der Lely [102]

completed in the mid 1970s to supplement the Hume Dam.

Rice growing began as a 'war effort' in 1942–1945, and 2000 ha were grown in the Wakool District, where the area expanded after the Second World War. It spread to Deniboota and Denimein in 1955 and to the Berriquin District in 1968. By 1971, 14 000 ha were under rice in the Murray Region; by the 1980s the area had tripled.

The intensity of rice growing has generally been much lower in the Murray Region than it is in the Murrumbidgee Region, due to the much lower availability of water. In 1988 only 5%–7% of the landscape was involved. Today, however, some farms in the Berriquin district have 30% of their land under rice. The light, porous soils which characterise this district are of the type which is least suited to rice, so the district's contribution to water-table rise is considerable.

An example of how the water-table has been rising is supplied by records kept on a farm near Deniliquin, where fine-wool merinos and growing a small amount of irrigated wheat are the main land uses. When the farm, **Bultarra**, was purchased in 1932, bores had to be sunk tens of metres to tap the mildly brackish groundwater. About 40 years later the water-table had risen so much that three exceptionally wet La Nina years in the early 1970s caused permanent wetlands in low-lying parts of the property. (See graph on page 38 which shows that this interval was one where Murray Valley encephalitis was prevalent because of the extra water lying about.) Some of the water was saltier than seawater and the few remaining old gum trees on the property started to die. Deep drains and big pumps sucked out more than half a million litres of water a day, every day for the next 20 years, getting it off the property and heading towards the river systems, across adjoining private and public land, until regulations on disposal of salty water and concern for the environment prompted the installation of an evaporation pond.

A program of tree planting and saltbush establishment was commenced in order to lower the water-table and to reclaim the badly salted and unproductive parts of the land. In the last five years, 13 000 trees and an amazing 800 000 saltbushes have been planted. The water-table has already dropped by an average of a metre, the 5000 sheep have had fodder throughout the latest drought and the productivity of the farm has gone up by 40%. Native grasses and shrubs have started to reappear between the saltbush rows. The cost of all this to the owner, Robert Meares, has been $160 000, which he says is equivalent to the price of a new tractor. The saltbush should still be thriving in 50 years' time, and maybe far longer, as saltbush is known to have reached 200 years old in the chenopod shrublands of South Australia.

A success story like this, in which adversity has been turned to positive advantage, must be an inspiration to many other landowners.

Not all of the irrigation area is visibly affected by the rising water-table and salinisation at present. The **Denimein Irrigation District**, which extends approximately 40 km in a north-westerly direction from the town of Deliniquin, has less than 1000 ha damaged as yet and the water-table is only rising at 8 cm a year. The district is bounded by the Edward River to the south and extends to the Billabong Creek system in the north, with Box Creek running through the middle. Its irrigation water comes via the Mulwala Canal from the Yarrawonga Weir. There are 234 km of supply channels in Denimein. (The Edward River is the abandoned northern course of the River Murray.) The Community Land and Water Management Plan for Denimein aims at introducing land management practices which will prevent steady rise of the water-table (which would affect 17% of the district by 2020 at

The Wakool Evaporation Basin, where salt water is stored — a practice which itself raises the water-table and adds salt to rivers and streams.

MARTIN DRIVER

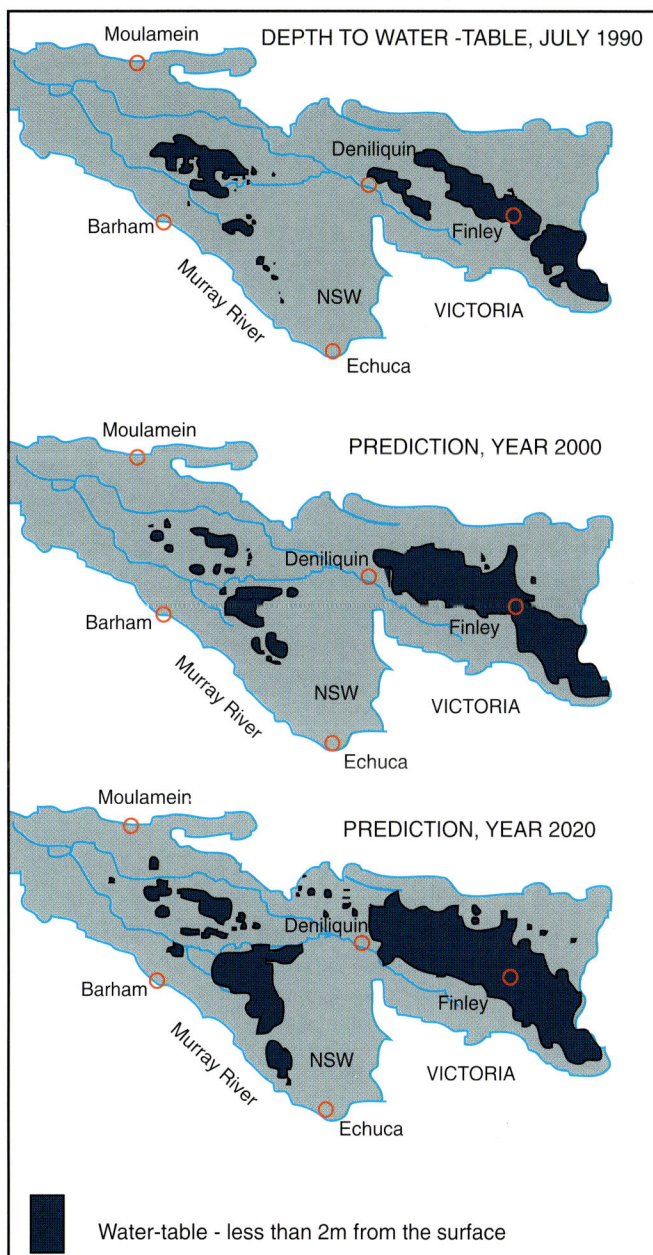

PREDICTIONS OF DEPTH OF WATER-TABLE IN THE MURRAY IRRIGATION AREA IN 1990, 2000 AND 2020

Water-table - less than 2m from the surface

After Beale [103]

(Murray Irrigation Ltd has given permission for the use of this diagram provided it is emphasised that it is 'indicative, not positive'.)

Planting saltbush at Barrabool Station.

MARTIN DRIVER

the present rate). The fact that the groundwater in Denimein is very salty makes prevention measures essential.

Throughout geological time the ancestral Murray (and the other ancestral rivers of the Riverine Plain) changed their courses.[97] In the case of the Edward River, it became an anabranch of the Murray in geologically very recent times, only about 8000 years ago, as the final chapter in changes to the Murray's course, which started with a tectonic event which occurred 25 000 years ago. A major fault, the **Cadell Fault**, runs between Echuca and Deniliquin. Movement on this fault resulted in the uplift and tilting of a block of land. The block was tilted to the west and its eastern edge was raised by between 8 and 12 m. The Murray used to flow across the top of the faulted block to join the Goulburn River north of Echuca. The abandoned river is still visible at the top of the block as **Green Gully**. The Goulburn formed Lake Kanyapella at the southern end of the fault block when the tilt occurred. Between 25 000 and 13 000 years ago this lake drained and the Goulburn River cut a new course across its dry bed. Meanwhile a fan of small streams formed in the low-lying area east of the fault block. This area has become the Barmah–Millewa redgum forest.

The Edward River, Gulpa Creek and the maze of small anabranches to the east of the Cadell Fault can divert over half of the Murray's flow into New South Wales during floods. The Edward runs hundreds of kilometres westward to join the Wakool River and to rejoin the Murray at the edge of the Mallee.

The ancient prior streams (much older than the course changes of the last 25 000 years) which underlie the modern landscape are important underground drainages. Mapping their distribution is an important prerequisite for dealing with local problems of drainage and land management, just as the recognition of the aeolian (wind-blown dune) systems which are features of the landscape is essential if land-use practices are to be matched to the capacity of the soil type to carry them sustainably.

The formation of **Lake Mulwala**, resulting from the construction of the Yarrawonga Weir on the Murray, and permanent flooding of part of the floodplain, drowned the grey box forest. The trunks of the dead trees in this vast expanse of water make a starkly beautiful picture. The **Mulwala Canal**, which takes the water from the Murray into the New South Wales Murray Region Irrigation District, is gravity fed. Its channel had to be constructed along the high parts of the landscape, following ridges. Because of the geological history of the region during the intensely dry and windy glacial stages of the Pleistocene, the ridges are mainly of aeolian sediments, permeable and not the best water-holders. The canal leaks and is a considerable contributor to the problem of rising water-tables even before its water is distributed for irrigation. It is said that when it was being constructed so much water disappeared down the wombat holes which were abundant in the soil of the ridge (and absent in the surrounding country where soil was less suitable for burrowing) that dynamite was used to destroy the warrens. Local extinction of the hairy-nosed wombats was hastened by this process.

Landcare groups have been active in planting trees along the sides of the canal to combat the rising water-table which is being compounded by its leaking. Recently the 'Angry Anderson Challenge' and Corridors of Green program led to a coordinated effort and planting of almost a quarter of a million trees.

Because the canal often runs through farmland where irrigation is limited to one side of the canal and dryland farming is carried out on the other, it is possible to see clearly that **irrigation leads to waterlogging and salinity problems while the dryland farming does not**. In many places, the actual construction of the canal has interfered with natural drainage, however, and created the same sort of problem areas. Laser levelling is increasingly used to keep areas prone to waterlogging in production, and, combined with draining this manages to achieve a temporary respite. The underlying problem remains.

In March 1995, the New South Wales government privatised management of the Murray Irrigation Area and Districts. **Murray Irrigation Limited**, based in Deniliquin, took over, becoming the largest privately owned irrigation supply and drainage company in Australia. Each irrigator is a shareholder in the company. Of the ten elected company directors, eight are irrigator member directors and two are directors with special skills in engineering and finance.

In April 1996, the NSW Minister for Land and Water Conservation launched the $498 million Land and Water Management plans for the Murray Irrigation Region (Community Land and Water Management Plans for: **Cadell**, including Deniboota; **Berriquin; Denimein; Wakool**) They are the first such plans to be put in place in New South Wales and the Murray Region leads in trying to implement environmentally responsible food production and 'sustainable' agriculture. **Implementation of the plans over the next 30 years** is confidently expected to improve conditions for agriculture. Farming communities will

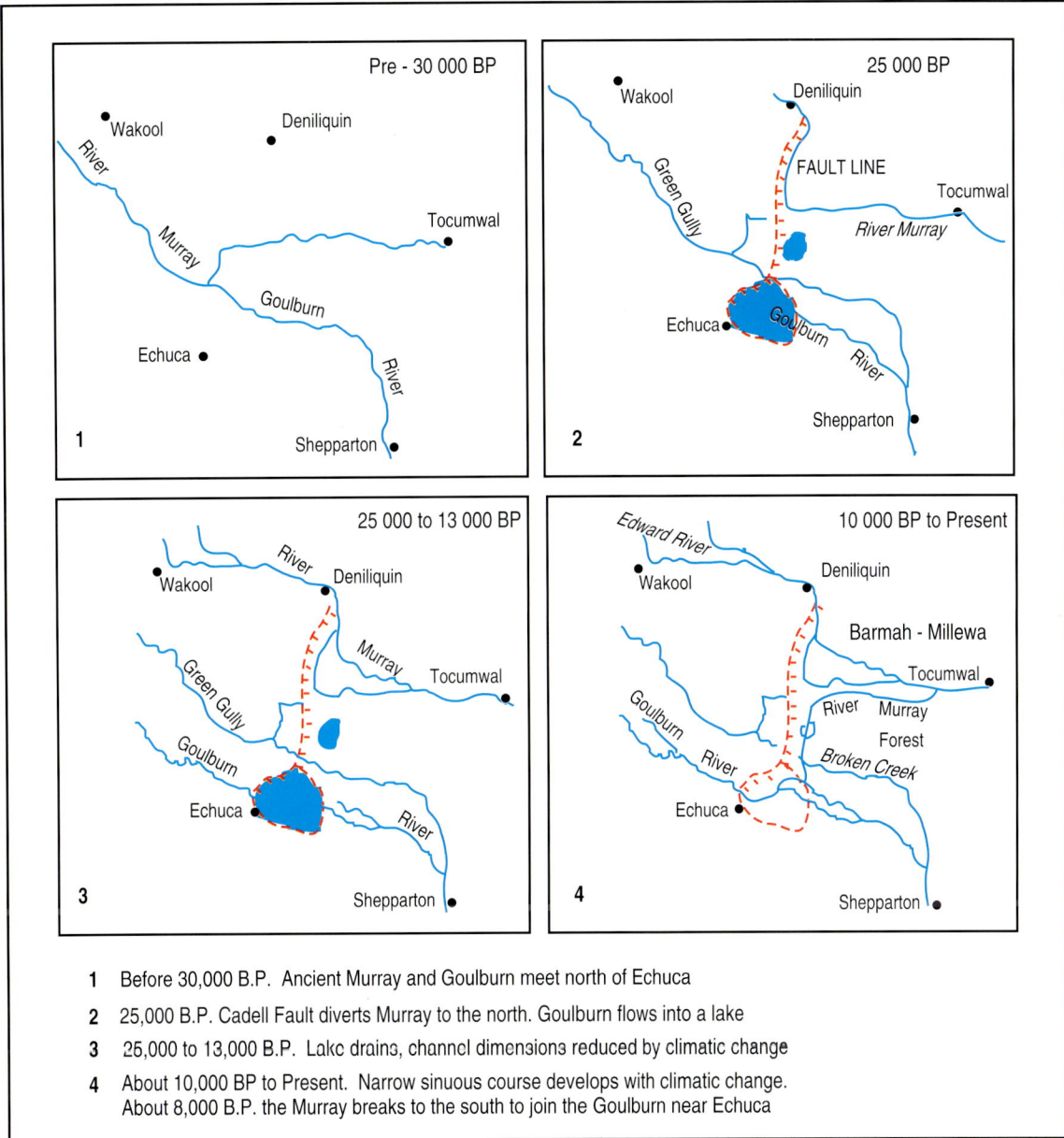

Map 1 (Pre - 30 000 BP): Wakool, Deniliquin, River Murray, Goulburn, Tocumwal, Echuca, River, Shepparton

Map 2 (25 000 BP): Wakool, Deniliquin, Green Gully, FAULT LINE, Tocumwal, River Murray, Echuca, Goulburn River, Shepparton

Map 3 (25 000 to 13 000 BP): Wakool, River, Deniliquin, Murray, Tocumwal, Green Gully, Goulburn, Echuca, River, Shepparton

Map 4 (10 000 BP to Present): Edward River, Wakool, Deniliquin, Barmah - Millewa, Tocumwal, River Murray, Goulburn, River, Forest, Broken Creek, Echuca, Shepparton

1 Before 30,000 B.P. Ancient Murray and Goulburn meet north of Echuca

2 25,000 B.P. Cadell Fault diverts Murray to the north. Goulburn flows into a lake

3 25,000 to 13,000 B.P. Lake drains, channel dimensions reduced by climatic change

4 About 10,000 BP to Present. Narrow sinuous course develops with climatic change.
   About 8,000 B.P. the Murray breaks to the south to join the Goulburn near Echuca

After Bowler [105]

Poor drainage and the rising water-table have killed the forest at Green Gully. (This gully used to be the bed of the Murray when it ran here on its way to join the Goulburn River before movement on the Cadell Fault raised a ridge and blocked the Murray's course, diverting it into its modern channel.)

BOB BEALE, SYDNEY MORNING HERALD [106]

contribute more than 70% of the cost of each plan by direct capital investment in farm works and a direct increase in water prices; the Commonwealth and State governments are expected to contribute 10%–15% each.

WHAT THE RIVERINE PLAIN WAS LIKE LAST CENTURY

The history of settlement of the region to the north of Deniliquin and its conversion to what today is seen as a treeless plain explains its present-day problems. Martin Driver, Regional Manager of Greening Australia in the South West Plains, has supplied information, including a copy of an article by 'Bruni' in The Australasian of 21 August 1886 and an article from the Pastoral Review of 1931 which show the evolution of properties in the region.

In the 1986 publication is a detailed account of the wildlife — roos, emus, dingoes being 'gradually destroyed', brolgas and wild turkeys, ducks in season and

... crested pigeons making a permanent home in the fine belts of woodland on this estate ... The flock of sheep reared on the pastures of Willurah are as profitable as any in the Riverina ... The wool is of excellent character and good quality ... The estate consists of a little over 100,000 acres, which is well subdivided and every paddock has a permanent water supply. In ordinary seasons about 70,000 sheep are shorn on this estate.

On a journey from the property to Deniliquin the writer describes the sandhill vegetation, which is of particular interest because the area described is the place where a fence today is superimposed on previous fences buried by wind-blown soil and sand. Bob Beale used a picture of the fence to illustrate his article in the *Sydney Morning Herald*[106] and has kindly supplied the photograph for use in this account.

A sad contrast exists between today's landscape and the description in 1886: '*At the Billabong we crossed some very pretty country. The sandhills here rise into mounds of considerable size, and among them are some very handsome trees. Pines, gums and willows attain a large size, and many of them are very handsome. Here I saw some honeysuckle trees which seemed strangely out of place in the Riverina*'.

(The trees referred to are: pines, *Callitris glaucophylla*; gums, *Eucalyptus camaldulensis*; willows, *Acacia salicina*; honeysuckle, *Banksia marginata*. The honeysuckle (Banksia) mentioned was also mentioned by Sturt in his journals but until recently was represented by one remaining plant, which has since been destroyed by fire. Fortunately seed had been collected from it and the genotype is now represented in the field again and in the Greening Australia seedbank.)

The article from the *Pastoral Review* of 16 November 1931 is reproduced in its original form, because it records changes induced by pastoral expansion, and the picture which it painted applied to

Above top: Waterlogging and salinity adjacent to the Mulwala Canal. Corridors of Green and the Angry Anderson Challenge planted 250 000 trees along the edge of the canal to lower the watertable in 1995.

Above middle: Laser levelling and draining of fields adjacent to the Mulwala Canal help with the problems of waterlogging and salinity, restoring productivity but not changing the underlying problems.

Above: The Mulwala Canal, dry in winter.

M.E.W

vast areas of today's 'breadbasket' — the most essential food-producing southern half of the Murray–Darling Basin.

NOTES ON THE EVOLUTION OF A RIVERINA PROPERTY

Changes in the Natural Flora

The Advent of the Rabbit and the Blowfly

Some interesting historical notes compiled by Mr R.G. Kiddle regarding changes in the pastures and other features of the country on Steam Plains, situated in the Riverina some 42 miles [68 km] from Deniliquin and 38 [61 km] from Jerilderie, having come under our notice, we have permission from Mr Kiddle to summarise and publish them.

Steam Plains is a oblong block about 15 miles [24 km] long by five miles [8 km] wide, and consisted of open plain lands intersected by pine ridges and belts of timber, a wide, very shallow creek and various shallow lignum swamps, which in very wet seasons fill and overflow and form other shallow creeks. The pine ridges, or sandhills as they were called, were covered with a forest of murray pines of all ages from seedlings to mature trees, interspersed with various kinds of acacias and similar trees, such as needlewood, wild irishman, hopbush, deadly nightshade, sandalwood and willows (cuba), and below these were numerous kinds of smaller blue and salt bushes. In this condition the sandhills were not good feeding grounds for sheep, as the grass was not as sweet nor as plentiful as in the open country. Also they were a great harbour for noxious animals, dogs and marsupials etc.

On the edges of the pine ridges, and extending out on to the plains, in some cases perhaps only two or three hundred yards [185–275 m], and in others two or three miles

[3–5 km], were timbered areas generally of a hard red soil, carrying grasses which were very sweet and quick growing after a dry period, and timbered with large quantities of edible trees, mostly boree (myall), cuba (willow), quandong and wilga etc. Beyond these timbered areas, and sometimes amongst them were swamps timbered with box (eucalyptus) and gum trees, and the balance of the country was open plain interspersed with swamps and depressions, the biggest of which grow large

Above: Steam Plains in 1994 — a man-made desert, in sad contrast to the landscape described in the historical account of this property.

Above right:Remnant vegetation on Steam Plains in a fenced area which was not degraded.

MARTIN DRIVER

quantities of lignum, growing in many cases 10 ft. high [3 m]. Such lignum swamps produced very little useful fodder. The wide shallow creek, generally dry, crossing the property was also heavily timbered with box, and it and similar box swamps produced very little grass. Towards the southern edge of the run there occurred one large and two small swamps filled with a heavy growth of cane grass.

The open plain country, which when dry is either crumbly red or grey clay, and the open boree hard red country, were generally bush country with annual and perennial grasses growing around and between the bushes. These bushes consisted mainly of Old Man saltbush, and considerable areas of blue bush and smaller saltbushes and cottonbush. At this time, taking a line from Narandera to Corowa, which would run along about 70 miles [112 km] east of Steam Plains, the

country all to the east was forest country. Today, so much timber has been killed that, generally speaking, that forest line is now one hundred miles [160 km] further to the east.

About 1850 fencing was started in the district and Steam Plains was fenced about then. This enabled more stock to be carried, but as a result the bush was more severely eaten during dry periods, and the less there was the more it was punished, so that by 1874 the bulk of the saltbush had been eaten out and killed and only certain areas of the cottonbush remained. The exception to this is that about 400 acres [162 ha] close to the homestead was preserved and still retains its original cover of Old Man saltbush, bluebush etc. However, large numbers of sheep were successfully carried, for though the bush was gone the country was not eaten out, and responded to rains quickly; also thousands of edible trees were continually dropping edible leaves and branches. Large sums of money were spent in killing the box trees in the creek and swamps, and the sandhills were cleared of much of the useless scrub (needlewood, hopwood, wild irishman) and the pine trees were pollarded to a height of 8 ft [2.4 m]. These operations meant a largely increased growth of grass in the timbered areas. Further, the water supplies were improved and the lignum was cut and killed in the swamps. This period of improvement lasted approximately till 1897.

Rabbits were first known on Steam Plains in 1880, and in the year 1882, 29 scalps were paid for at 2s.6d. each; in the same year 884 kangaroos and 136 emus were paid for at 1s. each. In 1890 the property was rabbit netted on the boundaries, and continual but ineffective methods of destroying the pest were adopted, and the whole district became very badly infested, it being nothing unusual to poison from ten to twelve thousand at one waterhole. The result was that during any dry period both the rabbits and the sheep were underfed and the country was being eaten out. It was not fully realised what damage the rabbits were doing, but many of the edible trees were ringbarked and killed, and practically all bush and perennial grasses were killed.

In 1897 the autumn was very dry, and over 13,000 lambing ewes were fairly successfully fed on branches of boree and cuba trees until June when the season broke. The years

GROUNDWATER SALINITY, DENIMEIN

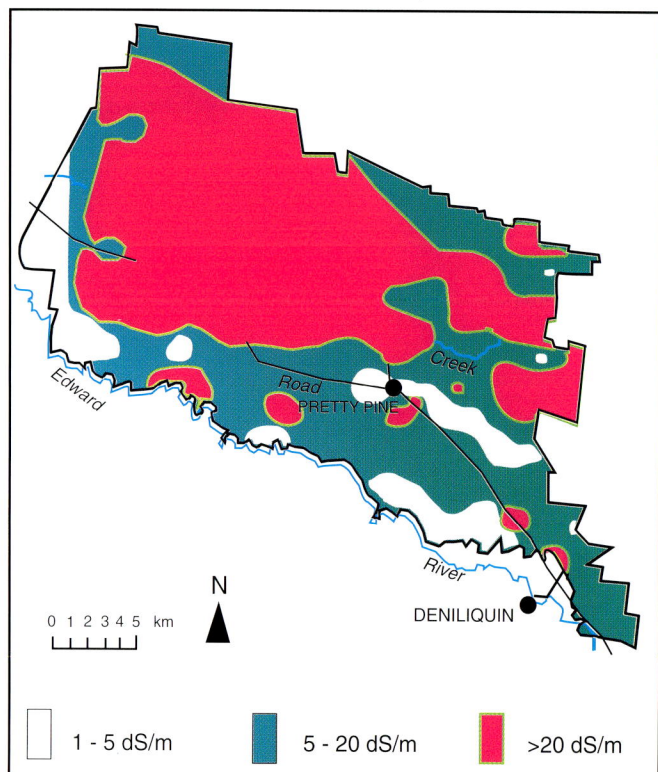

N

0 1 2 3 4 5 km

Edward
Road
Creek
PRETTY PINE
River
DENILIQUIN

| | 1 - 5 dS/m | | 5 - 20 dS/m | | >20 dS/m |

After Jones [104]

1898 and 1899 were dry, and the country became very bare and started to drift. During 1900 to 1901 the rabbit burrows were all dug out and all the rabbits destroyed, since then there have been practically none on the property. Unfortunately, before the country could recover in 1902–1903 drought started, and during that summer **the whole country was in effect a moving sand drift**, with most netted fences and yards covered with sand. Blinding sandstorms occurred frequently, and many of the excavated dams were practically filled with drift.

As mentioned previously, in 1897 13,000 sheep were satisfactorily fed on the leaves and branches of boree and cuba trees. In places these trees were so thick that in mustering sheep it was not possible to see more than 300 yards, but generally the boree country was more open than that. About this time it was first definitely noticed that the tent caterpillar (very hairy and living in woven bags during the day time) was attacking the boree trees and killing them by eating the leaves. The caterpillar has continued its destruction, and 90 per cent of the boree trees are now dead. A bush fire swept the property in 1918, burning many of the dead borees, and today it is practically clear country, where once it was possible to see only 300 yards [275 m]. Though there is an abundance of young boree trees growing, which would soon reforest the country if protected from sheep, such precautions would only result in fostering them for the benefit of the caterpillar.

Today the sandhills are clear of all useless scrub and the pines have been considerably thinned out, and the two principal sandhills have been fenced in paddocks by themselves. The result is that during the growing season they produce a heavy crop of herbage, mostly crowfoot and barley and corkscrew grasses, which can then be eaten, and the more suitable country reserved to a limited extent for summer use. The trees in the box swamp and the creek have nearly all been killed, and most of the dead timber has disappeared. This part is now the heaviest carrying country on the property, the growth generally being a mixture of trefoil and barley grass. The boree country is now mostly very open and forms the main area of the perennial grasses, such as whitetop and corkscrew, together with local herbage. The lignum swamps carry a good solo of herbages — mostly trefoil, barley, blue, and small crowfoot.

The open plains, where it has been possible to treat them generously, are now well covered with cottonbush to an extent of about 12,000 acres [4856 ha], and are growing the usual herbage and grasses, while in several areas large quantities of wild oats grow in good seasons to a height of 3 ft. [1 m] and to an extent of several hundreds of acres. The cane grass swamps have been burnt at times and are now producing more feed than in the past.

Where the sand drifts of 1902 covered the fences and other obstructions these drifts now grow similar grasses to the sandhills. This is the case, even to a large extent, where the drifts are held on fences crossing grey clay plains. About 1900, blowflies first became really troublesome and the position worse and worse...

(Plants mentioned, apart from the pines, gums, willows and honeysuckle already identified above are: needlewood, *Hakea leucoptera*; wild irishman *Bursaria spinosa*; hop bush, *Dodonaea viscosa*; deadly nightshade — possibly *Santalum* sp. according to Martin Driver; sandalwood, *Santalum lanceolatum*; cuba (cooba, native willow) *Acacia salicina*; blue bush, *Maireana sedifolia* & *pyramidata*; boree, *Acacia pendula*; quandong, *Santalum acuminatum*; wilga, *Geijera parviflora*; box, *Eucalyptus largiflorens*; gum, *Eucalyptus camaldulensis*; lignum, *Muehlenbeckia florulenta*; old man saltbush, *Atriplex nummularia*; cotton bush, *Maireana aphylla*.)

An account like this highlights attitudes to native animals (noxious, all to be killed), native vegetation (useless scrub); killing trees to make more grass; keeping animals on in drought by feeding them edible acacia trees; opening up more grazing when used parts are no longer productive. The droughts, drifting sand, dust storms, over-grazed pastures, rabbit and caterpillar plagues, degradation (and even the forgiving nature of the land where sand-drifts are recolonised and plants return to over-grazed pastures after rain, for a time at least) are all here. This account emphasises again that **the land inherited by today's farmers and their**

Above left: Callitris woodland (Callitris glaucophylla) and good grass understorey, on Barrabool Station, adjacent to Steam Plains.

Above right: Boree (Acacia pendula) and perennial grasses in a paddock on Barrabool Station which was destocked in 1918 and has regenerated to become like the original productive country which supported so many sheep in the 1800s.

MARTIN DRIVER

GREENING AUSTRALIA: ITS ACTIVITIES IN THE DENILIQUIN REGION

Greening Australia is involved in many issues and its activities in the Deniliquin region are an example of what it is achieving all over Australia.

Vegetation management or establishment, related land management and property planning and support all come within its ambit. Its current projects include:

- Managing remnants of native vegetation. In this connection its most significant contribution has been the initiation and ongoing management of incentives of $1200 per kilometre of fencing to private landholders who want to fence off remnant and regenerating vegetation on their properties. Without this sort of support, the required level of vegetation management cannot be achieved. It is only fair that all Australians should contribute (financially) in this way to maintaining biodiversity and sustainability of the ecosystem on which we all depend for survival. Greening Australia's role in making urban citizens realise that they, as well as the people on the land, have such a responsibility is one of its important functions. The Murray Catchment Management Committee has endorsed this **fencing incentive program** through Greening Australia as its highest priority Action Plan to address ongoing vegetation decline. Martin Driver, Regional Manager for Greening

Australia, hopes to see the program extended State-wide.
- Re-establishing and enriching native vegetation.
- Operating a local native seed bank.
- Running direct seeding programs.
- Managing saltbush and grasslands.
- Dealing with all vegetation-related enquiries and extension programs.
- Running workshops, field days; publications and media publicity. A recent seminar organised by Greening Australia and attended by directors of major food companies including Woolworths, Kellogs, Ridley Corporation and Clean Foods Marketing Australia, and the National Food Authority Executive Officer, highlights this important educational role. A number of important and basic points were raised and publicised:

    1. Caution is needed in promoting Australian products as 'clean, green and environmentally friendly.' Consumers were becoming increasingly concerned about chemical contamination of their food and there was growing concern about the environmental effects of intensive food production.

    2. Sooner or later the corporate world, and all of us (the consumers) will have to pay the full cost of production, which includes the cost of land degradation. Higher product prices are inevitable because the environmental factor has not been covered so far. Incentives will have to be paid for best management practices (sustainability).

    3. The corporate world, by sponsoring Landcare and environmental programs, has an opportunity for valuable public relations and advertising, and at the same time the final cost will be less because the longer the degradation goes on **the more expensive it becomes to fix**.

- Promoting and coordinating commercial farm forestry.
- Sponsorship programs. One such project, **Flightpaths of Green**, is an example of the role being increasingly played by commercial enterprises in conservation. **Cathay Pacific** has generously donated $750 000 towards projects aimed at saving the endangered Superb and Regent Parrots. These are the Green Gully Landcare Group's fencing program to protect woodland habitats of the Superb Parrot, and the planting of 200 000 native trees and shrubs by the Group; and the Superb Parrot Action Faction in Victoria in which the Barmah redgum forests are being extended by the planting of trees by 20 landholders.

---

fathers before them was already degraded almost beyond recognition, and management since has often been a struggle to restore productivity.

The bringing of irrigation to the dry, relatively barren and unproductive landscapes which the Riverine Plain had become, which was made possible after the completion of the Hume Dam in 1935, ushered in the modern era of massive production whose consequences are now evident. Today's generation of farmers may be responsible for the degradation which is now present and threatened, but where it involves irrigation they are as innocent of intent to harm the environment as the early settlers were. The world-wide Green Revolution after the Second World War, riding a wave of optimism offered by irrigation, fertilisers, better crop varieties and economic growth, believed in a future in which the increasing hordes of an overpopulated world would be fed and living standards would rise everywhere. Whether, in the fullness of present day knowledge of the situation and the prognosis, carrying on with practices which are manifestly unsustainable is still blameless behaviour is debatable.

*Right: An area in the Gulpa Creek forest, fenced by the Southern Riverina Field Naturalists, in which Murray pine (*Callitris preissii*) is regenerating.*

M.E.W.

THE MURRUMBIDGEE IRRIGATION AREA

The Murrumbidgee Irrigation Area lies in the centre of the **Murrumbidgee River Catchment**, which covers 84 000 km² and is one of New South Wales' most productive agricultural regions. The whole catchment is experiencing serious desertification.

In the **Upper Catchment**, escalating erosion of land in its headwaters, algal blooms in the river and tributaries, rising water-tables, increasing salt and nutriment in waterways, urban salinity in Yass, salinised land and dying trees are examples of the widespread effects of unsustainable agricultural practices. Downstream, in the **Middle Catchment**, the similar local problems are compounded by those of the Upper Catchment and water-tables have risen by 10 m in the 70 years of recording. Urban salinity in Wagga Wagga (see Chapter 5), which can no longer be ignored, is bringing the subjects of rising water-tables and salinity right 'home' to its population. (It is said that the reason why Griffith, in the centre of an area with very high water-tables, is not afflicted in the same way as Wagga is because its old sewerage system with leaking pipes is serving as a drainage system, carrying water-table water away with the sewage effluent. Apparently the amount of water carried in the sewerage system is far more than the amount which officially goes into it. So where Wagga needs to repair its sewers to lower water-tables under the urban area, Griffith will have escalating urban salinity problems if it mends its sewers!)

The **irrigation areas** downstream of the Middle Catchment inherit its salt and rising water-tables, and the increasing nutrients and silt in waterways, and then add their local contribution. In its turn, the Lower Murrumbidgee has to deal with the compounded problems from all the catchment upstream. Even the Billabong Creek portion of the catchment, a sub-catchment south of the Murrumbidgee, suffers raised water-tables and permanent waterlogging of many of its wetlands.

The **rivers** on which irrigation depends have to contend with altered flow regimes, semi-permanent drought, increased sediment and pollutants, and damage to their ecology and that of their wetlands.

The Murrumbidgee and Coleambally Irrigation Areas (the MIA and the CIA) receive their water from the Murrumbidgee River via large canals which feed into a network of smaller canals (mostly under gravity flow) to deliver the water to farm boundaries. Apart from the main irrigated crop, rice, the region produces large quantities of wheat, maize, soybeans, citrus fruits, grapes, stone fruits, and vegetables. Irrigated pasture produces prime lambs and beef cattle. Some rice farmers produce one crop per year in a paddock (rice, which is a summer crop, followed by fallow), while others make use of the stored water in the soil after the rice is harvested and plant a second crop, like winter wheat.

With the diverse cropping, very large amounts of pesticides, herbicides and fertilisers are used, and because of irrigation, high water-tables and the associated drainage, there are major problems of water contamination as well as build-up of contaminants in soils.

The contaminated drainage water has the potential to have consequences downstream of the irrigation areas, as run-off; via the streams, particularly **Mirrool Creek**, a natural waterway through the region; in the terminal wetland, **Barren Box Swamp**, into which

THE MURRUMBIDGEE CATCHMENT

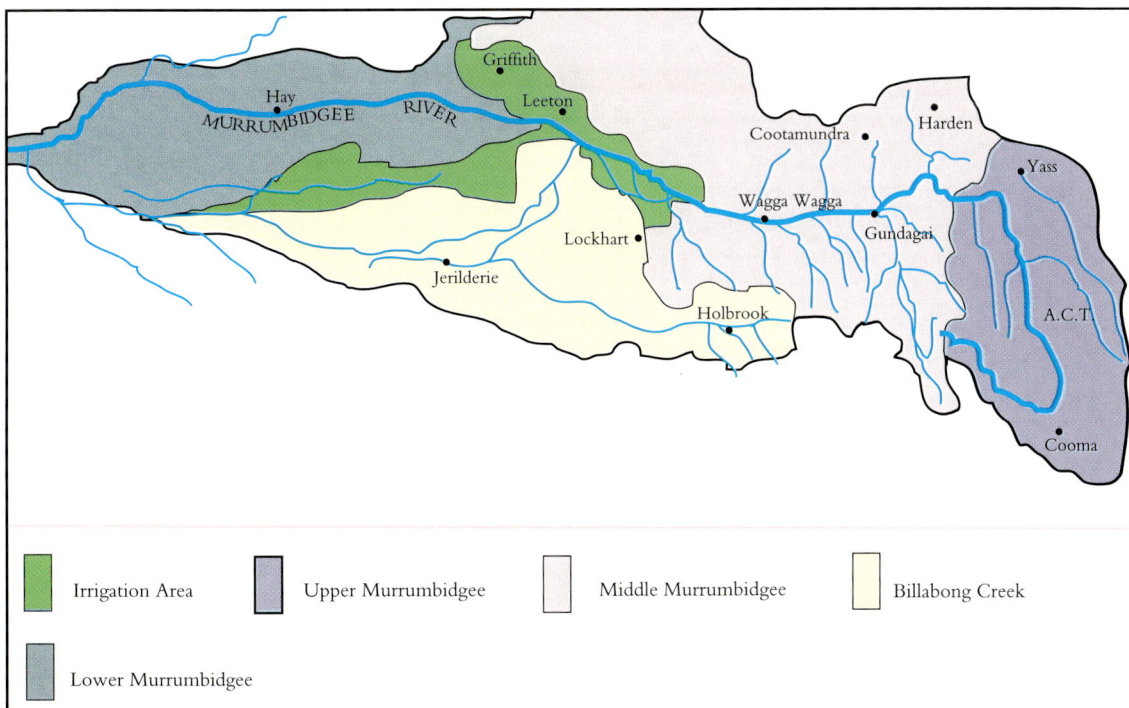

Legend:
- Irrigation Area
- Upper Murrumbidgee
- Middle Murrumbidgee
- Billabong Creek
- Lower Murrumbidgee

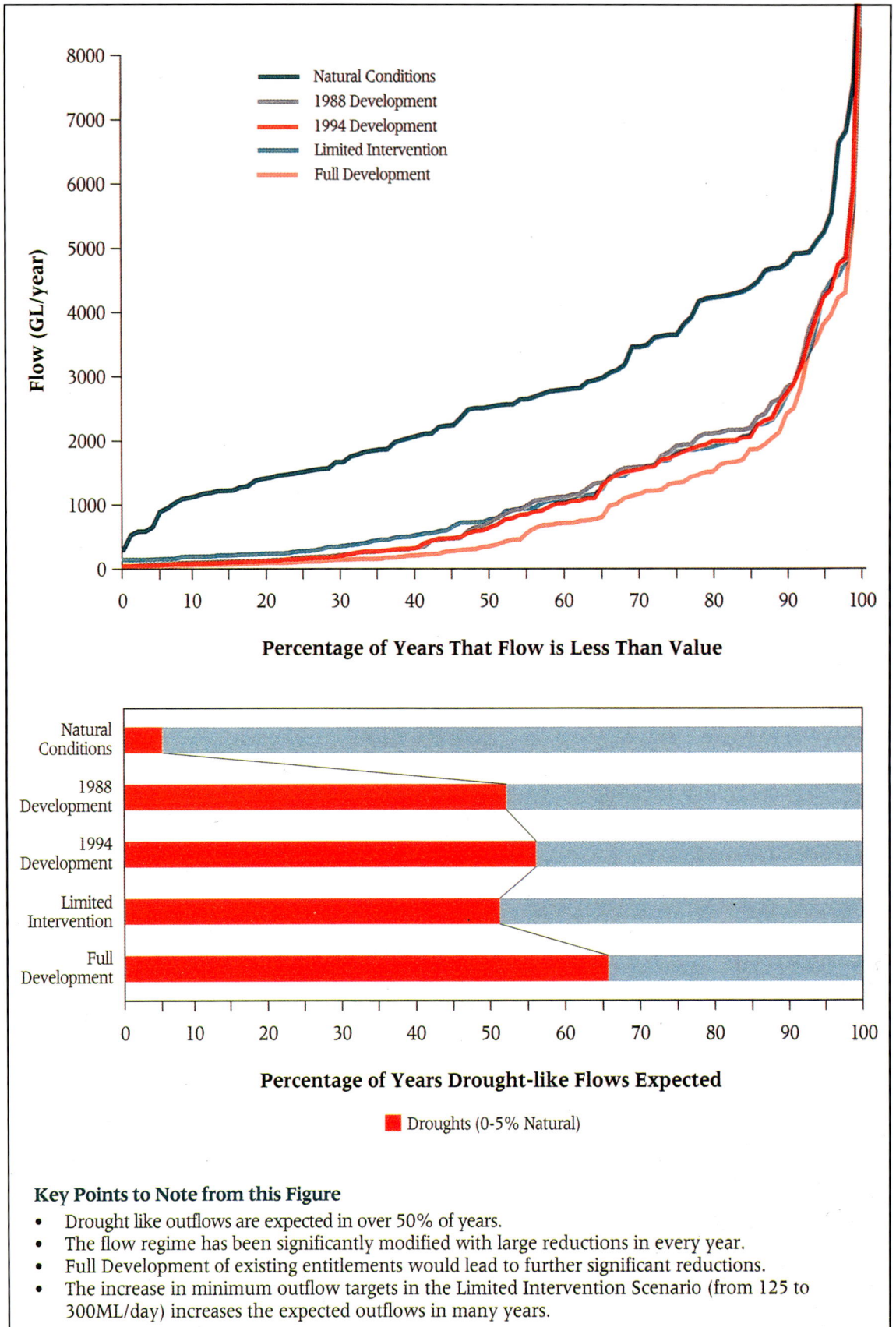

Key Points to Note from this Figure

- Drought like outflows are expected in over 50% of years.
- The flow regime has been significantly modified with large reductions in every year.
- Full Development of existing entitlements would lead to further significant reductions.
- The increase in minimum outflow targets in the Limited Intervention Scenario (from 125 to 300ML/day) increases the expected outflows in many years.

(From Audit of Water Use in the Murray-Darling Basin, [91] *with kind permission of the MDBC Ministerial Council)*

Above The Main Drain in Griffith.

Left: Furrow irrigation with siphon pipes.

M.E.W.

the complex drainage network drains; and even in the major rivers (Murrumbidgee, Murray, Lachlan) to which floodwaters can carry contaminated drainage water during extreme climatic events. Some drainage water is recycled and mixed with Murrumbidgee River water and is supplied to the Wah Wah and Benerembah Irrigation Districts (in the Lower Catchment) for stock and domestic purposes. By the time water reaches the Lower Catchment it has the potential to be salty and contaminated by chemicals and nutrients.

Waterlogging problems were already present in the Yanco irrigation area in the 1940s. Where high water-tables developed, salt started to appear towards the bottom of slopes, in low-lying areas, on channel edges and in areas underlain by surcharged shallow aquifers. Classification of land into types suitable and unsuitable for rice resulted, and the land types excluded were: sandhill formations; land with soils and drainage which made them suitable for horticulture; land underlain by shallow aquifers and prior streams; and most soils in the mallee landscape. In the 1960s it was decided that soil type was the more reliable classification, and certain soil types would be excluded because their infiltration rates were too great. The only soils to be used were the heavy clay floodplain soils, including red-brown earths and grey and brown clays. Compulsory soil profile examination was introduced for all new rice lands in the 1970s, and for any current rice lands suspected of having too much deep percolation.[98]

In 1980 an expert committee examined problems of rising water-tables and salinity, highlighting the rapidly rising water-tables in irrigated areas and the imminent threat of large areas of salinisation. In 1984 a working group, comprising representatives of the departments of Water Resources and Agriculture and the rice industry, instituted a program to phase out rice growing on unsuitable land. Rice growing would be restricted to paddocks where rice water use was less than 16 ML/ha per season. This was based on the premise that up to 12 ML/ha is evaporated and the total drainage (surface and deep percolation) should not exceed 4 ML/ha. (In the CIA about 30% of irrigated land is unsuitable for rice under this ruling.)

It has been realised that water use must be

Right: Electro-fishing for carp (the 'rabbits of the rivers') in Mirrool Creek near Griffith. A generator in the rear boat generates a current which is fed into the long-handled net which is used by an operator in the leading boat. When the net is plunged into the water, carp are zapped and shoot up to the surface, to be collected in the net. The operators are licenced and have to avoid areas where native fish are present. The fish are transported to Sydney Fish Markets overnight and there is a demand for carp, particularly among Asian Australians.

M.E.W.

Above: Barren Box Swamp, a silty-water graveyard of trees, is remembered as a wonderful live swamp with dense reed beds and abundant wildlife, particularly water birds, by local residents. It recently suffered a severe infestation with alligator weed, which was fortunately completely eradicated.

M.E.W.

diminished and that too much recharge results from acceptance of these figures. It has even been suggested, and not in jest, that the cost of water to the irrigator should be based on the amount of water which enters the drains after use, instead of the amount of water entering during irrigation. This would provide an incentive for water saving.

In 1985 it was predicted that the water-table would be within 2 m of the surface over 80% of the MIA-Benerembah within two decades. By 1991, in six years, not in twenty, 85% had water-tables within 2 m of the soil surface.[102] Salinity problems increased in some districts. In the Benerembah Irrigation District, salinisation increased from 2% of affected land in 1985, to 50% in 1988, with 20% seriously affected. Construction of surface drains began in 1990 in Benerembah.

The fertile landscapes, the new vineyards spreading

out around Griffith, neat citrus orchards like a child's drawing of round green trees covered with round orange fruit, give little visual evidence to anyone driving through (as I did in winter) that an environmental crisis exists in the region. Closer examination notes the white salt along road verges, where water pressure when the paddies were flooded forced salt to the surface. Treeless landscapes, a few dead skeletons, all so modified by agricultural activity and presenting the reassuring pastoral stereotype of a patchwork of fertile fields. It comes as a shock to read the scientific reports leading to the formulation of the Land and Water Management Plans for the district. That the overall situation is understood in depth, though much more information is needed about many of the problems, is the result of the efforts of various government agencies over the many years since irrigation began and problems began to manifest themselves.

In the case of the MIA and the CIA, the scientific groundwork needed to deal with the day-to-day problems faced by farmers, and the expertise needed to formulate plans which give temporary 'sustainability' to irrigated farming and other land use practices, has been supplied by locally based institutions and extension services. These in the MIA are representative of such decentralised agencies which form the backbone of the continent-wide professional network which cooperates with landholders, understanding the local problems better than any more 'ivory-tower' bodies in Canberra or in major cities could possibly do. As people living in catchments (and that is all of us!) increasingly take responsibility for *our* **environments and** *our* **problems**, these decentralised centres of scientific and managerial expertise become even more important.

Without liaison between the irrigators and the scientific and other agencies, no cooperative approach to dealing with problems would have been possible. The **Irrigation Research and Extension Committee (IREC)** has fulfilled this role since 1947, coordinating research and extension work in the MIA and CIA to enable the research scientist, the advisory officer and the farmer to work as a team. IREC finds out from farmers what problems they are having; evaluates the problems and recommends solutions; guides research towards solution of problems; sponsors and if necessary supports special research and advisory projects financially; and plans advisory programs to lift sustainable production. An executive committee handles administrative matters and determines policy, while a series of specialist sub-committees, consisting of irrigator representatives and research and advisory personnel, meet regularly to analyse problems and propose solutions.

The current government policies which limit and reduce rather than expand research which is basic to solving environmental problems and which gives hope of some measure of future viability for agriculture, particularly in key areas like the MIA, are self-defeating. Top-heavy bureaucracy, too little revenue going into getting on with the job and fixing the pressing on-ground problems, too much waiting around until every detail has been assessed before implementing measures which will at least prevent further deterioration, all add up to fiddling, not 'while Rome burns' but, for example, while the MIA drowns.

The activities and programs of the **CSIRO Division of Water Resources**, **Griffith Laboratory** are described briefly below, as an example of the sort of basic research which is being done in institutions which, as I see it, are often pared down to 'bare bones', starved for funds to implement their programs, and yet which are fundamental to the survival of agriculture.

Problems, Research and Solutions

'Sustainable irrigated agriculture' was identified by the CSIRO Division of Water Resources as a priority issue in 1991 and the activities of the division in Griffith have been focused on finding solutions to the local problems of rising water-tables and degradation of water and soil resources. (The Division of Irrigation and other organisations with different names had been undertaking research into different aspects for a long time before that.)

Professor Wayne Meyer, who divides his time between Charles Sturt University and the Division, sums up the dilemma underlying all the research in his foreword and summary to the research strategy position paper:[107]

*All Australians benefit, both directly and indirectly, from the food and fibre produced by the irrigation industry. However, **this production carries with it a significant cost in terms of land and water degradation. It is now apparent that our exploitation of natural resources for irrigated agriculture cannot be sustained.** Irrigators, extension workers and scientists must work together to halt the degradation of our land and water resources. However, this group alone cannot provide the solutions. Sustainable irrigated agriculture can only be achieved if supported by government policies; these must include a combination of financial and regulatory measures. The financial incentives to improve*

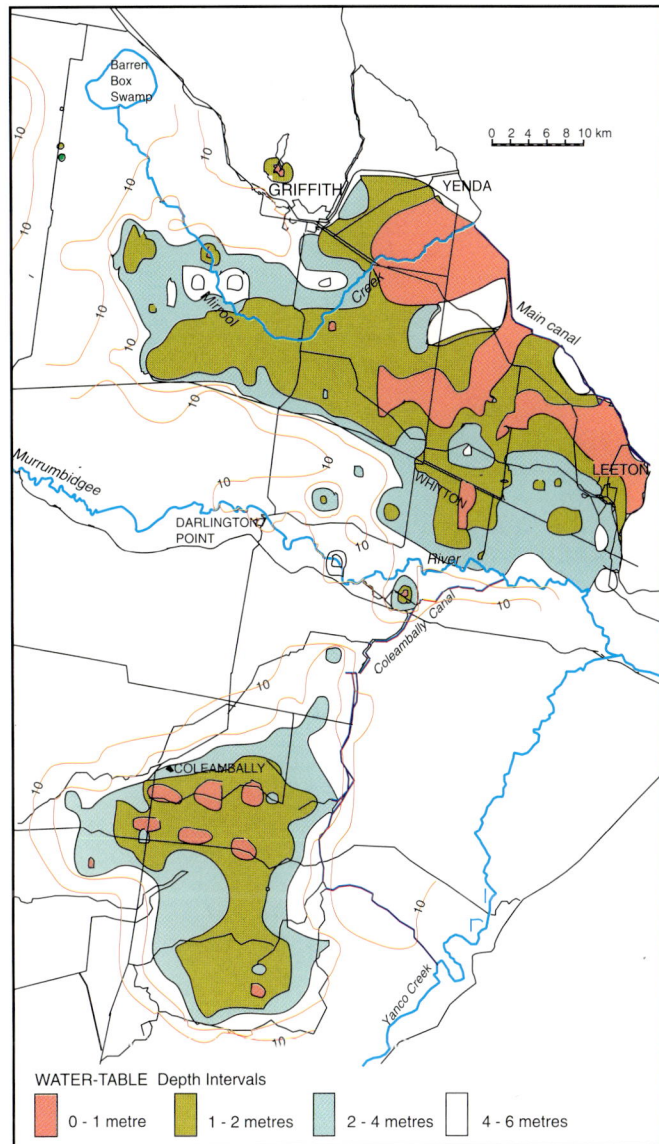

THE MURRUMBIDGEE AND COLEAMBALLY IRRIGATION AREAS
Water-table Depth Below Surface

WATER-TABLE Depth Intervals

| 0 - 1 metre | 1 - 2 metres | 2 - 4 metres | 4 - 6 metres |

After van der Lely [102]

The connection between high water-tables and irrigation is clearly demonstrated in this map.

View from a lookout across Griffith to the vineyards and irrigated plains devoid of natural vegetation and all looking fertile and productive. The rising water-table and problems with salinisation lurking just below the surface are hidden from casual view.

M.E.W.

THE MURRUMBIDGEE AND COLEAMBALLY IRRIGATION AREAS

Water-table Salinity

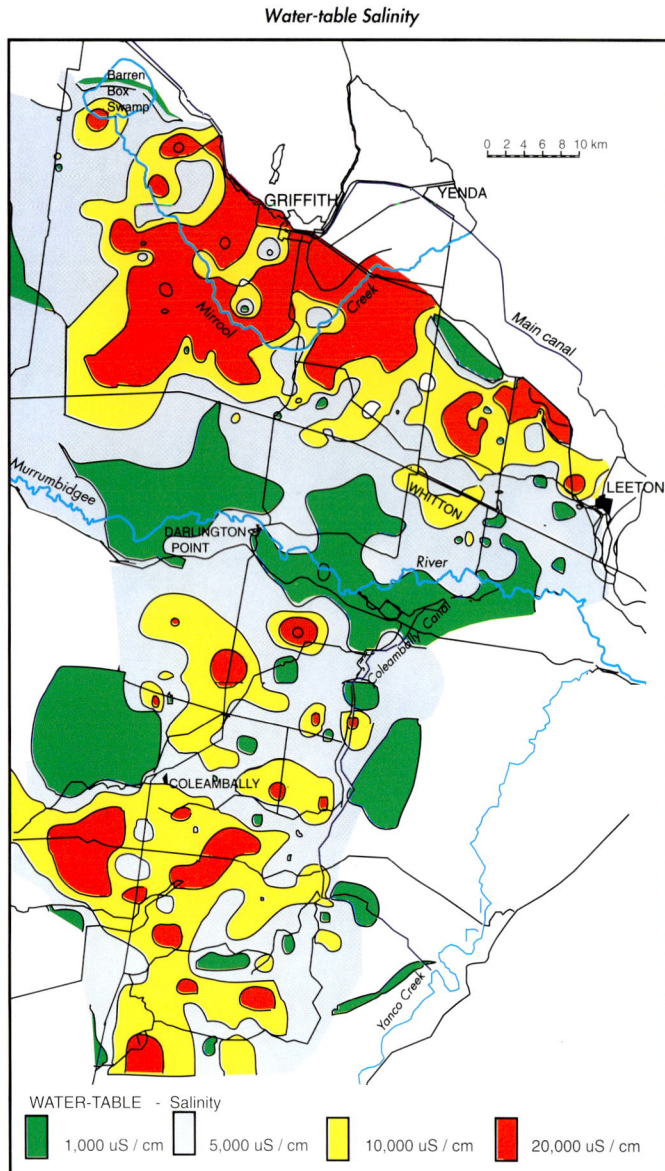

WATER-TABLE - Salinity

1,000 uS / cm	5,000 uS / cm	10,000 uS / cm	20,000 uS / cm

After van der Lely [102]

A highly saline water-table underlies the irrigation districts.

irrigation management practices are, at present, inadequate; whilst the penalties for poor management practices are virtually non-existent....The challenge for research is to present sustainable management options, for educators to take that information out to irrigators and the wider community, and for government to provide the incentives to act.

...Non-exploitive and restorative management practices are more costly than current practices. The cost of protection should be shared by everyone — an **'environmental levy'** on all food would be a direct and emphatic response. The levy could support restoration works, upgrade infrastructure, reward efficient resource use and fund research, education and training programs.

The challenge faced by researchers is to reduce degradation while improving productivity — incompatible bedfellows. However, this recognises the socio-economic-political aspects of the situation: that an industry which brings in nearly six billion dollars in a world in which the economy takes precedence over the environment is going to proceed, no matter what, even until it self-destructs; that if profitability is suppressed for too long, farm financial and physical assets will degrade more rapidly; that more sustainable management, encouraged by the provision of incentives, will at least buy time.

Six research priorities are addressed by the CSIRO Griffith Laboratory: sustainable irrigated agriculture; water use efficiency; surface and sub-surface drainage; pollution of surface waters and impact of changing flow regimes; salinity; and technology transfer and education.

Water use efficiency and drainage

In order to develop models for water balance under irrigated crops it is necessary to have data on evaporation, capillary upflow from shallow water-tables, drainage through soils and root water uptake. The **SWAGMAN Whatif** (**S**alt, **W**ater **A**nd **G**roundwater **MAN**agement) educational computer package was

Burnt rice stubble in a field near Griffith. The problem of what to do with rice stubble is a difficult one. The stubble has huge volume, breaks down slowly and is not useful as fodder, so burning is a preferred option and a lot of nutrient is lost, while erosion from bare fields is increased.

M.E.W.

developed from this data, helping people to understand the interaction between climate, soil types, water-table depth, irrigation management and water salinity. A more comprehensive package, **SWAGMAN Destiny**, is marketed and distributed by Charles Sturt University. It simulates water and salt balance in an irrigated cropping system over a 10–20 year time period, showing trends, likely variability in yields, soil salinity and water-table levels at points through time. An irrigation management package, **SIRAG Field**, is designed to help irrigators decide how much water to apply, and when. It is targeted at broadacre farmers (for wheat and maize) but can be used on a whole range of crops. (It was developed by CSIRO in conjunction with NSW Agriculture Department, private consultants and individual irrigators.)

A puddling technique for reducing deep percolation in rice culture has been developed. To date adoption has been poor. It appears that cooperating farmers have tried the technique, found that it works and then put it on the shelf to be used only when necessary — that is to keep water use below the 16 ML/ha target. (A large reduction in water loss by deep percolation has been achieved by the puddling technique, in which a rotary hoe or vibrating roller is used in flooded or wet soil, compacting and smearing a layer.[108, 109] Deep percolation can be reduced from 20 mm per day to 1–3 mm per day, resulting in a saving of 1–3 ML/ha over a rice season.

Research into the use of **sewerage effluent in irrigation** has resulted in the development of a surprisingly simple and efficient technique, **FILTER** (**F**iltration and **I**rrigated cropping for **L**and **T**reatment and **E**ffluent **R**euse[110]). Sewerage effluent is already used for irrigation worldwide, but can lead to waterlogging of low permeability soils, which occur extensively in eastern Australia. The high cost of effluent storage on urban lands during wet and winter periods, when crop irrigation requirements are low, make effluent irrigation less economically viable.

FILTER overcomes these problems. It enables year-round land application on soils with restricted drainage. The soil is physically loosened and chemically improved to a depth of 0.9 m to create and maintain porosity, allowing adequate flow rates for effluent through the loosened soil to a network of inter-connected drains, located just below the soil layer. The drainage network has control gates to allow regulation of leaching rates.

The FILTER technique combines using nutrient-rich effluent for intensive cropping, with filtration through the soil to a sub-surface drainage system during periods of low cropping activity and heavy rainfall. Effluent application and sub-surface drainage is regulated to ensure adequate nutrient removal, thereby producing low-nutrient drainage waters which meet Environment Protection Agency (EPA) criteria for discharge of treated effluent to surface water bodies. The **filtration phase** with high hydraulic loading could be followed, if required, by a **cropping phase**

THE MURRUMBIDGEE AND COLEAMBALLY IRRIGATION AREAS

Change in Water-table Depth between 1986 and 1991

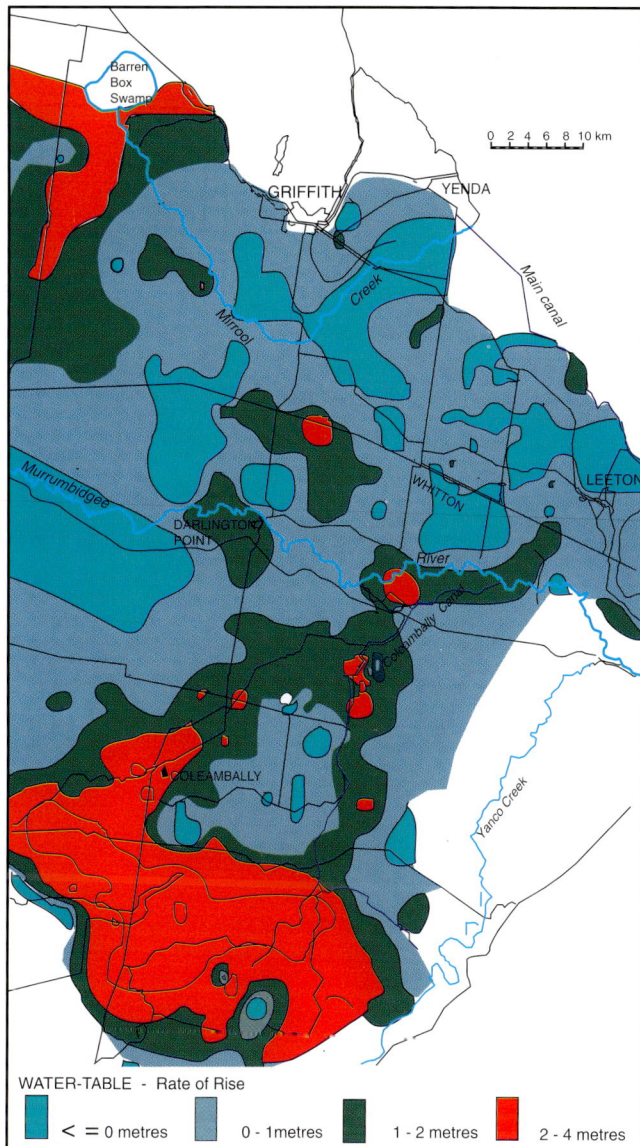

After van der Lely [102]

The rapid rate of water-table rise in five years is illustrated in this map. The area south of the CIA has recorded a water-table rise of about a metre a year, and the Barren Box Swamp area, which receives the tail waters of drainage from Mirrool Creek and the canals of the MIA, has suffered a similar rapid rise. Today the swamp is a starkly beautiful dead landscape of silty-grey water reflecting skeleton trunks of the eucalypts which have drowned in the permanently innundated, increasingly salty, wetland.

with reduced hydraulic loading to remove any nutrients stored in the soil, thus providing a sustainable system. The specific combinations of filtration and cropping phases used will depend on the site conditions.

Field trials are in progress to evaluate the FILTER technique in collaboration with the Griffith City Council, supported by the NSW Public Works Department and the Commonwealth Department of Primary Industry & Environment. Field data indicates that the technique meets its primary goals of lowering nitrogen and phosphorus concentrations below EPA limits, while maintaining adequate flow rates, crop yield

SCHEMATIC DIAGRAM OF FILTER PLOTS.

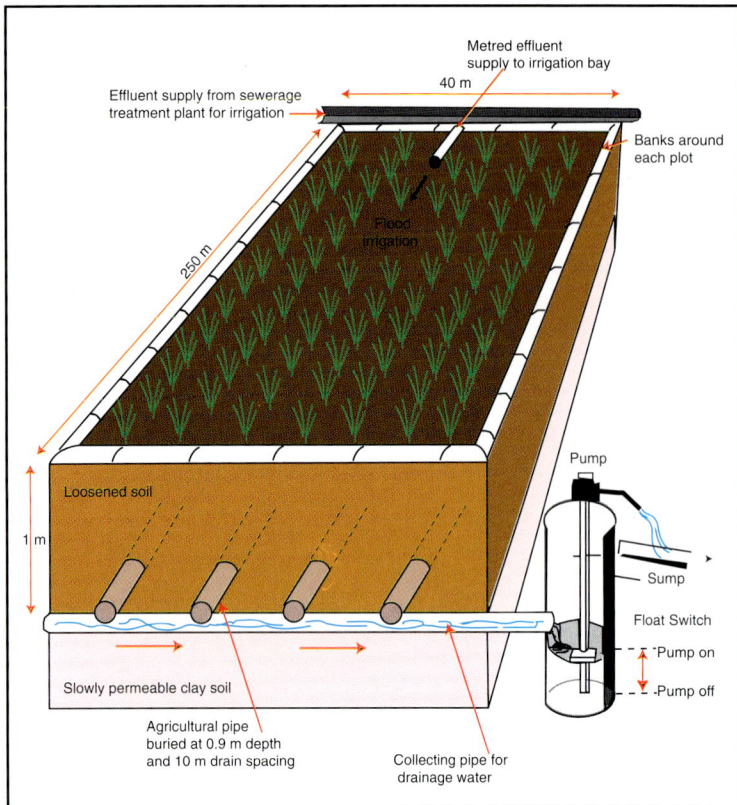

Effluent supply from sewerage treatment plant for irrigation

Metred effluent supply to irrigation bay

40 m

Banks around each plot

250 m

Flood irrigation

Loosened soil

1 m

Slowly permeable clay soil

Agricultural pipe buried at 0.9 m depth and 10 m drain spacing

Collecting pipe for drainage water

Pump

Sump

Float Switch

Pump on

Pump off

After Jayawardane [110]

and nutrient removal to provide a sustainable system.

The inspiration for developing the FILTER technique came from observing what happens in nature, where water is recycled through animals and filtered through soils many times before reaching the sea. Since urban land areas available to city councils for dealing with urban pollution concentrations is limited, the natural process is accelerated in the FILTER, using technological inputs of artificial drainage and intensive cropping.

Research into drainage has shown that mole drains, unlined tunnels in the soil profile made by a special cultivator tool, provide efficient drainage in the horticultural sector, which is already extensively drained by conventional pipe drains which do not cope with the very much raised water-table that exists now.[111, 112] Programs to minimise water use and thereby to decrease the amount of water entering drains, and to stop deep penetration from mobilising salt in the soil profile, are dealing with the twin problems of rising water-tables and salinity.

Disposal of salt from the drainage is essential in order to keep saline groundwater away from the root zone of plants, and to minimise downstream problems. Research into evaporation basins; salt concentration through irrigation of a series of increasingly salt-tolerant crops and eventual deposition of salt in **sacrificial areas** as an option; and recycling of surface drainage water, are all part of integrated programs which first have to understand the water balance, its relation to

different crops and many other factors. Where soils become very saline under vegetable growing, alternating rice crops on the land can push the salt deeper down because of the pressure exerted during flooding. This only moves the salt beyond the flooded bay, to cause problems elsewhere.

Improved irrigation systems, more modern and adjustable or automated (but expensive and beyond the financial capability of many irrigators to install), would go some way to improving the situation as regards rising water-tables and drainage problems.

The **Rivers and Wetlands Program** carries out research on aquatic ecosystems — rivers, lakes, storages, wetlands, irrigation canals and floodplains. Basic research on **toxic algal blooms**, essential for understanding and dealing with the problem in our water-starved rivers, where irrigation interferes with natural flows and creates 'drought' conditions perennially, are an important component. Testing how toxic the pesticides, herbicides and other chemicals which are entering the waterways are to the organisms which live in the water is vital to set allowable limits for their presence in drainage water. The increase in nutrients in waters as a result of agricultural fertiliser run-off, sewerage effluent and other sources, has to be monitored and related changes to ecosystems have to be assessed.

Research into water regimes in rivers; the flow patterns which result from regulation and the removal of so much water for irrigation; how much **'environmental flow'** is needed to maintain river and wetland health; and understanding of the fundamental functioning of aquatic ecosystems is essential if water resources are to be properly managed and not progressively degraded. Study of water plants, including introduced weeds of waterways and their control, is necessary if healthy aquatic systems are to be maintained. Alligator weed (*Alternanthera philoxeroides*), a 'feral plant' introduced from South America and capable of choking irrigation systems, rivers and wetlands, has been a prime target. It has recently been eradicated from Barren Box Swamp using techniques learnt at Williamstown in New South Wales. It is considered essential that it is completely eradicated from Australia. If it entered the river systems in the Murray Basin it would easily get out of control, with catastrophic results.

The Dilemma: Irrigation and the Exploitation of the Resource Base

In an inaugural address to Charles Sturt University (Riverina Campus) on 14 June 1994, Professor Wayne Meyer said:

Australia is one of the few countries of the world which produces a net surplus of food. We maintain a high standard of living because of what we produce. It makes no moral sense, nor is it economically rational to maintain this production and standard of living by exploiting our biological resource base.

Australian irrigation is caught in the dilemma of responding to the necessity to produce, but in so doing is demonstrably exploiting the land, soil and water resource base.

The dilemma is the essence of ecological balance. If the perceived right to produce is not balanced by an equal responsibility to look after the resource base, then the ecological system will collapse. There are healthy signs that we are beginning to grasp our responsibilities. We are moving from an attitude of pioneering exploiter to long-term custodian. We are considering ourselves as part of an inter-connected and inter-dependent ecological system. We are beginning to assign real dollar values to the intangibles and environmental quality and we are just beginning to recognise the importance of the ever present need to educate and transfer knowledge to the next generation.

THE POPLAR BOX LANDS OF MID-WESTERN NEW SOUTH WALES

A vast tract of waterless country in New South Wales, bounded by the Riverine Plain to the south, the black soil plains of the Bogan River to the north, the Darling River to the west and the Lachlan River in the east, was one of the last areas to be settled in New South Wales. Between 1840 and 1880, grazing rights were being taken up, properties were being progressively fenced, and tanks (government and private) were installed. Stocking followed the establishment of watering points.

The poplar box (*Eucalyptus populnea*) woodlands had a grassy understorey — kangaroo grass, star grass and others; mulga was interspersed; edible herbs and shrubs abounded in 1880 according to the Royal Commission of 1901. By 1895 silting of rivers, soil compaction, gully erosion were evident. **Woody weeds** were replacing edible pasture; edible species had disappeared in many areas. The rabbit plagues from 1880 onwards were devastating. Pastoral inspectors reported that in 1890 and 1891, which should have been splendid seasons as far as rainfall was concerned, 'drought' conditions applied as far as pasture was concerned. Rabbits had eaten the land out, the ground appeared incapable of growing anything but moss. Many people thought that the rabbits had actually poisoned the land because nothing grew after rain.[113]

Today the poplar box lands support **fair to very poor pastures** over much of their range. Damage done in the early days has not been healed. The carrying capacity of the land has been destroyed and the grazing of feral animals and increased numbers of kangaroos (as a result of water availability) continues to take its toll.

CHAPTER EIGHT

AUSTRALIA'S GRASSLANDS

THE TEMPERATE GRASSLANDS

The global biodiversity loss which results from human activity is alarming. It may come as a surprise to many to realise that the ecosystems which have been most drastically reduced and whose remnants are everywhere **most endangered are the prairie and steppe grasslands of the temperate zone**. They are very close to extinction, and their decline has been insidious, far less visible and commented upon than the disappearance of tropical rainforests which always springs to mind when ecosystem destruction is mentioned.

The earliest Hominids roamed the savanna grasslands of Africa; early *Homo sapiens* hunted on the grassy plains worldwide, grazed their animals there and cultivated their first gardens; and in time farmers grew grasses for their seeds when they graduated to cereal growing. The natural grassland systems, ecologically complex and species-rich, were ploughed up for crops or altered as improved pastures. Simple systems, poor in species, replaced rich native grassland wherever humans spread.

Australia has followed the world trend of temperate grassland destruction and now finds itself in a situation where only **0.5% of the original lowland grassland remains in even semi-natural condition**.[114] The original area was probably about two million hectares; the remnants that survived to 1992 amounted to 10 000 ha.

The grasslands of temperate south-eastern Australia are of two floristically and geographically distinct types:

- On the Monaro in New South Wales, in Victoria south of the ranges of the Great Divide, in the moister hill country of South Australia, and in Tasmania the grassland comprises deep-rooted perennial tussock grasses, dominated by *Themeda triandra* (kangaroo grass) or *Poa* species. *Stipa, Danthonia* and other perennial grasses are present, and the spaces between perennial grasses are occupied, according to season, by large numbers of species of herbs, some annual, others persisting between flowering seasons as rootstock or bulbs. Lichen crusts cover the soil between tussocks, and very few shrubs are found in the grassland.

- On the broad plains of the Murray River Valley and in parts of South Australia the grassland is dominated by *Danthonia* and *Stipa* and is more herb-field than grassland. On the Riverine Plains *Danthonia setacea*, wallaby grass, is most frequently dominant. Many arid zone species, which are at their eastern limit, are present in these herblands.

Of the 20 lowland grassland communities in south-eastern Australia, only three are adequately reserved. At least one community has become extinct in the last 100 years and most are reduced to small remnants (less than 1% of their former range). In Victoria and southern New South Wales most remnants are on private property, roadsides, travelling stock routes and reserves. Half of the most significant grassland sites in South Australia are on private land, one-third are on roadsides and the remaining sixth is on Crown land. In Tasmania, lowland grassland communities are better protected than most of the communities in mainland states. All eight of the community types which are found in Tasmania are represented in reserves, but only one is considered to be adequately reserved. The two most significant remnants are on private land. The fact that up to 2% of the remaining Tasmanian grassland is being cleared annually gives no room for complacency.

The fragmentation of remnant temperate grassland communities makes their preservation extremely difficult.

New South Wales

The protection and management of **'specified native grasslands'** has become a priority issue in New South Wales.[115] It has been realised, very late and perhaps in some cases too late, that native grassland ecosystems are a threatened species and will become extinct if nothing is done to protect them. They were the obvious areas to plough up for cropping and to graze with introduced animals, and their destruction, use and misuse goes back to the beginning of settlement.

To what extent native grasslands were in a 'natural' state when Europeans first saw them is a question which cannot be answered. The firing of the continent by Aborigines had created savanna and grassland where climate and soils predicated eucalypt woodland and dense scrub and heath in many regions along the eastern, better-watered sector. The grassy black-soil plains, which never supported trees because of their cracking clays, would also have been altered by the regular burning, not to the extent of changing the ecosystem type, but almost certainly in the species composition of the grasses and herbs.

How altered the native grassland remnants are today, compared with their status at the beginning of European use, is also unknown. Even the plant species they contained and the proportions in which they occurred before they were subjected to the influences of introduced animal grazing or other disturbance, is uncertain. The history of use of the Riverine Plains Grasslands given in Chapter 7 gives some insight into their alteration last century. Today's grasslands are the product of their past management and gross disturbance, derived from a mosaic of different pre-settlement communities. However, they are productive low-input, low-output systems which are co-adapted to natural climatic variation and they respond positively to management manipulations and to rest.

The 'specified native grasslands', for whose protection legislation is being drafted, are remnants of the once major ecosystems which remain:

- on the Hay Plains (western Riverina), in the local government areas of Berrigan, Carrathool, Conargo, Deniliquin, Griffith, Hay, Jerilderie, Leeton, Murray, Murrumbidgee, Wakool and Windouran;
- on the Liverpool Plains in the Gunnedah, Murrurundi, Parry and Quirindi shires;
- on The Monaro in the Bombala, Cooma– Monaro

and Snowy River local government areas; and

- in the Brewarrina, Moree Plains and Walgett shires.

The New South Wales Government has approved a self-regulating program of protection and management under the State Environmental Planning Policy, SEPP No. 46 — Protection and Management of Native Vegetation, namely: *To prevent inappropriate native vegetation clearing within NSW...ensuring that native vegetation is protected and managed in the environmental, social and economic interests of the State.* The proportion of remnant grassland which must be protected within a shire or a farm boundary is laid down.

The aims are to conserve biodiversity and ecological integrity and to avoid land degradation and minimise the need for rehabilitation. The program recognises that native vegetation protection is superior to replacement vegetation and it links native vegetation management to Total Catchment Management in which community involvement is essential.

The program, whose aims are laudatory, is in its draft phase (approved by the Minister in February 1996) and a period of six months has been set for review, with the draft being distributed to landowners, shires, agencies etc. for their input. There are problems inherent in self-regulation, just as there are in creating laws and being unable to police them. Because control is seen by some to threaten their autonomy on their own land, the response is to get in quickly and plough up the remnant grassland before anyone stops them. And this is certainly happening, but it is hoped that most of landowners are responsible and understand the link between biodiversity and sustainability.

It has been found that controlled grazing of the native grasslands has not been threatening to their survival, which should make acceptance of the protection legislation easier. Built into the policy are socio-economic provisions which should safeguard the rights of any farmer whose financial situation might be such that he can justify converting some of his native grassland to cash crops.

View to the hills between Warialda and Moree, across degraded grassland.

M.E.W.

South Australia

The disappearance of native tussock grasslands, which were in the southern, better-watered, winter rainfall region in South Australia, was rapid. As in New South Wales, the grassy areas were the first to be ploughed for crops.

The region from the Adelaide Plain to the North Mount Lofty Ranges was seen as prime agricultural land and was taken up in the early days of settlement for cropping or improved pasture. One of the casualties of this clearing was the **pygmy bluetongue lizard**, *Tiliqua adelaidensis*, which had been described in 1863 and was apparently once abundant.

The pygmy bluetongue was considered to be one of Australia's most endangered reptiles, if not already extinct, having not been seen for 33 years.[116,117] Its rediscovery in the Burra region, in remnant patches of native grassland on private land, has resulted in a program aimed at protecting it and finding out about its biology. It is now known from 10 spatially discrete sub-populations in the mid-north of South Australia on a line northwards from Burra to Hallett. The areas where it has been found have so far been preserved from ploughing only by the goodwill of the landowners. However, the Native Vegetation Branch of the SA Department of Environment and Natural Resources has been assisting in drafting a Heritage Agreement for these areas. Such an agreement will preserve the land from ploughing but will allow grazing. It is believed that medium level grazing has no ill effect on the lizards and may in fact be beneficial because it maintains diversity and prevents the invasion of introduced plants.

Research on the lizard is being funded by the Australian Nature Conservation Agency and the Endangered Species Program. It is hoped that a captive breeding program may be possible at the Adelaide Zoo when enough is known about the animal. Its survival in isolated grassland remnants is at best precarious in the wild. Adults are only up to 20 cm long; they occupy trapdoor spider holes, sometimes with the lid still attached, and do not dig their own; they eat cockroaches, ants, spiders, grasshoppers and beetles and some plant material; females give birth to one to four live young.

The *Lomandra dura–Lomandra effusa* (mat rush or irongrass) grassland habitat in which the pygmy bluetongues have all been found is itself listed as not conserved and 'very rare and endangered'. As a result of a conservation effort to save the little bluetongue, conservation of an endangered grassland ecosystem and its total biodiversity may result — which is very satisfactory from all perspectives.

SUBTROPICAL AND TROPICAL GRASSLANDS

An example of a grassland type which has become so altered as to have virtually disappeared is presented by the kangaroo grass (*Themeda* spp.) pastures which were widespread in southern Queensland. In the 1850s they provided good grazing, but selective over-grazing by sheep (combined with dry season burns) eradicated the kangaroo grass. Over a 40-year period, black speargrass (*Heteropogon contortus*) replaced it. The speargrass has seeds which have awls which burrow into sheep causing pain and even death. Farmers had to change over from sheep to cattle in consequence, and the continued heavy grazing pressure finally eradicated the speargrass, in only a few years, leaving an annual pasture of wire grasses (*Aristida* spp.) and herbs, much less productive than the original kangaroo grass perennial pasture.

The Mitchell Grass Plains

The Mitchell downs are flat to gently undulating plains with deep brown or grey, or sometimes red, cracking clay soils with strongly self-mulching surfaces. The downs are often open grassland but may be lightly wooded with bauhinia, vine tree (supplejack), whitewood, rosewood or boree (*Acacia tephrina*). They also grade into gidgee country (*Acacia cambagei*). In healthy pastures, the ground cover is Mitchell grass (*Astrebla* spp.) and other grasses and herbs.

The Mitchell grass rangelands cover 32.8 million hectares, 19% of Queensland. The cracking-clay soils on the plains which support the 'rolling downs' grasslands do not allow trees to become established. When they dry and crack, tree roots are broken, while the fibrous roots of grasses are suited to the conditions. The cracking-clay soils are derived from Cretaceous rocks of the Great Artesian Basin and of the Barkly Tableland region. Smaller areas of Mitchell grass occur scattered on black soils of river floodplains. A notable outlier is found on the Burt Plain north of the Macdonnell Ranges in Central Australia.

The use of the Mitchell grass plains as rangelands was largely made possible by the discovery of artesian water in the 1880s. There is little permanent surface water in the regions. The heavy and constant grazing

Eucalypt woodland with an understorey of Themeda triandra *(kangaroo grass) near the Nymboida River in northern New South Wales.*

M.E.W.

pressures imposed on the plains has resulted in a great thinning of the grass cover overall and in elimination of some species from the community. The 'forgiving' nature of the Mitchell grass plains, which have the ability to recover from over-grazing when given the chance, is an example of the sustainability of the native grassland ecosystem under conservative management.

Overstocking at times is virtually unavoidable, considering the vagaries of climate, the droughts, and fluctuations in markets. With changes in natural fire regimes and the imposed grazing practices, vast areas (43%) of Mitchell country are being invaded by native woody weeds and/or unpalatable pasture species. This is particularly the case in gidgee country (*Acacia cambagei*) where areas which were once lightly wooded now have a major problem. In addition, prickly acacia, *Acacia nilotica*, has invaded large areas of the Mitchell grass plains.

An account of one landowner's battle to restore his land near Longreach, and his comments on the history of grazing in the region, gives an insight into the problems suffered by the Mitchell grass rangelands in the Longreach region.

History of 'Strathdarr', Longreach, given by Frank Dean at the 'Landcare is People Care' Conference, Longreach, June 1995

Mr Dean was speaking in defence of tree clearing, and against the impending government regulations which prohibited clearing in the Mitchell grasslands (and elsewhere in Queensland) in order to maintain 'ecological and environmental sustainability'. This account emphasises: the problems which come from sweeping government regulations; the failure by authorities to understand the changes which have taken place due to changes in fire regimes; the battle that today's landholders have had because they inherited massive environmental problems caused by their predecessors; that woody weeds without groundcover understorey allow massive erosion; and the overall problems in the Mitchell grasslands. (When one travels through the Longreach region today, one sees many badly degraded properties, woody weed infested, or with scalds and sparse grass. Some stations up for sale and others advertise bed and breakfast, trying to make a living from tourism because their degraded lands are no longer productive.)

'Strathdarr' had been a famous merino stud and prior to 1950 contained a large area of open gidgee scrub in which they 'grew out' their sale rams.

In 1972, we purchased 'Strathdarr', a property of 60 000 acres [24 300 ha], 25 kilometres west of Longreach on the Darr River. At that time an area of 15 000 to 18 000 acres [6070–7284 ha] of what had been productive gidgee had been taken over by the proliferation of gidgee seedlings which had originated with the record rainfall year of 1950. As well, prickle bushes (algaroba, Acacia nilotica and parkinsonia) were present over the whole property, varying from isolated trees to dense masses along creeks and around some dams.

Every paddock had a gidgee, sandalwood and prickle bush problem. A determined campaign over 15 years saw the prickle bush problem eradicated and in 1987–88 the old scrub areas were pulled with all areas of invasion excluded; much of which has since been cleared using a tractor and stick rake, leaving all useful trees standing.

Dorothy Davidson[118] noted that gidgee seedlings were sometimes 60 to the square yard, which equates to 300 000 to the acre or 750 000 to the hectare. In parent scrubs, trees numbered 80–100 to the acre [200–250 ha].

The natural Mitchell grasslands were colonised by few trees; individual coolabahs round the edge of waterholes, in the creek and river systems. Open plains with isolated to scattered trees of various species, patches of open gidgee scrub; and all subject to intermittent huge summer grass fires in exceptional

Top: The Burt Plain, north of the Macdonnell Ranges in Central Australia, a Mitchell grass outlier.

Centre: Over-grazed land and termite mounds, Mt Isa district.

Bottom: Gidgee and Mitchell grass savanna near the Queensland–Northern Territory border.

M.E.W.

Above top left: 'Woody weed', Gidgee, spreading into Mitchell grass from a creek frontage.

Above top right: Woody weeds spreading into Mitchell grass plain, with prickle bushes in foreground.

Above left: Dingo Creek, near Longreach, with Mitchell grass and coolabahs.

JOHN REYNOLDS

seasons which created the total disturbance necessary for the ecological and environmental diversity and the stable productivity of the region.

The suggestion that over the entire Mitchell grasslands any tree clearing at all is not desirable because of the sparsity of trees portrays a dismal lack of first-hand knowledge of the changes to the composition of tree populations that have taken place since the record rainfall year of 1950 and the subsequent above average rainfall years of 1954–57.

*A local survey found that gidgee invasion showed up as a major concern and landholders perceived gidgee as a greater problem than exotics, and that some 3 million acres had been lost to woody weeds. Areas of gidgee seedling proliferation became a degraded wasteland, devoid of any pasture, subject to massive erosion and worthless as a habitat for native birds or animals. **It is a complete fallacy to suggest that a shrub canopy 3 to 5 feet [1–1.5 m] above the ground will control erosion where ground cover is absent.***

Mills[119] has suggested that 'the clearing of native vegetation is the precursor to all forms of accelerated erosion'. I refute this and state that on Strathdarr such gullying and erosion has taken place before clearing. Where time has allowed the regeneration of natural grass, erosion has practically ceased.

If ecological and environmental sustainability is defined as the long-term maintenance of the productive capacity of the land and degradation as the result of an undesirable change in one or more of the elements involved, then the continuing control of the proliferation and invasion of woody weeds must receive the full support and assistance of Government.

*In Queensland's 173 million hectares, the Department of Lands recognises 14 major pasture types with their attendant soil and tree structures… Any person who believes that they are capable of devising one set of criteria which would adequately cover the methods of controlling land development over such a vast and diverse area would either be arrogant or extremely naive. If control of land management by legislation is deemed necessary, then it must be **on an individual property basis,** supporting the requirements of the region and administered by persons with a hands-on knowledge of that region.*

*The time, money and effort that we have put into Strathdarr has been as a long-term goal to return the property as near as possible to its original state. **We have become an integral part of the natural system and, in our decisions as managers of the land and the treatment of our rangeland, must assume the role vacated by fire.***

*If now, by legislation, we and others like us are not permitted to continue to control invasive trees, then the stated aim of the government and the conservation movement, under the guise of 'ecological and environmental sustainability', is really to have **millions of acres of highly productive western Queensland Mitchell grasslands become a degraded wasteland.** If such is the case, then the government should not seek to compel lessees to remain captive but should be prepared to purchase all lands surrendered at fair market value; accept the loss of revenue from such grazing leases; and compensate Local Government and local businesses for their lack of income.*

Mr Dean comments on another property, 'Nogo', 13 km west of Longreach, selected by his grandfather in 1890. An old map shows some paddocks as 'good open boree Mitchell grass with patches of gidyea'. Massive seedling proliferation and invasion during the 1950s had reduced most of that area also to worthless scrub, impenetrable to sheep and devoid of pasture, and pulling in 1987–88 restored some of the land to pasture.

Since the Landcare conference at which the case for clearing was so competently put, Mr Dean (personal communication) notes that there has been a dramatic change in attitudes, not only by the Government but by the Queensland Conservation Council and the Department of Environment and Heritage, whose original attitudes and the statements they had made had greatly upset landholders.

(When legislation is introduced, or threatened,

The bare ground beneath gidgee, and erosion are seen in this picture of Dingo Creek, near Longreach. Woody weeds in thick infestations do not have groundcover beneath their canopy, and erosion continues below.

JOHN REYNOLDS

without full understanding and consultation, as so often happens when 'politics' and not 'government' determine actions by authorities, it can do a great deal of harm. Unnecessary stress is inflicted on people who are battling enough with the problems of their very survival as primary producers without the extra aggravation.)

About 6 million adult merino sheep are currently run on the Mitchell grass plains. The high variability of mean annual rainfall (about 50%) results in great fluctuations in forage production, therefore to manage the system sustainably requires tactical or adaptive stocking regimes. In order to take the guesswork out of management strategies a new computer software product (which is also available in printed format for farmers without computers) has been designed by the Queensland Department of Primary Industry. **GrazeOn** uses a feed budgeting approach to estimate the capability of Mitchell grasslands to run animals for defined but usually short (to three years) periods of time.

The pasture management program is designed so that pasture condition is controlled; grazing pressure is estimated using numbers of domestic and non-domestic animals; spatial aspects of grazing behaviour are used to estimate utilisation of paddocks by grazing animals; and animal intake is adjusted to physiological state and size of animals (dry, lactating, pregnant, lambs etc.) and to the greenness of pasture. Climatic and pasture-growth forecasts can be incorporated (*Climax, Rainman, Grasp*). The system is intended to increase preparedness for drought and generally reduce risks. In dry seasons, or when the pasture condition is poor, fewer domestic animals would be run, but productivity per head would be better; in good seasons or on pasture in good condition, more animals and higher production would result.

In theory, by using *GrazeOn,* pastoralists should be able to restore pasture to good condition and then maintain it in that state, reducing the need for supplementary feeding and destocking in dry times, and enabling higher income in good years. (Although the *GrazeOn* program has been designed for use on Mitchell grasslands, it is believed by its creators to be applicable to all arid and semi-arid areas with highly variable rainfall and defined periods of pasture growth. Therefore it has the potential to be developed for rangelands nationwide.) Whether in fact the system can work **in practice** is another matter. No generalised system can apply over the wide range of conditions and the diversified seasonal patterns which characterise the arid and semi-arid regions. The practical farmer who knows his own land and its specific characteristics sees many of the clever, high tec, programs created in research institutions as no substitute for experience, and useful only as a general guide to monitoring the on-ground situation.

The Spinifex Grasslands

Hummock grasslands cover nearly a quarter of Australia in the arid zone. The spinifex grasses belong to two endemic genera, *Triodia* and *Plectrachne*, which evolved in Australia after it had become an island continent and presumably in response to the establishment of aridity. Where hummock grasses spread over the vast plains of parts of the arid zone they dominate the perennial vegetation and only scattered *Grevillea* or other shrubs may be present; elsewhere spinifex may be associated with mallee eucalypts, with mulga or with saltbush and bluebush. It also inhabits the stony ridges and hillsides on the shallowest, poorest soils, completely adapted to the vagaries of climate.

Right: View from a lookout to the Cockburn Ranges (south of Wyndham in the Kimberley) across a spinifex plain, with Cochlospermum in flower in the foreground.

Below: Spinifex in the Tanami Desert.

Bottom:Spinifex hummocks along the road verge beyond Pooncarie.

M.E.W.

DISTRIBUTION OF SPINIFEX

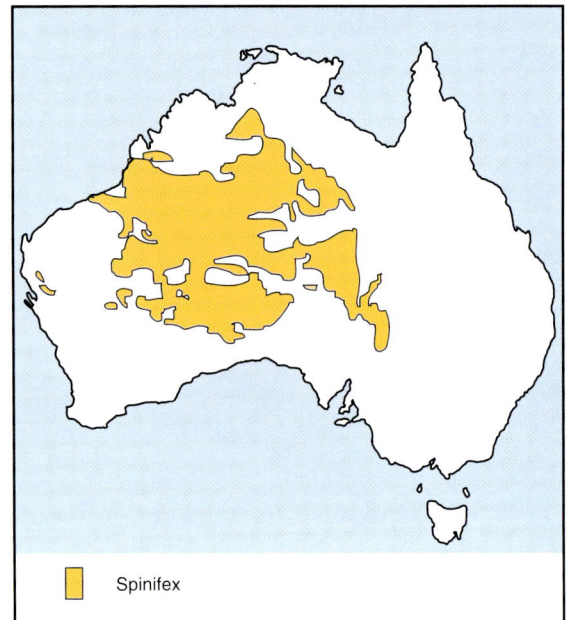

Spinifex

On the whole, the spinifex lands have not been subjected to over-grazing, either by native or introduced animals. They are at best capable of supporting very low numbers of grazers, and it is mainly the ephemerals that appear between hummocks after rain or the more palatable plants which form the succession after fire which are eaten. New young spinifex growth or the flowering growth and seed heads after rain are briefly palatable. **Termites are the main, year-round, grazers of spinifex.**

Burning, at fairly long intervals, rejuvenates spinifex ecosystems. The nature of the vegetation, in which hummocks are dotted on bare earth, tends to limit fire frequency, though good rains and growth of connecting vegetation can result in the landscape being able to burn before there is sufficient biomass of spinifex alone to allow fire to be carried more frequently than every five or six years.

TERMITES

The role of termites in the carbon cycle in arid regions is extremely significant. Their function is like that of the abundant soil micro-organisms in wetter regions. They consume organic matter and recycle nutrients, nitrogen in particular. **In our tropical savannas 16% of the organic nitrogen available to plants is recycled annually by termites**. When large tracts of semi-arid land are cleared of native vegetation and termitaria, nutrient recycling is significantly slowed.

Termites have specially adapted digestive systems which enable them to function on a diet of cellulose, which is indigestible to many other animals. Their salivary glands and mid-gut produce enzymes which make glucose for energy from cellulose, and which also make acetate as an (unusual) energy source. Termites can also create protein from atmospheric nitrogen, a process almost exclusively carried out by plants in photosynthesis and by nitrogen-fixing bacteria in root nodules. (A down-side of their efficient extraction of nutrient from cellulose is the amount of methane which they produce — estimated to be equivalent to that produced by all the cattle in the world on a global scale, and not good for the ozone layer!)

Termites do not have restrictive dietary requirements. Though the diets of different species vary and overlap, all seem to be capable of adapting to whatever is available. Research into harvester termites in the Alice Springs district showed that termites were taking the dry material and were not competing with the cattle and kangaroos which were grazing the experimental area.

Wood-eating termites (Amitermes spp.) facilitate the decomposition of fallen timber in arid landscapes. Substantial soil hummocks are developed round the timber, and these hummocks become 'islands', considerably more fertile than the surrounding soil, supporting productive plants and diverse faunal communities. Small-scale patchiness of the soil surface due to various biological activities is a characteristic of arid landscapes under natural conditions, and is vital for the maintenance of biodiversity.

The importance of termites as grazers in arid and semi-arid regions is something which one might not immediately recognise. In this continent, which is so different from other lands in the evolutionary path followed by its vertebrates, the absence of herds of grazing ungulates has provided niches for these colonial invertebrates as significant herbivores. They are able to survive the droughts and long seasonal dry periods which characterise so much of ENSO-dominated Australia because they live enclosed in structures which insulate them from the climate. They can be permanent inhabitants of drought-prone places because they eat dry plant material, where many other grazers are mainly opportunists which follow green pasture after rain.

Termites have been around since early Tertiary times (the last 60 million years) and some of the most anatomically primitive types, like *Mastotermes darwiniensis* are still found in near-coastal parts of tropical northern Australia, remnants of globally widespread populations known from fossils in Oligocene to Miocene rocks in Europe.[120]

Circumstantial evidence suggests that primitive forms were widespread in Tertiary Australia, being gradually replaced by more advanced forms. Their local abundance, as with all species, would have fluctuated with the

Mastotermes.

climatic changes which have characterised Australia during its northwards movement since it became an island continent, and particularly during the fluctuations which have characterised the Pleistocene. From Western Australia to Cape York, tropical northern Australia was arid during the late Pleistocene.

There are about 350 species of termites in Australia. Only 20% of these are mound-builders, the rest form underground nests. The numbers of individuals in a large mound-building colony are impressive and research at the Lansdown Research Station south of Townsville has shown that with up to a million termites per mound, and 24 mounds per hectare in the Charters Towers region, this represents a termite liveweight of 105 kg/ha,

Spinifex and termites, near the entrance to the Bungle Bungle National Park.

which is four times the cattle liveweight of 24 kg/ha. The termites there are responsible for consuming 20% of the annual above-ground vegetation, and most of the rest is broken down by soil-dwelling bacteria and fungi.

Less is known of the numbers of individuals involved in subterranean nests or the numbers of nests per hectare, though in some places they are very abundant and 1000 nests per hectare has been suggested in some mulga lands.

The clay mud with which all termites make their mounds, underground nests and galleries, is brought up from the subsoil layer

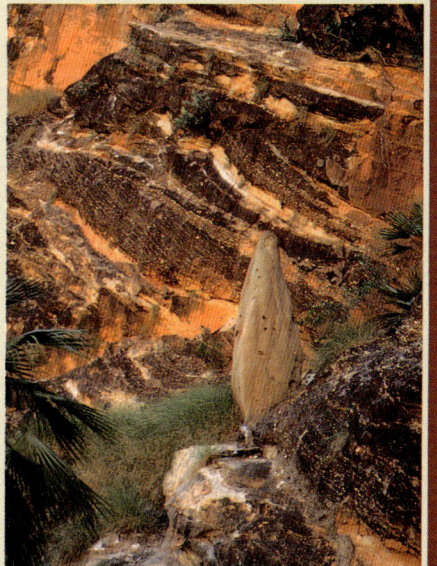

A termite tower, high on a cliff in the Bungle Bungles. Galleries run from the edifice down to the spinifex at the base of the cliff.

and mixed with saliva and faecal matter, creating a waterproof and exceedingly durable substance. It is nutrient-rich compared to the surrounding soil, and on breakdown (when the colony dies or as its structures are eroded by weathering) it supplies extra calcium, magnesium, potassium and organic matter to create enriched patches of soil. The material of mounds has 50 to 100 times more nitrogenous material than the surrounding soil.

The clay-rich subsoil may be brought up from considerable depths, disturbing and aerating the soil below the mound. It was carried up from a depth of 4 m in mound-building examples studied west of Charters Towers. The mound-building termites have a system of galleries running to food sources, and these increase the penetration of rainwater into the soil around the mound. The hard clay central mound below the soil surface in subterranean termitaria acts as an area where runoff is increased, while the areas through which gallery tunnels run allow increased rainfall entry deep into the soil.

In the Warrego region, underground nests have hard caps 2–3 m in diameter, covering 20% of the soil surface. The age of these nests was estimated at 70 years. Termite pavements are distinct soil surface features in many semi-arid woodlands, contributing to the high biomass of invertebrates which exist in semi-arid zones under natural conditions. The nutrient-rich patches and the areas of increased rainfall intake and runoff lead to a mosaic of subtly different environments which promote biodiversity. And biodiversity is, of course, required for a healthy, dynamic ecosystem.

Just as ants have been shown to be soil-makers by their underground activities, termites play a similar role. Studies near Brocks Creek in the Northern Territory[120] have shown that the rate of soil manufacture by termites in the sandy soils overlying granite equals the rate of natural erosion. Topsoil is constantly eroded in natural ecosystems by slope wash, erosion being a never-ending natural process. Where termites are present, their activity maintains an equilibrium, and only when factors like man-made fires create opportunity for erosion at an unnatural rate is this equilibrium upset. (Man-made fire is more frequent and often more damaging than natural fire which is part of dynamic natural systems in the tropical savannas.) The termites at Brocks Creek were also shown to have been responsible for creating a gravel layer at depth in the soil. Their activities in extracting the clay fragment from the weathering surface of the granite bedrock actually broke up the rock, leaving the hard siliceous parts as pebbles.

Spinifex termites create the largest mounds in Australia — up to 7 m high and perhaps 100 years old. The amount of bioturbation caused by their activity is obviously significant.

The 'magnetic' termites of the Northern Territory, with two species, one in regions near Darwin and the other in Arnhem Land, are equally amazing though they do not attain the

A five metre termite mound, between the Arthur and the Marshall Rivers in the Northern Territory.

M.E.W.

enormous size. They stand like gravestones in the landscape, narrow plates about a metre high, with flat vertical sides, slightly tapered and rounded at the top, all neatly aligned north–south. By so doing they get morning and evening sun on their wide flanks and the hot sun of the rest of the day only shines on their narrow ends and thin top. Their alignment appears to be achieved by positioning according to the sun but there may also be a direct response to the Earth's magnetic field. A strong magnet on the ground next to a nest has been shown to influence the internal pattern of tunnels, and it would seem logical that blind creatures building in the dark would require another sense, a genetic compass instinct, in order to achieve such uniformly exact alignment.

The purpose of the north-south alignment is to maintain temperature within the mound as close to the optimal 33°C as possible. It, and

the insulation of the mud and the activities of the occupants, successfully maintain constant temperature and the high humidity required for survival.

Research into the role of termites in mulga-lands which have suffered degradation has re-enforced the concept — the major tenet — which has emerged through the study of desertification presented in this book — that the key to the problems is loss of biodiversity (which is essential for maintaining equilibrium in ecosystems). In natural, pristine mulga communities with their complex web of interactions between animals and plants, soil and climate, a dynamic balance was maintained. Under natural conditions mulga suffers intermittent defoliation by grasshoppers, caterpillars and beetles; thrips cause galls; seeds are destroyed by weevils and wasps; bugs suck the sap of the trees; and termites and borers attack the wood. All this keeps the

Magnetic termite mounds, like gravestones in a landscape.

M.E.W.

A magnetic termite mound edge-on showing its narrow, flat shape; and 'ordinary' termite mounds, in a recently burnt swamp.

M.E.W.

dung on the ground; wood of trees; and annuals, as they die.[121]

When the mulga cover is lost by clearing or fire and introduced animals change the grazing pressures on remaining vegetation, the balance of the ecosystem is disturbed. With no mulga litter on the ground and increased competition for food, particularly in droughts, the activities of termites can become a serious degrading influence. In south-western Queensland, loss of mulga by fire followed by sheep grazing which deterred seedling re-establishment resulted in opening up of the tree cover and increase in grass pasture. More sheep were introduced, and harvester termites became more abundant. When a dry time returned, the combined efforts of sheep and termites denuded the region. The termites took to eating the bases out of the tussock grasses because there was no mulga leaf litter to see them through the drought, and the perennial grasses were unable to respond when rain returned.

mulga 'on its toes' — reacting to change in an ecosystem which is alive from the ground up — from its microbiological organisms and termites and other soil invertebrates to the birds and insects in its branches. The termites are busily cycling the dry litter and animal

A spinifex–Grevillea–termite community.

M.E.W.

COOPERS CREEK, PRIME 'ORGANIC' BEEF, FRAGILE ECOSYSTEMS, AND, PLEASE, NO IRRIGATED COTTON...

Floodplains of the Channel Country of western Queensland become highly productive grasslands after each flood-out. The cleanest, most 'organic' beef in the world is grown on the floodplains of Cooper Creek around Windorah — by default. The natural ecosystems of the floodplains in this part of the Channel Country are uncontaminated by pesticides and fertilisers, because there is no agriculture in a region where rainfall is inadequate and evaporation is enormous. About $100 million of export beef a year is produced from the grazing on the floodplains when they green up after the floodouts which turn the dry Channel Country into lush pasture.

Pastoralists in the Windorah region say that the country is the best in the world for fattening cattle. The grazing is produced by the annual, but very variable, flooding of the Cooper. Rain in the huge catchment changes the dry landscape, even when none occurs locally and the nearest falls may be hundreds of kilometres away. The Cooper is transformed from a chain of waterholes in a sinuous bed which winds across the flattest land imaginable to a running river in a network of running streams; then the waters spread across the countryside, replenishing the soil's water, revitalising it with silt. How far the floods flow each year depends on the height reached by the river, each flood being different, and sometimes not occurring, but the very flat terrain means that even a 10 cm difference in river height can mean that some of the pastures on which beef production depends will not be lush grass needed to fatten the cattle on certain properties. Country away from the floodplains is arid and unproductive.

The flowing of the ephemeral rivers and the flooding of the vast floodplains of the inward-draining river systems in the Lower Cooper (and Lower Diamantina further west), which sends water towards Lake Eyre, is dependent on sufficient water coming down from the upper reaches of the rivers. The Coongie Lakes and other wetlands owe their precarious survival to years when there is enough water to reach them in sufficient volume. In a dry land where rainfall fluctuates in the distant catchments of the rivers, **any interference with the natural flow and cycles of the rivers would be environmental vandalism. All the ecosystems are fragile and the fragility increases from the better-watered north to the nearly waterless dead heart of the continent.**

About 20 km north-north east from Windorah is a property 'Curravera', bought by cotton farmers from further east. They want to irrigate from the Cooper and claim that they will only be taking less than 2% of annual flow when they use 42 million megalitres a year. The Coopers Creek Protection Group opposes the project. Interfering with the fragile balance

Grey box on a grassy floodplain in the Channel Country.

M.E.W.

Coopers Creek.

M.E.W.

Mulga and termites in country between the channels of the Channel Country.

M.E.W.

of the natural (sustainable) ecosystems on which local pastoralism depends, and threatening the survival of ecosystems downstream by altering the hydrology is only one of their concerns. The excessive use of pesticides and fertilisers required in cotton production could put the clean, 'organic' quality of their beef at risk. The advocates of cotton argue that soon new, **genetically engineered cotton** will be available soon and it will hardly need any pesticides; and that because the property to be irrigated is slightly raised above the floodplain, levee banks can prevent contamination of water.

The battle lines are drawn...

CHAPTER NINE

THE FIVE FOCAL CATCHMENTS OF THE NATIONAL DRYLAND SALINITY PROGRAM

The National Dryland Salinity Program is focused on five catchments which have been chosen in order to spread research over a range of projects. The Catchments are: The Upper South East Catchment in South Australia; the Kent River Catchment in Western Australia; the Loddon–Campaspe Catchments in Victoria; the Upper Burdekin Catchment in Queensland; and the Liverpool Plains in New South Wales.

THE UPPER SOUTH EAST CATCHMENT, SOUTH AUSTRALIA

The Upper South East of South Australia has a large component of wetlands and old dune systems, being the region whose landscapes were produced by the flooding of the Murray Basin by the sea during the Tertiary, and by the sea-level changes of the Pleistocene. This catchment has an area of 700 000 ha, average rainfall of about 500 mm a year and evaporation rate of twice that amount. Low relief, with dune and limestone ridges parallel to the coast impeding drainage, combine to create a wet, fertile region which was eagerly developed for grazing. A total of 434 farming enterprises was based in the region in 1995, with grazing of cattle and sheep the main land use and some limited areas of cropping. However, the impacts of clearing and drainage have combined to culminate recently in a situation where surface flooding and rising groundwater are problems which have created about 400 000 ha of farmland salinisation.

The worst affected areas lie between Keith, Woods Well, Kingston and Desert Camp, and a further 200 000 ha are threatened.[95,123] Major State government and community investigations into salinity management are under way, prompted by financial losses to farmers. Stock carrying capacity is estimated to have fallen by 0.5 million dry sheep equivalents, with a further loss of over one million predicted over the next 25 years, a long-term productivity loss of 45%. Waterlogging during the winter rainy season affects most of the catchment, many rivers and wetlands are now in the high salinity category, and flood management has become an issue.

The proximity of agricultural enterprises in this catchment to inland freshwater wetlands and to the Coorong makes it a particularly sensitive area where any change in the water balance caused by land-use practices is potentially serious. The Coorong is listed as a *Wetland of International Importance* under the Ramsar Convention and several other regional wetlands also

THE FIVE FOCAL CATCHMENTS

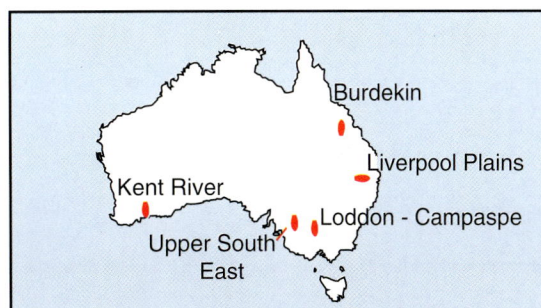

179

have high conservation value. Destruction of wetlands has been extensive since European settlement (which was rapid in the region between 1860 and 1879, see map p.14)

Since the first drain was constructed at Kingston in 1863, it is estimated that 4320 km^2 (or 88.8%) of the original 4900 km^2 of wetlands have been drained. (Twelve of the original 42 native mammal species of the area became locally extinct during this process, and eight became rare. Many bird species also became locally extinct or rare.) Many of the remaining wetlands are semi-permanent or temporary and flood only on a seasonal basis.[122]

The low hills and flats running parallel to the coast have been cleared for agriculture mostly in the last three or four decades, resulting in a rising water-table. The deep-rooted lucerne pastures which replaced native vegetation after clearing kept the water-table at near-natural levels until they were devastated in the 1970s by aphid attacks, and then groundwater recharge from rainfall started in earnest. Re-establishment of lucerne has been hampered by the non-wetting characteristics of soil on the rises. Surface flooding, compounded by altered drainage and run-on from neighbouring lands, as well as the higher water-tables, has increased the loss of pasture on low-lying land. As water-tables rise to within 2 m of the surface, evaporation draws the saline groundwater to the surface. Increasing areas of bare

ground have been prone to surface evaporation in summer, and therefore to salinisation.

Investigations have shown that the salinisation in this region cannot be managed by re-vegetation alone, and that surface drainage is necessary to dispose of the water which flows into the area during 'wet' winters. Provision will be made to maintain regional wetlands as part of the drainage scheme. Farmers will have to undertake on-farm practices which include pasture improvement on the rises and flats, and saltland plantings on salt-affected areas. Significant revegetation with native species is proposed to achieve a 20% cover in the region over 13 years, with the aim of reducing recharge of the local groundwater system.

In June 1995 the South Australian State Cabinet endorsed *the staged implementation of an integrated package of measures to address the twin problems of dryland salinity and surface flooding in the Upper South East*. The package includes surface water and wetland management, coordinated drainage, on-farm agricultural measures and revegetation. Details of the financing of the scheme are given below, because this example is typical of the sort of arrangements which are made between government agencies, landowners and community groups like Landcare.[123]

To finance the Upper South East Land Use Plan involves:

- State Government contributing 37.5% of the $24-million project over six years, with a matching contribution sought from the Commonwealth.
- The local community contributing 25% of the cost before the project could be implemented. The South Eastern Water Conservation and Drainage Board has developed a proposal to raise the required $1 million per year from the local community. The proposal recognises that the community levy should be raised from an area wider than that which is salinised and has defined a catchment which extends from the coast right to the Victorian border, an area of more than a million hectares. Within the catchment four zones are delineated according to the varying degrees of contribution to the problem and benefit to be received from implementation of the management plan. A different levy is imposed for each zone, from 10 cents per hectare per year for areas which receive no direct benefit, to $2.10 per hectare for areas receiving the greatest benefit. In this way landowners will contribute 90% of the community contribution.
- The remaining 10% will be collected from the six local government areas in recognition of the indirect benefit that urban dwellers in the service towns throughout the region will receive from healthier agricultural activity.

THE UPPER SOUTH EAST DRYLAND SALINITY AND FLOOD MANAGEMENT PLAN

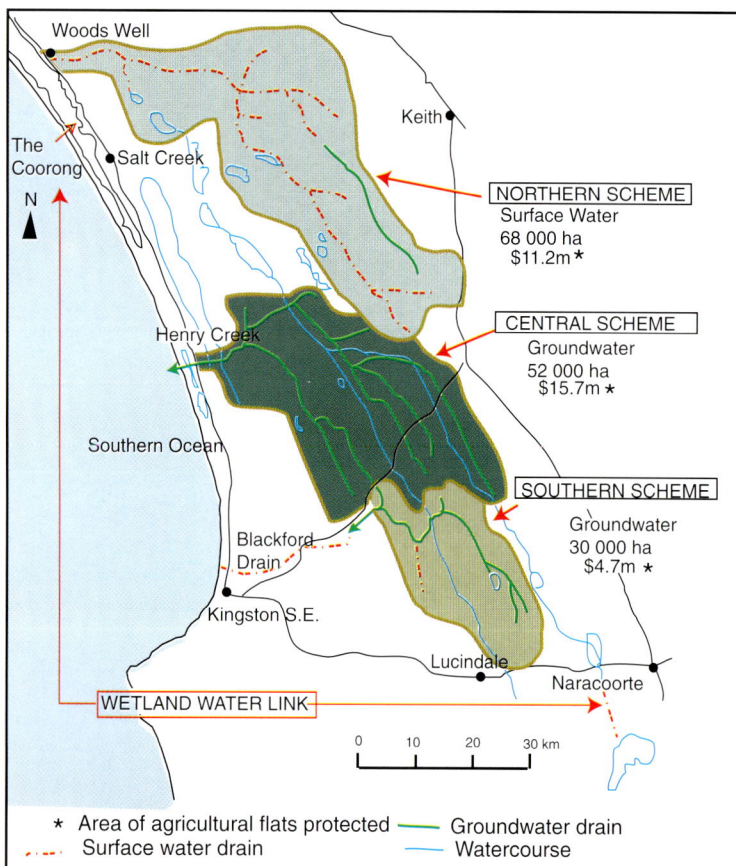

Woods Well
The Coorong
N
Salt Creek
Keith

NORTHERN SCHEME
Surface Water
68 000 ha
$11.2m *

Henry Creek

CENTRAL SCHEME
Groundwater
52 000 ha
$15.7m *

Southern Ocean

SOUTHERN SCHEME
Groundwater
30 000 ha
$4.7m *

Blackford Drain
Kingston S.E.
Lucindale
Naracoorte

WETLAND WATER LINK

0   10   20   30 km

* Area of agricultural flats protected
- - - Surface water drain
—— Groundwater drain
— Watercourse

After LWRRDC [123]

PROPOSED SOUTH EAST WETLANDS WATERLINK

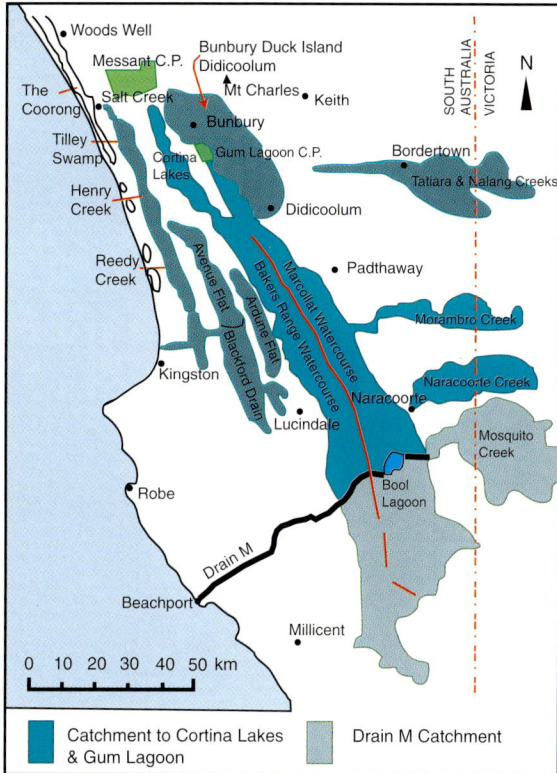

| Catchment to Cortina Lakes & Gum Lagoon | Drain M Catchment |

SOUTH EAST WATERCOURSES CATCHMENT AND LOCALITY PLAN

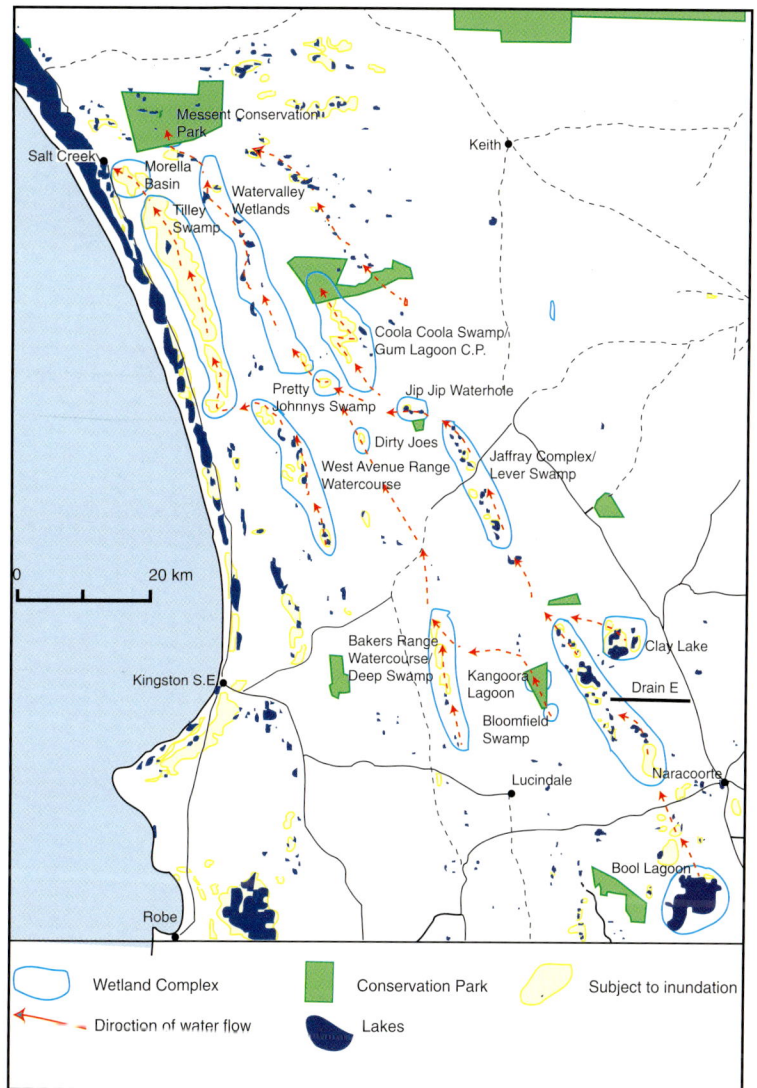

| Wetland Complex | Conservation Park | Subject to inundation |
| Direction of water flow | Lakes | |

After Watervalley Wetlands Management Plan

The Wetlands Waterlink Proposal for the South East: The Upper South East Salinity and Flood Management Plan

The Wetlands Management Program of the Department of Environment and Natural Resources considers that a major opportunity exists to create a chain of wetlands in the South East. This **'Wetlands Waterlink'** would stretch from Bool Lagoon to the Coorong, providing a habitat link between the two *Wetlands of International Importance* through corridor ribbons of swamps, marshes, lakes and native vegetation. The concept effectively balances the use of water in wetland management while protecting agricultural land from excessive flooding. It would create a mosaic of wetland and terrestrial habitats which would provide breeding grounds, wildlife corridors and refugia, thereby promoting the return of biodiversity and establishing the region as worthy of Ramsar International Listing. It would also become a tourist attraction.

Wetlands are the most biologically productive of all ecosystems and their importance is only now being recognised. Worldwide they have suffered a similar fate to those of the South East, with few remaining in pristine condition and their overall numbers drastically reduced. Now the opportunity exists to do something wonderfully positive to redress the situation at least in this special part of Australia. When the Waterlink would help with the flooding and salinity problems as well, one can only hope the plan will be accepted and implemented.

THE UPPER KENT RIVER CATCHMENT, WESTERN AUSTRALIA

The Upper Kent River Catchment in south-western Western Australia is the smallest catchment in the National Dryland Salinity Program, and it differs from the others in that it has no urban centres. It represents land which was originally forest and open woodland. State forests of karri and jarrah still comprise most of the 720 km^2 of the Lower Kent Catchment, where rainfall of 1400 mm in the Kenton area on the lower reaches of the river ensures that salt does not accumulate in soils. The Kent River flows into the ocean half way between the towns of Walpole and Denmark on the south coast.

The Upper Kent Catchment has an area of 185 000 ha. The jarrah, redgum and white gum forests have been cleared from 65% of the region, and remnant forest on private land totals 27% of the area. Rainfall of 550 to 900 mm a year and average evaporation of 1350 mm sets the stage for salinisation, while the large areas which are inward draining towards swamps and

THE WATERVALLEY WETLANDS: A PRIVATE CONSERVATION PROJECT

The Watervalley Wetlands is one of the most important wetland sites in Australia and it exists because of the vision and generosity of one man, Mr Tom Brinkworth, and his family. King of a pastoral empire, he bought Cortina Station in 1970 and has added a string of properties over the years, including Watervalley and Didicoolum. His land stretches for 150 km with the wetlands spread out from north of Kingston to south of Beachport. He has spent millions of dollars on earthworks, weirs, pipes and drains, creating a series of lakes and renewing wetlands on his property. Hundreds of thousands of waterbirds breed there, and many are migrants, some from the northern parts of the continent when wetlands have contracted during the dry season; others from distant lands.

The lakes are stocked with all the native fish species of the Murray–Darling system; the protected revegetation zones round the lakes are burgeoning with new life. The Watervalley Wetlands are regarded as being in the same class as Bool and Hacks Lagoons, or the Coorong, and Lakes Alexandrina and Albert (both listed under the Ramsar Convention which requires that the wetland concerned is home to more than 20 000 waterbirds).

Brolgas and magpie geese will probably be re-introduced to the wetlands. (Some magpie geese have already been returned to Bool Lagoon.) Mr Brinkworth believes that improving the drainage system in the South East is crucial to enhancing the wetlands. The biggest drain in the region, Drain M, carries the freshwater overflow from Bool Lagoon straight to the sea, and he wants to see it returned to its natural course, flooding the wetlands, and flowing into the Coorong as it used to do a hundred years ago.

Mr Brinkworth started the **Wetlands and Wildlife Trust,** a registered organisation which provides economic incentives for private sector conservation. The trust already owns 10 000 ha of wetlands and conservation lands, and its founder believes that if the Federal Government permitted an extension of the concept under the Income Tax Act, millions of hectares would be conserved for ever Australia-wide. (The Bush Heritage Trust started by Dr Bob Brown in Tasmania has similar aims to the Wetlands and Wildlife Trust, and the Victorian government has an Act enabling private individuals to put a covenant on their land.) The South Australian State government has backed the Wetlands and Wildlife Trust, endorsing a recommendation which waives State charges on land sold or donated to approved trusts or schemes dedicated for conservation purposes.[124]

JIP JIP LAKE, JULY 1992

Jip Jip Lake was created in 1984 by construction of a weir across the Marcollat Watercourse above Jip Jip waterhole. It is on private land and is part of the **Watervalley Wetlands** project of conservationist Tom Brinkworth. When the area was flooded some pockets of river redgums were drowned, but a large buffer zone around the lake is protected from grazing and regeneration of the river reds is occurring. Management of water levels since 1989 has been revised to allow seasonal drying, in order to stimulate the food chain for seasonal breeding of waterbirds, and to sustain the trees. The picture shows the lake in a drying phase where bleached sea tassel *(Ruppia megacarpa)* is exposed around the margins and areas of drowned vegetation are exposed in the lake bed, while strong regeneration is occurring in the protected riparian zone. *(Photograph and caption information kindly supplied by Anne Jensen)*

Jip Jip Lake, July 1992.

ANNE JENSEN

MANDINA MARSHES, JULY 1992

The Mandina Marshes were created in 1991 when Mr Tom Brinkworth built a flow-control structure to maintain an appropriate flow regime in this extensive wetland area. Regional drainage had reduced it to temporary, infrequently filled swamps, parts of which had been ploughed or grazed during dry seasons. The wetland now covers 1865 ha and supports major rookeries of ibis, egrets and cormorants. *(Photograph and caption information kindly supplied by Anne Jensen.)*

Mandina Marshes, July 1992.

ANNE JENSEN

lakes present problems of rising water-tables. Soil erosion and deterioration of remnant vegetation and its associated wildlife are additional problems.

Salinisation of the Kent River has become a major concern partly because the river is considered a potential water supply for future development in south-western Western Australia (where population is concentrated and quality drinking water is at a premium). The salinity levels of the water draining from the upper catchment have increased more than tenfold since the catchment was cleared, and are still rising, while the salinity levels of water draining the lower catchment have remained approximately constant. (This illustrates graphically the difference between forested and cleared land in maintaining water-tables at safe levels and reducing the threat of salinisation.) The salty water from the Upper Catchment mixes with the fresh water from the Lower Catchment, so that at its mouth, near Owingup Swamp, the Kent River is brackish. The Owingup Swamp has been recognised as important for biodiversity in the region and increasing salinity is threatening its rare waterfowl and fish populations.

Some clearing and development took place in the Upper Catchment in the 1800s but the main burst of activity was in the land settlement boom after the Second World War, when policies of almost total land clearance were the norm. Clearing bans were instituted in 1977 in response to the salinity problem which was developing in the rivers. **At present 20% of the catchment is affected by severe secondary salinisation, and the problem is still spreading and will affect 30% by early next century**. It is significantly reducing the agricultural productivity of the region and is ecologically destructive.

About 90 farms are operating in the Upper Kent Catchment today. The relatively long growing season makes them potentially valuable and though grazing sheep and cattle is the main land use and only 15% of farmland is cropped, a further 42% would be suitable for viticulture, horticulture and agroforestry if secure water supplies are constructed (as no fresh groundwater is available). An estimated 33% of the catchment is affected by waterlogging between May and October (in the winter rainfall season). Already the replacing of trees on areas of the Upper Catchment where rainfall is greater than 600 mm has been carried out by Landcare groups. Agro-forestry and hardwood enterprises are seen as remedies for land degradation problems and as possible solutions for the economic decline of the region. Plantations of bluegums had also been established on more than 6% of the cleared land by the end of 1995, in commercial enterprises, not as part of any planned Landcare initiative as such, and not necessarily sited in premium places for maximum impact on catchment hydrology.

The research being carried out under the National Dryland Salinity Program will aim at establishing land use practices which minimise waterlogging, salinisation and soil degradation (sodium level, soil acidity and

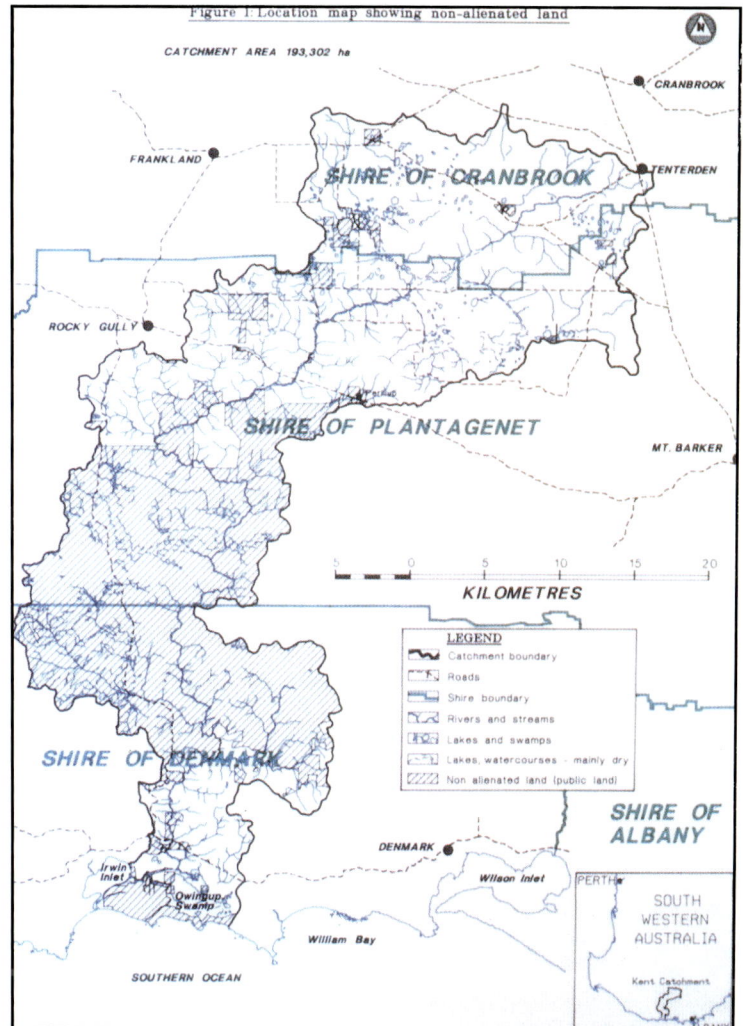

Figure 1 Location map showing non-alienated land

CATCHMENT AREA 193,302 ha

KILOMETRES

LEGEND
Catchment boundary
Roads
Shire boundary
Rivers and streams
Lakes and swamps
Lakes, watercourses - mainly dry
Non alienated land (public land)

The Kent River Catchment

Steve Porritt, AgWA

erosion). It will also address the problems of increased nutrient levels and salt in streams and counter the decline in area of natural vegetation remnants. Surveys of plants, native and introduced animals, birds, reptiles and amphibians have been carried out as a basis for the program.

The current approach to agriculture in the Upper Catchment is clearly unsustainable, and a shift to sustainable practices will have to include, among other things, the systematic planting of shelter belts, better soil husbandry, conservation of native vegetation remnants, and a focus on plant–microbe interactions and on species diversity in the agricultural ecosystem.

The first part of the program has aimed at identifying and describing **Land Management Units** (LMUs). A unit is essentially a piece of land which has similar production characteristics, as well as similar degradation hazards, for a given land use. Units provide an alternative to the traditional square paddock framework and allow land to be farmed according to its production capability rather than to arbitrary fenceline.[125] Strategies can then be developed for the best management practices for each unit type and advice given on what to plant, rotations, fertilisers and all the other factors which have to be considered if sustainability is to be achieved.

The 1995 Land Management Report for the Kent

Landsat TM August 1994 - bands 4, 5, 7 in R, G, B

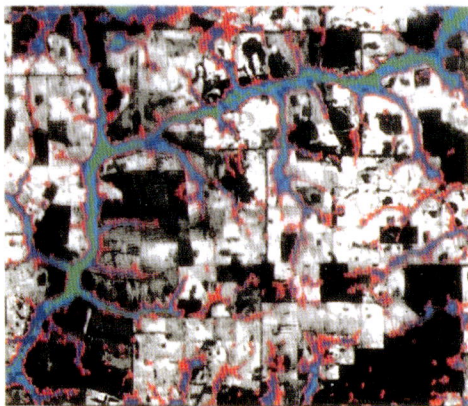

Salinity Change Map -

Top: Dryland salinity in the Kent Catchment. Salt encroachment has rendered one dam and its surrounding pasture useless, and another dam is threatened.

Above:Mapping Salinity, past, present and future
STEVE PORRITT, AGWA

River Catchment lists key recommendations for Total Catchment Management.

- Fencing to exclude stock from remnant bush, streams, wetlands and eroded areas; and to manage grazing of saltland planted to saltbush.
- Active management of remnant bush, streams and wetlands, and rehabilitation of eroded areas.
- Farming land according to its capability. Land Management Units provide a starting point.
- Landcare and other community meetings and workshops to organise farm planning and mapping according to LMUs and soils, and for exchange of information between farmers and agencies.
- Widespread and systematic planting of trees. Alley farming with 20% of agricultural area planted to shelter belts is the objective. Corridors linking remnant bush would advantage wildlife.
- Use of plants which have high rates of transpiration — perennial pastures rather than annual; deep-rooted crops; management for active growth which increases water up-take during the rainy season; and planting trees.
- Surface and sub-surface draining used in conjunction with alley farming.

All this sounds very progressive and upbeat. However, it says nothing about the people involved and the effort and sacrifices which are being made in an attempt to do a King Canute-sized job of holding back the tide of degradation which is engulfing the region. Because the same sort of human problems beset all Landcare efforts to some degree, and the Kent River example is about as difficult as they come, it highlights a number of social and economic issues.

When one reads the 1985–95 annual reports of the Kent River Soil Conservation District Committee and the Kent River Land Conservation District (LCD) Committee which preceded the Kent Focal Catchment Project, one cannot help being overwhelmed by the magnitude of the task facing the largely voluntary workers in regions where the degradation is severe. The same handful of people are the 'willing horses' and what they achieve is remarkable. Overworked, often under-appreciated, it is so easy to become discouraged, yet it is obvious that gains are slowly being made. Burn-out and disillusionment are two of the factors with which the core community members have to contend. A few quotes from reports by committee officers underline the problems:

1990: *I have observed a wide range of attitudes towards Landcare in the LCD, ranging from total involvement and co-operation on the one hand to scepticism on the other. Without involvement and co-operation by a majority of land users I question whether your representatives on the committee are going to continue to donate their valuable time and money to the LCD for little reward... Land users in the catchment that are involved in the sheep and wool industry have enjoyed several good years, but with very moderate amounts of money being spent on conservation work. It is my opinion that* **until the government of the day gives farmers more incentive through the taxation system nothing much will change, with respect to conservation work.** *With the prospect of gross income being reduced by around 40% in the coming year, I wonder what the future holds for conservation in the Kent.*

*1994–95: The LCD Committee has had a very active year representing and attempting to serve the needs of the community, as well as fulfilling the demands of the Kent Project...which after 15 months of meeting is going to attempt to address "The threats to sustainable agriculture caused by the rising saline water-table, also to improve ground and surface water use, distribution and quality." What we now have to decide is **who pays in human and monetary cost** to get up to 25% of the farm land back to a stable vegetated state, reclaimed degraded land and trees in a sustainable condition, and catchment drainage systems, if they are to be put in place. **With an aging and declining community of Stewards of a Natural Resource at our disposal,** we need to identify and put up proposals to achieve at least some of our goals and present them through the Kent Project. **It is beyond the capability of existing landholders to fund and maintain land management practices to correct generations of mistakes and provide a sustainable natural resource for future generations. Therefore what is required is clearly identified workable financial incentives for farmers with the will and ability to get on with the job. Such leadership does not appear to be forthcoming from Federal government.***

These comments emphasise several of the factors which influence the situation — the aging nature of the farming community, where comparatively few young people are taking up the challenges of the land, and where often the conservatism of the older generation makes the adoption of new practices unattractive; the fact that today's farmers are battling with environmental degradation caused by their predecessors on the land (and often being blamed for the worsening situation although it is not of their making); the financial difficulties which mean that there is no money to put into conservation when farming has become such a marginal pursuit; and the need for realistic incentives from government.

So much government money which is made available for land and water conservation is **perceived** to be supporting the bureaucracy, being spent on expensive glossy reports which mainly pass from Department to Department justifying their existence, when more used on the ground to deal with the everyday problems would solve some of them. Certainly the Federal government activities are seen by a great number of citizens involved in these matters as window-dressing for the next election. (We should not forget that all of us are voters and that through community movements like Landcare we have a voice and can change our world for the better.)

THE LODDON-CAMPASPE FOCAL CATCHMENTS, VICTORIA

The Loddon and Campaspe Rivers have their headwaters in the Great Divide, and they run through the Riverine Plain in northern Victoria to the Murray

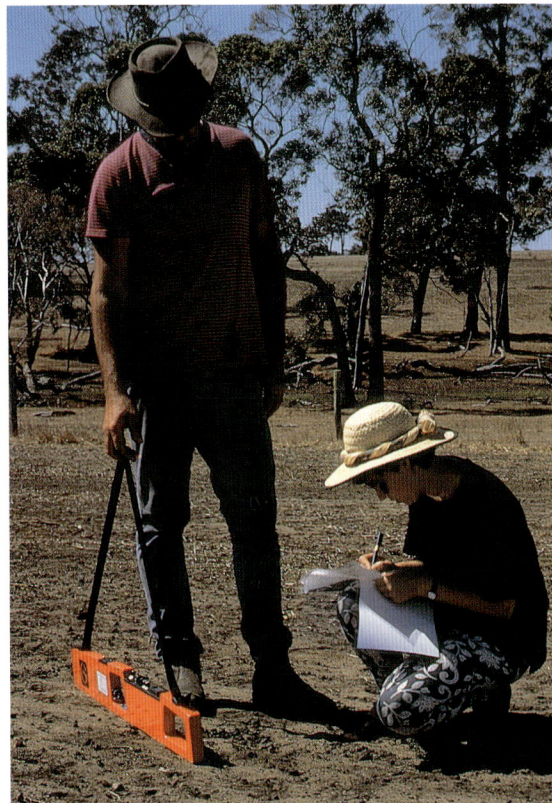

Kim and Susan Henderson taking salinity readings with an EM38.

LWRRDC

River. The Loddon Catchment has an area of 965 000 ha, the Campaspe 443 100 ha. The population of the region is higher than that in the four other focus catchments.

The dryland salinity problem in the Loddon–Campaspe catchments has been recognised for many years and it impacts significantly on agriculture in the uplands and on the plains. Apart from the salinisation problems, the productivity of the area is affected by soil acidification and erosion, and by waterlogging on the plains. The soils are derived from rocks which already have a high salt content, and that salinity is estimated to be augmented by salt from rainfall at 20 kg/ha each year in the upper part of the catchment. Rainfall over the catchment varies from 1300 to 380 mm, averaging about 500 mm per annum. Salt entering the Murray River from the catchments is estimated to comprise about 10% of the river's salt, measured at Morgan. The Bet Bet sub-catchment yields 20% of the Loddon's contribution from only 10% of the land area.

Irrigation on the plains compounds the problems. Large-scale irrigation started last century and within 20 years the region was experiencing high water-table and salinity problems. **Today, virtually the whole of the irrigation area on the Loddon Plains has a high, saline, water-table, with salinity problems extending into the surrounding dryland regions.** This area was part of what was a salt desert during the last glacial stage of the Pleistocene ice age, only 18 000 years ago, when sediments from dry salt lakes were blown across the landscape. Gypsum is abundant in the soils. An account of this horrendous stage is given in *After the Greening.*[6]

The sub-surface geology of the area, with deep leads in ancient river beds (prior streams), alternating marine and freshwater sediments with differing permeability, and other features, results in the northern Loddon Plain being a natural groundwater discharge zone. This northern part of the plain is drained by Barr Creek, which has an annual load of 170 000 tonnes of salt, mostly derived from saline groundwater. Barr Creek originated as a surface drain for groundwater discharge during past phases of high water-tables and salinisation during ice age climatic fluctuations, and today is a major 'point source' of salt discharge into the Murray River.

Irrigated agriculture and the physical conditions which exist on the Loddon Plain are so clearly incompatible that it seems outrageous that it continues at all.

In the upper parts of the catchment the salinity in streams varies from low to extremely high, and eutrophication (increased nutrient levels from agricultural run-off) contributes to algal blooms and problems for aquatic life.

There are about 1800 farming enterprises in the dual catchment with grazing (sheep and cattle); cropping (wheat, oats, barley, lupins, field peas, canola, safflower); and horticulture (apples, grapes, potatoes). The extensive clearing in the catchment raises concerns for the remnant natural vegetation and the maintenance of biodiversity.

Ten study sites have been selected for collection and correlation of data such as soil characteristics, groundwater, historical climate records, and site-specific biophysical information, in order to be able to model land-use options which can restore soil–water balance. The underlying research is more comprehensive than in any of the other focus catchments.

Three practical initiatives have been developed to help to achieve the Salinity Management Plan's major goal of *reducing the impacts of salinity and other forms of soil and water deterioration by using rain where it falls*. Financed by the Department of Conservation and Natural Resources, these innovative schemes are:

- The **Perennial Pasture Seed Rebate Scheme**, which offers an incentive to plant deep-rooted perennial pastures with a rebate of $2.00 a kilogram for seed of lucerne, phalaris or cocksfoot. Seed is purchased from private suppliers, not government agencies; the rebate is paid and an information kit which contains technical information on perennial pastures and the salinity management plan relevant to the farmer's district accompanies the payment. Deep-rooted, perennial pastures help to lower water-tables and to prevent erosion.

- The **Machinery Conversion Scheme** provides a grant towards the modifications needed to convert conventional combines to enable direct drilling (planting into last year's stubble) and minimum tillage. Stubble retention and minimum tillage are key elements of improved land management.

- A **Rate Rebate Scheme** gives 100% rebate of rates on land taken out of production for revegetation. It is given for one year to establish perennial pasture; for each year over 10 years to establish trees. The City of Greater Bendigo was the first Local Government area to introduce this incentive and is to be congratulated for taking positive steps to remedy salinity in its region.

THE UPPER BURDEKIN CATCHMENT, QUEENSLAND

The Burdekin River Catchment covers 15 million hectares, an area twice the size of Tasmania. It supports a quarter of Queensland's export beef cattle industry. Soil erosion caused by grazing had risen to five to 50 times the geological rate. **An estimated 20 million tonnes of topsoil, containing nitrogen and phosphorus worth $100 million, is deposited in the Burdekin Falls Dam annually, or out to sea.**

The **Upper Burdekin Catchment** is an area of 6.7 million hectares centred around Charters Towers. Gold mining and cattle are major industries. The catchment was chosen as a focal catchment in the National Dryland Salinity Research, Development and Extension program because it presents opportunities for assessing the dryland salinity risk in the semi-arid tropics. Rainfall averages 500–700 mm per year but is very variable, and restricted to summer, and evaporation is approximately 2000 mm — which suggests that a salinisation risk is present, although locals consider that it is only a problem 'down south'. The landscape is reasonably uncleared; problems relate to over-grazing and fire-management mainly on the 200 large grazing properties, and to irrigation in the newly emerging horticultural industries depending on the Burdekin Dam. The dam was designed as an emergency water supply for Townsville, but so far has not been called upon in that capacity.

The building of the dam might not be an unmitigated advantage to the region. Erosion due to over-grazing has been so severe that the river system carries a great load of sediment. Silting up of the dam is a problem, but the downstream effects are more serious than that.[126] The dam starves the river below it of the sediment required to maintain the delta on its coastal floodplain, which is where a large part of the sugar industry is located. In addition, the fine sediment fraction is washed over the wall and serves to clog up the intake areas for the aquifers which supply water for the cane in the delta. Through time the sand in the lower part of the river will be removed and with no more coming past the dam there will not be any to protect and maintain the delta. (Any sea-level rise due to the Greenhouse effect would be a serious additional problem.)

Rice growing is expanding in the Burdekin valley where the soils have a sandy or sandy-loam horizon overlying a clay horizon with high sodium content. Up to 19 rice crops have been produced on paddies flooded by water from the dam and changes to the soil have resulted, making it more suitable for rice cropping but rendering it unsuitable for other crops when not flooded for rice.

Catchments throughout the dry tropics have many similarities to the Upper Burdekin. They are in a generally under-developed state, and like the Upper Burdekin, have a highly seasonal and very variable rainfall pattern and are under extensive grazing by cattle. Considerable similarities exist between the Burdekin, the Northern Territory and the Kimberley. Most tropical catchments are facing pressures for vegetation clearing and intensification of land use. Part of the reasoning behind the choice of the Burdekin as a focal catchment is that a study of the situation there will provide information useful in dealing with other catchments in the north. A preliminary report on land degradation was produced in 1991 by CSIRO.

A project steering committee meeting in Charters Towers in October 1993 decided that the total Upper Burdekin Catchment was too large and that the study would be confined to the Dalrymple Shire. A major project report outlines the database on which the project will proceed.[127]

Gully erosion was found to be widespread and severe on one-third of the shire, and sheet erosion and scalding were widespread over the whole region. (Extrapolated over the dry tropical savannas, and added to the known state of the Ord River Catchment, and others in the Kimberley, a picture emerges of a **great deal of degradation in the northern rangelands**.)

The invasion of **exotic woody weeds** was a major concern.

- Rubber vine (Cryptostegia grandiflora) was prevalent on waterways.
- Chinee apple or jujube (Ziziphus mauritania) was thick on some disturbed areas.
- Parthenium weed (Parthenium hysterophorus) was spreading on some clay soils.
- Lantana (Lantana camara) and prickly acacia (Acacia nilotica) are also problems in some areas.
- Currant bush (Carissa ovata and C. lanceolata), native species, had become a serious weed problem because its sprawling habit enables it to cover much of the ground surface in some areas, restricting pasture growth.

Pasture decline was found to be severe although rainfall had been above average in the two years prior to the report. Change in pasture composition has been progressive since grazing began. The first herds of cattle and sheep had caused a decline in the percentage of kangaroo grass (Themeda triandra), and black spear grass (Heteropogon contortus) increased as it is more resistant to grazing. It declined in its turn, being replaced by the wire grasses (Aristida spp.) and annual grasses. In the west of the shire the spinifex-based pastures (Trioda

mitchellii) have declined. In recent years Indian couch (Bothriochloa pertusa) has spread in the eastern part of the shire. It protects the soil because of its creeping habit and withstands grazing but does not provide a bulk of standing food in the winter. Timber regrowth and thickening up of natural timber (woody weed invasion) are increasing problems in the area.

Salinity is confined to small areas in low places in the landscape locally where a great deal of clearing took place during mining operations, for mine props and fuel, last century. The depth of the water-table in the catchment is being mapped and places where it is within 6 m of the surface are considered to be at risk — mainly on the alluvial flats. Land clearing is officially only by permit so that rise of water-tables should not be contributed to by further tree removal.

Landcare and community involvement are important ingredients in programs which hope to bring sustainability to the pastoral industry in the Burdekin. The Dalrymple Landcare Committee was the first Landcare committee to be formed in an extensive grazing area in Australia, and its activities over the last nine years have led to a massive attitudinal change for the better in the region. Smaller groups are now forming to address problems and set goals for improvements in their immediate vicinities.

The **Balfes Creek Catchment Group,** formed in 1994, represents one of the tributary catchments in the Charters Towers region. The group comprises landholders of the 19 commercial properties that make up the catchment. They have identified woody weeds, in particular rubber vine and Parkinsonia, as their main focus, while all other land management issues relating to erosion, salinity awareness, soil fertility and fire are to be addressed in their action planning. Their goal is sustainable land management, in a region which is in the middle of a rural crisis with the cattle market in tatters and no rain yet this year (1996). **Rubber vine control** is recognised as being beyond the financial capacity of individual farmers where infestation is serious, but is feasible where it is in scattered pockets, and is being tackled on that basis. Community lobbying enables the obtaining of government assistance in subsidising chemicals and diesel, and in providing the training needed in using the herbicides safely and effectively.

A case history of one of the stations within the Balfes Creek catchment has been chosen to illustrate the history of land use, the changes through time and the present situation in the Burdekin. The Landsberg family of Trafalgar Station have generously supplied information on 83 years of management of the station by three generations.

Above top: The Balfes Creek Landcare Group has a program for monitoring groundwater levels in wells and bores.

Above: Trafalgar House.

ROGER LANDSBERG

Trafalgar Station

A history of 83 years of management of a cattle station in north Queensland.

(Facts regarding the station and its management only supplied by Roger Landsberg, grandson of the first owner. Integration into the context of this book and additions and comments by the author.)

Trafalgar is a 32 000 ha property. Its soils are mainly phosphate-deficient yellow earths, but alluvial flats along the three large creeks which dissect the land are more fertile, with blackwood and gidgee scrub (*Acacia melanoxylon* and *A. cambagei*) growing on brown cracking clay soils which have a higher phosphate content. These alluvial soils occur on about 25% of the property. The yellow earths are timbered with box, ironbark and other eucalypts, wattles and quinine (*Petalostigma pubescens*). Native pasture includes perennial Queensland blue, kangaroo and spear grasses; and a variety of soft annual grasses and herbaceous plants. A number of natural waterholes are scattered over the property, with one in each of the creeks being a '9-month' hole in normal seasons

Trafalgar was bought by Lovis James Landsberg in

1913, fully stocked with 3000 cattle and 300 horses, for ten thousand pounds sterling, half of which was borrowed. At the time of purchase there was only one man-made water facility, one divisional fence which halved the property, and one centrally positioned set of dip yards.

It must have been a difficult decade in which to take on a new property because between 1911 and 1917 there was a persistent El Nino episode and it had two peak drought periods — in 1912–13 and 1915–16 with hardly any relief between. Farm records show that the horses were sold to the Indian remount market and most of the male cattle were sold, so that when the disastrous 1915 drought came the farm was debt-free and could survive, although only 300 breeders survived that year. Recurrent deaths among the herd during the next ten years were finally diagnosed as botulism resulting from 'bone chewing' by the cattle. The phosphorus deficiency in native pasture on the yellow earth soils caused a craving which was satisfied by chewing bones of those that had died, and the spores of the disease were ingested. Once the disease was diagnosed, by CSIRO officers who had encountered it in South Africa, a program of supplementation with bone flour and the burning of all carcases reduced the number of deaths until better supplements and vaccination became available in the late 1960s.

The original herd was shorthorn and shorthorn–red poll cross until 1928, when it was replaced with 800 Hereford breeders. Improvements to the property between 1915 and 1946 consisted of four wells and seven dams to supplement natural waterholes. Water and yard facilities were further updated in the 1960s and pasture improvement on a large scale took place in the 1970s and 1980s.

Gordon James Landsberg took over management of the property in the early 1950s and in 1958 Brahman and Santa Gertrudis bloodlines were introduced, the latter being dropped after three years. The perceived optimum herd size was always 3000 mixed cattle. In the early days numbers had fluctuated greatly due to drought and botulism. Drought years 1919, 1923, 1926, 1935, 1948 and 1951 resulted in 20% of breeders dying and as much as an 80% decrease in brandings in the year following each drought year. The introduction of urea supplementation in 1965–66 resulted in an improvement in breeder performance and numbers of saleable animals.

A beef industry recession in the 1970s led to a dramatic rise in cattle numbers on Trafalgar (to over 5000 head) and throughout the Dalrymple Shire, where numbers increased from 300 000 to a million. Good rains, productive pastures and the new feeding technology, using hardy Brahman cattle and intensive management, resulted in high numbers being maintained. The dry years later in the decade resulted in rapid land degradation — over-stocking, pasture under stress from inadequate and unpredictable rainfall, no natural attrition of herds such as had occurred with animals dying in droughts and from disease — a recipe

RUBBER VINE

DISTRIBUTION OF RUBBER VINE

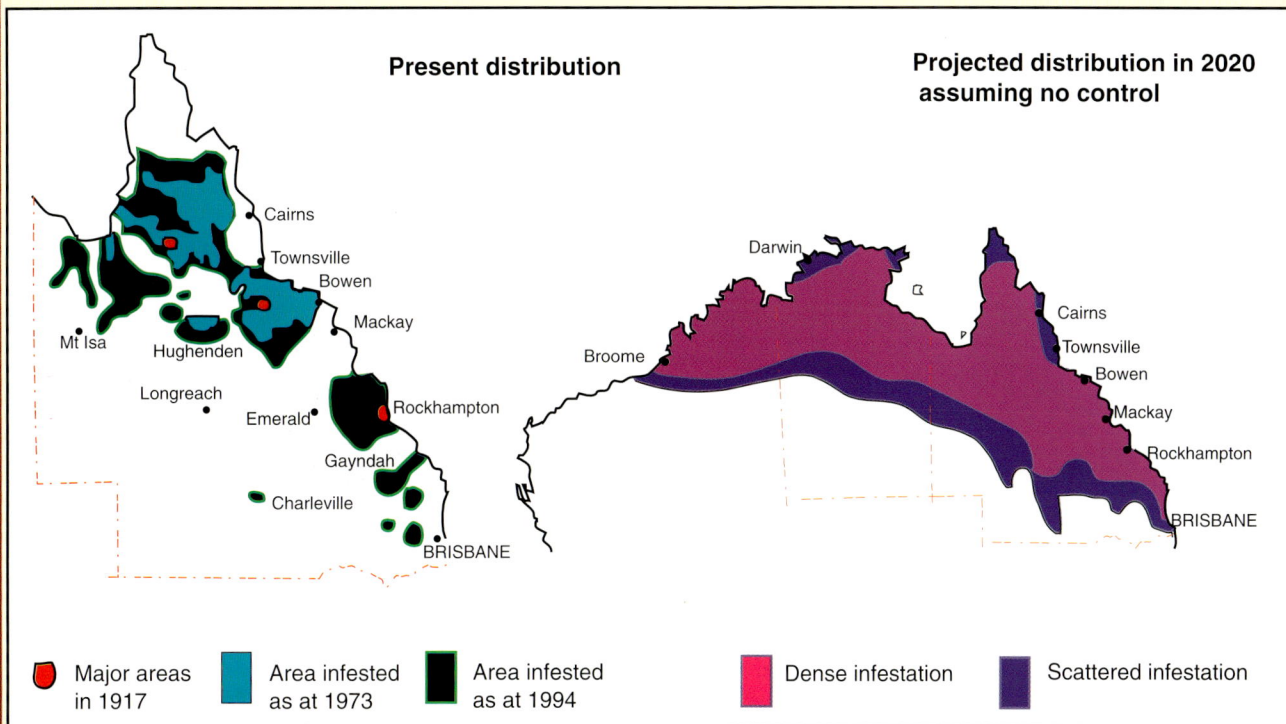

Present distribution

Projected distribution in 2020 assuming no control

Cairns
Townsville
Bowen
Mackay
Mt Isa
Hughenden
Longreach
Emerald
Rockhampton
Gayndah
Charleville
BRISBANE

Darwin
Broome
Cairns
Townsville
Bowen
Mackay
Rockhampton
BRISBANE

Major areas in 1917   **Area infested as at 1973**   **Area infested as at 1994**   **Dense infestation**   **Scattered infestation**

After QDPI Pamphlet

The Triffids of science fiction are rivalled by the all-enveloping, strangling, unstoppable *Cryptostegia grandiflora* which came to beautify north Queensland mining towns as a tame ornamental shrub from Madagascar in the mid 1870s and escaped to become one of the worst feral plants imaginable. A member of the Asclepiadaceae, it is aided and abetted in its invasion by the millions of parachute-suspended seeds which the wind carries far and wide from infested areas. Its pods can also float down rivers, releasing their seeds when they run aground far from their parent plants. Each pod contains about 300 seeds which can germinate to produce a hectare of solid rubbervine which will produce at least a billion seeds. With germination rates regularly attaining 95% and seeds having the ability to survive on the soil surface for a year (and longer if cultivated under) the magnitude of the problem becomes clearly visible.

Rubber vine has spread along the river systems, smothering other vegetation and forming impenetrable thickets, and outward into areas where competition has been reduced by over-grazing or drought. Where it has spread over hillsides and through pastures it has reduced grazing area and often is so thick that it causes difficulties in mustering and restricts access to water. It is poisonous to stock, though seldom eaten and then only when drought leaves little else.

Rubber vine is now found throughout the river systems from southern Cape York and the Gulf of Carpentaria and south along the coast to the Burnett River (on which Bundaberg is situated). Isolated infestations extend as far south as Gatton and as far west as the Northern Territory border, and are common throughout central Queensland west of the Great Divide. Infestations are present around Mt Isa, Longreach, Aramac, Blackall and Charleville. It is a declared noxious weed.

Control is difficult, labour-intensive and expensive. Some methods are: herbicides sprayed on leaves, on basal bark of stems, on cut surface of trunk when the plants have been slashed — from the ground, from helicopters when heavy infestation is along rivers; hot fires achieved by allowing grass to accumulate and dry prior to burning, which involves removal of stock for at least 12 months to allow fuel build-up, followed by herbicides on regrowth; mechanical means like ploughing and discing in suitable areas, followed by fire (but not bulldozing as the stems which are buried sprout again).

Research into biological control may one day provide an answer. The problem of rubber vine invasion is not confined to Australia, but is widespread in tropical lands, so many scientists are trying to find a solution.

Rubber vine festooning trees along a river.

M.E.W.

PASTURE MANAGEMENT ON TRAFALGAR

In 1936 Townsville stylo (Stylosanthes humilis) was introduced into pastures. It spread in moderate proportions until anthracnose (a fungal disease of legumes to which it was susceptible) wiped it out in the 1960s. Buffel grass (Cenchrus ciliaris) was introduced in small areas in 1954. In 1960, 2500 ha of eucalypt forest were ring-barked; in the late 1960s about 3000 ha were cleared by 'chaining' and sown to buffel grass and urochloa (Urochloa mosambicensis). Prolific grass growth followed, but eucalypt sucker regrowth was equally prolific, and re-chaining had to be carried out every six to eight years, costing about $4.5 per hectare. The cost of maintaining this clearing and the fact that it promotes dense woodland and woody weeds has led to a decision that no further eucalypt woodland will be managed in this way. Instead, smaller areas of gidgee and acacia scrub on the better soils are cleared and sown to pasture more profitably and without the problem of woody regrowth.

Under present-day management, care is taken to retain timber on water-intake areas of slopes and ridges, and along stream lines. Refuges are left for native fauna. The clearing and sowing of improved pastures (at a cost of $40 per hectare for clearing, $15 for seed in 1990) allows a high stocking rate in good years, and careful management of numbers, combined with 'locking up' each paddock

Brahman heifers on Trafalgar Station.

ROGER LANDSBERG

each five to eight years to allow enough grass growth to sustain a hot fire to control woody weeds, results in sustainable use. Fifteen to 20% of the property is 'locked up' each year on a rotational basis, and in drought years the rested paddocks can be used as reserve grazing. Native pasture is oversown with seca stylo (Stylosanthes scabra) in most years, and burnt-off paddocks are always resown.

for widespread over-grazing and its attendant ills, compounded by the changes in fire regimes which had occurred through the years. (Fire had maintained open savanna, controlled feral and native woody weeds, and restricted eucalypt seedling establishment in the early days.)

Throughout the grazing lands of north Queensland, degradation resulted from this general over-stocking and the carrying of too many cattle into drought. (Made possible by the hardy breeds, reduction in disease and higher productivity — the 'green revolution' equivalent in pastoralism of the improved plant varieties, irrigation and superphosphates in agriculture. In these regions landowners could not blame early settlers for most of their problems, unlike graziers in the Western Division of New South Wales whose land was permanently damaged by over-grazing by 1900, because it was only in the last two decades that most of the serious and permanent damage occurred.) On Trafalgar, careful management has prevented much of the degradation which has occurred elsewhere and it is interesting to see the 'evolution' which has occurred towards sustainable land use on this property. The critically dry spells of 1978–79, 1982–83 and 1987–88 were managed in an *ad hoc* fashion, each time employing a different drought strategy.

- 1978: agistment, which resulted in a high percentage of lost cattle;

- 1983: selling all adult breeders direct to slaughter and feeding 900 calves in homestead yards — successful, as the young stock went ahead after the April–May rains at an outlay of $17 per head.
- 1987: feeding, from as early as June 1987, until all cattle were involved by January 1988 when the rain came, an investment of $75 per head. When no follow-up rain came, 60% of the herd had to be sold at depressed prices, leaving 1200 head. The investment in feeding became a loss and land degradation continued, so this exercise was a failure.

Roger and Jenny Landsberg took over management of the station in 1986. It is no mere coincidence that they decided to rethink their whole operation at a time when the first Landcare committee in an extensive grazing area came into being. As a founding chairman of the Dalrymple Landcare Committee, Roger was instrumental in spreading its doctrine and applying it to Trafalgar Station. The way Landcare works — identifying problems, setting goals, planning strategies against the background of knowledge of the physical, biological and socio-economic factors involved — has been fundamental in the making of a new management plan. The plan integrates cattle, pasture and financial management within the parameters set by unpredictable climate, changed markets, and the limitations imposed by sustainability.

The emphasis is on low stocking rate, high quality cattle of specially selected cross-breed strains targeted specifically at the Japanese and south-east Asian market, and management to obtain optimum results in all facets of the enterprise. This management is flexible and is adjusted to suit the season, the state of pastures and the volatility of world markets, and it is capable of being opportunistic. Drought is managed, not just suffered, by setting dates for selling if it has not rained, thereby avoiding drought feeding or agistment. A careful watch is kept on the state of paddocks and a rotation is practiced which allows up to 20% to be spelled for seed generation, firing and/or drought mitigation. Noxious weed eradication is systematically carried out, and stream banks are being fenced off to protect water quality. An average cost for eradication of scattered rubber vine infestation is about $50 a hectare. (With land in the region worth about $40 to $80 a hectare and really dense infestations costing about $1500 a hectare to clear, it is obvious that control of the weed is beyond the capability of individuals or even groups, and government assistance is required.)

As a result of this re-structuring and focusing on sustainable development, herd efficiency has resulted in steers being saleable at a younger age; uniformity of quality and weight; being able to take advantage of premium market values; younger mating ages with increased calving percentages; and improved growth rates. Input costs on supplements and mustering have been reduced, and land degradation has been slowed and perhaps halted.

The dedication required to keep a property like Trafalgar going, when labour costs are so high that only one permanent employee and one casual are there to take some of the load off family, is amazing. As this book goes to press (September, 1996) the unbroken four-year drought in the region has once again brought Trafalgar and the Landsberg family to the edge — and nothing more can be done except to pray for rain before Christmas...

CATTLE NUMBERS IN DALRYMPLE SHIRE BASED ON LOCAL OBSERVATIONS

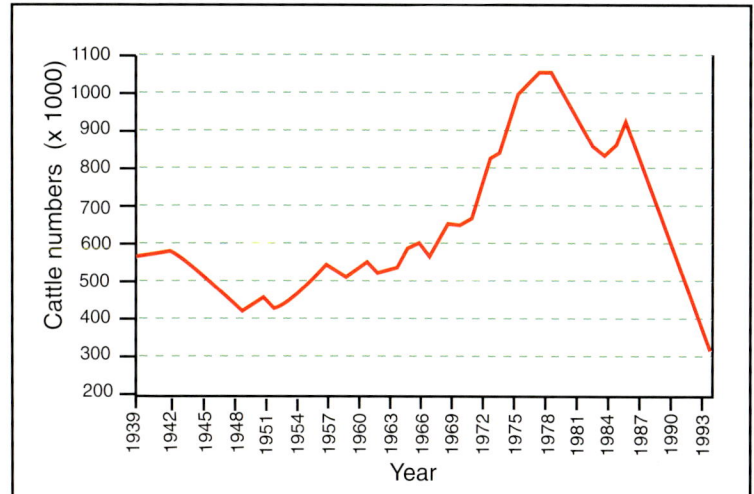

After Mortiss[127]

STOCKING RATES COMPARED WITH SAFE STOCKING RATES, 1945 TO 1985

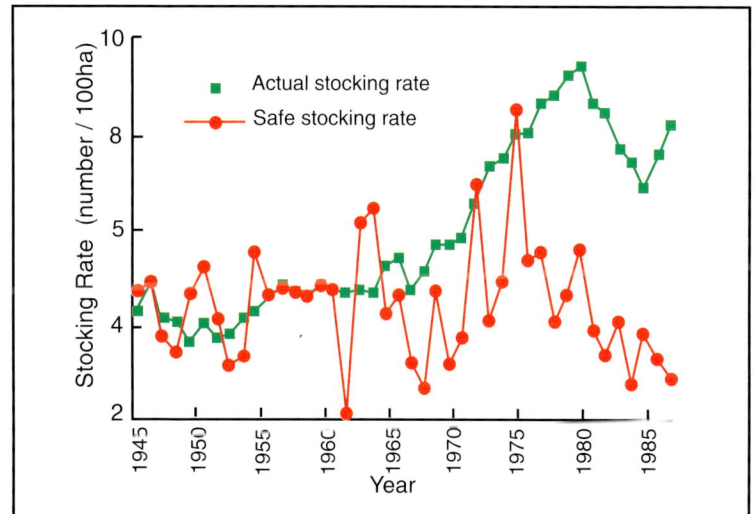

After QDP

Above left: Collecting water samples from the very low house dam to test the safety of the water for use, September 1996. Four years of drought have dried up most of the other dams on the property. If there is no rain by Christmas, the situation on Trafalgar is precarious. Above right: A dry dam, one of 10 on Trafalgar after four years of drought.

ROGER LANDSBERG

Above top: The degraded pasture on Trafalgar after four years of drought.

Above middle: Feeding supplement at a watering point on Trafalgar, September 1996.

Above: The prolonged drought on Trafalgar has caused the death of narrow-leaf ironbark trees. September 1996. The El Nino drought continued in western Queensland in particular, after the eastern margin and most other regions had drought-breaking rains.

ROGER LANDSBERG

THE LIVERPOOL PLAINS

The Liverpool Plains is part of the Namoi Catchment within the Murray–Darling Basin. Its catchment comprises 11 728 km^2 and can be divided into two sub-catchments — the Mooki River and the Coxs Creek.

The catchment can also be divided into three segments determined by their differing soil types, relief, and the prevailing land-use and farming practices. The sandstone and basalt ridges surrounding the plains country represent marginal grazing lands with native bushland remaining in only the most rugged and inaccessible places. The red-brown earths on the slopes support mixed farming, and intensive cropping is practiced on the productive black soils of the floodways and floodplains of the basin.

The Liverpool Plains is one of the most productive agricultural areas in Australia, comprising 1.2 million hectares. The fertile black soils and a climate with summer and winter rainfall allows cropping in both seasons. Land values of $1500 a hectare place a value of about $300 million on the plains. Agricultural primary production for the 1991–92 year totalled $186 million. Manufacturing turnover within the catchment was about $150 million with the predominate use of raw agricultural commodities for value-adding purposes.

Salinisation has become a potentially serious problem in the Plains. A recent comprehensive study[128] concludes that: *much of the Plains could be rendered worthless and incapable of any productivity if land management actions to address the rising water level problems are not undertaken.*

The sandstone and basalt hills and the red earth slopes of the catchment were extensively cleared for grazing in the early days of settlement, upsetting the water balance by removing the highest water-users (trees and perennial native grasses) from the landscape and starting the raising of water-tables by increasing the rate of groundwater recharge. Cropping of the lighter-textured red soils began in the 1880s with wheat, and soldier settlement after the First World War saw increased farming of the 'more valuable' red soils. The black soil plains were used for grazing until the mid 1950s. According to early records, they were originally savanna with deep-rooted perennial grasses (mainly the plains grass *Stipa aristiglumis*) and scattered trees — a high evapo-transpiring, perennial type of ecosystem. Their cracking clays largely preclude trees here as in other black soil plains.

From the 1950s onwards, the Green Revolution, resulting from introduction of new wheat and other plant varieties and better farm machinery capable of working the heavy clay soils, resulted in the intensive cropping of the black soil plains and replacement of native grass by improved pastures. The red soil slopes, which had been the major cropping areas, mainly reverted to grazing. The cropping was mainly wheat in back-to-back, short fallow systems involving stubble burning and deep tillage. In the 1970s, wheat prices and export demand fell and quotas were introduced.

Farmers started to grow sorghum and sunflowers as well as wheat. The bare fallow systems had taken their toll and widespread erosion and soil loss were evident. Practices like strip farming and retaining crop residues were introduced in the late 1970s and early 1980s to combat erosion and to trap soil moisture. Rigid long-fallow systems, like wheat-fallow-sorghum-fallow giving two crops in three years, were the norm.

Agricultural production in the Gunnedah and Quirindi Shires increased fourfold in the 15 years up to 1993. Cotton growing on the plains has recently increased with the introduction of new short-season growth varieties; intensive beef cattle production has escalated. Over the whole plains area, 95% of the income from agriculture is now from intensive land-use practices and the rate of water-table rise and associated waterlogging and salinisation has increased, according to Broughton's report.[128] (Some local farmers with records going back a generation believe that the rise in the water-table which was shown in the research for that report was directly due to higher rainfall and that nothing much has changed.)

The use of long-fallow crop rotations to maintain nutrients and moisture, and the fact that some of the crops, like wheat, are shallower-rooted and less efficient at evapo-transpiration than the native perennial pastures which they have replaced, are factors which affect the hydrology of the region. The increased run-off in the agriculturally modified Lake Goran sub-catchment has seen the lake less prone to drying up since the 1980s, and the water-table around it is raised, resulting in some waterlogging in the area. Some salinised areas surround the lake, but again locals argue that the doom and gloom about salinisation is unfounded and base their arguments on the fact that a prime crop of sunflowers was grown on the dried-up lake bed a couple of years ago, which does not imply high salt levels.

The hydrogeology of the plain's catchment is complex and geology is the critical factor which has determined the rate at which salinisation has proceeded under current land-use practices, and the potential severity of the problems. An underlying trough structure in the Gunnedah Basin below much of the Mooki River catchment forces the four aquifers in the region towards the surface in a northerly direction. All four aquifers carry saline water. Complex geology underlying the whole region results in many smaller troughs and bedrock rises which imprison groundwater locally and cause its pressurisation when recharge rates are too great. The aquifers are recharged by direct infiltration of rainwater, streambed infiltration and hill-slope run-off within local sub-catchments — from water taken in by the alluvium and from the de-vegetated ridges — according to the recent studies.[129,130]

THE LIVERPOOL PLAINS, IN THE MURRAY–DARLING BASIN

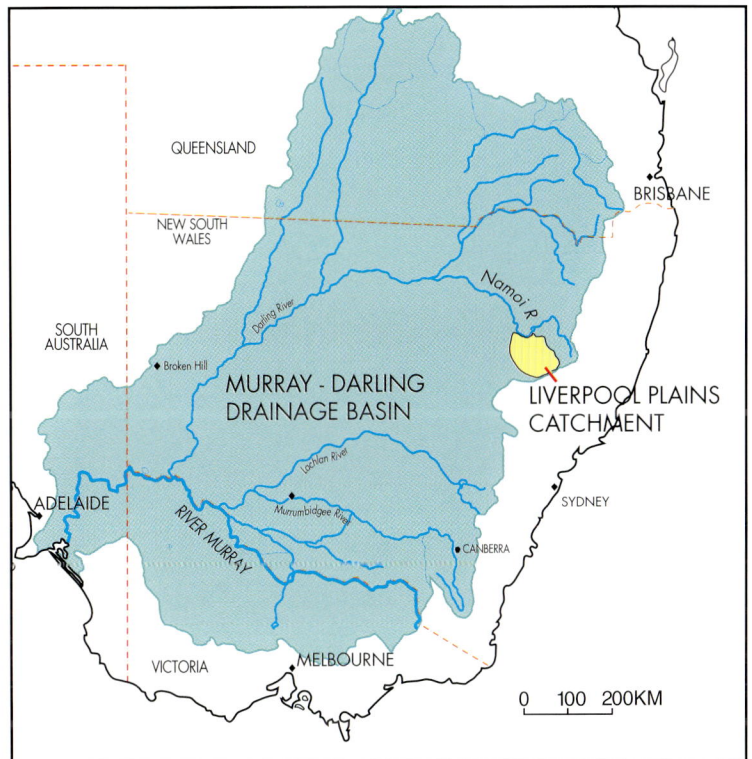

Strip cropping on the Liverpool Plains.
M.E.W.

Strip cropping on the Breeza Plain.
M.E.W.

Above: Saltbush planted on the Breeza Plain as a fodder reserve and to lower the watertable. Saltbush is very deep rooted.

Right: Massive earthworks for irrigated cotton on the Breeza Plain.

M.E.W.

In the Liverpool Plains, the degree to which an individual farm is affected by rising water-tables and salinity is, to a great extent, predetermined by its site-specific circumstances — whether its land is flat and badly drained or sloping and well-drained; its underground geological structure; and the depth and degree of pressurisation of the upper aquifer below its soil surface. On some parts of the black-soil plains, salinisation will increase no matter what on-farm remedial action is taken because of pressurised leakage from the upper aquifer. Sustainable farming may be a long-term impossibility both from a hydrological and socio-economic perspective in such cases.

The most recent report on dryland salinity in the Liverpool Plains, produced by Dr Romy Greiner,[129] now of the Australian Bureau of Agricultural and Resource Economics, for the National Soil Conservation Program, estimates that 195 000 ha of the plains has water-tables within 5 m of the ground surface, creating a high risk of salinisation in the very near future, and about 30 000 ha are already salinised. These figures are an increase on the estimates of the Dryland Salinity Management Group in 1993, which envisaged a sixth of the plains as being out of production because of salinity within 10 years.

The region is characterised by high variability in rainfall because of ENSO. The relatively dry years of the 1991–95 El Nino, which slowed the rise and even lowered the water-table in some regions, may have masked the seriousness of the situation. (Farmers who say that the water-table was always high, meaning over a generation, have discounted the time factor involved. The early clearing of the slopes for agriculture before the black soil plains were ploughed had already raised the water-table before their records commenced. Its increased salinity, from leakage upwards from salty aquifers under continuing pressure, increases the salinity risk.)

Scientists involved in the Climate Variability program, studying the effects of ENSO, are concentrating some of their efforts on the Liverpool Plains Catchment. They believe that a critical threshold has been reached and that a few La Nina years of better than average rainfall, or a big flood, could be disastrous because waterlogging of the plain would bring salt up into the root zone over wider areas, with an overwhelming impact on agricultural sustainability. By developing a model of the catchment they will be able to simulate a number of different scenarios, and hope to find out the maximum allowable rate of recharge of groundwater, and what cropping systems will minimise overall recharge. This should help farmers to make decisions on opportunistic cropping, and improve the timing of management decisions.

Because the problems are so immediate and serious it is hardly necessary to add speculations about what will happen in response to the comparatively slow changes due to global warming. They lurk as an increasing hazard in the future.

Recognition of the salinity and other problems — like soil erosion, fertility decline because of soil structure and nutrient loss, and decline in soil-microbiological and invertebrate populations — has prompted some changes in land-use and farming practices in the plains. The theoretical preferred options for salinisation control and dealing with all the other problems would be massive replanting of trees on the ridges and slopes and re-establishment of deep-rooted, perennial pasture understorey. The cracking clays of the black soil regions prevent the use of agroforestry on the plains as a tool to control groundwater rise, so different crops and rotations have to be used instead. Planting of saltbush in salinised areas turns non-productive land into a useful fodder resource.

A river on the Breeza Plain cutting down into the deep alluvium.

M.E.W.

THE LIVERPOOL PLAINS CATCHMENT

Conservation of remnants of woodland and native grassland in the Liverpool Plains is vital to preserve what little of their biodiversity is left. Integration of native tree replantings with the few natural vegetation remnants would assist in habitat preservation and expansion for native plants and animals and will benefit the koala population which is scattered on the plains in remnant habitats on private lands.

The switch to perennial pastures and more holistic resource management practices which is already occurring will go some way to improving matters by slowing the rate of deterioration of soil and water resources. A salinity awareness campaign conducted by CALM has seen the development of 13 Landcare groups. Piezometers, measuring the depth of water-table below the soil surface, are being used routinely on many farms, monitoring the situation, and sophisticated, computer-based land management is replacing older systems.

The assessment of dryland salinity in the Liverpool Plains, carried out and reported on by Dr Greiner, took into account all the socio-economic factors affecting farming in the region. The practical measures it advocated to control problems were those that were known to be within the capability of farmers to implement within the constraints of their current situations. Many farmers have shown great reluctance to alter their practices, particularly when their farms are reasonably problem-free at present (though often contributing to the symptoms of salinisation and waterlogging elsewhere by their non-cooperation in total catchment strategies). **For as long as land-use practices are heavily determined by socio-economic conditions of production, and a free market system prevails, compromises will have**

to be accepted between what would be best in the interests of long-term viability and what is practical now.

The changes in land-use suggested for use in different combinations according to the different conditions and circumstances on individual farms are:

- 'Traditional' long-fallow wheat–sorghum paddock sequences should be replaced by short-fallow rotations and opportunity

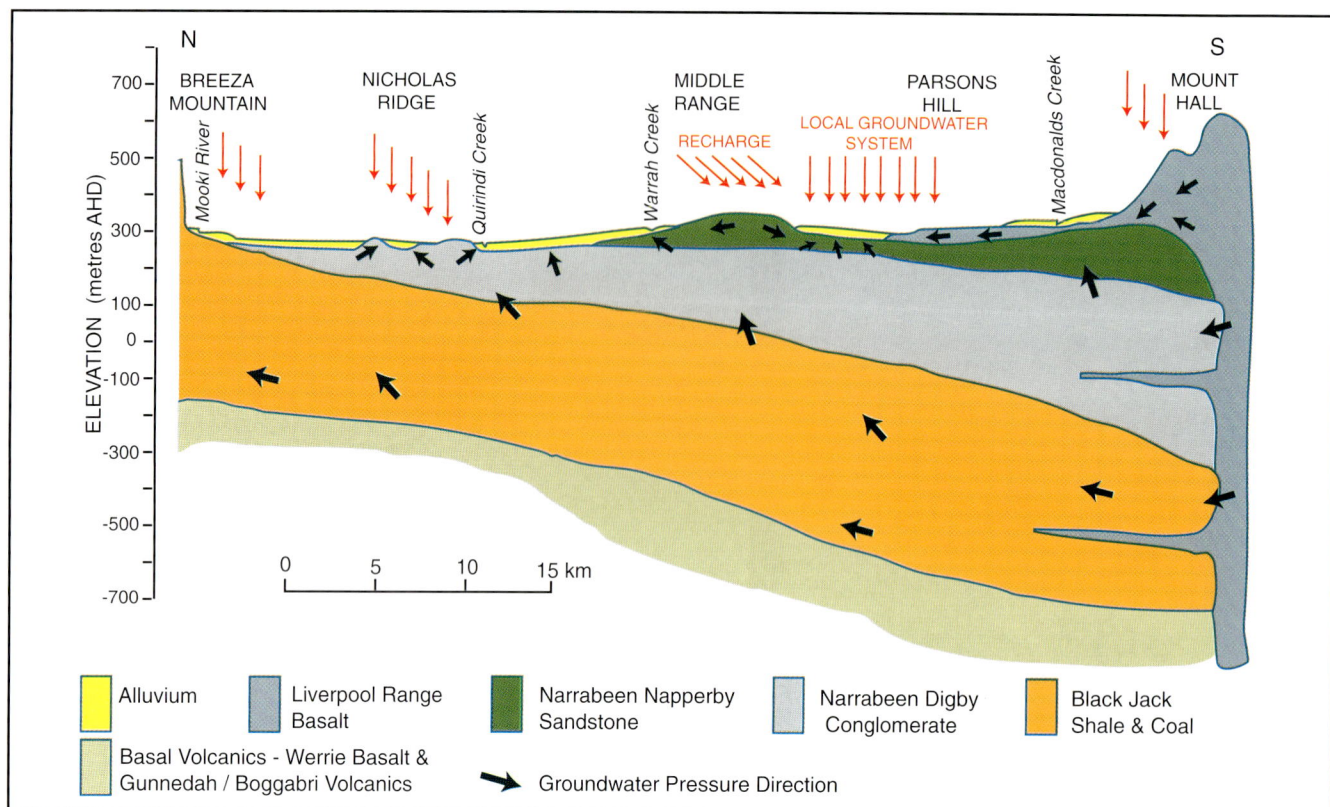

After Broughton[128]

Schematic longitudinal section showing aquifer relationships and groundwater flow direction from the Liverpool Range to Breeze Mountain
(The geological sections for the Liverpool plains were kindly supplied by the Hydrology Unit, NSW Department of Land and Water Conservation, Parramatta.)

The Liverpool Range basalts, age 38 to 35 million years, form the Liverpool Ranges of the Great Divide in the region. A hot-spot volcano poured the basalt out over the landscape, covering the Permian and Triassic rocks of an ancient plain from which younger (Jurassic) rocks had been largely stripped, leaving only localised ridges. Erosion of the basalt over time and spreading of the sediments derived from its erosion and from the deeper bedrock of the region has resulted in the deep alluvial black soils of the plain.

cropping. This latter management system aims to store soil water as quickly as possible and once there is enough stored, use it at the next sowing opportunity. A sowing opportunity occurs when the time is suitable for a profitable crop to be sown; soil is not too wet or too dry; 60 cm depth of wet soil is available for a winter crop, and 1 m of wet soil for a summer crop.

- **A range of summer and winter crops in both long and short fallowing rotations including lucerne** as a hay cash crop and in the improved pasture phase of rotations is preferred.
- **Barley and dryland cotton** grows satisfactorily on soil already somewhat salinised. Saltbush planted in highly salted areas offers a return after a year and is a useful drought-insurance pasture.

The conclusions of Greiner's report are:

The condition of the upper aquifer has been identified as a major variable for the emergence and extent of soil salinisation. While a pressurised aquifer can be managed both in an environmentally sustainable and financially viable manner, through the use of the land-use changes mentioned above, the prospects of long-term sustainable production on the

plains diminish with an increase in aquifer leakage, an increase in the salinity encroachment rate, high initial debt levels on the farm, and high household expenditures for consumption purposes. Where upward leakage exceeds 10 cm a year, this becomes the dominant factor so that no management strategy can prevent the salinisation of farmland…

This study reveals the possibility that a large number of farms in the Liverpool Plains might go bankrupt because soil salinisation, the causes of which are external to these farms, deprives them of the productivity of their land resource. The salinity problem necessitates that a new perspective on catchment management be taken and that innovative policies need to be considered which account for the large financial and social scale of the issue.

The Mooki River Catchment

The catchment has an area of $7648 \, km^2$. The Mooki River joins the Namoi River near Gunnedah. Water quality in the Mooki River deteriorates progressively between Caroona and Breeza as more salt, silt and agricultural runoff is added to the river. Tributaries of the Mooki River flow from the basalts of the Liverpool Range, whose peaks rise to 1200 m. The range is the remnant of the Liverpool Shield Volcano which was active during the Late Eocene and Early Oligocene, about 38 to 35 million years ago. Basalt poured out of the volcano and created flows which have since been eroded to form steep hills and mountains with long sloping foothills, striking in a north–south direction. The basalt flows were originally many hundreds of metres thick.

The eastern Mooki tributaries emerge from the range onto narrow valleys between resistant ridges of Triassic rocks down as far as Pine Ridge. Then they meander across the wide, flat alluvial plain, receiving tributaries draining the Melville Range. The western Mooki River Catchment is often referred to as the Lake Goran catchment because drainage channels and two major tributaries flowing across the long slopes and broad drainage plains between the hills and mountains (derived from Jurassic volcanics) all discharge into Lake Goran when there is heavy rainfall. Most of the smaller tributaries are ephemeral, many losing channel when they leave the steeper grades and reach the floodplain. Their water then percolates into the shallow groundwater system and during times of high evaporation some salinisation of the soil results.

Lake Goran dries (or used to dry) periodically. When the lake is full its water flows over the floodplain on its eastern side and makes its way to the Mooki River, via Native Dog Gully. The Mooki floodplain becomes constricted at Breeza, to a width of only 6 km, by resistant hills of Permian rocks on the west and Carboniferous rocks on the east. Downstream of Breeza the plains widen out again to 22 km, forming the Breeza Plain. They are bounded on the west by the Curlewis Hills, on the east by the Melville Range.

The Mooki River makes little contribution to the flow in the Namoi except during flooding events. Its deep Quaternary alluvials and those of the Namoi River floodplains constitute the Liverpool and Breeza Plains. The alluvium involved owes its exceptional volume to the uplift of the New England Plateau (as a result of movement on the Mooki thrust faults) in Pliocene times about five million years ago. Rapid erosion following uplift resulted in large alluvial fans being built by rivers emerging onto the plains, and the sediments were subsequently distributed by braided streams to form plain-wide alluvium.

Briefly, the geology of the catchment comprises two provinces, separated by the Hunter–Mooki Thrust Fault which was active in Late Carboniferous to Middle Permian times (290 to 260 million years ago). East of the fault are the rocks of the Werrie Syncline; to the west of the fault the Gunnedah Basin sediments and Oxley Basin sediments. Four water-bearing strata (aquifers) underlie the plains. Due to erosion over the ages the full sequence of strata is not uniformly present (as will be seen in the three geological sections chosen to illustrate this account.

The four aquifers are:
- Permian, Jurassic and Tertiary 'volcanic fractured rock aquifers';

THE MOOKI RIVER CATCHMENT

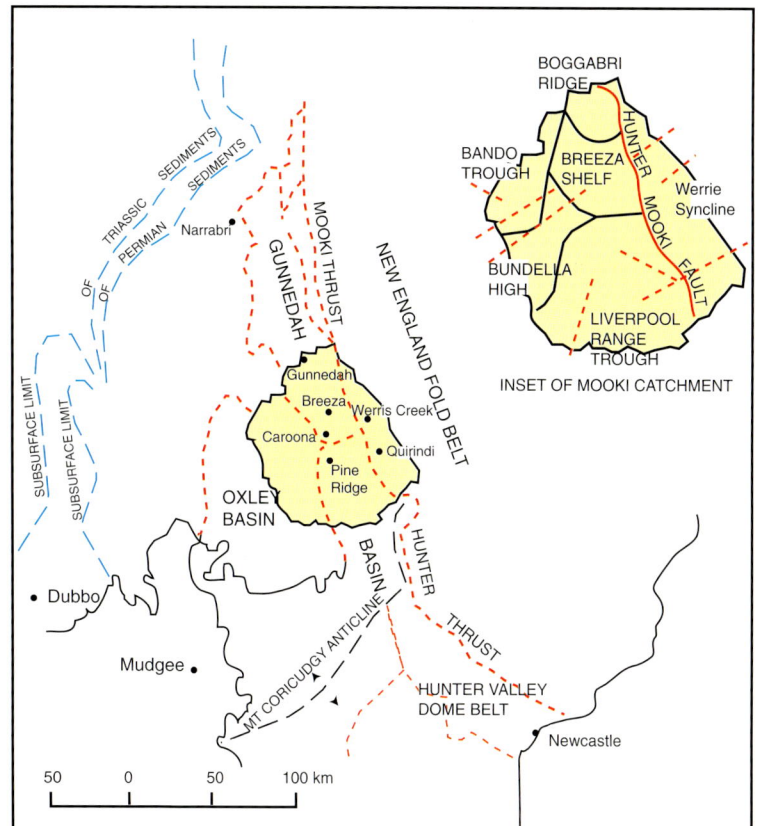

After Broughton[128]

- Triassic and Permian 'sedimentary fractured rock aquifers';
- Jurassic 'consolidated sedimentary rock aquifer';
- Quaternary 'unconsolidated sediment aquifer'.

A short history of a Breeza Plain property

This account, provided by the present owner of 'Denistone' is included because it gives the history and present status of the property as seen from the perspective of a landowner, while the preceding account of the plains was based on the perspective of scientific investigators, outsiders whose (unintentional) inferences appear to many on the land to have been judgemental and failing to acknowledge the good work being done by many of the very best farmers and resource managers here and throughout Australia. Warwick Fisher writes:

My grandfather purchased the property in 1938. It was regarded as having some of the poorer soils. Plant breeding was in its infancy and was only applied to wheat production. Markets for sorghum, sunflower and grain legumes had not even been sought. The tall introduced varieties of wheat grew best on the shallow red soils. On the deep black clay soils they grew so well that they tended to fall over, making them impossible to harvest. The cracking nature of the black clay soils made those soils susceptible to rapid drying and erosion. Tree root systems torn apart by cracking inhibited the establishment of native tree plantations.

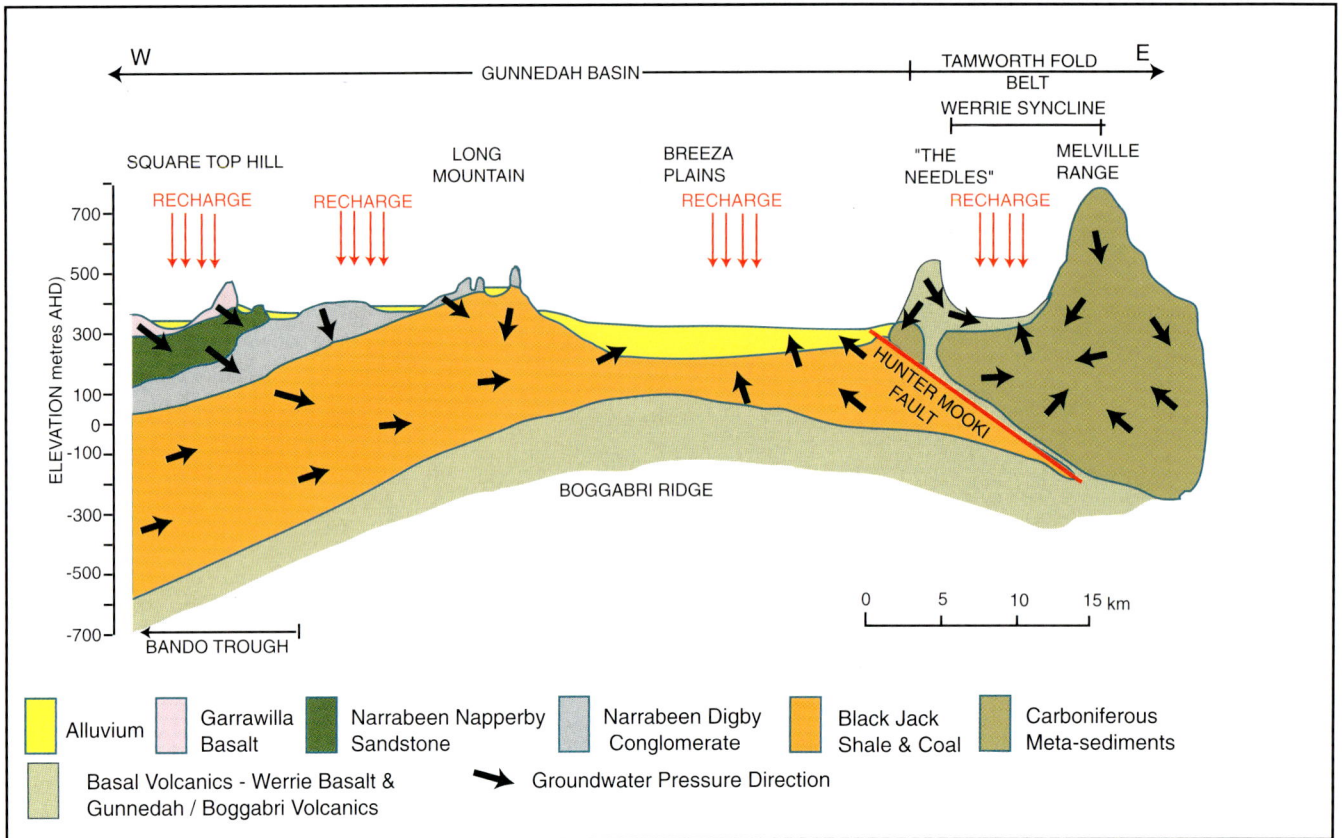

After Broughton[128]

Hydrogeology of the Breeza Plains
Schematic cross-section showing aquifer relationships and groundwater flow direction from Square Top Hill to Melville Range.
The Quaternary alluvium of the Breeza Plain is underlaid by Permian sediments (containing coal), resting on Permian volcanics. A Permian volcanic fractured rock aquifer (the water-bearing gravels) separates the two, and although this water-table is between 12 and 80 m below the ground it is pressurised, and water can leak upwards from it to within 4 m of the ground surface when excess recharge occurs. Irrigated cotton is becoming a growth industry on the Breeza Plain, using water from bores which tap the gravel aquifer.

Because of these characteristics and the absence of suitable varieties, the plains were largely used to run sheep for wool production (Australia ran on the sheep's back in those days). Bores and windmills were installed to tap the shallow aquifers to provide water for livestock. Fences were erected around artificial boundaries and across waterways with no regard for catchment flow. Often these were washed away in floods. Eventually, with assistance from the one-way plough, these fencelines became barriers to flood water, diverting the course of minor streams and causing rill erosion. The fencelines also became havens for noxious weeds and pests. It was not until the early 1980s, after the collapse of the wool market and a move to broad-scale grain production, that many fences became redundant and were finally removed.

Technology and politics intervened through the 1960s to carve the modern face of the Liverpool Plains. The first wheat variety, Gabo, bred to take advantage of the black soil plains, was released. Drought ravaged the early 1960s and wheat, which had become highly profitable, replaced wool which suffered a series of price crashes. The introduction of heavy machinery and the ubiquitous one-way plough removed more and more grassland. The marginal perimeters of the Plains were cleared and brought into grain production, thereby paving

the way for eventual dryland salinity and erosion. The technologies of the 1960s were so successful in increasing the production of wheat that Australian production quotas were introduced in the early 1970s.

Further technological developments saw groundwater discovered in quantities sufficient to enable the development of highly profitable irrigation farming; plant breeding and marketing programs saw development and production of new crops such as oilseeds and coarse grains; margarine displaced butter; fast-food outlets promoted the expansion of intensive livestock industries which sought barley, wheat and sorghum as primary sources of raw material.

The mid-1980s saw the arrival of cotton production on the Liverpool Plains. Varieties tolerant of the cooler, shorter seasons of the Plains were bred. Combined with the irrigation resources, cotton is now substantially displacing coarse grains and cereals whose gross margins (at the time of writing) are unable to complete with that of cotton. The intensive livestock industries, which were built up around an infrastructure of reliable supplies of cheap grain, are now finding that cotton is threatening the surety of that supply. They call for new marketing policies and relaxation of grain import controls to assist them to restore profitability to their domestic and export

industry. Importing grain would have the potential to bring in further weeds and diseases...

...Most farmers regard erosion as the greatest threat to the agricultural environment... and the soils most at risk are the most productive ones. Zero tillage and strip farming is practiced (on about 25% of the plains) and the availability of machinery capable of planting into heavy stubble residues will enhance the farmer's ability to change management practices. However, the machinery is expensive and 'you can't be green if you are in the red'.

Zero tillage has depended heavily on the use of herbicides to control weeds, which used to be ploughed under in traditional systems. It was confidently expected that the main chemical involved in these herbicides, glyphosate, had a chemical structure which would make it impossible for plants to develop resistance to it over time. Research at the William Farrer Centre for Conservation at Charles Sturt University has proved otherwise. The situation parallels the antibiotic-resistant bacteria which have emerged in medicine, and it is the over-use of herbicides, the cure-all, that is to blame. Return to full tillage would be disastrous for conservation and changed farming practices, like Holistic Resource Management [50], where animals are rotated in systems to eat weeds and recycle their nutrients may be the answer.

Landcare on the Breeza Plain

The Upper Breeza Landcare Group has fenced off and established a native tree plantation at Square Bush. The Siphon Hills Landcare Group has started to stabilise severe gully erosion on Tandara. Through the Liverpool Plains Land Management Committee, Landcare groups have been identifying, quantifying and mapping many of the problem areas.

The Coxs Creek Catchment

The Coxs Creek Catchment covers $4080\,km^2$. The river runs through a straight, narrow, well-defined valley before joining the Namoi near Boggabri. Flow from Coxs Creek only affects the Namoi during flood events.

Most of its tributaries drain from the Liverpool Ranges in the south and west portion of the catchment and there is little drainage from the mid to lower east portion. In the north-west the tributaries drain the Willala and Pilliga Scrub.

Geology controls the problems of rising water-tables in this catchment as it does in the Mooki River catchment. The Bando Trough underlying the plain confines the aquifers and they can become locally pressurised by the increased recharge where conformation of geological strata restricts flow.

An account of the history of land use in the Coxs Creek region has been supplied by John Strang of Tambar Springs:

Europeans first came to the district in the 1830s, with large flocks of sheep and cattle which were controlled by shepherds. Grazing pressure was concentrated near the river and then only in the wet season, with the stock being removed when it dried up. By about 1870 proper land title was granted, some timber was cleared from hillsides and most holdings were fenced. Most of the Coxs Creek area was part of the Bando Station owned by the White family from the Hunter River. Dams were constructed and wells were dug, many finding good sub-artesian water. By 1900, percussion drilling plants were available and good water could be reached in most areas. Windmills and storage tanks made reliable watering points and the whole area could be grazed in all seasons. Erosion and weeds became noticeable.

Just after 1900 the country suffered drought and a rabbit plague. Sheep numbers continued to build up because of good wool prices and the land was stressed to the limit. Gullies can be seen today on hillsides, caused by a single rainfall event in 1920 which washed away the soil from bare slopes. In 1925 Bando was sold and subdivided into five blocks. At that time the land was completely denuded of grass due to drought, overstocking and millions of rabbits. Conditions of sale stated that all blocks must have rabbit-proof boundary fences. This made it possible to control rabbits, at least partly, over the next 25 years. The land was managed slightly better, with more subdivision fencing, and, with the establishment of regular stock sales, sheep and cattle numbers could be adjusted to the feed available. Very little plains grass was left and pastures were largely herbs and weeds until 1950, which was the wettest for 30 years.

Above left: Irrigation of cotton on the Breeza Plain. Water is pumped from the gravel aquifer underlying the plain.

Above right: Mustard weed and other herbaceous weeds on the Breeza Plain. Under programs in Holistic Resource Management this landscape will be progressively grazed by cattle in cells created by using electric fencing. The nutrients in the weed crop are recycled via the animals and are available for the next crop, while the cattle are fattened. Expensive herbicides, the alternative before minimum till and replanting, are unnecessary in this land use system.

M.E.W.

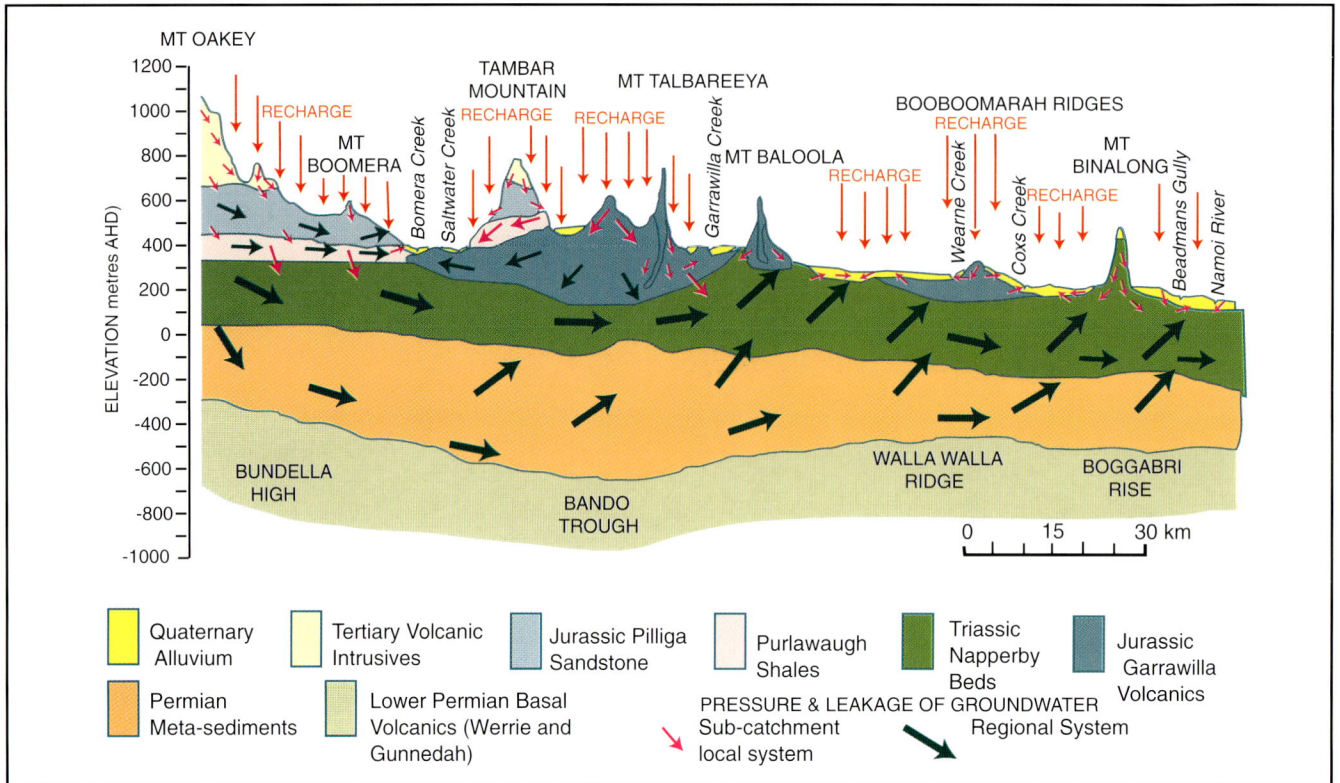

After Broughton[128]

With the wet year came mosquitos, and myxomatosis devastated the rabbit populations. Soldier settlement saw eight 400 ha blocks divided from Bando Station and grain production was encouraged on these subdivisions with part of the land to be sown to lucerne. Within two years it was realised that long-term stands of lucerne were not possible, the cracking clays broke the roots. The Gabo wheat and the coming of the strong diesel tractors which could work the heavy clay soils initiated the wheat boom. Wheat had taken over all the flat land and small numbers of stock were running on the hills by the early 1960s. Growing wheat year after year, burning stubble and removing nutrients from the soil with each crop led to depletion of organic matter and soil nutrients. Compaction of the soil by farm machinery had destroyed soil structure and decreased water penetration; ponding against fences, weeds on fencelines invading crops (and wild oats contaminating the wheat) were all problems.

By the 1970s, the development of hybrid sorghum allowed a rotational system (known as 'thirds') to be developed, with sorghum–fallow–wheat–fallow. It controlled weeds, allowed water storage in the soil and slowed the depletion of soil nitrogen. Grain prices rose dramatically; strip planting became fashionable; stubble retention and zero till became more widely accepted; fences disappeared and a period of good management and profitable farming continued until 1983.

Since 1983 the region has experienced two major droughts, a run of five extremely wet winters, and a constant decline in real commodity prices. Wheat could not be planted in a number of seasons, leading to a doubling up of summer cropping. Opportunity cropping has replaced strict rotations with short-term gains, but relying heavily on chemical weed control and artificial fertilisers. Zero till has had a lot of publicity but depends on huge applications of herbicides. The drought which has only recently ended lowered water-tables and gave the land a long fallow.

THE COXS CREEK CATCHMENT

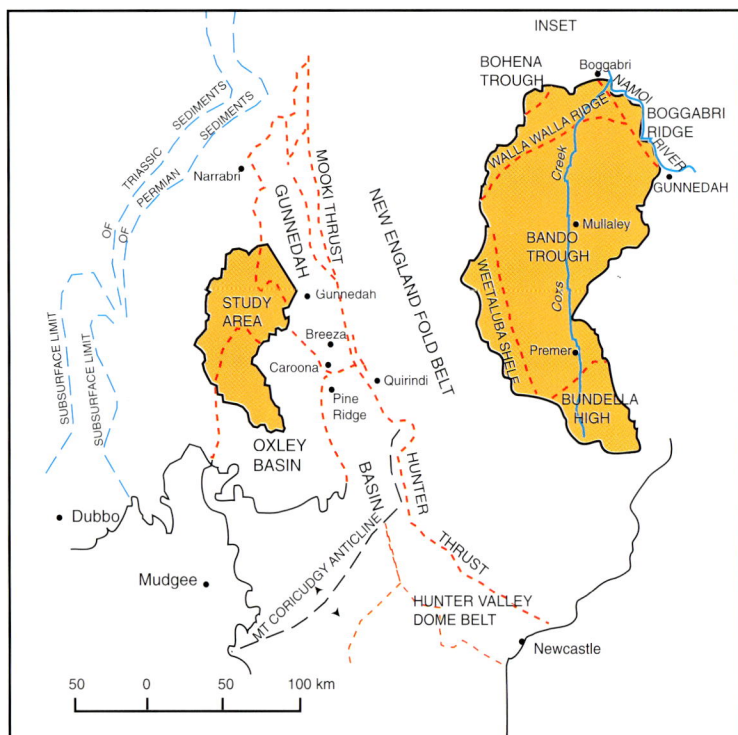

After Broughton[130]

GROUNDWATER IN THE NAMOI VALLEY

The deep alluvium of the Namoi Valley contains a vast groundwater resource. Alluvial aquifers supply high-yielding, low salinity groundwater for irrigation, for town and village water supply (to Gunnedah, Boggabri, Narrabri, Wee Waa, Quirindi and Nundle) and for stock and domestic water on farms. It is estimated that the 8000 km^2 area of the valley holds 30 million megalitres of water, with about 10 million megalitres available for extraction.

Licences are held for 1300 high-yield irrigation bores on 600 properties in the valley, meeting half of the irrigation requirements in a normal rainfall year and 80% to 90% of irrigation water in droughts. The irrigation industry in the Namoi Valley is more heavily dependent on groundwater than any other in New South Wales. During droughts, when recharge is much decreased, the rate of water usage is not sustainable. In the lower valley, below Narrabri, 70 000 ML are used in a normal rainfall year; in 1993–94 and 1994–95 usage was over 140 000 ML a year; the long-term sustainable yield is estimated to be 95 000 ML.

Above: Cattle grazing to eliminate weeds before proceeding with minimum till planting of the next crop on the Breeza Plain. The electric fences are simple battery powered ribbons; the cattle learn quickly to respect them and farmers say that to protect new tree plantings in areas where cattle graze it is only necessary to put the ribbon round the trees, without electrifying it, if the animals have been educated in the cells to expect a shock.

M.E.W.

CHAPTER TEN

OUT OF CONTROL

PROBLEMS WITH INTRODUCED ANIMALS AND PLANTS

AND WITH NATIVE SPECIES THAT HAVE RUN RIOT

Rabbits are desert-makers. *When everything else has been eaten they burrow and eat the roots of the dead plants. Strzelecki Desert.*

M.E.W.

The introduced domestic animals which have left the confines of the farm or town are the highly visible component of the army of ferals which has invaded Australia, displacing native animals and causing loss of biodiversity and enormous environmental degradation. Rabbits have made desert; goats have turned arid lands into dust bowls; buffalo and pigs have destroyed wetlands; foreign fish are destroying the ecology of rivers; foxes and cats are eating their way through our wildlife; and starlings, pigeons and other birds are creating their own set of problems — to mention only a few!

A less visible component of the invading hordes comprises insects and all sorts of invertebrates, some even taking over marine environments. The introduced honey bee, valuable for its honey and as a pollinator of introduced plants, competes for nest holes with wildlife when hives go feral, and competes with native bees for pollen and nectar. European wasps are dangerous and unwelcome invaders of our gardens; particularly destructive wood-eating termites have arrived in timber and are proving even more destructive than our native species; new and potentially disastrous fruitflies can arrive in spite of quarantine measures.

Feral plants, escapees from farms and gardens, and noxious weeds brought in with seed and produce, have invaded disturbed areas, penetrated our forests, woodlands and pastures, and in some instances have taken over whole ecosystems. Water weeds, foreign seaweeds, invaders of wetlands — both land and water — mean that these areas are under siege. Added to all these are introduced diseases of plants and animals.

Accounts of many of the individual invading species, plant and animal, additional to those discussed below, are included in the case studies of ecosystems or regions where they are presenting problems.

The high-tech age in which we live offers hope of finding solutions to many of the problems which involve ferals. Helicopters to pursue animals and enable shooting from the air; radio-tracking of herds; sophisticated poisons for animal and plant control; biological controls like calicivirus disease for rabbits and tip-moth caterpillars for bitou bush all have their place in the battle. Computers, with their ability to analyse data and to communicate information, are revolutionising agriculture and land management and already play a part in control of insect pests and feral animal and weed control.

Feral cattle on a pristine beach on Cape York.

JIM FRAZIER

Rabbit footprints and ripples in the sand of the Strzelecki desert.

M.E.W.

Computer modelling which looks at climatic variation — like **CLIMEX,** which monitors weekly variations and extremes which might favour the reproduction of a pest — will soon be able to monitor variations over longer periods. When it is possible to know what is likely to happen to the climate a season ahead with confidence, planning by farmers and graziers will no longer be subject to the unpredictables which have hampered them in the past. They will have a vital tool allowing them to have far more control over pests, weeds, and even diseases. It will become possible to target the optimum areas for releasing biological control agents for pests and weeds, as well as to understand the relationship of the large-scale ENSO fluctuations to pest problems.

The Cooperative Research Centre for Tropical Pest Management in Brisbane is working on creating software which will make insect pest control more efficient because it will be known in advance what species are likely to become a problem under the predicted climatic conditions for the next season. This will enable farmers to devise better control strategies for particular weeds or pests, minimising damage. For example: Studies of the Queensland fruitfly at the Centre, its biology and preferences, have enabled predictions to be made of the climatic conditions under which it will break out of its tropical haunts and invade southern orchards; and use of a computer program to predict the summer generation of the green vegetable bug on a pecan-nut farm at Moree enabled control at the start of infestation, saving the orchardist an estimated $1.9 million.

The **cane toad** *(Bufo marinus)* is a climatic opportunist. CLIMEX predictions, which integrate climatic fluctuations within zones and the biological requirements of a species, indicate that the potential range of the toad from infested areas in Queensland is southward as far as Port Macquarie, but that there are times in ENSO fluctuations when warmer and wetter years could see it spread to the Myall Lakes. (This means that under Greenhouse conditions its range will be considerably altered, as will that of many pest species.)

Cane toads were introduced in 1935 to control two insect pests of sugar cane. They had no effect on the pests and must rank as one of the worst failures of biological control experiments, because they have spread over 500 000 km^2. They are poisonous and none of our native species of birds or reptiles have any immunity to the toxins. They can live for up to 15 to 20 years and each female can lay 30 000 eggs a year (producing toxic tadpoles). It is impossible to poison the toads or the tadpoles in the water because all other aquatic life would be affected, so the only hope of control is to find a disease specific to cane toads, and research by the CSIRO continues.

Climate predictions will also be important in forecasting the spread of other exotic pests like the western flower thrip, the poinsettia white fly, the spiralling whitefly and the Changa mole cricket, all of which are recent arrivals in Australia and serious pests overseas.

THE OODNADATTA REGION, WEST OF LAKE EYRE AND NORTH TO THE NORTHERN TERRITORY BORDER

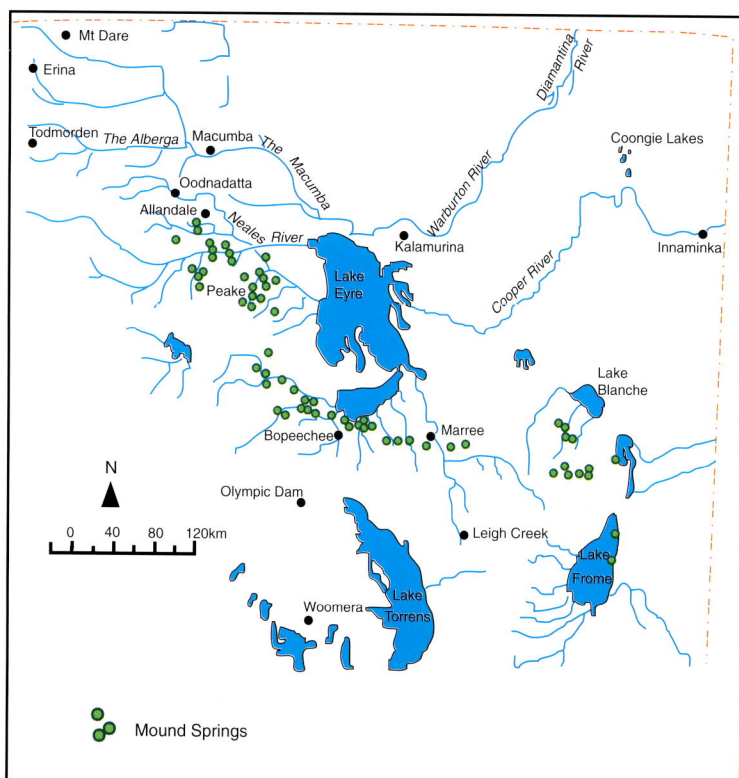

Radio-tracking and helicopters, two technological aids to elimination of feral livestock, gives hope that the feral problems in the arid rangelands may soon be under control.

The control of **feral donkeys** in the Kimberley started in earnest in 1982 when numbers were about one million, twice as many as cattle in the region. Shooting from helicopters reduced numbers by 90% over the years and it became increasingly difficult and expensive to complete elimination of the 10% remaining. The Agriculture Protection Board of Western Australia chose two properties where the grazing is good and where there is adequate fencing as pilot projects to try out 'Judas donkeys', fitted with radio collars, as a means of tracking the elusive remnant herds in order to eliminate them efficiently. Donkeys are social animals and when one had been shot with a tranquilliser dart and had a collar attached it returned to the herd. Then it was an easy matter to locate the animals even in wooded country where they would not have been visible from the helicopter. Choosing well-fenced properties for the experiment has meant that the results in those areas are permanent and the expenses, shared equally by the board and landowners, was considered reasonable (about $10 per animal culled).

In the Oodnadatta District, South Australia, between 25 September and 5 October 1995, a donkey shoot on Peake, Macumba, Allandale, Todmorden, Eringa and Mt Dare Stations, using helicopters and sharp-shooters, resulted in 2342 donkeys being killed. Almost half the total were removed from Macumba Station. The supervisor, Garry Paige, from the Pastoral Management Branch (DENR SA) noted that the area was drought afflicted and cattle were being moved out to Queensland.[131]

The Mt Dare Station is in the Witjira National Park and Mr Paige's comments on the operation show the impact that feral animals have on native pastures:

I was pleased to note the improvement in conditions on Mt Dare which has been subject to overstocking, especially with feral animals, since the 1930s. Long before I first became familiar with this property in 1947, every blade of grass was removed by the hordes of donkeys, horses and cattle. There has been a period of very light stocking since 1984 when I removed most of the feral animals during the BTEC program [Brucellosis-Tuberculosis Eradication Campaign]. Mitchell grass is now established along all creeks and watercourses, along with other perennials such as Eragrostis *sp., and light to medium stands of Mitchell were noted across the open stony tablelands where, in the bad old days, we could never find feed for our horses.*

It is nice to have a good news story from that arid part of the continent and to know that degradation, though severe, may not always be irreversible.

Mr Paige's comments on migration of ferals in the region are also of interest and give some idea of the magnitude of the feral problem and the unlikely places where feral grazing is impacting:

There are two flowing bores north of Mt Dare in the N.T. (Annacoora and McDills) These waters are in desert

Mitchell grass, gibbers and feral horses near Lake Eyre.

M.E.W.

Camel tracks down a Strzelecki Desert dune.

M.E.W.

country outside of leases and are a haven for feral donkeys and horses. Migration of these animals on to Mt Dare is inevitable. Horses apparently have moved across the top of Lake Eyre from Kalamurina to Macumba this summer, following the dry conditions along the lower Warburton. The presence of considerable numbers of horses, donkeys and camels is also being reported from the western side of Eringa.

Mr Paige concluded his report by saying that shooting from helicopters achieved such a degree of success that numbers could be reduced to bearable levels and eventual total eradication could be possible if the pressure was maintained.

Domestic goats are present on all continents except Antarctica, yet New Zealand, Australia and small islands are the only places where **feral goats** have become a significant problem. According to Dr Robert Henzell, senior research officer at the Animal and Plant Control

Commission in Adelaide, it is lack of sufficient predators which is the main factor underlying their success. In the vast and sparsely inhabited arid and semi-arid sheep-grazing lands in southern Australia where feral goats abound, dingoes have been largely controlled, reducing predation, and water has been provided for stock, enabling spread into areas which would have been limiting because of goats' need for drinking water. Smaller numbers of goats occur in isolated groups of up to one or two hundred in agricultural areas, in and around patches of native scrub or other dense vegetation.

Goats are social animals and are usually found in groups whose size and composition varies according to the time of year and environmental factors. An unusually large flock of 1000 animals has been recorded from the Northern Flinders Ranges. Usually numbers are highest in areas where hilly terrain and shrub and tree density makes mustering or shooting (human predation) difficult[132] The use of 'Judas goats', radio-collared and able to be followed on their return to the group is possible because of this herd instinct.

The high reproductive rate and early maturing of goats can result in a population increase of 75% in a year. (Therefore it is necessary to remove about 45% of a population annually to keep it at stable numbers — making goat eradication a formidable task.) Females three months old can breed, bearing one kid at the first pregnancy and usually twins thereafter. Triplets are not uncommon but mortality rate of very young triplets is higher than for twins. Young kids are always susceptible to depredation when they are left in 'safe' places under bushes while their mothers feed. There is a five-month gestation period and an average female produces twin kids every eight months.

In addition, goats are hardy and relatively free from parasites and disease; they are highly mobile and they eat a wide range of plant material, preferring the nutritious growing tips, buds and seeds; their browsing and ability to reach high off the ground, and even to climb, results in most plant material in arid lands being within their reach, so the damage they do in droughts is enormous; on the whole they withstand drought well because they eat plants not touched by other herbivores when all else is gone; they cause erosion, particularly during droughts by their destruction of vegetation and their trampling of the fragile soils which characterise the semi-arid zone.

Their one weakness, which makes their control somewhat easier, is their dependence on drinking water. Trapping and mustering at water points exploits this weakness.

THE EFFECT OF FERAL ANIMALS ON MULGA REGENERATION

The fragility of mulga ecosystems was underlined by the research programs into feral animal control and mulga regeneration in the Flinders Ranges.[133] Euros were the most obvious natural grazers of the region, feral goats and rabbits the introduced grazers. Rabbits were in plague numbers in 1980–81, according to a study which had started in 1977. By using enclosures which excluded rabbits only, or goats and euros but not rabbits, the different effects of feral grazing were assessed.

Mulga regenerates by seed only and germination only occurs in the infrequent, La Nina, years of high rainfall. Rabbits are a particular menace to seedlings, and where they were excluded from experimental plots, young plants survived in large numbers. Goats had a less serious effect on seedling survival. However, the study showed that the growth of seedlings was exceedingly slow and they were at risk for many years. At the same time, unless there was reasonable follow-up summer

rain over several years following germination, young plants did not survive anyway. This emphasises that rehabilitation of mulga-lands is not simply a case of removing grazers, though control of rabbits is essential if there is to be any chance for the mulga. The combination of mulga's specific requirements for germination and survival and the imposition of the unpredictable climate swings resulting from ENSO have created a highly sensitive system whose balance is precarious.

FERAL GOATS AND THE YELLOW-FOOTED ROCK WALLABY

The survival of the yellow-footed rock wallaby is often said to be threatened by feral goats. Reasons given are competition for food and for safe rock ledges and caves, and competition for scarce water in times of drought. A full analysis of facts about populations of both animals[34] refutes or at least sheds doubt on most of the arguments.

The dramatic decline in numbers of the wallaby, in the Flinders Ranges at least, occurred between 1880 and 1920, when the numbers of feral goats were negligible. Hunting by landowners, the effects of sheep and particularly of rabbits, and predation by foxes which were widespread by the end of the period, are likely reasons. Recovery after hunting was stopped has not restored pre-settlement numbers. The continuing pressures exerted by rabbits, sheep and foxes have not been considered as reasons for this failure to thrive, and it has been customary to blame the goats. While goats appear to compete more directly with rock wallabies, there is no proof that this is usually the case. They are often seen together in the rocky areas to which the wallabies are specifically adapted, eating some of the same things, and both occupy caves. However, goats have far wider grazing ranges, are too large for most of the crevices and small caves chosen by wallabies, and would have to be present in far larger numbers than have yet been known in the rocky areas to have a limiting effect.

From 1960 onwards goat numbers increased dramatically in the northern Flinders, and at the same time the density of the wallabies increased,[135] which suggests that they were not in direct competition or that competition was minor compared with other factors operating. In Weetootla Gorge in the Gammon Ranges, a healthy colony of rock wallabies co-exists with a population of feral goats of above average density. An aerial survey in 1979 in the rugged area of the Gammon Ranges National Park, Arkaroola, Balcanoona and Moolawatana where most of the yellow-footed rock wallabies are located, found an average density of 12 goats per square kilometre over the 3000 km^2 surveyed. This was within the range of carrying capacity for sheep, and since that time culling and mustering have reduced numbers dramatically.

Control of rabbits and of foxes has improved, and it is hoped that the yellow-footed rock wallabies are secure in the Flinders Ranges. (The acquisition of a large area in the Flinders by Earth Sanctuaries has probably ensured their survival. 'Buckaringa' will be cleared of ferals, in accordance with the practices of the organisation, and its fencing will prohibit re-entry.)

Remnant populations of rock wallabies in the Olary Ranges in South Australia and in New South Wales are in considerable danger. Dr Henzell warns against killing off all the goats thought to be competing in the Olary Ranges without addressing the culling of foxes and dingoes. With young goats off the menu (and with rabbits probably disappearing due to the new virus) the wallabies, and much other remnant wildlife, could be the victims of predators which had lost their preferred prey.

Goats as weed-control machines Goats have been shown to be very useful in weed control. At Myrtleford in Victoria they have been used to clear blackberry and to eat other weeds like thistle and even castor-oil plants, saving expensive back-breaking labour or chemicals. A herd of cashmere goats let loose on 10 ha of solid blackberry ate all the edible parts, flattened the canes and opened up what had been impenetrable thicket in four months, thriving on the blackberry leaves which are as nutritious as spring pasture. Maintaining a goat herd and rotating it for weed control becomes an attractive option, provided fencing is adequate — goats can get out of most paddocks, which explains their tendency to become feral.

Feral pigs are the most serious pests of agricultural lands and of wetlands. They require surface water and thick cover for shelter from heat and sun, and this largely restricts them from the rangelands. Their numbers Australia-wide can only be guessed at because they are often congregated in remote areas, but it is likely that they run to many millions. In parts of the Macquarie Marshes, 80 pigs per square kilometre have been counted. In agricultural areas they are often the greatest predator of lambs, and have been known to take 40% of lambs in a season on some properties, costing the sheep industry a great deal of money. Hunting with pig dogs (dangerous and barbaric), shooting, trapping and poisoning are all control methods, but the pigs' very rapid breeding defeats most efforts.

Control of feral pigs in the fertile Oberon district of New South Wales has recently involved the use of radio collars and 'Judas' individuals. Some farms in the district have major control problems because they back onto National Park and areas of pine plantations which were sanctuaries for the pigs, so a cooperative effort was required. Radio collars fitted mainly to sows, which are group animals, unlike boars which tend to be solitary, enabled the habits of the groups to be studied so that the best places could be chosen to establish feeding stations. The aim was to attract as many pigs as possible to cook-up stations where grain and molasses were boiled in big barrels and left out in increasing amounts over some

weeks. This was done in winter, when the animals were hungry, and they became used to the easy feeding. When it was decided that sufficient animals were attending the stations, 1080-poisoned grain was put out instead of grain and molasses. It was served in a feeder barrel so that the poison would not get into the environment, and it was hoped with a fair amount of confidence that native animals would not be involved in the kill because they shun the areas in which pigs congregate regularly. About 90% of the pigs in the trial area were eliminated in this way, making it a much easier job for landholders to trap, shoot or bait the strays.

Feral pigs are a major problem in the rainforests and on the tropical fruit farms around Tully and Mission Beach, about 150 km south of Cairns in Queensland, damaging crops, digging wallows and uprooting plants. The area includes the Cassowary Coast, famous for its big birds which, however, have declined in numbers until only about 70 remain. A major reason for their decline is the feral pigs which eat eggs and chicks. In order to trap pigs (there is now a market in Germany for gamy-flavoured pork) traps had to be designed which could not trap cassowaries. A great deal of damage is done by pigs in World Heritage Rainforests in Queensland as well, and the fact that the pigs are omnivores poses a threat to native animals in the ancient forests, where some are listed as endangered.

Rosy dock, a beautiful introduced weed which adds a splash of colour throughout the Centre, growing with mulla mulla (Ptilotus) on a granite hillside at Alice Springs.

M.E.W.

ENVIRONMENTAL WEEDS: INTRODUCED PLANTS WHICH HAVE BECOME FERAL

About 10% to 15% of plant species growing wild in Australia are introduced. A quarter of them are weeds posing serious or very serious environmental risks, according to a recent study funded by the Endangered Species Program of the National Parks and Wildlife Service and the CSIRO. The study finds that the damage caused to native fauna and flora throughout

Australia by introduced plants is so serious and poses such formidable management problems and control difficulties as to require a national approach. A top 18, worst weed list, has been compiled and the species involved have been allocated to five groups according to the relative urgency of need for action against them.[136]

- **Group 1** species require action as soon as possible; the need is critical. **Rubber vine** is the worst in this category (it is described in the Upper Burdekin study in Chapter 9). The three 'ponded pasture' grasses introduced into wetlands of the tropical north are considered potentially as serious. They are **hymenachne, aleman grass** and **para grass** (described in Chapter 11). The **giant sensitive plant,** *Mimosa pigra,* which is taking over the northern floodplains is another species whose control is critical (Chapter 11). The **Athel Pine**, *Tamarix aphylla,* is regarded as a threat to all watercourses in arid Australia and is in Group 1 for this reason. A tropical vine, blue thunbergia (*Thunbergia grandiflora*) completes Group 1. It is native to northern India and was introduced as an ornamental plant. It is a threat to the tropical lowland forest remnants of far north Queensland, smothering trees and killing them. Infestations are widely scattered and are mostly on private land. (If this list was written now it would start with **alligator weed** (*Altenanthera philoxeroides),* now regarded as the most dangerous of all weeds, potentially capable of ruining the irrigation industry and spreading uncontrollably along rivers, over wetlands and wherever soil is damp. Dr Kath Bowmer of the CSIRO Division of Water Resources warns that it could become the dominant aquatic plant from Broome, through the Kimberley, Northern Territory, Cape York and all down the east coast and across the Murray Basin. A major outbreak in Barren Box Swamp on the MIA was eradicated, and heavy fines are imposed if the plant is not controlled on sight wherever it appears.)

- **Group 2** species require action within two years. Included are the **buffel grass,** *Cenchrus ciliaris,* which has been planted through much of Central Australia and is now considered among the worst weeds. **Mission grass** in the Top End is another introduced pasture species which now poses a threat. In southern Australia the **bridal creeper,** *Myrsiphyllum asparagoides,* is regarded as a serious threat in a range of habitats where it smothers the ground and shrub layer and prevents regeneration of native species. In the ocean along the eastern Tasmanian coast a variety of kelp, *Undaria pinnatifida,* introduced in ballast water, is out of control and threatens to spread along most of the southern Australian coastline.

- Lower down the urgency scale, some worst weeds are classified as **Group 3**, requiring attention within two to five years; and **Group 4**, within six to 10 years.

- **Group 5** worst weeds comprise the water weeds *Salvinia* (water fern) and the water hyacinth, for both of which control measures are in hand.

Australia's capacity to control environmental weeds is limited. The prognosis for their spread on a continental scale is grim. Economically and even technically the problems are too large, and there is a political element arising from conflict between conservation and agriculture or horticulture which also constrains. **Government agencies continue to promote environmentally unacceptable pasture species; there is a lack of controls on the import of ornamental plants; and the continuing maintenance of grazing on marginal lands predisposes them to weed invasion**. Prevention of further non-essential introductions should be given top priority and the plant import legislation has to be updated to prevent further ecological and economic disasters.

Native Plants which Attain 'Weed' Status

Woody Weeds

The term 'woody weeds' has become generally used to describe native species of shrubs which assume dominant and weed-like numbers in a disturbed and degraded ecosystem. (It would be preferable to restrict the use of the word weed to introduced species, making a distinction.)

The semi-arid rangelands of the Western Divisions of the Eastern States are much altered by native woody weeds. The core woody weed country comprises woodlands (largely mulga) on red earths (often calcareous) where wind and water erosion are widespread. A large percentage of the ground surface is bare and there is little organic matter in the top soil layer. Pasture biomass is very meagre in dry times, and characteristically there is no response of perennial pasture species to rain, even during optimal seasonal conditions.

Recent estimates of the situation in western New South Wales are of 20 million hectares virtually lost to woody weeds, and the spread continuing at 4% a year.

The **Royal Commission of 1901** into the plight of Crown tenants in the Western Division of New South Wales recorded the loss of palatable species and the **proliferation of woody shrubs,** leading to greatly reduced productivity, which resulted from the boom days of early settlement. The rush by pastoralists to take up the grazing lands with their perennial grass understorey, palatable herbs and scattered shrubs, and the numbers of stock which selectively over-grazed regardless of seasonal conditions, started the degradation. Changed fire regimes played their part and rabbit plagues devastated the land, and boom had turned to bust in a couple of decades.

The serious ecological problems which have been suffered by the fragile marginal lands during about 100 years of our management, and the social problems which stem from trying to make a living on progressively degrading country, have now reached crisis point. A significant number of pastoral enterprises in this sort of country in north-western New South Wales and south-western Queensland are no longer viable. In December 1993, the mean debt burden of the 135 clients who used the Bourke Rural Counselling Service was greater than $400 000. (Instead of calling a Royal Commission into the plight of farmers, like in 1901, a flurry of intensive agency-community inquiries has ensued: West 2000 in New South Wales, the South West Strategy of Queensland and the National Strategy for Rangeland Management.)

The density of shrubs in woody weed country can be amazingly high. *Eremophila*, *Dodonaea* and *Senna* species can reach densities of 7000 stems per hectare. Such country would be capable of supporting one dry

A mulga woody weed infestation near Quilpie.

M.E.W.

sheep equivalent to 25 ha, giving a farmer a gross margin for woody weed country of $0.16 per hectare in average years. Even in 1989 at the peak of wool prices the gross margin would have been less than a dollar a hectare.

It is now known that it is **economically not feasible to rehabilitate country which has been taken over by woody weeds in the Western Division**. The problem is simply too large. Fire is not effective when the infestation is over vast areas, post-fire management to achieve results is beyond financial capabilities. Destocking alone does not work; feral animal control, particularly goats and rabbits, has to be incorporated.

The solution, then, would seem to be to use the no-longer-productive woody weed country differently. Land management reform would be required on a grand scale and whether the rural sector is ready for such reform yet is uncertain. One proposal is to turn woody weed areas which are no longer productive into **Multiple Use Reserves.**[137,138] Under this scheme, Crown Leases could be relinquished on a voluntary basis by farmers whose operations were no longer viable. Tenure would be changed to Reserve at point of transfer; all stock would be removed; stewards would be appointed to maintain certain improvements, control weeds and ferals and coordinate activities of the different land-users. The original lessee would have the option of staying on in this managerial capacity. Kangaroos and goats would be controlled and harvested for sale; according to the capacity of the land in good seasons, stock owners might bid for the grazing rights in set areas for certain set periods; recreation and tourism, managing non-grazed flora for bush foods, cabinet timbers and cut flowers might be additional uses.

Landholders faced with woody weed invasion of their Mitchell grass pastures by gidgee (*Acacia cambagei*) in the Longreach district of Queensland are still fighting, and in some cases controlling, the spread which resulted from two episodes (in the 1950s and 1970s) when wetter than usual periods promoted massive germination of seeds.

Above: A gidgee clump, showing classes (cohorts) — parent plants and young from the exceptionally wet years in the 1950s and 1970s.
Above right: Gidgee encroachment into Mitchell grass near Longreach.

JOHN REYNOLDS

If the dynamics of climate and of the response of the woody plants had been understood, or if it had been possible to predict the weather patterns which enabled the proliferation of the invaders, the present situation might not have arisen on such a scale. Fortunately it may be possible in the future to manage rangelands which have recently started to degrade in a way which does not allow more pasture to be lost to woody weeds.

Mass germination of seedlings of woody shrubs occurs during La Nina wetter-than-usual years and now that it is becoming possible to predict the climatic fluctuations of ENSO it should be possible to be prepared to take measures at the right time which will prevent woody weed establishment. The Cooperative Research Centre for Pest Management in Brisbane suggests that shrub seedlings should be allowed to grow through the first year, and the land should then be destocked and fire or biological control used while the seedlings are most vulnerable. A return of stock and heavy grazing pressure will eliminate remaining seedlings in the following seasons.

NATIVE FAUNA: INCREASED POPULATIONS AS A RESULT OF HUMAN ACTIVITIES

Kangaroos and emus have multiplied greatly, assuming plague proportions in some places, because of the availability of water in areas which were waterless before settlement, and the provision of so much grazing country when woodland was cleared. Many other native animals have taken advantage of the changes made by humans and prospered. To mention only a few: **possums** are pests in Tasmanian orchards; **cockatoos, corellas and galahs** enjoy the grain in the wheatfields; **magpie geese** destroyed a complete rice-growing scheme near Darwin and make agriculture difficult in the whole Top End; **kurrawongs** have become disproportionately abundant in some parts of eastern Australia where introduced camphor laurel trees have provided a source of food during seasons which used to be lean and limiting to their numbers; **seagulls** are present in enormous numbers on waste dump sites; native **noisy miners** have proliferated in Sydney, displacing smaller birds in urban gardens.

DISTRIBUTION OF WOODY WEEDS

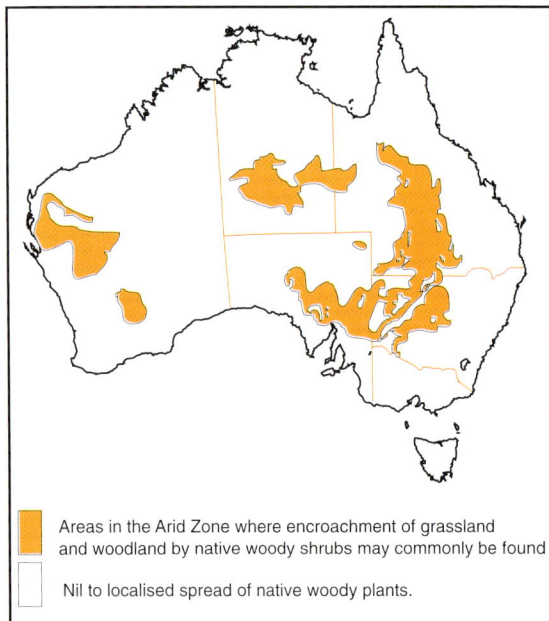

Areas in the Arid Zone where encroachment of grassland and woodland by native woody shrubs may commonly be found

Nil to localised spread of native woody plants.

THE VALUE OF VOLUNTEERS IN REHABILITATING URBAN BUSHLAND

Survey of programs in the Greater Sydney Region

Urban bushland in the Sydney area is a diminishing resource, in quality and quantity. As population grows and the urban sprawl proceeds relentlessly, protection and rehabilitation of remnant bushland becomes increasingly important. The Sydney flora is one of the richest in Australia, comprising 2500 native species. Over 500 introduced species now pose a threat to natural ecosystems.

A survey was conducted for the 1994–95 financial year of all local government agencies and national park districts in the greater Sydney region to determine the number of bushland rehabilitation programs operating and the number of people involved in them. It was found that 4787 volunteers were working in 468 groups or individually in Sydney's bushland. They carried out a staggering 93 732 hours of work, which can be commercially valued at over $2 million. In the last four years there has been a 450% increase in volunteer participation, with 64% of the programs commencing during this time. Local government is leading the way in volunteer bushland rehabilitation with 77% of councils which have bushland in their municipalities managing such programs. Sydney's national park districts are relative newcomers to volunteer bush regeneration programs, becoming involved during the last two years.[139]

The geographic distribution of volunteer effort is very uneven, being concentrated in a small number of municipalities. Six councils, representing 17% of all councils with bushland (four in the north, one in the south, and one on the western rim), manage over 75% of volunteer groups, over 70% of all volunteers, and their residents contribute about 50% of all volunteer hours. (A high percentage of the city's bushland is found in the six council areas, and socio-economic factors contribute to the distribution of volunteers, the six being higher status areas with higher incomes and educational levels.) From the purely conservation point of view, it is ironic and disappointing that all these six areas with high volunteer input are located on Hawkesbury Sandstone, which has the bushland type which is the most comprehensively protected and conserved vegetation type in New South Wales. (This is not to say that every possible effort should not be made to preserve every remnant!) It is the rarer and more threatened and endangered vegetation types like the Cumberland Plain Woodland, Eastern Suburbs Banksia Scrub and Castlereagh Woodland which are crying out for protection and rehabilitation of fast disappearing remnants.

Volunteers in the Sydney region are mainly engaged in weed control, but a holistic approach to weeds and other management problems is increasingly apparent in their activities. Many are involved in mapping; flora and fauna surveys; and attending to problems arising from stormwater runoff with high nutrient loads, and from rubbish dumping. Bush remnants are subject to many pressures — from changed fire regimes to theft of bushrock and flora and fauna; from feral animals to damage caused by incursions of essential services like roads, sewers, power lines and fire tracks.

A consistent rise in volunteer numbers can be expected as environmental education courses, such as are run by TAFE and community colleges in bushland management, and programs to involve the unemployed are increased.

The Lane Cove National Park Community Bush Regeneration Project

The Lane Cove National Park comprises 400 ha in a major bushland valley in northern metropolitan Sydney. It is a long, narrow, fragmented area of bushland fringing 10 km of the Lane Cove River, totally surrounded by urban development with 2000 residential and commercial neighbours. The park was a casualty of the bushfires which caused havoc in greater Sydney in January 1994. During a few horrifying days, 83% of the park burnt.

The public **Lord Mayor's Bushfire Appeal** and substantial sponsorship from **Westpac** provided the funding to create **the Community Bush Regeneration Program**, which began in May 1994. Over 150 people volunteered to rehabilitate the Park. The **Friends of Lane Cove National Park** (originally a small group of volunteer bush regenerators who had been working in the park for a number of years) was established as a community support group for post-fire recovery. The $330 000 donated to the park was used to establish a formal volunteer program to undertake post-fire rehabilitation over a three-year period, managed by two full-time staff.

In the two years since the Program started, volunteer membership has grown to about 250, with people working in 26 groups throughout the park. Most groups work in a chosen site of about 1.5 ha, on a weekly, fortnightly or monthly basis. A nursery is also managed by staff and volunteers, and is producing the native species which occur naturally in the park for planting in areas where weeds have been removed and revegetation is necessary.

Community education is a high priority in the park. Volunteers have the opportunity to participate in regular workshops and training courses, ranging from bush regeneration, weed ecology and identification, fauna identification and first aid. All volunteers attend an introductory four-hour training workshop which includes principles of bush regeneration, catchment management, occupational health and safety, and weeding techniques. This workshop is followed up by regular field-based training. Volunteers are sponsored to undertake industry-recognised training courses in bushland management with the National Trust, TAFE and community colleges. Each group has a trained volunteer bush regenerator who acts as a trainer–coordinator, resulting in a highly trained and supervised volunteer workforce. A quarterly newsletter is produced (also with volunteer participation).

The program has a very positive effect on the local community. It provides opportunities for its volunteers and staff and also for employment programs, students, the unemployed and people required to work under Community Service Orders, all of whom gain valuable work experience.

CHAPTER ELEVEN

THE

TROPICAL NORTH

THE NORTHERN FLOODPLAINS

Where magpie geese thrive and the buffalo roamed

A key feature of northern Australia's palaeogeography and climate evolution has been the effect of lower sea-level and drier times with increased wind intensity during glacial stages of the Pleistocene ice age (the last 2.6 million years). Direct evidence of the changes involved is only available for the period from the last interglacial 125 000 years ago up to the present. By inference similar situations characterised some of the other 16 glacial–interglacial fluctuations as well.

The land bridge which existed between Australia and New Guinea, and which continued up through the islands of south-east Asia, interrupted the warm ocean current which now flows westwards through the Torres Strait between Australia and the Indonesian archipelago. This deprived the northern coast of moist maritime air and hence of potential rainfall. Sea surface temperature was lower in the Indian Ocean adjacent to Northern Australia and Indonesia, perhaps below the threshold

Wetlands on the northern floodplain: view from Obiri Rock in Kakadu National Park. Waterbirds move from one wetland to another seeking preferred conditions. The margin communities, including paperbark and monsoon forests, are important as waterfowl habitats with birds moving into them seasonally or daily, and several species of ducks nesting in woodland. Crocodiles are numerous, and Barramundi populate the rivers and larger water bodies.

M.E.W.

(26–27°C) required for tropical cyclones to form. With the northern coastline about 400 km further away, rainfall would probably have been affected (even without restriction of cyclones) because today rainfall decreases sharply as the distance from the coast increases (from 1600 mm at Darwin to 750 mm 400 km inland, which is a decrease in average annual rainfall of 2 mm for every kilometre travelled south).

A large freshwater to brackish lake occupied the area where the Gulf of Carpentaria is today between 35 000 and 12 000 years ago. Pollen records in cores taken from the sediments which had accumulated in the prehistoric Lake Carpentaria indicate that sedges dominated on the surrounding plains which merged into drier grasslands with paperbarks, scattered *Callitris* and *Casuarina* and some eucalypts.[141]

There is now a great deal of evidence that **intertropical aridity** was a feature of the period between 20 000 and about 11 000 years ago in Australia, India, tropical South America and large parts of Indonesia.[142] The rapid melting of the northern ice sheets after 18 000 years ago saw sea-level rising fast at first, and it has been estimated[143] that horizontal loss of land to the sea on the northern floodplains would have been nearly one metre per week until 10 000 years ago. (The rate of vertical encroachment was about 15 mm per year.) Such changes would have been visible to northern coast-dwelling Aboriginals as they were forced back towards the once barren Arnhem Land Plateau, where evidence of some prior occupation is dated at 25 000 years.

Aboriginal legend has stories of a great flood which no doubt have their origins in the rapid inundation of the flat plains which existed all around the continent on the continental shelf, particularly those connecting Australia to lands to its north, and also the Bass Plain which connected Tasmania to the mainland. People would have been largely inhabitants of coastal regions and the exposed continental shelf during the extremely inhospitable last glacial stage. Then every small present-day island, like Kangaroo, Rottnest, Fraser, and a host of others on the shelf, were elevations on the flat plains on which they lived, and the sea was many kilometres further out than it is today.

With rising sea-levels and retreat of coastlines the moist maritime airflow returned, rainfall increased and penetrated inland, and the duration of the summer monsoon increased. Vegetation responded to the changes and the northern boundary of the arid zone moved towards the centre of the continent. By 14 000 years ago, the sea had started to flood Lake Carpentaria, and it had risen sufficiently to flood Torres Strait by 9000 years ago. Warm currents could then lap the northern coastline. A 'greenhouse' phase between 9000 and 7000 years ago saw warmer and wetter conditions than apply today and the maximum size attained by the rainforest pockets which had survived the aridity of the glacial stage by being situated in localities whose microclimates were determined by local topography.

It must be evident from this account that

SEA-LEVEL CHANGES DURING THE LAST 125 000 YEARS

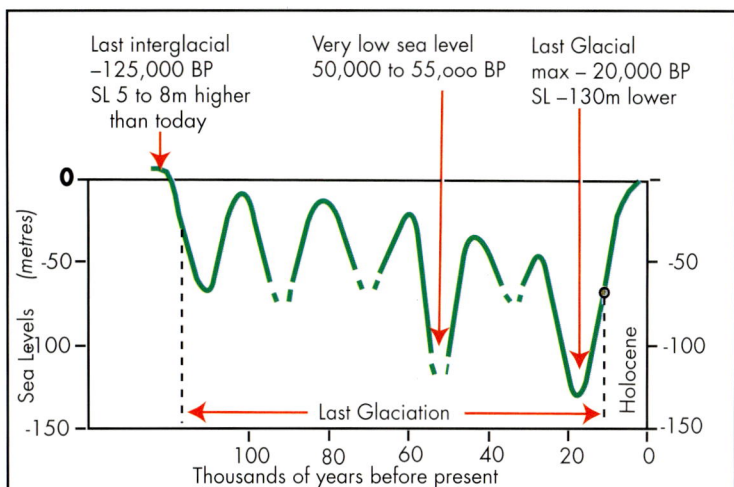

CHANGES IN THE COASTLINE OF NORTHERN AUSTRALIA AND PAPUA NEW GUINEA RELATIVE TO THE LAST GLACIAL MAXIMUM.

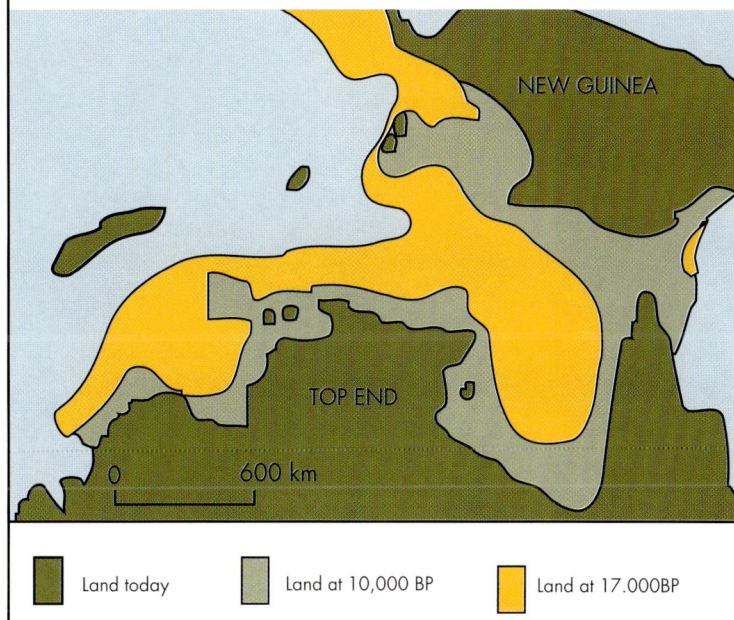

After Williams[140]

the myth of a uniformly 'rainforested' tropical north any time within the last two million years, or right back to Early Miocene for that matter, is well and truly debunked!

Sea-level stabilised by 6000 to 7000 years ago and the coastal plains of the tropical north began to form. The ancient 'raised beaches' and inland dune ridges which are features of the seaward edges of the coastal plains provide evidence of the sea-level fluctuations of the Pleistocene, and of its stabilising then, without significant fluctuation since.[143] The coastal valleys of the larger rivers became estuaries, mangroves colonised the tidal mudflats and were at their most extensive between 7500 and 6000 years ago. This **'big swamp'** phase is particularly well dated in the South Alligator plains, and is clearly evident in a number of other localities along the northern coastline. The big mangrove swamps acted as efficient sediment traps and the fine sediment which came down the rivers during the wet season eventually buried the mangroves. By about 4000 years ago the coastal plain was traversed by sinuous tidal rivers and mangroves were confined to the coastal fringe and to river margins, much as they are today. By 2000 years ago many of the meandering channels had been cut off from their parent rivers, leaving them with a characteristic cuspate form in the lower valleys of the South and East Alligator Rivers.

This history of mangroves and brackish water far inland must surely imply the presence of acid sulphate soils underlying the northern part of the floodplains wherever the big swamp previously extended, unless the volumes of water which percolate in the monsoon have leached the acid over time. If such soils do in fact exist at depth they would be a factor militating against any agricultural or land use schemes such as those occasionally brought up to substantiate arguments about use of northern floodplains for intensive agriculture.

The black clays of the wetlands are young and rich in nutrients. They are the accumulation of the eroded sediments from sandstone escarpment areas inland and mud from flooding of the catchments in the monsoon, mixed with some from the river and marine floodplain, a product of the few thousand years since sea-levels stabilised. They produce lush growth in the wet; in the dry they become massively cracked and their vegetation is reduced to dried stems and the underground organs of plants, and seeds, waiting for the rain. The clay soils swell as they absorb water, the cracks close and the native rodents, snakes and other animals which have been hiding within their protective depths emerge.

When the monsoon arrives, the floodplains of the north-flowing rivers are flooded by run-off from the slightly higher savanna country. Slight levee banks separate the often brackish river waters from the fresh water of the floodplains. Billabongs, havens for water birds whose habitat has declined significally in the southern half of the continent, are replenished.

The coastal plains for the most part are dynamic and salt water penetrates far up valleys so that a salty water-table renders some alluvial soils many kilometres inland unsuitable for agriculture. Extensive flooding during the wet season sees many of the coastal plains under water for half the year, restricting their vegetation to sedges and some grasses. The plains form a buffer zone between the salty tidal flats and the paperbark forests which are often situated in perennially flooded areas on the inland edge of the plains. In the past, buffalo damage in the wetlands has allowed salt water to penetrate into the paperbark swamps, killing the trees. **Feral buffalo** have been largely eradicated in the national Brucellosis and Tuberculosis Eradication Campaign, and the remaining buffalo are controlled in herds with cattle. Buffalo did not do such wholesale damage as feral goats or donkeys have done elsewhere because they require a particular combination of food, water and shade, which restricts their distribution. Their conflict with native fauna has thus been patchier,

as has their grazing impact. In addition their damage by trampling in boggy soils has been concentrated on the black soil cracking clays which are remarkable in their ability to recover once the animals are removed.

Feral pigs are still a destructive agent in the northern wetlands. Pigs can attain very high numbers in good years and are a health risk to domestic livestock as carriers of brucellosis. Feral pigs from the northern wetlands are supplied to the European game-meat market (Germany in particular), but not in numbers which would solve the feral problem. (When cane toads reach the northern coastal wetlands on their relentless 30 km a year advance across tropical Australia from the east they will be ideally suited to the environments they find there, and one can only speculate on their impact on the native fauna.)

The productivity of the wetlands is great during the wet season, but is decimated during the dry, and subject to the ENSO fluctuations which affect the intensity of the monsoon and result in great annual rainfall variability. The main native herbivore, whose populations fluctuate according to the amount of herbage and the degree of flooding of the plains, is the dusky rat, *Rattus colletti*. It can reach plague proportions in some years. Relatively few species of plants and animals are involved in the floodplain ecology compared with the nearby savannas and wet forests, whose inmates use the floodplains when food there is plentiful. Magpie geese, grasshoppers and snakes are often abundant. **Magpie geese**, which feed largely on the corms of sedges and seeds of wild rice, require large territories in order to find sufficient areas with satisfactory water levels which enable them to probe the mud for the corms, or to find enough seed. They are no longer found in southern Australia because of the loss of suitably extensive wetland habitats there.

Use of the seasonal wetlands by Aboriginals has been considerable for a very long time. Assuming that Aboriginals arrived from the north, and knowing that there is evidence of their presence in the Australian continent for 60 000 years, it is possible that they have hunted, gathered food and fished on the northern floodplains for up to 60 000 years, at first in small numbers, and in increasing numbers as time went by. For part of that time they fired the flood plains just as they fired the monsoonal savanna. The low erodibility of the soils, the productivity of the land in the wet season, and the prevalence of short-lived plants would have enabled the ecosystems to be forgiving and to bounce back under fire management, just as recovery has been rapid and generous after removal of the grazing and trampling pressures of the feral buffalo. (Where the trampling by buffalo has allowed the entry of salt water into freshwater paperbark swamps the effects are less easily remedied and the damage is more long lasting.)

The human impact which has caused the most serious and ongoing degradation of the northern floodplains has been indirect — due to the introduction of feral plants.[144] The spread of *Mimosa pigra* today

Left: Mimosa pigra spreading in a massive invasion of a wetland, where a few remaining feral buffalo still graze.

Below: Buffalo damage to a river bank being contained with a wooden barrier in Kakadu.

M.E.W.

presents major problems. Mimosa has invaded at least 800 km^2 of wetlands, where it forms solid stands which look from a distance like a metres-high lawn, so densely are the bushes packed together. It is a rampant invader, as its colonisation of 30 000 ha of wetlands on the Adelaide River near Darwin in three years indicates. There, open sedge and grass country, ideal waterbird habitat, was transformed into shrubland so dense that no native vegetation survives under it. The mimosa invaded land over-grazed by buffalo where its floating seeds, carried on floodwaters, could germinate without local competition. (The soil beneath mimosa plants can contain up to 12 000 seeds per square metre.)[145]

Mimosa has been declared a noxious weed and research is being carried out on control. A combination of biological control agents and a fire regime to reduce competition and allow sedges and grasses to re-establish looks like being the best recipe, although massive chemical spraying is used in dense infestations as a containment measure to slow the spread to new areas. The threat of mimosa is ever present in the thinking of managers of Kakadu National Park where four full-time rangers seek it out and aim to destroy localised infestations before they spread and take over. The very existence of magpie geese is threatened by spread of mimosa, for more than 60% of the Australian population of these birds relies on the permanent wetlands in the park for survival in the dry season, and the rest are now confined to northern wetlands. One native animal — the red-cheeked dunnart — benefits from the invasion and thrives in the mimosa thickets in some areas.

Even open water is vulnerable to invasion by weeds. The floating fern, **Salvinia,** can cover a billabong in a matter of weeks, doubling its biomass every 2.5 days. Biological control, using a South

THE SPREAD OF *MIMOSA PIGRA* IN THE TROPICAL NORTH

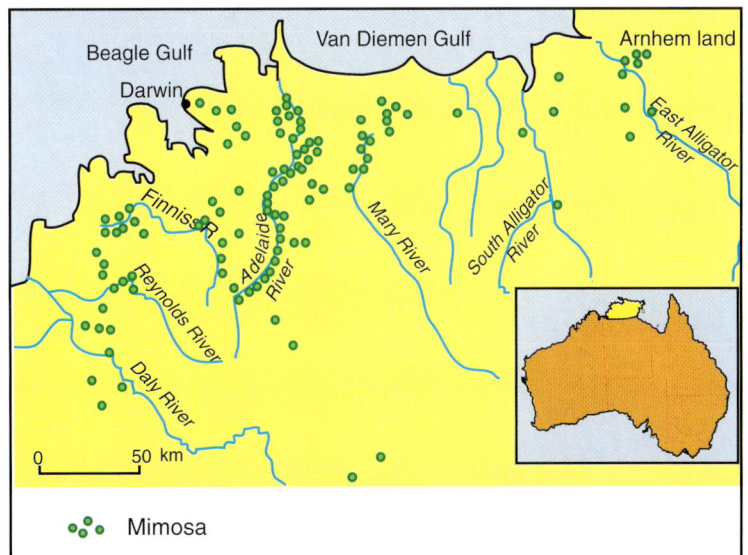

•°• Mimosa

American weevil which eats and sinks the leaf mats, is used successfully in some places, but outbreaks in Kakadu have sometimes been beyond the power of available weevils to control them.

Para Grass *(Brachiaria mutica)* has invaded several thousand hectares on the East Alligator floodplain and is spreading rapidly. It is being promoted as an improved pasture species for wetland grazing. It becomes a monoculture, greatly affecting the biodiversity of the wetlands when it replaces the vastly more complex natural ecosystems.

In the northern tropical wetlands, as in other ecosystems, control of weed species can lead to another set of problems, and post-eradication management while balance is being restored to an ecosystem is a vital, but little understood, part of any rehabilitation process. Often attempts to control one weed only result in the rapid establishment of another. The history of introduced pasture species turning feral and taking over should act as a warning against such introductions, particularly when it has been shown in the north that native perennial grasses and properly managed grazing routines result in equally good productivity.

Land-use and the Tropical Wetlands

Grazing

In the Top End it is normal grazing practice to move stock from the upland savanna woodland onto the floodplains, as soon as they are dry enough after the Wet, to take advantage of the rich seasonal grassy vegetation. It is becoming an increasingly common practice to plant exotic grasses like para grass and **hymenachne** *(Hymenachne amplexicaulis)*, which grow readily in flooded conditions, to improve the pastures and eliminate the almost barren later dry stage. These alien grasses displace native species and do not supply the corms or the rice-grass seed required by magpie geese, and do not maintain the less visible elements of the wetlands' biodiversity either. Considerable debate is current on the merits of using 'ponded pasture' species. In the course of time they may so radically change the ecosystems that many species will become extinct.

Aleman grass *(Echinochloa amplexicaulis)*, from Central America, a ponded pasture species capable of growing in deep water and spreading rapidly to choke waterways and wetlands, is a recent import whose spread should be stopped before it takes over.

Two other introduced grasses which are not wetland grasses but are spreading and causing problems and are so potentially dangerous that their elimination and noxious status declaration are suggested are:

- **Mission Grass** *(Pennisetum polystachion)* which is one of the world's worst weeds. It was introduced from West Africa in 1970 as a potential fodder crop. It has been declared a noxious weed in the Northern Territory where it invades bushland as well as disturbed areas, out-competing native plants. It cures (dries out at the end of its life cycle)

later and has greater biomass than native grasses, and has the potential to change fire regimes.

- **Gamba grass** *(Andropogon gayanus)*, also from West Africa, is encroaching on the savannas of Kakadu. It is a giant grass which also cures later than native species, changing fire regimes.[146]

The whole question of management of the floodplain country may be academic within the next generation. With a greenhouse sea-level rise of only half a metre, saltwater invasion will render this wide strip of northern Australia a salt-marsh terrain. (Parts of the north of the continent are known to be presently sinking, so this geological phenomenon is going to compound the problems of sea-level rise.)

Mining

The impacts of mining within the boundaries of Kakadu National Park are discussed in the section on uranium mining in Chapter 13. Objections to mining in general are largely political, whether they be about uranium and the morality of mining it at all; or about Aboriginal rights and Mabo; or about conflicting land use as in National Parks. The risk of off-site environmental degradation is so much reduced by the constraints and regulations within which mining is carried out these days as to be almost negligible, or at least to compare favourably with degradation caused by some agricultural land use, except perhaps in some extremely sensitive areas.

Agriculture in the Northern Floodplains

The 1953 Humpty Doo rice-growing experiment, based on irrigation from the specially constructed Fogg Dam south-east of Darwin, was a failure. The native fauna (magpie geese, rats and insects in particular), responded to the sudden bountiful food supply by eating the project to death. It had been unwisely placed right on top of the second largest magpie goose breeding area in the continent. The venture was abandoned, but the wildlife triumphed and today the Fogg Dam has become a world famous waterbird and wetland habitat and a magnet for birdwatchers.

The magpie geese have turned their attention to other crops, attacking the mangoes and melons in two newly emerging industries. It is now strongly argued that horticultural projects in the Top End should only attract support if they can remain commercially viable in the face of crop losses to wildlife, so large and unsolvable are the problems of controlling native species in pest situations.

The **Ord River Scheme** is the subject of a case study later in this chapter. It is another scheme which proved an expensive mistake, but it is now being resurrected.

KAKADU NATIONAL PARK

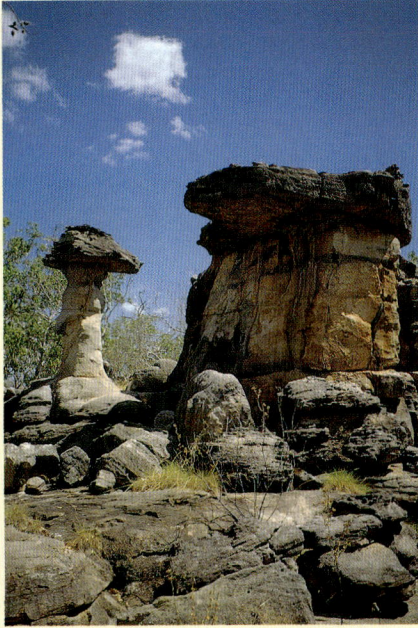

Pillars of eroded sandstone in the escarpment portion of Kakadu at Obiri. The rocky sandstone plateau supports dry woodland and grassland, with closed forest in ravines and low shrubland on sandy outwash areas. The closed forest remnants are dominated by Allosyncarpia in the gullies. The flora and fauna contain many endemic species: 11% of plant species are endemic; and there are 5 bird species, 4 marsupials, 6 reptiles and 2 frogs endemic to the whole plateau.

M.E.W.

Kakadu is the second largest National Park in Australia. The first section was declared in 1979, and since then three other sections have been added, resulting in a total of 19 700 km². It is World Heritage Listed and functions mainly as Aboriginal land leased back to the Commonwealth Government, with some areas excised, notably the Ranger and Jabiluka uranium leases.

The park includes almost the entire South Alligator River catchment, and the West Alligator River catchment, so park management represents a total catchment management program. The park comprises the western edge of the sandstone country of the Arnhem Land Plateau and its drainage, which gives rise to the large rivers and wetlands on the northern coastal plain. With the geologically complex region of Pine Creek Geosyncline rocks to the south, the result is great landscape diversity with a magnificent range of habitats and much biodiversity. Woodland and open forest savannas occupy 60% of the park and represent the highly flammable component, with 85% of the former burnt annually and 48% of the latter burnt in two of every three years.

Because of the size of the park, its diversity and the fact that it is ecologically intact, it is unique. It is representative of the ecosystems of a vast area of northern Australia, and its flora and fauna are largely intact, with no known extinctions. It has low numbers of feral plant and animal species, and continual vigilance and eradication programs aim to improve even this situation.

The ancient Aboriginal art galleries in the sandstone caves, and the ongoing Aboriginal involvement and cultural input add an extra dimension to this wonderful park.

The large size of the park is critical to maintaining its biodiversity and only one of this size would be viable over the long term in northern Australia where climatic fluctuations, fire and other factors require access to refuge areas and patch diversity on a grand scale for survival of species. Worldwide there has been a recognition, sadly too late, that most national parks are too small and that loss of biodiversity in them is inevitable over time.

KAKADU NATIONAL PARK

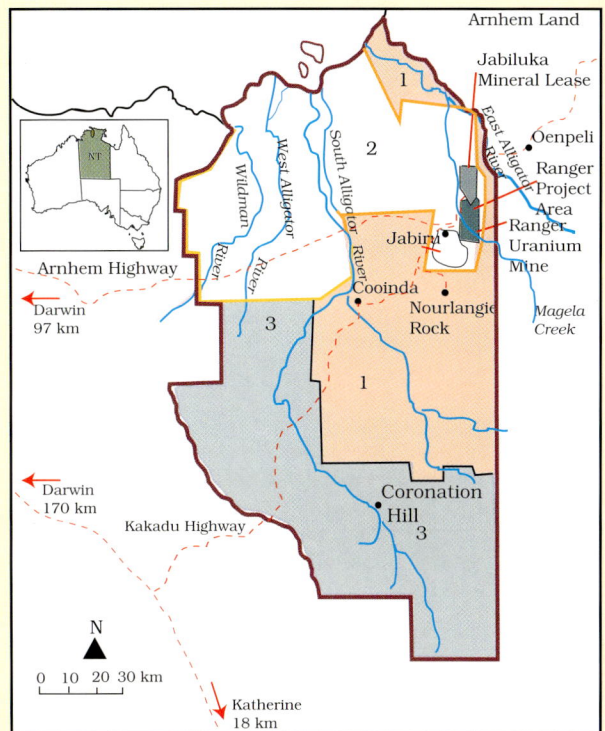

After Braithwaite and Werner[147]

The wet-dry tropics worldwide are under threat of habitat destruction with its attendant biodiversity loss. The problem is made more serious by the fact that only a small proportion of the species in tropical ecosystems have been described. (Only 2% of the original dry forest in Central America remains and no one knows how many undescribed species have gone forever with it.) Australia, with large areas of its wet-dry tropics in a relatively natural state, has the opportunity (and the responsibility?) to do something which is no longer possible in other parts of the world — to perpetuate a truly viable park in the wet-dry tropics and maintain its biodiversity. **Whether we have the wisdom to manage fire in a way compatible with this aim is the question.**

The regular, almost annual, burning that is carried out under the 'wisdom' of Aboriginal

Right: Sandstone vegetation at Nourlangi Rock. The sandstone plateau region shares the highest goanna species density with the Kimberley.

M.E.W

Far right: Aboriginal art galleries decorate the sandstone overhangs and caves.

M.E.W

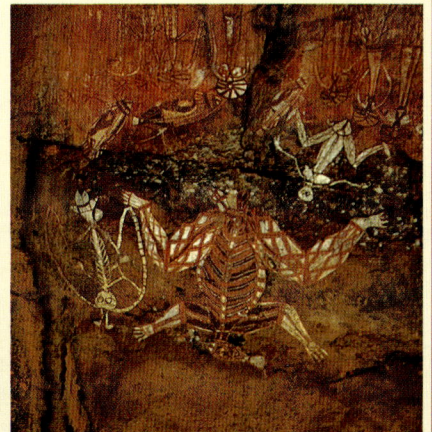

advisers may prove to be the factor which destroys the dream of sustainable management. Politically correct or not, fire management has to be based on scientific grounds rather than on how we think the Aboriginals used to do it. The pyromaniac that lurks inside the entire human race may be putting the whole concept of sustainability at risk.

The development of tourism in Kakadu has been a model for other countries to emulate. In fact, as many visitors to the Top End will agree, the Northern Territory excels in the infrastructure it supplies for tourists in the whole region, and in Kakadu in particular. The partnership between Aboriginal and non-Aboriginal Australians which results in the excellence of the enterprise is another model worth emulating elsewhere.

Yellow Waters, where tourists take boat trips to see crocodiles and the peaceful beauty of the wetlands. Migratory birds frequent the northern wetlands: 30 species breed in eastern Asia and spend the other season in northern Australia; increasing numbers of water birds are using the area as a stopping-off point on their migrations.

M.E.W.

Eucalypt woodland savanna, the widespread vegetation type of the tropical north.

M.E.W.

THE TROPICAL SAVANNAS

Savannas are the dominant ecosystems of tropical and subtropical regions throughout the world where rainfall is highly seasonal, and they are in fact *the product of that climate where extreme alternation of wet and dry seasons occurs.*[148,149] Fire and herbivory are seen as secondary determinants or modifying factors. In northern Australia, herbivory by native mammals is low, and according to experts, 99% is by invertebrates (particularly by grasshoppers and termites).[150] This is in sharp contrast to the ungulate-dominated grazing patterns in other savannas of the world. **The fact that coevolution of the flora and fauna in Australia has not resulted in plants having the defence of thorns is one of the reasons why the introduction of hoofed animals has had such an impact on the vegetation.** Seedlings of species of *Acacia* in Africa, for instance, are protected by their vicious thorns, while species of the genus in Australia (mulga etc.) have no such protection and sheep and other introduced stock

seek them out and eat them with impunity, preventing regeneration. Acacias in Australia, evolving from the same Gondwanan stock as those in Africa, India and South America, chose the phyllode and not the thorn line of modification of their structures and only a few native species are spiny.

In tropical Australia, savanna is the dominant ecosystem, covering a vast area — about a quarter of the continent, yet very lightly populated. Some local areas within wet-dry savannas may contain other vegetation types, where surface water or groundwater accumulations exist, or where microclimates are contained within landscape features determined by geology or topography. (Aboriginals make up about half the population of the tropical savannas — 43% in the Kimberley; 57% in the Gulf; and 46% in Cape York, and their population is increasing rapidly, as is their land tenure.) In contrast, tropical savannas in the rest of the world support nearly a fifth of the world's population. In Australia, pastoralism is the main land-use in the tropical savannas, but **the main income**

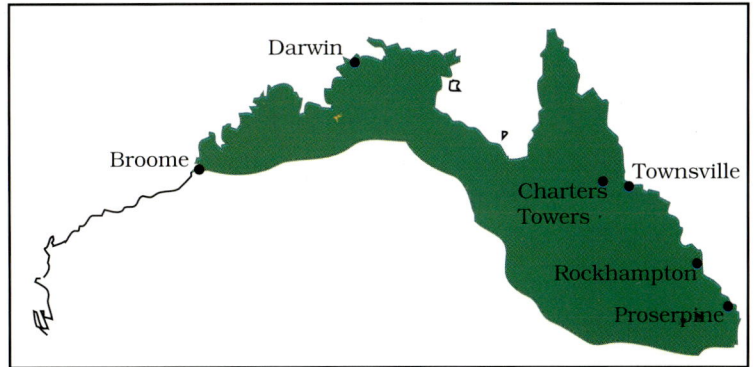

Darwin
Broome
Townsville
Charters Towers
Rockhampton
Proserpine

earners are mining and tourism, and together about $7.5 billion is contributed to the National economy by the tropical north.

The 'sustainable' nature of tourism and mining, which do not run down the life-supporting soil and water resources of the nation, is now seen by many of us as making them preferred industries for supporting the national economy. It is unlikely, however, that there will be a ready acceptance of the concept that Australia should **not** see itself as an agricultural nation; that by feeding multi-millions of people (of whom only 18 million live in Australia) we are destroying our resource base; that with careful management and keeping our population within bounds set by our ecological footprint we can feed and maintain *Australians* sustainably; and that we have an alternative approach available to us which would guarantee the well-being of the continent into the future and the security of our lifestyle for future generations...

Very small areas of wet tropics, where rainfall is evenly distributed throughout the year and where tropical rainforest grows, exist in Australia. (See Rainforest Map, p.265.) In Africa and South America, on the other hand, large areas are present, and when they are cleared, or burnt frequently, a derived form of savanna results and it will revert to rainforest over time. **Australian savannas are *not* derived from rainforest by fire or any other factor** and would not revert to rainforest if fire or grazing or clearing ceased. The small areas of **monsoon forest** in Kakadu, confined to areas with locally wet microclimates, represent only 0.5% of the northern Stages I and II, and it is believed that in the wetter times between 9000 and

about 5000 years ago there may have been four times as much monsoonal forest, but still only involving 2% of the area.

A wet-dry climate predisposes vegetation to fire, and natural fires are inevitable. The highest annual incidence of lightning in Australia occurs in the northern savannas, concentrated in the build-up to the wet season, when vegetation is at its driest and most flammable. However, there is no way of knowing how frequently areas were subjected to natural fire in the past, when there is a history of Aboriginal fire altering fire regimes for perhaps 60 000 years.

Prolific growth occurs each wet season in the tropical ecosystems and plants like the annual spear grass, *Sorghum intrans,* produce sufficient biomass to

Above top left: Baobabs are found in the savanna of the western Kimberley. Above top right: Cooktown ironwood (Erythrophleum chlorostachys) dominates the savanna on black soil of swamps in the western Kimberley. Above: Palms form groves in the savanna in areas bordering swamps. M.E.W.

carry a fire each year. This means that fire is inevitable in the long run because of the prevalence of lightning at the end of the dry season when grass fuel is abundant and ready for easy ignition.

Fire 'management' is the most contentious land management issue in the tropical north. Over the whole region, more than 70% of the savanna woodlands and open forests which dominate the landscape are now burnt annually (and more than 85% in Kakadu). A further large percentage of the remainder burns in two years out of three. The fires are almost exclusively lit by people. It is acknowledged by the scientists working on effects of fire that very little is known about the long-term ecological consequences of such frequent burning. (This should surely be a valid reason for caution and for a more conservative approach to the subject.)

One argument goes that by allowing excessive build-up of fuel, hotter and more damaging fires would occur under 'natural' regimes, and it is on this assumption that the almost annual burning is justified. Dr Braithwaite (personal communication) says that fuel does not build up beyond two to three years and the argument is more about fire weather times and when fires are unstoppable. Thus the prevention of such late season fires is, officially, the dominant motivation for contemporary fire management, and 'cool' burning early in the season after the Wet in patches 'like the Aboriginals used to do' is accepted as the best way to

go. (That a very large percentage of 'contemporary regime fires' were burning just before the monsoon was due to arrive in 1995 when I travelled extensively through these areas, shows a **gaping hole between what is known or thought to be best practice and what is actually happening. The country was in flames, bare scorched earth ready to be washed away, and it looked like irresponsible vandalism to me!**)

The assumption that frequent low-intensity burning is better from an ecological point of view than less frequent but more intense burning is unsubstantiated. There may even be some evidence that increased habitat diversity followed a particularly intense late dry season fire in Kakadu.[151] The savanna ecosystems evolved before people started lighting fires to 'manage' them, and logic suggests that they must be adapted to higher intensity, lower frequency, late dry season fire regimes.

Those who credit Aboriginals with all wisdom in the matter are forgetting that a contemporary Aboriginal in a 4WD (and with special fire-lighters provided by NPWS) can and does burn out hundreds of square kilometres, while a tribal person living off the land took care not to render the whole area over which he could walk to obtain his food a scorched earth landscape. **Those who are not concerned with political correctness are increasingly admitting that Aboriginals used fire for many reasons and**

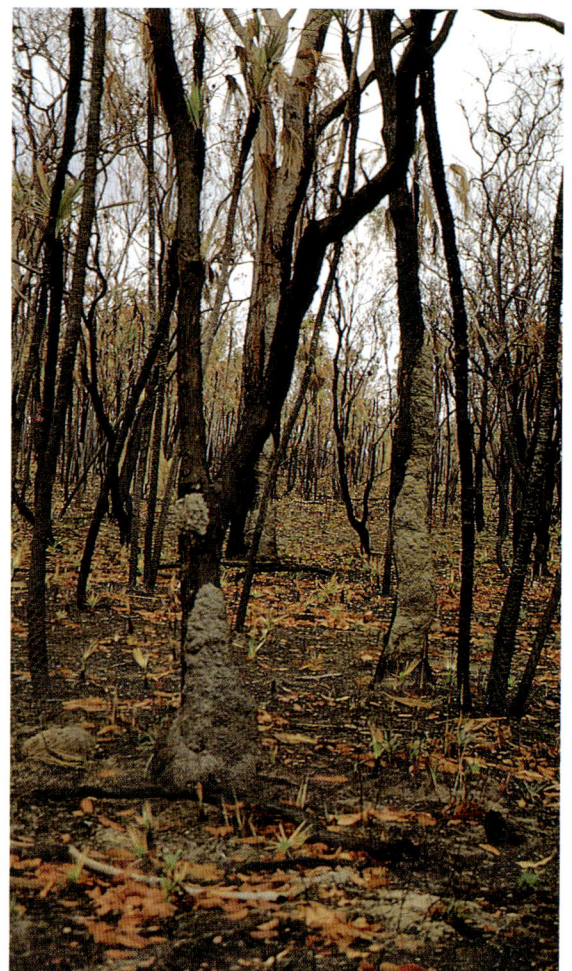

Right: A late season fire, just before the onset of the monsoon, leaves ground bare and exposed to erosion, while trees, already stressed by the long dry, are often killed by such a late burn.

Far right: A late-season, very hot fire has damaged tree trunks and made them vulnerable to termite invasion.

M.E.W.

SATELLITE SEQUENCE SHOWING TOP END BURNING IN 1990.

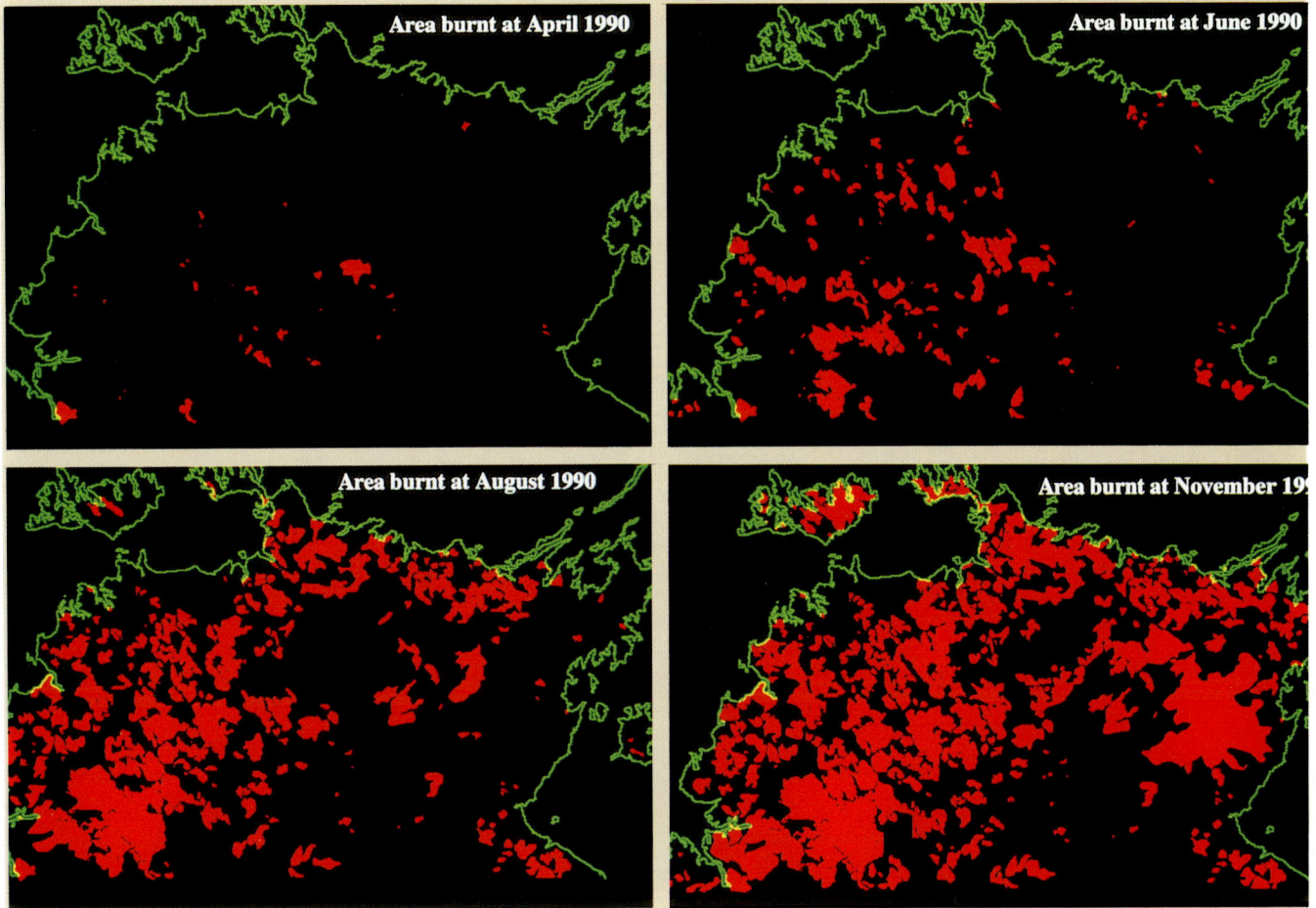

Area burnt at April 1990

Area burnt at June 1990

Area burnt at August 1990

Area burnt at November 19[90]

DEAN GRAETZ

that conservation in the full sense of maintaining biodiversity and the sustainability of ecosystems was not within their vocabulary, and was not a deliberate intention. Today's wholesale burning of tropical savannas based on, and officially validated by, what amounts to the cultural connection between Aboriginals and fire has to be seen as unjustifiable. It is not scientific or logical to insist that because Aboriginals burnt the land, deliberate burning must be right.

The deliberate burning practiced today is to protect property which would be at risk from uncontrolled wildfire; to improve pastures; for various reasons by Aboriginals who now own or lease a large proportion of the Top End; and it has a complement of some accidental or purely vandalistic fires as well. Accepting that natural fire is inevitable, unpredictable and not compatible with the present-day land uses, some fire 'management' becomes necessary. The critical issue becomes not whether savannas should be burnt at all but how frequently and at what time(s) of the year. Until certain knowledge is available of the long-term effects of annual burning there should be regulations at least about when burning is *not* allowed so that the most damaging fires (in terms of soil erosion) are avoided.

The problems of enforcing regulations are obviously going to be enormous and may be insurmountable, partly because of the dual legal systems involved.

A major problem is the difference in the laws which govern Aboriginal and non-Aboriginal behaviour. Aboriginals may burn where and when they like on land they own and lease; they can range over country held by others as well as over that which they own in the course of their hunting and foraging; they are allowed by law to kill animals which are protected, even endangered, and which non-Aboriginal Australians are prohibited from killing, and they use high-powered modern guns, not traditional hunting methods to do so.[152] This situation has to be addressed. It creates a divided nation and a great deal of resentment.

A mosaic of patches at different successional stages after fire is one of the factors which is stated in scientific literature as contributing to the *biodiversity* of a region. If biodiversity of the savannas is the number of species which exist in its ecosystems when they are in a state of natural balance, then under the normal dynamics with fires caused by lightning affecting different areas at different longer intervals, this requirement for the

Regeneration, particularly of cycads, after fire.

M.E.W.

maintenance of biodiversity was met before humans intervened. The actual biodiversity does not change by supplying *more* burnt patches by adding human-induced fires. Does it not mean that certain species become much more abundant in the greater number of burnt patches which are undergoing successional stages and *apparent* biodiversity is greater? To think otherwise is to imply that human intervention is necessary to preserve biodiversity.

The heterogeneity of the large savanna ecosystem depends on its recent fire history, but on a smaller scale within specific areas it depends on differences in soil fertility, caused in part by local activities of termites, ants, other invertebrates, and sometimes vertebrates; in water availability; and in topography. The way the vital faunal link in nutrient recycling is affected by the very frequent fire regimes has to be taken into account, and very little is known about the long-term effects of different fire regimes.

Nutrient-deficient soils characterise much of the savanna country, so rapid release of nutrients from organic matter is critical. Fires, termites and micro-organisms are the three main agents that mineralise organic matter in savannas.[153] Fires may cause direct losses through the transfer to the atmosphere of nutrients as gases and particulates, while indirect losses may result from erosion of ash and soil from burnt ground in storms. Research at Kapalga in the Kakadu

National Park showed that in grassy woodland fires, 54% to 94% of all measured nutrients in the fuel were transferred to the atmosphere, but that rainfall accession and the deposition of particulates would replace most of the losses of nutrients with the exception of nitrogen. Estimated rates of biological fixation of nitrogen appeared to be insufficient to replace the annual loss. The researchers concluded that a regime of annual fires that completely burnt the available grassy fuel would deplete nitrogen reserves in the savannas, but more recent research has suggested that free-living soil bacteria are probably maintaining the levels.

Ants are one of the most important faunal groups in tropical savannas, being closely linked with soil, vegetation and other fauna, and they are also involved in nutrient recycling. Their responses to different aspects of environmental change have been investigated and found to be useful in assessing the health of ecosystems and in monitoring the success of rehabilitation in areas which are degraded. Ants have been found to be sensitive to different fire regimes[154] and fire-free intervals of only a few years have been found to be ecologically beneficial. Too frequent fire, like the annual burning now being inflicted on much of the land, results in destruction of forest and biomass litter which would otherwise have its nutrients recycled by ants and termites. Fire management policies should take into account the wellbeing and optimum conditions of its ant fauna if balance is to be maintained in ecosystems.

Two CSIRO researchers into fire ecology in the Northern Territory argue that the reasons commonly given for today's burning practices are either logically suspect, or are aimed at protecting vegetation types other than savannas.[155] It is well known that in southern Australia many plants have their reproductive biology geared to fire. They are 'fire dependent', in that high volume seed dispersal depends on, and is promoted by fire; germination is assisted by the ashbed nutrients; and establishment of the young plants which 'renew' the vegetation is aided by reduced competition for space and/or light when 'over-mature' plants are removed. This does not apply to the species in savanna woodland where the eucalypts, for instance, shed their seeds after flowering and do not retain them in persistent capsules that only open completely after fire; and where most perennial plant species in savannas regenerate vegetatively after fire and are not replaced by fresh plants. Even the nature of savanna fires is different, with the low concentrations of volatile oils in tropical eucalypt foliage precluding the crown fires which are so devastating in south-eastern and southern Australia. Even if some species in savannas are fire-dependent, they certainly do not need to be burnt every year.

To quote Allan Andersen and Dick Braithwaite:[155]

The notion that fire is "good" for vegetation hardly leads to the conclusion that the more frequently it is burned the better! In short, most savanna plants are well-adapted to cope with frequent burning, but they are unlikely to "need" fires at the frequency prevailing under current management.

There is no doubt that some plant species are particularly sensitive to too-frequent fire.[156] The native cypress pine *Callitris intratropica* is fire sensitive. It is typically restricted to sandstone escarpments which offer protection from fire, but it is also extremely drought-tolerant and it expands into eucalypt savanna in the absence of fire. It can survive low intensity fires but not if they are too frequent. *Allosyncarpia ternata*, the Arnhem Land endemic relative of eucalypts (in the Eucalyptopsis alliance of Myrtaceae) which forms monospecific stands on and around the sandstone escarpment of the Kakadu region, is also drought-tolerant and capable of some vegetative regeneration if fire penetrates its usually fire-excluding habitat, but repeated burning eliminates it.

Frequent burning of savanna also gradually penetrates the boundaries of the monsoon forest pockets; it gradually thins out the woody sprouts of eucalypts which follow fire, and kills the saplings which are fire-sensitive until they attain a certain size; and it therefore has the potential to cause long-term structural degradation of the woodlands and open forests. It has been suggested that fire-free intervals of three to five years are required to prevent such degradation.

In order to obtain more detailed information on Australian tropical savannas, a new scientific project has recently begun. The International Geosphere-Biosphere Program has established *transects* in major ecosystems of the world. Each transect is a series of study sites (research areas) spread along an imaginary line, allowing for information from a relatively small number of sites to be extrapolated across a large geographic area (in other words, a sampling line). The **North Australian Tropical Transect (NATT)** follows a rainfall gradient, extending from the northern coastline just east of Darwin due south to about 1000 km inland (from 1600 mm to 500 mm of annual rainfall). The aim is to provide the ecological information required for the sound management of savanna resources. Three research themes are involved at the five study sites along the NATT line:

- The structure of savanna ecosystems in relation to variation in rainfall and soil type.
- The impacts of human use of the land on savanna structure.
- Indicators of the impacts of land-use on biodiversity, which can be readily incorporated into land assessment and monitoring programs.

NATT was established by the CSIRO Division of Wildlife & Ecology with funding from the Land and Water Rural Research Development Commission. It involves the Co-operative Research Centre for the Sustainable Development of Tropical Savannas, a partnership of land management and research institutions from throughout northern Australia. Researchers from other institutions in Australia and overseas also have an input. Surely with availability of so much expertise it should be possible to determine what land management practices are sustainable. A

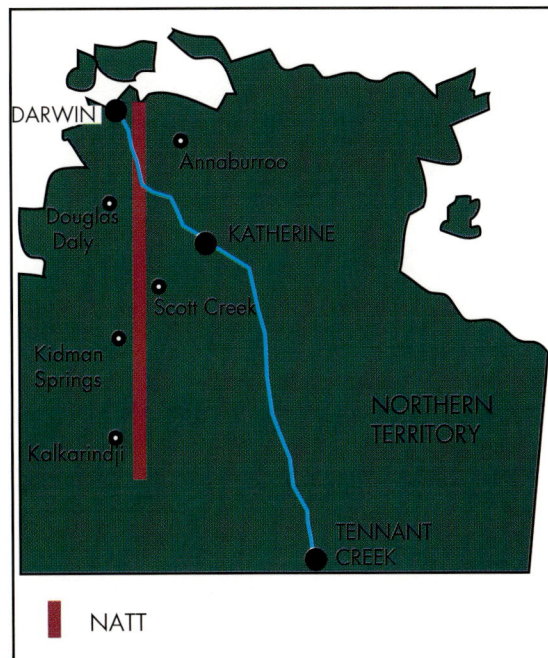

holistic approach is obviously necessary, and a reassessment of all land-use options and management practices, particularly fire management and how it affects biodiversity in the long term.

THE ORD RIVER SCHEME

A Study in Catchment Rehabilitation

The Ord River Scheme, like the Snowy Scheme, was a brain-child of the heady post-war days of the Green Revolution when mammoth 'Projects', big ideas of making Australia a big producer by introducing irrigation schemes, and of developing the north, were all the go. The schemes had another factor in common — both focused attention on the extremely degraded nature of their catchments, which posed serious threats of siltation to their proposed dams. And because this meant a threat to the all-powerful economy, money and resources for rehabilitation were made available in both cases. In the Snowy, the massive erosion of the High Country had been caused by snow-lease over-grazing; in the Ord it was 'open range' grazing, which was concentrated in areas adjacent to the river systems. The worst degradation was therefore focused on the most productive pasture land of the river frontages and floodplains where the tussock grass perennial pastures grew.

Rangeland management in the tropical north had always been 'cattle hunting' without fences, where the river frontages took the brunt of grazing, since the early days of pioneering settlement by the Durack family and others in the 1880s. A rapid build-up in 'official' cattle numbers, and in feral cattle, donkeys and horses, put great

Right: The Argyle Dam, its wall and the pressurised outflow at the bottom of the wall. A Brachychiton flowering in the foreground.

M.E.W.

Above: A view across the arid landscape to the green irrigated fields of the Ord River Scheme.

M.E.W.

pressure on pastures and by the 1930s most of the more productive land was severely degraded and eroded. A number of reports in the 1940s documented the erosion, but it was the realisation that **22 million tonnes of sediment were being carried annually in the Ord** (according to estimates at that time), and that 90% of the Ord catchment was above the proposed dam, that started a series of projects to re-stabilise the worst-affected areas.

The Ord River catchment has an area of 46 000 km^2. The catchment supports diverse rangelands:

- Extensive hummock grasslands (spinifex), which have remained in good condition as they have not been subjected to significant grazing pressures.
- Acacia woodlands with hummock grasses and a small component of palatable grasses and herbs.
- Open savanna woodlands, often degraded by grazing, fire and drought.
- Black soil plains which, though close to water and supporting palatable pasture, are generally in good range condition because they are naturally resistant to erosion.

- Tussock grasslands, composed of mid-height perennials, mainly on very friable calcareous soils particularly prone to erosion.

The areas which contributed most silt to the river systems were identified as being associated with one soil type, derived from ancient limestones and shales which weather down to fine-textured calcareous soils which are highly erodible by both wind and water. The original vegetation has been described as grassland and grassy savanna,[158] but the species involved and the structure of ecosystems was not recorded before degradation altered them.[159]

The worst affected areas were concentrated principally on the Ord River Station, Turner Station and Flora Valley Station, with smaller areas on the Elvire and Ruby Plains Stations (all in the eastern Kimberley Division of Western Australia). Large areas occurred on Mistake Creek Station in the Northern Territory, which adjoins Ord River Station in the north and east.[157] A scheme of cooperative rehabilitation between lessees of the Western Australian stations and the government began in 1960. Lessees were to remove cattle and contribute towards fencing programs, while the Agriculture Department began cultural and reseeding treatments on the most severely degraded areas. Rehabilitation was also carried out in the adjoining Northern Territory under an agreement with the Territory Administration.

The cooperative program did not work, and in 1967 the whole of the Ord River and Turner River Stations and parts of Flora Valley, Ruby Plains and Elvire Stations near Halls Creek, comprising about a million hectares, were resumed. The land became a Water Catchment Reserve — the **Ord River Regeneration Reserve** (which came under the control of the Minister for Lands) and the Ord River Regeneration Project began.

An eroding plain where soil loss is occurring between the tussock grasses and their surrounding biotic crusts.

M.E.W.

Irrigation area:
Ivanhoe Plain
Designated irrigation area

Regeneration Reserve
Area of most severe erosion

Bungle Bungle National Park

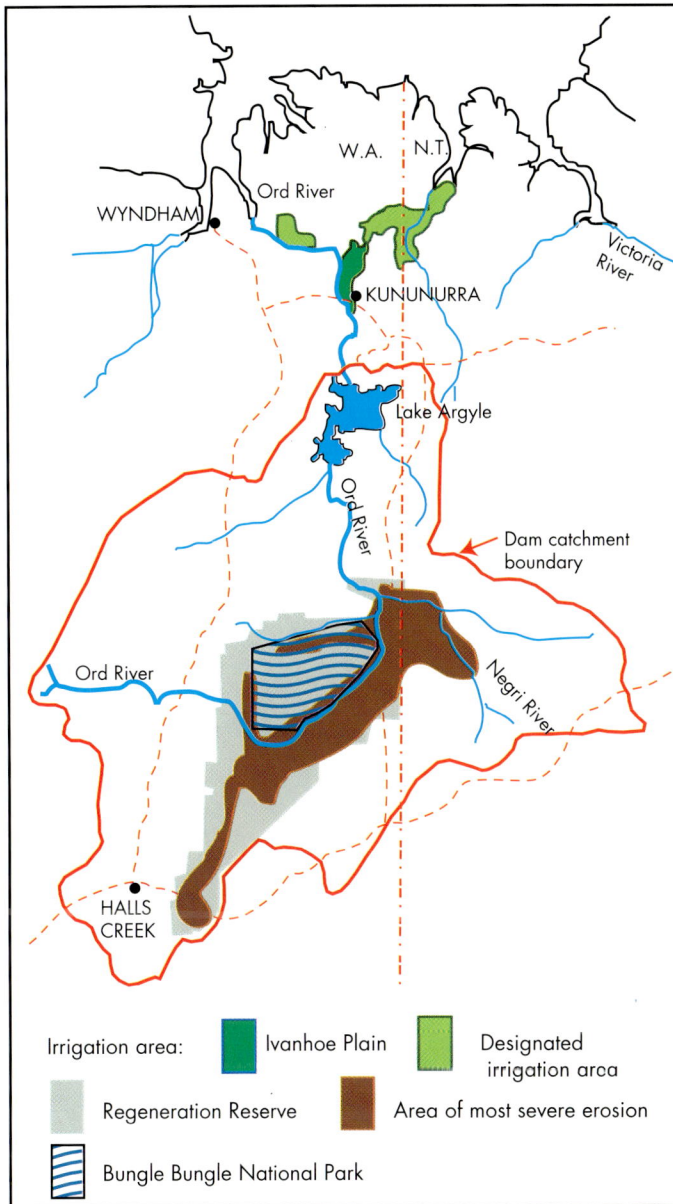

After deSalis. **157**

The regeneration program has involved destocking, strip contour cultivation and reseeding in the most degraded areas, with extensive fencing to facilitate destocking. A special Act was gazetted in 1967 and amended in 1969, vesting ownership of all remaining cattle in the reserve in the Crown.

Since 1975 a complete destocking policy has been in place, though in practice considerable grazing pressure remained because of the difficulty in eradicating more animals than were being replaced by their breeding. Improved mustering and helicopter hunting has been winning the battle recently.

Plants used in the rehabilitation programs were the kapok bush *(Aerva javanica),* which had been introduced into Australia by Afghan camel drivers, and which was already widespread in the degraded areas; birdwood grass *(Cenchrus setiger)* and buffel grass *(Cenchrus ciliaris).* The kapok bush produces masses of woolly seeds which

form mats on the ground below the bushes (and clog up car radiators!). All three plants are highly successful colonisers of bare soil and the use of such introduced plants (which have become serious weeds in a wider context) is justifiable. **In many extremely degraded situations the only plants which will grow, hold the soil and act as starters of successions are such introduced 'weed' species**.

The succession consists of three stages:
- A kapok bush-dominant stage. The seeds accumulate in gutters, rills and around obstacles and kapok bush is virtually the only species in this primary stage of colonisation. Many areas in the reserve are still at this stage, due largely to the fact that degradation has continued because the removal of animals, particularly ferals, has been incomplete.

Above: Speargrass growing in deep sand in the dry bed of the Ord River.

Right: The kapok weed (Aerva javanica) on roadsides in the East Kimberley where it is a widespread weed.

Right: The poisonous calotrope weed is spreading rapidly in the tropical north.

M.E.W.

- The second stage of the succession exhibits diversity. The major species, kapok bush and birdwood grass, are complemented by other introduced species, such as buffel grass, and a number of native annuals. These include camel bush (Trichodesma zeylanicum), tall mulla mulla (Ptilotus exaltatus), smelly bush (Pterigeron odorus) and roly poly (Salsola kali). The introduced and poisonous Calotrope weed (Calotropis procera) often forms thickets.

- A third stage can be a pure stand of birdwood grass, though its distribution is still very restricted.

Between 1960 and 1980, management policy revolved largely around regeneration works, fencing and annual cattle mustering. Donkey control was carried out as far as possible. By the early 1980s parts of the reserve had recovered sufficiently to be used as a research centre for a series of cattle grazing and management trials. The trials demonstrated the advantages of weaning, and of Brahman infusion into herds, but at the same time showed up the fragility of the vegetation cover and the great difficulty involved in managing a complex mixture of partly recovered and still badly degraded country.

In 1989 the amount of sediment still being carried into Lake Argyle annually was estimated to be 23.5 million tonnes,[159] about the same as before rehabilitation had begun! At this rate the storage volume of the dam would be reduced by about 40% in 100 years, and it was suggested that greater emphasis should be given to treatment of the extensive areas of active gullies in the project area, and to degraded areas in the rest of the catchment. In 1993, an official report stated:

There are no definitive data, since the initiation of the regeneration program, indicating a proportional reduction in sediment loads from the Regeneration Reserve corresponding with the increase in vegetation cover. However, as cover is the only effective means of manipulating river silt loads, it must be assumed that increased vegetative cover will eventually reduce silt loads. There has been no consideration given to the problems of silt accretions resulting from slumping of nearly perpendicular walls of major gullies nor from the new erosion rills and gutters referred to previously.[157]

The magnitude of the task in an area as large as this is emphasised by this statement. One is reminded of the situation in Homestead Creek in Western New South Wales (Chapter 4) where gullying and stripping was virtually unstoppable. **Fragile soils, once destabilised, erode progressively until a new stable state is reached, and whether it is economically feasible to do anything about it or not, in view of the size of the area which needs rehabilitation, will remain a question.**

In 1987 a large part of the area in the west of the reserve was gazetted as National Park and Conservation Reserve and became the Purnululu National Park (the Bungle Bungles National Park) managed by CALM. A large proportion of this area is rugged, inaccessible hills; the savannas surrounding them lead down to the degraded river frontages, and expensive fencing would be required to protect degraded areas and the monsoon forest pockets in the region if it were to be opened up again for grazing. A policy of total eradication of ferals should leave the wonderful Bungles area in pristine condition, and the degraded areas on the rivers around it continuing to recover. Tourism in the area is being most carefully managed, with limited access on bad roads which require special vehicles and thus limit access; designated camping sites; walking trails and a policy of closing off areas whenever it is thought wise to do so. The area is anyway only accessible in the dry season.

The regeneration reserve is not the only part of the catchment which supplies sediment to the Argyle Dam, so management practices and rehabilitation of the rest, which is leased and continues to be grazed, is also vital.

The final stage of the Ord River Dam, opened in 1972, stored a volume of water about nine times that of Sydney Harbour. It had the potential to irrigate 75 000 ha of land. It was planned to grow cotton, maize, barley, wheat, safflower, soybeans and pasture. Only cotton was grown, unsuccessfully, for about 10 years, and on only 5000 ha. The scheme proved to be one of Australia's most costly failures.

However, things are looking up and the hydroelectric power station which was part of the original concept is now being completed. (With the unstoppable silting of the dam its life may be limited?) Irrigated crops are being produced, including sugar and a great variety of melons; commercial seed production is proving viable and the remoteness of the area is favourable for this enterprise because there is no risk of contamination of strains of the seeds being grown by cross-pollination, there being no crops outside the irrigation area; a leguminous fodder tree, leucaena, is being trialled.

Leucaena *(Leucaena leucocephala)* is an import from tropical South America. As forage it contains about 30% protein. However, it contains an unusual amino acid called mimosine which forms a toxic compound in the rumen of cattle. Goats are able to detoxify it, and research has shown that it is possible to innoculate cattle with the gut bacteria which goats have in their rumens, solving the toxidity problem. A large area of northern Australia is climatically suitable for leucaena, wherever there is a patch of deep, well-drained, non-acid soil.

Top left and top right: The Bungle Bungles are a wonderland of sandstone architecture and palm-filled gorges.

Above middle: The hydroelectric power plant under construction in 1995 at the base of the Argyle Dam wall. The turbines are driven by the pressurised water from the outflow tunnel at the wall base.

Above: The river below the dam is an amazing deep green colour.

M.E.W.

THE EMPTY SILO WHICH WAITS IN VAIN FOR GRAIN... AND THE SEA WHICH IS SILTING-UP FOR THE SAME REASONS AS IS THE ARGYLE DAM.

Ill-conceived agricultural schemes to bring prosperity to the tropical north are not confined to the past and one can only wonder why the lessons of past failures are not learnt. A modern silo stands unused near the wharf at Broome. It is incongruous in this essentially arid landscape — the schemes for growing grain to supply it have not eventuated.

The unused white elephant silo at Broome Wharf.

Apricot-coloured sands and an azure sea which owes its amazing colour to the suspended sediment in it. The sediment is the product of the annual floods of the Fitzroy River, which is among the biggest in the world if measured by the volume of water which it carries into the sea during the monsoon, and other rivers. The increased quantities of sediment entering the sea each year now come from the river frontages and floodplains which have suffered degradation from over-grazing and are eroding rapidly.

M.E.W.

CHAPTER TWELVE

THE

ARID RANGELANDS

Apart from the area covered by the central deserts, a great deal of arid Australia is rangeland. Pastoral leases cover most of the country, excluding National Parks, Aboriginal Land and Reserves. Grazing is not only by 'official' introduced animals, but also by the millions of feral animals which are established all over the continent (even in the deserts where no pastoral activities take place — rabbits at Lake Eyre, camels in the red dunefields of the Strzelecki Desert). Even the tropical north, where monsoonal rainfall results in a wet season with a lot of rain near the coast and decreasing amounts towards the centre, is largely 'arid rangeland' because more than half of the year is dry with very high rates of evaporation.

Before settlement, the vegetation of the rangelands was adapted to light and irregular grazing by soft-footed native animals whose numbers were controlled by the availability of water and the occasional natural fire. **Europeans brought: year-round water,** encouraging increased numbers of kangaroos; **hooved animals,** cutting up the ground and imposing constant heavy grazing pressure; **fences** which concentrated the impact of grazing; and **changed fire regimes.** In the arid zone they suppressed fire to conserve fodder; in the seasonally wetter tropics they commonly burnt annually to promote green pick. Unrealistic expectations of the carrying capacity of the land; no concept of the fragility of the arid ecosystems and the soils; and optimism about a land of unlimited possibilities, all conspired to see the boom days of early pastoralism replaced by bust. The failure to control grazing and feral animals has resulted in loss of biodiversity, with palatable vegetation

AREA OF AUSTRALIA SUBJECT TO GRAZING

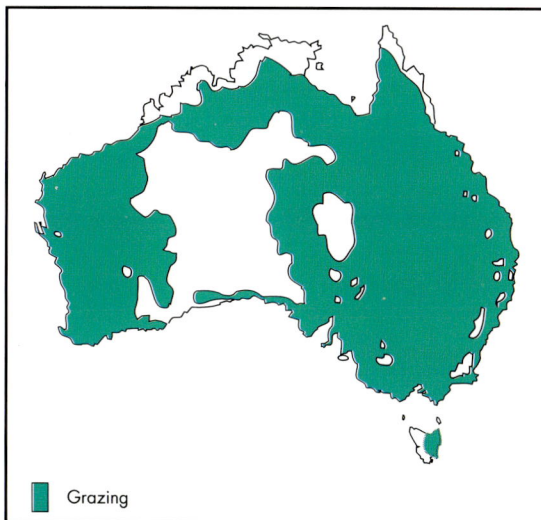

Grazing

The savanna in good order away from the river, in the Victoria River district of the Northern Territory.

M.E.W.

Rangeland degraded beyond redemption, at Renner Springs, Northern Territory.

M.E.W.

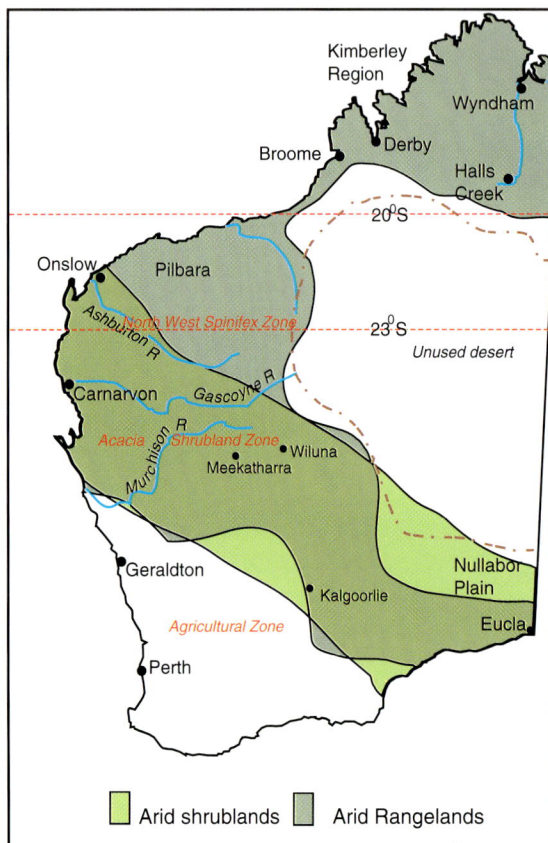

WESTERN AUSTRALIA
LATITUDES, DIVISIONS, ARID SHRUBLANDS

Kimberley Region

Wyndham

Broome Derby

Halls Creek

20°S

Onslow Pilbara

Ashburton R *North West Spinifex Zone*

23°S *Unused desert*

Carnarvon *Gascoyne R*

Murchison R *Acacia Shrubland Zone* Wiluna

Meekatharra

Geraldton

Nullabor Plain

Kalgoorlie

Eucla

Agricultural Zone

Perth

☐ Arid shrublands ☐ Arid Rangelands

After Holm and Burnside [163]

declining and soil washing and blowing away.

Today the rangelands which have had even moderate grazing pressures from stock are all degraded. **Losses to the pastoral industry caused by land degradation have been estimated at 50% to 80% of animal production, or 30% to 40% of economic productivity. The resource base of the pastoral industry has literally been eroded.**[160]

The same sort of problems result from grazing similar country where the major vegetation types are associated with the same general soil types, wherever they may be on the continent. The degradation from over-grazing described in Chapter 11, The Tropical North, and in the case study on the Burdekin catchment in Chapter 9 approximates that in the north west; mulga growing on hardpan soils in western Queensland is adapted to its environment and faces the same problems under pressures of grazing as the mulgalands of the arid shrubland region of Western Australia; sandplain floras have different species composition in different regions, but their perennial plants and ephemeral herbs have the same problems presented by the uncertainty of rainfall, low nutrient soil and drought, and their responses to grazing, and to over-grazing, are similar.

Therefore, to give an idea of the scope of degradation caused by grazing, the rangelands of Western Australia are presented here as an example, representative of the rangelands of the driest vegetated continent.

THE RANGELANDS OF WESTERN AUSTRALIA

The Arid Shrublands of Western Australia

Much of the information on the arid shrublands has been obtained from *Reading the Rangeland,* a book produced by officers of Agriculture WA and financed by the National Landcare Program.[161]

In Western Australia about $960\,000\,km^2$ of arid and semi-arid land is used as rangeland. These rangelands south of the Pilbara are arid shrublands, covering about $850\,000\,km^2$. Rainfall is unreliable and very variable, occurring mainly in winter when depressions stray north and eastward from the agricultural areas of the south-western corner of the continent, but with heaviest falls resulting from tropical cyclones straying south in summer. The perennial vegetation is drought and heat adapted; ephemerals take advantage of rain whenever it falls. Average rainfall ranges from 150 to 250 mm, varying between seasons, both in distribution and amount.

Soil moisture is normally the limiting factor for plant growth. Soil fertility tends to be secondary. Native vegetation is adapted to the infertility of rangeland soils, most of which have very low nitrogen and phosphorus levels (less than half of the average found in arid zones of other continents). Rangeland soils support sparse vegetation, which in turn supports low animal populations. Different parts of landscapes have access to different amounts of **effective rainfall** from the overall regional amount. For example, stony hillsides may only absorb half of the rain which falls on them, and the rest runs off down the slope, while depressions at the foot of the slope may receive the equivalent of two or three times the regional rainfall. Thus a region is a patchwork of areas with different soil moisture possibilities.

The ecosystems which comprise the rangelands are fragile and **biodiversity** is the key to their successful

CYCLONES, FLOODS AND ERODED CATCHMENTS
— MUD, MUD, GLORIOUS MUD!

When cyclones travel down the Western Australian coast, bringing dramatic flooding and damage far inland, the eroded catchments of rivers are stripped and massive amounts of silt make their way to the sea. Cyclone Bobby, in February 1995, crossed the coast at Onslow in the early morning of the 25th and was level with Carnarvon early next day. Fortunately Carnarvon, at the mouth of the Gascoyne River, was not directly in its path, but the vast catchment of the Gascoyne ensured that the river started to run, and it was in full spate within a couple of days.

The river at Carnarvon is a dry trench for about 50 of the 52 weeks of the year, and water from heavy rain as far away as Meekatharra can take weeks to reach the coast. When it is dry, pumps on shallow bores in its bed draw water from under its sand for irrigation of the banana, tomato and other horticultural enterprises. The full flood from Cyclone Bobby ran for two or three weeks after the passage of the cyclone. Flooding with red-muddy water occurred over wide areas. After the floods subsided and the river retreated to its channel a large mud delta remained, stretching for several kilometres along the coast and out to sea.

Top right: The Gascoyne River in flood following Cyclone Bobby. The posts are what is left of railings on a high-level bridge and the depth of water was more than 8 m when the photograph was taken — capturing the awesome power of a mud flood.

TIM BARTON

Middle right: A red-mud flood from the Gascoyne River, inundating farmland and leaving banana plantations looking like lawns in the flooded landscape.

PHOTO TAKEN FROM AN ULTRALITE PLANE BY CHRIS JONES.

Right: The mud delta at the mouth of the Gascoyne River after Cyclone Bobby.

PHOTO TAKEN FROM AN ULTRALITE PLANE BY CHRIS JONES.

The mulgalands of the Murchison region stretch across the plains from one low range of hills to the next, extending for hundreds of kilometres.

JOHN BEARD **162**

existence. Having many species comprising the vegetation assures that some will have the attributes which enable them to survive through heat and drought, or to regenerate, to seed or to germinate, whatever the fickle conditions, and that a degree of landcover will be maintained, preventing erosion. Biodiversity gives the systems **resilience**. Grazing of fragile ecosystems tends to reduce their biodiversity and to destabilise them.

The arid shrublands stretch from the Indian Ocean between Kalbarri and Exmouth in a broad arc through the goldfields to the Nullarbor and the Southern Ocean. Pastoral leases occupy 85% of the area and it has been known as 'station country' since the first arrival of settlers in the 1870s. The discovery of gold in the late 1890s stimulated further interest and by 1910 most of the suitable grazing country had been allocated. Sheep numbers peaked in the 1930s and over-grazing, particularly severe around rivers and watering points, resulted. Mining also affected the landscape with timber taken for fuel and building purposes, and local over-grazing by the meat, dairy and draft animals around mining settlements damaging the vegetation. Permanent damage to the most used parts of the area, the mulga shrublands of the western half of the region, and to the vegetation on the Nullarbor (see map p.18) are evidence of the fragility of the ecosystems when grazing pressure from introduced animals has been applied to them.

Three main soil and vegetation types comprise the arid shrublands.

1. Mulga Shrubland with open mulga (*Acacia aneura*) and low shrubs on shallow, non-saline soils. Mulga represents 60% of the total shrublands, occupying $500\,000\,km^2$ in the Murchison, Gascoyne and Goldfields districts. (On a continental scale the mulgalands cover 20% of Australia.) The mulgalands were often the first to be developed for pastoralism because good quality water is frequently available through bores or wells less than 10 m deep. Grazing (and frequently over-grazing) by sheep and cattle, which in some parts has been going on for a hundred years, has resulted in thinning of tree cover and degradation of much of the country. Three distinctive types of mulga shrubland occur:

- **Granitic shrubland** in hilly or undulating country with outcropping granite and soil surface of coarse sand and some cryptogamic soil crusts. Water infiltration is rapid on granitic soils. Even when in good condition, this country will not support high stocking rates.
- **Stony hardpan plains,** gently undulating with distinct drainage lines, stony or gravelly soil surface and slow water infiltration rate. The stony plains are the least productive. Soils beneath the stony mantle are very thin. Trees and large shrubs are scattered, and medium shrubs are largely unpalatable. Rain produces a rush of annuals.

- **Hardpan plains,** above river floodplains, with no obvious drainage lines, and slow water infiltration. Cryptogamic crusts are common. These 'wash plains' occupy extensive areas of the Gascoyne, Murchison and north-eastern Goldfields between the low hills and the river floodplains or salt lakes. They are the most widespread country type in the rangelands of Western Australia and often extend for up to 60 km without change. The shallow soil overlies the hardpan layer, a clay-rich 'coffee rock' known also as Murchison cement, which separates the soil from a good groundwater province where water is only between 6 and 16 m below the surface. Mulga roots manage to penetrate the hardpan, as do those of a few smaller shrubs. The cryptogamic crusts are important in preventing erosion between the shrubs, and a few small annuals grow after rain.

- **Groving** is a common feature on the hardpan plains. Dense patches of mulga and other shrubs form 'contour lines' across the gentle slopes, sometimes continuous for up to a kilometre and visible from satellites. Run-off in the intergroves is intercepted by the groves, and organic matter and seeds accumulate, resulting in the more fertile, elongated patches of denser vegetation. **Cryptogamic crusts** are very important as protectors of bare soil between scattered bushes and perennial grasses in the arid shrublands and their destruction leads to erosion.

2. Saltbush and bluebush, low bluebush or saltbush shrubs on saline, often eroded soils. This is some of the most fertile and productive grazing country, though it occupies only about 150 000 km². Perennial saltbush plants usually live for up to 25 years, with seedlings established in most years; bluebushes, such as pearl bluebush *(Maireana sedifolia)*, establish new plants rarely but may live for 300 years. Gascoyne bluebush *(M. polypterygia)* may live from 150 to 200 years.

Five soil/landscape groups commonly occur in this type of country:

- **Breakaway slopes,** high in the landscape, on sandy, grey-white shallow soils. Laterite protects the plateaux, but the breakaway slopes erode rapidly when their vegetation is damaged by grazing. Over-grazing has occurred in these extra-fragile parts of the landscape, and the cryptogamic crusts have suffered severely.

- **Undulating plains,** on stony lower slopes with brown or red-brown shallow soils, below the breakaway slopes and adjacent to the major rivers. Stony mantles protect the soil, but if disturbed by removal of vegetation through grazing, erosion is rapid. Over-grazing results in the replacement of palatable species with woody weeds.

- **Flood plains and river frontages,** on sandy red-brown to red-grey soils of variable depth. This type of country includes the flood plains of the major river systems, the Gascoyne, Murchison, Ashburton, Greenough, Minilya and Wooramel which flow westward into the Indian Ocean. The flood plains vary from narrow to up to 20 km wide. The north-eastern Goldfields region lacks rivers, but similar vegetation and soils occur around major ephemeral creeks. The soils are relatively fertile but river frontages have been extensively used for grazing since the earliest days, and mostly have been over-grazed, and when vegetation cover is damaged, erosion follows.

The hardpan layer in the soil is exposed in this profile in mulgaland where the taller trees are minnieritchie (Acacia grasbyi).

John Beard

DISTRIBUTION OF MULGA SHRUBLAND

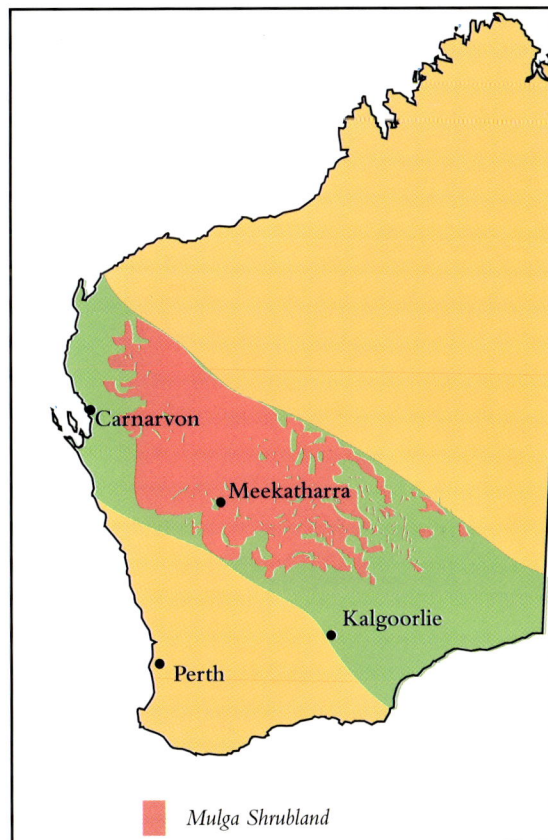

Carnarvon

Meekatharra

Kalgoorlie

Perth

Mulga Shrubland

After Burnside et al.[161]

DISTRIBUTION OF MULGA AND SALTBUSH IN AUSTRALIA

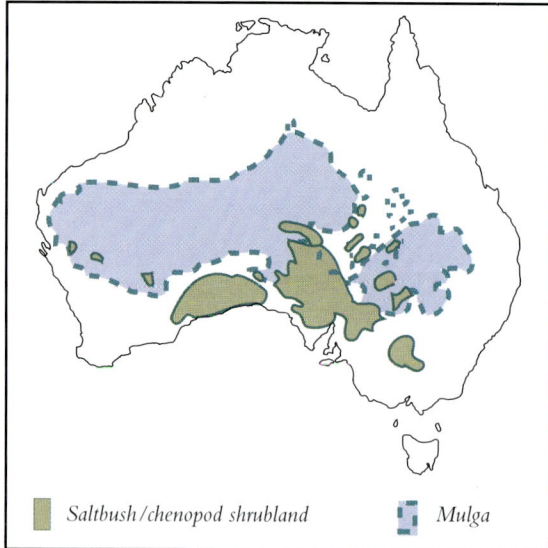

Below: A satellite image of eroded river frontages on Victoria River Downs Station N.T.

DEAN GRAETZ

Saltbush/chenopod shrubland   Mulga

Above: Aerial photograph showing mulga growing.

DEAN GRAETZ

DISTRIBUTION OF SALTBUSH AND BLUEBUSH

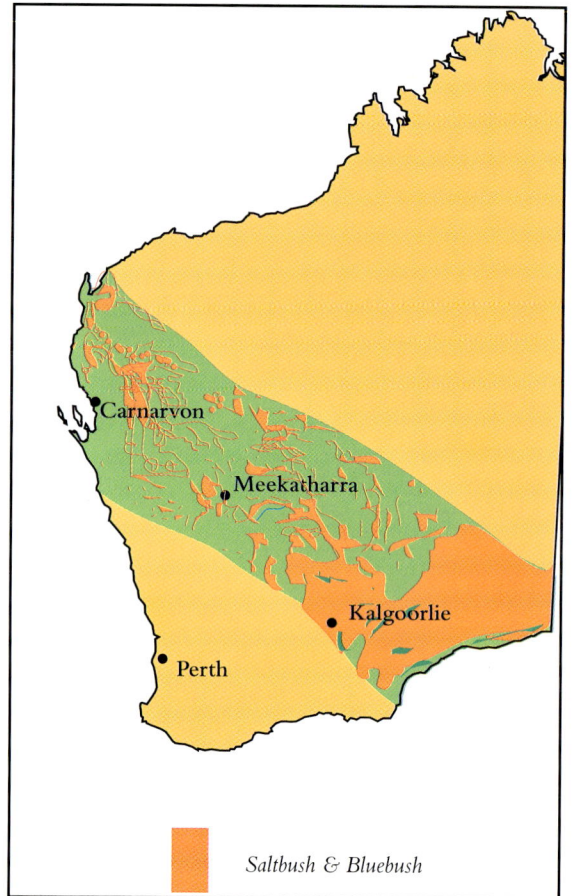

Carnarvon

Meekatharra

Kalgoorlie

Perth

Saltbush & Bluebush

After Burnside et al.[161]

Severe degradation, woody weed invasion, spread of introduced grasses and weeds, bare scalds and loss of the vital cryptogamic crusts are evidence of the overuse of these fragile ecosystems. When the rivers flood they carry vast amounts of sediment to the sea.

- **Level plains and lake frontages,** on deep red soils with cryptogamic crusts covering more than half of the soil surface. Dense saltbush and bluebush shrubs are the dominant plants of the plains in the pastoral lands to the north and south of Carnarvon and in the ancient drainage systems through the Murchison and the Goldfields. These ancient drainages flow eastwards into salt lakes. Some of the salt lakes are very large, up to 70 km long. Soils are saline, particularly close to the lakes. Fresh water is very scarce, limiting pastoral activities.

- **The Nullarbor Plain,** a geographically distinct area, gently undulating with shallow soils over limestone, and common cryptogamic crusts. Rainfall infiltration is low, and run-off is mainly into dongas, shallow depressions on the Bunda Plateau (an ancient seabed). Round the edges of the plain a belt of woodland occurs, dominated by western myall *(Acacia papyrocarpa),* a species which only regenerates from seed a couple of times a century when periods of unusual rainfall provide the right conditions. Replacement of lost adult plants is impossible when rabbits are there to eat seedlings in the first few years after germination.

- Rabbits have had a profound effect on the Nullarbor, where they have lived in vast numbers since 1900, grazing on the saltbush and the ephemerals. In 1991 warren densities were between 100 and 200 per square kilometre (compared with three to 12 in other arid areas). In addition to the damage caused by rabbits, frequent fires resulting from sparks from steam trains, after the building of the Transcontinental Railway during the First World War, altered large areas from saltbush plain to annual prairie-herbfield. The change to grassy pastures results in increased natural fires started by lightning, so fire frequency has remained higher than it used to be before settlement, even after steam was replaced by diesel power in trains.

(Saltbush covers about 10% of Australia. Grazing by stock and rabbits has resulted in thinning of the vegetation of the chenopod shrublands, in most areas to half its pre-settlement density. The carrying capacity of these lands is now a fraction of what it used to be.)

3. Sandplain, dense tall shrubs and perennial grasses on non-saline, deep and sandy soils. Sandplain occurs interspersed with other country such as mulga shrubland, or covers large areas on its own. About a fifth of the arid shrubland is sandplain, and many areas produce spectacular wildflowers. There are four basic sandplain types:

● **Spinifex** on plains, or on banks on hardpan plains; on sandy soil with rapid infiltration of water. Tracts of spinifex occur in the eastern Goldfields, parts of the Gascoyne and Ashburton. Very extensive tracts occur to the north and east of the arid shrublands in the Pilbara and towards the desert centre. Marble gum (*Eucalyptus gongylocarpa*), mulga and gidgee (*Acacia pruinocarpa* in WA) are scattered in the spinifex. Spinifex country's value for stock is greatest about a year after fire and subsequent rain when diverse ephemerals (grasses and herbs) germinate. Their numbers decrease as the spinifex again attains dominance during the next five years.

● **Wanderrie** (tussock grass, *Eragrostis* spp.) on plains, or banks on hardpan plains, vegetation of many perennial tussock grasses and some shrubs, on sandy soil with rapid water infiltration rate. The 'wanderrie grasses' are of several different tussock genera. They provide good grazing and occur either as featureless grassy plains or as 'wanderrie banks' which are very slightly raised, elongated (up to a kilometre) and narrow, on mulga hardpan plains. They are probably remnants of dune sand from the Pleistocene, like the 'sandhills' on the Riverine Plain in the Murray Basin, though reduced to even lower ridges. Because of their good infiltration rate, the banks make good use of summer rains and produce a flush of ephemerals and summer grasses, predisposing them to selective grazing. Over-grazing results in invasion by woody weeds, particularly poverty bushes (*Eremophila*),

decrease in perennial grasses and ultimately in scalding.

● **Bowgada** (*Acacia ramulosa* or *A. linophylla*) on gently undulating plains; vegetation of low trees or tall shrubs, with fewer perennial grasses than in wanderrie; soils sandy with rapid infiltration. The acacia shrubs grow to 4 m high, dominating the vegetation and suppressing smaller shrubs. The pods are the only parts of the bowgada eaten by stock, and pastoralists call bowgada lands 'hungry country'. While the vegetation type is usually known as bowgada, a large area in the west Gascoyne and Shark Bay region is called 'wanyu'. (There it occupies a third of the Carnarvon Basin, an area of about 25 000 km^2.) The absence of understorey in mature bowgada shrub country

An extensive scald on the alluvial flat in the Ashburton valley, surrounded by land with scattered acacias.

JOHN BEARD

THE NULLARBOR PLAIN

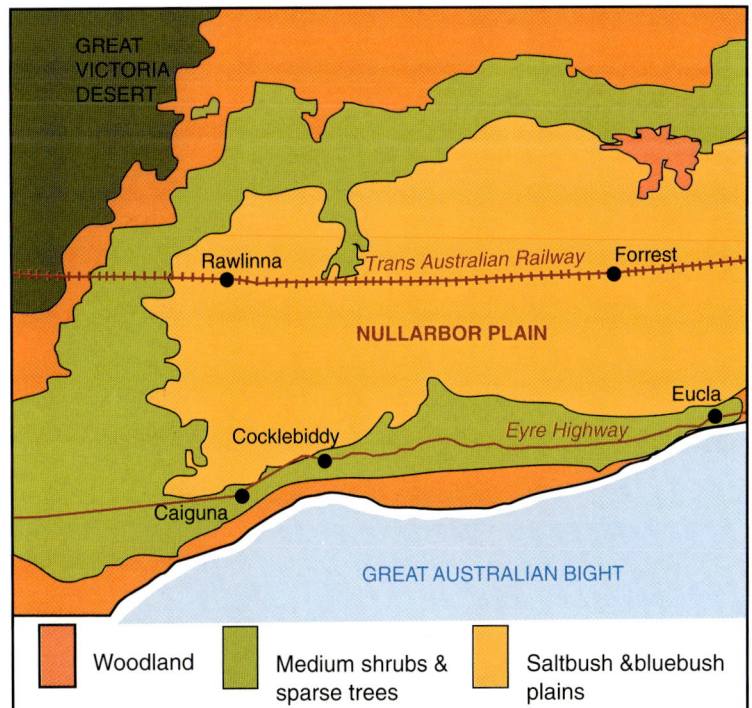

| Woodland | Medium shrubs & sparse trees | Saltbush & bluebush plains |

After Burnside et al.[161]

DISTRIBUTION OF BOWGADA

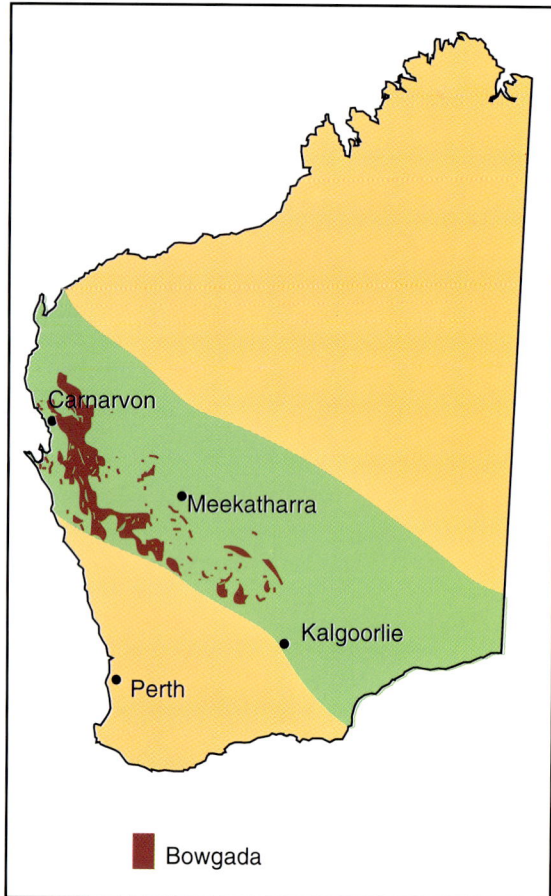

Bowgada

After Burnside et al.[161]

DISTRIBUTION OF WANDERRIE GRASSES AND CURRANT BUSH

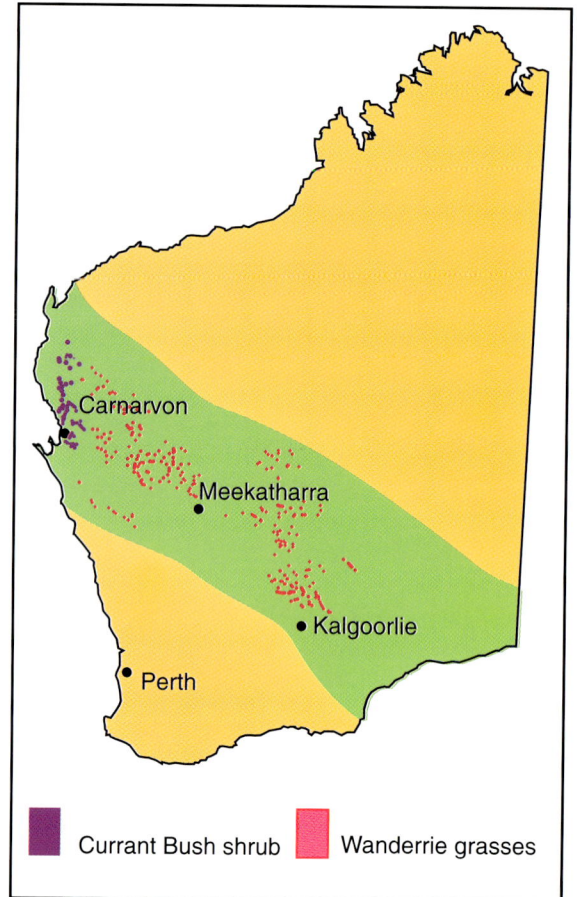

Currant Bush shrub   Wanderrie grasses

After Burnside et al.[161]

Below: Ironstone hills rise from the Ashburton plain in a transitional zone between mulga-dominated and spinifex-dominated vegetation. Spinifex and mulga in the foreground; in the rear spinifex spreads on the dry slopes and snakewood covers the flats.

JOHN BEARD

results in a low capacity to carry fires, but if unusually good rainfall results in grass and ephemerals and they dry out, fire can sweep through the country. Such fires normally occur once every 30 or 50 years. The last one in the Carnarvon region was in 1964. Fire eliminates the bowgada and a long succession follows, with cottonbush, fire bush, desert poplar and fire wattle. It takes about 30 years for the mature bowgada assemblage to be established again.

- **Currant bush mixed shrub** *(Scaevola spinescens)* which only occurs in locally dominant stands on the sandy soils of the land systems flanking the erodible floodplains in the Carnarvon area. It occupies $4000\,km^2$ on less sandy soils, which are mostly stable, often alternating with patches of wanyu. The soil surface is thinly crusted and water infiltration rate is moderate.

The main vegetation is medium to tall mixed shrubs, including currant bush. In the natural state it comprises an unusually diverse range of low shrubs, many of which are palatable, with occasional taller shrubs including needlebush *(Hakea preisii)* and snakewood *(Acacia xiphophylla)*. Currant bush is an important forage plant. Grazing has a major impact on the vegetation and in drier years it eliminates the less hardy species like cotton bush, bluebushes and the younger currant bushes. When this happens, space is left for invasion of less palatable shrubs like cassias (whose seeds can lie in soil for very long periods waiting for an opportunity to germinate). Heavy grazing pressure results in bare and sealed soils and wind erosion. Fire is rare, the discrete shrubs without interconnecting groundcover do not carry fires, and when it occurs under exceptional circumstances it completely alters the vegetation, promoting massive growth of needlebush.

Managing Western Australia's Arid Shrublands

Most of the arid shrublands are leased to pastoralists, with 330 leases current and not due to expire until 2015. (Some of the less accessible and less productive grazing areas remain Crown Land; and some specific areas are national parks, nature reserves or Aboriginal reserves.) The Pastoral Board administers the land, collects annual rent and requires compliance with various statutes and conditions which have been set to ensure acceptable standards of land use, directed towards conservation and regeneration of vegetation.

Pastoral Lease Reports are prepared for each property on a five-yearly schedule by inspectors from the Department of Agriculture; **Range Condition Reports** are also prepared when an application for lease sale is received and these are made available to intending purchasers. They make recommendations on management to address specific land degradation problems. The two reports cover information on stocking history, current stock numbers, seasonal conditions and the effectiveness of fences and waters in management. Concerns about land degradation and erosion are referred to the Commissioner for Soil and Land Conservation who can issue notices requesting destocking, fencing and attention to other issues.

The average size of a pastoral lease is $172\,000$ ha $(1720\,km^2)$. Those on the fringes of the agricultural areas in the south-western corner of the continent are small, mainly less than $50\,km^2$; those on the Nullarbor can be up to $5000\,km^2$. With the all-natural pasture on stations, the **stocking rates range from one sheep to 5–6 ha on good saltbush or bluebush country to one sheep to 30–40 ha on poor condition stony hardpan plains.** Cattle are also run in some areas, and some properties have changed from sheep to cattle and back again, depending on fluctuations in profitability.

Average paddock size is about 7000 ha, water points (troughs adjacent to windmills or earth dams) are provided about every 4000 ha of country. Most paddocks are stocked perennially, but some are spelled

Baobabs are one of the special attractions of the western Kimberley. They are protected plants and are used as street trees in Derby.

M.E.W.

Above top: Over-grazed rangeland in breakaway country.
Above: The Victoria River in the Northern Territory.

in either winter or summer to allow recovery. The contribution of feral animals to grazing pressures has probably been under-estimated; and kangaroos and emus, which are able to breed up with the availability of water from troughs and dams, are considerable additions to grazing.

Feral Animals in the Arid Rangelands

Besides the introduced stock, donkeys, wild horses, goats, rabbits, foxes and wild dogs are abundant. Pastoralists are required to contribute to a 'vermin rate' which finances control and eradication programs. It was estimated in 1990 that **a million goats** were present, contributing 12% of the total grazing pressure on the vegetation. Kangaroos were exerting 50% of the grazing pressure, and sheep were responsible for the remaining 38%. During 1992–93, major feral goat control programs removed more than 900 000 animals, but the rapid rate of increase resulted in 750 000 goats still being present in June 1993.

Wild dogs are mainly present in the drier outlying areas and half a million poison baits have been dropped annually for some years to control numbers. In the Murchison, more than 14 000 fresh meat baits were laid to control foxes in 1992–93, but the breeding rate of foxes is such that lethal baiting has to be repeated consistently until some sort of biological control is discovered.

The main problem weeds in the arid rangelands are saffron thistle, mesquite *(Prosopis)* and horehound.

Right: Eucalypt woodland on the Gibb River Road.

M.E.W.

The Kimberley Region of Western Australia

The Kimberley region lies north of 20°S in a tropical monsoon zone. Almost all useful rainfall is in summer, December to March (from 1150 mm on the north coast to 500 mm and less inland). The most valuable pastures are those on the extensive grassy plains adjacent to the Ord, Fitzroy and Margaret Rivers where they comprise Mitchell grasses *(Astrebla* spp.), ribbon grasses *(Chrysopogon* spp.) and the introduced buffel and birdwood grasses *(Cenchrus* spp.). Low quality spinifex pastures are widespread and only provide grazing after burning late in a dry season.[163]

About 600 000 cattle are grazed in the Kimberley and most are open range herds (up to 40 000 per station).

An analysis of the situation in the **north-west of Australia** in 1985 noted that:[164]

- reclamation and rehabilitation of the Ord River catchment had taken two decades to partially achieve. (It has still not been even partially achieved 10 years on, see Chapter 11);
- 80% of the **west Kimberley** area was in **poor to fair** condition;
- 41% of the grazed areas in the Victoria River District suffer from erosion.

The most serious erosion and degradation problems in northern Australia are concentrated along river frontages and around watering points. The major rivers of the north carry huge amounts of water during the monsoon and have wide, fertile floodplains. The surrounding savannas have shallow, easily eroded soils, damaged by trampling and selective grazing. Fire, too frequent and at the wrong time of year, poses extra risks of erosion. The silt load carried by the northern rivers is enormous as a result of catchment erosion. The azure colour of the ocean at Broome results from the suspended sediment which is carried out to sea each year when the rivers are in flood.

Noogoora burr *(Xanthium* spp.), the dreaded weed with burrs which ruin wool, infests the Fitzroy River system. The Agricultural Protection Board is anxious to prevent its spread to other parts of the Kimberley, so all stations from Fitzroy Crossing to the river mouth have been placed in quarantine. No unauthorised people may enter quarantine areas; stock and fodder have to be inspected before leaving the properties; all excavation and earthmoving machinery must be cleaned and inspected before leaving; mining and exploration companies require permits to enter, and their vehicles and equipment are subject to inspection.

This may seem like a lot of fuss over a weed, but the nature of the burrs ensures that the plant spreads everywhere, carried by people, animals, machinery or in fodder. The plant is one of the most widespread weeds in the world. Its growth can be so dense that cattle and sheep cannot get access to watering places; it is a major weed of irrigated soybeans, maize, sunflowers and cotton.

The Pilbara lies between the Kimberley and 23°S (where the arid shrublands begin). Rainfall is unreliable, a spin-off from some cyclones, and the area is arid. The absence of permanent water away from the coastal fringe, and the predominance of spinifex make this a poor area for grazing, unable to support animals in large numbers. The tablelands of the Chichester and Hamersley Ranges support perennial tussock grasses like the pastures of the Kimberley and these areas are lightly stocked.

Above top: Eroding tussock grassland in the Ord River catchment.

Above: Red rocks, azure sea at Ganthaume Point, Broome.

M.E.W.

THE WEST KIMBERLEY LAND CONSERVATION DISTRICT

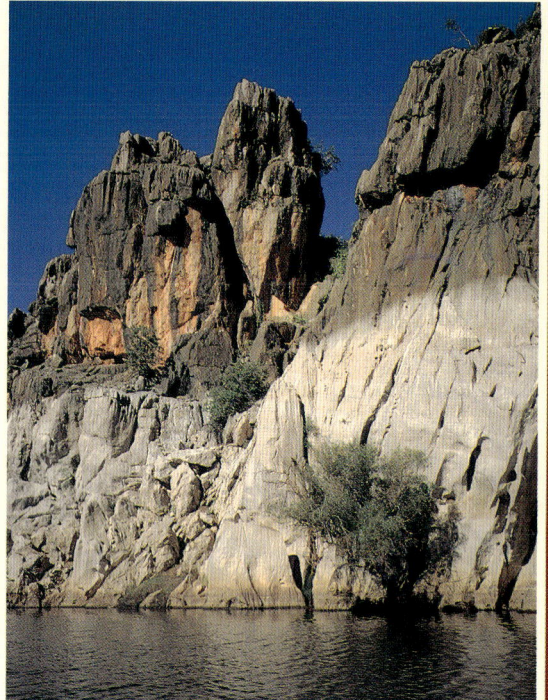

The Fitzroy and Meda Rivers and their tributaries are the life-support of the West Kimberley Land Conservation District where 33 stations run 140 000 cattle (1992 figures). The Fitzroy catchment covers 8.8 million hectares.

The Fitzroy is one of the largest rivers in Western Australia and, like other major rivers of the north runs seasonally during the wet season. Then it is a raging torrent for a few months and its floodplain, up to 35 km wide, can be completely inundated.

The best pasture is found on the floodplains and levees, and since the beginning of pastoralism in the region grazing pressures have been concentrated here, relying on the river water. This fragile environment has suffered severe damage over time and the pastoral industry today is investing a great deal of money in trying to rehabilitate the river frontage lands. Measures include: fencing of paddocks so that grazing can be controlled; destocking badly degraded areas (300 000 ha of frontage land destocked and allowed to rest for up to five years in 1992); 200 km of river fenced on both sides to protect the banks; 200 000 ha of floodplain used only on a seasonal basis; establishing watering points away from the river.

Geike Gorge on the Fitzroy River. Sandbanks are nesting sites for crocodiles, and the limestone cliff shows the high-water mark of annual floods.

M.E.W.

The Fitzroy River at the Old Crossing is largely sand in winter, and becomes a mighty river which spreads out over floodplains up to 35 km wide in the monsoon.

M.E.W

CHAPTER THIRTEEN

MINING AND THE ENVIRONMENT

Mining has had a bad reputation as an environmental destroyer, a polluter, and an industry which exploits and moves on, leaving a trail of permanent damage. When one looks at Mt Lyell in Tasmania and at the vast area affected by the Leigh Creek Coal Mine in South Australia it is only too obvious that that **used to be** the case. However, mining in Australia today is carried out within such strict environmental constraints and subject to so much monitoring that it is now perhaps the most environmentally conscious of all land-users — and let us not forget that $40 billion annually of our nation's wealth (which underpins our standard of living) comes from our mineral exports. Certainly it is not *sustainable*, in that the minerals being removed are

Leigh Creek, South Australia
The mining at Leigh Creek has proceeded without progressive rehabilitation, and now a completely changed landscape of mountains of spoil and flooded pits extends over an area about 16 km long and up to 6 km wide, without vegetation on the dumps.
M.E.W.

THE ALLIGATOR RIVERS REGION AND KAKADU NATIONAL PARK

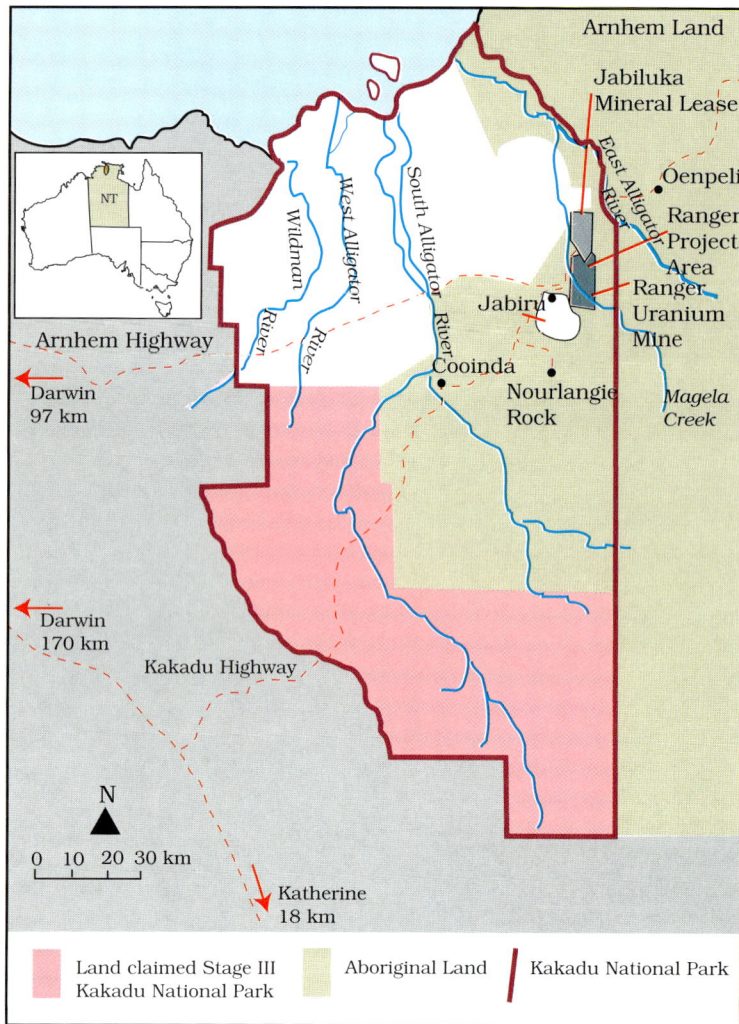

Arnhem Land

Jabiluka Mineral Lease

Oenpeli

Ranger Project Area

Ranger Uranium Mine

Jabiru

Cooinda

Nourlangie Rock

Magela Creek

NT

Wildman River

West Alligator River

South Alligator River

East Alligator River

Arnhem Highway

Darwin 97 km

Darwin 170 km

Kakadu Highway

N

0 10 20 30 km

Katherine 18 km

| Land claimed Stage III Kakadu National Park | Aboriginal Land | Kakadu National Park |

not renewable, but if we and all the rest of the world demand or aspire to a technology-based lifestyle this is the price we have to pay. The day will come, if the human race survives long enough to see it (which is doubtful when its life support systems are based on *equally unsustainable resources of soil and water)* when the oceans will have to be mined.

Uranium is clearly the substance which excites the most alarm, and uranium mining is the most controversial of all mining activities — and no wonder, when the bomb, radiation hazards which last thousands of years, and all the other horrors are known, and when ethical and political issues are added to the brew. Leaving aside the emotive and highly politicised issues which are beyond the scope of this book, in terms of safe and responsible management of the mining of uranium, Australia leads the world.

In 1978, as a direct outcome of the Ranger Uranium Environmental Inquiry, and the Fox Report which resulted from it, the **Office of the Supervising Scientist (OSS)** was set up to protect the environment of the Alligator Rivers Region. (The *Environmental Protection (Alligator Rivers Region) Act 1978* required the Supervising Scientist to provide an annual report to

Parliament on the operation of the Act and on certain related matters.) The expertise which OSS has developed over the years since in what is one of the most environmentally sensitive areas of the continent made it a focal point when the Commonwealth Government began to examine the concept of ecologically sustainable development in relation to the mining industry.

In 1993, the Supervising Scientist and his support organisation were amalgamated with the Environmental Protection Agency (EPA) in the Department of the Environment, Sport and Territories (DEST). OSS is now a small but highly specialised branch whose primary purpose is *to encourage the development and adoption of environmental excellence in the mining industry.* Its core activities are still protection of the Alligator Rivers Region, where it undertakes six-monthly environmental performance reviews and works with mine operators to achieve continual improvement. It also continues to carry out scientific research to develop better ways of monitoring environmental performance and detecting impacts. Its role in disseminating information, and backing up the Northern Territory Department of Mines and Energy, which is the main body policing compliance with regulations, ensures that the impact of mining and exploration on the region is controlled.

The situation in the Alligator Rivers Region is immensely complicated because several individually controversial elements are amalgamated here — uranium mining, Aboriginal land, National Park and World Heritage classification. Two committees are now established so that everyone with an interest (Government, industry, special interest groups, general community) can have an input into policy and research-related matters, and be fully informed. The Alligator Rivers Region Advisory Committee reflects the principle of the community's right to know; and the Alligator Rivers Region Technical Committee provides a forum for discussion on the research needed to maintain environmental protection.

Under the provisions of the amended Act, OSS it is now involved in other issues including the Mt Lyell rehabilitation project in Tasmania; in supervising environmental management in Christmas and Cocos Islands, and in advising the Minister for the Environment on matters relating to mining and radiation issues (including Maralinga, nuclear waste storage, hazards etc.).

It also is involved with the Environmental Protection Agency's production, in association with the mining industry, of an excellent series of educational booklets and a video on *Best Practice Environmental Management in Mining* [165] which should be in every school and library. (The booklets are being translated into several foreign languages.)

The **Three Uranium Producers** policy of the Hawke Labor Government (1983) approved Nabarlek and Ranger in the Northern Territory and Olympic Dam in South Australia. **Nabarlek** was mined and stockpiled when operations began in 1979 and the ore has now all been processed and Nabarlek is no longer operating. Decommissioning of the mine was completed in December–January 1995 and the mine site has been reshaped, contoured and revegetated. Monitoring is continuing to assess the effectiveness of rehabilitation.

Olympic Dam, 200 km north of Port Augusta, began operations in 1988. It is potentially one of the world's largest uranium producers, with two billion tonnes of ore containing 30 million tonnes of copper, over a million tonnes of uranium and significant quantities of gold and silver. It is an underground mine, not open-cut like Ranger. Its environmental impact is stringently controlled and its township is a model of excellent planning and design, retaining as much native vegetation as possible. The only arguments on environmental grounds against the mine and its township relate to its water supply, not its potential polluting activities. It depends entirely on a **bore field drawing water from the Great Artesian Basin** and is using massive quantities of water. There is some doubt whether such use is sustainable because of the problems of recharge.

Recharge of the aquifers of the Great Artesian Basin is mainly from the distant eastern margins of the basin, mainly in northern New South Wales and Queensland on the western slopes of the Great Divide. The water has to travel, at a metre a year, in the pores between grains in the sandstone aquifers. The water which comes to the surface in the **mound-springs** west of Lake Eyre is up to two million years old. Already extraction by the thousands of bores which have tapped the artesian water since its discovery in the 1880s has resulted in a considerable drop in water pressure. Water no longer gushes to the surface, it has to be pumped. The fall in pressure is starving some mound-springs, and further pressure decline will put the rest in serious trouble. Mound-springs are a lifeline in the desert on which animals depend for survival, and they contain a unique biota which is facing extinction.

When too much water is removed locally from a water-bearing stratum by bores, the danger is that fine clay particles start to clog the pores and the aquifer becomes impermeable. Because of the recharge rate, too rapid removal of water could exhaust an aquifer (of which there are many, representing different layers of sedimentary rock) and impair its ability to be recharged.

The **bore field at Olympic Dam** is closely monitored, and as at July 1996 was supplying **14 million litres a day**. No one has any experience of the consequences of removal of such huge volumes of water in a restricted area, and there are those who are very concerned about the outcome. The announcement by Western Mining Corporation on 15 July 1996 of a $1.25 billion expansion of mining now adds a new dimension. Water consumption could rise **to 42 million litres a day**. Logic alone tells us that this is not sustainable. The Federal Government, which controls the mining licence, is naturally overjoyed at

the economic advantages that come from the mine now, and the prospect of a greatly expanded windfall in the future. There has been no commitment to an environmental impact assessment in respect of water use. Even if one is carried out, it would still be largely guesswork. Extreme caution should be the watchword when the consequences of making a decision to allow such expansion could be so serious for the whole region, and for water supply in other, possibly quite remote, parts of the basin.

The Bubbler, a mound-spring in the Mound Spring National Park.

M.E.W.

RANGER URANIUM MINE AND THE ENVIRONMENT

The Ranger Uranium Mine is owned by ERA (Energy Resources of Australia Ltd) a company 75% Australian owned. It is situated in the 'Top End' of the Northern Territory, about 260 km east of Darwin. The ERA lease of 79 km^2 is surrounded by the Kakadu National Park, which has World Heritage status. The mine-site covers about 5 km^2, which is about the size of a small mixed farm. (For those who like comparisons this area is about twice the size of a metropolitan racecourse!) The mine is on the undulating lowlands of the East Alligator River and a tributary, Magela Creek, runs through the lease area.

Since mining began in 1980, sales of $2.8 billion have been generated. Ranger pays 4.25% of its gross revenue to the Commonwealth, which passes it on to the Aboriginal Benefits Trust Account. In addition, the cost of rehabilitating the mine site is assessed by the Commonwealth Government, and ERA must maintain sufficient money in a trust fund to meet this assessed cost. Ongoing rehabilitation with revegetation of areas no longer required has resulted in 100 ha already attended to since operations began.

Ranger is one of the most highly regulated mines in the world. It is subject to no less than 50 separate Acts of the Commonwealth and the Northern Territory. These regulations, backed up by a very

Right: The Ranger No. 1 Pit, which is now mined out.

Below left: Ranger Mine buildings, across an artificial freshwater lake in which rainwater from the mine site is held and regularly tested, to ensure that no contaminated water enters the river systems.

Below right: One of the artificial lakes on the Ranger lease. The sandstone escarpment is visible in the distance.

M.E.W.

impressive array of diverse and productive research programs, ensure that the uranium ore is mined and processed safely. Ranger has a team of 35 environmental officers, of whom 24 have professional qualifications. A great deal of their work concerns water management, because it is recognised that water is the main means of carrying contaminants off the site. Their work is monitored by the Northern Territory Department of Mines and Energy and the Office of the Supervising Scientist. Leading environmental scientists from the CSIRO and ANSTO are also consulted by Ranger so that best practicable management results, and supervising authorities agree that mining has had no adverse effect on the surrounding environment. Much of the research is of positive use and benefit to Kakadu Park management, because it involves understanding wetland and other ecosystems, preventing erosion, maintaining biodiversity and other issues fundamental to maintaining a healthy environment. ERA spends approximately $1.5 to $2 million a year on environmental research in the region.

Two factors make safe management difficult and require constant vigilance — the monsoonal climate which is also very variable; and the sensitivity of the area with its wetlands, rivers and the high water-table of the floodplain landscape which extends from Van Diemen Gulf to the sandstone escarpment south of the minesite. Rainfall during the wet season can vary from 700 mm to 2200 mm in different years, and the dry season is a drought when waterways become sandy creek beds with all but the largest rivers and waterholes drying up.

The aim is to keep all rainwater which falls on the

site within the confines of the site until it has been treated and/or tested and found to pose no significant risk to the environment. Run-off from ore dumps and waste rock piles is all contaminated and is fed into dams and artificial wetlands, which have been found to be efficient cleansers; or it may be irrigated onto bushland in the mine project area which is monitored to ensure that there is no significant impact on vegetation. In very wet seasons when the dams collecting runoff from ore-stockpiles are likely to overflow, the main No.1 pit, which has been mined out, is used for temporary storage. The supervising authorities will only allow contaminated water to be released from the site after testing to ensure its safe levels of uranium and other elements, and then only on a one-in-ten year basis and when the river systems in the area are in spate and such dilution would occur as would render the levels insignificant. This situation occurred for the first time in the 1994–95 wet season, but following protest from some downstream Aboriginal groups, the proposed release did not take place.

The **tailings dam** is a closed circuit, completely separate from stockpile runoff, and is managed in such a way that it will not overflow, even in an extreme wet event like a cyclone. Its water is recycled for use in the process plant, as is some of the water from the stockpile run-off.

If the rehabilitation which has been carried out in the area so far is any indication, there need be no doubts about the commitment of the mining company and its ability to restore the land to a natural state in time. Jabiru East was the first township, housing 2000 people, with a school, police station, medical centre, supermarket, two caravan parks and a recreation centre and swimming pool. Today when you drive through the site of the town you would find difficulty in believing that it had so recently been so intensively occupied. The bush has been restored and all signs of human occupation have gone. The permanent town of Jabiru, seven kilometres away, has replaced Jabiru East.

When the Ranger landscape is finally rehabilitated after all the mining is over, there will be a low hill rising to about 24 m above the surrounding area at the site of the tailings dam. The slope of the land will be compatible with the existing landscape, and will ensure that run-off will pass through wetlands before filtering into nearby waterways.

The **Jabiluka** lease adjoins the Ranger lease within the Kakadu National Park, and if permission is granted for mining to go ahead, it is possible that the ore will be processed at Ranger. (The Aboriginals are objecting and there is more than one option currently being considered.)

The new ERA plan is for underground mining, which entails minimum surface disturbance. With a proven record of safe management of the processing plant and tailings dam at Ranger, and the standards of environmental control and monitoring, there is no reason why this new mine will be any more of a threat to the wider environment than Ranger has been. The concept of biosphere reserves under UNESCO accepts that use and development by people has to be part of the equation and it can and must be integrated with the aims of maintaining biodiversity and protection of a region, so mining and the national park which surrounds it are not necessarily incompatible.

THE RANGER MINE-SITE

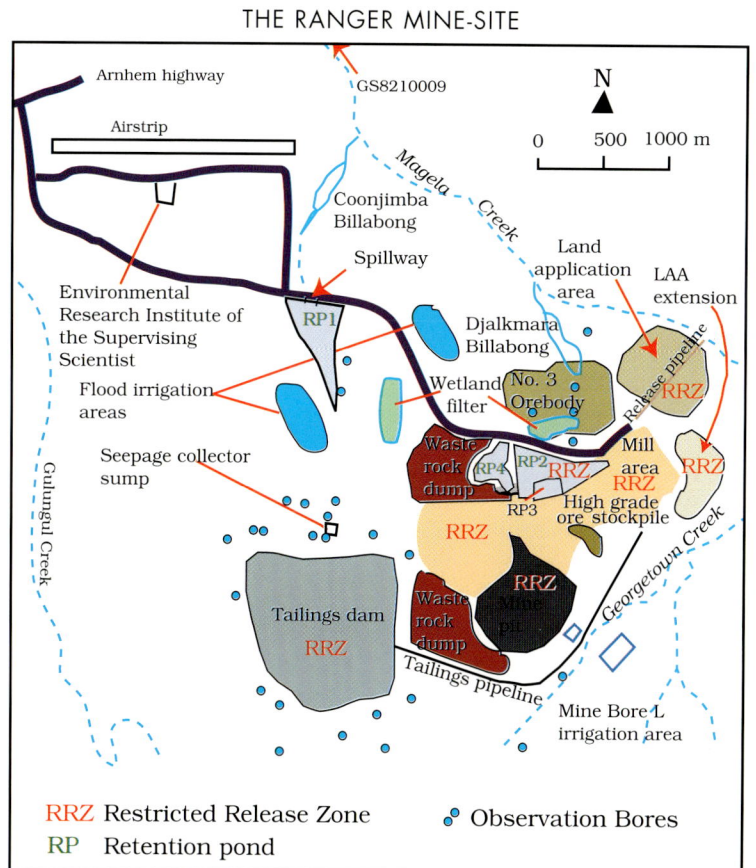

RRZ Restricted Release Zone   Observation Bores
RP Retention pond

Kindly supplied by OSS

Aerial View of the Ranger Uranium Mine (with tracing).

PHOTOGRAPH AND TRACING KINDLY SUPPLIED BY OSS, CANBERRA

This Project, starting in 1996 and to be completed in 2000, and costing $104.4 million, is aimed at reducing the radiological hazards at Maralinga and Emu where Britain carried out atomic bomb and warhead tests between 1953 and 1963, in order to allow a resumption of traditional Aboriginal land use. Britain and Australia reached an agreement in 1993 by which Britain is contributing 20 million pounds Sterling to the clean-up program. The claims of the Tjarutja Aboriginals against the Commonwealth Government have been settled by the provision of $13.5 million to assist them to *re-establish their traditional links with the land*. The issues are complex and divisive with two different arguments, for and against pouring many millions into rehabilitation:

1. With compensation paid, and most modern Aboriginals no longer interested in hunter-gatherer tribal living in remote desert areas, many Australians think that taxpayers' money would be better spent on solving pressing environmental problems in areas where people live and work productively. The damage caused by mistakes of the past, like allowing part of our land to be destroyed by another nation, is low on the list of priority for repair when seen in the context of the crisis situation which exists in areas whose sustainable use is essential for the future of all Australians, of Aboriginal or non-Aboriginal origins. Even to think like this is today considered `racist', which it is not; and it is certainly not politically correct, but some sort of *triage* system of assessment of which areas require attention now and which can wait will have to be formulated because there is never enough money.

2. The argument for decontamination and rehabilitation of the area, at whatever cost, is put by officers of the Department of Primary Industries and Energy in Canberra who refer to the Outstation Movement in which traditional peoples have been actively establishing new homeland centres as part of a concerted effort to re-establish cultural links with traditional lands (personal communication). The Maralinga Tjarutja use the Oak Valley outstation as a base to support semi-traditional use of lands which surround the former test site area. They want to use the Maralinga Village as a community resource after the rehabilitation work is completed. Their compensation money is held in a trust fund, tied to improvement of outstation infrastructure.

Just as the official line would see the first argument as racist, so the official argument could be seen as creating an *apartheid* system in what is supposed to be a multicultural society.

Approaching the Marcoo blast crater. Tree trunks still standing (2 December 1956).

Above top: An Operation Buffalo blast in 1956 at Maralinga. *A burst of intense gamma and neutron radiation occurs on detonation, followed by the mushroom cloud of highly radioactive material. Fallout from the cloud can rise to great heights and also be carried large distances down-wind, becoming a global, not local, problem. Contamination of the ground close to the site results from 'close-in fallout' and from 'neutron activation' of elements in the soil. These products have a short half-life so radiation levels close to eight of the nine ground zeros at Maralinga and Emu are now very low, and are insignificant beyond a 200 m radius. By 2030 these sites will be safe for permanent occupancy. One test site, Tadje, has plutonium in a narrow plume NNE from the site as a result of the different nature of the device tested, and an area extending for about a kilometre from the blast site will remain contaminated for 25 000 years. People are warned not to 'souvenir' glassy fragments of fused sand, created by the heat of the blast, because they contain radioactive material.*

Above middle: The Marcoo blast crater. *Vertical view from an Anson flying at 1500 feet, on 27 February 1956. This blast was carried out at ground level and was one of the smaller ones, about 1.5 kilotons. (Six of the others were from devices mounted on 30 m towers, one was an airdrop at 150 m, and one was from a balloon at 300 m.) The crater was used to bury machinery, including an aeroplane, during the cleanup.*

The **Maralinga and Emu sites** are located in South Australia in an area south of the Great Victoria Desert and north of the Nullarbor Plain. (Maralinga is 270 km north-west of Ceduna; Emu Field is about 190 km north-east of Maralinga.) Nine major nuclear trials involving atomic explosions, and several hundred 'minor trials' which dispersed radioactive materials, were carried out. The British Operation Brumby clean-up of 1967, in which contaminated material was ploughed back into the soil to 'dilute contamination', has made effective clean-up more difficult. Now this material has to be excavated and re-buried in engineered disposal trenches under a minimum 5 m thick protective cover.[166]

One of the methods being considered for stabilising the plutonium in these burial pits is the use of large electrical currents which will melt the pit contents into a vitrified mass. The plutonium has a half-life of about 25 000 years and obviously presents significant hazards for anyone involved in the clean-up, and it is admitted that even when the job is completed there will be areas to the north and north-west of the test site which will be unsuitable for more than transitory access. The major risk is of inhaling dust which is from surfaces contaminated with radioactive fallout, and in these permanently arid regions dust is a permanent environmental factor. The aim of the cleanup is to reduce the risk of contracting cancer from exposure to dust to an 'acceptable' level, and to clean up and bury deeply any contaminated fragments or larger-than-dust fallout.

It is no wonder that Britain did not speak up in condemnation of France in the recent tests in the South Pacific. The record of British testing in Australia and in the Monte Bello Islands is shameful, and its attitude to cleaning up the damage no less so. It is interesting to see how attitudes have changed in 30 years — with Australia vocal in condemnation of nuclear testing now, while it was only too happy to invite the 'mother country' to destroy part of its territory then.

Above top: Inside the protective fence which surrounds the Taranaki site where the balloon-borne test with a 27 kiloton force was carried out in October 1957. The photograph was taken in January 1994. This test caused very little local contamination, but presumably plenty of global radiation, and the reason why the Taranaki site is fenced and controlled is the 12 Vixen B trials which were carried out between 1960 and 1963. Plutonium, beryllium and uranium-235 were dispersed over several hundred hectares. A great deal of the area was 'ploughed' in Operation Brumby, burying the contaminated surface. Beyond the ploughed area, the plutonium contamination is on the surface, so dust is potentially lethal and will remain so for a very long time. The ground is littered with fragments of machinery, steel plate, plastic and bitumen, all radioactive and a hazard because people might `souvenir' them.

Above middle: The concrete capping on a debris pit, one of 21 in which contaminated material is buried. Person-proof fences surround the pits.

Above: Aboriginal women bringing seeds of local plants to a collection point. Replanting of native vegetation follows decontamination.

Left: **The Marcoo Monolith,** photographed in November 1994, showing how the vegetation has regenerated. The ground zeros of all nine major blasts (the positions of the devices before explosion) are marked by monoliths.

MT LYELL, QUEENSTOWN, TASMANIA

The lunar landscapes of Mt Lyell, where all the vegetation has gone from an area of $15\,km^2$ in the $50\,km^2$ which are suffering environmental damage, are so notorious that the tourist trade and residents of Queenstown who benefit from it do not want the bare hills to be re-vegetated.

Mt Lyell has been mined for copper and gold for over a hundred years and processing on the minesite has been more or less continuous. For the first 30 years the sulphur dioxide emissions from smelting literally burnt any vegetation not already removed by timber felling, soil erosion and wildfires. For the following 70 years the discharge of copper-rich sulphidic tailings, slag and acid drainage has had a devastating effect on 50 km of the Queen and King Rivers downstream of the mine, virtually eliminating aquatic life and killing streamside vegetation. A huge 400 ha delta of tailings has built up in Macquarie Harbour at the mouth of the King River, with approximately 250 ha above water. An infrastructure of derelict railway lines, bridges, product dumps and wharves add further to the environmental degradation.

In 1994 the Mount Lyell Mining and Railway Company renounced its lease and all operations ceased in December. Copper Mines of Tasmania took over the lease in 1995, and an Act of Parliament was passed to exclude it from liability for pre-existing damage and pollution. It was required to build a tailings dam to prevent further environmental problems caused by dumping wastes into the rivers, and all its activities will be stringently controlled and monitored.

The Tasmanian Government approached the Commonwealth Minister for the Environment about assistance in developing a remediation strategy for the Queenstown area and for the King and Queen Rivers. The Supervising Scientist was directed to undertake a joint study program with the Tasmanian Government, and the Mount Lyell Remediation Research and Demonstration Program came into being, funded by $1.5 million from the Commonwealth and $0.5 million from Tasmanian Government.[167-72]

Projects to date include:
- Identifying the source of acid leakage from the mine site and reduction of acid drainage. One of the waste dumps was covered with clay as an experiment.
- Fluvial processes in the King River were monitored. A report indicates that there will be little further erosion of the tailings embankments which are found in the lower reaches of the river. After a burst of erosion activity when the discharge of tailings into the river ceased in 1944, and combined with the change to a more regulated flow regime because of the Hydro Electric Commission dam built further up the river, the situation is much less dynamic. There are estimated

Above top: The bare, acid burnt hills around the Mt Lyell Mine are testimony to a hundred years of smelting and activities which took no account of the damage being done to the environment.

PHOTO KINDLY SUPPLIED BY COPPER MINES OF TASMANIA, THE NEW PROPRIETORS OF THE MINE

Above: A huge delta has been formed from mine tailings at the mouth of the King River in Macquarie Harbour.

PETER WAGGITT, OSS DARWIN

Left: Mount Owen, from Queenstown airstrip, showing regrowth, August 1996.

Below: The King River, August 1996, with a bank of old crushings from the mine.

Below bottom: The King River, upstream from the junction with the Queen River.

DICK BURNS

to be 9.4 million tonnes of mine wastes in the river, which represent 60 days' discharge from the mine, and which indicate that less than 10% of discharges have been deposited in the river, with most passing through to form the delta in Macquarie Harbour.

● Sampling of the materials and waters of the tailings banks in the King River show that up to 10 kg of copper and 300 kg of sulphuric acid are still being added to the river and harbour waters daily. This is only between 1% and 5% of the quantities entering the system from the lease site upstream.

● The addition of the major proportion of these materials to surface and groundwaters will continue for thousands of years, and the report advises minimal disturbance of tailings and mine dumps because increased oxidation means increased acid.

● The option of reprocessing the delta tailings and extracting gold and other minerals is uneconomic (producing $10 per tonne and costing $200 a tonne for the extraction). The most interesting and possibly viable options would be dredging the top off the delta to ensure that what remains stays wet and anaerobic, and locating the dredged material elsewhere in the harbour; or sealing the surface of the delta to reduce oxidation, and dredging channels across it.

● Biological investigations of life in the river and harbour, tolerance of different organisms to acid, suitable plants for revegetating acid ground, etc. are all parts of the research program. The fishing industry in Macquarie Harbour is naturally concerned about the toxic delta.

The program is likely to provide a role-model for tackling industrially polluted sites elsewhere in the world, so eventually good may come out of what has been an environmental disaster of the sort usually only

seen in Third World countries where mineral resources are exploited by foreigners.

Mt Lyell presents a dramatic picture of what copper mining without environmental controls can do to its immediate vicinity and to a very large area around the mine site. Advanced technology and all the

Right: The King River — the dead section near the mouth, looking upstream, August 1996.

DICK BURNS

Above: The Queen River running through Queenstown, downstream of the copper works, August 1996 — still highly acidic.

DICK BURNS

regulations today ensure that mines operating now, and new ones coming into production, will not pollute the wider environment and will limit disturbance to natural ecosystems around them.

ALCOA OF AUSTRALIA LTD

A World Giant in Aluminium Production

Its Mining and its Conservation Programs

Since the commencement of its mining operations, Alcoa, in association with government agencies and tertiary institutions, has developed effective rehabilitation techniques for its mined areas. For many years the company has been sharing its resources with the Australian community to help address wider environmental issues, such as vegetation decline and land degradation.

Alcoa is used here as a case study to show how modern mining can be environmentally responsible and how a company not only contributes to the economy of the nation (and thus to our standard of living) but also makes an enormous contribution to conservation and the development of sustainable land-use through practical measures and through education and example. Between 1982 and 1992 Alcoa gave away 3.5 million tree seedlings and made horticultural and other technical advice freely available, in addition to its projects supporting Landcare and Greening Australia.

Alcoa's bauxite mines, refineries and aluminium smelters

The world's largest aluminium producer, the Aluminium Company of America (ALCOA) and Western Mining are joint owners of **Alcoa of Australia** which currently mines bauxite at three sites in Western Australia. These are in the Darling Range south of Perth, on Crown land which is mostly jarrah forest. The jarrah forests of the south-western corner of Western Australia are very much reduced in extent due to the inroads made by clearing for agriculture and logging and in addition suffer the problems associated with the dreaded dieback fungus, *Phytophthora cinnamomi*.

The region is environmentally sensitive, containing catchments for Perth's water supply and the valuable forests. The bauxite occurs in pockets on the slopes of the hills, separated by valleys, ridges or areas of iron-rich laterite. The average size of a deposit is 20 ha, which, depending on the depth of the deposit (2–10 m), could be mined for between one and four years. Mining is being carried out at Jarrahdale for the refinery at Kwinana; at Huntly for the Pinjarra refinery; and at Willowdale for the Wagerup refinery. (Alcoa also has a gold mine near Boddington.)

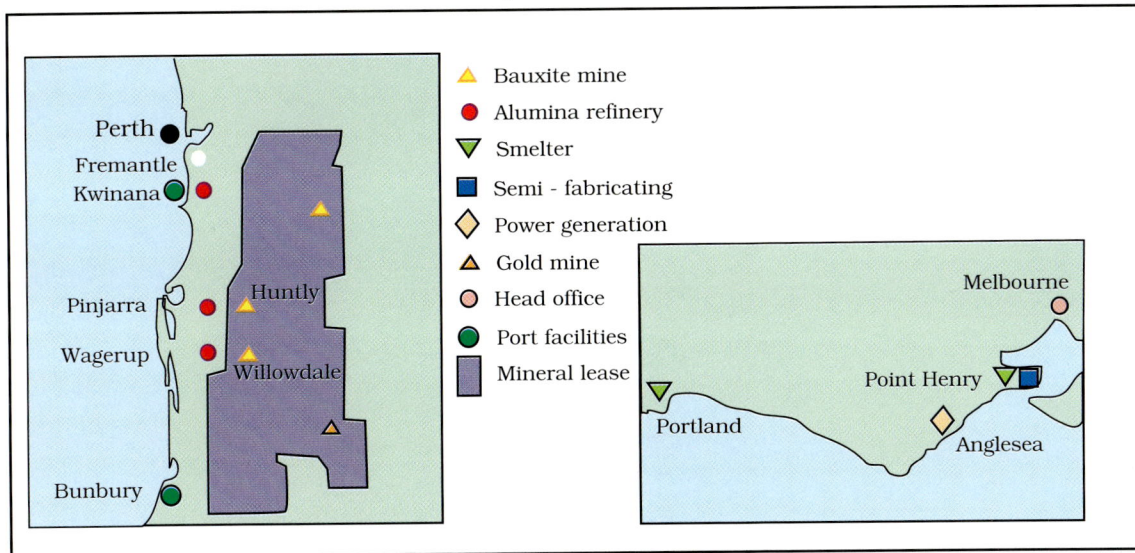

Bauxite mine
Alumina refinery
Smelter
Semi - fabricating
Power generation
Gold mine
Head office
Port facilities
Mineral lease

Courtesy Alcoa

When an ore body has been mapped and detailed plans have been prepared and approved by government agencies and all the committees involved in Darling Range management and resource development, right up to the Minister for Resource Development, mining can begin. The planning phase entails an assessment of the vegetation so that when mining is finished the land can be restored to almost its original condition over time.[173]

In the first stage of mining, CALM oversees the extraction of commercial timber; then site clearing occurs, and the surface soil with its local seed content is separated from the rest of the overburden and both are stockpiled. The caprock, which contains bauxite, is blasted and together with friable material is removed. A fleet of 85-tonne dump trucks carries the ore on specially constructed roads to the crushing facilities, from which it travels by rail or conveyor belts to the three refineries.

In the course of 35 years of mining, less than 0.5% of the jarrah forest has been cleared, and the rehabilitation which follows mining restores the land. (This is possible where the forest is eucalypt, in this case dominated by two species, while restoration would not have been possible if rainforest with its enormously complicated biodiversity had been the vegetation type.) Alcoa has a specialised environmental team of 30 full-time employees and its rehabilitation program has been so successful that it has been recognised by the United Nations Environment Programme through listing on the **Global 500 Roll of Honour.** The citation recognises that: ... *the Company has carried out a mine reforestation programme in the South West of Western Australia. This covers four bauxite mining areas in a unique forest, and three associated alumina refineries. The successful plan integrates overall environmental protection and industrial development.*

A total of $12 million a year is spent on rehabilitation, planning, operations and research. Alcoa and CALM have pioneered the rehabilitation program

KALGOORLIE, WESTERN AUSTRALIA

People living in Kalgoorlie and Boulder in the goldfields of Western Australia have been involved in ambitious tree planting programs to improve their environment. Dust from the mining operations and the bare ground they have created, and in particular from the slime dumps from the tailings dams, has been a major problem and a potential health hazard. The stabilising and revegetating of old slime dumps has been perfected by the Goldfields Dust Abatement Committee over the last decade. Surface run-off is controlled by surveying contour lines and grading absorption banks. Then fertiliser containing superphosphate and trace elements is spread and locally collected seed of several varieties of saltbush is broadcast. Nickel smelter slag is spread over the whole area at a rate of 300 tonnes per hectare to act as a mulch and stabilise the area. Where the surface has a high salinity level, the amount of slag is doubled. The method has proved highly successful.

which the company now operates. The jarrah forest ecosystem with its associated shrubs and wildflowers is being successfully restored. Die-back research, in cooperation with the State Government and universities, continues and all operations in the lease area are carried out in ways which minimise the risk of spread of the disease. Water quality in the lease area is monitored continuously.[174]

Visitors are encouraged to tour Alcoa's mining and rehabilitation operations. Up to 25 000 take advantage of the free tours each year.

The **refineries** use the latest anti-pollution technology; energy requirements at each refinery are supplied by on-site powerhouses, burning clean natural gas; dust control, drainage systems and noise reduction are all designed to minimise off-site impact.

Alcoa's **smelter** and semi-fabricating plant was positioned at Point Henry near the entrance to Port Philip Bay in Victoria because it required a deep water port and a local source of energy for smelting. The brown coal deposits at Anglesea are on a lease owned by the company and the coal is used to fuel Alcoa's own power station, which is built adjacent to the open cut

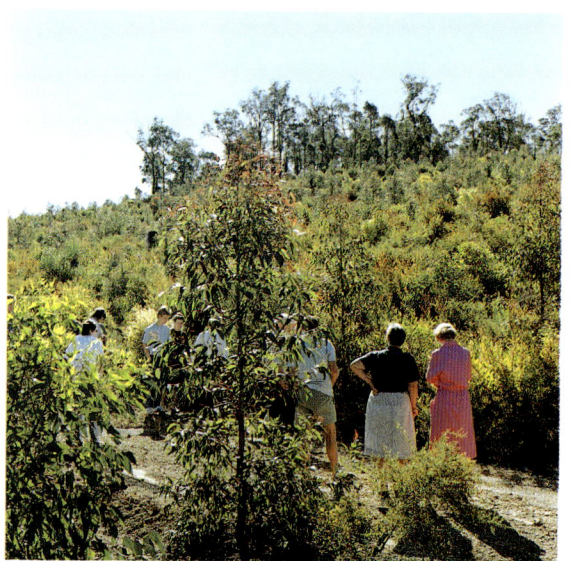

*Far right and right:
A mine pit
immediately after
mining, and the same
site three years after
rehabilitation.*

ALCOA

*Right: Bauxite
mining in the
Darling Range,
Western Australia.*

ALCOA

*Far right: Visitors
inspect a rehabilitated
mine site.*

ALCOA

operation, to supply power to Point Henry. The second smelter in Victoria, at Portland, is a joint venture between Alcoa (45%), the Victorian government (25%), Eastern Aluminium Ltd (10%), Marubeni Australia Ltd (10%), and the China International Trust and Investment Corporation (10%).[175]

Red mud, a byproduct of refining of bauxite

More than 14 million tonnes of bauxite residue result from the refineries in Western Australia, presenting major disposal problems. In 1982, Dr Jim Barrow at the CSIRO in Perth showed that it could be used to improve sandy soils in the State's south-west. When spread on the ground at 2000 t/ha (20 cm thick) it virtually eliminated the leaching of phosphorus from the soil. Ongoing research has proved that in addition to binding phosphorus it can increase the growth of pasture and vegetables. It is strongly alkaline (and therefore useful where soil acidification has resulted from fertiliser use, as in much agricultural land) and it improves soil water retention and reduces water repellence.[176]

Used at only 80 t/ha in the coastal plain lands of the

Peel Harvey catchment, it decreased the amount of phosphorus in run-off water by 70%. (Phosphorus from gardens, farm land, piggeries, dairies and sewage treatment plants poses a huge problem in this region, resulting in algal blooms in the inlet. Recent opening of the Dawesville Channel to the sea means that application of only 20 t/ha to the sands of the catchment will keep phosphorus levels low enough to prevent most algal blooms.) A large sub-catchment at Meredith, west of Harvey, comprising 4000 ha, has been treated with red mud as a trial, funded by Alcoa and a National Landcare Grant. It is expected to halve the amount of phosphorus leaching from the catchment.

The ALCOA Landcare Project

In 1989, Alcoa committed $6.5 million to support the National Decade of Landcare in Western Australia and in Victoria, where it has operations.

In the west, its activities involve on-ground demonstration of rehabilitation techniques in agricultural and wetland situations, as well as public awareness and educational activities. Its contribution to the establishment of six sub-catchment demonstration

THE WHITE CLIFFS OPAL FIELD

An aerial view of the Opal Field at White Cliffs looks like funnel-ant activity. The underground houses complement the illusion.

PICTURE SUPPLIED BY GWEN ROWE, A LONG-TIME RESIDENT OF WHITE CLIFFS

sites in the wheatbelt, the assistance program to Lake Toolibin and the 'Avon Ascent' have been described in Chapter 5. The Tammin Alcoa Landcare Education Centre in the heart of a major farming area is used by over 800 students as well as other visitors each year, teaching about salinity, erosion, land management and Landcare.

In Victoria, Alcoa is providing $1.5 million to support a range of Landcare projects, including: establishing native seed banks in Melbourne and Portland for community revegetation programs; assisting urban revegetation in association with Greening Australia; supporting community programs for wetland rehabilitation at Leopold and Lake Connewarre; providing direct seeding machines to enable The Australia Trust for Conservation Volunteers, Greening Australia and Landcare Groups to initiate projects more quickly and efficiently; and sponsorship of a Postgraduate Diploma in Landcare at the Ballarat University College.[174]

Left: Radio collars are fitted to koalas to monitor their movements. The Koala research program at Blair Athol is carried out in collaboration with the University of Queensland.

COAL MINING AND THE ENVIRONMENT

The Blair Athol Coalmine, Clermont, Queensland

First mining of coal at Blair Athol, by underground methods, commenced in 1890, followed by small-scale open-cut mining in 1923. In the late 1960s the potential of the area was recognised, but major expansion only occurred after the oil crisis of 1973, when electricity producers were confronted by the

uncertainties of oil supplies and started looking around for alternatives. The high quality, low ash-low sulphur coal from Blair Athol met the requirements of power stations in Japan, Asia and Europe where tightening emission controls required such qualities in their fuel. A joint venture, led by CRA Limited, developed the new open cut mine and despatched its first consignment to

Above: Rehabilitated land at Blair Athol.

JAMES SULLIVAN

THE BOWEN BASIN COAL MEASURES AND LOCATION OF BLAIR ATHOL MINE

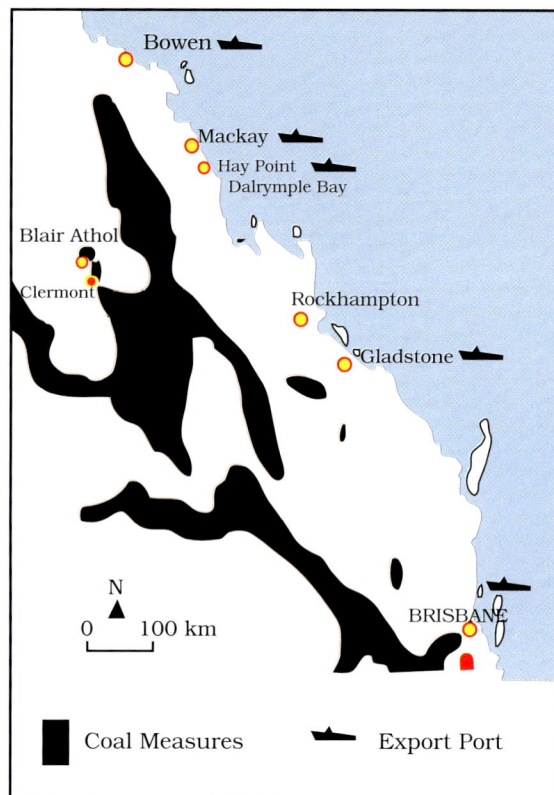

Bowen

Mackay

Hay Point
Dalrymple Bay

Blair Athol

Clermont

Rockhampton

Gladstone

N

0   100 km

BRISBANE

■ Coal Measures   ⊷ Export Port

Above top: Pollution control equipment is installed at the Blair Athol Mine workshop. An oil separator and collection sumps ensure that run-off water from the workshop area does not pollute the environment.

Above: An experiment in association with the University of Queensland simulates rainfall on mined land to determine erosion parameters.

JAMES SULLIVAN

Japan in 1984. Recoverable reserves are currently estimated at 150 million tonnes, with the mine expected to produce until 2010. After that it is intended that the site, fully rehabilitated, will become a wildlife reserve. (Before mining started it was marginal pastoral and agricultural land.)

Development of the modern mining operations by the joint venture in the early 1980s included rehabilitation of the old mining areas, existing open cut mine spoil, underground shafts and processing facilities. Domestic and feral animals were removed from the mining lease and a substantial forested buffer zone was retained around the new mine.

Mining is carried out by traditional strip-mining techniques. Before it begins the existing vegetation is analysed and an inventory of wildlife is taken. Trees used by the resident koala population are marked, and they are initially left standing when the surrounding areas are cleared by bulldozers in 100 m wide strips. This gives the koalas time to relocate into the bush nearby. Then the topsoil is removed and stockpiled for immediate and future use. Overburden is removed by dragline, exposing the coal, and mining commences. The coal is taken by trucks to the plant to be crushed and quality tested, then it is stockpiled to be taken to Dalrymple Bay for export. Throughout the mining process water is sprayed over the mine to prevent dust pollution.

After the coal has been removed, overburden previously removed is used to regrade the land to blend in with the natural landscape and to minimise erosion. Topsoil is replaced and native vegetation replanted. Progressive re-establishment of native fauna habitat and native commercial timber species (principally rosewood) on a stable landform are the major goals of mine rehabilitation. Eucalypt seedlings are specially planted by local school children to be a future food supply for koalas.

The **Koala research project**, conducted in collaboration with experts from the University of Queensland, is an important part of operations. It has been found that koalas often sit in trees which they do not use for food, so replanting food trees only would not be satisfactory. The intensive study has already shown that older revegetated areas are being recolonised.

Since 1993, Blair Athol has been involved in educational activities with schools and a manual has been produced covering a structured program of activities in earth sciences, ecology and social studies. The aim is to share resources, skills and opportunities with children from the local community, and to let people see for themselves the mine's performance on environmental issues.

For such a large coal producer (10 million tonnes per year, earning about $350 million in 1993–94) the mine has minimal impact on the local environment. In all, about 800 ha will be disturbed, far less than other similar-sized producers, and it is being progressively rehabilitated.

COAL MINING IN THE HUNTER VALLEY

The Hunter Valley is a broad, gently undulating valley about 30 km wide and extending about 150 km north-west from Newcastle to the Liverpool Ranges (part of the Great Divide). Coal mining has been taking place in the valley over the past 200 years in three regions: The Newcastle or Tomago coal measures near the coast; the Greta coal measures round Cessnock and Maitland; and the Singleton coal measures in the upper part of the valley.

Although coal mining in the Upper Hunter dates back to early settlement, production was almost negligible until the late 1960s when the Liddell power station was commissioned. At about the same time the demand for coking coal by the Japanese steel mills began to rise dramatically. In 1962, total coal production was only 1.9 million tonnes. By 1992 this was 51 million tonnes, of which some 10 million tonnes per annum is consumed locally by two of the State's largest coal-fired power stations.[177]

Since the 1980s, coal production has been dominated by open-cut mines working the Singleton coal measures and a northern outcropping of the Greta measures. Virtually all mining activity is currently contained within a roughly triangular area of land, bounded by Singleton in the south, Muswellbrook and Aberdeen in the north, and Denman and Jerrys Plains in the west.[178] Within this mining triangle, the landscape is rolling hills, bisected by the Hunter River, whose floodplains are prime agricultural land. Dairying is the main use, with market gardens and oil seed production under spray irrigation. Very little of the original native vegetation remains in the valley, clearing for agriculture was almost total, and such unimproved pasture as remains has lost its valuable perennial grass species and has a mixture of less palatable grasses.

The country away from the floodplain is 'unimproved' grazing land, used for beef production. Soils are typically shallow and infertile and the pastures which replaced native vegetation have suffered from over-grazing by stock and rabbits, causing sheet erosion.

Salinisation of low-lying sites is common, due to removal of native vegetation and rising of the saline water-table. The Hunter River has suffered from high salinity during droughts since the earliest days of settlement (and in its natural state before that).In the last 20 years, attempts have been made at fully integrating environmental management with production and development operations at coal mines in the Hunter. During this time, the number of mines has doubled and annual raw coal production has grown from 22 million to 75 million tonnes, with surface mines producing 68% of the total. In open-cut mining, the average ratio of overburden stripped to coal is 4:1, and roughly 200 million cubic metres of soil and broken rock is excavated, transported and dumped each year in the Hunter Valley. The fact that this is done in close proximity to towns and villages, to dairy farms, vineyards and market gardens (with very few complaints) attests to the effectiveness of the environment management systems which have been developed and the attention which mine management pays to ensuring that those systems are applied and maintained.

Technology has been developed to control air, water and noise emissions; land disturbed by surface mining is progressively rehabilitated. Without these environmental protection measures an industry as large as the Hunter coal industry would never have been able to develop in the region. Land rehabilitation involves restoring the landscape to its original rolling form, replacing the overburden and the topsoil and planting native trees and improved pastures. The pasture restored on minesites has proved to have several times

Above: Aerial view of Hunter Valley No 1, showing progressive rehabilitation. The mine started in 1987 near buildings in the background and has progressed towards the bottom of the picture, where part of the current low-wall can be seen. Rehabilitation has followed. Dark areas are young, direct-seeded trees; the dams serve as part of erosion control in early stages, then as water supply for cattle as areas return to grazing.

Left: Cattle grazing on mature rehabilitation at the Hunter Valley No. 1 Mine, coal stockpiles in the background.

JOHN HANNAN

Right top Coal & Allied's Hunter Valley No 1 Open Cut Mine: photo taken of a section of the open cut in 1982.

Right: The same area in 1992, after rehabilitation. The mine is still operating but the active area of workings has moved from left to right, and is now located off the right hand side of the picture. Drought has caused the browning of the pasture.

JOHN HANNAN

the carrying capacity of the unimproved, often degraded, pastures of the region.

A major problem in the Hunter coal mines has been the disposal of saline groundwater. The water-table in the region is naturally saline and it has risen because of land clearing. Mining intercepts the water-table and it was necessary to develop management practices which did not affect river salinity and the quality of water downstream of mining operations.

Water management and disposal at coal mines

- Run-off from areas of undisturbed land is diverted round the active mining and disturbed areas. This water can be discharged from the mine lease because it is no different from run-off from non-mine land, or it can be stored in dams to augment the mine's water supply.

- Where soil and vegetation has been disturbed, run-off water contains clay and silt, so it has to be held in settlement dams before release from the site.

- Run-off from 'hardstand' areas and water used for cleaning equipment often contains oils and it has to pass through filters; the effluent from the sewerage treatment plant (and the hardstand areas) is used on site for dust suppression or to irrigate rehabilitation areas. The EPA does not allow its off-site disposal.

- Water which collects in active mining areas, as a result of rainfall or groundwater seepage, is collected and pumped into holding dams which are isolated from other run-off. If the mine workings receive substantial amounts of groundwater seepage, this water is likely to be highly saline and priority is given for it use in dust suppression, including road watering and spray installations on conveyor belts, dump stations and stockpiles. Some of the more recently constructed coal preparation plants are able to use saline water in their circuits.

The Contribution by Mining to Hunter River Salinity

Under average seasonal conditions and river flows, natural groundwater accessions amount to 7.5% of annual salt load. Normal surface run-off accounts for about 87% of the total, although seepage and tailwater from irrigation is included in this figure. Mines currently contribute around 5% to 7% of the annual salt load. (Of the 19 mines currently operating in the Upper Hunter, only 10 have the need to discharge under average seasonal conditions.)

Two major studies showed that **under drought conditions**, groundwater accessions were the most important source of salinity and that coal mining, either surface or underground, had virtually no effect on groundwater flow or quality, but that the pumping of saline groundwater to the surface from active mine workings had the potential to affect surface water quality, if it was discharged to the river at times when the environment could not absorb the impact. A 'nil dry weather discharge' policy was the EPA's first reaction, but it proved unworkable and the severe drought of 1992 forced the coal industry to develop discharge schemes and protocols which maintain river water quality within acceptable limits in respect of both the natural ecosystem and downstream users.

A simple and effective method has been arrived at in collaboration with irrigation farmers and the two major power stations in the Upper Hunter, which are major water users in the region. Mines and the power stations are required to build sufficient storage dams to contain up to six months of excess saline water. Discharges of this water to the river are permitted only in times of high flows, when very little use is being made of the river and there is sufficient volume of flow to dilute the salinity of the mine and power station discharges. In average rainfall years, these river 'freshes' occur about three times per year. The rate of discharge from each mine and power station is carefully controlled, so that salinity in the river is kept below levels that have been agreed upon with the local community and the EPA. A monitoring system, both in the river and at each discharge point, measuring flow and salinity, is connected by telemetry to the computer system at the Department of Land and Water Resources at Muswellbrook, which is able to tell each mine how much they can discharge while maintaining river salinity at acceptable levels.

ANTS: THEIR ROLE IN ECOSYSTEMS AND AS BIO-INDICATORS

Australia could well be called the Continent of the Ants. In the semi-arid and seasonally arid regions of the continent up to 150 species can occur in one hectare; in cooler, wetter parts the figure might be well over 50. Their importance in ecosystems cannot be overstated. They are involved in:

- bioturbation of soils in the course of their nest building;
- recycling of nutrients by collecting vegetable and animal matter in their scavenging and feeding;
- acting as predators;
- collecting and storing seeds and a close associations with plants. The role of harvester ants in granivory in the arid zone is vital. Seeds are one of the most stable resources available to consumers there, and they are often abundant in the soils of arid ecosystems. In other parts of the world granivory is the province of rodents first, with birds and ants second. The paucity of animals in the rodent niche in Australia has led to an enhanced role for ants in seed collecting, and with the climatic fluctuations experienced by vegetation of our arid lands the availability of seed in the soil when rain comes is very important;[179]
- tunnelling, which causes water to be absorbed by the soil profile.

They are obviously important in ecosystems as judged by the number of spiders, hemipterans, beetles, mantids and other invertebrates which mimic them.

It has been discovered that the environmental health of ecosystems can be assessed by monitoring the activity of ant colonies. As **bio-indicators** they are useful because they are diverse and abundant everywhere; they interact in many ways with other parts of ecosystems; they are readily sampled and processed; and they are highly sensitive to environmental variables. Though Australian ants are poorly known at species level they can be classified into functional groups whose relative abundances vary predictably with climate, vegetation type and level of disturbance. The relative abundance of functional groups is sensitive to environmental change and provides insights into processes underlying such change. Therefore they can be used to evaluate degradation and restoration processes objectively.

Experiments to assess their value as bio-indicators were carried out on 30 **bauxite mines** undergoing rehabilitation. It was found that the species richness of ants correlated with species richness of termites and springtails in the soil, and also with the invertebrate species richness on the vegetation. In the Myall Lakes National Park in rehabilitation after **sand mining** the ant succession matched the small mammal succession. Another experiment showed that the stages of rehabilitation on eight sites at the **Ranger Uranium Mine** in the Northern Territory could be objectively determined by using ant populations as bio-indicators.[180] The first colonisers of wasteland were species which scavenge on open ground. As plant regeneration proceeded so a succession of ant groups suited to the changing environment returned. The speed at which they re-colonised, and the number build-up involved was found to relate to the distance of the area being rehabilitated from areas with established natural vegetation.

Ants as agricultural pests: Ants are one of the most serious pests currently affecting citrus production in Australia. They do not do direct damage to fruit or trees, but because every ant has a sweet tooth, the effect is the same. They feed on the honeydew produced by scale insects, aphids or whiteflies and their presence protects those insects from predators.

It has been found in the Murrumbidgee Irrigation Area, one of Australia's major citrus producing regions, that controlling ants results in a return of predatory and parasitic insects and a reduction of soft scale and other honeydew-producing insect populations to low, non-damaging numbers.

THE STORY OF AN ENVIRONMENT CENTRE

The Sutherland Shire Environment Centre has been so successful in promoting environmental awareness and acting as a nucleus for all sorts of programs aimed at sustainable development in the Shire that I requested its founder, chairman and benefactor, R.D. (Bob) Walshe to write an account of its origins and evolution. Perhaps this story might inspire people seeking to leave a legacy which will help to ensure a better world for their grandchildren to help to finance similar ventures?

Bob Walshe writes:

Think Locally — and Act Locally

'Think globally, act locally' ... so runs the well-known maxim. But let me tell you the story of Sutherland Shire Environment Centre and why its six years of intense activity have led us to change those words radically.

We know the global threats. I'd say the Top Eight are: ozone depletion, Greenhouse warming, forest destruction, soil loss, air-land-sea pollution by toxins and radiation, nuclear hazards, fresh water shortage and, underlying all, the relentless thrust of population growth and ever-improving exploitive technology.

But individuals, confronted by these enormities, feel powerless and disinclined to join — let alone form — a green resistance organisation. No wonder there is so much green talk around and so little action. ('All I can do is send Greenpeace a donation.')

The little band that formed our Shire Environment Centre did so chiefly to confront local problems. The Shire has a population of nearly 200 000, it's the second largest of Sydney's 43 local government areas. Even its famous historical corner, Kurnell on Botany Bay, has been shamefully degraded — despite its millennia of Aboriginal occupation and its triple distinction as Captain Cook's first landfall, the First Fleet's anchorage, and the site of Australia's first environmental protest when Aborigines remonstrated with sailors who were cutting down trees.

Kurnell? Sydney inflicted its huge oil refinery on it in the 1950s and forty years later is inflicting the worst aircraft noise suffered by any suburb. Nearby Cronulla? Its majestic sandhills were trucked away for building sand, its lovely beachfront uglified by incongruous high-rise. Botany Bay and Georges River? Both grossly polluted.

At the other end of the Shire, Lucas Heights not only hosts Australia's two nuclear reactors but serves as the nation's de facto radioactive waste repository, close to which is a radioactive waste dump, and the largest putrescible waste landfill on the continent.

Though the Shire's blackspots contrast sharply with its many lovely features — water views, tracts of bushland, greenery in urban areas — there was little concerted resident action before 1991. The problems were left to the Shire Council. But councils come and go, varying in quality, often manipulated by developers, and seldom effectively driven by the electors, who complain mightily of council bumbling but (except for a noble few) won't give an evening a month to civic or political organisations that should keep an eye on council performance.

Early in 1991 a handful of residents moved to set up some sort of environment centre. There aren't many of these across New South Wales. In Sydney, apart from the CBD-based Total Environment Centre, there is only Manly's active Centre (partly subsidised by its Council), Sutherland's (not subsidised), and a couple of others struggling to be born. There are perhaps a dozen more in country towns, mostly coastal. All vary, and all have strongly local features. There is no formula, except that all share a spiritual base in idealism, initiative and stickability of one, two or a handful of core activists.

Our Centre emerged unpredictably from an evening course, 'Writing for the Environment', attended by 55 Shire residents. A dozen went on meeting for weeks afterwards till someone said impatiently, 'Let's set up an environment centre'. In its early chaotic months, survival depended on three enthusiasts: a businessman in his late sixties, an unemployed engineer in his twenties, and a woman with excellent office skills who gave many hours a day while running a family. No help came from the local press.

Money was a headache. But a few solid donations trickled in. We arranged raffles, street stalls, even a launch trip down the Georges and around Botany Bay (it raised $900), and a sympathetic businessman took over some early debts. We rented a room — our present shopfront-office in Sutherland's main arcade — furnished and equipped it largely by donations, and settled to sustained fund-raising to meet bills for rent, phone, photocopier, word-processor, stamps, stationery, light, power and the rest, adding up to $500–$600 a month.

In short, a big internal effort while externally the Shire's many problems fell upon us. But there was toughness from the start. We survived, and now there are many helping hands. Our 1995 Report announced a doubling of the work-volume in that year. The 1996 Report recorded an even wider spread of activities. We've added a full-time director to our secretary, both deeply committed, energetic and able officers.

A working structure has evolved, based on 15 committees: Holsworthy airport protest, Environmental education, Nuclear issues, Urban planning, Transport/roads, Water/sewerage, Nature conservation, Electromagnetic fields, Marine protection, Kurnell–Towra rehabilitation, Hacking River, Waste management, Population stabilisation, Fundraising, Newsletter. The committees function with high autonomy, each headed by a convenor, with a network of helpers. The Centre also sends representatives to about 20 Council/Government/community committees.

Success has attended many Centre efforts. We've been prominent (with others) in campaigns to avert a 'megatip' (1992), to defer a new nuclear reactor (1993), to prevent near-shore sand mining (1994), and to defeat urban expansion around Helensburgh which would have sent pollution into the Royal National Park (1994–95). In 1996–97 we are among the leaders of the popular struggle against airport construction on our doorstep, at Holsworthy.

Fund-raising never ceases to weigh on us, but we accord it top status as environmental work, part of our lifeblood. Each month a great team sets up a stall in a shopping-centre, sells donated goods, hands out brochures and raises over $500 to offset overheads. Membership subs of course help, but not greatly. We have a few generous donors and hope to find more (there are people and businesses out there who could make large donations). We think too that our Council could help us, as Manly Council helps its Centre.

We've grown in our Shire and grown steeply in local knowledge. But we haven't lost sight of those global threats. We know the planet is being rushed towards breakdowns in its food chains, biodiversity ... ecology in general. The worsening ozone depletion, greenhouse warming, toxic-pollution and other separate spoiling agents flow increasingly into confluence — a lethal synergy or whole which will be tragically more destructive than the sum of the separate agents.

Yet we must think locally and act locally. So we never lose touch with our community and its felt environment. For now we see that this is the only way we can send a grassroots message up the line, to Council, to State government, to Federal government, to the world at large. The local path turns out to be the only path to the global.

Every local community the world over should have some form of environment centre (by whatever name), an articulate community leadership above party politics, to shield it against the degrading forces rampant in these headlong times. Yes, indeed: 'Think and act locally' — and for God's sake and the planet's ACT URGENTLY!

CONSERVATION PROTECTION ON PRIVATE LAND

The range of National Parks and Reserves throughout Australia protects and conserves examples of many of the continent's ecosystems, but in order to provide an integrated range and a functional habitat for Australian fauna it is necessary to complement them with conservation areas on privately owned land. Within Australia, several organisations provide permanent conservation protection on private land that resides with the property title and provides a legally binding agreement with the current owner and all future owners.

- In **South Australia,** the Department of Environment and Natural Resources enters into **Heritage Agreements.** These can be voluntary but have been used to protect land when applications to clear land for farming have been refused. Rate relief and compensation have been offered as part of the package. The scheme had cost over $70 million to 1996 and had protected 550 000 ha of conservation land.

- In **Tasmania,** the Department of Environment and Land Management issues **Conservation Covenants** (enabling legislation was passed in 1994).
- In **New South Wales,** the National Parks and Wildlife Service enters into **Voluntary Conservation Agreements.** The scheme had been dormant, but was re-activated in 1993.
- In **Queensland,** the Department of Environment and Heritage has **Nature Refuges with a Conservation Agreement,** with legislation passed in 1993.
- In **Victoria,** the **Trust for Nature (Victoria)** provides permanent conservation through **Conservation Covenants.** It is an independent body established by Act of Parliament (*Victorian Conservation Trust Act 1972*, amendments 1978 & 1986)

Conservation Achievements on Private Land in Victoria

Victoria, the smallest mainland State, has three million hectares managed under the National Parks Act — 13% of Victoria, and almost a third of all public land. However, 65% of the State is privately owned, and conservation of native vegetation on private land is a major area of activity for government and non-government organisations.[181]

Vegetation clearing in Victoria since settlement has been on a gigantic scale. In 1869, **forest and woodland** covered 88% of the State (20 million hectares). Over the next 100 years the area was reduced to eight million hectares, or 35% of the State. (No wonder the State has massive salinity problems!) Of the area which now remains,

only 5% is on private land — and this 5% is important because it often represents ecosystems and habitats not represented in national parks and reserves. **Grasslands and grassy woodlands** used to cover 7.5 million hectares, and 95% of these ecosystems have been destroyed or degraded by the rapid development of agricultural and pastoral enterprises. Only 0.3% remain conserved in original condition without modification through fertiliser application or contamination with introduced pasture species.

Clearing the land for agriculture was very rapid in the 40 years between 1866 and 1906 in response to the demand for food created by the goldrush — agricultural land increased from 12% to 61% of the State. Clearing continued steadily as urban development and primary production required ever more land, and between 1972 and 1987 was still occurring at 15 000 ha a year, with 87% taking place on privately owned land. A consequence of the massive clearance is that now one in three of Victoria's vertebrate animals and one in four of its plant species are considered rare, threatened or extinct. The loss of biodiversity is matched by the increase in land degradation. According to a report by the Catchment and Land Management Division of the Department of Conservation and Natural Resources (1996):

- By 1991, salinity had affected 140 000 ha of irrigated land and 120 000 ha of dryland farming areas and these areas were expected to increase by 400% by the year 2040.
- A further 3.2 million hectares are considered affected by erosion, soil acidity and soil compaction, and 7.8 million hectares have a high risk of degradation.

In response to the serious situation a number of Acts were introduced:

- 1975: *Wildlife Act; Wildlife Sanctuaries, Management Co-Operative Sanctuaries*
- 1987: *Conservation, Forests and Lands Act Land Management Co-Operative Agreements*
- 1988: *Flora and Fauna Guarantee Act Interim Conservation Orders Critical Habitat* — which lists taxa and communities of threatened flora and fauna and is the reference for decisions on clearance. It currently lists 250 species of plants and animals, 15 communities and 13 potentially threatening processes.
- 1994: *Catchment and Land Protection Act*

(Under the Wildlife and Conservation Acts of 1975 and 1987, cooperative areas and cooperative agreements can be established for conservation on private land. However, in practice very few such agreements have been established and it has been left to a non-government body to fill the niche.)

The Department of Conservation and Natural Resources administers the control approach, implementing the various Acts, and a number of government projects and programs supplement it.

- **Land for Wildlife**, a very successful program initiated in 1981 to establish voluntary agreement with landholders to provide habitat for wildlife on their properties. By 1995 there were 3100 participating properties covering 319 000 ha, of which 69 000 ha were identified as managed for wildlife. The program is expanding by 550 properties a year and is supported by two full-time staff and 13 part-time extension officers drawn from the local community.
- **Tree Victoria** encourages various community groups and organisations in tree growing, direct seeding and remnant vegetation/regeneration activities in rural areas. The aim is to plant five million trees a year over the next 20 years.
- **Botanic Guardians** provides assistance to local community groups in the conservation of rare and threatened native plant species or vegetation communities on public land.
- The **Good Neighbour Program** provides protection to private landholders adjacent to public land from pest plants and animals transferring across boundaries.
- The **Land Protection Incentive Scheme** provides financial support to individual landholders to undertake work on land and soil degradation.
- **Coast Action** and **Landcare** are part of the national programs.

A large number of statutory authorities and non-government organisations support conservation work on private land in Victoria. These include:

- *The Threatened Species Network* and *The Indigenous Flora & Fauna Association (IFFA)* — advising;
- The *Australian Bird Environment Foundation* and the *Royal Australasian Ornithologists Union* — raising funds to support conservation of habitat;
- The *Victorian National Parks Association* — fencing workshops and conservation strategies;

- Roadside Conservation Advisory Committee — protection of roadside habitats;
- Greening Australia (Victoria) — information, guidance, financial support; River Murray Corridors of Green;
- Landcare Groups and Australian Trust for Conservation Volunteers — hands-on conservation work;
- Victorian Wetlands Trust — promoting better wetland conservation and management;
- Tree Project — plant propagation for rural landholders;
- Victorian Farmers Federation — Wetlands Advisory Officer, Landcare publications;
- Shire Conservation Officers & The Australian Bush Heritage Fund — land purchase;
- **The Trust for Nature — covenants. Permanent protection of conservation areas on private land is offered by this unique organisation, as detailed below.**

The Victorian success in reducing native vegetation clearance is reflected in the reduction of areas cleared since the introduction of clearing controls in 1989. From an annual clearance rate of 15 000 ha in 1987, the area cleared on private land declined to 4250 ha a year by 1992, including illegal clearing. Over the same period, annual clearing approvals declined from 5800 to 3000.

TRUST FOR NATURE (VICTORIA)

Formerly the **Victorian Conservation Trust,** this statutory authority was established in 1972 under its own Victorian Conservation Trust Act. The Act was amended in 1995 to change the name to **Trust for Nature (Victoria)** to avoid the trust being confused with a government department and other conservation organisations. The new name relates more specifically to the trust's work in the natural environment.[181-183]

The objects of the trust as described in the Act are:

1. For scientific and educational purposes the Trust shall encourage and assist in:
   a. Preservation of areas which are ecologically significant; of natural interest or beauty; of historical interest
   b. Conservation of wildlife and native plants
   c. Conservation and creation of areas for scientific study of matters in a. and b.
2. The Trust shall encourage and assist in conservation and creation of areas of natural beauty or interest for use by the public for enjoyment, recreation and education.

The trust has a full-time staff of seven in Melbourne, with six part-time regional coordinators located throughout rural Victoria. Its operations comprise:

- **Voluntary covenants with landowners.** The covenant details the area of land to be covenanted, and the activities that can occur on the land. These usually include fencing to prevent grazing by domestic livestock, exclusion of cats and dogs, control of feral animals and weeds. Each covenant is different, to meet the needs of individual landholders. The trust develops conservation management and monitoring programs for each, in consultation with the owners. Covenants can only be revoked by agreement of the trust and approval of the Minister for Conservation and Environment, as well as the Governor-in-Council. By 1996, 170 covenants had been registered, covering more than 6000 ha, and a further 120 were being negotiated to protect an additional 5000 ha.
- **Land purchase.** The trust can purchase land and retain the title, or, under the Act, transfer it to the Crown. The trust has purchased 93 properties with a total area of 7000 ha. Currently it owns 53 properties. It has also purchased significant conservation land on behalf of the Federal and State government, and this land is subsequently transferred to the national parks system.
- **Public appeals.** Local community interest in saving a valuable piece of land frequently leads to the establishment of a public appeal. The trust can assist by providing advice, collection of funds and offering tax deductibility. In many cases the trust purchases the land for the appeal and can also approach government for financial support.
- **Buying and selling conservation land through a revolving fund.** The trust has established a fund to enable it to purchase land that has a conservation significance. A covenant is placed on the land to protect it permanently, and it is on-sold to conservation-minded people. The proceeds return to the fund for further purchases. Seven properties have been bought and then sold with covenants to date.
- **Conservation training and education.** The staff of the trust conduct training programs on conservation management, and educational activities focusing on conservation. These are often held in conjunction with another conservation organisation to maximise public participation and benefit.
- **Membership program.** Through membership, people can actively participate in programs on trust properties and covenants. The trust receives donations and bequests, including property, and it can assist with the sale of members' covenanted properties with advertising in its publications. Its Conservation Bulletin keeps members in touch, as does its Nature News booklet.

The Trust for Nature is the sort of organisation that should be established in every State and Territory.

CHAPTER FOURTEEN

FORESTS AND WILDERNESS

The extent of tree clearing in Australia in the 200 years of European occupation has been on a scale almost beyond comprehension. Before settlement, forests covered 10% of the continent and woodlands occupied a further 23%. The area covered by tall and medium forest has been halved, and three-quarters of the rainforest component has gone. More than 35% of woodlands have been cleared or severely modified. And the clearing goes on relentlessly.

The **Global Landcover Change Project**, using satellites to monitor the changing vegetation, watches and records the destruction of tropical rainforests in South America, and world media protest at the destruction. It also monitors the clearing of woodland and forest which is currently taking place in south-eastern Queensland where the almost total removal of brigalow is proceeding. It is depressing to know that the speed at which land is being cleared there matches the rate of destruction in Brazil, and there is no outcry, not even in Australia.

An enormous environmental price is now being paid for the massive destruction of trees, particularly in the catchments which contain Australia's agriculturally productive Murray–Darling Basin in the east and the Western Australian wheatbelt and agricultural lands of the south-west. The dryland salinity, rising water-tables, waterlogging and salinisation of soil, erosion and degradation of land and water resources, are symptoms of the hydrological changes which have largely been caused by removing the high-transpiring components of the vegetation (followed by land-use practices which compound the problems).

In a world in which the tropical forests are disappearing and old-growth forests are threatened everywhere, global biodiversity is declining at an alarming rate. Australia can no longer afford to destroy its remaining old growth forests — they are a priceless resource. Few of our tall forests of any type remain in pristine condition, and particularly where they have not been degraded they should be protected. **The practice of destroying old-growth forest in order to replace it with plantation is criminal vandalism. Plantations should be established on already degraded agricultural land.**

Research into production of 'super wattles' by the CSIRO, the Queensland Forest Research Institute and

Native forests, including rainforests, are cleared, chipped and then replaced by plantations of eucalypts (destined for wood pulp) by North Forest Products in north-west Tasmania (on North's privately owned land).

G.LAW

EXTENT OF THE BIG SCRUB

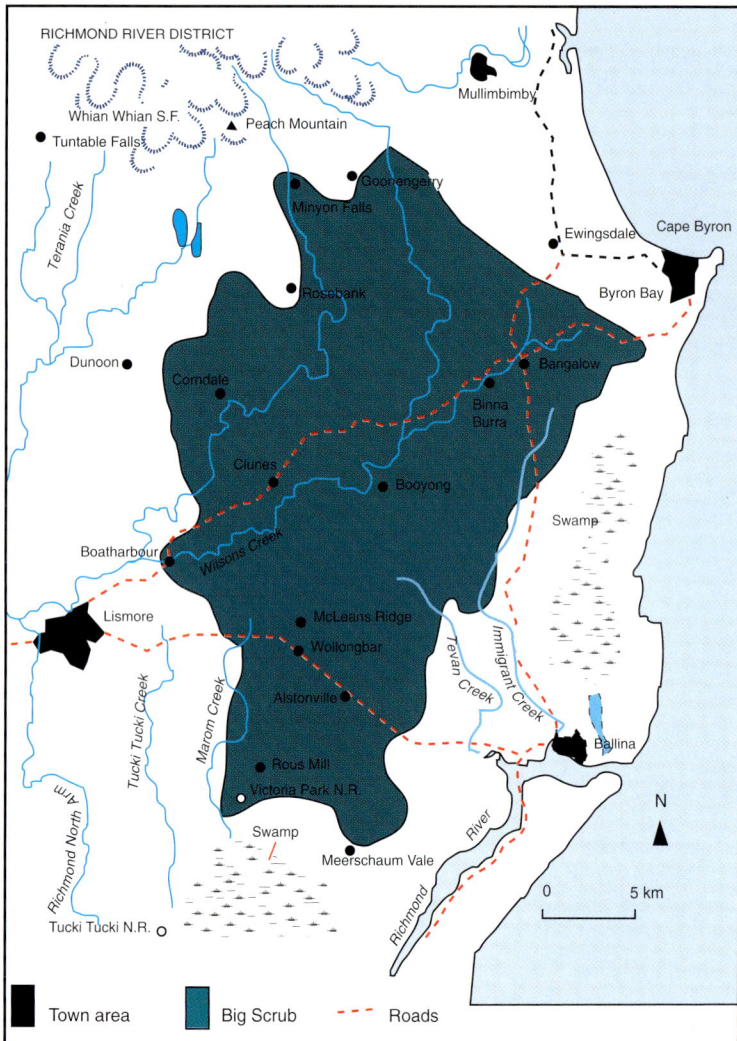

RICHMOND RIVER DISTRICT

Whian Whian S.F.
Tuntable Falls
Peach Mountain
Mullumbimby
Goonengerry
Minyon Falls
Ewingsdale
Cape Byron
Rosebank
Byron Bay
Dunoon
Corndale
Bangalow
Binna Burra
Clunes
Booyong
Swamp
Boatharbour
Wilsons Creek
Lismore
McLeans Ridge
Wollongbar
Tevan Creek
Immigrant Creek
Alstonville
Marom Creek
Tucki Tucki Creek
Ballina
Rous Mill
Victoria Park N.R.
Richmond North Arm
Swamp
Meerschaum Vale
Richmond River
N
0   5 km
Tucki Tucki N.R.
Terania Creek

■ Town area   ■ Big Scrub   - - - Roads

After NPWS **184**

the Northern Territory Conservation Commission is showing the way towards protecting native forests by producing timber which rivals rainforest species for furniture manufacture. Breeding experiments with the northern black wattle, *Acacia auriculiformis*, have produced a fast-growing variety which grows straight, producing timber of red-gold colour with interesting grain and with strength and durability similar to teak. The super acacia grows two or three times faster than teak, and because it is a legume with nitrogen-fixing root nodules it enriches the soil it grows in. Trials of the timber production are currently under way on Melville Island, involving the resident Tiwi community.

Other rainforest substitutes being researched are *Acacia aulocarpa* as a substitute for red cedar; *Acacia mangium* for pulpwood; and the quick-growing *Acacia crassicarpa* and *Eucalyptus pellita* for their rot-resistant characteristics. It is hoped that by breeding the best and fastest growing substitutes for rainforest timber, the time will come when furniture designers no longer import (or use local) rainforest timber. The trees also offer a promising new enterprise for northern Aboriginal communities.

Several forest types are 'endangered species' and remnants are particularly in need of conservation. In New South Wales and Queensland, for instance:

- The remnant **Gondwanan rainforests,** little changed in composition from the ancestral forests which evolved during the warm and wet Late Cretaceous and Early Tertiary, are unique, of enormous scientific importance, and require total protection. Large areas in north Queensland have World Heritage status and protection, and national parks protect some others.

- Most of the **lowland tropical rainforests** have disappeared to accommodate sugar production in northern Queensland.

- The **subtropical lowland forests** of northern New South Wales' river valleys, like the Clarence, which were the magnet for cedar-getters last century, have gone apart from small pockets like the Wingham Brush near Tarree. The cedar was 'cut out' on the Clarence by 1842. Clearing of forests in the Tweed Valley was also total and the dairy farms which replaced them have become more marginal over time. Now many are no longer viable and a plantation policy, in which State Forests is buying up weed-infested paddocks and planting eucalypts, is being implemented. Landowners can enter into joint venture deals with Forestry to turn parts of their properties into plantation forest.

- The **Big Scrub** which used to extend from the bend in the Richmond River between Lismore and Meerschaum Vale, through the hinterland between Ballina and Byron Bay and northwards to near Mullumbimby is now infertile, rolling grassland — it had been completely destroyed by 1900.

- The **wet sclerophyll forests of tall eucalypts,** like the mountain ash forests of Victoria, and of O'Sullivans Gap in New South Wales and elsewhere, have been decimated.

- **Littoral rainforest,** rich in palms, survives as a small protected patch at Port Macquarie.

- Remnant forests on the escarpment of the Southern Highlands near Robertson are **transitional between subtropical and temperate** types, and therefore unique. The Robertson Environmental Protection Society Inc. has produced a booklet on the **Yarrawa Brush** (funded by the *Save the Bush* grants program) and members are replanting rainforest trees, creating corridors between remnants where possible, and managing the forest remnants.

- ...the list is endless, with small fragments of **vine forests** surviving the relentless advance of development along the eastern seaboard.

Victoria, the smallest mainland State, has lost between 70% and 100% of its trees over most of its area; as has the winter rainfall agricultural region of South Australia. The tall eucalypt forests of south-western Western

Extent of clearing: ■ Intensive   ■ Moderate   ■ Minimal

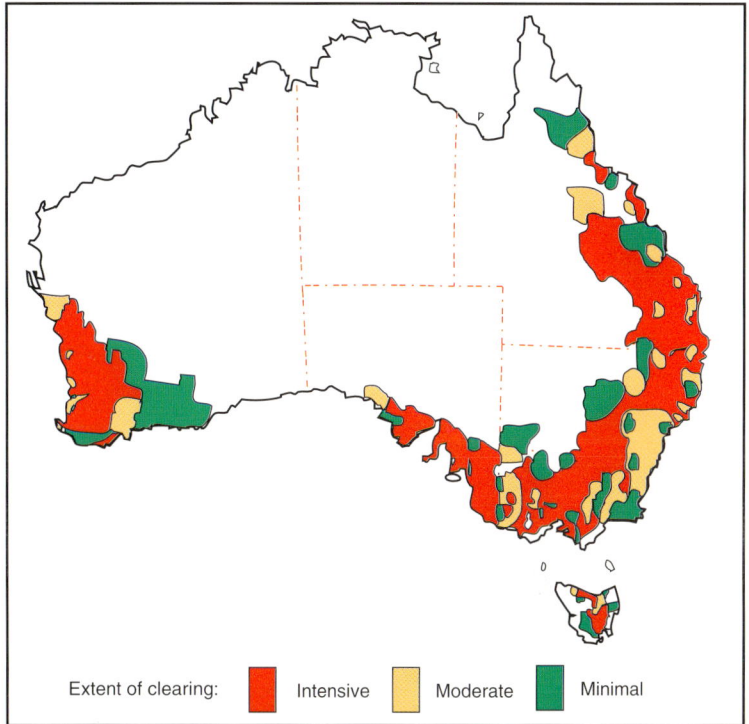

After Cocks[185]

Australia have greatly decreased in extent and die-back poses a serious threat to those remaining.

Tasmania, the Island State, with a cool temperate climate, was about three-quarters forested before settlement though Aboriginal burning had created button-grass plains around forests and along ridges, reducing the potential forest area. A great deal of forest has been cleared for agriculture and logging has been widespread. The Huon Pine forests have virtually disappeared from the Huon Valley and the timber is now so valuable that it is being 'mined' — logs which ended up buried in the mud as a result of the practice of floating logs down rivers have remained in perfect condition and are now being collected. Some major wilderness areas and forests remain in pristine condition, and are used here as an example to show what we must protect at all costs.

Above: A beautiful natural forest of eucalypts with an understorey of native broome, on the road from Robertson to Bowral, New South Wales.

M.E.W.

Above top: Buttress of a huge rainforest fig in the Wingham Brush, a small remnant of the original forest in the Manning River Valley.

Above: Palm forest in a remnant of littoral rainforest at Port Macquarie.
M.E.W.

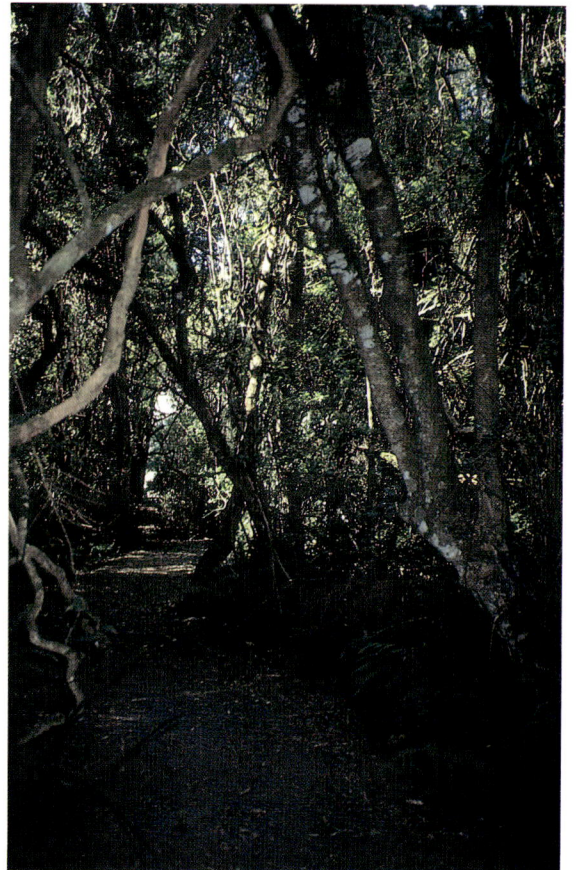

Right: A strangler fig beginning its destruction of its host in the littoral rainforest at Port Macquarie.

Far right: The Yarrawa Bush rainforest fragment at Robertson.

Below: Tall eucalypts in wet sclerophyll forest near Bulahdelah (O'Sullivans Gap).

Below right: Rainforest at O'Reillys in the Border Ranges.

M.E.W.

REMNANT RAINFORESTS

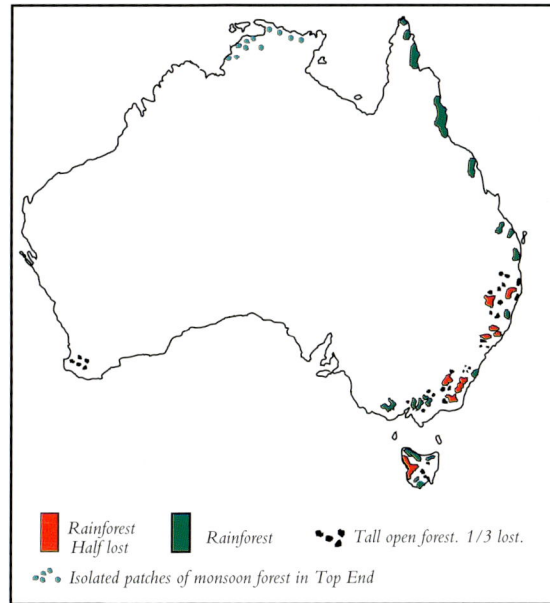

🟥 Rainforest Half lost	🟩 Rainforest	•▪• Tall open forest. 1/3 lost.
•ᵃ• Isolated patches of monsoon forest in Top End		

Far left: Cloud forest, lichen festooned, on Ebor volcano in northern NSW.

M.E.W.

TASMANIA'S FORESTS

Tasmania has the tallest forests in the Southern Hemisphere, some of the greatest remaining areas of pristine temperate rainforest and some of the world's oldest trees. An ancient huon pine, growing on Mt Read near Rosebery, is believed to be at least 10 500 years old. In only a few years from now these facts could make Tasmania unique and a mecca for ever more overseas tourists, scientists and Australians from other States. Yet Tasmania is a State torn apart by the logging–woodchipping–conservation debate. It exports more woodchips than all the other States put together. The industry has the two largest woodchip-export mills in Australia, the North Forest Products' mill at Hampshire, and the Boral mill at Longreach.

Over 90% of timber extracted from native forests is woodchipped, and only 5% of logged trees end up as sawn timber. (So much for the *only forest waste is chipped* nonsense!)

Private companies get the profits from cutting down public native forests, and it is usually Forestry Tasmania (the State, using public money) that has to replant the forests. The royalties paid by the companies fall far short of covering the costs of forest management, regrowth, and the infrastructure costs (roads, fire fighting, and cleaning up after the destruction). The **forests are being sold off at a loss** as evidenced by the Forestry Commission's $500 million debt, which was a significant contributor to the Tasmanian financial crisis of the early 1990s. Job losses attributable to woodchipping were estimated at 4000 by 1995. (So

much for the furphy about the industry providing jobs!)

On public land, and also on private land, over 70% of forests logged are clear-felled. This destroys whole habitats and most of the wildlife they support. The 'regenerated forests' cannot supply habitat to many of the creatures dislodged by the clear-felling. The soil erosion, siltation of streams and downstream effects of clear-felling are serious consequences. The method of burning the felled coupes to get rid of the mountains of 'unusable' wood (which ought to be the only fraction woodchipped) from the edges in towards the centre results in total slaughter of reptiles and other small animals and organisms — a scorched earth policy which completes the vandalism.

Tasmania has some of the world's largest remaining tracts of temperate wilderness. Destruction and logging of the tall forests of the south-west and the Tarkine is threatened or already occurring. Logging operations are penetrating up more of the untouched valleys. Experts agree that forests of World Heritage value are being destroyed, and that the integrity of the World Heritage sites themselves is being compromised.

Only 19% of Tasmanian forests is protected in reserves. This figure includes 34% of the rainforests, but only 15% of eucalypt forests. A further 5% are recommended for protection. However, even protection in National Parks is not a guarantee that the forests will remain protected. The case of forests in the **Hartz Mountains National Park**, east of the Picton River in the south-west illustrates this.

The Park was declared in 1939. In 1979, 2150 ha of forest were removed from the National Park. In 1989, the Labor-Green Accord said logging and building roads could not proceed in these forests, which had been assessed by experts as having high conservation values. But the Field Government ignored this and let the bulldozers into the Hartz forests. In 1993 the Federal Environment Minister was warned

Right: A clearfelled coupe in the Tarkine.

Below: Road through the Tarkine.

PETER SIMS

Picton River (where rafting companies take 4000 visitors a year); the Great Western Tiers and north-east highlands; in the middle of the Wielangta area on the east coast; on the Dempster Plains, Olympic Ridge and Netherby Plains in the Tarkine Wilderness; in the Weld Valley and on Brown Mountain near Ellendale; on the slopes of Wylds Craig; on the lower slopes of Ben Lomond and in the upper Mersey; in the central highlands; and in many other areas.

At a convention on Biodiversity in Rio de Janeiro in 1992, Australia and many other countries signed an agreement not to use rainforest timber. How then is rainforest timber woodchipped in Tasmania and sold for as little as $7.60 a tonne?

The Tarkine

The Tarkine was placed on the National Wilderness Register in 1995 by the Australian Heritage Commission as a significant temperate wilderness. The wilderness occupies 350 000 ha. Logging operations, including clear-felling, presently take place on the Tarkine Wilderness perimeter, close to the boundary as identified by the Interim Listing of the National Estate (May 1995). The boundary had to be modified as logging activities over the past four years have seriously degraded some significant high conservation areas which were originally recommended by the Wilderness Society in its World Heritage submission. These forest areas contain a high percentage of rainforest species, including *Nothofagus cunninghami*, myrtle beech, which is woodchipped and exported to Japan to make high quality fax paper among other things. A huge pile of myrtle woodchips is currently waiting (and rotting) on Burnie wharf.

that logging would threaten the World Heritage Area, yet woodchipping was approved. In 1995, the Prime Minister (Keating) said that his government would do *everything within its power* to protect 72 forests in Tasmania. Although the Hartz forests were on his list, destruction of the forest commenced, logging roads were built. A number of Labor members in the Tasmanian House of Representatives then lobbied the Federal Government to allow logging (and it is believed they threatened to resign from the Party if they were not heard) and on 30 March 1995, Cabinet agreed. The forests have been clear-felled.

The promise to protect 72 forests was reduced to two (!) in December 1995, and 42 areas on the list were released for logging, in addition to the hundreds of logging areas already approved. The casualties of that decision include forests along the

THE TARKINE WILDERNESS
AND THE ROAD WHICH VIOLATES IT

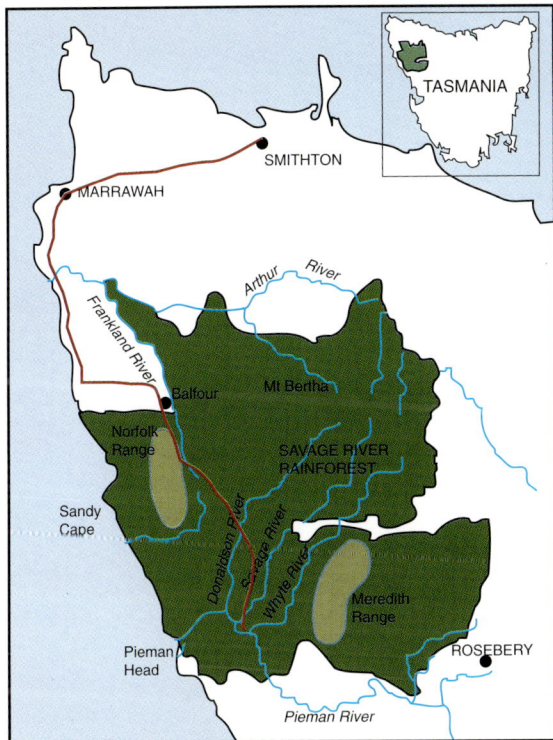

The Interim Listing provides no legislative protection and full assessment has been delayed until at least late 1997, because of a concerted campaign by the Forest (Industries) Protection Society and local communities that rely on jobs from forestry objecting to the Wilderness classification and the Listing.

A road, suitable for 4WDs, through the Tarkine Wilderness was completed and opened in January 1996. Its construction was contested every bit of the way, both legally, as the project did not meet planning requirements, and through 35 separate actions involving 1000 protesters (and 100 arrests). The Australian Heritage Commission protested that the road: *would reduce the wilderness value of a substantial portion of the Mount Vero–Tarkine Wilderness area as well as dividing a large contiguous area of high wilderness value in two.* It would also allow the spread of wildfires, weeds, feral animals and diseases such as die-back fungus, into an untouched area. (Fires caused by Forestry burnt out

10 000 ha of Tarkine heath and woodland in 1988 and devastated more than 5000 ha of forest and heath in 1995.)

The road is: *a great white scar ripped across the exposed ridges of open moorlands, and giant slashes through the former grand rainforests in the river gorges* according to the Tarkine Pamphlet produced by the Wilderness Society and the Tarkine National Coalition. The Donaldson River, one of the few Australian rivers whose catchments had not been violated, has now had its valley opened up by the road, and land slippage, tree falls, serious erosion and peoples' rubbish have come to this recently pristine area.

The purpose of the road, according to the government, is to enable 10 to 15 tourist vehicles a day; its cost, including the roads linking the wilderness track to Smithton, $35 million; its perceived real purpose to open the area up for logging and mining.

The Tasmanian Wilderness Society and the Tarkine National Coalition are actively campaigning to protect the Tarkine. Every Australian who appreciates the heritage value of forests and wilderness and wants future generations to have access to them can support the campaigns to persuade government that the area has to become a fully protected National Park with World Heritage status without delay. To sell the forests off as woodchips, which amounts to exploitation by a foreign nation, is treason.

THE AUSTRALIAN
BUSH HERITAGE FUND

Buying Back the Bush

Bush Heritage is a non-profit organisation, registered nationally, whose sole aim is to acquire and manage private land of outstanding conservation significance. Much of the habitat of Australia's unique flora and fauna is on privately owned land, outside national parks or reserves, unprotected and increasingly threatened by the expansion of human activities. Sometimes the only way to protect the natural value of such land is to buy

Above left: Massive clear-felling operations push deeper into Tasmania's famed south-west wilderness in the Huon Valley, adversely affecting the integrity of the adjacent World Heritage Area.

Above right: Clearfelling in the Picton Valley, adjacent to a World Heritage Area.

G. LAW

Above: The Savage River Mine's pipeline track cuts a scar across Australia's largest temperate rainforest.

G. LAW

Above top right: Myrtle Beech woodchips on Burnie Wharf, July 1996. Some of the mountains of chips were kept waiting for so long for a ship that they were reported to be unsuitable for export to Japan, their fate instead to be boiler fuel.

LYLE RUBOCK

Above right: The so-called tourist road (which carries three or four cars per day in winter) has violated the Donaldson River wilderness rainforest.

PETER SIMS

Right: A loaded log train at Wiltshire Junction, loaded with old-growth forest logs from the Tarkine area. Such trains run six days a week, taking logs to Boral's chip mill at Longreach (on the Tamar). The chips are exported to Japan.

LYLE RUBOCK

Below right: The Savage River iron-ore mine has destroyed and blighted a large area of the largest temperate rainforest remaining in the Southern Hemisphere. Will the Tarkine road allow this sort of destruction to occur in other places in the pristine Tarkine Wilderness?

G. LAW

Above: Rainforest of myrtle beech and blackwood clear-felled for woodchips at Horton Loop in the Tarkine. The Rio Agreement of 1992, signed by Australia, prohibits the commercial use of rainforest timbers.

LYLE RUBOCK

Above right: The old-growth eucalypt in the foreground has been felled to provide access to myrtle beech rainforest in the Tarkine which is to be clear-felled for woodchipping.

ARNOLD ROWLANDS

Right: Rainforest bordering the Tarkine area, clear-felled and massive amounts of timber burnt. The myrtle beech forest adjacent to the clear-felling burnt as well.

PETER SIMS

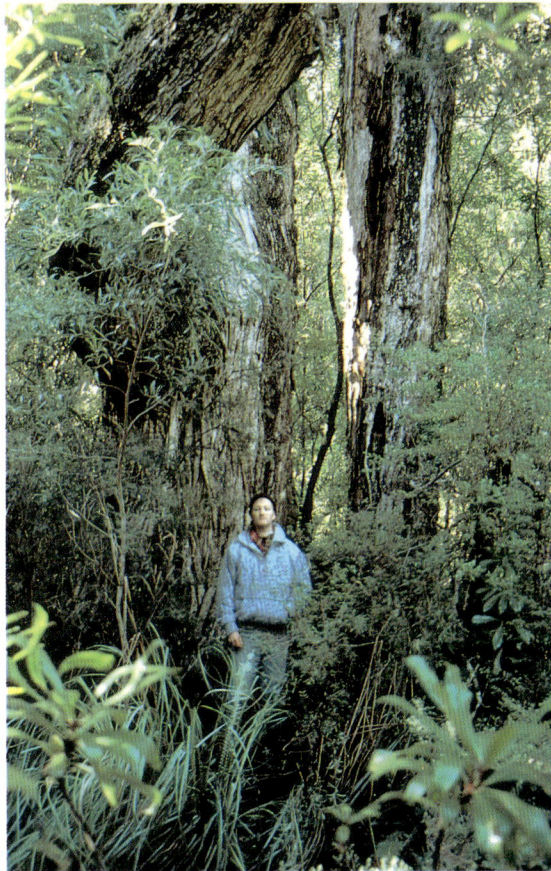

Far left: The residue of logging of a myrtle beech rainforest wasted on the forest floor. This waste timber should be the only material being woodchipped when rainforest timber is felled. Myrtle beech is a magnificent timber for cabinet making.

Left: An ancient Huon pine (over 3000 years old) in the Tarkine Wilderness. Such ancient trees are not protected.

PETER SIMS

Right: Lowland redgum forest in the Brogo property, a remnant in the Bega Valley.

GREG BLAKE

Below: The Liffey Valley, site of Bush Heritage's first purchase, has beautiful forest, rivers and waterfalls.

JIM FRAZIER

it. The **Australian Bush Heritage Fund** was set up to do just that.[186,187]

The fund was established in 1990 to save 241 ha of threatened **forest in the Liffey Valley** on the edge of the Great Western Tiers in northern **Tasmania**. The land, which adjoins the Tasmanian Wilderness World Heritage Area, was up for auction, the forest destined for woodchips. Dr Bob Brown used the money he had just received as the Goldman Environmental Prize (USA), borrowed from a bank and from private individuals, and secured the land. Friends and associates rallied to support his effort and the fund was established. It is funded by tax-deductible donations and is modelled broadly on the United States' *Nature Conservancy,* the largest private, non-profit owner of nature reserves in the world.

Bush Heritage is doing on a national scale what many small groups of concerned citizens, and some individuals, are doing to protect important blocks of land. In New South Wales alone, National Parks and Wildlife has hundreds of important blocks on its priority list, but government money will never be available to secure all or even many of them, nor will they have the resources to manage them. Therefore, to a large extent, it is up to 'people power' to achieve the conservation of Australia's biodiversity, by achieving a change in attitude (as in Landcare initiatives) from expecting the government to do things, to finding ways of doing them ourselves.

Bush Heritage is governed by a Board of Directors, with a panel composed of prominent academics to oversee land selection and management. The organisation is receiving growing support, from overseas as well as from Australians. Even in 1993–94, when many other environmental and community organisations were feeling the pinch, Bush Heritage's income doubled. It is one way that concerned citizens can do something positive for the environment, confident that scientific and financial management of the organisation are such that their contribution will not be wasted and what they are doing is protecting biodiversity as well as the amenity of wonderful, pristine areas of our world.

(This love of nature, expressed in positive action, is, as I see it, the new 'religion' essential for the maintenance of Gaia, the Living Planet, provider of the life-support systems on which our very survival depends.)

The purchase of the forest in the Liffey Valley ensures safe refuge for 60 bird species, including several Tasmanian endemics. The swift parrot, which breeds only in Tasmania and which is endangered is just one of the many species, which include six raptors, which will benefit.

In 1993, Bush Heritage made its second purchase — this time 8.17 ha in the **Palm Road** area north of the **Daintree River in Queensland,** an area famous for its beautiful fan palms *(Licuala ramsayii),* adjoining the World Heritage Area. The cassowary is the most visible beneficiary in this purchase. This bird is now a Permanently Protected Species, which has shown from a CSIRO survey to be reduced to only 54 adults in the Daintree Lowlands, and threatened by dogs, feral pigs, speeding vehicles and habitat destruction. The cassowary's diet is mainly fleshy fruit, and it is a vitally important distributor of seeds for more than 100 rainforest tree species. For seeds to germinate in rainforest they need to be deposited in areas away from the parent tree in order to have light and space to grow. Thus cassowaries are essential in the tropical rainforest ecosystem, being the only dispersers of some large-fruited trees.

In 1995 the fund acquired 120 ha of land comprising one of the largest and best preserved areas of native bushland remaining in the heavily cleared **Bega Valley in New South Wales**. Situated on the **Brogo River,** north-west of Bega, it comprises undulating land sloping down to the river with its old sheoaks and pockets of dry rainforest. Only between 5% and 6% of this productive farming region retains its natural vegetation, mainly as very small, isolated patches. The large-enough-to-remain-viable remnant of lowland redgum grassy woodland with remnant pockets of forest purchased by the fund is a vital refuge for native flora and fauna, including the rare powerful owl.

Very little of this sort of ecosystem remains intact after 200 years of settlement, and several of the plant species and communities represented are at the southernmost limits of their geographical distribution. The lowland redgum *(Eucalyptus tereticornis)* grassy woodland ecosystem is considered to be of national importance, and only very small areas of this vegetation type are represented in other reserves. Remnants of the once widespread Bega Valley dry rainforests, rich in Port Jackson Figs, have survived in the fund area because the granite boulders have protected them from the fires which were used to clear vegetation as agriculture advanced. Rock orchids are abundant. Sugar gliders, wallabies, possums, wombats, echidnas, bandicoots, lace monitors, eastern grey kangaroos, platypus and water dragons, and at least 45 species of birds live in this refuge.

The 1996 purchase by the fund is of 333 ha of remnant native vegetation on land near **Kojonup in Western Australia** (in the southern part of the Upper Middle catchment zone of the Blackwood River Catchment, see Chapter 5). The block lies in the transition zone between the wheat belt and the south-western forests. The surrounding area has been extensively cleared. The vegetation is wandoo woodland dominated by *Eucalyptus wandoo,* an endemic Western Australian species, with many other endemics as understorey. The vegetation on the block is in good to very good condition. It is adjacent to an established nature reserve and thus extends the area of protection for flora and fauna.

The wandoo is very important for the survival of various vertebrate species, being a tree which forms nesting hollows, and locally the only species which does

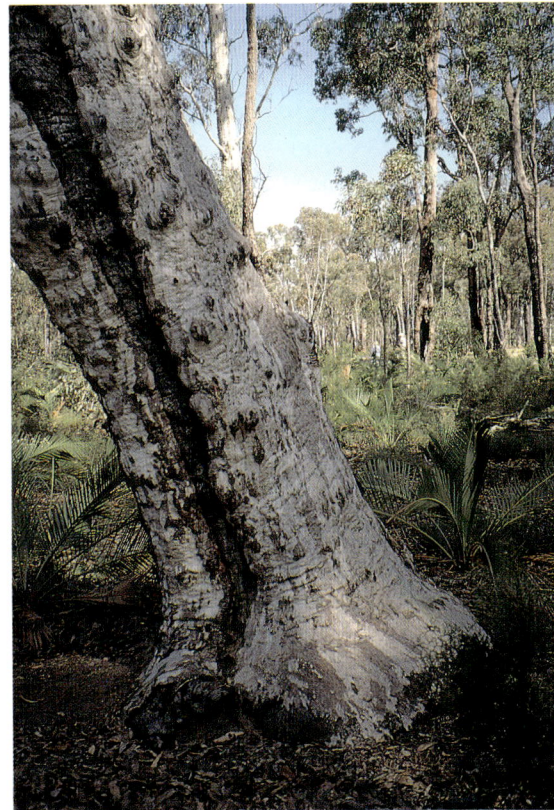

Far left: Fan palms in the Daintree where Bush Heritage has purchased land on Palm Road.

JIM FRAZIER

Left: Wandoo woodland is the main ecosystem on the Kojonup property acquired by Bush Heritage in Western Australia. Eucalyptus wandoo has wonderful white, grey-flecked trunks, and old trees have hollows suitable for nesting holes.

M.E.W.

Waratahs, grown for export, on Mt Murray near Robertson.

M.E.W.

so to any extent. The competition for nesting sites limits the ability of many species to breed, and areas without nesting trees are devoid of the animals which need hollow trees. The block is potential habitat for 80 species of birds, 44 of which were observed in the brief survey so far carried out, including five rare species — the peregrine falcon, the barking owl, Carnaby's black cockatoo, the freckled duck and the crested shrike-tit. It is potential habitat for the numbat (now being returned after captive breeding to the Dryandra Forest), the brushtail bettong and the red-tailed wambenger, three species classified as nationally endangered. It offers refuge to the honey possum, the brush wallaby, the western pygmy possum, the mardo, the common dunnart, the southern brown bandicoot and several species of bats; as well as 25 species of reptiles, including the carpet python which is rare in Western Australia, and four species of frogs.

Bush Heritage's approach is, like Landcare, about community involvement. Their Land Management Officer organises local committees of volunteers and coordinates planning and management at each location. The aim is preservation of natural values while allowing access for educational purposes, and so that donors can see 'their' protected land. The Daintree management committee works with the assistance of the Daintree Rainforest Foundation. At Liffey the management committee consists of local residents and landowners. It works in consultation with government agencies managing the Tasmanian Wilderness World Heritage Area and the Liffey Falls State Reserve. The fund forests at Liffey and Daintree require little intervention to maintain their natural state, but the Brogo property is surrounded by grazing land, frequented by feral animals and liable to weed invasion and other degrading forces and its bushland management and protection is being planned. A committee of local experts, neighbours and other interested people is being formed. The Western Australian property, just acquired, is in the process of being assessed.

Bush Heritage is a shining example of putting into practice 'what *we* can do for the country we love' instead of complaining that '*they* (the government)

ought to do something about preserving our heritage'.

(The contact address for the Australian Bush Heritage Fund is GPO Box 101, Hobart 7001.)

THE SOCIETY FOR GROWING AUSTRALIAN PLANTS (SGAP)

Each State has an SGAP branch, with many local groups, whose members are dedicated to growing native plants in their gardens; propagating them for distribution to others; building up numbers of rare and endangered species; educating their members and the general public by lectures, conferences and botanical ecotours; and becoming involved in projects to save the bush, preserve the forests and regenerate degraded natural vegetation in their vicinities. With water a commodity increasingly under pressure as the urban spread continues in the better-watered parts of the continent where most Australians live, and always a limiting factor in the arid 75% of the land, it makes sense to have gardens adapted to water-saving and the inevitable droughts. Native plant nurseries, and a whole horticultural industry involved in breeding new varieties, promoting them and also supplying the cut flower industry, are all part of a booming sector of the economy. A large and expanding export industry in cut flowers and Australian plants has developed.

Members of SGAP who are botanically minded and want to be more involved in the scientific and research issues can join study groups and specialise in genera of their choice (like *Acacia, Banksia, Grevillea*) or in grasses, or rainforest trees, or Australian food plants. The society produces a beautifully illustrated periodical, *Australian Plants;* publishes books on native plants; and has a library service for members of local groups.

An example of a major SGAP project which now involves a number of other organisations and groups is the **Opossum Creek–Springfield Project** at Goodna in Queensland.[188] The Ipswich Branch of SGAP and the Springfield Land Corporation, who are developing a satellite city for an expected 60 000 people, are working together to preserve, rehabilitate and expand remnant vegetation. Opossum, Woogaroo and Mountain Creeks are major drainage lines within the Springfield development. A fringing rainforest known as the **Woogaroo or Goodna Scrub** once extended from the Brisbane River at Goodna upstream for about 6 km, according to a survey map dated 1869. Red cedar *(Toona australis),* black bean *(Castanospermum australe),* native frangipani *(Hymenosporum flavum),* rose satinash *(Syzygium francisii)* and a host of other wonderful trees like lillipillis, figs and silky oaks *(Grevillea robusta)* were components of the riverine rainforest of the moist alluvial loams. The hoop pine scrub *(Araucaria cunninghamii)* of the drier and less fertile sites was a rich assemblage including kamala *(Mallotus phillipensis),* yellow tulip *(Drypetes australasica),* hard quandong *(Elaeocarpus obovatus)*, cheese tree *(Glochidion ferdinandi)* and many others, with a diversity of woody vines.

The spread of settlement in the Brisbane River valley resulted in the elimination of most of the forest. The Goodna region, between Brisbane and Ipswich, was rapidly cleared as the cities expanded. Timber from the region was shipped from a wharf at Goodna according to the *Queensland Times* of 1878, downstream to Brisbane, upstream to Ipswich. The remnants in gullies and fringing the floodplains of the creeks, and patches on rocky sandstone outcrops, have since been selectively logged, removing most of the valuable timber trees. Disturbance by logging and clearing around remnants has resulted in major problems of weed invasion by trees such as camphor laurel *(Cinnamomum camphora)* and Chinese elm *(Celtis sinensis)*; by lantana *(Lantana camara)*; and by numerous herbaceous weeds.

More than 200 native species, mostly of the riverine forest assemblage, have been identified in the largest, Opossum Creek, remnant which is a main focus of the SGAP–Springfield program. Several rare and endangered endemic species have been found. Considering the rarity of any remnants of vine forests on sandstone outcrops, and the almost complete elimination of the riverine rainforests in the area, the work being done is of great significance and importance. It involves preservation of wildlife corridors between forest remnants and development of greenbelts which will add greatly to the amenity of the satellite city.

As is so often the case in conservation exercises, it was largely the passion and enthusiasm of one person, in this case Lloyd Bird, an amateur botanist–ex-miner–conservationist, which started the fight to save the bush he loves. The Springfield Corporation supplied funds for access roads and continues with financial support. Most work is carried out by volunteers from the many groups now involved. These are the Ipswich SGAP, which has received a Landcare grant of $21 000 over three years; the Ipswich Shire Council; Nature Search 2001; the Moreton area Scouts; the Claremont Special School and the Australian Trust for Conservation Volunteers. (The ATCV involves international visitors who wish to make a contribution to environmental improvement, working with unemployed youth from Brisbane and Ipswich who want to do something more positive than passively accepting the dole and who register with LEAP, the Landcare and Environmental Action Program.) The Redbank Plains High School students are propagating plants from material gathered during field trips to Opossum Creek, and their plants are used in replanting areas from which lantana and other feral plants have been removed.

Projects like this demonstrate how much can be achieved by local people when they become aware of conservation issues in their region to which they can relate. It is such grass-roots efforts and achievements that give us hope that our grandchildren will have forests to enjoy and will understand their value.

WORLD WIDE FUND FOR NATURE AUSTRALIA

(Formerly World Wildlife Fund)

The World Wide Fund For Nature Australia is currently involved in the **WWF South-East Queensland Vineforests Project**. It funded a publication, *Vineforest Atlas of South-East Queensland,* which describes the distribution and conservation status of vineforest plants throughout the region. Its new project aims to raise awareness of vineforest conservation issues, and to assist landholders and land managers with the conservation of significant vineforests. The successful 'Woogaroo Scrub' project described in the Opossum Creek–Springfield Project serves as a successful model of what the WWF project aims to achieve.

The project will see WWF working with landholders to protect and manage remnant scrub on their privately owned land, without compromising any of their rights. WWF believes they should be rewarded financially for keeping and managing their scrub, and assisted in overcoming major problems like weed infestations and feral animals. Councils and the State and Federal Governments will be asked to contribute to the financial incentives. The Queensland Department of Environment and the Queensland Department of Natural Resources are already helping the project by providing WWF's Vineforest Liason Officer with office facilities, mapping facilities and transport. WWF will assist individual property owners and landholder groups, like Landcare Groups, with management issues using funding from donations, corporate sponsorship or government grants. A series of demonstration projects is being established to show landholders how WWF can assist them.

Property owners who want to give their scrub long-term protection can enter into a voluntary **Nature Refuge Agreement** with the State Government. The WWF will seek funds to assist with the preparation of the agreement. The **Berlin Scrub in the Lockyer Valley** is being established as a demonstration project. Its owner, Dick Scanlan, is a Lockyer Landcare member. He has signed a Nature Refuge Agreement and WWF plans to assist him by constructing a 4WD track, fencing an area of scrub and starting weed control in the fenced-off area. The work is to be carried out jointly with Lockyer

THE AUSTRALIAN FLORA FOUNDATION

This foundation is an independent, national organisation which was set up to foster research into the biology and cultivation of Australian plants. The main aim of the research is conservation, through studying endangered plants, the cultivation of native plants in wildflower farms and plantations to replace bush harvesting, and investigating regeneration in pastoral areas and the viability of reserves. The Foundation raises funds for research (donations, bequests and government grants) for which researchers apply. Projects are assessed by the Foundation's Scientific Research Committee. A student prize is awarded annually to encourage young scientists to study Australian plants. The Foundation can be contacted through GPO Box 205, Sydney 2001.

ANGLESEA, AIREYS INLET SOCIETY FOR THE PROTECTION OF FLORA AND FAUNA (ANGAIR INC.)

This society was formed in 1968 in an effort to preserve the native flora and fauna in this beautiful coastal region of Victoria. A local schoolteacher, Edith Lawn, founded the society and one of its leading members, until her death in April 1996, was Mary D. White (sometimes confused with the author of this book) who will be sadly missed.

The society is involved in freeing the area of introduced weed species which have invaded the heathlands and coastal areas. Every Monday morning, except for one Monday a month when community walks are arranged, members meet and about a dozen regularly tackle weeds. An annual weed week sees many more members participating in the removal of boneseed, sollya, coastal tea tree, coastal wattle, Spanish heath and other invasive weeds. The group's nature walks give people an appreciation of the beauty of the area, and knowledge of its biota and its problems.

ANGAIR also works with the community to encourage the planting of indigenous trees, shrubs and grasses. Their present projects involve working with Victoria Roads and Barwon Water on plantings near the town centre and around the Barwon Water Pumping Station. They are also working with Alcoa Australia and the Department of Natural Resources and the Environment in supporting the Anglesea Primary School in revegetating a large gravel pit. This has turned out to be an exciting and rewarding project and valuable in teaching children about nature and conservation.

The society has collaborated with Deakin University, the Geelong Environmental Council, Department of Natural Resources and Environment, the Surf Coast Shire and Alcoa in formulating a management plan for Alcoa lease land; it has published books on wildflowers and coastal vegetation (written by Mary D. White); has an annual Wildflower and Art Show in September; members are working to restore the original dam at the Ironbark Basin to provide water for birdlife in the area; and the group has acquired public land for the community, including 'O'Donohue's' at Anglesea which will soon become part of the Angahook-Lorne Forest Park.

ANGAIR is another example of a voluntary group and individuals who have taken responsibility for *their* environment and are protecting and enhancing the things which they value. Members find great satisfaction in their achievements and pleasure in the friendship and community spirit which results from their activities.

Top right: Anglesea Primary School children working in the disused gravel pit, which they are rehabilitating and planting with native plants.

Above right: Pultenaea mollis, the gold or soft bush pea, with creamy yellow myrtle wattle (Acacia myrtifolia) and the white-flowered cypress daisy bush (Olearia teretifolia) in the heathland which is looked after by members of ANGAIR.

Right: Stackhousia monogyna, creamy candles, a beautiful wildflower of the coastal heathland at Anglesea.

MARGARET MACDONALD

Landcare and the Lockyer Watershed Management Association Inc.

Mr Scanlan has written an account of how he came to establish his nature refuge, and he reflects on the changes which the Lockyer Valley has undergone through time and also on his changed attitude to land management — from axeman to conservationist.

The valley was forested when the early settlers selected land in the 1880s and 1890s. At that time 80% of the forest was eucalypt and the remainder was 'softwood scrub' (vineforest) mainly on the hills to the south of the valley. The settlers ring-barked the forest eucalypts, but the scrubs were felled by axe, fired and grassed, giving good pasture for beef and dairy cattle. Mr Scanlan used to listen to his father's stories of his days as an axeman and dreamed of one day owning land in the valley and felling the scrub like his father had done. Not much of the scrub was left by the time that he acquired his 180 ha in 1950, but the land he bought was mostly vineforest-covered, with a small amount of brigalow. During the next 15 years, with some help, the forest was felled, leaving only 28 ha untouched, and lantana was spreading. By 1970, soil erosion and landslip were problems and it was obvious that land clearing had caused serious degradation.

Mr Scanlan's later involvement with the Lockyer Watershed Management Association, concerned with soil conservation, water quality, pasture improvement and restoration of natural vegetation, completely changed his attitudes to land management. The LWMA were interested in the 28 ha of virgin scrub remaining on his land and in other patches in the valley. A 'Remnant Vegetation Sub-committee' was established. In 1992 the Nature Conservation Act was passed, enabling 'Nature Refuge' conservation agreements with landholders to be drawn up by the Department of Environment and Heritage. The agreements are legally binding and protect flora and fauna in perpetuity, but the landholder retains ownership of the property. When an application is made for such an agreement, the scrub (or other vegetation to be protected) is assessed to establish if its ecological value is suitable.

In Mr Scanlan's case, 45 ha was to become the refuge, containing the virgin scrub. Boundaries were agreed and the name **Berlin Scrub** decided upon. The agreement requires that reasonable efforts be made to prevent spread of weeds or invasion by feral animals; certain animals, including some cattle, may be allowed to enter in certain situations; special interest groups, with the landholders permission, can have access to the land for nature-based recreation; no trees may be removed but fallen branches can be taken for domestic firewood, excluding hollow logs and limbs; only local indigenous trees may be planted; no trail bikes or 4WDs are allowed in the scrub.

The Berlin Scrub Refuge shows others how they may protect important ecosystems on their properties in perpetuity.

Also in the Lockyer Valley, an **'activity trail'** has been established. Called **'A Touch of Paradise'** it takes tour groups through remnant brigalow–vineforest scrub on a private property owned by Rob and Bonnie Bauer. The trail and an accompanying booklet have been produced by Lockyer Landcare (the Lockyer Watershed Management Association) funded by the National Landcare Program, 1994. Guided tours are available by prior arrangement as part of the **Catchment Care Education Project** which aims to give as many people as possible a better understanding of the need for all of us *to look after our own patch,* no matter how big or how small.

THE 'EARTH SANCTUARY' PROJECTS OF JOHN WAMSLEY

John Wamsley is fanatical about the elimination of feral animals, particularly cats and foxes. His fanaticism and the public image he often presents of an angry man full of hate has tended to obscure his **enormous contribution to conservation, to breeding rare and endangered species, and to promoting public ownership of environmentally significant areas where native animals are protected from competition with, and predation by, ferals.** The fact that most of the shares in Earth Sanctuary are owned by the Wamsleys (10 million of the 14 million shares) is another perceived disadvantage for many conservationists and for governments uneasy at the buying power which aims to spend $20 million a year purchasing ecologically significant land. (Australia is famous for cutting down its tall poppies.)

The concept of the sanctuaries is simple. The land is bought, special fencing which defeats the efforts of feral animals to enter is constructed at $20 000 per kilometre, and feral animals are eradicated from inside the sanctuary. Then locally extinct or endangered animals are re-introduced and can multiply in safety. (Some purist conservationists object to the introduction of species to areas in which they are not native. Perhaps they should look back in time to a green and largely forested land, which was Australia when it became an island continent, and see today's faunal distribution in a longer perspective. As the continent dried with the approach of the Pleistocene ice age, distribution of species changed. Today's distribution is the product of the intense drying of the continent which took place in the Pleistocene, particularly during the last glacial stage. Many animals now restricted to small ranges are living in what amounts to refugia, and if other, man-made, refugia are provided they may be saved from extinction.)

Extinction is permanent. Surely saving species from extinction is the first imperative, and if it depends on an animal having a safe place to breed then John Wamsley cannot be criticised. As to his attitude to cats, which has confronted and upset a lot of people who love and respect domestic cats, (and I am a cat person and some of my best friends and companions are cats), when the magnitide of the feral cat problem is understood his crusade to eradicate cats becomes less unreasonable.

Earth Sanctuary's properties are:

- the **Warrawong Sanctuary** near Adelaide, where platypus breed and brush-tailed bettongs, long-nosed potoroos and the southern brown bandicoot are thriving.
- **Yookamurra** in the Murray Mallee, 2774 ha, the largest feral-free area in mainland Australia, with populations of numbats, sticknest rats, bilbies, boodies (kangaroo rats) and woylies (burrowing bettongs).
- **Scotia Sanctuary** in the far west of New South Wales near Wentworth, 650 km^2 containing some of the least disturbed land which still survives in the Western Division.
- **Buckaringa** in the Flinders Ranges, where the largest wild populations of the yellow-footed wallaby exist.
- **Tiparra**, 1000 ha on the Yorke Peninsula in South Australia, where it is proposed to fence off 20 km of coast.

URBAN BUSHLAND RESTORATION

As an example of the sort of project in which city people can participate, the following account of activities in a Sydney suburb has been supplied by Alfred Bernhard, Bushland Manager for the Willoughby City Council.

Flat Rock Gully, a once-pristine valley with waterfalls, between Northbridge and Naremburn on Sydney's Lower North Shore, is a site which incorporates all the elements for a worst-case scenario of environmental degradation. It was used as a rubbish tip over a 50-year period, with landfill continuing as late as the 1980s. Major despoilation of the gully occurred, involving loss of flora and fauna; contamination of the creekline with fill and leachate; stormwater runoff carrying pollutants from the highly urbanised catchment which has a significant industrial area; and sewer overflows polluting the watercourses and increasing soil nutrient levels, resulting in proliferation of weeds such as privet and lantana.

The rubbish tip embankment and other areas of physical disturbance have been inundated with weeds, many of which have spread to adjacent bushland. The tree canopy in many places is smothered with morning glory, balloon vine or Madiera vine. Absence of fire for long periods has resulted in senescence and a lack of regeneration of some species, as well as favouring soft-leaved species such as *Pittosporum undulatum*.

Members of the local community had worked to redress some of these issues over the years, but it was not until 1994 that a detailed plan of management was prepared. After lengthy public consultation the plan was adopted by Willoughby Council in 1996. In adjacent areas, at Pyalla Street and Cliff Avenue, dedicated groups of residents have been working as part of council's Bushcare Volunteer Program in order to regenerate bushland sites.

Since the adoption of the plan of management, major initiatives in rehabilitation have commenced, including the establishment of a contract for bush regeneration work and a training program for the local unemployed, also focused on bushland rehabilitation. As part of this program, initial priorities have included the control of invasive vines; manual and mechanical removal of noxious weeds such as pampas grass and blackberry; and selective poisoning of camphor laurel and privet using glyphosate. Mosaic clearing has been carried out to avoid undue disruption to habitat, and fauna surveys and water quality monitoring have begun.

Access tracks have been constructed or maintained, facilitating work in new areas, and these will form the basis of interpretive walks based on natural and historical features. (Old sandstone walls, ruins of huts and a cave said to be where Henry Lawson slept when he was too drunk to walk home, are part of the history of the valley where orchards were planted in the early days.)

Participants in the New Work Opportunities program for local unemployed people, receiving Certificates of Attainment from the Mayor of Willoughby, Councillor Eunice Raymond, following a six-month training period.

ALFRED BERNHARD

Rehabilitation of the former rubbish tip site will create a park for passive recreation, complementing the sporting facilities nearby.

ALFRED BERNHARD

On the rubbish tip fill platform, the re-contouring of the mounds of rubble and construction fill has formed the basis for a new park with a bushland character. Several thousand plants have been propagated from seed collected in adjacent bushland and these will ultimately form part of the green link along the whole Flat Rock Creek catchment. The walking tracks will be part of the regional connection from Artarmon to the Middle Harbour foreshore. Ongoing bushland management work must be linked to principles of total catchment management (particularly as this small catchment is part of the larger Middle Harbour catchment). Improvements in water quality, control of gross pollutants such as plastics and polystyrene must be addressed urgently, to enhance the creek ecosystem. The physical work of weed control and other management processes is to be complemented by a program of public education about the need to control domestic pets; control noxious weeds and create bush-friendly gardens; and to cease dumping garden waste in bushland. The bushland which will be managed in the area is an asset of inestimable value.

Flat Rock Gully is an example of the sort of restoration work being initiated in many reserves and patches of remnant bush within local government areas in Sydney and other cities and towns. Councils can supply information to would-be participants about projects in their areas; Landcare groups, environment centres and many societies, clubs and other environmentally oriented groups can also direct and advise anyone interested in helping.

CHAPTER FIFTEEN

COASTAL AND MARINE ENVIRONMENTS AND THE EASTERN GREEN CRESCENT

THE COASTAL ZONE

For the purposes of this book, the environments and ecosystems which have been described are terrestrial and the vast area of sea under Australia's control is outside its focus and can only receive brief mention. A major **State of the Marine Environment Report (SOMER) was produced in 1995 as part of the Ocean Rescue 2000 Program,**[189] forming part of the overall national **State of the Environment Report (SOE '96)** released in September 1996.[190] It provides a readable and comprehensive assessment of the marine environment. The information in the SOMER report is intended to form a basis for the **Australian Marine Conservation Plan,** a Commonwealth initiative to achieve sustainable use and development of Australia's seas and coastal zone.[191]

A quarter of Australia's population lives within 3 km of the sea, and two-thirds reside in our coastal cities and towns, which underlines the nature of our dry continent — only the fringes, particularly the eastern margin, where a disproportionate number of Australians are concentrated, are uniformly fairly green and inviting. The impact of humans on the fragile coastal environments, the urban sprawl which engulfs coastal wetlands, mangrove swamps and fertile floodplains at river mouths, is concentrated around population centres, so a great deal of the coastal fringe is in relatively untouched condition.

Little, however, is completely unaffected by human impact, direct or indirect, even far away from the major cities and towns and their sprawl. The networks of coastal roads, with their drainage; farms with altered land-use and tree clearing affecting the water balance; the spread of feral plants like boneseed changing dune ecology; physical damage to fragile dune systems by recreational vehicles — all expand the areas suffering direct change. Even in remote and apparently untouched regions, the coastal fringe is affected if its river catchments are degraded. Feral animals are everywhere on the land, including in remote coastal environments where stock may not be officially grazing; the degradation of catchments by grazing of fragile ecosystems affects rivers; and rivers carry sediment into the sea, changing the conditions on the continental shelf and posing threats to coral reefs and other marine life. The effects of high sediment levels in water are reduction of light penetration, which affects photosynthesis, and the smothering of seabed organisms. High levels of nutrients are often carried with the sediments, and these increase the likelihood of algal blooms, some of which are toxic. Estuaries and coastal wetlands and lakes are particularly vulnerable. The pollution from chemicals and fertilisers can be concentrated in them before it eventually reaches the marine environment.

The **regulation of rivers** affects the amount of water reaching the sea, the build-up of nutrients in them when there is insufficient water to flush them out, and the timing of their cycles (which may be tied to fish breeding cycles). The sea has its own feral invaders, the introduced marine fauna and flora, mainly brought in ballast water by ships, which spread and compete with the native biota.

Dawn on a stony beach near Forster, New South Wales.

M.E.W.

The ocean which surrounds Australia, like the continent it encircles, is infertile. The overall infertility of our dry and time-worn land provides low-fertility run-off to the sea, and there are no major upwellings of nutrient-rich deep water in the region. The relatively low fisheries production is tied to this infertility — the seas, like the land, have most of their more fertile areas round the margins and most is very lightly populated considering the volume of water involved. Even the ENSO climatic fluctuations, which affect the productivity of the land, affect the productivity of the sea. Diminished run-off in major droughts causes 'drought' in the estuaries and decreased productivity.

Of the **estuaries** which were studied for SOMER, 64% in New South Wales and 22% in Victoria were considered to have poor water quality. Catchments in the tropical north are less affected by human activities, but may carry heavy sediment loads as a result of soil erosion, like the Ord and Fitzroy Rivers for instance, where over-grazing of river frontages has destabilised the land. Poor water quality and loss of habitat have caused a decline in estuarine fisheries, which are thought to be threatened in 21% of estuaries in New South Wales, and in 23% in Victoria. However, the increased nutrient levels in some estuaries has enhanced their value for oyster farming. (On the down side, the Georges River oyster industry has been destroyed by an introduced virus QX, Queensland Unknown, which fortunately has not yet spread to the Botany Bay oyster leases; in September 1996, Tweed River oysters were contaminated and produced an outbreak of gastroenteritis when their water was enriched with faecal bacteria as well as nutrients.)

The **temperate seagrass beds** are under particular threat. Their massive dieback in many areas is linked to the increased sediment and nutrients which comes from degraded catchments. They are ecologically important because of their high productivity, their ability to trap and stabilise sediments, their importance as fisheries habitats and breeding grounds, and their habitat for turtles and dugongs.

- New South Wales has lost half of the *Zostera* seagrass beds in its estuaries. Lake Macquarie has lost 700 ha of seagrass, representing 44%; Tuggerah Lakes have lost 1300 ha; Botany Bay has lost 257 ha, which represents 58% of the original seagrass area; and the Clarence River estuary has lost 445 ha, 60% of the total area.
- In Victoria, 85% of the total biomass of seagrass in Westernport Bay (17 800 ha) has been lost; in the Gippsland Lakes 'major losses' have occurred.
- In Tasmania, declines in seagrass in the Hobart and D'Entrecasteaux area, Triabunna and St Helens on the east coast, Tamar and Port Sorell in the north-east and Smithton (Duck Bay) in the north-west, are cause for concern.
- In South Australia's St Vincent Gulf, over 5000 ha of seagrass has been lost; and 7000 ha in Holdfast Bay.
- In Western Australia, 97% of seagrass in Cockburn Sound (3300 ha) has been lost; at Princess Royal Harbour 810 ha have gone, representing 66% of the total area; and at Oyster Harbour 46% of the seagrass area (720 ha) has been lost.
- In Queensland at Hervey Bay, serious loss of tropical seagrass has led to high mortality in dugongs; 100 000 ha were lost in the 1992–93 floods of the Mary and Burum Rivers which caused high turbidity. In Moreton Bay near Brisbane some seagrass losses have occurred.

In south-eastern and south-western Australia, decline in water quality and high nutrient levels are of great concern in **coastal lakes and lagoons**. Those that are not adequately flushed by the sea are particularly affected (like Tuggerah Lakes and Lake Macquarie in

A birdsfoot delta in the wetlands of the coastal plain, seen from a lookout on North Brother, an ignimbrite volcano, at Laurieton, New South Wales.

M.E.W.

View from Diamond Head in the Crowdy Bay National Park.

M.E.W.

New South Wales, the Gippsland Lakes in Victoria, and the Peel-Harvey system in Western Australia). As coastal lakes are a feature largely restricted to the south-eastern coastal strip, which is the densely inhabited sector of the coastline, a significant proportion of the nation's coastal lakes has been degraded.

Coastlines and shores are vulnerable to human impact. In the more populous south-east, south and south-west, significant areas around coastal cities and towns have been reclaimed, altered by sea-walls or port developments, industry, housing, tourism and recreational facilities. The Swan Coastal Plain in southern Western Australia has lost most of its native vegetation as Perth's urban spread has advanced.

Salt marshes in populated areas are frequently reclaimed, and such areas also frequently become the rubbish dumps with their pollutants and toxins readily entering the watertable. The **intertidal zone** is often damaged, or over-harvested for molluscs or sea urchins or bait; **fishing in the coastal zone,** which involves an enormous recreational component, urgently needs a national management policy and controls; **dune systems** are easily damaged and their specialised flora and fauna may be under threat. The invasion by bitou bush (boneseed), which was introduced as a dune stabiliser and has run riot, has resulted in a great decrease in dune biodiversity in many east coast areas. **Sand mining,** even when it is followed by rehabilitation, can grossly alter dune areas and their ecosystems.

A wealth of sand lies on the continental shelf, and subject to its being mined responsibly and at sufficient distance from the coast, it could (and should) be exploited to reduce the pressure on terrestrial sand deposits. The technology exists to do this.

Sewage and storm water run-off are major polluters of the ocean in urban areas. Each year 10 000 tonnes of phosphorus and 100 000 tonnes of nitrogen are discharged through Australia's sewerage systems, much of which finds its way into the marine environment, directly through marine outfalls, or indirectly via rivers. Australia can no longer afford to

COMMERCIAL FISHING AND OVER-FISHING

The Australian Fishing Zone has an area of nearly 9 million square kilometres (the third largest in the world). The low productivity of the oceans surrounding Australia accounts for the comparatively low fish catch from such a large area — 200 000 tonnes a year. This includes a number of high value export fisheries such as abalone, rock lobsters and prawns, and a large cultured pearl industry. Annual exports of marine products were valued at $1.1 billion in 1992–93. Some 200 fish species, 60 crustacean species and 30 mollusc species are fished by about 10 000 vessels.

Australia has seriously over-fished southern blue-fin tuna, southern sharks, gemfish and orange roughy. Of the 100 fisheries investigated,[192] nine were considered to be overfished, 23 were fully or heavily fished, nine were underfished and 59 were of `unknown status'. We have learnt nothing from the demise of the cod and herring fisheries and others in the Northern Hemisphere. The cultivation of a demand and a taste for exotic seafoods of all sorts which we see happening in Australia in our Yuppie-driven urban society is inexcusable. We have no idea how the resources should be managed because the biology of the creatures involved and the functioning of their ecosystems is not understood.

The use of non-selective fishing gear, like the huge bottom trawl nets which have decimated the biota in the prawn fisheries in Torres Strait, is one of the reasons for decline in catch. The 'by-catch' and the damage to the seafloor habitats is disgraceful. Some trawlers even drag chains along the bottom to reduce snags which would damage their nets. Loss of habitat by the sedimentation of estuaries, loss of seagrass and other human-induced changes all contribute to falling catches. We have all heard of the long-line fishing which kills dolphins and albatross as a by-catch, and the albatross is now an endangered species. Out of sight is largely out of mind where the ocean is concerned, and it is obvious that **we exploit the sea as we exploit the land, on a grander scale as more technology is developed, with an eye on larger profits and with no real worry that we are destroying the resource.**

Aquaculture, a growing industry, is one satisfactory answer. In the last decade it has expanded from a $50 million to more than $260 million per year industry. The South Australian tuna farming enterprises catch wild fish and fatten them up for sale to Japan, so the sea is still being robbed of a fish which is so overfished that its survival may be threatened.

Mangroves fringe the meandering river on the coastal plain near Cardwell, Queensland (opposite Hinchinbrook Island).

JIM FRAZIER

use its waterways and ocean as sewers. The increased nutrients which enter the sea in the increased sediments which come from degraded catchments pose enough of a problem without deliberate additions from sewers.

Estimations of sediment and nutrient entering the sea in Queensland indicate that the amount of sediment, nitrogen and phosphorus is at least four times what it was in pre-settlement times. Queensland is comparatively lightly populated, its nutrients in run–off come largely from agriculture. The rivers of Queensland's east coast catchments are estimated to deliver about 14 million tonnes of sediment to estuaries and coastal marine waters annually. The factor by which the nutrient enrichment has been increased compared with pre-settlement times in the ocean off Sydney, for instance, where 4700 million litres of 'treated sewage' are discharged into the sea each day, must be astronomical. In addition, the rubbish and pollutants delivered by stormwater drains in urbanised parts of the coastal strip is a major concern. Industrial

chemicals, pesticides, heavy metals, pathogens, and everything from street drains including dog droppings, oil and petrol, end up in the sea.

Delegates to an oil industry conference in Perth in 1995, were informed that 37% of **oil pollution in the oceans of the world** was contributed by urban run-off from gutters and stormwater drains; 33% by transport vessel operation (largely bilge water); accidents involving tankers contributed 12% and off-shore oil production 2%; while natural sources and absorption from the atmosphere accounted for 7% and 9% respectively. Better management of urban run-off and control of bilge water release by shipping would therefore make a most significant improvement.

The Ports Corporation of Queensland has become involved in doing something about the sediment load which ends up in the sea. Most Queensland ports are situated in sensitive Great Barrier Reef, Gulf of Carpentaria or Torres Strait areas. The Corporation in 1995 gave $50 000 towards Integrated Catchment Management projects surrounding the ports of Lucinda, Mourilyan and Weipa, and it collects baseline environmental data about its ports which will be available in future projects.

Mangrove forests are productive ecosystems of major economic and ecological importance. They provide habitats and nurseries for many fish, form a buffer for estuaries from sediments and for coastlines from storm waves, are natural nutrient filters and are critical habitats for many birds and other wildlife. Significant areas of mangroves have been cleared or killed around metropolitan areas, though most mangrove areas remain relatively untouched. About 20% of the mangroves have been cleared in Moreton Bay near Brisbane and there has been significant die-back of mangroves near Adelaide. Only Western

COASTAL ENVIRONMENT INITIATIVES

Coastcare is a community coastal action program established by the Commonwealth Government in association with State and Local governments. The Commonwealth is providing over $23 million in funding over the next four years, as part of the $53 million Coastal Action Program.

Coastcare provides opportunities and resources for residents, volunteers, business and interest groups to take part in coastal management through such activites as: rehabilitation and protection of dunes, estuaries and wetlands; controlling feral animals and weeds; community-based monitoring of coastal environments and implementation of management plans; ensuring that recreational and tourism activities are sustainable and do not degrade the environment; and educating the community in environmental science and management.

The Coastcare program provides funding for community group projects; technical support and training; and links between government agencies, land and marine managers, universities and community groups to share knowledge and technical skills. Special events like Ocean Care Day are educational (and fun) and schools are encouraged to learn about coastal environments and how to protect them as part of the curriculum.

Regional Coastcare facilitators have been appointed to help groups to identify problems and possible solutions and to plan projects. They can assist in preparing applications for funding, and in organising contacts with advisers and experts.

Dunecare, involving coastal communities looking after and rehabilitating sensitive dune systems, preceded Landcare in New South Wales.

A pilot Dunecare program was initiated by the Soil Conservation Service on the north coast of New South Wales in 1988, where four groups were chosen to participate in sand dune reclamation projects. Dunecare has since expanded all along the coast and has spread to other States. Landcare now supports Dunecare projects, where voluntary labour is backed by councils, local business and service clubs. Schools are often involved, learning environmental science while helping to stabilise dunes and promote sustainable use and management of coastal regions.

The **Sydney Coastal Councils Group** is an example of cooperation between a number of councils whose districts include harbour and sea foreshores. A shared concern for water quality has prompted a combined effort in order to have the lobbying power to insist that the Environmental Protection Authority (the EPA), Sydney Water and the State Government protect and manage the waterways in accordance with 'water quality goals which require that they are safe to swim in and that aquatic ecosystems are protected'. In August 1996, the Chairman of Sydney Coastal Councils, Dr Peter Macdonald, launched *Water Quality Guidelines for Sydney's Estuarine, Fresh and Ground Waters: A Vision for Sydney's Waterways.*

The councils which came together in 1989 to form the group are Botany, Leichardt, Manly, Mosman, North Sydney, Pittwater, Randwick, Rockdale, South Sydney, Sutherland, Sydney, Warringah, Waverley, Willoughby and Woollahra — representing over a million Sydney residents.

Sydney Coastal Councils is currently mapping the state of waterways in its region, using a geographical information system, and is preparing a 'State of the Waters' report. This will be used to lobby those responsible to identify, reduce and prevent the sources of pollution. Sydney Water licences for sewage overflow, to be determined by the EPA, will be influenced by the group's findings. Stormwater management, and guidelines for cleaning tidal harbour and sea rock pools, and for coastal risk management are within the scope of the group's activities.

Australia protects all mangroves; only very small areas are within reserves elsewhere.

Coral reefs are under threat globally, and the Great Barrier Reef is no exception. It has been estimated that about 70% of the world's coral reefs are degraded in some way, and coral is dying worldwide. Already a tenth of the world's coral has died; by 2000, a third will be gone; and by 2030 it is estimated that 70% of all coral reefs will have been lost. Nutrient enrichment appears to be the culprit. Phosphorus interferes with the formation of the calcareous skeletons of the corals.

The Great Barrier Reef is threatened by increased sediment and nutrients; by effects of fishing and tourism; and by the risk of oil spills because of the major shipping lanes which lie so close to it. Specific threats include elevated nutrients and sediments in the inner Great Barrier Reef, outbreaks of crown-of-thorns starfish in the outer central and northern parts of the reef, and damage from the passage of tropical cyclones.

Early signs of damage from siltation are appearing in the inner reef areas, according to Dr Frank Talbot, Chairman of the Coral Reef Research Institute, and human contact is altering and degrading the parts of the reef where tourists walk or boat anchors interfere with the coral. A study of historic photographs has shown that there has been a decline of hard corals on half of the 12 locations identified in photographs taken up to 100 years ago.

THE EASTERN GREEN CRESCENT

The Great Divide, the watershed which runs down the eastern margin of the continent, separates the tablelands to its west, with their westward flowing rivers, from the ranges of the Great Escarpment and the catchments of rivers flowing eastwards to the sea. Examples of land use and their consequences in the western sector of the green crescent have largely been covered in other chapters of this book. They included the clearing of forest, woodland and native grassland to make way for agriculture and improved pasture; the dryland salinity that results from altered hydrology; the degradation of soil and water; and the loss of biodiversity.

Much of the farm land east of the Divide was also cleared and, apart from the areas with better soils like alluvium in valleys or basaltic patches, the unimproved pasture which replaced forest and woodland has proved to be disappointingly unproductive. Signs of erosion following clearing are everywhere in landscapes and although they are not as dramatic as those in the more marginal regions where harsher climate has contributed to rapid degradation, productivity losses have resulted in many farming enterprises becoming unprofitable.

The storage dams, like the Warragamba which supplies Sydney, suffer the same complaints as inland water storages west of the Divide, with eroded catchments supplying excessive volumes of sediment, and agriculture supplying nutrients and pollutants to the water.

Farmland in the Nymboida Valley. Clearing of trees from the valley has opened it up for pasture, but the unimproved pasture is poor quality and the shallow soils away from the river alluvium are unproductive.

M.E.W.

THE EASTERN GREEN CRESCENT:
Distribution of introduced and sown pastures and crops

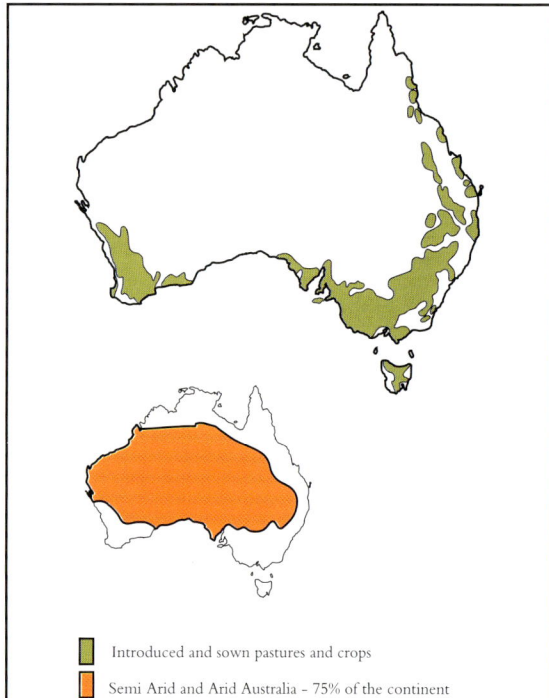

Introduced and sown pastures and crops

Semi Arid and Arid Australia - 75% of the continent

The **Warragamba Dam** (also known as Lake Burragorang) was constructed in the 1960s and it is estimated that in the 30 years since, 60 million tonnes of sediment have accumulated in it. Its catchment covers an area of $9500\,km^2$, and four rivers enter the reservoir — the Wollondilly, Cox's and Nattai Rivers and Werriberri Creek. Mud deltas have built up at the points at which the rivers enter the dam and extend for up to 10 km from entry points. (The dam is 50 km long and up to 95 m deep.) The sediment comes from eroding gullies and stream beds; the erosion here, as elsewhere on the continent, is linked to land management practices, with some of the blame for practices like excessive tree clearing and over-grazing going back to early days of settlement. About a million tonnes of sediment per year come from the Wollondilly catchment, 700 000 t from the Cox's River catchment and 330 000 t from the Nattai River catchment. The

size of the dam is such that it will take a very long time to fill with sediment, but the location of off-take points for the Sydney water supply may be affected because of the build-up near them.

Sediment is not the only problem — it transports nutrients. The sediment which comes from Werriberri Creek in particular results from erosion of fertilised farmland, and all the rivers are bringing in extra nitrogen and phosphorus from sewage effluent as well. At times of drought and low water levels there is an increasing risk of eutrophication (nutrient enrichment) to a critical level at which outbreaks of blue-green algae (cyanobacteria) could occur. An outbreak of toxic organisms sufficient to render the water supply of Australia's major city unsafe for drinking does not bear thinking about, but under Greenhouse and the unknown changes that it will bring to rainfall distribution, it is not beyond the bounds of possibility.

Our rivers are in trouble. Those within cities like, for instance, the Yarra in Melbourne, the Swan in Perth, the Derwent in Hobart, the Cooks and Hawkesbury-Nepean in Sydney, obviously have a great deal to contend with as they receive urban and industrial run-off, debris and pollutants from stormwater drains, oil and rubber from roadways, dog droppings and in some cases sewage effluent on top of their quotas of sediment and nutrients from their further catchments. Most rivers outside large cities flow through towns or settlements because water is the lifeblood of the land and rivers dictated where settlements would be established in the first place. Continent-wide, rivers have been used as drains and sewers. Where they are dammed or regulated the riverine environment suffers from unnatural cycles; riparian vegetation, essential for river health, is often grossly altered or destroyed; floodplains are protected by levees and wetlands are starved of water.

Population: its effects on the eastern margin

The eastern sector, from the Great Divide to the Pacific coastline, with more reliable rainfall, has the major concentration of population in an arc from southern Queensland to coastal South Australia, including Tasmania. About 11.5 million of the total Australian population of 18 million live in Brisbane, Sydney, Melbourne, Hobart and Adelaide. (With Perth's 1.26 million, about 71% of population are in the State capital cities; more with Canberra included.) The spread of urbanisation and its infrastructure in and between major cities alienates good agricultural land, and that is a limited resource which needs protection, particularly when so much is degraded and becoming decreasingly productive. The impact of people is felt everywhere by the environment, in the changes that occur, the run-off from changed areas to rivers, the disposal of waste, destruction of habitat for native fauna and flora and consequent loss of biodiversity, and all the other disturbances that follow humans wherever they go.

Urban bushland in and around cities and towns is

increasingly under threat and although Councils are officially committed to Agenda 21 and the introduction of ecologically sustainable development, which involves the management of their catchments and remaining natural vegetation, there is a considerable gap between avowed intention and implementation.

In the country, Landcare and other grass-roots movements are active, and rural people are taking responsibility for the problems in their environments, and are increasingly doing so in an organised way on a catchment basis. They cannot be expected to do it alone. The urban population has to take responsibility not only for its local environmental problems, but must also admit its responsibility for problems which result from its unrealistic expectations which drive the rural sector and result in land and water degradation. Someone, and that is us, has to pay the bill for conservation and rehabilitation when the standard of living we demand, the economic philosophies which we allow to govern and run our society, are responsible for the damage to basic, life-supporting resources.

In our urban sphere, unless we want to see artificial environments wall-to-wall along the eastern margin of the continent, there has to be coordinated planning and regulation which protects the pockets of natural vegetation which remain. Urban sprawl cannot go on, with developers clearing new land instead of re-developing run-down or dysfunctional residential and commercial land in and around large population centres; and the most stringent environmental constraints must be put on new areas opening up for housing and its attendant services.

The involvement of all citizens is required — **each one of us lives in a catchment and everything we do has a effect on the environment**. In urban living (and that is what 86% of the Australian population is doing) we are disconnected from the environment — the out-of-sight, out-of-mind syndrome applies. We do not give much thought to what happens to what goes away down the drain or sewers, or in the garbage or the clean-up; nor do we consider that by wasting water we are putting pressure on our dams, demanding that more rivers are starved of normal flow to satisfy our needs; or that by using more electricity than we need we are causing more burning of coal in power stations; or that by using our cars when we could walk or use public transport we are contributing to the global greenhouse effect and declining air quality in our city.

Above all, Government has to be made to realise that pursuit of the almighty dollar and putting the *economy* ahead of the health of the *environment* is running down the basic resources of soil and water on which Australia's future depends. To repeat the quotation which started the chapter on soil degradation:

A nation that destroys its soils destroys itself.

(President Roosevelt, 1937 during the United States 'dustbowl' era)

Above top right: A cleared hillside where forest has been replaced by pasture, destabilising the soil cover, so that slumping and erosion are cutting back into the hill from a roadway.

Above top left: Erosion in a cleared gully beside the road from Gloucester to Nowendock, New South Wales.

Above: Urban bushland in Sydney's harbour-side suburbs adds greatly to the amenity of the city and provides refuge for native animals and plants.

M.E.W.

EPILOGUE

GAIA AND THE GREED OF MAN

Since the beginning of time, the Earth has seen co-evolution of life and the inanimate environment, resulting in the living, life-friendly biosphere which makes Earth unique in our solar system. The acceptance of the principle of Gaia, the Living Earth, behaving like an enormous organism with all its components and systems in dynamic balance, is fundamental to maintaining the ability of the Earth to sustain life. Only humans, by virtue of their technology, have had the ability to live outside the rules which apply to all other creatures — natural laws which forced them to operate within bounds which maintain the balance. We are now so remote from the values which sustain Gaia, exploiting the Earth to sustain economy-driven systems which are intrinsically unsustainable, that 'development', as it is perceived today, is incompatible with maintaining that balance. It is not going too far to say that **'sustainable development' is an oxymoron.** 'Ecologically sustainable *development'*, the much vaunted ESD, is no less an oxymoron if the underlying motive is first and foremost the welfare of the economy.

For as long as the aim is to manage and redesign nature in order to keep economic growth going, 'sustainability' is a meaningless concept. At best we can hope to slow the decline in ecosystem health, and the overall health of the planet, and buy a little more time. Even the Rio Summit of 1992, whose aim was the promotion of sustainability, had to admit that the environmental degradation and inappropriate development which was so clearly evident worldwide was largely the result of 50 years of unbridled corporate industrial expansion. Nothing has changed in the world attitude since, and all the good efforts to start rehabilitation of the environment 'from the bottom up', like the wonderful Landcare and other movements in Australia, will be limited to temporary gains against a tide which can only be turned when environmental concerns are given precedence over economic aspirations.

This is a fundamental truth which is decidedly **not** politically correct, neither is it palatable to governments whose eyes are fixed on the global economy, on free trade and the holy grail of economic growth. This truth may not be recognised and acted upon until the world is *in extremis* with its natural resources of land and water barely able to support life, and with the human species heading rapidly towards extinction...

This is not to say that we may as well give up the fight. Australia could be a world leader in bringing about the necessary change in attitudes which offer hope to an embattled Earth. Australians must demand that their elected government plans for a long-term future for its citizens by acknowledging that fundamental change is necessary to guarantee any future at all.

BIBLIOGRAPHY

1. Lovelock J. 1988: *The Ages Of Gaia*. Oxford University Press.
2. La Riviere JWM. 1989: Threats to the world's water. *Scientific American* Sept: 48-55.
3. DEST. 1996: *Australia. State of the Environment 1996*. CSIRO Publishing, Melbourne.
4. Dregne H, Kassas M, Razanov B. 1991: A new assessment of the world status of desertification. *Desertification Control Bulletin* (UN Environmental Program) 20: 6-18.
5. UNCED. 1992: *Earth Summit Agenda 21: Programme of action for sustainable development*. UN Department of Public Information, New York.
6. White ME. 1994: *After the Greening. The Browning of Australia*. Kangaroo Press, Sydney.
7. WA Legislative Assembly. 1991: *Final report of the Select Committee into Land Conservation*. State Printer, WA.
8. Williams M, McCarthy M, Pickup G. 1995: Desertification, drought and landcare: Australia's role in an international convention to combat desertification. *Australian Geographer* 26(1): 23-32.
9. Ehrlich PR, Holdren JP. 1971: Impact of population growth. *Science* 171:1212-1217.
10. Young ARM. 1996: *Environmental Change in Australia since 1788*. Oxford University Press, Melbourne.
11. Graetz RD, *et al.* 1995: Landcover disturbance over the Australian continent. A contemporary assessment. *Biodiversity Series 7*. Biodiversity Unit, DEST, Canberra.
12. Graetz *et al.* 1992: *Looking back. The changing face of the Australian continent 1972–1992*. CSIRO, Canberra.
13. NSW NPWS. 1991: *Kosciusko grazing. A history*. Sydney: NSW NPWS.
14. Kasper J. 1987: The impact of man on the flora of the Mount Kosciusko alpine area. Thesis. Narrabundah College, Canberra.
15. Leigh JH, *et al.* 1987: Effects of rabbit grazing and fire on a subalpine environment. 1. Herbaceous and shrubby vegetation. *Aust J Bot* 35.
16. Brain CK, Sillen A. 1988: Evidence from the Swartkrans cave for the earliest use of fire. *Nature* 336: 464-466.
17. IPCC WG1. 1995. Summary for policymakers. Intergovernmental panel on climate change.
18. Bell A. 1986: What air bubbles trapped in Antarctic ice tell us. *Ecos* 47; 23-26.
19. Beattie AJ, ed. 1995: *Biodiversity. Australia's Living Wealth*. Reed Books Australia, Sydney.
20. Cook GD, Hurst D, Griffith D. 1995: Atmospheric trace gas emissions from tropical savannah fires. *CALMScience Supplement* 4: 123-128.
21. Selkirk PM. 1992: Climate change and the Subantarctic. In: DASET. *Impact of Climate Change. Antarctica, Australia*. Government Printer, Canberra.
22. Adamson DA, *et al.* 1988: An analysis of air temperature records for Macquarie Island: decadal warming, ENSO cooling and Southern Hemisphere circulation patterns. *Pap Proc Roy Soc Tas* 122(1): 107-112.
23. Gillieson D, *et al.* 1991: Flood history of the limestone ranges in the Kimberley region, Western Australia. *Applied Geography* 11: 105-123.
24. Stevens T, *The Australian* 5 June 1995.
25. O'Neill G. 1995: Coping with Climate. *Ecos* 84; winter.
26. Williams MAJ. 1986: The Creeping Desert. What can be done? *Current Affairs Bulletin* 63: 24-31.
27. Nicholls N. 1989: How old is ENSO? *Climate Change* 14: 111-115.
28. de Wit M, *et al.* 1988: Geological map of sectors of Gondwana. *American Association of Petrol Geology and Witwatersrand University*.
29. Wray RAL, *et al.* 1993: Cainozoic heritage in the modern landscape near Bungonia, southern New South Wales. *Aust Geographer* 24(1): 45-61.
30. Ollier C. 1982: The Great Escarpment of Eastern Australia: tectonic and geomorphic significance. *J Geol Soc Aust* 29: 13-23.
31. Prentice ML, Denton GH. 1988: The deep-sea oxygen isotope record, the global ice sheet system, and Hominid evolution. In: *Evolutionary History of the "robust" Australopithicines*. Aldino de Gruyter, Rotterdam.
32. Hope G, Kirkpatrick J. 1988: The ecological history of Australian forests. In: *Australia's Everchanging Forests*. Special Publication 1, Department of Geography and Oceanography, Australian Defence Force Academy, Canberra.
33. Chappell J. 1983: Sea-level changes, 0-40 KA. *Proc CLIMANZ 1*. Canberra 1981.
34. Veevers JJ, *et al.* 1991. Review of seafloor spreading round Australia. 1. Synthesis of the patterns of spreading. *Aust J Earth Sci* 38: 373-389.
35. Habermehl MA. 1980: The Great Artesian Basin. *BMR J Aust Geol Geophys* 5: 9-38.
36. Stephenson AE, Brown CM. 1989: The ancient Murray River system. *BMR J Aust Geol & Geophys* 11: 387-395.
37. Wilson EO, ed. 1988: *Biodiversity*. National Academy Press, Washington.
38. Kitching RL. 1994: Biodiversity and taxonomy: impediment or opportunity? In: Moritz & Kikkawa, eds. *Conservation Biology in Australia and Oceania*. Surrey Beatty and Sons, Sydney.
39. DASET 1992: *A national strategy for the conservation of Australia's biological diversity: Draft for public comment*. DEST, Canberra.
40. Beattie AJ, *et al.* 1992: Changes in Australian terrestrial biodiversity since European settlement and into the future. *Proc Bur Rural Res & CSIRO Plant Industry 14*.
41. Morton SR, *et al.* 1995: Refugia for biological diversity in arid and semi-arid Australia. *Biodiversity Series 4*. Biodiversity Unit, DEST, Canberra.
42. Morton SR. 1990: The impact of European settlement on the vertebrate animals of arid Australia: a conceptual model. *Proc Ecol Soc Aust* 16: 201-213.
43. Noble JC. 1994: Bettong (*Bettongia* spp.) biocontrol of shrubs in semi-arid mulga (*Acacia aneura*) rangelands: an hypothesis. In: Page & Bentel, eds. *Ecological Research and Management in the Mulgalands*. University of Queensland.
44. Noble JC. 1995: Mesomarsupial ecology in Australian rangelands: burrows, bettongs (*Bettongia* spp.) and biocontrol of shrubs. *Proc 5th IRC* Salt Lake City, Utah.
45. Rogers RW. 1989: Blue-green algae in southern Australian rangeland soils. *Aust Rangel J* 11(2): 67-73.
46. Smith GD, *et al.* 1990: Cyanobacterial nitrogen fixation in arid soils in Central Australia. *FEMS Microbiol Ecol* 74: 79-90.
47. Eldridge DJ, *et al.* 1995: Distribution, characteristics and management of sealing, crusting and hardsetting soils under rangeland conditions in Australia. In: *Sealing, Crusting and Hardsetting Soils: Productivity and Conservation*. Aust Soc Soil Sci, Qld Branch.
48. McTainsh G. 1990: Wind erosion in eastern Australia. *Aust J Soil Res* 28: 323-339.
49. Greene RSB. 1992: Soil physical properties of three geomorphic zones in a semi-arid mulga woodland. *Aust J Soil Res* 30: 55-69.
50. Savory A. 1988: *Holistic Resource Management*. Island Press, Washington.
51. Eldridge DJ. 1994: Cryptogam cover and soil surface condition: effects on hydrology on a semiarid woodland soil. *Arid Soil Res Rehab* 7: 203-217.
52. Eldridge DJ. 1993: Effects of ants on sandy soils in semi-arid eastern Australia: Local distribution of nest entrances and their effect on infiltration of water. *Aust J Soil Res* 31: 309-318.
53. Eldridge DJ. 1994: Nests of ants and termites influence infiltration in a semi-arid woodland. *Pedobiologia* 38: 481-492.
54. Eldridge DJ, Greene RSB. 1994: Microbiotic soil crusts: a review of their roles in soil and ecological processes in the rangelands of Australia. *Aust J Soil Res* 32: 389-415.
55. Rogers RW. 1972: Soil surface lichens in arid and subarid

southeastern Australia: the relationship between distribution and environment. *Aust J Bot* 20:301-316.

56. Mucher HJ, *et al.* 1988: Micromorphology and significance of the surface crusts of soils in the rangelands near Cobar, Australia. *Geoderma* 42: 227-244.

57. Greene RSB, *et al.* 1990: The effect of fire on the soil in a degraded semi-arid woodland. 1. Cryptogam cover and the physical micromorphological properties. *Aust J Soil Res* 28: 755-777.

58. Watson J. 1995: Community involvement in the Fitzgerald Biosphere Reserve. Success Story. *Proc World Congress on Biosphere Reserves* Sevilla, Spain.

59. Watson J. 1993: Fostering community support for the Fitzgerald River Biosphere Reserve, Western Australia. *Nature & Resources* 29(1-4): 24-28.

60. Adamson DA, *et al.* In press: Pleistocene uplift and palaeoenvironments of Macquarie Island: from palaeobeaches and sedimentary deposits. *Pap Proc Roy Soc Tas.*

61. Jones TD, McCue KF. 1988: The seismicity and tectonics of the Macquarie Ridge. In: Banks & Smith, eds. *Proceedings of the Symposium on Macquarie Island.* Royal Society of Tasmania.

62. Copson G, *et al.* 1994: Far out — the possibilities for Macquarie Island Biosphere Reserve. In: Brunckhorst D, ed. *Marine Protected Areas: Biodiversity, Biogeography and Biosphere Reserves.* Proc Internat Workshop, Canberra.

63. DELM Tas. 1993: *One of the Wonder Spots of the World. Macquarie Island Nature Reserve.* NPWS Tasmania.

64. Copley P, Williams S. In press: Distribution, relative abundance and conservation of the malleefowl in South Australia.

65. Williams SL. 1995: Malleefowl as a flagship for conservation on farms in the Murray Mallee of South Australia. In: *Nature Conservation 4: The Role of Networks.* Surrey Beatty & Sons, Sydney.

66. Noble JC. 1993: Relict surface-soil features in semi-arid mulga (*Acacia aneura*) woodlands. *Rangeland J* 15(1): 48-70.

67. Eldridge DJ, *et al.* 1994: Effects of ants on sandy soils in semi-arid eastern Australia.II. Relocation of nest entrances and consequences for bioturbation. *Aust J Soil Res* 32: 323-333.

68. Nix HA. 1978: Land Resources: Area suitable for agriculture. *Proc 2nd Int. Symp Aust Acad Tech Sci,* Sydney: 25-38.

69. Pimentel D. 1995: Environmental and economic costs of soil erosion and conservation benefits. *Science* 267: 1117-1123.

70. Fanning P. 1994: Long-term contemporary erosion rates in the arid rangelands environment in western New South Wales, Australia. *J Arid Envir* 28: 173-187.

71. McTainsh G. 1985: Dust processes in Australia and West Africa. A comparison. *Search* 16(3-4): 104-106.

72. McTainsh G. 1989: Quaternary aeolian dust processes and sediments in the Australian region. *Quat Sci Rev* 8: 235-253.

73. McTainsh G, *et al.* 1989: Aridity, drought and dust storms in Australia (1960–84). *J Arid Environments* 16: 11-22.

74. McTainsh G, Pitblado JR. 1987: Dust storms and related phenomena measured from meteorological records in Australia. *Earth Surface Processes and Landforms* 12: 415-424.

75. Kiefert L, McTainsh G. In press: Oxygen isotope abundance in the quartz fraction of aeolian dust: implications for soil and ocean sediment formation in the Australasian region.

76. Carter D. 1995: Storm. *WA J Agric* 36: 82-87.

77. Freebairn DM. 1992: Managing resources: the soil resource: erosion, stubble management and catchment. *Proc 6th Aust Agronomy Conference,* Armidale.

78. Freebairn DM, *et al.* 1986: Effects of catchment management on runoff, water quality and yield potential from vertisols. *Agricultural Water Management* 12: 1-19.

79. Freebairn DM, Wockner GH. 1986: A study of soil erosion on vertisols of the eastern Darling Downs, Queensland. 1. Effects of surface conditions on soil movement within contour bay catchments. *Aust J Soil Research* 24: 135-158.

80. Freebairn DM, Wockner GH. 1986: A study of soil erosion on vertisols of the eastern Darling Downs, Queensland. 2. The effect of soil, rainfall and flow conditions on suspended sediment losses. *Aust J Soil Research* 24: 135-158.

81. Eckersley R. 1989: Regreening Australia. The environmental,

economic and social benefits of reforestation. *CSIRO Occasional Paper No.3*

82. Chartres C, *et al.* 1992: Land degradation as a result of European settlement of Australia and its influence on soil properties. In: *Australia's renewable resources: sustainability and global change.* International Geosphere-Biosphere Program, UNESCO.

83. Ghassemi F, Nix HA, Jakeman AJ. 1995: *Salinisation of Land and Water Resources.* Human causes, extent, management and case studies. UNSW Press, Sydney.

84. Hamilton S. 1995: Urban salinity investigations in Wagga Wagga. *AGSO Record* 1995/61

85. Christiansen G. 1995: An economic report on the costs of urban salinity in the city of Wagga Wagga. *Economic Notes, CALM.*

86. Macfarlane D. 1991: A review of secondary salinity in agricultural areas of W.A. *Land and Water Research News* 11: 7-16.

87. Peck AJ. 1983: Response of groundwater to clearing in Western Australia. In: *Papers of the International Conference on Groundwater and Man.* Aust. Water Research Council, Canberra, 2: 327-335.

88. Robertson G. 1995: The National Dryland Salinity Program. *Proc `Making Catchment Management Happen' conference,* Gunnedah. Liverpool Plains Land Management Committee.

89. Van Der Moezel PG, Bell DT. 1990: Saltland reclamation: selection of superior tree genotypes for discharge sites. *Proc Ecol Soc Aust* 16: 545-549.

90. BCCG. 1996: Blackwood Catchment Regional Initiative. *National Landcare Program Report.*

91. MDBCMC. 1995: *An audit of water use in the Murray-Darling Basin.* MDBC Ministerial Council, Canberra.

92. Arthington A. 1995: State of the rivers in cotton growing areas. Northern NSW and the border rivers with Queensland. *LWRRDC Occasional Paper 02/95.*

93. NSW DLWC *State of the Water Storages.*

94. Madden C. 1995: The Goulburn Broken Catchment experience. *Proc `Making Catchment Management Happen' conference,* Gunnedah. Liverpool Plains Land Management Committee.

95. LWR RDC 1994: *Management Strategy 1994-1998.* National Dryland Salinity Research Development & Extn Program.

96. Jensen A. 1996: Water allocations for South Australian Wetlands. *WATERways Newsletter.*

97. Mackay N, Eastburn D, eds. 1990: *The Murray.* MDBC, Canberra.

98. Humphreys L, *et al.* 1994: The development of on-farm restrictions to minimise recharge from rice in New South Wales. *Aust J Soil & Water Conserv* 7(2): 11-20.

99. van der Lely A. 1993: Present and future salinity conditions in the MIA. *NSW Dept. Water Res Tech report 5TR370.*

100. Gutteridge Haskin & Davey Pty Ltd 1985: Waterlogging and land salinisation in irrigated areas in NSW. Vol.1. GH & D, Sydney.

101. Swinton R. 1994: *Issues in Irrigation.* Thesis. MAS. University of Western Sydney, Hawkesbury.

102. van der Lely A. 1992: Groundwater in the MIA, CIA & Murray Valley IREC. *Farmers Newsletter* 140.

103. Beale B. 1995: Rising water threatens irrigation areas. Billions of skeletons in our backyard. *Sydney Morning Herald* March 18.

104. Jones A. 1995: *Denimein Community's Land & Water Management Plan.* LWMP Working Group.

105. Bowler JM. 1978: Quarternary climate and tectonics in the evolution of the Riverine Plain, SE Australia. In: Davies JL, Williams MAJ. *Landform Evolution in Australia.* ANU Press, Canberra.

106. Beale B. 1995: Growing problem ignored at our peril. *Sydney Morning Herald* November 15.

107. Meyer WS. 1992: Sustainability of land & water resources used for Australian irrigated agriculture. A research strategy position paper. *CSIRO Water Res Series No. 8.*

108. Humphreys L, Muirhead W. 1996: Puddling. *Farmers Newsletter Large Area* No. 147. June, 1996.

109. Humphreys L, *et al.* 1992: Minimising deep percolation from rice. *Farmers Newsletter, Large Area* No. 140. December.

110. Jayawardane NS. 1995: *Wastewater treatment and reuse through irrigation, with special reference to the Murray Basin and adjacent coastal areas.* CSIRO Div Water Res, Griffith NSW. Rep. 95/1.

111. Muirhead WA, *et al,* 1992: Waterlogging: its cause and amelioration with mole drains. *Farmers Newsletter, Large Area* 140.

112. Moll J. 1996: Is sub-surface drainage financially attractive for

vegetable growers? *Farmers Newsletter* 177.

113. Harrington GL, *et al.* 1979: The effects of European settlement and domestic livestock on the biological system in poplar box (*Eucalyptus populnea*) lands. *Aust Rangel J* 1(4): 271-279.

114. Kirkpatrick J, *et al.* 1995: *Australia's Most Threatened Ecosystems: the southeastern lowland native grasslands*. Surrey Beatty and Sons, Sydney.

115. SEPP 46 1996: *Protection and Management of Native Vegetation*. Department of Land & Water Conservation, Draft legislation.

116. Hutchinson M, Milne T. 1994: Research plan for the pygmy bluetongue lizard *Tiliqua adelaidensis* (Peters 1863). Unpublished Draft report ANCA & ESP.

117. Hutchinson MN. 1995: Redescription and ecological notes on the pygmy bluetongue, *Tiliqua adelaidensis* (Squamata: Scincidae) *Trans Roy Soc SA* 118(4): 217-226.

118. Davidson D. 1954: The Mitchell grass association of the Longreach district. *Botany Paper III*, University of Qld.

119. Mills JR. 1989: Cited in: *Tree clearing in the rangelands of Queensland*. Qld Conservation Council, March 1995.

120. Williams MAJ. 1978: Termites, soils and landscape equilibrium in the Northern Territory of Australia. In: Davies JL, Williams MAJ. *Landform Evolution in Australasia*. ANU Press, Canberra.

121. Watson JAL, *et al.* 1973: Termites in mulga lands. *Tropical Grasslands* 7(1): 121-126.

122. Jensen A, *et al.* 1996: *Preservation and Management of natural wetlands in the South Australian Murray Valley*.

123. LWR RDC 1996: Local community contribution to Upper South East land use plan. *Focus*, 5 (Feb): 2.

124. Austin N. 1995: Baron of the bush. *The Advertiser* 9 December.

125. Kelly S. 1995: Land management report for the Kent River Catchment. *WA Department of Agriculture*.

126. Nix HA. 1990: *Water/Land/Life: The Eternal Triangle. Jack Beale Water Resources Lecture*. Water Research Foundation of Australia, ANU, Canberra.

127. Mortiss PD. 1995: The environmental issues of the Upper Burdekin Catchment. *Progress Report QO95017*. Department of Primary Industry, Qld.

128. Broughton A. 1994: Mooki River Catchment. *Hydrogeological Investigations and Dryland Salinity Studies*. Water Resources, Liverpool Plains NSW.

129. Greiner R. 1994: *Economic Assessment of dryland salinity in the Liverpool Plains*. Project report. Department of Agriculture and Resource Economics, University of New England, Armidale.

130. Broughton A. 1994: Coxs Creek Catchment. *Hydrogeological Investigations and Dryland Salinity Studies*. Water Resources, Liverpool Plains NSW.

131. Paige G. 1995: Report on feral animal eradication Oodnadatta District. Unpublished report to DPI, SA.

132. Henzell R. 1993: The ecology of feral goats. *Proc Nat Workshop, Feral Goat Management*. Bureau of Resource Sciences, Canberra.

133. Henzell R. 1991: Rabbits, feral goats, mulga and rangeland stability. *Working document, Australian Vertebrate Pest Control Conference, 1991*.

134. Henzell R. 1990: Feral goats and yellow-footed rock wallabies. *Proc Yellow-footed Rock Wallaby Workshop*. Port Augusta, SA NPWS.

135. Copley P. 1981: Distribution and status of the Yellow-footed Rock Wallaby, *Petrogale xanthopus* in the Flinders Ranges, South Australia. World Wildlife Fund Aust.

136. CSIRO WLE. 1992/93: Environmental weeds — a massive problem. *Ecos* 74(Summer): 6-8.

137. Anon. 1993: Woody weed management strategy. *Proceedings of National Workshop*. Cobar NSW. Woody Weeds Task Force, 70-73.

138. Freudenberger D. 1993: Wooded rangelands in the decade of 2040. *Range Management Newsletter* 93(2): 8-9.

139. Rees LM, Smith MG. 1996: *The value of volunteers in rehabilitating Sydney's urban bushland. 1994 survey results*. NPWS, Sydney.

140. Williams MAJ. 1991: Evolution of the landscape. In: *Monsoonal Australia: landscape, ecology and Man in the northern lowlands*. Balkema, Rotterdam: 5-17.

141. DeDekker P, *et al.* 1991: Late Pleistocene record of cyclic aeolian activity from tropical Australia suggesting the Younger Dryas is not an unusual climate event. *Geology* 19: 602-605.

142. Williams MAJ. 1985: Pleistocene aridity in tropical Africa, Australia and Asia. In: Douglas & Spence, eds. *Environmental Change and Tropical Geomorphology*. George, Allen & Unwin, Sydney: 219-233.

143. Clarke MF. 1979: Point Stuart Chenier and Holocene sea levels in Northern Australia. *Search* 10(3): 90-92.

144. Cook G, Setterfield S. 1995: Ecosystem dynamics and the management of environmental weeds in wetlands. *Proc Wet-Dry Tropics Management workshop*. Jabiru, NT.

145. Lonsdale M, Braithwaite R. 1988: The shrub that conquered the bush. *New Scientist*, Oct: 52-55.

146. McKaige B. 1994: Inviting trouble. Introduced pasture species. *Australasian Science* Spring: 31-33.

147. Braithwaite RW, Werner PA. 1987: The biological value of Kakadu National Park. *Search* 18(6): 296-301.

148. Frost P, *et al*, eds. 1986: Responses of savannas to stress and disturbance: a proposal for a collaborative program of research. *Biology International* Special issue: 10.

149. Mott JJ, *et al.* 1985: Australian savanna ecosystems. In: Tothill & Mott, eds. *Ecology and Management of the World's Savanna*. Australian Acadamy of Science, Canberra: 56-82.

150. Andersen AN, Lonsdale WM. 1990: Herbivory by insects in Australian tropical savannas. *J Biogeog* 17: 433-444.

151. Lonsdale M. 1991: Assessing the effects of fire on vegetation in tropical savannas. *Aust J Ecol* 16: 363-374.

152. Pearce D, *et al.* 1996: Aboriginal people of the tropical savannas: resource utilization and conflict resolution. In: Ash, ed. *The Future of Tropical Savannas: An Australian Perspective*. CSIRO Australia.

153. Cook GD. 1994: The fate of nutrients during fires in a tropical savanna. *Aust J Ecol* 19: 359-365.

154. Andersen AN. 1991: Responses of ground-foraging ant communities to three experimental fire regimes in the savanna forest of tropical Australia. *Biotropica* 23: 575-585.

155. Andersen AN, Braithwaite RW. 1992: Burning for conservation of the Top End's Savannas. In: Moffat & Webb, eds. *Conservation and Development Issues in North Australia*. NARU.

156. Andersen AN. In press: Fire ecology and Management.

157. de Salis J. 1993: *Ord River Regeneration Reserve*. Miscellaneous Publication. WA Department of Agriculture.

158. Fitzgerald K. 1968: The Ord River Catchment Regeneration Project. *Bulletin 399*, WA Department of Agriculture.

159. Watson AN. 1989: *The Ord River Regeneration Project 20 years on*. Report. WA Department of Agriculture.

160. Morton SR, *et al.* 1994: The stewardship of arid Australia. Ecology and landscape management. *J Environ Managem* 41.

161. Burnside D, *et al.* 1995: *Reading the Rangeland*. Department of Agriculture, WA.

162. Beard JS. 1990: *Plant Life of Western Australia*. Kangaroo Press, Sydney.

163. Holm A, Burnside D. 1992: *Rangeland Management in Western Australia*. Miscellaneous Publication, Department of Agriculture, WA.

164. Foran BD, *et al.* 1985: The pasture dynamics and management of two rangeland communities in the Victoria River District of the Northern Territory. *Aust Rangel J* 7(2): 107-115.

165. EPA 1995: *Best Practice Environmental Management in Mining*. 9 booklets. AFED, Canberra.

166. DPIE. 1994: *Maralinga Rehabilitation Project*. Statement of evidence to be presented to the Parliamentary Standing Committee on Public Works. Australian Construction Services, Canberra.

167. Waggitt P, Jones W. 1996: The Mount Lyell Remediation Research and Demonstration Program — The half time picture. *OSS Report*.

168. DELM 1995: Mt Lyell. RRDP Newsletter 1; July.

169. DELM 1996: Mt Lyell. RRDP Newsletter 4; Feb.

170. OSS 1994: *Annual Report 1993-1994*.

171. OSS 1995: *Annual Report 1994-1995*.

172. Needham S, Jones W. 1996: Tackling the remediation of a century of mining impact at Mount Lyell, Tasmania. Abstract 41. *Geol Soc Aust 13th Geology Convention*, Camberra.

173. Ward SC, *et al.* 1990: Bauxite mine rehabilitation in the Darling Range W.A. *Proc Ecol Soc Aust* 16: 557-565.

174. Alcoa Landcare Project. Brochure

175. Alcoa 1992: Alcoa Australia. Brochure
176. Summers R. 1994: Red mud — cutting pollution, boosting yields. *WA J Agric* 2: 55-59.
177. Hannan JC. 1993: Management of saline waters in the Upper Hunter Valley — A shared process. *Proc Aust Mining Ind Counc 18th Ann Workshop,* Burnie, Tasmania.
178. Hannan JC, Gordon RM. 1996: Environmental management of surface coal mines in the Hunter Valley, NSW. In: *Environmental Management in the Australian Mining Industry.* Aust Min & Energy Envir Foundation, Sydney.
179. Morton SR. 1982: Granivory in the Australian arid zone: diversity of harvester ants and structure of their communities. In: *Evolution of Flora and Fauna of Arid Australia.* (Barker & Greenslade, eds.) Peacock, Adelaide.
180. Andersen AN. 1993: Ants as indicators of restoration success at a uranium mine in tropical Australia. *Restoration Ecology* Sept: 156-167.
181. Whelan BR. 1995: Victorian overview of conservation achievements on private land. From Conflict to Conservation. Native vegetation management in Australia. Seminar proceedings. Adelaide 21 November.
182. Whelan BR. 1996: The advantages of a Trust in conservation for private lond owners. In: *Conservation Outside Nature Reserves.* University of Queensland, 5-8 February.
183. Safstrom R. 1995: In trust; working with people to achieve conservation on private land in Victoria. In: *Nature Conservation. The Role of Networks.* Surrey Beatty and Sons, Sydney.
184. NSW NPWLS. 1977: *Rainforests.* Reprint from *Parks & Wildlife* 2:1.
185. Cocks D. 1992: Use with Care. NSW University Press, Sydney.
186. Bird J. 1995: Buying back the bush. *ANH* Summer.
187. Bird J. 1995: Buying back the bush. The Australian Bush Heritage Fund. *The Bird Observer* 3.
188. Bird LH. 1993: The Woogaroo Scrub Project. *Growing Idea* 10-11.
189. DEST. 1995: *Our Sea, Our Future.* SOMER, Commonwealth of Australia.
190. DEST. 1996: Australia. State of the Environment 1996. CSIRO Publishing, Melbourne.
191. DEST. 1995: *Living on the Coast.* Commonwealth of Australia.
192. Kailola P, *et al.* 1993: *Australian Fisheries Resources.* Bur Res Sci & Fisheries R & DC.

ACKNOWLEDGMENTS

I acknowledge with gratitude the help, advice and encouragement I have received from the more than two hundred people who have sent me their publications, supplied slides and photographs, checked draft text and helped me in many other ways. I have been amazed, and touched, by everyones' enthusiastic response to my requests. I have tried to thank each person by mail when their contribution was received, and hope that no one has been overlooked.

The names of those who kindly supplied slides and photographs are given in the captions. Their contribution has been invaluable, enabling all aspects and subjects to be illustrated, and I thank them again. I also thank those individuals and organisations who have given permission for me to base some of my maps and diagrams (also credited in captions) on ones used in their publications. The availability of some base maps and diagrams on disk has been a great help, and I thank the Murray-Darling Basin Commission; the NSW Department of Land and Water Conservation, Parramatta; and the Department of Water Resources at Leeton.

Those who kindly helped me by sending publications and information, answering my letters, and checking and advising are listed below by State:

IN THE ACT:
Helen Alexander, Doug Cocks, John Casey, Andrew Campbell, P.J. Davoren, David Eastburn, Richard Eckersley, Romy Greiner, Dean Graetz, John Lovering, Stewart Needham, Jim Noble, Henry Nix, Cliff Ollier, Richard Price, Roger Rawson, Brad Russell, Sue Salmon, Dingle Smith

IN THE N.T.:
Alan Anderson, Dick Braithwaite, Graham Griffin, Ken Hodgkinson, Barbie McKaige, Peter Waggitt

IN W.A.:
Alcoa, Jim Addison, John Beard, John Bennett, Greg Beeston, N.M.Beech, Dan Carter, Jenny Crisp, Mandy Curnow, Andrew Craig, John Collett, Susanne Denning, Kingsley Dixon, Noel Dodd, Kate Davey, Glenn Gates, Gordon Graham, Alan Grosse, Alex Holm, Murray Hall, Terri Lloyd, Alan Lloyd, Jill Maugham, Kate McLeod, Susan Masterson, Bob Nulsen, Steve Porritt, David Reid, Martin Revell, Lyn Slade, Angela Sanders, Greg Street, Martine Scheltema

IN QUEENSLAND:
Bruce Boyes, Lloyd Bird, David Cobon, Frank Dean, David Freebairn, Doug Fishburn, Peter Jeffrey, Sandy Kidd, Roger Kitching, Roger Landsberg, Bruce Lawrie, Jenny Milson, Lorna Murray, Grant McTainsh, Bernie Pegram, John Reynolds, Roger Shaw, James Sullivan, Alan Smith, Bill Wilkinson

IN SOUTH AUSTRALIA:
Nicola Barnes, Alwin Clements, Peter Copley, Phil Cole, Sandy Gunter, R. Henzell, Anne Jensen, Michael Michelmore, Tim Milne, Scott Nicholls, Beverley Overton, Lynn Pedler, Garry Paige, Stephanie Williams, Martin A.J. Williams, Leith Yelland

IN VICTORIA:
John Cranmer, Cherree Densley, Craig Madden, Margaret Macdonald, W.J. O'Kane, Jan Palmer, Jane Williams, Brian Whelan, John Wolseley, Mike Young

IN TASMANIA:
Dick Burns, Greg Blake, Bob Brown, Janice Bird, Geoff Copson, Simon Finnis, Jamie Kirkpatrick, Geoff Law, Stuart Newman, Patrick Quilty, Peter Sims, Isobel Stanley

IN NEW SOUTH WALES:
John Anderson, Gail Abbott, John Blackwell, Andrew Beattie, Bob Beale, Alan Brink, Bill Currans, Dick Condon, Densey Clyne, Martin Driver, Diana Day, Tony Dare-Edwards, P.J. Davies, ERA, Dick Evans, David Eldridge, Michael Elvins, John Egan, Trish Fanning, Warwick Fisher, Joan Ferguson, Terry Francis, Cate Gillies, Angus Gidley-Baird, Liz Humphries, Sue Hamilton, John Hannan, Bruce Hooper, Peter Halliday, Nihil Jayawardane, Sue Lennox, Kevin Mills, David Mitchell, Warren Muirhead, John Merrick, Wayne Meyer, Geoff McLeod, Murray Irrigation Ltd., Brian Marshall, Gillian Napier, Nancy Pallin, Jenny Quealy, Meredith Ryan, Lynn Rees, Chris Roach, Gwen Rowe, Judy Reizes, David Roots, John Strang, Greg Sinclair, Pat Selkirk, Patrick Soars, Richard Swinton, Bryan Short, Ron Soutar, Bill Templeman, Geoff White, Gary Wells, John Warren, Michael Williams, Wagga Wagga Council, Val Williams, Ed Wilson, Liz Webb, Bryce Wauchope, Ann Young

A particular thank you to: Barbara Eckersley who made the maps and diagrams and met an almost impossible deadline while maintaining the highest professional standard; Professor Jim Rose who read, edited and checked the whole book for scientific accuracy; Bob Walshe who was my "cutting service" over two years, providing me with hundreds of bits from newspapers to keep me up-to-date; Dean Graetz for the satellite imagery which adds a new dimension; David Roots and John Casey who enabled me to travel on ecotours to obtain the photographs and first-hand information and impressions of the real Australia; Van McCune who has encouraged me when the job seemed too big; family and friends who have taken an interest; and last but not least, the designer Linda Robertshaw who has brought the final product to life..

INDEX OF BOXES

INDEX OF MAPS AND DIAGRAMS